# Hands-On System Programming with Linux

Explore Linux system programming interfaces, theory, and practice

Kaiwan N Billimoria

**Packt>**

BIRMINGHAM - MUMBAI

# Hands-On System Programming with Linux

Copyright © 2018 Packt Publishing

All rights reserved. No part of this book may be reproduced, stored in a retrieval system, or transmitted in any form or by any means, without the prior written permission of the publisher, except in the case of brief quotations embedded in critical articles or reviews.

Every effort has been made in the preparation of this book to ensure the accuracy of the information presented. However, the information contained in this book is sold without warranty, either express or implied. Neither the author, nor Packt Publishing or its dealers and distributors, will be held liable for any damages caused or alleged to have been caused directly or indirectly by this book.

Packt Publishing has endeavored to provide trademark information about all of the companies and products mentioned in this book by the appropriate use of capitals. However, Packt Publishing cannot guarantee the accuracy of this information.

**Commissioning Editor:** Gebin George
**Acquisition Editor:** Rohit Rajkumar
**Content Development Editor:** Priyanka Deshpande
**Technical Editor:** Rutuja Patade
**Copy Editor:** Safis Editing
**Project Coordinator:** Drashti Panchal
**Proofreader:** Safis Editing
**Indexer:** Rekha Nair
**Graphics:** Tom Scaria
**Production Coordinator:** Arvindkumar Gupta

First published: October 2018

Production reference: 1311018

Published by Packt Publishing Ltd.
Livery Place
35 Livery Street
Birmingham
B3 2PB, UK.

ISBN 978-1-78899-847-5

www.packtpub.com

# Mapt

mapt.io

Mapt is an online digital library that gives you full access to over 5,000 books and videos, as well as industry leading tools to help you plan your personal development and advance your career. For more information, please visit our website.

## Why subscribe?

- Spend less time learning and more time coding with practical eBooks and Videos from over 4,000 industry professionals

- Improve your learning with Skill Plans built especially for you

- Get a free eBook or video every month

- Mapt is fully searchable

- Copy and paste, print, and bookmark content

## Packt.com

Did you know that Packt offers eBook versions of every book published, with PDF and ePub files available? You can upgrade to the eBook version at www.packt.com and as a print book customer, you are entitled to a discount on the eBook copy. Get in touch with us at customercare@packtpub.com for more details.

At www.packt.com, you can also read a collection of free technical articles, sign up for a range of free newsletters, and receive exclusive discounts and offers on Packt books and eBooks.

# Contributors

## About the author

**Kaiwan N Billimoria** taught himself programming on his dad's IBM PC back in 1983. He was programming in C and Assembly on DOS until he discovered the joys of Unix (via Richard Steven's iconic book, *UNIX Network Programming*, and by writing C code on SCO Unix).

Kaiwan has worked on many aspects of the Linux system programming stack, including Bash scripting, system programming in C, kernel internals, and embedded Linux work. He has actively worked on several commercial/OSS projects. His contributions include drivers to the mainline Linux OS, and many smaller projects hosted on GitHub. His Linux passion feeds well into his passion for teaching these topics to engineers, which he has done for over two decades now. It doesn't hurt that he is a recreational ultra-marathoner too.

> *Writing a book is a lot of hard work, tightly coupled with teamwork. My deep gratitude to the team at Packt: Rohit, Priyanka, and Rutuja, as well as the technical reviewer, Tigran, and so many other behind-the-scenes workers. Of course, none of this would have been remotely possible without support from my family: my parents, Diana and Nadir; my brother, Darius; my wife, Dilshad; and my super kids, Sheroy and Danesh! Heartfelt thanks to you all.*

## About the reviewer

**Tigran Aivazian** has a master's degree in computer science and a master's degree in theoretical physics. He has written BFS and Intel microcode update drivers that have become part of the official Linux kernel. He is the author of a book titled *Linux 2.4 Kernel Internals*, which is available in several languages on the Linux documentation project. He worked at Veritas as a Linux kernel architect, improving the kernel and teaching OS internals. Besides technological pursuits, Tigran has produced scholarly Bible editions in Hebrew, Greek, Syriac, Slavonic, and ancient Armenian. Recently, he published *The British Study Edition of the Urantia Papers*. He is currently working on the foundations of quantum mechanics in a branch of physics called quantum infodynamics.

## Packt is searching for authors like you

If you're interested in becoming an author for Packt, please visit `authors.packtpub.com` and apply today. We have worked with thousands of developers and tech professionals, just like you, to help them share their insight with the global tech community. You can make a general application, apply for a specific hot topic that we are recruiting an author for, or submit your own idea.

# Table of Contents

**Preface** — 1
**Chapter 1: Linux System Architecture** — 9
  **Technical requirements** — 9
  **Linux and the Unix operating system** — 10
  **The Unix philosophy in a nutshell** — 11
    Everything is a process – if it's not a process, it's a file — 12
    One tool to do one task — 15
    Three standard I/O channels — 17
      Word count — 18
      cat — 19
    Combine tools seamlessly — 21
    Plain text preferred — 23
    CLI, not GUI — 24
    Modular, designed to be repurposed by others — 24
    Provide mechanisms, not policies — 25
      Pseudocode — 25
  **Linux system architecture** — 27
    Preliminaries — 27
      The ABI — 27
      Accessing a register's content via inline assembly — 31
      Accessing a control register's content via inline assembly — 33
      CPU privilege levels — 34
        Privilege levels or rings on the x86 — 35
    Linux architecture — 38
      Libraries — 39
      System calls — 40
      Linux – a monolithic OS — 41
        What does that mean? — 42
  **Execution contexts within the kernel** — 46
    Process context — 47
    Interrupt context — 47
  **Summary** — 48
**Chapter 2: Virtual Memory** — 49
  **Technical requirements** — 49
  **Virtual memory** — 50
    No VM – the problem — 51
      Objective — 52
    Virtual memory — 54
      Addressing 1 – the simplistic flawed approach — 58
      Addressing 2 – paging in brief — 61

Table of Contents

        Paging tables – simplified — 63
        Indirection — 65
        Address-translation — 65
    Benefits of using VM — 66
        Process-isolation — 66
        The programmer need not worry about physical memory — 67
        Memory-region protection — 68
        SIDEBAR :: Testing the memcpy() C program — 69
**Process memory layout** — 73
    Segments or mappings — 74
        Text segment — 76
        Data segments — 76
        Library segments — 77
        Stack segment — 78
            What is stack memory? — 78
            Why a process stack? — 78
            Peeking at the stack — 81
    Advanced – the VM split — 84
**Summary** — 89

# Chapter 3: Resource Limits — 91
**Resource limits** — 91
**Granularity of resource limits** — 93
    Resource types — 94
        Available resource limits — 94
**Hard and soft limits** — 96
    Querying and changing resource limit values — 99
        Caveats — 101
        A quick note on the prlimit utility — 102
            Using prlimit(1) – examples — 102
    API interfaces — 105
        Code examples — 107
    Permanence — 112
**Summary** — 113

# Chapter 4: Dynamic Memory Allocation — 115
**The glibc malloc(3) API family** — 116
    The malloc(3) API — 116
        malloc(3) – some FAQs — 119
        malloc(3) – a quick summary — 124
    The free API — 124
        free – a quick summary — 126
    The calloc API — 126
    The realloc API — 127
        The realloc(3) – corner cases — 128
        The reallocarray API — 129
**Beyond the basics** — 130
    The program break — 130
    Using the sbrk() API — 130

[ ii ]

How malloc(3) really behaves — 134
Code example – malloc(3) and the program break — 135
Scenario 1 – default options — 135
Scenario 2 – showing malloc statistics — 136
Scenario 3 – large allocations option — 137
Where does freed memory go? — 138
Advanced features — 138
Demand-paging — 139
Resident or not? — 141
Locking memory — 142
Limits and privileges — 143
Locking all pages — 147
Memory protection — 148
Memory protection – a code example — 149
An Aside – LSM logs, Ftrace — 157
LSM logs — 157
Ftrace — 158
An experiment – running the memprot program on an ARM-32 — 158
Memory protection keys – a brief note — 161
Using alloca to allocate automatic memory — 161
Summary — 165

## Chapter 5: Linux Memory Issues — 167
Common memory issues — 168
Incorrect memory accesses — 170
Accessing and/or using uninitialized variables — 171
Test case 1: Uninitialized memory access — 171
Out-of-bounds memory accesses — 173
Test case 2 — 173
Test case 3 — 174
Test case 4 — 175
Test case 5 — 176
Test case 6 — 177
Test case 7 — 178
Use-after-free/Use-after-return bugs — 179
Test case 8 — 180
Test case 9 — 181
Test case 10 — 182
Leakage — 185
Test case 11 — 185
Test case 12 — 187
Test case 13 — 190
Test case 13.1 — 191
Test case 13.2 — 192
Test case 13.3 — 194
Undefined behavior — 195
Fragmentation — 196
Miscellaneous — 197
Summary — 198

## Chapter 6: Debugging Tools for Memory Issues — 199
Tool types — 200

[ iii ]

*Table of Contents*

Valgrind — 201
    Using Valgrind's Memcheck tool — 201
    Valgrind summary table — 213
    Valgrind pros and cons : a quick summary — 213
Sanitizer tools — 214
    Sanitizer toolset — 215
    Building programs for use with ASan — 216
    Running the test cases with ASan — 217
    AddressSanitizer (ASan) summary table — 230
    AddressSanitizer pros and cons – a quick summary — 231
Glibc mallopt — 233
    Malloc options via the environment — 235
**Some key points** — 236
    Code coverage while testing — 236
    What is the modern C/C++ developer to do? — 237
    A mention of the malloc API helpers — 237
**Summary** — 239

**Chapter 7: Process Credentials** — 241
  **The traditional Unix permissions model** — 242
    Permissions at the user level — 243
    How the Unix permission model works — 243
        Determining the access category — 246
    Real and effective IDs — 248
        A puzzle – how can a regular user change their password? — 251
    The setuid and setgid special permission bits — 253
        Setting the setuid and setgid bits with chmod — 254
        Hacking attempt 1 — 255
  System calls — 258
    Querying the process credentials — 258
        Code example — 259
        Sudo – how it works — 260
        What is a saved-set ID? — 261
    Setting the process credentials — 261
        Hacking attempt 2 — 262
    An aside – a script to identify setuid-root and setgid installed programs — 266
        setgid example – wall — 268
        Giving up privileges — 271
        Saved-set UID – a quick demo — 272
        The setres[u|g]id(2) system calls — 275
    Important security notes — 277
  **Summary** — 278

**Chapter 8: Process Capabilities** — 279
  **The modern POSIX capabilities model** — 280
    Motivation — 280
    POSIX capabilities — 281
    Capabilities – some gory details — 284
        OS support — 284

[ iv ]

| | |
|---|---|
| Viewing process capabilities via procfs | 284 |
| Thread capability sets | 286 |
| File capability sets | 287 |
| Embedding capabilities into a program binary | 288 |
| Capability-dumb binaries | 292 |
| Getcap and similar utilities | 292 |
| Wireshark – a case in point | 293 |
| Setting capabilities programmatically | 294 |

## Miscellaneous — 300
| | |
|---|---|
| How ls displays different binaries | 300 |
| Permission models layering | 301 |
| Security tips | 302 |
| FYI – under the hood, at the level of the Kernel | 302 |

## Summary — 303

## Chapter 9: Process Execution — 305
### Technical requirements — 305
### Process execution — 306
| | |
|---|---|
| Converting a program to a process | 306 |
| The exec Unix axiom | 307 |
| Key points during an exec operation | 308 |
| Testing the exec axiom | 309 |
| Experiment 1 – on the CLI, no frills | 310 |
| Experiment 2 – on the CLI, again | 310 |
| The point of no return | 311 |
| Family time – the exec family APIs | 312 |
| The wrong way | 315 |
| Error handling and the exec | 315 |
| Passing a zero as an argument | 315 |
| Specifying the name of the successor | 316 |
| The remaining exec family APIs | 319 |
| The execlp API | 319 |
| The execle API | 321 |
| The execv API | 321 |
| Exec at the OS level | 322 |
| Summary table – exec family of APIs | 323 |
| Code example | 324 |

### Summary — 327

## Chapter 10: Process Creation — 329
### Process creation — 330
| | |
|---|---|
| How fork works | 330 |
| Using the fork system call | 333 |
| Fork rule #1 | 334 |
| Fork rule #2 – the return | 335 |
| Fork rule #3 | 341 |
| Atomic execution? | 343 |
| Fork rule #4 – data | 343 |
| Fork rule #5 – racing | 344 |
| The process and open files | 345 |

## Table of Contents

| | |
|---|---|
| Fork rule #6 – open files | 347 |
| Open files and security | 349 |
| Malloc and the fork | 350 |
| COW in a nutshell | 352 |
| Waiting and our simpsh project | 353 |
| The Unix fork-exec semantic | 354 |
| The need to wait | 355 |
| Performing the wait | 356 |
| Defeating the race after fork | 356 |
| Putting it together – our simpsh project | 357 |
| The wait API – details | 361 |
| The scenarios of wait | 364 |
| Wait scenario #1 | 365 |
| Wait scenario #2 | 365 |
| Fork bombs and creating more than one child | 366 |
| Wait scenario #3 | 368 |
| Variations on the wait – APIs | 368 |
| The waitpid(2) | 368 |
| The waitid (2) | 371 |
| The actual system call | 372 |
| A note on the vfork | 374 |
| More Unix weirdness | 374 |
| Orphans | 374 |
| Zombies | 375 |
| Fork rule #7 | 376 |
| The rules of fork – a summary | 377 |
| **Summary** | 377 |
| **Chapter 11: Signaling - Part I** | 379 |
| **Why signals?** | 380 |
| The signal mechanism in brief | 380 |
| **Available signals** | 383 |
| The standard or Unix signals | 384 |
| **Handling signals** | 387 |
| Using the sigaction system call to trap signals | 388 |
| Sidebar – the feature test macros | 389 |
| The sigaction structure | 389 |
| Masking signals | 394 |
| Signal masking with the sigprocmask API | 394 |
| Querying the signal mask | 395 |
| Sidebar – signal handling within the OS – polling not interrupts | 398 |
| Reentrant safety and signalling | 398 |
| Reentrant functions | 398 |
| Async-signal-safe functions | 400 |
| Alternate ways to be safe within a signal handler | 400 |
| Signal-safe atomic integers | 401 |
| Powerful sigaction flags | 404 |
| Zombies not invited | 405 |
| No zombies! – the classic way | 406 |
| No zombies! – the modern way | 407 |
| The SA_NOCLDSTOP flag | 409 |

[ vi ]

| | |
|---|---|
| Interrupted system calls and how to fix them with the SA_RESTART | 409 |
| The once only SA_RESETHAND flag | 411 |
| To defer or not? Working with SA_NODEFER | 412 |
| Signal behavior when masked | 412 |
| Case 1 : Default : SA_NODEFER bit cleared | 413 |
| Case 2 : SA_NODEFER bit set | 414 |
| Running of case 1 – SA_NODEFER bit cleared [default] | 418 |
| Running of case 2 – SA_NODEFER bit set | 419 |
| Using an alternate signal stack | 422 |
| Implementation to handle high-volume signals with an alternate signal stack | 423 |
| Case 1 – very small (100 KB) alternate signal stack | 425 |
| Case 2 : A large (16 MB) alternate signal stack | 426 |
| Different approaches to handling signals at high volume | 427 |
| **Summary** | **427** |
| **Chapter 12: Signaling - Part II** | **429** |
| **Gracefully handling process crashes** | **430** |
| Detailing information with the SA_SIGINFO | 430 |
| The siginfo_t structure | 431 |
| Getting system-level details when a process crashes | 435 |
| Trapping and extracting information from a crash | 436 |
| Register dumping | 441 |
| Finding the crash location in source code | 445 |
| **Signaling – caveats and gotchas** | **447** |
| Handling errno gracefully | 447 |
| What does errno do? | 447 |
| The errno race | 448 |
| Fixing the errno race | 449 |
| Sleeping correctly | 450 |
| The nanosleep system call | 451 |
| **Real-time signals** | **454** |
| Differences from standard signals | 455 |
| Real time signals and priority | 456 |
| **Sending signals** | **460** |
| Just kill 'em | 460 |
| Killing yourself with a raise | 461 |
| Agent 00 – permission to kill | 461 |
| Are you there? | 462 |
| Signaling as IPC | 463 |
| Crude IPC | 463 |
| Better IPC – sending a data item | 464 |
| Sidebar – LTTng | 469 |
| **Alternative signal-handling techniques** | **471** |
| Synchronously waiting for signals | 471 |
| Pause, please | 472 |
| Waiting forever or until a signal arrives | 472 |
| Synchronously blocking for signals via the sigwait* APIs | 473 |
| The sigwait library API | 473 |
| The sigwaitinfo and the sigtimedwait system calls | 478 |
| The signalfd(2) API | 479 |

*Table of Contents*

| | |
|---|---|
| Summary | 482 |
| **Chapter 13: Timers** | **483** |
| Older interfaces | 484 |
| The good ol' alarm clock | 484 |
| Alarm API – the downer | 487 |
| Interval timers | 487 |
| A simple CLI digital clock | 491 |
| Obtaining the current time | 493 |
| Trial runs | 495 |
| A word on using the profiling timers | 496 |
| The newer POSIX (interval) timers mechanism | 498 |
| Typical application workflow | 499 |
| Creating and using a POSIX (interval) timer | 499 |
| The arms race – arming and disarming a POSIX timer | 502 |
| Querying the timer | 504 |
| Example code snippet showing the workflow | 504 |
| Figuring the overrun | 507 |
| POSIX interval timers – example programs | 508 |
| The reaction – time game | 508 |
| How fast is fast? | 508 |
| Our react game – how it works | 509 |
| React – trial runs | 511 |
| The react game – code view | 513 |
| The run:walk interval timer application | 517 |
| A few trial runs | 518 |
| The low – level design and code | 520 |
| Timer lookup via proc | 524 |
| A quick mention | 525 |
| Timers via file descriptors | 525 |
| A quick note on watchdog timers | 527 |
| Summary | 528 |
| **Chapter 14: Multithreading with Pthreads Part I - Essentials** | **529** |
| Multithreading concepts | 530 |
| What exactly is a thread? | 530 |
| Resource sharing | 531 |
| Multiprocess versus multithreaded | 535 |
| Example 1 – creation/destruction – process/thread | 536 |
| The multithreading model | 537 |
| Example 2 – matrix multiplication – process/thread | 539 |
| Example 3 – kernel build | 544 |
| On a VM with 1 GB RAM, two CPU cores and parallelized make -j4 | 544 |
| On a VM with 1 GB RAM, one CPU core and sequential make -j1 | 546 |
| Motivation – why threads? | 547 |
| Design motivation | 547 |
| Taking advantage of potential parallelism | 547 |
| Logical separation | 548 |
| Overlapping CPU with I/O | 548 |
| Manager-worker model | 549 |
| IPC becoming simple(r) | 549 |

[ viii ]

| | |
|---|---|
| Performance motivation | 549 |
| Creation and destruction | 549 |
| Automatically taking advantage of modern hardware | 549 |
| Resource sharing | 550 |
| Context switching | 550 |
| A brief history of threading | 551 |
| POSIX threads | 551 |
| Pthreads and Linux | 552 |
| **Thread management – the essential pthread APIs** | **553** |
| Thread creation | 554 |
| Termination | 557 |
| The return of the ghost | 559 |
| So many ways to die | 562 |
| How many threads is too many? | 562 |
| How many threads can you create? | 564 |
| Code example – creating any number of threads | 566 |
| How many threads should one create? | 568 |
| Thread attributes | 570 |
| Code example – querying the default thread attributes | 571 |
| Joining | 574 |
| The thread model join and the process model wait | 579 |
| Checking for life, timing out | 580 |
| Join or not? | 581 |
| Parameter passing | 582 |
| Passing a structure as a parameter | 583 |
| Thread parameters – what not to do | 585 |
| Thread stacks | 587 |
| Get and set thread stack size | 587 |
| Stack location | 588 |
| Stack guards | 590 |
| **Summary** | **594** |
| **Chapter 15: Multithreading with Pthreads Part II - Synchronization** | **595** |
| **The racing problem** | **596** |
| Concurrency and atomicity | 597 |
| The pedagogical bank account example | 597 |
| Critical sections | 600 |
| **Locking concepts** | **601** |
| Is it atomic? | 603 |
| Dirty reads | 607 |
| Locking guidelines | 608 |
| Locking granularity | 610 |
| Deadlock and its avoidance | 611 |
| Common deadlock types | 612 |
| Self deadlock (relock) | 612 |
| The ABBA deadlock | 612 |
| Avoiding deadlock | 613 |
| **Using the pthread APIs for synchronization** | **614** |
| The mutex lock | 615 |

[ ix ]

| | |
|---|---|
| Seeing the race | 618 |
| Mutex attributes | 621 |
| Mutex types | 621 |
| The robust mutex attribute | 623 |
| IPC, threads, and the process-shared mutex | 625 |
| Priority inversion, watchdogs, and Mars | 631 |
| Priority inversion | 631 |
| Watchdog timer in brief | 633 |
| The Mars Pathfinder mission in brief | 635 |
| Priority inheritance – avoiding priority inversion | 636 |
| Summary of mutex attribute usage | 638 |
| Mutex locking – additional variants | 639 |
| Timing out on a mutex lock attempt | 639 |
| Busy-waiting (non-blocking variant) for the lock | 640 |
| The reader-writer mutex lock | 640 |
| The spinlock variant | 642 |
| A few more mutex usage guidelines | 644 |
| Is the mutex locked? | 645 |
| Condition variables | 646 |
| No CV – the naive approach | 647 |
| Using the condition variable | 647 |
| A simple CV usage demo application | 649 |
| CV broadcast wakeup | 653 |
| **Summary** | 655 |

## Chapter 16: Multithreading with Pthreads Part III — 657

| | |
|---|---|
| **Thread safety** | 657 |
| Making code thread-safe | 660 |
| Reentrant-safe versus thread-safe | 660 |
| Summary table – approaches to making functions thread-safe | 662 |
| Thread safety via mutex locks | 662 |
| Thread safety via function refactoring | 665 |
| The standard C library and thread safety | 667 |
| List of APIs not required to be thread-safe | 667 |
| Refactoring glibc APIs from foo to foo_r | 668 |
| Some glibc foo and foo_r APIs | 670 |
| Thread safety via TLS | 671 |
| Thread safety via TSD | 673 |
| **Thread cancelation and cleanup** | 674 |
| Canceling a thread | 674 |
| The thread cancelation framework | 675 |
| The cancelability state | 675 |
| The cancelability type | 676 |
| Canceling a thread – a code example | 679 |
| Cleaning up at thread exit | 681 |
| Thread cleanup – code example | 682 |
| **Threads and signaling** | 684 |
| The issue | 685 |
| The POSIX solution to handling signals on MT | 685 |
| Code example – handling signals in an MT app | 686 |
| **Threads vs processes – look again** | 688 |

*Table of Contents*

| | |
|---|---|
| The multiprocess vs the multithreading model – pros of the MT model | 689 |
| The multiprocess vs the multithreading model – cons of the MT model | 690 |
| **Pthreads – a few random tips and FAQs** | **691** |
| Pthreads – some FAQs | 691 |
| Debugging multithreaded (pthreads) applications with GDB | 692 |
| **Summary** | **694** |
| **Chapter 17: CPU Scheduling on Linux** | **695** |
| **The Linux OS and the POSIX scheduling model** | **695** |
| The Linux process state machine | 696 |
| The sleep states | 697 |
| What is real time? | 699 |
| Types of real time | 700 |
| Scheduling policies | 701 |
| Peeking at the scheduling policy and priority | 703 |
| The nice value | 704 |
| CPU affinity | 705 |
| **Exploiting Linux's soft real-time capabilities** | **708** |
| Scheduling policy and priority APIs | 708 |
| Code example – setting a thread scheduling policy and priority | 710 |
| Soft real-time – additional considerations | 715 |
| **RTL – Linux as an RTOS** | **716** |
| **Summary** | **717** |
| **Chapter 18: Advanced File I/O** | **719** |
| **I/O performance recommendations** | **720** |
| The kernel page cache | 721 |
| Giving hints to the kernel on file I/O patterns | 722 |
| Via the posix_fadvise(2) API | 722 |
| Via the readahead(2) API | 723 |
| MT app file I/O with the pread, pwrite APIs | 724 |
| Scatter – gather I/O | 726 |
| Discontiguous data file – traditional approach | 726 |
| Discontiguous data file – the SG – I/O approach | 728 |
| SG – I/O variations | 731 |
| File I/O via memory mapping | 731 |
| The Linux I/O code path in brief | 732 |
| Memory mapping a file for I/O | 735 |
| File and anonymous mappings | 738 |
| The mmap advantage | 740 |
| Code example | 742 |
| Memory mapping – additional points | 742 |
| DIO and AIO | 744 |
| Direct I/O (DIO) | 744 |
| Asynchronous I/O (AIO) | 745 |
| I/O technologies – a quick comparison | 746 |
| Multiplexing or async blocking I/O – a quick note | 747 |
| I/O – miscellaneous | 748 |

[ xi ]

*Table of Contents*

   Linux's inotify framework   748
   I/O schedulers   748
   Ensuring sufficient disk space   750
   Utilities for I/O monitoring, analysis, and bandwidth control   751
 **Summary**   752

## Chapter 19: Troubleshooting and Best Practices   753
 **Troubleshooting tools**   754
  perf   754
  Tracing tools   755
  The Linux proc filesystem   755
 **Best practices**   756
  The empirical approach   756
  Software engineering wisdom in a nutshell   756
  Programming   757
   A programmer's checklist – seven rules   757
   Better testing   758
   Using the Linux kernel's control groups   758
 **Summary**   759

## Other Books You May Enjoy   761

## Index   765

[ xii ]

# Preface

The Linux OS and its embedded and server applications are critical components of today's key software infrastructure in a decentralized and networked universe. Industry demand for proficient Linux developers is ever-increasing. This book aims to give you two things: a solid theoretical base, and practical, industry-relevant information—illustrated by code—covering the Linux system programming domain. This book delves into the art and science of Linux system programming, including system architecture, virtual memory, process memory and management, signaling, timers, multithreading, scheduling, and file I/O.

This book attempts to go beyond the use API X to do Y approach; it takes pains to explain the concepts and theory required to understand the programming interfaces, the design decisions, and trade-offs made by experienced developers when using them and the rationale behind them. Troubleshooting tips and industry best practices round out the book's coverage. By the end of this book, you will have the conceptual knowledge, as well as the hands-on experience, needed for working with Linux system programming interfaces.

## Who this book is for

*Hands-On System Programming with Linux* is for Linux professionals: system engineers, programmers, and testers (QA). It's also for students; anyone, really, who wants to go beyond using an API set to understand the theoretical underpinnings and concepts behind the powerful Linux system programming APIs. You should be familiar with Linux at the user level, including aspects such as logging in, using the shell via the command-line interface, and using tools such as find, grep, and sort. A working knowledge of the C programming language is required. No prior experience with Linux systems programming is assumed.

## What this book covers

`Chapter 1`, *Linux System Architecture*, covers the key basics: the Unix design philosophy and the Linux system architecture. Along the way, other important aspects—CPU privilege levels, the processor ABI, and what system calls really are—are dealt with.

Preface

Chapter 2, *Virtual Memory*, dives into clearing up common misconceptions about what virtual memory really is and why it is key to modern OS design; the layout of the process virtual address space is covered too.

Chapter 3, *Resource Limits*, delves into the topic of per-process resource limits and the APIs governing their usage.

Chapter 4, *Dynamic Memory Allocation*, initially covers the basics of the popular malloc family of APIs, then dives into more advanced aspects, such as the program break, how malloc really behaves, demand paging, memory locking and protection, and using the alloca function.

Chapter 5, *Linux Memory Issues*, introduces you to the (unfortunately) prevalent memory defects that end up in our projects due to a lack of understanding of the correct design and use of memory APIs. Defects such as undefined behavior (in general), overflow and underflow bugs, leakage, and others are covered.

Chapter 6, *Debugging Tools for Memory Issues*, shows how to leverage existing tools, including the compiler itself, Valgrind, and AddressSanitizer, which is used to detect the memory issues you will have seen in the previous chapter.

Chapter 7, *Process Credentials*, is the first of two chapters focused on having you think about and understand security and privilege from a system perspective. Here, you'll learn about the traditional security model – a set of process credentials – as well as the APIs for manipulating them. Importantly, the concepts of setuid-root processes and their security repercussions are delved into.

Chapter 8, *Process Capabilities*, introduces you to the modern POSIX capabilities model and how security can benefit when application developers learn to use and leverage this model instead of the traditional model (seen in the previous chapter). What capabilities are, how to embed them, and practical design for security is also looked into.

Chapter 9, *Process Execution*, is the first of four chapters dealing with the broad area of process management (execution, creation, and signaling). In this particular chapter, you'll learn how the (rather unusual) Unix exec axiom behaves and how to use the API set (the exec family) to exploit it.

Chapter 10, *Process Creation*, delves into how exactly the `fork(2)` system call behaves and should be used; we depict this via our seven rules of fork. The Unix fork-exec-wait semantic is described (diving into the wait APIs as well), orphan and zombie processes are also covered.

Chapter 11, *Signaling – Part I*, deals with the important topic of signals on the Linux platform: the what, the why, and the how. We cover the powerful `sigaction(2)` system call here, along with topics such as reentrant and signal-async safety, sigaction flags, signal stacks, and others.

Chapter 12, *Signaling – Part II*, continues our coverage of signaling, what with it being a large topic. We take you through the correct way to write a signal handler for the well-known and fatal segfault, working with real-time signals, delivering signal to processes, performing IPC with signals, and alternate means to handle signals.

Chapter 13, *Timers*, teaches you about the important (and signal-related) topic of how to set up and handle timers in real-world Linux applications. We first cover the traditional timer APIs and quickly move onto the modern POSIX interval timers and how to use them to this end. Two interesting, small projects are presented and walked through.

Chapter 14, *Multithreading with Pthreads Part I – Essentials*, is the first of a trilogy on multithreading with the pthreads framework on Linux. Here, we introduce you to what exactly a thread is, how it differs from a process, and the motivation (in terms of design and performance) for using threads. The chapter then guides you through the essentials of writing a pthreads application on Linux, covering thread creation, termination, joining, and more.

Chapter 15, *Multithreading with Pthreads Part II – Synchronization*, is a chapter dedicated to the really important topic of synchronization and race prevention. You will first understand the issue at hand, then delve into the key topics of atomicity, locking, deadlock prevention, and others. Next, the chapter teaches you how to use pthreads synchronization APIs with respect to the mutex lock and condition variables.

Chapter 16, *Multithreading with Pthreads Part III*, completes our work on multithreading; we shed light on the key topics of thread safety, thread cancellation and cleanup, and handling signals in a multithreaded app. We round off the chapter with a discussion on the pros and cons of multithreading and address some FAQs.

*Preface*

Chapter 17, *CPU Scheduling on Linux*, introduces you to scheduling-related topics that the system programmer should be aware of. We cover the Linux process/thread state machine, the notion of real time and the three (minimal) POSIX CPU scheduling policies that the Linux OS brings to the table. Exploiting the available APIs, you'll learn how to write a soft real-time app on Linux. We finish the chapter with a brief look at the (interesting!) fact that Linux *can* be patched to work as an RTOS.

Chapter 18, *Advanced File I/O*, is completely focused on the more advanced ways of performing IO on Linux in order to gain maximum performance (as IO is often the bottleneck). You are briefly shown how the Linux IO stack is architected (the page cache being critical), and the APIs that give advice to the OS on file access patterns. Writing IO code for performance, as you'll learn, involves the use of technologies such as SG-I/O, memory mapping, DIO, and AIO.

Chapter 19, *Troubleshooting and Best Practices*, is a critical summation of the key points to do with troubleshooting on Linux. You'll be briefed upon the use of powerful tools, such as perf and tracing tools. Then, very importantly, the chapter attempts to summarize key points on software engineering in general and programming on Linux in particular, looking at industry best practices. We feel these are critical takeaways for any programmer.

Appendix A, File I/O Essentials, introduces you to performing efficient file I/O on the Linux platform, via both the streaming (stdio library layer) API set as well as the underlying system calls. Along the way, important information on buffering and its effects on performance are covered.

For this chapter refer to: https://www.packtpub.com/sites/default/files/downloads/File_IO_Essentials.pdf.

Appendix B, Daemon Processes, introduces you, in a succinct fashion, to the world of the daemon process on Linux. You'll be shown how to write a traditional SysV-style daemon process. There is also a brief note on what is involved in constructing a modern, new-style daemon process.

For this chapter refer to: https://www.packtpub.com/sites/default/files/downloads/Daemon_Processes.pdf.

# To get the most out of this book

As mentioned earlier, this book is targeted at both Linux software professionals—be they developers, programmers, architects, or QA staff members—as well as serious students looking to expand their knowledge and skills with the key topics of system programming on the Linux OS.

We assume that you are familiar with using a Linux system via the command-line interface, the shell. We also assume that you are familiar with programming in the C language, know how to use the editor and the compiler, and are familiar with the basics of the Makefile. We do *not* assume that you have any prior knowledge of the topics covered in the book.

To get the most out of this book—and we are very clear on this point—you must not just read the material, but must also actively work on, try out, and modify the code examples provided, and try and finish the assignments as well! Why?
Simple: doing is what really teaches you and internalizes a topic; making mistakes and fixing them being an essential part of the learning process. We always advocate an empirical approach—don't take anything at face value. Experiment, try it out for yourself, and see.

To this end, we urge you to clone this book's GitHub repository (see the following section for instructions), browse through the files, and try them out. Using a **Virtual Machine (VM)** for experimentation is (quite obviously) definitely recommended (we have tested the code on both Ubuntu 18.04 LTS and Fedora 27/28). A listing of mandatory and optional software packages to install on the system is also provided within the book's GitHub repository; please read through and install all required utilities to get the best experience.

Last, but definitely not least, each chapter has a *Further reading* section, where additional online links and books (in some cases) are mentioned; we urge you to browse through these. You will find the *Further reading* material for each chapter available on the book's GitHub repository.

# Download the example code files

You can download the example code files for this book from your account at `www.packt.com`. If you purchased this book elsewhere, you can visit `www.packt.com/support` and register to have the files emailed directly to you.

*Preface*

You can download the code files by following these steps:

1. Log in or register at `www.packt.com`.
2. Select the **SUPPORT** tab.
3. Click on **Code Downloads & Errata**.
4. Enter the name of the book in the **Search** box and follow the onscreen instructions.

Once the file is downloaded, please make sure that you unzip or extract the folder using the latest version of:

- WinRAR/7-Zip for Windows
- Zipeg/iZip/UnRarX for Mac
- 7-Zip/PeaZip for Linux

The code bundle for the book is also hosted on GitHub at `https://github.com/PacktPublishing/Hands-on-System-Programming-with-Linux`. We also have other code bundles from our rich catalog of books and videos available at `https://github.com/PacktPublishing/`. Check them out.

# Download the color images

We also provide a PDF file that has color images of the screenshots/diagrams used in this book. You can download it here: `https://www.packtpub.com/sites/default/files/downloads/9781788998475_ColorImages.pdf`

# Conventions used

There are a number of text conventions used throughout this book.

`CodeInText`: Indicates code words in text, database table names, folder names, filenames, file extensions, pathnames, dummy URLs, user input, and Twitter handles. Here is an example: "Let's check these out via the source code of our `membugs.c` program."

A block of code is set as follows:

```
include <pthread.h>
int pthread_mutexattr_gettype(const pthread_mutexattr_t *restrict
attr,     int *restrict type);
int pthread_mutexattr_settype(pthread_mutexattr_t *attr, int type);
```

When we wish to draw your attention to a particular part of a code block, the relevant lines or items are set in bold:

```
include <pthread.h>
int pthread_mutexattr_gettype(const pthread_mutexattr_t *restrict
attr,       int *restrict type);
int pthread_mutexattr_settype(pthread_mutexattr_t *attr, int type);
```

Any command-line input or output is written as follows:

```
$ ./membugs 3
```

**Bold**: Indicates a new term, an important word, or words that you see onscreen. For example, words in menus or dialog boxes appear in the text like this. Here is an example: "Select **C** as the language via the drop-down."

> Warnings or important notes appear like this.

> Tips and tricks appear like this.

# Get in touch

Feedback from our readers is always welcome.

**General feedback**: Email `customercare@packtpub.com` and mention the book title in the subject of your message. If you have questions about any aspect of this book, please email us at `customercare@packtpub.com`.

**Errata**: Although we have taken every care to ensure the accuracy of our content, mistakes do happen. If you have found a mistake in this book, we would be grateful if you would report this to us. Please visit www.packt.com/submit-errata, selecting your book, clicking on the Errata Submission Form link, and entering the details.

**Piracy**: If you come across any illegal copies of our works in any form on the Internet, we would be grateful if you would provide us with the location address or website name. Please contact us at `copyright@packt.com` with a link to the material.

**If you are interested in becoming an author**: If there is a topic that you have expertise in and you are interested in either writing or contributing to a book, please visit `authors.packtpub.com`.

# Reviews

Please leave a review. Once you have read and used this book, why not leave a review on the site that you purchased it from? Potential readers can then see and use your unbiased opinion to make purchase decisions, we at Packt can understand what you think about our products, and our authors can see your feedback on their book. Thank you!

For more information about Packt, please visit `packt.com`.

# 1
# Linux System Architecture

This chapter informs the reader about the system architecture of the Linux ecosystem. It first conveys the elegant Unix philosophy and design fundamentals, then delves into the details of the Linux system architecture. The importance of the ABI, CPU privilege levels, and how modern **operating systems** (**OSes**) exploit them, along with the Linux system architecture's layering, and how Linux is a monolithic architecture, will be covered. The (simplified) flow of a system call API, as well as kernel-code execution contexts, are key points.

In this chapter, the reader will be taken through the following topics:

- The Unix philosophy in a nutshell
- Architecture preliminaries
- Linux architecture layers
- Linux—a monolithic OS
- Kernel execution contexts

Along the way, we'll use simple examples to make the key philosophical and architectural points clear.

## Technical requirements

A modern desktop PC or laptop is required; Ubuntu Desktop specifies the following as recommended system requirements for installation and usage of the distribution:

- 2 GHz dual core processor or better
- RAM
    - **Running on a physical host**: 2 GB or more system memory
    - **Running as a guest**: The host system should have at least 4 GB RAM (the more, the better and smoother the experience)

- 25 GB of free hard drive space
- Either a DVD drive or a USB port for the installer media
- Internet access is definitely helpful

We recommend the reader use one of the following Linux distributions (can be installed as a guest OS on a Windows or Linux host system, as mentioned):

- Ubuntu 18.04 LTS Desktop (Ubuntu 16.04 LTS Desktop is a good choice too as it has long term support as well, and pretty much everything should work)
    - Ubuntu Desktop download link: https://www.ubuntu.com/download/desktop
- Fedora 27 (Workstation)
    - Download link: https://getfedora.org/en_GB/workstation/download/

Note that these distributions are, in their default form, OSS and non-proprietary, and free to use as an end user.

> There are instances where the entire code snippet isn't included in the book. Thus the GitHub URL to refer the codes: https://github.com/PacktPublishing/Hands-on-System-Programming-with-Linux.
> Also, for the *Further reading* section, refer to the preceding GitHub link.

# Linux and the Unix operating system

Moore's law famously states that the number of transistors in an IC will double (approximately) every two years (with an addendum that the cost would halve at pretty much the same rate). This law, which remained quite accurate for many years, is one of the things that clearly underscored what people came to realize, and even celebrate, about the electronics and the **Information Technology** (**IT**) industry; the sheer speed with which innovation and paradigm shifts in technology occur here is unparalleled. So much so that we now hardly raise an eyebrow when, every year, even every few months in some cases, new innovations and technology appear, challenge, and ultimately discard the old with little ceremony.

Against this backdrop of rapid all-consuming change, there lives an engaging anomaly: an OS whose essential design, philosophy, and architecture have changed hardly at all in close to five decades. Yes, we are referring to the venerable Unix operating system.

Organically emerging from a doomed project at AT&T's Bell Labs (Multics) in around 1969, Unix took the world by storm. Well, for a while at least.

But, you say, this is a book about Linux; why all this information about Unix? Simply because, at heart, Linux is the latest avatar of the venerable Unix OS. Linux is a Unix-like operating system (among several others). The code, by legal necessity, is unique; however, the design, philosophy, and architecture of Linux are pretty much identical to those of Unix.

# The Unix philosophy in a nutshell

To understand anyone (or anything), one must strive to first understand their (or its) underlying philosophy; to begin to understand Linux is to begin to understand the Unix philosophy. Here, we shall not attempt to delve into every minute detail; rather, an overall understanding of the essentials of the Unix philosophy is our goal. Also, when we use the term Unix, we very much also mean Linux!

The way that software (particularly, tools) is designed, built, and maintained on Unix slowly evolved into what might even be called a pattern that stuck: the Unix design philosophy. At its heart, here are the pillars of the Unix philosophy, design, and architecture:

- Everything is a process; if it's not a process, it's a file
- One tool to do one task
- Three standard I/O channel
- Combine tools seamlessly
- Plain text preferred
- CLI, not GUI
- Modular, designed to be repurposed by others
- Provide the mechanism, not the policy

Let's examine these pillars a little more closely, shall we?

*Linux System Architecture*

# Everything is a process – if it's not a process, it's a file

A process is an instance of a program in execution. A file is an object on the filesystem; beside regular file with plain text or binary content; it could also be a directory, a symbolic link, a device-special file, a named pipe, or a (Unix-domain) socket.

The Unix design philosophy abstracts peripheral devices (such as the keyboard, monitor, mouse, a sensor, and touchscreen) as files – what it calls device files. By doing this, Unix allows the application programmer to conveniently ignore the details and just treat (peripheral) devices as though they are ordinary disk files.

The kernel provides a layer to handle this very abstraction – it's called the **Virtual Filesystem Switch** (**VFS**). So, with this in place, the application developer can open a device file and perform I/O (reads and writes) upon it, all using the usual API interfaces provided (relax, these APIs will be covered in a subsequent chapter).

In fact, every process inherits three files on creation:

- **Standard input** (`stdin`: **fd 0**): The keyboard device, by default
- **Standard output** (`stdout`: **fd 1**): The monitor (or terminal) device, by default
- **Standard error** (`stderr`: **fd 2**): The monitor (or terminal) device, by default

> **fd** is the common abbreviation, especially in code, for **file descriptor**; it's an integer value that refers to the open file in question.
>
> Also, note that we mention it's a certain device by default – this implies the defaults can be changed. Indeed, this is a key part of the design: changing standard input, output, or error channels is called **redirection**, and by using the familiar <, > and 2> shell operators, these file channels are redirected to other files or devices.

On Unix, there exists a class of programs called **filters**.

> A filter is a program that reads from its standard input, possibly modifies the input, and writes the filtered result to its standard output.

Filters on Unix are very common utilities, such as `cat`, `wc`, `sort`, `grep`, `perl`, `head`, and `tail`.

Filters allow Unix to easily sidestep design and code complexity. How?

Let's take the `sort` filter as a quick example. Okay, we'll need some data to sort. Let's say we run the following commands:

```
$ cat fruit.txt
orange
banana
apple
pear
grape
pineapple
lemon
cherry
papaya
mango
$
```

Now we consider four scenarios of using `sort`; based on the parameter(s) we pass, we are actually performing explicit or implicit input-, output-, and/or error-redirection!

**Scenario 1**: Sort a file alphabetically (one parameter, input implicitly redirected to file):

```
$ sort fruit.txt
 apple
 banana
 cherry
 grape
 lemon
 mango
 orange
 papaya
 pear
 pineapple
$
```

All right!

Hang on a second, though. If `sort` is a filter (and it is), it should read from its `stdin` (the keyboard) and write to its `stdout` (the terminal). It is indeed writing to the terminal device, but it's reading from a file, `fruit.txt`.

This is deliberate; if a parameter is provided, the sort program treats it as standard input, as clearly seen.

Also, note that `sort fruit.txt` is identical to `sort < fruit.txt`.

**Scenario 2**: Sort any given input alphabetically (no parameters, input and output from and to stdin/stdout):

```
$ sort
mango
apple
pear
^D
apple
mango
pear
$
```

Once you type `sort` and press the *Enter* key, and the sort process comes alive and just waits. Why? It's waiting for you, the user, to type something. Why? Recall, every process by default reads its input from standard input or stdin – the keyboard device! So, we type in some fruit names. When we're done, press *Ctrl + D*. This is the default character sequence that signifies **end-of-file** (**EOF**), or in cases such as this, end-of-input. Voila! The input is sorted and written. To where? To the `sort` process's stdout – the terminal device, hence we see it.

**Scenario 3**: Sort any given input alphabetically and save the output to a file (explicit output redirection):

```
$ sort > sorted.fruit.txt
mango
apple
pear
^D
$
```

Similar to Scenario 2, we type in some fruit names and then *Ctrl + D* to tell sort we're done. This time, though, note that the output is redirected (via the > meta-character) to the `sorted.fruits.txt` file!

So, as expected is the following output:

```
$ cat sorted.fruit.txt
apple
mango
pear
$
```

**Scenario 4**: Sort a file alphabetically and save the output and errors to a file (explicit input-, output-, and error-redirection):

```
$ sort < fruit.txt > sorted.fruit.txt 2> /dev/null
$
```

Interestingly, the end result is the same as in the preceding scenario, with the added advantage of redirecting any error output to the error channel. Here, we redirect the error output (recall that file descriptor 2 always refers to `stderr`) to the `/dev/null` special device file; `/dev/null` is a device file whose job is to act as a sink (a black hole). Anything written to the null device just disappears forever! (Who said there isn't magic on Unix?) Also, its complement is `/dev/zero`; the zero device is a source – an infinite source of zeros. Reading from it returns zeroes (the first ASCII character, not numeric 0); it has no end-of-file!

## One tool to do one task

In the Unix design, one tries to avoid creating a Swiss Army knife; instead, one creates a tool for a very specific, designated purpose and for that one purpose only. No ifs, no buts; no cruft, no clutter. This is design simplicity at its best.

*"Simplicity is the ultimate sophistication."*

*- Leonardo da Vinci*

Take a common example: when working on the Linux **CLI (command-line interface)**, you would like to figure out which of your locally mounted filesystems has the most available (disk) space.

## Linux System Architecture

We can get the list of locally mounted filesystems by an appropriate switch (just df would do as well):

```
$ df --local
Filesystem            1K-blocks      Used Available Use% Mounted on
rootfs                 20640636   1155492  18436728   6% /
udev                      10240         0     10240   0% /dev
tmpfs                     51444       160     51284   1% /run
tmpfs                      5120         0      5120   0% /run/lock
tmpfs                    102880         0    102880   0% /run/shm
$
```

To sort the output, one would need to first save it to a file; one could use a temporary file for this purpose, tmp, and then sort it, using the sort utility, of course. Finally, we delete the offending temporary file. (Yes, there's a better way, piping; refer to the, *Combine tools seamlessly* section)

Note that the available space is the fourth column, so we sort accordingly:

```
$ df --local > tmp
$ sort -k4nr tmp
rootfs                 20640636   1155484  18436736   6% /
tmpfs                    102880         0    102880   0% /run/shm
tmpfs                     51444       160     51284   1% /run
udev                      10240         0     10240   0% /dev
tmpfs                      5120         0      5120   0% /run/lock
Filesystem            1K-blocks      Used Available Use% Mounted on
$
```

Whoops! The output includes the heading line. Let's first use the versatile sed utility – a powerful non-interactive editor tool – to eliminate the first line, the header, from the output of df:

```
$ df --local > tmp
$ sed --in-place '1d' tmp
$ sort -k4nr tmp
rootfs                 20640636   1155484  18436736   6% /
tmpfs                    102880         0    102880   0% /run/shm
tmpfs                     51444       160     51284   1% /run
udev                      10240         0     10240   0% /dev
tmpfs                      5120         0      5120   0% /run/lock
$ rm -f tmp
```

So what? The point is, on Unix, there is no one utility to list mounted filesystems and sort them by available space simultaneously.

Instead, there is a utility to list mounted filesystems: `df`. It does a great job of it, with option switches to choose from. (How does one know which options? Learn to use the man pages, they're extremely useful.)

There is a utility to sort text: `sort`. Again, it's the last word in sorting text, with plenty of option switches to choose from for pretty much every conceivable sort one might require.

> **The Linux man pages:** **man** is short for **manual**; on a Terminal window, type `man man` to get help on using man. Notice the manual is divided into 9 sections. For example, to get the manual page on the stat system call, type `man 2 stat` as all system calls are in section 2 of the manual. The convention used is cmd or API; thus, we refer to it as `stat(2)`.

As expected, we obtain the results. So what exactly is the point? It's this: we used three utilities, not one. `df`, to list the mounted filesystems (and their related metadata), `sed`, to eliminate the header line, and `sort`, to sort whatever input its given (in any conceivable manner).

`df` can query and list mounted filesystems, but it cannot sort them. `sort` can sort text; it cannot list mounted filesystems.

Think about that for a moment.

Combine them all, and you get more than the sum of its parts! Unix tools typically do one task and they do it to its logical conclusion; no one does it better!

> Having said this, I would like to point out – a tiny bit sheepishly – the highly renowned tool Busybox. Busybox (`http://busybox.net`) is billed as The Swiss Army Knife of Embedded Linux. It is indeed a very versatile tool; it has its place in the embedded Linux ecosystem – precisely because it would be too expensive on an embedded box to have separate binary executables for each and every utility (and it would consume more RAM). Busybox solves this problem by having a single binary executable (along with symbolic links to it from each of its applets, such as ls, ps, df, and sort).
> So, nevertheless, besides the embedded scenario and all the resource limitations it implies, do follow the *One tool to do one task* rule!

## Three standard I/O channels

Several popular Unix tools (technically, filters) are, again, deliberately designed to read their input from a standard file descriptor called **standard input** (**stdin**) – possibly modify it, and write their resultant output to a standard file descriptor **standard output** (**stdout**). Any error output can be written to a separate error channel called **standard error** (**stderr**).

In conjunction with the shell's redirection operators (> for output-redirection and < for input-redirection, 2> for stderr redirection), and even more importantly with piping (refer section, *Combine tools seamlessly*), this enables a program designer to highly simplify. There's no need to hardcode (or even softcode, for that matter) input and output sources or sinks. It just works, as expected.

Let's review a couple of quick examples to illustrate this important point.

## Word count

How many lines of source code are there in the C `netcat.c` source file I downloaded? (Here, we use a small part of the popular open source `netcat` utility code base.) We use the `wc` utility. Before we go further, what's wc? **word count** (**wc**) is a filter: it reads input from stdin, counts the number of lines, words, and characters in the input stream, and writes this result to its stdout. Further, as a convenience, one can pass filenames as parameters to it; passing the `-l` option switch has wc only print the number of lines:

```
$ wc -l src/netcat.c
618 src/netcat.c
$
```

Here, the input is a filename passed as a parameter to `wc`.

Interestingly, we should by now realize that if we do not pass it any parameters, `wc` would read its input from stdin, which by default is the keyboard device. For example is shown as follows:

```
$ wc -l
hey, a small
quick test
 of reading from stdin
by wc!
^D
4
$
```

Yes, we typed in 4 lines to stdin; thus the result is 4, written to stdout – the terminal device by default.

Here is the beauty of it:

```
$ wc -l < src/netcat.c > num
$ cat num
618
$
```

As we can see, wc is a great example of a Unix filter.

## cat

Unix, and of course Linux, users learn to quickly get familiar with the daily-use `cat` utility. At first glance, all cat does is spit out the contents of a file to the terminal.

For example, say we have two plain text files, `myfile1.txt` and `myfile2.txt`:

```
$ cat myfile1.txt
Hello,
Linux System Programming,
World.
$ cat myfile2.txt
Okey dokey,
bye now.
$
```

Okay. Now check this out:

```
$ cat myfile1.txt myfile2.txt
Hello,
Linux System Programming,
```

```
World.
Okey dokey,
bye now.
$
```

Instead of needing to run `cat` twice, we ran it just once, by passing the two filenames to it as parameters.

In theory, one can pass any number of parameters to cat: it will use them all, one by one!

Not just that, one can use shell wildcards too (`*` and `?`; in reality, the shell will first expand the wildcards, and pass on the resultant path names to the program being invoked as parameters):

```
$ cat myfile?.txt
Hello,
Linux System Programming,
World.
Okey dokey,
bye now.
$
```

This, in fact, illustrates another key point: any number of parameters or none is considered the right way to design a program. Of course, there are exceptions to every rule: some programs demand mandatory parameters.

Wait, there's more. `cat` too, is an excellent example of a Unix filter (recall: a filter is a program that reads from its standard input, modifies its input in some manner, and writes the result to its standard output).

So, quick quiz, if we just run `cat` with no parameters, what would happen? Well, let's try it out and see:

```
$ cat
hello,
hello,
oh cool
oh cool
it reads from stdin,
it reads from stdin,
and echoes whatever it reads to stdout!
and echoes whatever it reads to stdout!
ok bye
ok bye
^D
$
```

Wow, look at that: `cat` blocks (waits) at its stdin, the user types in a string and presses the Enter key, `cat` responds by copying its stdin to its stdout – no surprise there, as that's the job of cat in a nutshell!

One realizes the commands shown as follows:

- `cat fname` is the same as `cat < fname`
- `cat > fname` creates or overwrites the `fname` file

There's no reason we can't use cat to append several files together:

```
$ cat fname1 fname2 fname3 > final_fname
$
```

There's no reason this must be done with only plain text files; one can join together binary files too.

In fact, that's what the utility does – it concatenates files. Thus its name; as is the norm on Unix, is highly abbreviated – from concatenate to just cat. Again, clean and elegant – the Unix way.

> **TIP**
>
> cat shunts out file contents to stdout, in order. What if one wants to display a file's contents in reverse order (last line first)? Use the Unix `tac` utility – yes, that's cat spelled backward!
>
> Also, FYI, we saw that cat can be used to efficiently join files. Guess what: the `split (1)` utility can be used to break a file up into pieces.

## Combine tools seamlessly

We just saw that common Unix utilities are often designed as filters, giving them the ability to read from their standard input and write to their standard output. This concept is elegantly extended to seamlessly combine together multiple utilities, using an IPC mechanism called a **pipe**.

Also, we recall that the Unix philosophy embraces the do one task only design. What if we have one program that does task A and another that does task B and we want to combine them? Ah, that's exactly what pipes do! Refer to the following code:

```
prg_does_taskA | prg_does_taskB
```

> A pipe essentially is redirection performed twice: the output of the left-hand program becomes the input to the right-hand program. Of course, this implies that the program on the left must write to stdout, and the program on the read must read from stdin.

An example: sort the list of mounted filesystems by space available (in reverse order).

As we have already discussed this example in the *One tool to do one task* section, we shall not repeat the same information.

**Option 1**: Perform the following code using a temporary file (refer section, *One tool to do one task*):

```
$ df --local | sed '1d' > tmp
$ sed --in-place '1d' tmp
$ sort -k4nr tmp
rootfs 20640636 1155484 18436736 6% /
tmpfs 102880 0 102880 0% /run/shm
tmpfs 51444 160 51284 1% /run
udev 10240 0 10240 0% /dev
tmpfs 5120 0 5120 0% /run/lock
$ rm -f tmp
```

**Option 2** : Using pipes—clean and elegant:

```
$ df --local | sed '1d' | sort -k4nr
rootfs            20640636 1155492   18436728   6% /
tmpfs               102880       0     102880   0% /run/shm
tmpfs                51444     160      51284   1% /run
udev                 10240       0      10240   0% /dev
tmpfs                 5120       0       5120   0% /run/lock
$
```

Not only is this elegant, it is also far superior performance-wise, as writing to memory (the pipe is a memory object) is much faster than writing to disk.

One can extend this notion and combine multiple tools over multiple pipes; in effect, one can build a super tool from several regular tools by combining them.

As an example: display the three processes taking the most (physical) memory; only display their PID, **virtual size (VSZ)**, **resident set size (RSS)** (RSS is a fairly accurate measure of physical memory usage), and the name:

```
$ ps au | sed '1d' | awk '{printf("%6d %10d %10d %-32s\n", $2, $5, $6, $11)}' | sort -k3n | tail -n3
 10746     3219556     665252 /usr/lib64/firefox/firefox
 10840     3444456    1105088 /usr/lib64/firefox/firefox
  1465     5119800    1354280 /usr/bin/gnome-shell
$
```

Here, we've combined five utilities, `ps`, `sed`, `awk`, `sort`, and `tail`, over four pipes. Nice!

Another example: display the process, not including daemons*, taking up the most memory (RSS):

```
ps aux | awk '{if ($7 != "?") print $0}' | sort -k6n | tail -n1
```

> A daemon is a system background process; we'll cover this concept in *Daemon Process* here: https://www.packtpub.com/sites/default/files/downloads/Daemon_Processes.pdf.

# Plain text preferred

Unix programs are generally designed to work with text as it's a universal interface. Of course, there are several utilities that do indeed operate on binary objects (such as object and executable files); we aren't referring to them here. The point is this: Unix programs are designed to work on text as it simplifies the design and architecture of the program.

A common example: an application, on startup, parses a configuration file. The configuration file could be formatted as a binary blob. On the other hand, having it as a plain text file renders it easily readable (invaluable!) and therefore easier to understand and maintain. One might argue that parsing binary would be faster. Perhaps to some extent this is so, but consider the following:

- With modern hardware, the difference is probably not significant
- A standardized plain text format (such as XML) would have optimized code to parse it, yielding both benefits

Remember, simplicity is key!

## CLI, not GUI

The Unix OS, and all its applications, utilities, and tools, were always built to be used from a **command-line-interface** (**CLI**), typically, the shell. From the 1980s onward, the need for a **Graphical User Interface** (**GUI**) became apparent.

Robert Scheifler of MIT, considered the chief design architect behind the X Window System, built an exceedingly clean and elegant architecture, a key component of which is this: the GUI forms a layer (well, actually, several layers) above the OS, providing libraries for GUI clients, that is, applications.

> The GUI was never designed to be intrinsic to applications or the OS—it's always optional.

This architecture still holds up today. Having said that, especially on embedded Linux, performance reasons are seeing the advent of newer architectures, such as the frame buffer and Wayland. Also, though Android, which uses the Linux kernel, necessitates a GUI for the end user, the system developer's interface to Android, ADB, is a CLI.

A huge number of production-embedded and server Linux systems run purely on CLI interfaces. The GUI is almost like an add-on feature, for the end user's ease of operation.

> **TIP**
> Wherever appropriate, design your tools to work in the CLI environment; adapting it into a GUI at a later point is then straightforward.
> Cleanly and carefully separating the business logic of the project or product from its GUI is a key to good design.

## Modular, designed to be repurposed by others

From its very early days, the Unix OS was deliberately designed and coded with the tacit assumption that multiple programmers would work on the system. Thus, the culture of writing clean, elegant, and understandable code, to be read and worked upon by other competent programmers, was ingrained.

Later, with the advent of the Unix wars, proprietary and legal concerns overrode this sharing model. Interestingly, history shows that the Unix's were fading in relevance and industry use, until the timely advent of none other than the Linux OS – an open source ecosystem at its very best! Today, the Linux OS is widely acknowledged as the most successful GNU project. Ironic indeed!

## Provide mechanisms, not policies

Let's understand this principle with a simple example.

When designing an application, you need to have the user enter a login `name` and `password`. The function that performs the work of getting and checking the password is called, let's say, `mygetpass()`. It's invoked by the `mylogin()` function: `mylogin() → mygetpass()`.

Now, the protocol to be followed is this: if the user gets the password wrong three times in a row, the program should not allow access (and should log the case). Fine, but where do we check this?

The Unix philosophy: do not implement the logic, if the password is specified wrongly three times, abort in the `mygetpass()` function. Instead, just have `mygetpass()` return a Boolean (true when the password is right, false when the password is wrong), and have the `mylogin()` calling function implement whatever logic is required.

## Pseudocode

The following is the wrong approach:

```
mygetpass()
{
    numtries=1

    <get the password>
    if (password-is-wrong) {
        numtries ++
        if (numtries >= 3) {
            <write and log failure message>
            <abort>
        }
    }
}
<password correct, continue>
```

# Linux System Architecture

```
}
mylogin()
{
    mygetpass()
}
```

Now let's take a look at the right approach: the Unix way! Refer to the following code:

```
mygetpass()
{
    <get the password>

    if (password-is-wrong)
        return false;

    return true;
}
mylogin()
{
    maxtries = 3

    while (maxtries--) {
        if (mygetpass() == true)
            <move along, call other routines>
    }

    // If we're here, we've failed to provide the
    // correct password
    <write and log failure message>
    <abort>
}
```

The job of `mygetpass()` is to get a password from the user and check whether it's correct; it returns success or failure to the caller – that's it. That's the mechanism. It is not its job to decide what to do if the password is wrong – that's the policy, and left to the caller.

Now that we've covered the Unix philosophy in a nutshell, what are the important takeaways for you, the system developer on Linux?

Learning from, and following, the Unix philosophy when designing and implementing your applications on the Linux OS will provide a huge payoff. Your application will do the following:

- Be a natural fit on the system; this is very important
- Have greatly reduced complexity

- Have a modular design that is clean and elegant
- Be far more maintainable

# Linux system architecture

In order to clearly understand the Linux system architecture, one needs to first understand a few important concepts: the processor **Application Binary Interface (ABI)**, CPU privilege levels, and how these affect the code we write. Accordingly, and with a few code examples, we'll delve into these here, before diving into the details of the system architecture itself.

## Preliminaries

If one is posed the question, "what is the CPU for?", the answer is pretty obvious: the CPU is the heart of the machine – it reads in, decodes, and executes machine instructions, working on memory and peripherals. It does this by incorporating various stages.

Very simplistically, in the Instruction Fetch stage, it reads in machine instructions (which we represent in various human-readable ways – in hexadecimal, assembly, and high-level languages) from memory (RAM) or CPU cache. Then, in the Instruction Decode phase, it proceeds to decipher the instruction. Along the way, it makes use of the control unit, its register set, ALU, and memory/peripheral interfaces.

## The ABI

Let's imagine that we write a C program, and run it on the machine.

Well, hang on a second. C code cannot possibly be directly deciphered by the CPU; it must be converted into machine language. So, we understand that on modern systems we will have a toolchain installed – this includes the compiler, linker, library objects, and various other tools. We compile and link the C source code, converting it into an executable format that can be run on the system.

The processor **Instruction Set Architecture (ISA)** – documents the machine's instruction formats, the addressing schemes it supports, and its register model. In fact, CPU **Original Equipment Manufacturers (OEMs)** release a document that describes how the machine works; this document is generally called the ABI. The ABI describes more than just the ISA; it describes the machine instruction formats, the register set details, the calling convention, the linking semantics, and the executable file format, such as ELF. Try out a quick Google for x86 ABI – it should reveal interesting results.

> The publisher makes the full source code for this book available on their website; we urge the reader to perform a quick Git clone on the following URL. Build and try it: https://github.com/PacktPublishing/Hands-on-System-Programming-with-Linux.

Let's try this out. First, we write a simple `Hello, World` type of C program:

```
$ cat hello.c
/*
 * hello.c
 *
 ***************************************************************
 * This program is part of the source code released for the book
 *  "Linux System Programming"
 *  (c) Kaiwan N Billimoria
 *  Packt Publishers
 *
 * From:
 *  Ch 1 : Linux System Architecture
 ***************************************************************
 * A quick 'Hello, World'-like program to demonstrate using
 * objdump to show the corresponding assembly and machine
 * language.
 */
#include <stdio.h>
#include <unistd.h>
#include <stdlib.h>

int main(void)
{
    int a;

    printf("Hello, Linux System Programming, World!\n");
    a = 5;
    exit(0);
}
$
```

We build the application via the `Makefile`, with `make`. Ideally, the code must compile with no warnings:

```
$ gcc -Wall -Wextra hello.c -o hello
hello.c: In function 'main':
hello.c:23:6: warning: variable 'a' set but not used [-Wunused-but-set-variable]
   int a;
      ^
$
```

> Important! Do not ignore compiler warnings with production code. Strive to get rid of all warnings, even the seemingly trivial ones; this will help a great deal with correctness, stability, and security.

In this trivial example code, we understand and anticipate the unused variable warning that `gcc` emits, and just ignore it for the purpose of this demo.

> The exact warning and/or error messages you see on your system could differ from what you see here. This is because my Linux distribution (and version), compiler/linker, library versions, and perhaps even CPU, may differ from yours. I built this on a x86_64 box running the Fedora 27/28 Linux distribution.

Similarly, we build the debug version of the `hello` program (again, ignoring the warning for now), and run it:

```
$ make hello_dbg
[...]
$ ./hello_dbg
Hello, Linux System Programming, World!
$
```

We use the powerful `objdump` utility to see the intermixed source-assembly-machine language of our program (`objdump`'s `--source` option switch `-S, --source Intermix source code with disassembly`):

```
$ objdump --source ./hello_dbg
./hello_dbg:     file format elf64-x86-64

Disassembly of section .init:

0000000000400400 <_init>:
  400400:       48 83 ec 08             sub    $0x8,%rsp
```

```
[...]
int main(void)
{
  400527:       55                      push    %rbp
  400528:       48 89 e5                mov     %rsp,%rbp
  40052b:       48 83 ec 10             sub     $0x10,%rsp
    int a;

    printf("Hello, Linux System Programming, World!\n");
  40052f:       bf e0 05 40 00          mov     $0x4005e0,%edi
  400534:       e8 f7 fe ff ff          callq   400430 <puts@plt>
    a = 5;
  400539:       c7 45 fc 05 00 00 00    movl    $0x5,-0x4(%rbp)
    exit(0);
  400540:       bf 00 00 00 00          mov     $0x0,%edi
  400545:       e8 f6 fe ff ff          callq   400440 <exit@plt>
  40054a:       66 0f 1f 44 00 00       nopw    0x0(%rax,%rax,1)
[...]
$
```

> **TIP**: The exact assembly and machine code you see on your system will, in all likelihood, differ from what you see here; this is because my Linux distribution (and version), compiler/linker, library versions, and perhaps even CPU, may differ from yours. I built this on a x86_64 box running Fedora Core 27.

Alright. Let's take the line of source code `a = 5;` where, `objdump` reveals the corresponding machine and assembly language:

```
    a = 5;
  400539:       c7 45 fc 05 00 00 00    movl    $0x5,-0x4(%rbp)
```

We can now clearly see the following:

| C source | Assembly language | Machine instructions |
|----------|-------------------|----------------------|
| a = 5;   | movl $0x5,-0x4(%rbp) | c7 45 fc 05 00 00 00 |

So, when the process runs, at some point it will fetch and execute the machine instructions, producing the desired result. Indeed, that's exactly what a programmable computer is designed to do!

Though we have shown examples of displaying (and even writing a bit of) assembly and machine code for the Intel CPU, the concepts and principles behind this discussion hold up for other CPU architectures, such as ARM, PPC, and MIPS. Covering similar examples for all these CPUs goes beyond the scope of this book; however, we urge the interested reader to study the processor datasheet and ABI, and try it out.

## Accessing a register's content via inline assembly

Now that we've written a simple C program and seen its assembly and machine code, let's move on to something a little more challenging: a C program with inline assembly to access the contents of a CPU register.

> Details on assembly-language programming are outside the scope of this book; refer to the *Further reading* section on the GitHub repository.

x86_64 has several registers; let's just go with the ordinary RCX register for this example. We do make use of an interesting trick: the x86 ABI calling convention states that the return value of a function will be the value placed in the accumulator, that is, RAX for the x86_64. Using this knowledge, we write a function that uses inline assembly to place the content of the register we want into RAX. This ensures that this is what it will return to the caller!

Assembly micro-basics includes the following:

```
at&t syntax:
        movq <src_reg>, <dest_reg>
Register         : prefix name with %
Immediate value  : prefix with $
```

For more, see the *Further reading* section on the GitHub repository.

Let's take a look at the following code:

```
$ cat getreg_rcx.c
/*
 * getreg_rcx.c
 *
 ****************************************************************
 * This program is part of the source code released for the book
```

```
 *   "Linux System Programming"
 *   (c) Kaiwan N Billimoria
 *   Packt Publishers
 *
 * From:
 * Ch 1 : Linux System Architecture
 ***************************************************************
 * Inline assembly to access the contents of a CPU register.
 * NOTE: this program is written to work on x86_64 only.
 */
#include <stdio.h>
#include <unistd.h>
#include <stdlib.h>

typedef unsigned long u64;

static u64 get_rcx(void)
{
    /* Pro Tip: x86 ABI: query a register's value by moving its value
into RAX.
     * [RAX] is returned by the function! */
    __asm__ __volatile__(
            "push %rcx\n\t"
            "movq $5, %rcx\n\t"
            "movq %rcx, %rax");
                /* at&t syntax: movq <src_reg>, <dest_reg> */
    __asm__ __volatile__("pop %rcx");
}

int main(void)
{
    printf("Hello, inline assembly:\n [RCX] = 0x%lx\n",
                get_rcx());
    exit(0);
}
```
```
$ gcc -Wall -Wextra getreg_rcx.c -o getreg_rcx
getreg_rcx.c: In function 'get_rcx':
getreg_rcx.c:32:1: warning: no return statement in function returning
non-void [-Wreturn-type]
 }
 ^
$ ./getreg_rcx
Hello, inline assembly:
 [RCX] = 0x5
$
```

There; it works as expected.

# Accessing a control register's content via inline assembly

Among the many fascinating registers on the x86_64 processor, there happen to be six control registers, named CR0 through CR4, and CR8. There's really no need to delve into detail regarding them; suffice it to say that they are crucial to system control.

For the purpose of an illustrative example, let's consider the CR0 register for a moment. Intel's manual states: CR0—contains system control flags that control operating mode and states of the processor.

> Intel's manuals can be downloaded conveniently as PDF documents from here (includes the Intel® 64 and
> IA-32 Architectures Software Developer's Manual, Volume 3 (3A, 3B and 3C): System Programming Guide):
>
> https://software.intel.com/en-us/articles/intel-sdm

Clearly, CR0 is an important register!
We modify our previous program to access and display its content (instead of the ordinary `RCX` register). The only relevant code (which has changed from the previous program) is the function that queries the `CR0` register value:

```
static u64 get_cr0(void)
{
    /* Pro Tip: x86 ABI: query a register's value by moving it's value into RAX.
     * [RAX] is returned by the function! */
    __asm__ __volatile__("movq %cr0, %rax");
        /* at&t syntax: movq <src_reg>, <dest_reg> */
}
```

Build and run it:

```
$ make getreg_cr0
[...]
$ ./getreg_cr0
Segmentation fault (core dumped)
$
```

It crashes!

Well, what happened here? Read on.

[ 33 ]

## CPU privilege levels

As mentioned earlier in this chapter, the essential job of the CPU is to read in machine instructions from memory, decipher, and execute them. In the early days of computing, this is pretty much all the processor did. But then, engineers, thinking deeper on it, realized that there is a critical issue with this: if a programmer can feed an arbitrary stream of machine instructions to the processor, which it, in turn, blindly and obediently executes, herein lies scope to do damage, to hack the machine!

How? Recall from the previous section the Intel processor's CR0 control register: Contains system control flags that control operating mode and states of the processor. If one has unlimited (read/write) access to the CR0 register, one could toggle bits that could do the following:

- Turn hardware paging on or off
- Disable the CPU cache
- Change caching and alignment attributes
- Disable WP (write protect) on memory (technically, pages) marked as read-only by the OS

Wow, a hacker could indeed wreak havoc. At the very least, only the OS should be allowed this kind of access.

Precisely for reasons such as the security, robustness, and correctness of the OS and the hardware resources it controls, all modern CPUs include the notion of privilege levels.

The modern CPU will support at least two privilege levels, or modes, which are generically called the following:

- Supervisor
- User

*Chapter 1*

You need to understand that code, that is, machine instructions, runs on the CPU at a given privilege level or mode. A person designing and implementing an OS is free to exploit the processor privilege levels. This is exactly how modern OSes are designed. Take a look at the following table Generic CPU Privilege Levels:

| Privilege level or mode name | Privilege level | Purpose | Terminology |
|---|---|---|---|
| Supervisor | High | OS code runs here | kernel-space |
| User | Low | Application code runs here | user-space (or userland) |

Table 1: Generic CPU Privilege Levels

## Privilege levels or rings on the x86

To understand this important concept better, let's take the popular x86 architecture as a real example. Right from the i386 onward, the Intel processor supports four privilege levels or rings: **Ring 0**, **Ring 1**, **Ring 2**, and **Ring 3**. On the Intel CPU's, this is how the levels work:

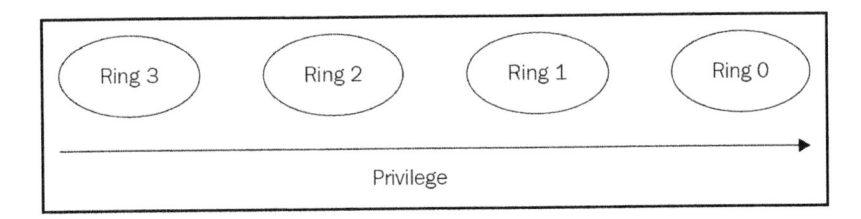

Figure 1: CPU ring levels and privilege

Let's visualize this *Figure 1* in the form of a *Table 2: x86 privilege or ring levels*:

| Privilege or ring level | Privilege | Purpose |
|---|---|---|
| Ring 0 | Highest | OS code runs here |
| Ring 1 | < ring 0 | <Unused> |
| Ring 2 | < ring 1 | <Unused> |
| Ring 3 | Lowest | Application code runs here (userland) |

Table 2: x86 privilege or ring levels

*Linux System Architecture*

> Originally, ring levels 1 and 2 were intended for device drivers, but modern OSes typically run driver code at ring 0 itself. Some hypervisors (VirtualBox being one) used to use Ring 1 to run the guest kernel code; this was the case earlier when no hardware virtualization support was available (Intel VT-x, AMD SV).
>
> The ARM (32-bit) processor has seven modes of execution; of these, six are privileged, and only one is the non-privileged mode. On ARM, generically, the equivalent to Intel's Ring 0 is Supervisor (SVC) mode, and the equivalent to Intel's Ring 3 is User mode.
>
> For interested readers, there are more links in the *Further reading* section on the GitHub repository.

The following diagram clearly shows of all modern OSes (Linux, Unix, Windows, and macOS) running on an x86 processor exploit processor-privilege levels:

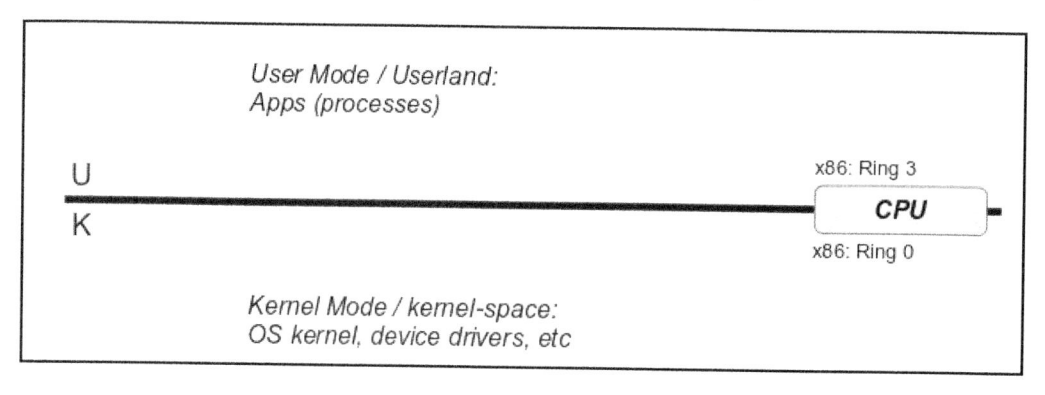

Figure 2: User-Kernel separation

Importantly, the processor ISA assigns every machine instruction with a privilege level or levels at which they are allowed to be executed. A machine instruction that is allowed to execute at the user privilege level automatically implies it can also be executed at the Supervisor privilege level. This distinguishing between what can and cannot be done at what mode also applies to register access.

To use the Intel terminology, the **Current Privilege Level** (**CPL**) is the privilege level at which the processor is currently executing code.

For example, that on a given processor shown as follows:

- The foo1 machine instruction has an allowed privilege level of Supervisor (or Ring 0 for x86)
- The foo2 machine instruction has an allowed privilege level of User (or Ring 3 for x86)

So, for a running application that executes these machine instructions, the following table emerges:

| Machine instruction | Allowed-at mode | CPL (current privilege level) | Works? |
|---|---|---|---|
| foo1 | Supervisor (0) | 0 | Yes |
|  |  | 3 | No |
| foo2 | User (3) | 0 | Yes |
|  |  | 3 | Yes |

Table 3: Privilege levels – an example

> So, thinking about it, foo2 being allowed at User mode would also be allowed to execute with any CPL. In other words, if the CPL <= allowed privilege level, it works, otherwise it does not.

When one runs an application on, say, Linux, the application runs as a process (more on this later). But what privilege (or mode or ring) level does the application code run at? Refer to the preceding table: User Mode (Ring 3 on x86).

Aha! So now we see. The preceding code example, `getreg_rcx.c`, worked because it attempted to access the content of the general-purpose `RCX` register, which is allowed in User Mode (Ring 3, as well as at the other levels, of course)!

But the code of `getreg_cr0.c` failed; it crashed, because it attempted to access the content of the `CR0` control register, which is disallowed in User Mode (Ring 3), and allowed only at the Ring 0 privilege! Only OS or kernel code can access the control registers. This holds true for several other sensitive assembly-language instructions as well. This approach makes a lot of sense.

> Technically, it crashed because the processor raised a **General Protection Fault (GPF)**.

[ 37 ]

# Linux architecture

The Linux system architecture is a layered one. In a very simplistic way, but ideal to start on our path to understanding these details, the following diagram illustrates the Linux system architecture:

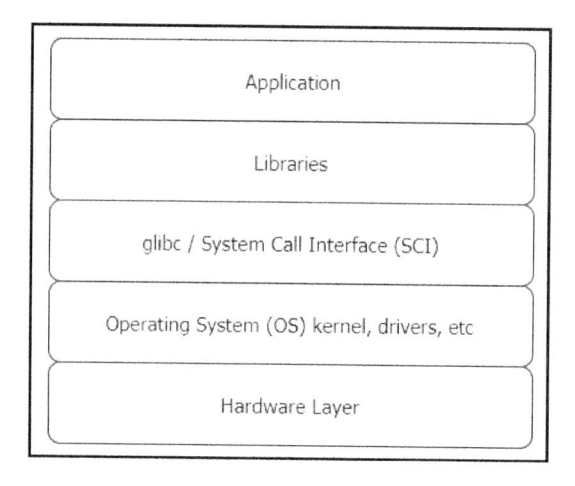

```
┌─────────────────────────────────────────────┐
│  ┌───────────────────────────────────────┐  │
│  │            Application                │  │
│  └───────────────────────────────────────┘  │
│  ┌───────────────────────────────────────┐  │
│  │             Libraries                 │  │
│  └───────────────────────────────────────┘  │
│  ┌───────────────────────────────────────┐  │
│  │   glibc / System Call Interface (SCI) │  │
│  └───────────────────────────────────────┘  │
│  ┌───────────────────────────────────────┐  │
│  │ Operating System (OS) kernel, drivers, etc │
│  └───────────────────────────────────────┘  │
│  ┌───────────────────────────────────────┐  │
│  │           Hardware Layer              │  │
│  └───────────────────────────────────────┘  │
└─────────────────────────────────────────────┘
```

Figure 3: Linux – Simplified layered architecture

Layers help, because each layer need only be concerned with the layer directly above and below it. This leads to many advantages:

- Clean design, reduces complexity
- Standardization, interoperability
- Ability to swap layers in and out of the stack
- Ability to easily introduce new layers as required

> On the last point, there exists the FTSE. To quote directly from Wikipedia:
>
> The "**fundamental theorem of software engineering (FTSE)**" is a term originated by Andrew Koenig to describe a remark by Butler Lampson attributed to the late David J. Wheeler
>
> We can solve any problem by introducing an extra level of indirection.

Now that we understand the concept of CPU modes or privilege levels, and how modern OSes exploit them, a better diagram (expanding on the previous one) of the Linux system architecture would be as follows:

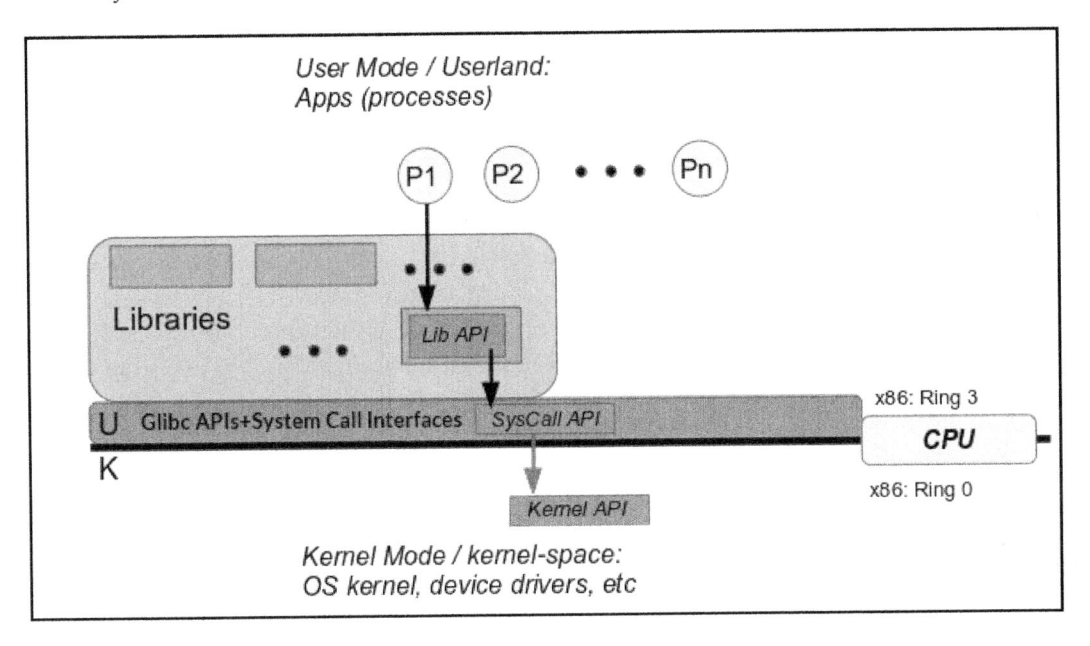

Figure 4: Linux system architecture

In the preceding diagram, **P1, P2, ..., Pn** are nothing but userland processes (Process 1, Process 2) or in other words, running applications. For example, on a Linux laptop, we might have the vim editor, a web browser, and terminal windows (gnome-terminal) running.

## Libraries

Libraries, of course, are archives (collections) of code; as we well know, using libraries helps tremendously with code modularity, standardization, preventing the reinvent-the-wheel syndrome, and so on. A Linux desktop system might have libraries numbering in the hundreds, and possibly even a few thousand!

The classic K&R `hello, world` C program uses the `printf` API to write the string to the display:

```
printf("hello, world\n");
```

Obviously, the code of `printf` is not part of the `hello, world` source. So where does it come from? It's part of the standard C library; on Linux, due to its GNU origins, this library is commonly called **GNU libc (glibc)**.

Glibc is a critical and required component on a Linux box. It not only contains the usual standard C library routines (APIs), it is, in fact, the programming interface to the operating system! How? Via its lower layer, the system calls.

## System calls

System calls are actually kernel functionality that can be invoked from userspace via glibc stub routines. They serve a critical function; they connect userspace to kernel-space. If a user program wants to request something of the kernel (read from a file, write to the network, change a file's permissions), it does so by issuing a system call. Therefore, system calls are the only legal entry point to the kernel. There is no other way for a user-space process to invoke the kernel.

> For a list of all the available Linux system calls, see section 2 of the man pages (`https://linux.die.net/man/2/`). One can also do: man 2 syscalls to see the man page on all supported system calls

Another way to think of this: the Linux kernel internally has literally thousands of APIs (or functions). Of these, only a small fraction are made visible or available, that is, exposed, to userspace; these exposed kernel APIs are system calls! Again, as an approximation, modern Linux glibc has around 300 system calls.

> On an x86_64 Fedora 27 box running the 4.13.16-302.fc27.x86_64 kernel, there are close to 53,000 kernel APIs!

Here is the key thing to understand: system calls are very different from all other (typically library) APIs. As they ultimately invoke kernel (OS) code, they have the ability to cross the user-kernel boundary; in effect, they have the ability to switch from normal unprivileged User mode to completely privileged Supervisor or kernel mode!

How? Without delving into the gory details, system calls essentially work by invoking special machine instructions that have the built-in ability to switch the processor mode from User to Supervisor. All modern CPU ABIs will provide at least one such machine instruction; on the x86 processor, the traditional way to implement system calls is to use the special int 0x80 machine instruction. Yes, it is indeed a software interrupt (or trap). From Pentium Pro and Linux 2.6 onward, the sysenter/syscall machine instructions are used. See the *Further reading* section on the GitHub repository.

From the viewpoint of the application developer, a key point regarding system calls is that system calls appear to be regular functions (APIs) that can be invoked by the developer; this design is deliberate. The reality: the system call APIs that one invokes – such as `open()`, `read()`, `chmod()`, `dup()`, and `write()` – are merely stubs. They are a neat mechanism to get at the actual code that is in the kernel (getting there involves populating a register the accumulator on x86 – with the system call number, and passing parameters via other general-purpose registers) to execute that kernel code path, and return back to user mode when done. Refer to the following table:

| CPU | Machine instruction(s) used to trap to Supervisor (kernel) Mode from User Mode | Allocated Register for system call number |
|---|---|---|
| x86[_64] | int 0x80 or syscall | EAX / RAX |
| ARM | swi / svc | R0 to R7 |
| Aarch64 | svc | X8 |
| MIPS | syscall | $v0 |

Table 4: System calls on various CPU Architectures for better understanding

## Linux – a monolithic OS

Operating systems are generally considered to adhere to one of two major architectural styles: monolithic or microkernel.

Linux is decidedly a monolithic OS.

## What does that mean?

The English word monolith literally means a large single upright block of stone:

Figure 5: Corinthian columns – they're monolithic!

On the Linux OS, applications run as independent entities called **processes**. A process may be single-threaded (original Unix) or multithreaded. Regardless, for now, we will consider the process as the unit of execution on Linux; a process is defined as an instance of a program in execution.

When a user-space process issues a library call, the library API, in turn, may or may not issue a system call. For example, issuing the atoi(3) API does not cause glibc to issue a system call as it does not require kernel support to implement the conversion of a string into an integer. <api-name>(n) ; n is the man page section.

To help clarify these important concepts, let's check out the famous and classic K&R Hello, World C program again:

```
#include <stdio.h>
main()
{
    printf("hello, world\n");
}
```

Okay, that should work. Indeed it does.
But, the question is, how exactly does the printf(3) API write to the monitor device?

The short answer: it does not.
The reality is that printf(3) only has the intelligence to format a string as specified; that's it. Once done, printf actually invokes the write(2) API – a system call. The write system call does have the ability to write the buffer content to a special device file – the monitor device, seen by write as stdout. Go back to our discussion regarding *The Unix philosophy in a nutshell* : if it's not a process, it's a file! Of course, it gets really complex under the hood in the kernel; to cut a long story short, the kernel code of write ultimately switches to the correct driver code; the device driver is the only component that can directly work with peripheral hardware. It performs the actual write to the monitor, and return values propagate all the way back to the application.

Linux System Architecture

In the following diagram, **P** is the `hello, world` process at runtime:

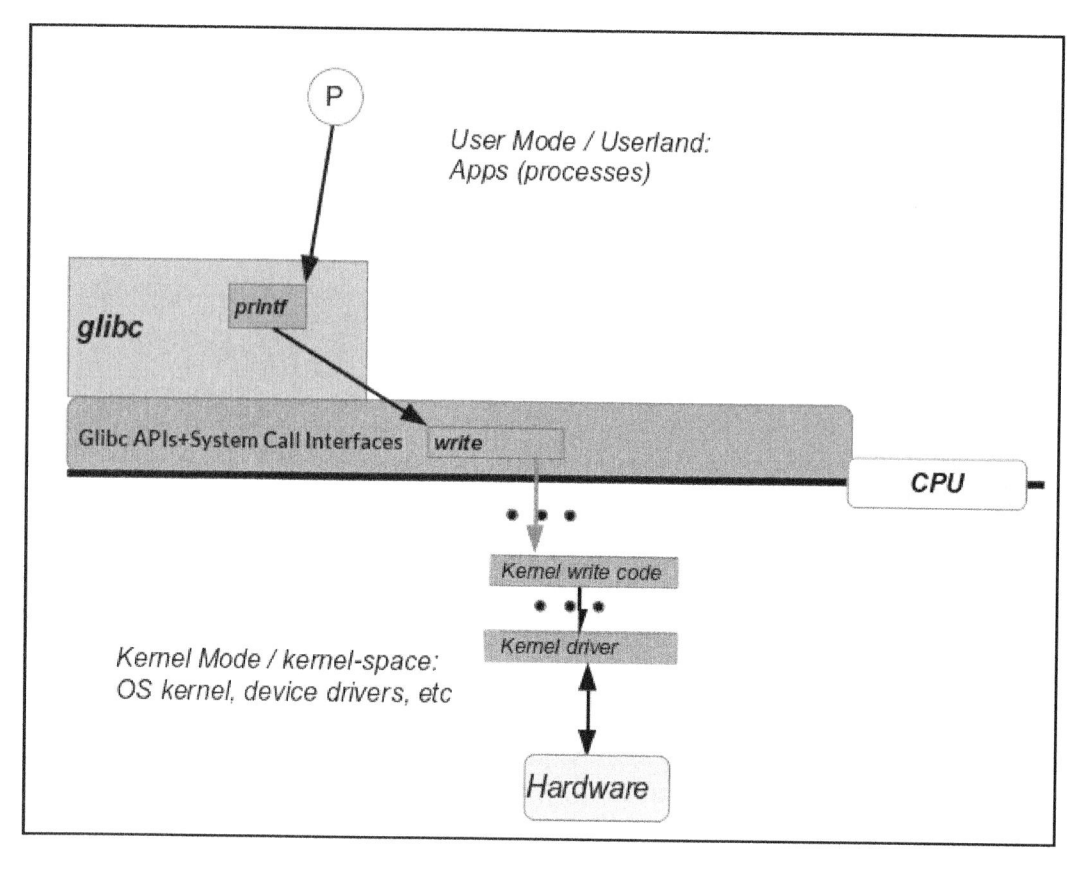

Fig 6: Code flow: printf-to-kernel

Also, from the diagram, we can see that **glibc** is considered to consist of two parts:

- **Arch-independent glibc**: The regular libc APIs (such as [s|sn|v]printf, memcpy, memcmp, atoi)
- **Arch-dependent glibc**: The **system call** stubs

> Here, by arch, we mean CPU.
> Also the ellipses (...) represent additional logic and processing within kernel-space that we do not show or delve into here.

Now that the code flow path of `hello, world` is clearer, let's get back to the monolithic stuff!

[ 44 ]

*Chapter 1*

It's easy to assume that it works this way:

1. The `hello, world` app (process) issues the `printf(3)` library call.
2. `printf` issues the `write(2)` system call.
3. We switch from User to Supervisor (kernel) Mode.
4. The kernel takes over – it writes `hello, world` onto the monitor.
5. Switch back to non-privileged User Mode.

Actually, that's NOT the case.

The reality is, in the monolithic design, there is no kernel; to word it another way, the kernel is actually part of the process itself. It works as follows:

1. The `hello, world` app (process) issues the `printf(3)` library call.
2. printf issues the `write(2)` system call.
3. The process invoking the system call now switches from User to Supervisor (kernel) Mode.
4. The process runs the underlying kernel code, the underlying device driver code, and thus, writes `hello, world` onto the monitor!
5. The process is then switched back to non-privileged User Mode.

To summarize, in a monolithic kernel, when a process (or thread) issues a system call, it switches to privileged Supervisor or kernel mode and runs the kernel code of the system call (working on kernel data). When done, it switches back to unprivileged User mode and continues executing userspace code (working on user data).

This is very important to understand:

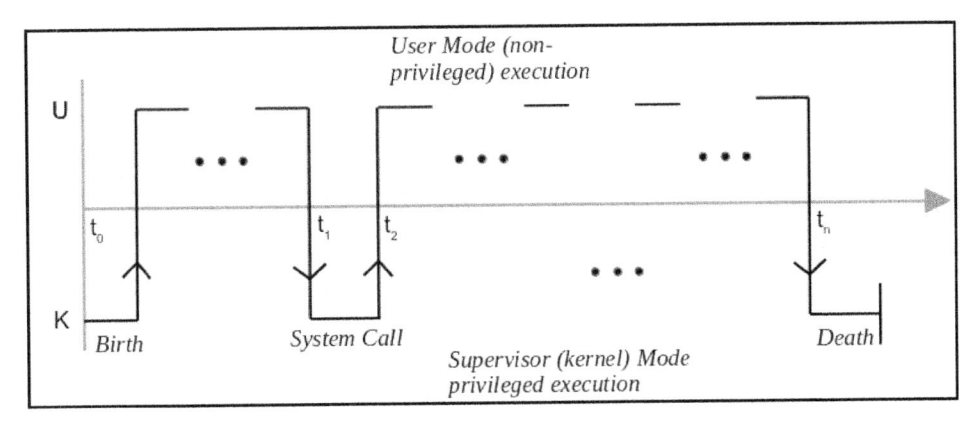

Fig 7: Life of a process in terms of privilege modes

[ 45 ]

The preceding diagram attempts to illustrate that the **X axis** is the **timeline**, and the **Y axis** represents **User Mode** (at the top) and **Supervisor (kernel) Mode** (at the bottom):

- **time $t_0$**: A process is born in kernel mode (the code to create a process is within the kernel of course). Once fully born, it is switched to User (non-privileged) Mode and it runs its userspace code (working on its userspace data items as well).
- **time $t_1$**: The process, directly or indirectly (perhaps via a library API), invokes a system call. It now traps into kernel mode (refer the table *System Calls on CPU Architectures* shows the machine instructions depending on the CPU to do so) and executes kernel code in privileged Supervisor Mode (working on kernel data items as well).
- **time $t_2$**: The system call is done; the process switches back to non-privileged User Mode and continues to execute its userspace code. This process continues, until some point in the future.
- **time $t_n$**: The process dies, either deliberately by invoking the exit API, or it is killed by a signal. It now switches back to Supervisor Mode (as the exit(3) library API invokes the _exit(2) system call), executes the kernel code of _exit(), and terminates.

In fact, most modern operating systems are monolithic (especially the Unix-like ones).

> Technically, Linux is not considered 100 percent monolithic. It's considered to be mostly monolithic, but also modular, due to the fact that the Linux kernel supports modularization (the plugging in and out of kernel code and data, via a technology called **Loadable Kernel Modules (LKMs)**).
> Interestingly, MS Windows (specifically, from the NT kernel onward) follows a hybrid architecture that is both monolithic and microkernel.

## Execution contexts within the kernel

Kernel code always executes in one of two contexts:

- Process
- Interrupt

*Chapter 1*

> It's easy to get confused here. Remember, this discussion applies to the context in which kernel code executes, not userspace code.

## Process context

Now we understand that one can invoke kernel services by issuing a system call. When this occurs, the calling process runs the kernel code of the system call in kernel mode. This is termed **process context** – kernel code is now running in the context of the process that invoked the system call.

Process context code has the following attributes:

- Always triggered by a process (or thread) issuing a system call
- Top-down approach
- Synchronous execution of kernel code by a process

## Interrupt context

At first glance, there appears to be no other way that kernel code executes. Well, think about this scenario: the network receive path. A network packet destined for your Ethernet MAC address arrives at the hardware adapter, the hardware detects that it's meant for it, collects it, and buffers it. It now must let the OS know; more technically, it must let the **Network Interface Card** (**NIC**) device driver know, so that it can fetch and process packets as they arrive. It kicks the NIC driver into action by asserting a hardware interrupt.

Recall that device drivers reside in kernel-space, and therefore their code runs in Supervisor or kernel Mode. The (kernel privilege) driver code **Interrupt service routine** (**ISR**) now executes, fetches the packet, and sends it up the OS network protocol stack for processing.

The NIC driver's ISR code is kernel code, and it is has run but in what context? It's obviously not in the context of any particular process. In fact, the hardware interrupt probably interrupted some process. Thus, we just call this *interrupt context*.

[ 47 ]

*Linux System Architecture*

The interrupt context code has the following attributes:

- Always triggered by a hardware interrupt (not a software interrupt, fault or exception; that's still process context)
- Bottom-up approach
- Asynchronous execution of kernel code by an interrupt

> **TIP**: If, at some point, you do report a kernel bug, it helps if you point out the execution context.

Technically, within interrupt context, we have further distinctions, such as hard-IRQs and softirqs, bottom halves, and tasklets. However, this discussion goes beyond the scope of this book.

# Summary

This chapter started by explaining the Unix design philosophy, including the central principles or pillars of the Unix philosophy, design, and architecture. We then described the Linux system architecture, where we covered the meaning of CPU-ABI (Application Binary Interface), ISA, and toolchain (using `objdump` to disassemble a simple program, and accessing CPU registers with inline assembly). CPU privilege levels and their importance in the modern OS were discussed, leading in to the Linux system architecture layers – application, libraries, system calls, and the kernel. The chapter finished with a discussion on how Linux is a monolithic OS and then explored kernel execution contexts.

In the next chapter, the reader will delve into the mysteries of, and get a solid grasp of, virtual memory – what exactly it means, why it's in all modern OSes, and the key benefits it provides. We will discuss relevant details of the making of process virtual address space.

# 2
# Virtual Memory

Coming back to this chapter, we will look at the meaning and purpose of **virtual memory** (**VM**) and, importantly, why it is a key concept and required one. We will cover the meaning and importance of VM, paging and address-translation, the benefits of using VM, the memory layout of a process in execution, and the internal layout of a process as seen by the kernel. We shall also delve into what segments make up the process virtual address space. This knowledge is indispensable in difficult-to-debug situations.

In this chapter, we will cover the following topics:

- Virtual memory
- Process virtual address space

## Technical requirements

A modern desktop PC or laptop is required; Ubuntu Desktop specifies the following as recommended system requirements for installation and usage of the distribution:

- 2 GHz dual core processor or better
- RAM
    - **Running on a physical host**: 2 GB or more system memory
    - **Running as a guest**: The host system should have at least 4 GB RAM (the more, the better and smoother the experience)

- 25 GB of free hard drive space
- Either a DVD drive or a USB port for the installer media
- Internet access is definitely helpful

We recommend the reader use one of the following Linux distributions (can be installed as a guest OS on a Windows or Linux host system, as mentioned):

- Ubuntu 18.04 LTS Desktop (Ubuntu 16.04 LTS Desktop is a good choice too as it has long term support as well, and pretty much everything should work)
    - Ubuntu Desktop download link: https://www.ubuntu.com/download/desktop
- Fedora 27 (Workstation)
    - Download link: https://getfedora.org/en_GB/workstation/download/

Note that these distributions are, in their default form, OSS and non-proprietary, and free to use as an end user.

> There are instances where the entire code snippet isn't included in the book. Thus the GitHub URL to refer the codes: https://github.com/PacktPublishing/Hands-on-System-Programming-with-Linux.
> Also, for the further reading section, refer to the preceding GitHub link.

# Virtual memory

Modern operating systems are based on a memory model called VM. This includes Linux, Unixes, MS Windows, and macOS. Truly understanding how a modern OS works under the hood requires a deep understanding of VM and memory management – not topics we delve into in intricate detail in this book; nevertheless, a solid grasp of VM concepts is critical for Linux system developers.

# No VM – the problem

Let's imagine for a moment that VM, and all the complex baggage it lugs around, does not exist. So, we're working on a (fictional) pure flat physical memory platform with, say, 64 MB RAM. This is actually not that unusual – most old OSes (think DOS) and even modern **Real-Time Operating Systems** (RTOSes) operate this way:

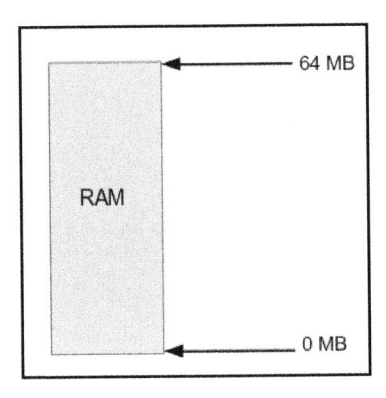

Figure 1: Flat physical address space of 64 MB

Obviously, everything that runs on this machine must share this physical memory space: the OS, device drivers, libraries, and applications. We might visualize it this way (of course, this is not intended to reflect an actual system – it's just a highly simplified example to help you understand things): one OS, several device drivers (to drive the hardware peripherals), a set of libraries, and two applications. The physical memory map (not drawn to scale) of this fictional (64 MB system) platform might look like this:

| Object | Space taken | Address range |
| --- | --- | --- |
| Operating system (OS) | 3 MB | 0x03d0 0000 - 0x0400 0000 |
| Device Drivers | 5 MB | 0x02d0 0000 – 0x0320 0000 |
| Libraries | 10 MB | 0x00a0 0000 – 0x0140 0000 |
| Application 2 | 1 MB | 0x0010 0000 – 0x0020 0000 |
| Application 1 | 0.5 MB | 0x0000 0000 – 0x0008 0000 |
| Overall Free Memory | 44.5 MB | <various> |

Table 1: The physical memory map

Virtual Memory

The same fictional system is represented in the following diagram:

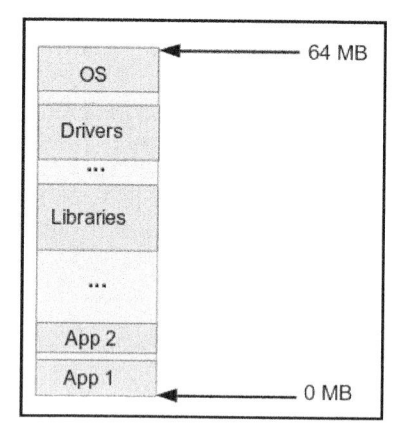

Fig 2: The physical memory map of our fictional 64 MB system

Normally, of course, the system will undergo rigorous testing before release and will perform as expected; except, there's this thing you might have heard of in our industry called bugs. Yes, indeed.

But let's imagine a dangerous bug creeps into Application 1, say, within the use of the ubiquitous memcpy(3) glibc API, due to either of the following:

- Inadvertent programming errors
- Deliberate malicious intent

As a quick reminder, the usage of the memcpy library API is shown as follows:

```
void *memcpy(void *dest, const void *src, size_t n).
```

## Objective

This C program snippet as follows intends to copy some memory, say 1,024 bytes, using the usual memcpy(3) glibc API, from a source location 300 KB into the program to a destination location 400 KB into the program. As Application 1 is the program at the low end of physical memory (see the preceding memory map), it starts at the 0x0 physical offset.

# Chapter 2

> We understand that on a modern OS nothing will start at address `0x0`; that's the canonical NULL memory location! Keep in mind that this is just a fictional example for learning purposes

First, let's see the correct usage case.

Refer to the following pseudocode:

```
phy_offset = 0x0;
src = phy_offset + (300*1024);      /* = 0x0004 b000 */
dest = phy_offset + (400*1024);     /* = 0x0006 4000 */
n = 1024;
memcpy(dest, src, n);
```

The effect of the preceding code is shown in the following diagram:

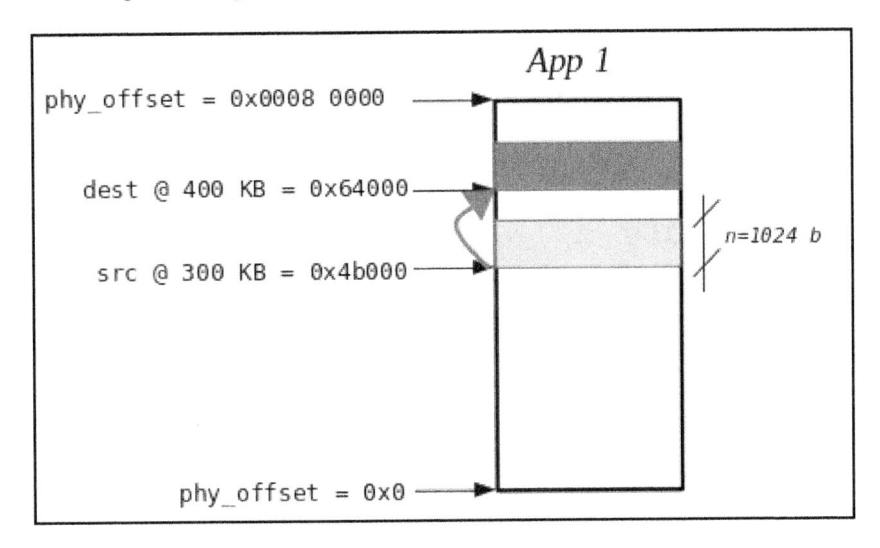

```
                           App 1
phy_offset = 0x0008 0000 ─────┐
                              ▼
                           ┌─────────┐
                           │░░░░░░░░░│
dest @ 400 KB = 0x64000 ──▶├─────────┤
                           │         │ n=1024 b
src @ 300 KB = 0x4b000 ───▶├─────────┤
                           │         │
                           │         │
                           │         │
phy_offset = 0x0 ──────────▶└─────────┘
```

Fig 3: Zoomed into App 1: the correct memcpy()

As can be seen in the preceding diagram, this works! The (big) arrow shows the copy path from source to destination, for 1,024 bytes. Great.

Now for the buggy case.

All remains the same, except that this time, due to a bug (or malicious intent), the `dest` pointer is modified as follows:

```
phy_offset = 0x0;
src = phy_offset + (300*1024);        /* = 0x0004 b000 */
dest = phy_offset + (400*1024*156);   /* = 0x03cf 0000  !BUG! */
n = 1024;
memcpy(dest, src, n);
```

The destination location is now around 64 KB (0x03cf0000 – 0x03d00000) into the operating system! The best part: the code itself does not fail. `memcpy()` does its job. Of course, now the OS is probably corrupted and the entire system will (eventually) crash.

Note that the intent here is not to debug the cause (we know); the intent here is to clearly realize that, in spite of this bug, memcpy succeeds.
How come? This is because we are programming in C – we are free to read and write physical memory as we wish; inadvertent bugs are our problem, not the language's!

So what now? Ah, this is one of the key reasons why VM systems came into existence.

## Virtual memory

Unfortunately, the term **virtual memory** (**VM**) is often misunderstood or hazily understood, at best, by a large proportion of engineers. In this section, we attempt to clarify what this term and its associated terminologies (such as memory pyramid, addressing, and paging) really mean; it's important for developers to clearly understand this key area.

First, what is a process?

A process is an instance of a program in execution.
A program is a binary executable file: a dead, disk object. For example, take the `cat` program:
```
$ ls -l /bin/cat
-rwxr-xr-x 1 root root 36784 Nov 10 23:26 /bin/cat
$
```
When we run `cat` it becomes a live runtime schedulable entity, which, in the Unix universe, we call a process.

*Chapter 2*

In order to understand deeper concepts clearly, we start with a small, simple, and fictional machine. Imagine it has a microprocessor with 16 address lines. Thus, it's easy to see, it will have access to a total potential memory space (or address space) of $2^{16}$ = 65,536 bytes = 64 KB:

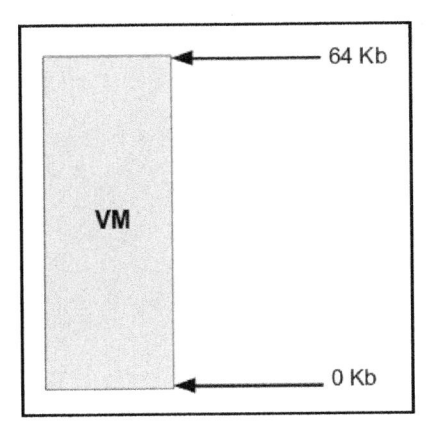

Fig 4: Virtual memory of 64 KB

But what if the physical memory (RAM) on the machine is a lot less, say, 32 KB? Clearly, the preceding diagram depicts virtual memory, not physical. Meanwhile, physical memory (RAM) looks as follows:

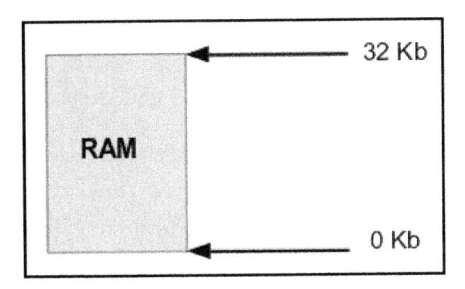

Fig 5: Physical memory of 32 KB

## Virtual Memory

Still, the promise made by the system to every process alive: every single process will have available to it the entire virtual address space, that is, 64 KB. Sounds absurd, right? Yes, until one realizes that memory is more than just RAM; in fact, memory is viewed as a hierarchy – what's commonly referred to as the memory pyramid:

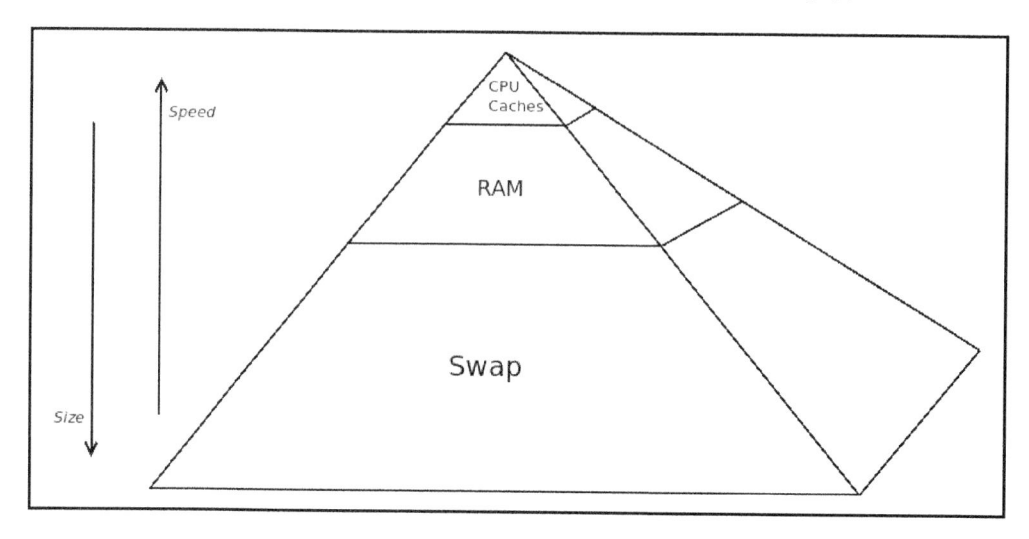

Fig 6: The Memory pyramid

As with life, everything's a trade-off. Toward the apex of the pyramid, we gain in **Speed** at the cost of size; toward the bottom of the pyramid, it's inverted: **Size** at the cost of speed. One could also consider CPU registers to be at the very apex of the pyramid; as its size is almost insignificant, it has not been shown.

*Swap* is a filesystem type – a raw disk partition is formatted as swap upon system installation. It's treated as second-level RAM by the OS. When the OS runs out of RAM, it uses swap. As a rough heuristic, system administrators sometimes configure the size of the swap partition to be twice that of available RAM.

To help quantify this, according to *Computer Architecture, A Quantitative Approach, 5th Ed*, by Hennessy & Patterson, fairly typical numbers follow:

| Type | CPU registers | CPU caches ||| RAM | Swap/storage |
|---|---|---|---|---|---|---|
|  |  | L1 | L2 | L3 |  |  |
| Server | 1000 bytes | 64 KB | 256 KB | 2 - 4 MB | 4 - 16 GB | 4 - 16 TB |
|  | 300 ps | 1 ns | 3 - 10 ns | 10 - 20 ns | 50 - 100 ns | 5 - 10 ms |
| Embedded | 500 bytes | 64 KB | 256 KB | - | 256 - 512 MB | 4 - 8 GB Flash |
|  | 500 ps | 2 ns | 10 - 20 ns | - | 50 - 100 ns | 25 - 50 us |

Table 2: Memory hierarchy numbers

> Many (if not most) embedded Linux systems do not support a swap partition; the reason is straightforward: embedded systems mostly use flash memory as the secondary storage medium (not a traditional SCSI disk as do laptops, desktops, and servers). Writing to a flash chip wears it out (it has limited erase-write cycles); hence, embedded-system designers would rather sacrifice swap and just use RAM. (Please note that the embedded system can still be VM-based, which is the usual case with Linux and Win-CE, for example).

The OS will do its best to keep the working set of pages as high up the pyramid as is possible, optimizing performance.

> It's important for the reader to note that, in the sections that follow, while this book attempts to explain some of the inner workings of advanced topics such as VM and addressing (paging), we quite deliberately do not paint a complete, realistic, real-world view.
>
> The reason is straightforward: the deep and gory technical details are well beyond the scope of this book. So, the reader should keep in mind that several of the following areas are explained in concept and not in actuality. The *Further reading* section provides references for readers who are interested in going deeper into these matters. Refer it on the GitHub repository.

*Virtual Memory*

## Addressing 1 – the simplistic flawed approach

Okay, now to the memory pyramid; even if we agree that virtual memory is now a possibility, a key and difficult hurdle to overcome remains. To explain this, note that every single process that is alive will occupy the entire available **virtual address space** (**VAS**). Thus, each process overlaps with every other process in terms of VAS. But how would this work? It wouldn't, by itself. In order for this elaborate scheme to work, the system has to somehow map every virtual address in every process to a physical address! Refer to the following mapping of virtual address to physical address:

**Process P:virtual address (va) → RAM:physical address (pa)**

So, the situation is something like this now:

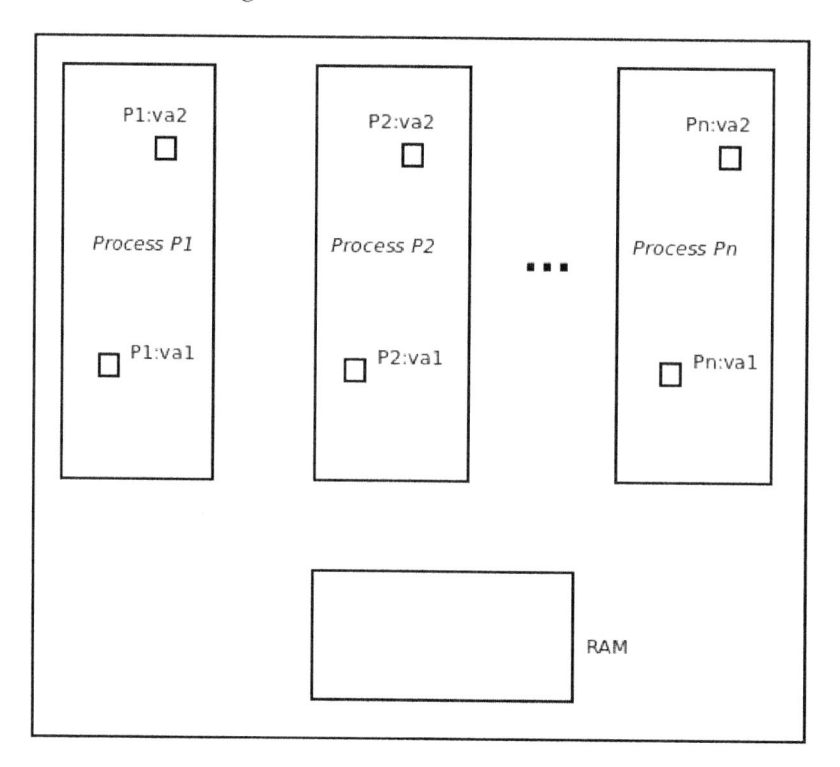

Fig 7: Processes containing virtual addresses

*Chapter 2*

Processes **P1**, **P2**, and **Pn**, are alive and well in VM. Their virtual address spaces cover 0 to 64 KB and overlap each other. Physical memory, **RAM**, of 32 KB is present on this (fictional) system.

As an example, two virtual addresses for each process are shown in the following format:

`P'r':va'n'`; where `r` is the process number and `n` is 1 and 2.

As mentioned earlier, the key now is to map each process's virtual addresses to physical addresses. So, we need to map the following:

```
P1:va1 → P1:pa1
P1:va2 → P1:pa2
...

P2:va1 → P2:pa1
P2:va2 → P2:pa2
...

[...]

Pn:va1 → Pn:pa1
Pn:va2 → Pn:pa2
...
```

*Virtual Memory*

We could have the OS perform this mapping; the OS would then maintain a mapping table per process to do so. Diagrammatically and conceptually it looks as follows:

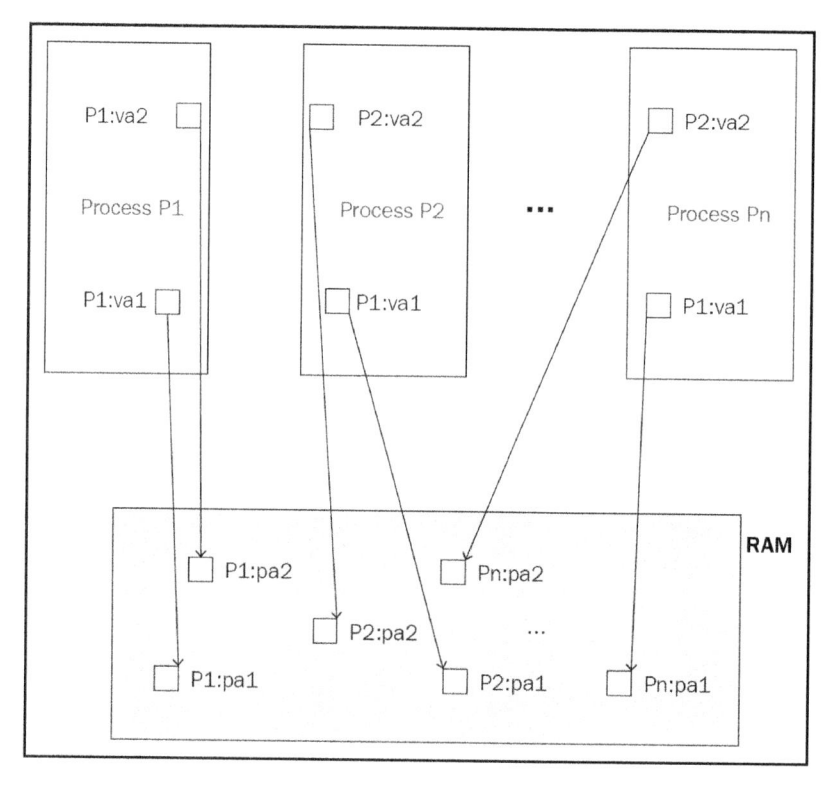

Fig 8: Direct mapping virtual addresses to physical RAM addresses

So that's it, then? Seems quite simple, actually. Well, no, it won't work in reality: to map all the possible virtual addresses per process to physical addresses in RAM, the OS would need to maintain a **va**-to-**pa** translation entry per address per process! That's too expensive, as each table would possibly exceed the size of physical memory, rendering the scheme useless.

A quick calculation reveals that we have 64KB virtual memory, that is, 65,536 bytes or addresses. Each of these virtual addresses need to be mapped to a physical address. So each process would require:

- 65536 * 2 = 131072 = 128 KB, for a mapping table. per process.

It gets worse in reality; the OS would need to store some metadata along with each address-translation entry; let's say 8 bytes of metadata. So now, each process would require:

- 65536 * 2 * 8 = 1048576 = 1 MB, for a mapping table. per process.

Wow, 1 megabyte of RAM per process! That's far too much (think of an embedded system); also, on our fictional system, there's a total of 32 KB of RAM. Whoops.

Okay, we can reduce this overhead by not mapping each byte but mapping each word; say, 4 bytes to a word. So now, each process would require:

- (65536 * 2 * 8) / 4 = 262144 = 256 KB, for a mapping table. per process.

Better, but not good enough. If there are just 20 processes alive, we'd require 5 MB of physical memory to store just the mapping metadata. With 32 KB of RAM, we can't do that.

## Addressing 2 – paging in brief

To address (pun intended) this tricky issue, computer scientists came up with a solution: do not attempt to map individual virtual bytes (or even words) to their physical counterpart; it's far too expensive. Instead, carve up both physical and virtual memory space into blocks and map them.

A bit simplistically, there are broadly two ways to do this:

- Hardware-segmentation
- Hardware-paging

**Hardware-segmentation:** Carves up the virtual and physical address space into arbitrary-sized chunks called **segments**. The best example is Intel 32-bit processors.

**Hardware-paging:** Carves up the virtual and physical address space into equal-sized chunks called **pages**. Most real-world processors support hardware-paging, including Intel, ARM, PPC, and MIPS.

Actually it's not even up to the OS developer to select which scheme to use: the choice is dictated by the hardware MMU.

# Virtual Memory

> Again, we remind the reader: the intricate details are beyond the scope of this book. See the *Further reading* section on the GitHub repository.

Let's assume we go with the paging technique. The key takeaway is that we stop attempting to map all possible virtual addresses per process to physical addresses in RAM, instead, we map virtual pages (just called pages) to physical pages (called page frames).

> **Common Terminology**
>
> **virtual address space** : **VAS**
> Virtual page within the process VAS : page
> Physical page in RAM : **page frame (pf)**

> Does NOT work: **virtual address (va)** → **physical address (pa)**
> Does work: (virtual) page → page frame
>
> The left-to-right arrow represents the mapping.

As a rule of thumb (and the generally accepted norm), the size of a page is 4 kilobytes (4,096 bytes). Again, it's the processor **Memory Management Unit (MMU)** that dictates the page size.

So how and why does this scheme help?

Think about it for a moment; in our fictional machine, we've got: 64 KB of VM, that is, 64K/4K = 16 pages, and 32 KB of RAM, that is, 32K/4K = 8 page frames.

Mapping 16 pages to corresponding page frames requires a table of only 16 entries per process; this is viable!

> As in our earlier calculations:
> 16 * 2 * 8 = 256 bytes, for a mapping table per process.

The very important thing, it bears repeating: we map (virtual) pages to (physical) page frames!

This is done by the OS on a per-process basis. Thus, each process has its own mapping table that translates pages to page frames at runtime; it's commonly called the **Paging Table (PT)**:

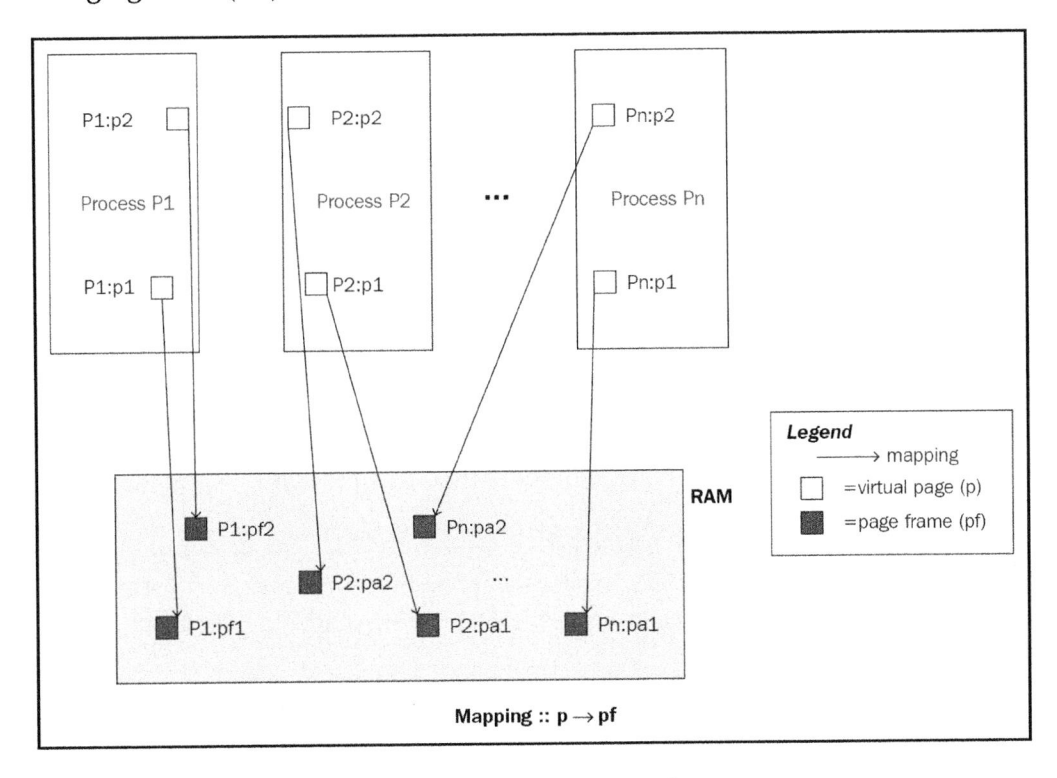

Fig 9: Mapping (virtual) pages to (physical) page frames

## Paging tables – simplified

Again, in our fictional machine, we've got: 64 KB of VM, that is, 64K/4K = 16 pages, and 32 KB of RAM, that is, 32K/4K = 8 page frames.

Mapping the 16 (virtual) pages to corresponding (physical) page frames requires a table of only 16 entries per process, which makes the whole deal viable.

## Virtual Memory

Very simplistically, the OS-created PT of a single process look as follows:

| (Virtual) page | (Physical) page frame |
|---|---|
| 0 | 3 |
| 1 | 2 |
| 2 | 5 |
| [...] | [...] |
| 15 | 6 |

Table 3: OS-created PT

Of course, the astute reader will notice that we have a problem: we've got 16 pages and just eight page frames to map them into – what about the remaining eight pages?

Well, consider this:

- In reality, every process will not use every available page for code or data or whatever; several regions of the virtual address space will remain empty (sparse),
- Even if we do require it, we have a way: don't forget the memory pyramid. When we're out of RAM, we use swap. So the (conceptual) PT for a process might appear like this (as an example, pages 13 and 14 are residing in swap):

| (Virtual) page | (Physical) page frame |
|---|---|
| 0 | 3 |
| 1 | 2 |
| 2 | 5 |
| [...] | [...] |
| 13 | <swap-address> |
| 14 | <swap-address> |
| 15 | 6 |

Table 4: Conceptual PT

> Again, please note that this description of PTs is purely conceptual; actual PTs are more complex and highly arch (CPU/MMU) dependent.

## Indirection

By introducing paging, we have actually introduced a level of indirection: we no longer think of a (virtual) address as an absolute offset from zero, but rather as a relative quantity: `va = (page, offset)`.

We think of each virtual address as associated with a page number and an offset from the beginning of that page. This is called using one level of indirection.

So each time a process refers to a virtual address (and of course, note that this is happening almost all of the time), the system must translate the virtual address to the corresponding physical address based on the PTs for that process.

## Address-translation

So, at runtime, the process looks up a virtual address which is, say, 9,192 bytes from 0, that is, its virtual address: `va = 9192 = 0x000023E8`. If each page is 4,096 bytes in size, this implies the va address is on the third page (page #2), at an offset of 1,000 bytes from the start of that page.

So, with one level of indirection, we have: `va = (page, offset) = (2, 1000)`.

Aha! Now we can see how address-translation works: the OS sees that the process wants an address in page 2. It does a lookup on the PT for that process, and finds that page 2 maps to page frame 5. To calculate the physical address shown as follows:

```
pa = (pf * PAGE_SIZE) + offset
   = (5 * 4096) + 1000
   = 21480 = 0x000053E8
```

Voila!

The system now places the physical address on the bus and the CPU performs its work as usual. It looks quite simple, but again, it's not realistic—please see the information box as follows as well.

Another advantage gained by the paging schema is the OS only needs to store a page-to-page-frame mapping. This automatically lets us translate any byte in the page to the corresponding physical byte in the page frame by just adding the offset, as there is a 1:1 mapping between a page and a page frame (both are of identical size).

*Virtual Memory*

In reality, it's not the OS that does the actual calculations to perform address-translation. This is because doing this in the software would be far too slow (remember, looking up virtual addresses is an ongoing activity happening almost all the time). The reality is that the address lookup and translation is done by silicon – the hardware **Memory Management Unit** (**MMU**) within the CPU!

Keep the following in mind:
- The OS is responsible for creating and maintaining PTs for each process.
- The MMU is responsible for performing runtime address-translation (using the OS PTs).
- Beyond this, modern hardware supports hardware accelerators, such as the TLB, use of CPU caches, and virtualization extensions, which go a long way toward getting decent performance.

## Benefits of using VM

At first glance, the sheer overhead introduced due to virtual memory and the associated address-translation would seem to warrant not using it. Yes, the overhead is high, but the reality is given as follows:

- Modern hardware-acceleration (via TLBs/CPU caches/prefetching) mitigates this overhead and provides decent enough performance
- The benefits one derives from VM outweigh the performance issues

On a VM-based system, we get the following benefits:

- Process-isolation
- The programmer need not worry about physical memory
- Memory-region protection

It's important to understand these a bit better.

## Process-isolation

With virtual memory, every process runs inside a sandbox, which is the extent of its VAS. The key rule: it cannot look outside the box.

So, think about it, it's impossible for a process to peek or poke the memory of any other process's VAS. This helps in making the system secure and stable.

Example: we have two processes, A and B. Process A wants to write to the `0x10ea` virtual address in process B. It cannot, even if it attempts to write to that address, all it's really doing is writing to its own virtual address, `0x10ea`! The same goes for reading.

So we get process-isolation – each process is completely isolated from every other process.
Virtual address X for process A is not the same as virtual address X for process B; in all likelihood, they translate to different physical addresses (via their PTs). Exploiting this property, the Android system is designed to very deliberately use the process model for Android apps: when an Android app is launched, it becomes a Linux process, which lives within its own VAS, isolated and thus protected from other Android apps (processes)!

- Again, don't make the mistake of assuming that every single (virtual) page within a given process is valid for that process itself. A page is only valid if it's mapped, that is, it's been allocated and the OS has a valid translation for it (or a way to get to it). In fact, and especially true for the enormous 64-bit VAS, the process virtual address space is considered to be sparse, that is, scanty.
- If process-isolation is as described, then what if process A needs to talk to process B? Indeed, this is a frequent design requirement for many, if not most, real Linux applications – we need some mechanism(s) to be able to read/write the VAS of another process. Modern OSes provide mechanisms to achieve this: **Inter-Process Communication** (**IPC**) mechanisms. (A little on IPC can be found in `Chapter 15`, *Multithreading with Pthreads Part II - Synchronization*.)

# The programmer need not worry about physical memory

On older OSes and even modern RTOSes, the programmer is expected to understand the memory layout of the entire system in detail and use memory accordingly (recall *Fig 1*). Obviously, this places a major burden on the developer; they have to ensure that they work well within the physical constraints of the system.

# Virtual Memory

Most modern developers working on modern OSes never even think this way: if we want, say, 512 Kb of memory, do we not just allocate it dynamically (with `malloc(3)`, seen later in detail in Chapter 4, *Dynamic Memory Allocation*), leaving the precise details of how and where it's done to the library and OS layers? In fact, we can do this kind of thing dozens of times and not worry about stuff such as, "Will there be enough physical RAM? Which physical page frames should be used? What about fragmentation/wastage?"

We get the added benefit that the memory returned to us by the system is guaranteed to be contiguous; of course, it's just virtually contiguous, it need not be physically contiguous, but that kind of detail is exactly what the VM layers take care of!

All is handled, really efficiently, by the library layer and the underlying memory-management system in the OS.

## Memory-region protection

Perhaps the most important benefit of VM is this: the ability to define protections on virtual memory and have them honored by the OS.

Unix and friends (including Linux), allow four protection or permission values on memory pages:

| Protection or permission type | Meaning |
|---|---|
| None | No permission to do anything on the page |
| Read | Page can be read from |
| Write | Page can be written to |
| Execute | Page (code) can be executed |

Table 5: Protection or permission values on memory pages

Let's consider a small example: we allocate four pages of memory in our process (numbered 0 to 3). By default, the default permission or protections on the pages is **RW (Read-Write)**, which means the pages can be both read from and written to.

[ 68 ]

With virtual memory OS-level support, the OS exposes APIs (the mmap(2) and mprotect(2) system calls) with which one can change the default page protections! Kindly take a look at the following table:

| Memory page # | Default protections | Changed protections |
|---|---|---|
| 0 | RW- | -none- |
| 1 | RW- | Read-only (R--) |
| 2 | RW- | Write-only (-W-) |
| 3 | RW- | Read-Execute (R-X) |

With powerful APIs such as this, we can set memory protections to the granularity of a single page!

Applications (and indeed the OS) can, and do, leverage these powerful mechanisms; in fact, that's precisely what is done on particular regions of process address space by the OS (as we'll learn in the next section, *SIDEBAR :: Testing the memcpy() 'C' program*).

Okay, fine, we can set certain protections on certain pages, but what if an application disobeys them? For example, after setting page #3 (as seen in the preceding table) to read-execute, what if the app (or OS) attempts to write to that page?

This is where the real power of virtual memory (and memory management) is seen: the reality is that on a VM-enabled system, the OS – more realistically, the MMU – is able to trap into every single memory access and determine whether the end user process is obeying the rules or not. If it is, the access proceeds successfully; if not, the MMU hardware raises an exception (similar, but not identical, to an interrupt). The OS now jumps into a code routine called the exception (or fault) handler. The OSes exception-handling routine determines whether the access is indeed illegal, and if so, the OS immediately kills the process attempting this illegal access.

How's that for memory protection? In fact, this is pretty much exactly what a Segmentation Violation or segfault is; more on this in Chapter 12, *Signaling - Part II*. The exception-handler routine is called the OSes fault-handler.

## SIDEBAR :: Testing the memcpy() C program

Now that we better understand the what and why of a VM system, let's go back to the buggy pseudocode example we considered at the beginning of this chapter: the case where we used memcpy(3) to copy some memory but specified the wrong destination address (and it would have overwritten the OS itself in our fictional physical-memory-only system).

## Virtual Memory

A conceptually similar C program, but which runs on Linux—a full-fledged virtual-memory-enabled OS—is shown and tried out here. Let's see how the buggy program works on Linux:

```
$ cat mem_app1buggy.c
/*
 * mem_app1buggy.c
 *
 ******************************************************************
 * This program is part of the source code released for the book
 *  "Linux System Programming"
 *  (c) Kaiwan N Billimoria
 *  Packt Publishers
 *
 * From:
 *  Ch 2 : Virtual Memory
 ******************************************************************
 * A simple demo to show that on Linux - full-fledged Virtual
 * Memory enabled OS - even a buggy app will _NOT_ cause system
 * failure; rather, the buggy process will be killed by the
 * kernel!
 * On the other hand, if we had run this or a similar program in a flat purely
 * physical address space based OS, this seemingly trivial bug
 * can wreak havoc, bringing the entire system down.
 */
#define _GNU_SOURCE
#include <stdio.h>
#include <unistd.h>
#include <stdlib.h>
#include <string.h>
#include "../common.h"

int main(int argc, char **argv)
{
    void *ptr = NULL;
    void *dest, *src = "abcdef0123456789";
    void *arbit_addr = (void *)0xffffffffff601000;
    int n = strlen(src);

    ptr = malloc(256 * 1024);
    if (!ptr)
        FATAL("malloc(256*1024) failed\n");

    if (argc == 1)
        dest = ptr;            /* correct */
    else
        dest = arbit_addr;     /* bug! */
```

```
        memcpy(dest, src, n);

        free(ptr);
        exit(0);
}
```

The `malloc(3)` API will be covered in detail in the next chapter; for now, just understand that it is used to dynamically allocate 256 KB of memory to the process. Also, of course, `memcpy(3)` is used to copy memory from a source to a destination pointer, for n bytes:

```
void *memcpy(void *dest, const void *src, size_t n);
```

The interesting part is that we have a variable called `arbit_addr`; it's set to an arbitrary invalid (virtual) address. As you can see from the code, we set the destination pointer to `arbit_addr` when the user passes any argument to the program, making it the buggy test case. Let's try running the program for both the correct and buggy cases.

Here is the correct case:

```
$ ./mem_app1buggy
$
```

It runs fine, with no errors.

Here is the buggy case:

```
$ ./mem_app1buggy buggy-case pass-params forcing-argc-to-not-be-1
Segmentation fault (core dumped)
$
```

It crashes! As described earlier, the buggy memcpy causes the MMU to fault; the OSes fault-handling code realizes that this is indeed a bug and it kills the offending process! The process dies because it's at fault, not the system. Not only is this correct, the segfault caused also alerts the developer to the fact that their code is buggy and must be fixed.

> **TIP**
>
> 1. What's a core dump anyway?
> A core dump is a snapshot of certain dynamic regions (segments) of the process at the time it crashed (technically, it's a snapshot of minimally the data and stack segments). The core dump can be analyzed postmortem using debuggers such as GDB. We do not cover these areas in this book.
>
> 2. Hey, it says (core dumped) but I don't see any core file?
> Well, there can be several reasons why the core file isn't present; the details lie beyond the scope of this book. Please refer to the man page on `core(5)` for details: https://linux.die.net/man/5/core.

Think about what has happened here in a bit more detail: the destination pointer's value is `0xffffffffff601000`; on the x86_64 processor, this is actually a kernel virtual address. Now we, a user mode process, are trying to write some memory to this destination region, which is protected against access from userspace. Technically, it's in the kernel virtual address space, which is not available to user mode processes (recall our discussion of *CPU privilege levels* in `Chapter 1`, *Linux System Architecture*). So when we – a user mode process – attempt to write to kernel virtual address space, the protection mechanism spins up and prevents us from doing this, killing us in the bargain.

Advanced: How does the system know that this region is protected and what kind of protection it has? These details are encoded into the **Paging Table Entry** (**PTEs**) for the process, and are checked by the MMU on every access!

This kind of advanced memory protection would be impossible without support in both hardware and software:

- Hardware support via the MMU found in all modern microprocessors
- Software support via the operating system

There are many more benefits that VM provides, including (but not limited to) making powerful technologies, such as demand paging, **copy-on-write** (**COW**) handling, defragmentation, memory overcommit, memory-compaction, **Kernel Samepage Merging** (**KSM**), and **Transcendent Memory** (**TM**), possible. Within this book's scope, we will cover a couple of these at later points.

# Process memory layout

A process is an instance of a program in execution. It is seen as a live, runtime schedulable entity by the OS. In other words, it's the process that runs when we launch a program.

The OS, or kernel, stores metadata about the process in a data structure in kernel memory; on Linux, this structure is often called the **process descriptor**—though the term *task structure* is a more accurate one. Process attributes are stored in the task structure; the process **PID (process identifier)** – a unique integer identifying the process, process credentials, open-file information, signaling information, and a whole lot more, reside here.

From the earlier discussion, *Virtual memory*, we understand that a process has, among many other attributes, a VAS. The VAS is the sum-total space potentially available to it. As in our earlier example, with a fictional computer with 16 address lines, the VAS per process would be $2^{16}$ = 64 KB.

Now, let's consider a more realistic system: a 32-bit CPU with 32 lines for addressing. Clearly, each process has a VAS of $2^{32}$, a fairly large quantity of 4 GB.

4 GB in hexadecimal format is `0x100000000`; so the VAS spans from the low address of `0x0` to the high address of `4GB - 1 = 0xffff ffff`.

However, we have yet to learn more details (see the *Advanced: VM split*) regarding the exact usage of the high end of the VAS. Therefore, for the time being at least, let's just refer to this as the high address and not put a particular numerical value to it.

*Virtual Memory*

Here is its diagrammatic representation:

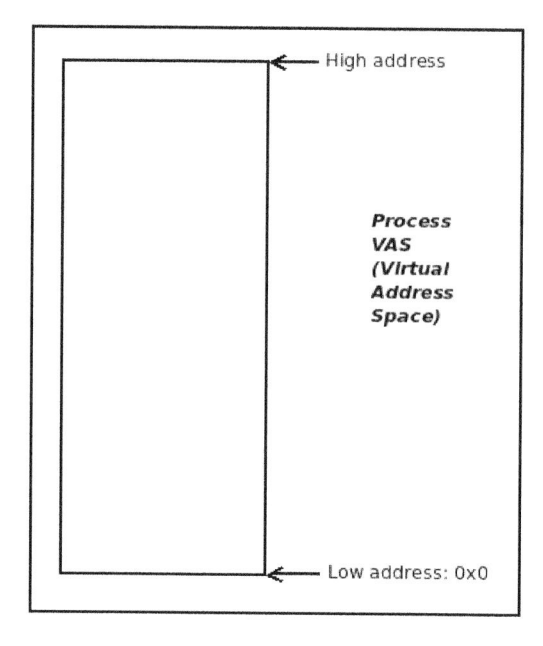

Fig 10: Process virtual address space (VAS)

So, the thing to understand for now is that on a 32-bit Linux, every process alive has this image:
**0x0** to 0xffff ffff = 4 GB of virtual address space.

## Segments or mappings

When a new process is created (details in `Chapter 10`, *Process Creation*), its VAS must be set up by the OS. All modern OSes divide up the process VAS into homogeneous regions called **segments** (don't confuse these segments with the hardware-segmentation approach mentioned in the, *Addressing 2 – paging in brief* section).

A segment is a homogeneous or uniform region of the process VAS; it consists of virtual pages. The segment has attributes, such as start and end addresses, protections (RWX/none), and mapping types. The key point for now: all pages belonging to a segment share the same attributes.

Technically, and more accurately from the OS viewpoint, the segment is called a **mapping**.

[ 74 ]

*Chapter 2*

> From now on, when we use the word segment, we also mean mapping and vice versa.

Briefly, from the lower to high end, every Linux process will have the following segments (or mappings):

- Text (code)
- Data
- Library (or other)
- Stack

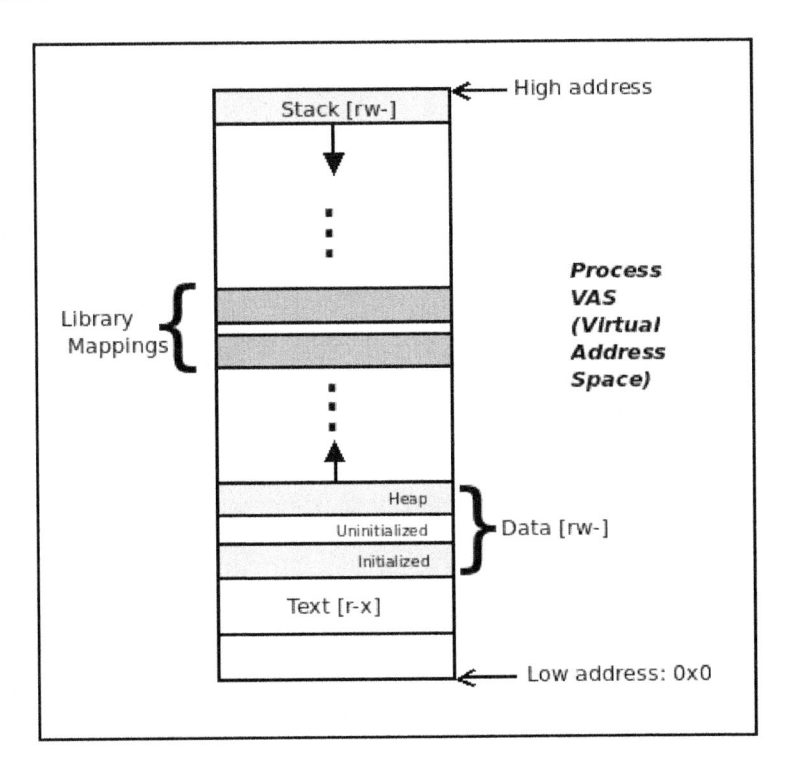

Fig 11: Overall view of the process VAS with segments

Read on for more details about each of these segments.

[ 75 ]

## Text segment

Text is code: the actual opcodes and operands that make up the machine instructions that are fed to the CPU to consume. Readers may recall the `objdump --source ./hello_dbg` we did in `Chapter 1`, *Linux System Architecture*, showing C code translated into assembly and machine language. This machine code resides within the process VAS in a segment called **text**. For example, let's say a program has 32 KB of text; when we run it, it becomes a process and the text segment takes 32 KB of virtual memory; that's 32K/4K = 8 (virtual) pages.

For optimization and protection, the OS marks, that is, protects, all these eight pages of text as **read-execute (r-x)**. This makes sense: code will be read from memory and executed by the CPU, not written to it.

The text segment on Linux is always toward the low end of the process VAS. Note that it will never start at the `0x0` address.

> **TIP**: As a typical example, on the IA-32, the text segment usually starts at `0x0804 8000`. This is very arch-specific though and changes in the presence of Linux security mechanisms like **Address Space Layout Randomization (ASLR)**.

## Data segments

Immediately above the text segment is the data segment, which is the place where the process holds the program's global and static variables (data).

Actually, it's not one mapping (segment); the data segment consists of three distinct mappings. In order from the low address, it consists of: the initialized data segment, the uninitialized data segment, and the heap segment.

We understand that, in a C program, uninitialized global and static variables are automatically initialized to zero. What about initialized globals? The initialized data segment is the region of address space where explicitly initialized global and static variables are stored.

The uninitialized data segment is the region of address space where, of course, uninitialized globals and static variables reside. The key point: these are implicitly initialized to zero (they're actually memset to zero). Also, older literature often refers to this region as the BSS. BSS is an old assembler directive – Block Started by Symbol – that can be ignored; today, the BSS region or segment is nothing but the uninitialized data segment of the process VAS.

The heap should be a term familiar to most C programmers; it refers to the memory region reserved for dynamic memory allocations (and subsequent free's). Think of the heap as a free gift of memory pages made available to the process at startup.

A key point: the text, initialized data, and uninitialized data segments are fixed in size; the heap is a dynamic segment – it can grow or shrink in size at runtime. It's important to note that the heap segment grows toward higher virtual addresses. Further details on the heap and its usage can be found in the next chapter.

## Library segments

When linking a program, we have two broad choices:

- Static linking
- Dynamic linking

Static linking implies that any and all library text (code) and data is saved within the program's binary executable file (hence it's larger, and a bit faster to load up).

Dynamic linking implies that any and all shared library text (code) and data is not saved within the program's binary executable file; instead, it is shared by all processes and mapped into the process VAS at runtime (hence the binary executable is a lot smaller, though it might take a bit longer to load up). Dynamic linking is always the default.

Think about the `Hello, world` C program. You invoked `printf(3)`, but did you write the code for it? No, of course not; we understand that it's within glibc and will be linked into our process at runtime. That's exactly what happens with dynamic linking: at process load time, all the library text and data segments that the program depends upon (uses) are *memory-mapped* (details in Chapter 18, *Advanced File I/O*) into the process VAS. Where? In the region between the top of the heap and the bottom of the stack: the library segments (refer to the preceding diagram).

Another thing: other mappings (besides library text and data) may find their way into this region of address space. A typical case is explicit memory mappings made by the developer (using the `mmap(2)` system call), implicit mappings such as those made by IPC mechanisms, such as shared memory mappings, and the malloc routines (refer to Chapter 4, *Dynamic Memory Allocation*).

# Stack segment

This section explains the process stack: what, why, and how.

## What is stack memory?

You probably remember being taught that stack memory is just memory but with a special push/pop semantic; the memory you push last resides at the top of the stack, and if you perform a pop operation, that memory gets popped off – removed from – the stack.

The pedagogical example of visualizing a stack of dinner plates is a good one: the plate you place last is at the top, and you take the top plate off to give it to your dinner guest (of course, you could insist that you give them the plate from the middle or bottom of the stack, but we think that the plate on the very top would be the easiest one to pop off).

Some literature also refers to this push/pop behavior as **Last In First Out** (**LIFO**). Fair enough.

The high end of the process VAS is used for the stack segment (refer to *Fig 11*). Okay, fine, but what exactly is it for? How does it help?

## Why a process stack?

We're taught to write nice modular code: divide your work into subroutines, and implement them as small, easily readable, and maintainable C functions. That's great.

The CPU, though, does not really understand how to invoke a C function, how to pass parameters, store local variables, and return a result to the calling function. Our savior, the compiler, takes over, converting C code into an assembly language that is capable of making this whole function thing work.

The compiler generates assembly code to invoke a function, passes along parameters, allocates space for local variables, and finally, emits a return result back to the caller. To do this, it uses the stack! So, similar to the heap, the stack is also a dynamic segment.

Every time a function is called, memory is allocated in the stack region (or segment or mapping) to hold metadata that has the function call, parameter passing and the function return mechanism work. This metadata region for each function is called the stack frame.

The stack frame holds the metadata necessary to implement the function call-parameter use-return value mechanism. The exact layout of a stack frame is highly CPU (and compiler) dependent; it's one of the key areas addressed by the CPU ABI document.

On the IA-32 processor, the stack frame layout essentially is as follows:

```
[ <-- high address
   [ Function Parameters ... ]
   [ RET address ]
   [ Saved Frame Pointer ] (optional)
   [ Local Variables ... ]
 ]  <-- SP: lowest address
```

Consider some pseudocode:

```
bar() { jail();}
foo() { bar();}
main() { foo();}
```

The call graph is quite obvious:

```
main --> foo --> bar --> jail
```

The arrow drawn like --> means calls; so, main calls foo, and so on.

The thing to understand: every function invocation is represented at runtime by a stack frame in the process's stack.

If the processor is issued a push or pop instruction, it will go ahead and perform it. But, think about it, how does the CPU know where exactly – at which stack memory location or address – it should push or pop memory? The answer: we reserve a special CPU register, the **stack pointer** (usually abbreviated to **SP**), for precisely this purpose: the value in SP always points to the top of the stack.

The next key point: the stack segment grows toward lower virtual addresses. This is often referred to as stack-grows-down semantics. Also note that the direction of stack growth is a CPU-specific feature dictated by the ABI for that CPU; most modern CPUs (including Intel, ARM, PPC, Alpha, and Sun SPARC) follow the stack-grows-down semantic.

*Virtual Memory*

The SP always points to the top of the stack; as we use a downward-growing stack, this is the lowest virtual address on the stack!

For clarity, let's check out a diagram that visualizes the process stack just after the call to `main()` (`main()` is invoked by a `__libc_start_main()` glibc routine):

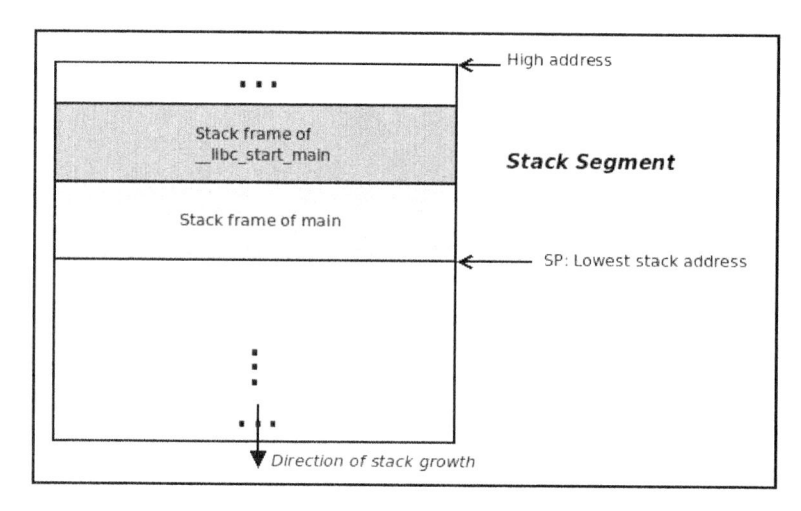

Figure 12: Process stack after main() is called

The process stack upon entry to the `jail()` function:

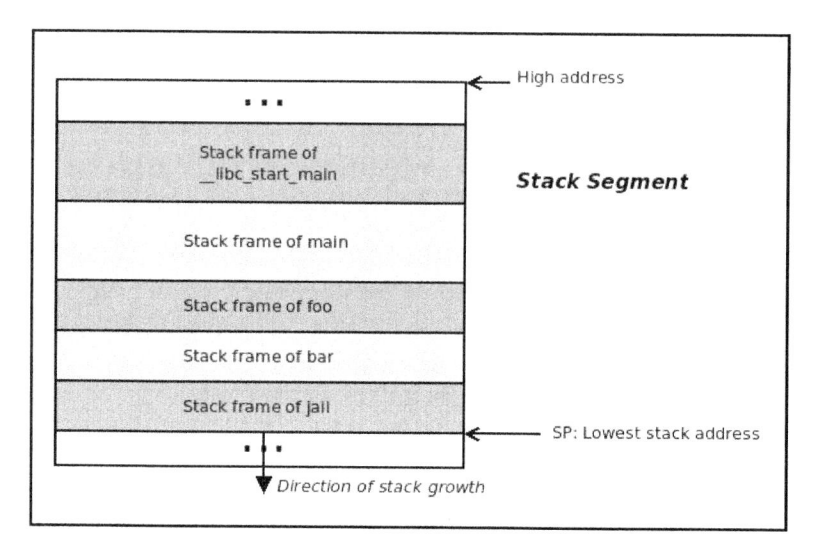

Figure 13: Process stack after jail() is called

## Peeking at the stack

We can take a peek into the process stack (technically, the stack of `main()`) in different ways. Here, we show two possibilities:

- Automatically via the `gstack(1)` utility
- Manually with the GDB debugger

Peek at the usermode stack, first, via `gstack(1)`:

> **TIP:** WARNING! Ubuntu users, you might face an issue here. At the time of writing (Ubuntu 18.04), gstack does not seem to be available for Ubuntu (and its alternative, pstack, does not work well either!). Please use the second method (via GDB), as follows.

As a quick example, we look up the stack of `bash` (the parameter is the PID of the process):

```
$ gstack 14654
#0  0x00007f3539ece7ea in waitpid () from /lib64/libc.so.6
#1  0x000056474b4b41d9 in waitchld.isra ()
#2  0x000056474b4b595d in wait_for ()
#3  0x000056474b4a5033 in execute_command_internal ()
#4  0x000056474b4a52c2 in execute_command ()
#5  0x000056474b48f252 in reader_loop ()
#6  0x000056474b48dd32 in main ()
$
```

The stack frame number appears on the left preceded by the `#` symbol; note that frame `#0` is the top of the stack, (the lowest frame). Read the stack in a bottom-up fashion, that is, from frame `#6` (the frame for the `main()` function) up to frame `#0` (the frame for the `waitpid()` function). Also note that, if the process is multithreaded, `gstack` will show the stack of *each* thread.

Peek at the Usermode Stack, next, via GDB.

The **GNU Debugger (GDB)** is a renowned, very powerful debug tool (if you don't already use it, we highly recommend you learn how to; check out the link in the *Further reading* section). Here, we'll use GDB to attach to a process and, once attached, peek at its process stack.

## Virtual Memory

A small test C program, that makes several nested function calls, will serve as a good example. Essentially, the call graph will look as follows:

```
main() --> foo() --> bar() --> bar_is_now_closed() --> pause()
```

The `pause(2)` system call is a great example of a blocking call – it puts the calling process to sleep, waiting (or blocking) on an event; the event it's blocking upon here is the delivery of any signal to the process. (Patience; we'll learn more in `Chapter 11`, *Signaling - Part I*, and `Chapter 12`, *Signaling - Part II*).

Here is the relevant code (`ch2/stacker.c`):

```c
static void bar_is_now_closed(void)
{
    printf("In function %s\n"
    "\t(bye, pl go '~/' now).\n", __FUNCTION__);
    printf("\n Now blocking on pause()...\n"
        " Connect via GDB's 'attach' and then issue the 'bt' command"
        " to view the process stack\n");
    pause(); /*process blocks here until it receives a signal */
}
static void bar(void)
{
    printf("In function %s\n", __FUNCTION__);
    bar_is_now_closed();
}
static void foo(void)
{
    printf("In function %s\n", __FUNCTION__);
    bar();
}
int main(int argc, char **argv)
{
    printf("In function %s\n", __FUNCTION__);
    foo();
    exit (EXIT_SUCCESS);
}
```

Note that, for GDB to see the symbols (names of functions, variables, line numbers), one must compile the code with the `-g` switch (produces debug information).

Now, we run the process in the background:

```
$ ./stacker_dbg &
[2] 28957
In function main
In function foo
In function bar
In function bar_is_now_closed
 (bye, pl go '~/' now).
 Now blocking on pause()...
 Connect via GDB's 'attach' and then issue the 'bt' command to view the process stack
$
```

Next, open GDB; within GDB, attach to the process (the PID is displayed in the preceding code), and view its stack with the **backtrace ( bt)** command:

```
$ gdb --quiet
(gdb) attach 28957 # parameter to 'attach' is the PID of the process to attach to
Attaching to process 28957
Reading symbols from <...>/Hands-on-System-Programming-with-Linux/ch2/stacker_dbg...done.
Reading symbols from /lib64/libc.so.6...Reading symbols from /usr/lib/debug/usr/lib64/libc-2.26.so.debug...done.
done.
Reading symbols from /lib64/ld-linux-x86-64.so.2...Reading symbols from /usr/lib/debug/usr/lib64/ld-2.26.so.debug...done.
done.
0x00007fce204143b1 in __libc_pause () at ../sysdeps/unix/sysv/linux/pause.c:30
30 return SYSCALL_CANCEL (pause);
(gdb) bt
#0 0x00007fce204143b1 in __libc_pause () at ../sysdeps/unix/sysv/linux/pause.c:30
#1 0x00000000004007ce in bar_is_now_closed () at stacker.c:31
#2 0x00000000004007ee in bar () at stacker.c:36
#3 0x000000000040080e in foo () at stacker.c:41
#4 0x0000000000400839 in main (argc=1, argv=0x7ffca9ac5ff8) at stacker.c:47
(gdb)
```

> On Ubuntu, due to security, GDB will not allow one to attach to any process; one can overcome this by running GDB as root; then it works well.

*Virtual Memory*

How about looking up the same process via `gstack` (at the time of writing, Ubuntu users, you're out of luck). Here it is on a Fedora 27 box:

```
$ gstack 28957
#0  0x00007fce204143b1 in __libc_pause () at
../sysdeps/unix/sysv/linux/pause.c:30
#1  0x00000000004007ce in bar_is_now_closed () at stacker.c:31
#2  0x00000000004007ee in bar () at stacker.c:36
#3  0x000000000040080e in foo () at stacker.c:41
#4  0x0000000000400839 in main (argc=1, argv=0x7ffca9ac5ff8) at
stacker.c:47
$
```

> Guess what? It turns out that `gstack` is really a wrapper shell script that invokes GDB in a non-interactive fashion and it issues the very same `backtrace` command we just used!
> As a quick learning exercise, check out the `gstack` script.

## Advanced – the VM split

What we have seen so far is actually not the complete picture; in reality, this address space needs to be shared between user and kernel space.

> This section is considered advanced. We leave it to the reader to decide whether to dive into the details that follow. While they're very useful, especially from a debug viewpoint, it's not strictly required for following the rest of this book.

Recall what we mentioned in the *Library segments* section: if a `Hello, world` application is to work, it needs to have a mapping to the `printf(3)` glibc routine. This is achieved by having the dynamic or shared libraries memory-mapped into the process VAS at runtime (by the loader program).

*Chapter 2*

A similar argument could be made for any and every system call issued by the process: we understood from `Chapter 1`, *Linux System Architecture*, that the system call code is actually within the kernel address space. Thus, if issuing a system call were to succeed, we would need to re-vector the CPU's **Instruction Pointer** (**IP** or PC register) to the address of the system call code, which, of course, is within kernel address space. Now, if the process VAS consists of just text, data, library, and stack segments, as we have been so far suggesting, how would it work? Recall the fundamental rule of virtual memory: you cannot look outside the box (available address space).

In order for this whole scheme to succeed, therefore, even kernel virtual address space—yes, please note, even the kernel address space is considered virtual – must somehow be mapped into the process VAS.

As we saw earlier, on a 32-bit system, the total VAS available to a process is 4 GB. So far, the implicit assumption is that the top of the process VAS on 32-bit is therefore 4 GB. That's right. As well, again, the implicit assumption is that the stack segment (consisting of stack frames) lies here—at the 4 GB point at the top. Well, that's incorrect (please refer to *Fig 11*).

The reality is this: the OS creates the process VAS, and arranges for the segments within it; however, it reserves some amount of virtual memory at the top end for the kernel or OS-mapping (meaning, the kernel code, data structures, stacks, and drivers). By the way, this segment, which contains kernel code and data, is usually referred to as the kernel segment.

How much VM is kept for the kernel segment? Ah, that's a tunable or a configurable that is set by kernel developers (or the system administrator) at kernel-configuration time; it's called **VMSPLIT**. This is the point in the VAS where we split the address space between the OS kernel and user mode memory – the text, data, library, and stack segments!

*Virtual Memory*

In fact, for clarity, let's reproduce Fig 11 (as Fig 14), but this time, explicitly reveal the VM Split:

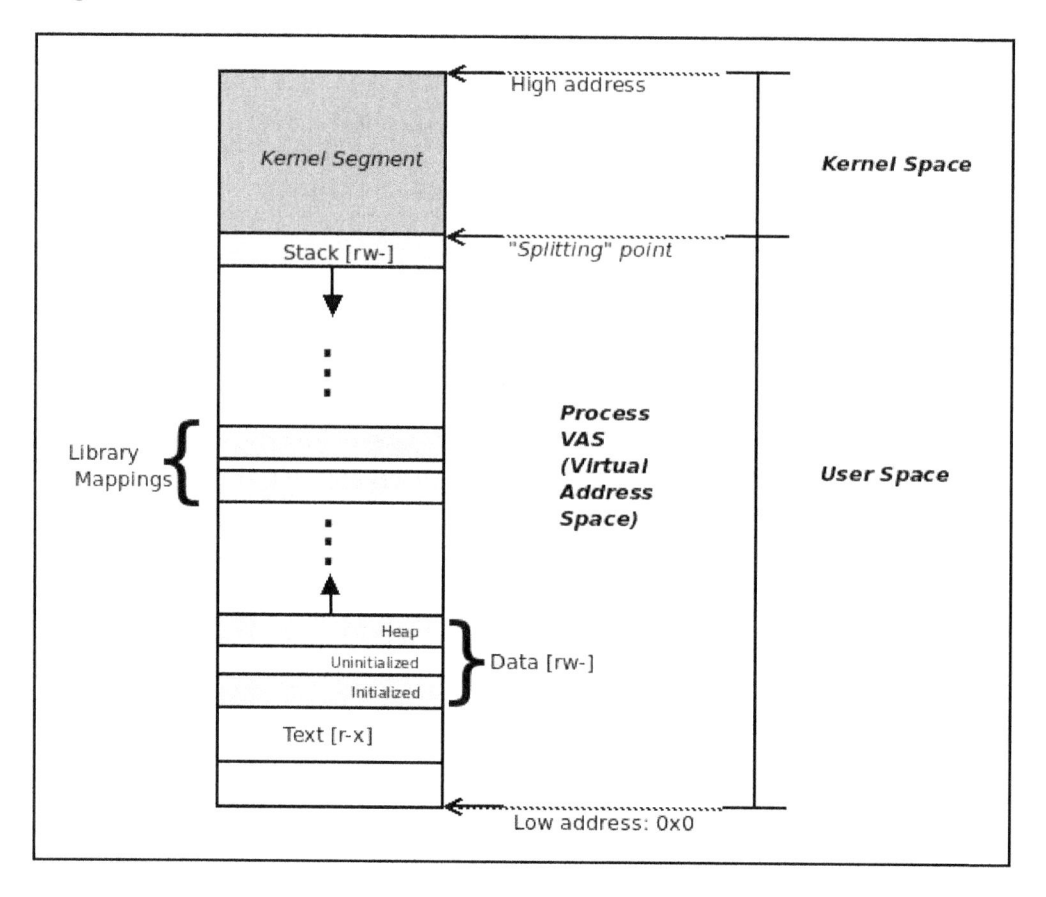

Figure 14: The process VM Split

Let's not get into the gory details here: suffice it to say that on an IA-32 (Intel x86 32-bit), the splitting point is typically the 3 GB point. So, we have a ratio: *userspace VAS : kernel VAS :: 3 GB : 1 GB   ; on the IA-32*.

Remember, this is tunable. On other systems, such as a typical ARM-32 platform, the split might be like this instead: *userspace VAS : kernel VAS :: 2 GB : 2 GB   ; on the ARM-32*.

On an x86_64 with a gargantuan `2^64` VAS (that's a mind-boggling 16 Exabytes!), it would be: *userspace VAS : kernel VAS  ::  128 TB : 128 TB  ; on the x86_64.*

Now one can clearly see why we use the term monolithic to describe the Linux OS architecture – each process is indeed like a single, large piece of stone!

Each process contains both of the following:

- Userspace mappings
    - Text (code)
    - Data
        - Initialized data
        - Uninitialized data (BSS)
        - Heap
    - Library mappings
    - Other mappings
    - Stack
- Kernel segments

Every process alive maps into the kernel VAS (or kernel segment, as it's usually called), in its top end.

This is a crucial point. Let's look at a real-world case: on the Intel IA-32 running the Linux OS, the default value of `VMSPLIT` is 3 GB (which is `0xc0000000`). Thus, on this processor, the VM layout for each process is as follows:

- **0x0** to **0xbfffffff** : userspace mappings, that is, text, data, library and stack.
- **0xc0000000** to **0xffffffff** : kernel space or the kernel segment.

*Virtual Memory*

This is made clear in the following diagram:

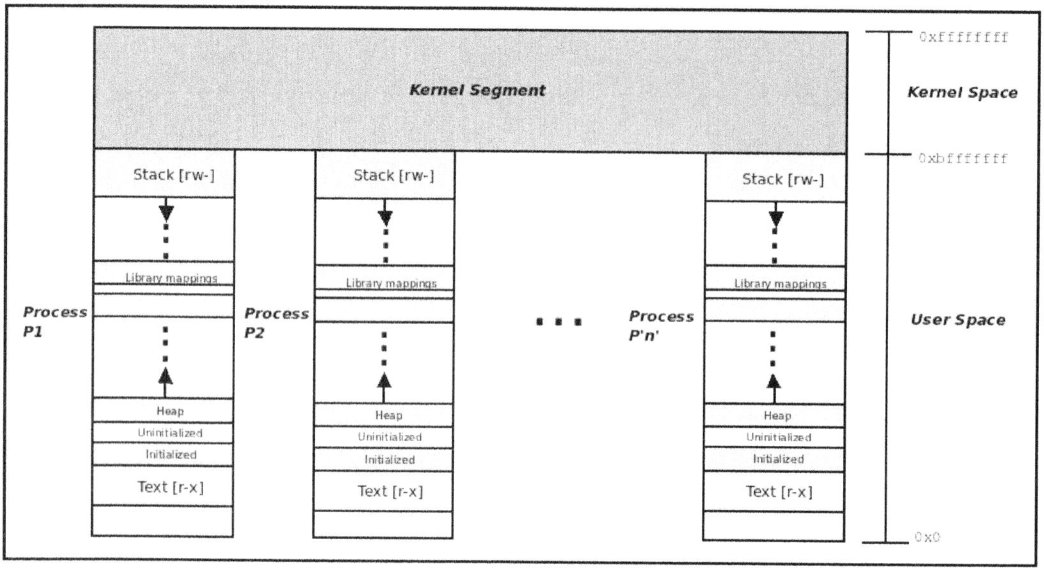

Fig 15: Full process VAS on the IA-32

Notice how the top gigabyte of VAS for every process is the same – the kernel segment. Also keep in mind that this layout is not the same on all systems – the VMSPLIT and the size of user and kernel segments varies with the CPU architecture.

Since Linux 3.3 and especially 3.10 (kernel versions, of course), Linux supports the prctl(2) system call. Looking up its man page reveals all kinds of interesting, though non-portable (Linux-only), things one could do. For example, prctl(2), used with the PR_SET_MM parameter, lets a process (with root privileges) essentially specify its VAS layout, its segments, in terms of start and end virtual addresses for text, data, heap, and stack. This is certainly not required for normal applications.

# Summary

This chapter delved into an explanation of VM concepts, why VM matters, and its many benefits to modern operating systems and the applications running on them. We then covered the layout of the process virtual address space on the Linux OS, including some information on the text, (multiple) data, and stack segments. The true reasons for the stack, and its layout, were covered as well.

In the next chapter, the reader will learn about per-process resource limits: why they are required, how they work, and of course, the programmer interfaces required to work with them.

# 3
# Resource Limits

In this chapter, we will look at per-process resource limits—what they are, and why we require them. We will go on to describe the granularity and the types of resource limits, distinguishing between soft and hard limits. Details on how a user (or system administrator) can query and set the per-process resource limits using appropriate CLI frontends (`ulimit`, `prlimit`) will be covered.

The programming interfaces (APIs)—practically speaking, the key `prlimit(2)` system call API—will be covered in detail. Two detailed code examples, querying the limits and setting a limit on CPU usage, will give the reader hands-on experience of working with resource limits.

In this chapter, with regard to resource limits, we will cover the following topics:

- Necessity
- Granularity
- Types—soft and hard
- The resource limits APIs, with example code

## Resource limits

A common hack is the **(Distributed) denial-of-service ((D)DoS)** attack. Here, the malicious attacker attempts to consume, indeed overload, resources on the target system to such an extent that the system either crashes, or at the very least, becomes completely unresponsive (hung).

Interestingly, on an untuned system, performing this type of attack is quite easy; as an example, let's imagine we have shell access (not root, of course, but as a regular user) on a server. We could attempt to have it run out of disk space (or at least run short) quite easily by manipulating the ubiquitous `dd(1)` (disk dump) command. One use of `dd` is to create files of arbitrary lengths.

## Resource Limits

For example, to create a 1 GB file filled with random content, we could do the following:

```
$ dd if=/dev/urandom of=tst count=1024 bs=1M
1024+0 records in
1024+0 records out
1073741824 bytes (1.1 GB, 1.0 GiB) copied, 15.2602 s, 70.4 MB/s
$ ls -lh tst
-rw-rw-r-- 1 kai kai 1.0G Jan  4 12:19 tst
$
```

What if we bump the blocksize (`bs`) value to `1G`, like this:

```
dd if=/dev/urandom of=tst count=1024 bs=1G
```

`dd` will now attempt to create a file that is 1,024 GB—a terabyte—in size! What if we run this line (in a script) in a loop? You get the idea.

To control resource-usage, Unix (including Linux) has a resource limit, that is, an artificial limit imposed upon a resource by the OS.

A point to be clear on from the very beginning: these resource limits are on a per-process basis and not system-wide globals—more on this in the next section.

Before diving into more detail, let's continue with our hack example to eat up a system's disk space, but this time with the resource limit for the maximum size of a file set in place beforehand.

The frontend command to view and set resource limits is a built-in shell command (these commands are called **bash-builtins**): `ulimit`. To query the maximum possible size of files written to by the shell process (and its children), we set the `-f` option switch to `ulimit`:

```
$ ulimit -f
unlimited
$
```

Okay, it's unlimited. Really? No, unlimited only implies that there is no particular limit imposed by the OS. Of course it's finite, limited by the actual available disk space on the box.

Let's set a limit on the maximum file size, simply by passing the -f option switch and the actual limit. But what's the unit of the size? bytes, KB, MB? Let's look up its man page: by the way, the man page for ulimit is the man page for bash(1). This is logical, as ulimit is a built-in shell command. Once in the bash(1) man page, search for ulimit; the manual informs us that the unit (by default) is 1,024-byte increments. Thus, 2 implies *1,024\*2 = 2,048* bytes. Alternatively, to get some help on ulimit, just type help ulimit on the shell.

So, let's try this: reduce the file size resource limit to just 2,048 bytes and then test with dd:

```
$ ulimit -f
unlimited
$ ulimit -f 2
$ ulimit -f
2
$ dd if=/dev/urandom of=tst count=2048 bs=1
2048+0 records in
2048+0 records out
2048 bytes (2.0 kB, 2.0 KiB) copied, 0.00688134 s, 298 kB/s
$ dd if=/dev/urandom of=tst count=2049 bs=1
File size limit exceeded (core dumped)
$
```

Figure 1: A simple test case with ulimit -f

As can be seen from the preceding screenshot, we reduce the file size resource limit to 2, implying 2,048 bytes, and then test with dd. As long as we create a file at or below 2,048 bytes, it works; the moment we attempt to go beyond the limit, it fails.

> As an aside, note that dd does *not* attempt to use some clever logic to test the resource limit, displaying an error if it were to attempt to create a file over this limit. No, it just fails. Recall from Chapter 1, *Linux System Architecture*, the Unix philosophy principle: provide mechanisms, not policies!

## Granularity of resource limits

In the previous example with dd(1), we saw that we can indeed impose a limit upon the maximum file size. An important question arises: what is the *scope* or *granularity* of the resource limit? Is it system-wide?

[ 93 ]

*Resource Limits*

The short answer: no, it's not system-wide, it's *process-wide*, implying that the resource limits apply at the granularity of a process and not the system. To clarify this, consider two shells—nothing but the `bash` process—shell A and shell B. We modify the maximum file-size resource limit for shell A (with the usual `ulimit -f <new-limit>` command), but leave the resource limit for maximum file size for shell B untouched. If now they both use `dd` (as we did), we would find that the `dd` process invoked within shell A would likely die with the `'File size limit exceeded (core dumped)'` failure message, whereas the `dd` process invoked within shell B would likely continue and succeed (provided, of course, there's sufficient disk space available).

This simple experiment proves that the granularity of a resource limit is per process.

> When we delve into the inner details of multithreading, we'll revisit the granularity of resource limits and how they apply to individual threads. For the impatient, all resource limits-except for the stack size are shared by all threads within the process

## Resource types

So far, we've only checked out the maximum file size resource limit; are there not others? Yes, indeed, there are several others.

## Available resource limits

The following table enumerates the available resource limits on a typical Linux system (alphabetically ordered by the `ulimit option switch` column):

| Resource limit | ulimit option switch | Default value | Unit |
|---|---|---|---|
| `max core file size` | `-c` | unlimited | KB |
| `max data segment size` | `-d` | unlimited | KB |
| `max scheduling priority` (nice) | `-e` | 0 | Unscaled |
| `max file size` | `-f` | unlimited | KB |
| `max (real-time) pending signals` | `-i` | <varies> | Unscaled |
| `max locked memory` | `-l` | <varies> | KB |
| `max memory size` | `-m` | unlimited | KB |
| `max open files` | `-n` | 1024 | Unscaled |

| max pipe size | -p | 8 | 512-byte increments |
|---|---|---|---|
| max POSIX message queues | -q | <varies> | Unscaled |
| max real-time scheduling priority | -r | 0 | Unscaled |
| max stack segment size | -s | 8192 | KB |
| max CPU time | -t | unlimited | Seconds |
| max user processes | -u | <varies> | Unscaled |
| address space limit or max virtual memory | -v | unlimited | KB |
| max file locks held | -x | unlimited | Unscaled |

There are a few points to note:

- At a glance, some of the resource limit meanings are quite obvious; several may not be. Most of them are not explained here, some of them will be touched upon in subsequent chapters.
- The second column is the option switch to pass to ulimit to display the current value for the particular resource limit in that row; for example, ulimit -s to print out the current value of the stack size resource limit (unit: KB).
- The third column is **Default value**. This, of course, could vary across Linux platforms. In particular, enterprise-class servers may tune their default values to be much higher than, say, an embedded Linux system. Also, quite often the default value is a calculation (based on, say, amount of RAM installed on the box); hence, the entry *<varies>* in some cases. Also, as mentioned earlier, unlimited does not mean infinite—it implies that no artificial upper limit has been enforced.
- Regarding the fourth column, **Unit**, the (bash(1)) man page (source: https://linux.die.net/man/1/bash) states the following:

  > [...] If limit is given, it is the new value of the specified resource (the -a option is display only). If no option is given, then -f is assumed. Values are in 1024-byte increments, except for -t, which is in seconds, -p, which is in units of 512-byte blocks, and -T, -b, -n, and -u, which are unscaled values. The return status is 0 unless an invalid option or argument is supplied, or an error occurs while setting a new limit. [...]

# Resource Limits

> Also, `unscaled` implies it's just a number.

One can display all resource limits via the `-a` option switch; we leave it to you to try out the `ulimit -a` command.

Note that `ulimit -a` orders the resource limits alphabetically by option switch, just as we did in the table.

Also, it's really important to understand that these resource limits are with respect to a single process—the shell process (Bash)—that invoked the `ulimit` command.

## Hard and soft limits

Unixes make a further distinction: in reality (under the hood), the resource limit for a given type is not one number—it's two:

- A value for the hard limit
- A value for the soft limit

The hard limit is the true maximum; as a regular user, it's impossible to exceed this limit. What if a process attempts this? Simple: it gets killed by the OS.

The soft limit, on the other hand, can be breached: in the case of some resource limits, the process (that exceeds the soft limit) will be sent a signal by the kernel. Think of this as a warning: you're nearing the limit kind of thing. Again, don't worry, we take a deep dive into signaling in Chapter 11, *Signaling - Part I*, and, Chapter 12, *Signaling - Part II*. For example, if a process exceeds the soft limit for file size, the OS responds by delivering the `SIGXFSZ` signal—`SIGnal: eXceeding FileSiZe`—to it! Overstep the soft limit for CPU and guess what? You will be the proud recipient of the `SIGXCPU` signal.

> Well, there's more to it: the man page on `prlimit(2)` shows how, on Linux, with regard to the CPU limit, `SIGKILL` is sent after multiple warnings via `SIGXCPU`. The right behavior: the application should clean up and terminate upon receiving the first `SIGXCPU` signal. We will look at signal-handling in Chapter 11, *Signaling – Part I*!

It's instructive to think of the hard limit as a ceiling value for the soft limit; in effect, the range of the soft limit for a given resource is [0, hard-limit].

To view both the hard and soft limits on your shell process, use the -S and -H option switches on ulimit, respectively. Here's the output of ulimit -aS on our trusty Fedora 28 desktop system:

```
$ ulimit -aS
core file size          (blocks, -c) unlimited
data seg size           (kbytes, -d) unlimited
scheduling priority             (-e) 0
file size               (blocks, -f) unlimited
pending signals                 (-i) 63260
max locked memory       (kbytes, -l) 64
max memory size         (kbytes, -m) unlimited
open files                      (-n) 1024
pipe size            (512 bytes, -p) 8
POSIX message queues     (bytes, -q) 819200
real-time priority              (-r) 0
stack size              (kbytes, -s) 8192
cpu time               (seconds, -t) unlimited
max user processes              (-u) 63260
virtual memory          (kbytes, -v) unlimited
file locks                      (-x) unlimited
$
```

When we run ulimit with both the following:

- -aS: Display all Soft resource limit values
- -aH: Display all Hard resource limit values

A question comes up: where exactly do the soft and hard limits (for the Bash process) differ? Instead of trying to manually interpret it, let's use a super GUI frontend to diff (well, it's more than just a diff frontend actually), called meld:

```
$ ps
  PID TTY          TIME CMD
23843 pts/6    00:00:00 bash
29305 pts/6    00:00:00 ps
$

$ ulimit -aS > ulimit-aS.txt
$ ulimit -aH > ulimit-aH.txt
$ meld ulimit-aS.txt ulimit-aH.txt &
```

[ 97 ]

*Resource Limits*

Screenshot of meld comparing the soft and hard limit resource values shown as follows:

```
                         ulimit-aS.txt — ulimit-aH.txt                        _  □  ×
File  Edit  Changes  View
 ○   💾  Save  ⟲  Undo  ⇆   ↑  ⬥  ●
  ulimit-aS.txt...ulimit-aH.txt  ×
 ⬇   ulimit-aS.txt                      📄    ⬇   ulimit-aH.txt                      📄
core file size          (blocks, -c) unlimited    core file size          (blocks, -c) unlimited
data seg size           (kbytes, -d) unlimited    data seg size           (kbytes, -d) unlimited
scheduling priority              (-e) 0           scheduling priority              (-e) 0
file size               (blocks, -f) unlimited    file size               (blocks, -f) unlimited
pending signals                  (-i) 63260       pending signals                  (-i) 63260
max locked memory       (kbytes, -l) 64           max locked memory       (kbytes, -l) 64
max memory size         (kbytes, -m) unlimited    max memory size         (kbytes, -m) unlimited
open files                       (-n) 1024     →  ← open files                    (-n) 4096
pipe size           (512 bytes, -p) 8              pipe size           (512 bytes, -p) 8
POSIX message queues    (bytes,  -q) 819200        POSIX message queues    (bytes,  -q) 819200
real-time priority               (-r) 0            real-time priority               (-r) 0
stack size              (kbytes, -s) 8192      →  ← stack size             (kbytes, -s) unlimited
cpu time               (seconds, -t) unlimited    cpu time               (seconds, -t) unlimited
max user processes               (-u) 63260       max user processes               (-u) 63260
virtual memory          (kbytes, -v) unlimited    virtual memory          (kbytes, -v) unlimited
file locks                       (-x) unlimited    file locks                       (-x) unlimited

                                                                        Ln 8, Col 1  INS
```

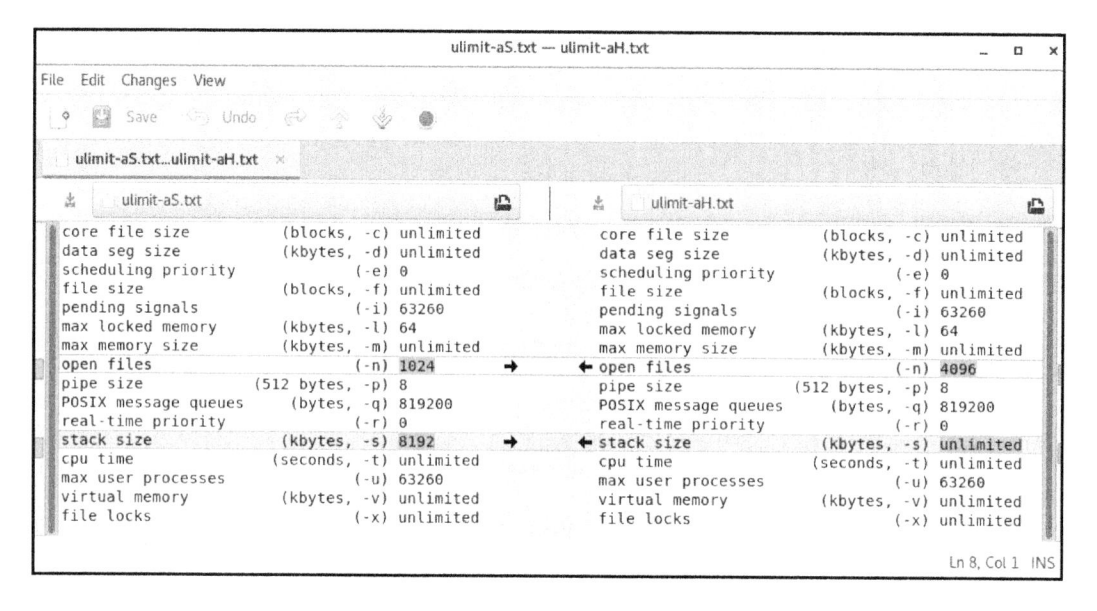

Figure 2: Screenshot showing meld comparing the soft and hard limit resource values

Note that we run `ps`; this is to reiterate the fact that the resource limit values we're seeing / are with respect to it (PID 23843). So, meld clearly shows us that, by default on a typical Linux system, only two resource limits differ in their soft and hard values: the max open files (soft=1024, hard=4096), and max stack size (soft=8192 KB = 8 MB, hard=unlimited).

> **TIP**: `meld` is extremely valuable to developers; we often use it to (peer-) review code and make changes (merges via the right- and left-pointing arrows). In fact, the powerful Git SCM uses `meld` as one of the available tools (with the `git mergetool` command). Install `meld` on your Linux box using the appropriate package manager for your distribution and try it out.

# Querying and changing resource limit values

We now understand that it's the kernel (the OS) that sets up resource limits per process and tracks usage, even killing the process if necessary—if it attempts to exceed a resource's hard limit. This raises the question: is there a way one can change the soft and hard resource-limit values? We've already seen it in fact: `ulimit`. More than that, though, the deeper question is: are we allowed to set any hard/soft limits?

The kernel has certain preset rules regarding the changing of a resource limit. Querying or setting a process's resource limits can only be done by the calling process upon itself or upon a process that it owns; more correctly, for any other process besides itself, the process must have the `CAP_SYS_RESOURCE` capability bit set (worry not, detailed coverage on process capabilities can be found in Chapter 8, *Process Capabilities*):

- **Querying**: Anyone can query the resource limits hard and soft (current) values of the processes they own.
- **Setting**:
    - A hard limit, once set, cannot be further increased (for that session).
    - A soft limit can be increased up to the hard limit value only, that is, soft limit range = [0, hard-limit].
    - When one sets the resource limit using `ulimit`, the system internally sets *both the hard and soft limits*. This has important consequences (see the preceding points).

Permissions for setting resource limits is given as follows:

- A privileged process (such as `superuser/root/sysadmin`, or one with the aforementioned `CAP_SYS_RESOURCE` capability) can increase or decrease both hard and soft limits.
- A non-privileged process (non-root):
    - Can set the soft limit of a resource in the range [0, hard-limit] for that resource.
    - Can irreversibly decrease a resource's hard limit (once reduced, it cannot ever increase it, but can only continue to decrease it). More precisely, the hard limit can be decreased to a value greater than or equal to the current soft limit.

Resource Limits

> **TIP:** Every good rule has an exception: a non-privileged user *can* decrease and/or increase the *core file* resource limit. This is usually to allow developers to generate a core dump (which can be subsequently analyzed via GDB).

A quick test case to demonstrate this is in order; let's manipulate the max open files resource limit:

```
$ ulimit -n
1024
$ ulimit -aS |grep "open files"
open files                      (-n) 1024
$ ulimit -aH |grep "open files"
open files                      (-n) 4096
$
$ ulimit -n 3000
$ ulimit -aS |grep "open files"
open files                      (-n) 3000
$ ulimit -aH |grep "open files"
open files                      (-n) 3000
$ ulimit -n 3001
bash: ulimit: open files: cannot modify limit: Operation not permitted
$ ulimit -n 2000
$ ulimit -n
2000
$ ulimit -aS |grep "open files"
open files                      (-n) 2000
$ ulimit -aH |grep "open files"
open files (-n) 2000
$ ulimit -n 3000
bash: ulimit: open files: cannot modify limit: Operation not permitted
$
```

The preceding command are explained as follows:

- The current soft limit is 1,024 (the default)
- The soft limit is 1,024, the hard limit is 4,096
- Using `ulimit`, we set the limit to 3,000; this, internally, has caused both the soft and hard limits to be set to 3,000
- Attempting to set the value higher (to 3,001) fails
- Reducing the value (to 2,000) succeeds
- Realize though, that again, both the soft and hard limits have been set to 2,000
- Attempting to go back to a previously valid value fails (3,000); this is because the valid range now is [0, 2,000]

Testing this with root access is left as an exercise to the reader; see the *Caveats* section that follows, though.

## Caveats

Things to consider, and exceptions that apply:

- Even if one can, increasing a resource limit may do more harm than good; think through what you are trying to achieve here. Put yourself in the malicious-hacker mindset (recall (DDoS attacks). On both server class, as well as on highly resource-constrained systems (often an embedded one), setting resource limits appropriately can help mitigate risk.
- Setting a resource limit to a higher value requires root privilege. For example: we wish to increase the max open files resource limit from 1,024 to 2,000. One would assume that using `sudo` should do the job. However, at first surprisingly, something such as `sudo ulimit -n 2000` will not work! Why? Well, when you run it, `sudo` expects that `ulimit` is a binary executable and thus searches for it in the `PATH`; but of course, that's not the case: `ulimit` is a built-in shell command and thus fails to launch. So, try it this way:

```
$ ulimit -n
1024
$ sudo bash -c "ulimit -n 2000 && exec ulimit -n"
[sudo] password for kai: xxx
2000
$
```

Don't worry, if you don't fully understand why we use the *exec* in the preceding snippet; the precise details regarding *exec* semantics will be covered in `Chapter 9`, *Process Execution*.

- Exception—you cannot seem to change the max pipe size resource limit.

> **TIP**
> Advanced: The default maximum pipe size is actually in `/proc/sys/fs/pipe-max-size` and defaults to 1 MB (from Linux 2.6.35). What if the programmer must change the pipe size? To do so, one could use the `fcntl(2)` system call, via the `F_GETPIPE_SZ` and `F_SETPIPE_SZ` parameters. Refer to the *fcntl(2)* man page for details.

# A quick note on the prlimit utility

Besides using `ulimit`, another frontend to querying and displaying resource limits is the `prlimit` utility. `prlimit` differs from `ulimit` in the following ways:

- It's a newer, modern interface (Linux kernel version 2.6.36 onward)
- It can be used to modify limits as required *and* launch another program that will inherit the new limits (a useful feature; see the following examples)
- It's a binary executable program in itself, not a built-in like `ulimit` is

Without any parameters, `prlimit` displays the resource limits of the calling process (itself). One can optionally pass resource limit `<name=value>` pairs to set the same, the PID of the process to query/set resource limits, or a command to be launched with the newly set resource limits. Here is the synopsis from its man page:

```
prlimit [options] [--resource[=limits] [--pid PID]
prlimit [options] [--resource[=limits] command [argument...]
```

Note how the `--pid` and `command` options are mutually exclusive.

## Using prlimit(1) – examples

Example 1—querying limits:

```
$ prlimit
```

Output for the preceding command is as follows:

```
RESOURCE   DESCRIPTION                              SOFT       HARD UNITS
AS         address space limit                 unlimited  unlimited bytes
CORE       max core file size                          0  unlimited blocks
CPU        CPU time                            unlimited  unlimited seconds
DATA       max data size                       unlimited  unlimited bytes
FSIZE      max file size                            2048       2048 blocks
LOCKS      max number of file locks held       unlimited  unlimited
MEMLOCK    max locked-in-memory address space      65536      65536 bytes
MSGQUEUE   max bytes in POSIX mqueues              819200     819200 bytes
NICE       max nice prio allowed to raise              0          0
NOFILE     max number of open files                 2000       2000
NPROC      max number of processes                  7741       7741
RSS        max resident set size               unlimited  unlimited pages
RTPRIO     max real-time priority                      0          0
RTTIME     timeout for real-time tasks         unlimited  unlimited microsecs
SIGPENDING max number of pending signals            7741       7741
STACK      max stack size                        8388608  unlimited bytes
```

```
$ ps
  PID TTY          TIME CMD
 2917 pts/7    00:00:00 bash
```

```
 3339 pts/7    00:00:00 ps
$ prlimit --pid=2917
RESOURCE   DESCRIPTION                      SOFT      HARD
UNITS
AS         address space limit              unlimited unlimited
bytes
CORE       max core file size               unlimited unlimited
bytes
CPU        CPU time                         unlimited unlimited
seconds
[...]
$
```

Here, we have abbreviated the output for better readability.

Example 2—set the resource limits for max file size and max stack size for the (preceding) shell process:

```
$ prlimit --pid=2917 --fsize=2048000 --stack=12582912
$ prlimit --pid=2917 | egrep -i "fsize|stack"
FSIZE    max file size    2048000   2048000  bytes
STACK    max stack size   12582912  12582912 bytes
$
```

Example 3—a program, `rlimit_primes`, that generates prime numbers; have it generate a large number of primes but give it only two seconds of CPU time to do so.

> Note that the `rlimit_primes` program, along with its source code, is described in detail in the *API interfaces* section.

For now, we just run it within the scope of the built-in `prlimit` program, ensuring that the `rlimit_primes` process only gets the CPU bandwidth (in seconds) that we pass via the `prlimit --cpu=` option switch. In the example, we ensure the following:

- We give our prime number generator process two seconds (via `prlimit`)
- We pass -2 as the second parameter; this will cause the `rlimit_primes` program to skip setting the CPU resource limit itself

*Resource Limits*

- We ask it to generate primes up to the number 8,000,000:

```
$ ./rlimit_primes
Usage: ./rlimit_primes limit-to-generate-primes-upto CPU-time-
limit
 arg1 : max is 10000000
 arg2 : CPU-time-limit:
  -2 = don't set
  -1 = unlimited
   0 = 1s
$ prlimit --cpu=2 ./rlimit_primes 8000000 -2
  2, 3, 5, 7, 11, 13, 17, 19, 23, 29, 31, 37, 41, 43, 47, 53,
  59, 61, 67, 71, 73, 79, 83, 89, 97, 101, 103, 107, 109, 113,
127, 131,

  [...]

  18353, 18367, 18371, 18379, 18397, 18401, 18413, 18427,
18433, 18439,
  18443, 18451, 18457, 18461, 18481, 18493, 18503, 18517,
18521, 18523,
  18539, 18541, 18553, 18583, 18587, 18593,
Killed
$
```

Note how, once it's out of its newly constrained CPU time resource (two seconds, in the preceding example), it gets killed by the kernel! (Technically, by the SIGKILL signal; a lot more on signals follows in Chapter 11, *Signaling - Part I*, and Chapter 12, *Signaling - Part II*). Note how the word Killed appears, indicating that the OS has killed the process.

Refer to the man page on prlimit(1) for further details.

> A practical case: When running fairly heavy software such as Eclipse and Dropbox, I have found it necessary to bump up the resource limits for them (as advised); otherwise, they abort as they run out of resources.
>
> Advanced: From the Linux kernel version 2.6.24 onward, one can look up the resource limits for a given process PID via the powerful proc filesystem: /proc/<PID>/limits.

# API interfaces

Querying and/or setting resource limits programmatically can be achieved with the following APIs—the system calls:

- `getrlimit`
- `setrlimit`
- `prlimit`

Of these, we will only focus on `prlimit(2)`; `[get|set]rlimit(2)` is an older interface, has quite a few issues (bugs), and is generally considered outdated.

> For `prlimit(2)` to work properly, one must be running on Linux kernel version 2.6.36 or later.

> How does one determine the Linux kernel version one is running on?
> Simple: use the `uname` utility to query the kernel version:
> ```
> $ uname -r
> 4.14.11-300.fc27.x86_64
> $
> ```

Let's get back to the `prlimit(2)` system call API:

```
#include <sys/time.h>
#include <sys/resource.h>

int prlimit(pid_t pid, int resource,
            const struct rlimit *new_limit, struct rlimit *old_limit);
```

The `prlimit()` system call can be used to both query and set a given resource limit—only one resource limit per call—for or on a given process. It receives four arguments; the first argument, `pid`, is the PID of the process to act upon. The special 0 value implies that it acts upon the calling process itself. The second argument, resource, is the name of the resource limit we wish to query or set (refer to the following table for the full list). Both the third and fourth arguments are pointers to `struct rlimit`; the third parameter, if non-NULL, is the new value we want to set (which is why it is marked `const`); the fourth parameter, if non-NULL, is the structure where we will receive the previous (or old) limit.

> Experienced C programmers will realize how easy it is to create bugs. It's the programmer's responsibility to ensure that the memory for the *rlimit* structures (third and fourth parameters), if used, must be allocated; the OS certainly does not allocate memory for these structures.

The `rlimit` structure contains two members, the soft and hard limits (`rlim_cur` and `rlim_max`, respectively):

```
struct rlimit {
     rlim_t rlim_cur;    /* Soft limit */
     rlim_t rlim_max;    /* Hard limit (ceiling for rlim_cur) */
};
```

Back to the second argument, resource, which is the programmatic name of the resource limit we wish to query or set. The following table enumerates all of them:

| Resource limit | Programmatic name (use in API) | Default value | Unit |
|---|---|---|---|
| max core file size | RLIMIT_CORE | unlimited | KB |
| max data segment size | RLIMIT_DATA | unlimited | KB |
| max scheduling priority (*nice*) | RLIMIT_NICE | 0 | unscaled |
| max file size | RLIMIT_FSIZE | unlimited | KB |
| max (real-time) pending signals | RLIMIT_SIGPENDING | <varies> | unscaled |
| max locked memory | RLIMIT_MEMLOCK | <varies> | KB |
| max open files | RLIMIT_NOFILE | 1024 | unscaled |
| max POSIX message queues | RLIMIT_MSGQUEUE | <varies> | unscaled |
| max real-time priority | RLIMIT_RTTIME | 0 | microseconds |
| max stack segment size | RLIMIT_STACK | 8192 | KB |
| max CPU time | RLIMIT_CPU | unlimited | seconds |
| max user processes | RLIMIT_NPROC | <varies> | unscaled |
| address space limit or max virtual memory | RLIMIT_AS (AS = Address Space) | unlimited | KB |
| max file locks held | RLIMIT_LOCKS | unlimited | unscaled |

Points to note are given as follows:

- The `RLIM_INFINITY` value for a resource value implies that there is no limit.
- Alert readers will notice that there is no entry for `max pipe size` (as there was in the previous table); this is because this resource cannot be modified via the `prlimit(2)` API.
- Technically, to modify a resource limit value, a process requires the `CAP_SYS_RESOURCE` capability (capabilities is explained in details in Chapter 8, *Process Capabilities*). For now, let's just use the traditional approach and say that in order to change a process's resource limit, one needs to own the process (or be root; being root or superuser is pretty much a shortcut to all the rules).

## Code examples

The following two C programs are used to demonstrate the usage of the `prlimit(2)` API:

- The first program, `rlimits_show.c`, queries all resource limits for the current or calling process and prints out their values.
- The second, given a CPU resource limit (in seconds), runs a simple prime number generator under the influence of that limit.

> For readability, only the relevant parts of the code are displayed. To view and run it, the entire source code is available at https://github.com/PacktPublishing/Hands-on-System-Programming-with-Linux.

Refer to the following code:

```
/* From ch3/rlimits_show.c */
#define ARRAY_LEN(arr) (sizeof((arr))/sizeof((arr)[0]))
static void query_rlimits(void)
{
    unsigned i;
    struct rlimit rlim;
    struct rlimpair {
        int rlim;
        char *name;
    };
    struct rlimpair rlimpair_arr[] = {
        {RLIMIT_CORE, "RLIMIT_CORE"},
```

## Resource Limits

```
            {RLIMIT_DATA, "RLIMIT_DATA"},
            {RLIMIT_NICE, "RLIMIT_NICE"},
            {RLIMIT_FSIZE, "RLIMIT_FSIZE"},
            {RLIMIT_SIGPENDING, "RLIMIT_SIGPENDING"},
            {RLIMIT_MEMLOCK, "RLIMIT_MEMLOCK"},
            {RLIMIT_NOFILE, "RLIMIT_NOFILE"},
            {RLIMIT_MSGQUEUE, "RLIMIT_MSGQUEUE"},
            {RLIMIT_RTTIME, "RLIMIT_RTTIME"},
            {RLIMIT_STACK, "RLIMIT_STACK"},
            {RLIMIT_CPU, "RLIMIT_CPU"},
            {RLIMIT_NPROC, "RLIMIT_NPROC"},
            {RLIMIT_AS, "RLIMIT_AS"},
            {RLIMIT_LOCKS, "RLIMIT_LOCKS"},
        };
        char tmp1[16], tmp2[16];

        printf("RESOURCE LIMIT                 SOFT                 HARD\n");
        for (i = 0; i < ARRAY_LEN(rlimpair_arr); i++) {
            if (prlimit(0, rlimpair_arr[i].rlim, 0, &rlim) == -1)
                handle_err(EXIT_FAILURE, "%s:%s:%d: prlimit[%d] failed\n",
                    __FILE__, __FUNCTION__, __LINE__, i);

            snprintf(tmp1, 16, "%ld", rlim.rlim_cur);
            snprintf(tmp2, 16, "%ld", rlim.rlim_max);
            printf("%-18s:  %16s  %16s\n",
                rlimpair_arr[i].name,
                (rlim.rlim_cur == -1 ? "unlimited" : tmp1),
                (rlim.rlim_max == -1 ? "unlimited" : tmp2)
            );
        }
    }
```

Let's try it out:

```
$ make rlimits_show
[...]
$ ./rlimits_show
RESOURCE LIMIT            SOFT              HARD
RLIMIT_CORE         :    unlimited         unlimited
RLIMIT_DATA         :    unlimited         unlimited
RLIMIT_NICE         :            0                 0
RLIMIT_FSIZE        :    unlimited         unlimited
RLIMIT_SIGPENDING   :        63229             63229
RLIMIT_MEMLOCK      :        65536             65536
RLIMIT_NOFILE       :         1024              4096
RLIMIT_MSGQUEUE     :       819200            819200
RLIMIT_RTTIME       :    unlimited         unlimited
```

```
RLIMIT_STACK         :           8388608      unlimited
RLIMIT_CPU           :         unlimited      unlimited
RLIMIT_NPROC         :             63229          63229
RLIMIT_AS            :         unlimited      unlimited
RLIMIT_LOCKS         :         unlimited      unlimited
$ ulimit -f
unlimited
$ ulimit -f 512000
$ ulimit -f
512000
$ ./rlimits_show | grep FSIZE
RLIMIT_FSIZE         :         524288000      524288000
$
```

We first use the program to dump all the resource limits. Then, we query the file-size resource limit, modify it (lower it from unlimited to about 512 KB using `ulimit`), and run the program again, which reflects the change.

Now for the second program; given a CPU resource limit (in seconds), we run a simple prime number generator under the influence of that CPU resource limit.

For readability, relevant parts of the source code (the relevant source file is `ch3/rlimit_primes.c`) are shown.

Here is the simple prime number generator function:

```
#define MAX    10000000        // 10 million
static void simple_primegen(int limit)
{
    int i, j, num = 2, isprime;

    printf("  2,  3, ");
    for (i = 4; i <= limit; i++) {
        isprime = 1;
        for (j = 2; j < limit / 2; j++) {
            if ((i != j) && (i % j == 0)) {
                isprime = 0;
                break;
            }
        }
        if (isprime) {
            num++;
            printf("%6d, ", i);
         /* Wrap after WRAP primes are printed on a line;
          * this is crude; in production code, one must query
          * the terminal window's width and calculate the column
          * to wrap at.
```

[ 109 ]

## Resource Limits

```
             */
#define WRAP 16
            if (num % WRAP == 0)
                printf("\n");
        }
    }
    printf("\n");
}
```

Here is the function to set up the CPU resource limit to the parameter passed, which is the time in seconds:

```
/*
 * Setup the CPU resource limit to 'cpulimit' seconds
 */
static void setup_cpu_rlimit(int cpulimit)
{
    struct rlimit rlim_new, rlim_old;

    if (cpulimit == -1)
        rlim_new.rlim_cur = rlim_new.rlim_max = RLIM_INFINITY;
    else
        rlim_new.rlim_cur = rlim_new.rlim_max = (rlim_t)cpulimit;

    if (prlimit(0, RLIMIT_CPU, &rlim_new, &rlim_old) == -1)
         FATAL("prlimit:cpu failed\n");
    printf
        ("CPU rlimit [soft,hard] new: [%ld:%ld]s : old [%ld:%ld]s (-1 = unlimited)\n",
         rlim_new.rlim_cur, rlim_new.rlim_max, rlim_old.rlim_cur,
         rlim_old.rlim_max);
}
```

In the following code, we first just do a quick test run—we print the first 100 primes and leave the CPU resource limit value untouched (it typically defaults to infinite). Then we invoke it to print the first 90,000 primes with five seconds of CPU time available to it. As expected (on modern hardware), both succeed:

```
$ prlimit | grep "CPU time"
CPU        CPU time          unlimited unlimited seconds
$ ./rlimit_primes
Usage: ./rlimit_primes limit-to-generate-primes-upto CPU-time-limit
 arg1 : max is 10000000
 arg2 : CPU-time-limit:
  -2 = don't set
  -1 = unlimited
   0 = 1s
$ ./rlimit_primes 100 -2
  2, 3, 5, 7, 11, 13, 17, 19, 23, 29, 31, 37, 41, 43, 47, 53,
    59, 61, 67, 71, 73, 79, 83, 89, 97,
$
$ ./rlimit_primes 90000 5
CPU rlimit [soft,hard] new: [5:5]s : old [-1:-1]s (-1 = unlimited)
  2, 3, 5, 7, 11, 13, 17, 19, 23, 29, 31, 37, 41, 43, 47, 53,
  59, 61, 67, 71, 73, 79, 83, 89, 97, 101, 103, 107, 109, 113, 127,

[...]

89753, 89759, 89767, 89779, 89783, 89797, 89809, 89819, 89821, 89833,
89839, 89849, 89867, 89891, 89897, 89899, 89909, 89917, 89923, 89939,
89959, 89963, 89977, 89983, 89989,
$
```

Now for the fun part: we invoke `rlimit_primes` to print the first 200,000 primes with only one second of CPU time available to it; this time it fails (note that we redirect standard output to a temporary file, so that we are not distracted by all the output):

```
$ prlimit | grep "CPU time"
CPU          CPU time           unlimited unlimited seconds
$ ./rlimit_primes 200000 1 > /tmp/prm
Killed
$ tail -n1 /tmp/prm
 54727, 54751, 54767, 54773, 54779, 54787, 54799, 54829, 54833, 54851,
 54869, 54877, 54881, $
```

[ 111 ]

Why did it fail? Obviously, the CPU resource limit—just one second—was too small a time for it to complete the given task; when the process attempted to exceed this limit, it was killed by the kernel.

> A note to advanced readers: one can use the very powerful and versatile `perf(1)` Linux utility to see this too:
>
> ```
> $ sudo perf stat ./rlimit_primes 200000 1 >/tmp/prm
> ./rlimit_primes: Killed
>
> Performance counter stats for './rlimit_primes 200000 1':
>
>    1001.917484      task-clock (msec)     #    0.999 CPUs utilized
>             17      context-switches      #    0.017 K/sec
>              1      cpu-migrations        #    0.001 K/sec
>             51      page-faults           #    0.051 K/sec
>  3,018,577,481      cycles                #    3.013 GHz
>  5,568,202,738      instructions          #    1.84 insn per cycle
>    982,845,319      branches              #  980.964 M/sec
>         88,602      branch-misses         #    0.01% of all branches
>
>    1.002659905 seconds time elapsed
>
> $
> ```

## Permanence

We've demonstrated that, within its operational framework, one can indeed query and set per-process resource limits using frontends, such as `ulimit`, `prlimit(1)`, as well as programmatically via library and system call APIs. However, the changes we wrought are temporary—for that process's life or the session's life only. How does one make a resource limit value change permanent?

The Unix way is to use (ASCII-text) configuration files that reside on the filesystem. In particular, on most Linux distributions, editing the `/etc/security/limits.conf` configuration file is the answer. We shall not delve further into the details here; if interested, check out the man page on `limits.conf(5)`.

# Summary

This chapter initially delved into the motivation behind per-process resource limits and why we require them. We also explained the granularity and the types of resource limits, distinguishing between soft and hard limits. Then we looked at how a user (or system administrator) can query and set the per-process resource limits using appropriate CLI frontends (ulimit(1), prlimit(1)).

Finally, we explored the programming interfaces (APIs)—practically speaking, the prlimit(2) system call—in detail. Two detailed code examples, querying the limits and setting a limit on CPU usage, rounded out the discussion.

In the next chapter, we will learn about the crucial, dynamic memory-management APIs and their correct usage. We'll go well beyond the basics of using the typical malloc() API, delving into a few subtle and important inner details.

# 4
# Dynamic Memory Allocation

In this chapter, we will delve into a key aspect of system programming on a modern OS—the management of dynamic (runtime) memory allocation and deallocation. We'll first cover the basic glibc APIs used to allocate and free memory dynamically. We'll then move beyond these basics, examining the program break within the VAS and the behavior of malloc(3) under differing circumstances.

We will then immerse the reader in a few advanced discussions: demand-paging, memory locking and protection, and the usage of the alloca API.

Code examples provide the reader with an opportunity to explore these topics in a hands-on manner.

In this chapter, we will cover the following topics:

- Basic glibc dynamic memory-management APIs and their correct usage in code
- The program break (and its management via the sbrk(3) API)
- The internal behavior of malloc(3) when allocating differing amounts of memory
- Advanced features:
    - The demand-paging concept
    - Memory locking
    - Memory region protection
    - Using the alloca(3) API alternative

# The glibc malloc(3) API family

In Chapter 2, *Virtual Memory*, we learned that there are regions or segments meant for the use of dynamic memory-allocation within the process of **Virtual Address Space** (**VAS**). The **heap segment** is one such dynamic region—a free gift of memory made available to the process for its runtime consumption.

How exactly does the developer exploit this gift of memory? Not just that, the developer has to be extremely careful with matching memory *allocations* to subsequent memory *frees*, otherwise the system isn't going to like it!

The **GNU C library** (**glibc**) provides a small but powerful set of APIs to enable the developer to manage dynamic memory; the details of their usage is the content of this section.

As you will come to see, the memory-management APIs are literally a handful: malloc(3), calloc, realloc, and free. Still, using them correctly remains a challenge! The subsequent sections (and chapters) will reveal why this is the case. Read on!

## The malloc(3) API

Perhaps one of the most common APIs used by application developers is the renowned malloc(3).

> **TIP:** The foo(3) syntax indicates that the foo function is in section 3 of the manual (the man pages) – a library API, not a system call. We recommend you develop the habit of reading the man pages. The man pages are available online, and you can find them at https://linux.die.net/man/.

We use malloc(3) to dynamically allocate a chunk of memory at runtime. This is as opposed to static—or compile-time – memory-allocation where we make a statement, such as:

```
char buf[256];
```

In the preceding case, the memory has been statically allocated (at compile-time).

So, how exactly do you use malloc(3)? Let's check out its signature:

```
#include <stdlib.h>
void *malloc(size_t size);
```

The parameter to `malloc(3)` is the number of bytes to allocate. But what is the `size_t` data type? Obviously, it's not a C primitive data type; it's a `typedef` – `long unsigned int` on your typical 64-bit platform (the exact data type does vary with the platform; the important point is that it's always unsigned – it cannot be negative. On a 32-bit Linux, it will be `unsigned int`). Ensuring that your code precisely matches the function signature and data types is crucial in writing robust and correct programs. While we're at it, ensure that you include the header file that the man page displays with the API signature.

> **TIP**
> To print a variable of the `size_t` type within a `printf`, use the `%zu` format specifier:
> ```
> size_t sz = 4 * getpagesize();
> [...]
> printf("size = %zu bytes\n", sz);
> ```

In this book, we will not delve into the internal implementation details regarding how `malloc(3)` and friends actually store, allocate, and free memory (refer the *Further reading* section on the GitHub repository.) Suffice to say, the internal implementation strives to be as efficient as can be; using these APIs is usually considered the right way to perform memory-management.

The return value is a pointer to the zeroth byte of the newly-allocated memory region on success, and NULL on failure.

> **TIP**
> You will come across, shall we say *optimists*, who say things such as, "Don't bother checking malloc for failure, it never fails". Well, take that sage advice with a grain of salt. While it's true that malloc would rarely fail, the fact is (as you shall see), it could fail. Writing defensive code – code that checks for the failure case immediately – is a cornerstone of writing solid, robust programs.

So, using the API is very straightforward: as an example, allocate 256 bytes of memory dynamically, and store the pointer to that newly allocated region in the `ptr` variable:

```
void *ptr;
ptr = malloc(256);
```

Dynamic Memory Allocation

As another typical example, the programmer needs to allocate memory for a data structure; let's call it `struct sbar`. You could do so like this:

```
struct sbar {
    int a[10], b[10];
    char buf[512];
} *psbar;

psbar = malloc(sizeof(struct sbar));
// initialize and work with it
[...]
free(psbar);
```

Hey, astute reader! What about checking the failure case? It's a key point, so we will rewrite the preceding code like so (and of course it would be the case for the `malloc(256)` code snippet too):

```
struct [...] *psbar;
sbar = malloc(sizeof(struct sbar));
if (!sbar) {
    <... handle the error ...>
}
```

Let's use one of the powerful tracing tools `ltrace` to check that this works as expected; `ltrace` is used to display all library APIs in the process-execution path (similarly, use `strace` to trace all system calls). Let's assume that we compile the preceding code and the resulting binary executable file is called `tst`:

```
$ ltrace ./tst
malloc(592)              = 0xd60260
free(0xd60260)           = <void>
exit(0 <no return ...>
+++ exited (status 0) +++
$
```

We can clearly see `malloc(3)` (and the fact that the example structure we used took up 592 bytes on an x86_64), and its return value (following the = sign). The `free` API follows, and then it simply exits.

It's important to understand that the *content* of the memory chunk allocated by `malloc(3)` is considered to be random. Thus, it's the programmer's responsibility to initialize the memory before reading from it; if you fail to do so, it results in a bug called **Uninitialized Memory Read** (UMR) (more on this in the next chapter).

[ 118 ]

> malloc(3) always returns a memory region that is aligned on an 8-byte boundary. Need larger alignment values? Use the posix_memalign(3) API. Deallocate its memory as usual with free(3).
> Details can be found on the man page at https://linux.die.net/man/3/posix_memalign.

Examples of using the posix_memalign(3) API can be found in the *Locking memory* and *Memory protection* sections.

## malloc(3) – some FAQs

The following are some FAQs that will help us to learn more about malloc(3):

- FAQ 1 : How much memory can malloc(3) allocate with a single call?

    A rather pointless question in practical terms, but one that is often asked!

    The parameter to malloc(3) is an integer value of the size_t data type, so, logically, the maximum number we can pass as a parameter to malloc(3) is the maximum value a size_t can take on the platform. Practically speaking, on a 64-bit Linux, size_t will be 8 bytes, which of course, in bits is 8*8 = 64. Therefore, the maximum amount of memory that can be allocated in a single malloc(3) call is $2^{64}$!

    So, how much is it? Let's be empirical (it's important to read in Chapter 19, *Troubleshooting and Best Practices*, and the brief discussion there on *The empirical approach*).and actually try it out (note that the following code snippet has to be linked with the math library using the -lm switch):

```
int szt = sizeof(size_t);
float max=0;
max = pow(2, szt*8);
printf("sizeof size_t = %u; "
       "max value of the param to malloc = %.0f\n",
       szt, max);
```

# Dynamic Memory Allocation

The output, on an x86_64:

```
sizeof size_t = 8; max param to malloc = 18446744073709551616
```

Aha! That's a mighty large number; more readably, it's as follows:

```
2^64 = 18,446,744,073,709,551,616 = 0xffffffffffffffff
```

That's 16 EB (exabytes, which is 16,384 PB, which is 16 million TB)!

So, on a 64-bit OS, `malloc(3)` can allocate a maximum of 16 EB in a single call. In theory.

> **TIP**: As usual, there's more to it: please see *FAQ 2*; it will reveal that the *theoretical* answer to this question is **8 exabytes** (8 EB).

In practice, obviously, this would be impossible because, of course, that's the entire usermode VAS of the process itself. In reality, the amount of memory that can be allocated is limited by the amount of free memory contiguously available on the heap. Actually, there's more to it. As we shall soon learn (in the *How malloc(3) really behaves* section), memory for `malloc(3)` can come from other regions of the VAS, too. Don't forget there's a resource limit on data segment size; the default is usually unlimited, which as we discussed in this chapter, really means that there's no artificial limit imposed by the OS.

So, in practice, it's best to be sensible, not assume anything, and check the return value for NULL.

As an aside, what's the maximum value a `size_t` can take on a 32-bit OS? Accordingly, we compile on x86_64 for 32-bit by passing the -m32 switch to the compiler:

```
$ gcc -m32 mallocmax.c -o mallocmax32 -Wall -lm
$ ./mallocmax32
*** max_malloc() ***
sizeof size_t = 4; max value of the param to malloc =
4294967296
[...]
$
```

Clearly, it's 4 GB (gigabytes) – again, the entire VAS of a 32-bit process.

- FAQ 2: What if I pass malloc(3) a negative argument?

    The data type of the parameter to malloc(3), size_t, is an unsigned integer quantity – it cannot be negative. But, humans are imperfect, and **Integer OverFlow (IOF)** bugs do exist! You can imagine a scenario where a program attempts to calculate the number of bytes to allocate, like this:

    num = qa * qb;

    What if num is declared as a signed integer variable and qa and qb are large enough that the result of the multiplication operation causes an overflow? The num result will then wrap around and become negative! malloc(3) should fail, of course. But hang on: if the num variable is declared as size_t (which should be the case), the negative quantity will turn into some positive quantity!

    The mallocmax program has a test case for this.

Here is the output when run on an x86_64 Linux box:

```
*** negative_malloc() ***
size_t max     = 18446744073709551616
ld_num2alloc   = -288225969623711744
szt_num2alloc  = 18158518104085839872
1. long int used:   malloc(-288225969623711744) returns (nil)
2. size_t used:     malloc(18158518104085839872) returns (nil)
3. short int used: malloc(6144) returns 0x136b670
4. short int used: malloc(-4096) returns (nil)
5. size_t used:     malloc(18446744073709547520) returns (nil)
```

## Dynamic Memory Allocation

Here are the relevant variable declarations:

```
const size_t onePB     = 1125899907000000; /* 1 petabyte */
int qa = 28*1000000;
long int ld_num2alloc = qa * onePB;
size_t szt_num2alloc  = qa * onePB;
short int sd_num2alloc;
```

Now, let's try it with a 32-bit version of the program.

> Note that on a default-install Ubuntu Linux box, the 32-bit compile may fail (with an error such as `fatal error: bits/libc-header-start.h: No such file or directory`). Don't panic: this usually implies that the compiler support for building 32-bit binaries isn't present by default. To get it (as mentioned in the Hardware-Software List document), install the `multilib` compiler package: `sudo apt-get install gcc-multilib`.

Compile it for 32-bit and run it:

```
$ ./mallocmax32
*** max_malloc() ***
sizeof size_t = 4; max param to malloc = 4294967296
*** negative_malloc() ***
size_t max     = 4294967296
ld_num2alloc  = 0
szt_num2alloc = 1106247680
1. long int used:    malloc(-108445696) returns (nil)
2. size_t used:      malloc(4186521600) returns (nil)
3. short int used:   malloc(6144) returns 0x85d1570
4. short int used:   malloc(-4096) returns (nil)
5. size_t used:      malloc(4294963200) returns (nil)
$
```

To be fair, the compiler does warn us:

```
gcc -Wall   -c -o mallocmax.o mallocmax.c
mallocmax.c: In function 'negative_malloc':
mallocmax.c:87:6: warning: argument 1 value '18446744073709551615' exceeds maximum object size 9223372036854775807 [-Walloc-size-larger-than=]
  ptr = malloc(-1UL);
  ~~~~^~~~~~~~~~~~~~
In file included from mallocmax.c:18:0:
/usr/include/stdlib.h:424:14: note: in a call to allocation function 'malloc' declared here
 extern void *malloc (size_t __size) __THROW __attribute_malloc__
```

[ 122 ]

```
__wur;
    ^~~~~
[...]
```

Interesting! The compiler answers our *FAQ 1* question now:

```
[...] warning: argument 1 value '18446744073709551615' exceeds maximum
object size 9223372036854775807 [-Walloc-size-larger-than=] [...]
```

> The maximum value you can allocate as per the compiler seems to be 9223372036854775807.
>
> Wow. A little calculator time reveals that this is 8192 PB = 8 EB! So, we must conclude that the correct answer to the previous question: *How much memory can malloc allocate with a single call? Answer: 8 exabytes.* Again, in theory.

- FAQ 3: What if I use `malloc(0)`?

  > Not much; depending on the implementation, `malloc(3)` will return NULL, or, a non-NULL pointer that can be passed to free. Of course, even if the pointer is non-NULL, there is no memory, so don't attempt to use it.
  >
  > Let's try it out:
  >
  > ```
  > void *ptr;
  > ptr = malloc(0);
  > free(ptr);
  > ```

We compile and then run it via `ltrace`:

```
$ ltrace ./a.out
malloc(0)                                   = 0xf50260
free(0xf50260)                              = <void>
exit(0 <no return ...>
+++ exited (status 0) +++
$
```

[ 123 ]

*Dynamic Memory Allocation*

Here, `malloc(0)` did indeed return a non-NULL pointer.

- FAQ 4: What if I use `malloc(2048)` and attempt to read/write beyond 2,048 bytes?

  This is a bug of course – an out-of-bounds memory-access bug, further defined as a read or write buffer overflow. Hang on please, the detailed discussion of memory bugs (and subsequently, how to find and fix them) is the subject of Chapter 5, *Linux Memory Issues*, and Chapter 6, *Debugging Tools for Memory Issues*.

## malloc(3) – a quick summary

So, let's summarize the key points regarding usage of the `malloc(3)` API:

- `malloc(3)` dynamically (at runtime) allocates memory from the process heap
    - As we shall soon learn, this is not always the case
- The single parameter to `malloc(3)` is an unsigned integer value—the number of bytes to allocate
- The return value is a pointer to the start of the newly allocated memory chunk on success, or NULL on failure:
    - You must check for the failure case; don't just assume it will succeed
    - `malloc(3)` always returns a memory region that is aligned on an 8-byte boundary
- The content of the newly allocated memory region is considered to be random
    - You must initialize it before reading from any part of it
- You must free the memory you allocate

## The free API

One of the golden rules of development in this ecosystem is that programmer-allocated memory must be freed.

Failure to do so leads to a bad situation – a bug, really – called **memory leakage**; this is covered in some depth in the next chapter. Carefully matching your allocations and frees is essential.

> **TIP**: Then again, in smaller real-world projects (utils), you do come across cases where memory is allocated exactly once; in such cases, freeing the memory is pedantic as the entire virtual address space is destroyed upon process-termination. Also, using the *alloca(3)* API implies that you do not need to free the memory region (seen later in, *Advanced features* section). Nevertheless, you are advised to err on the side of caution!

Using the `free(3)` API is straightforward:

```
void free(void *ptr);
```

It accepts one parameter: the pointer to the memory chunk to be freed. `ptr` must be a pointer returned by one of the `malloc(3)` family routines: `malloc(3)`, `calloc`, or `realloc[array]`.

`free` does not return any value; don't even attempt to check whether it worked; if you used it correctly, it worked. More on free is found in the *Where does freed memory go?* section. Once a memory chunk is freed, you obviously cannot attempt to use any part of that memory chunk again; doing so will result in a bug (or what's called **UB – undefined behavior**).

A common misconception regarding `free()` sometimes leads to its being used in a buggy fashion; take a look at this pseudocode snippet:

```
void *ptr = NULL;
[...]
while(<some-condition-is-true>) {
    if (!ptr)
        ptr = malloc(n);

    [...
    <use 'ptr' here>
    ...]

    free(ptr);
}
```

This program will possibly crash in the loop (within the `<use 'ptr' here>` code) in a few iterations. Why? Because the `ptr` memory pointer is freed and is attempting to be reused. But how come? Ah, look carefully: the code snippet is only going to `malloc(3)` the `ptr` pointer if it is currently NULL, that is, its programmer has assumed that once we `free()` memory, the pointer we just freed gets set to NULL. This is not the case!!

Be wary and be defensive in writing code. Don't assume anything; it's a rich source of bugs. Importantly, our `Chapter 19`, *Troubleshooting and Best Practices*, covers such points)

## free – a quick summary

So, let's summarize the key points regarding the usage of the *free* API:

- The parameter passed to `free(3)` must be a value returned by one of the `malloc(3)` family APIs (`malloc(3)`, `calloc`, or `realloc[array]`).
- `free` has no return value.
- Calling `free(ptr)` does not set `ptr` to `NULL` (that would be nice, though).
- Once freed, do not attempt to use the freed memory.
- Do not attempt to *free* the same memory chunk more than once (it's a bug – UB).
- For now, we will assume that freed memory goes back to the system.
- For Heaven's sake, do not forget to free memory that was dynamically allocated earlier. The forgotten memory is said to have *leaked out* and that's a really hard bug to catch! Luckily, there are tools that help us catch these bugs. More in `Chapter 5`, *Linux Memory Issues*, and `Chapter 6`, *Debugging Tools for Memory Issues*.

# The calloc API

The `calloc(3)` API is almost identical to `malloc(3)`, differing in two main respects:

- It initializes the memory chunk it allocates to the zero value (that is, ASCII 0 or NULL, not the number 0)
- It accepts two parameters, not one

The `calloc(3)` function signature is as follows:

```
void *calloc(size_t nmemb, size_t size);
```

The first parameter, `nmemb`, is n members; the second parameter, `size`, is the size of each member. In effect, `calloc(3)` allocates a memory chunk of (nmemb*size) bytes. So, if you want to allocate memory for an array of, say, 1,000 integers, you can do so like this:

```
int *ptr;
ptr = calloc(1000, sizeof(int));
```

Assuming the size of an integer is 4 bytes, we would have allocated a total of (1000*4) = 4000 bytes.

Whenever one requires memory for an array of items (a frequent use case in applications is an array of structures), `calloc` is a convenient way to both allocate and simultaneously initialize the memory.

> **TIP**: Demand paging (covered later in this chapter), is another reason programmers use `calloc` rather than `malloc(3)` (in practice, this is mostly useful for realtime applications). Read up on this in the up coming section.

## The realloc API

The `realloc` API is used to *resize* an existing memory chunk—to grow or shrink it. This resizing can only be performed on a piece of memory previously allocated with one of the `malloc(3)` family of APIs (the usual suspects: `malloc(3)`, `calloc`, or `realloc[array]`). Here is its signature:

```
void *realloc(void *ptr, size_t size);
```

The first parameter, `ptr`, is a pointer to a chunk of memory previously allocated with one of the `malloc(3)` family of APIs; the second parameter, `size`, is the new size of the memory chunk—it can be larger or smaller than the original, thus growing or shrinking the memory chunk.

A quick example code snippet will help us understand `realloc`:

```
void *ptr, *newptr;
ptr = calloc(100, sizeof(char)); // error checking code not shown here
newptr = realloc(ptr, 150);
```

*Dynamic Memory Allocation*

```
if (!newptr) {
    fprintf(stderr, "realloc failed!");
    free(ptr);
    exit(EXIT_FAILURE);
}
< do your stuff >
free(newptr);
```

The pointer returned by `realloc` is the pointer to the newly resized chunk of memory; it may or may not be the same address as the original `ptr`. In effect, you should now completely disregard the original pointer `ptr` and regard the realloc-returned `newptr` pointer as the one to work with. If it fails, the return value is NULL (check it!) and the original memory chunk is left untouched.

A key point: the pointer returned by `realloc(3)`, `newptr`, is the one that must be subsequently freed, *not* the original pointer (`ptr`) to the (now resized) memory chunk. Of course, do not attempt to free both pointers, as that to is a bug.

What about the contents of the memory chunk that just got resized? They remain unchanged up to `MIN(original_size, new_size)`. Thus, in the preceding example, `MIN(100, 150) = 100`, the contents of memory up to 100 bytes will be unchanged. What about the remainder (50 bytes)? It's considered to be random content (just like `malloc(3)`).

## The realloc(3) – corner cases

Consider the following code snippet:

```
void *ptr, *newptr;
ptr = calloc(100, sizeof(char)); // error checking code not shown here
newptr = realloc(NULL, 150);
```

The pointer passed to `realloc` is NULL? The library treats this as equivalent to a new allocation – `malloc(150)`; and all the implications of the `malloc(3)` That's it.

Now, consider the following code snippet:

```
void *ptr, *newptr;
ptr = calloc(100, sizeof(char)); // error checking code not shown here
newptr = realloc(ptr, 0);
```

The size parameter passed to `realloc` is 0? The library treats this as equivalent to `free(ptr)`. That's it.

# The reallocarray API

A scenario: you allocate memory for an array using `calloc(3)`; later, you want to resize it to be, say, a lot larger. We can do so with `realloc(3)`; for example:

```
struct sbar *ptr, *newptr;
ptr = calloc(1000, sizeof(struct sbar)); // array of 1000 struct sbar's
[...]
// now we want 500 more!
newptr = realloc(ptr, 500*sizeof(struct sbar));
```

Fine. There's an easier way, though—using the `reallocarray(3)` API. Its signature is as follows:

```
void *reallocarray(void *ptr, size_t nmemb, size_t size);
```

With it, the code becomes simpler:

```
[...]
// now we want 500 more!
newptr = reallocarray(ptr, 500, sizeof(struct sbar));
```

The return value of `reallocarray` is pretty identical to that of the `realloc` API: the new pointer to the resized memory chunk on success (it may differ from the original), `NULL` on failure. If it fails, the original memory chunk is left untouched.

`reallocarray` has one real advantage over `realloc` – safety. From the man page on *realloc(3)*, see this snippet:

> ... However, unlike that realloc() call, reallocarray() fails safely in the case where the multiplication would overflow. If such an overflow occurs, reallocarray() returns NULL, sets errno to ENOMEM, and leaves the original block of memory unchanged.

Also realize that the `reallocarray` API is a GNU extension; it will work on modern Linux but should not be considered portable to other OSes.

*Dynamic Memory Allocation*

Finally, consider this: some projects have strict alignment requirements for their data objects; using `calloc` (or even allocating said objects via `malloc(3)`) can result in subtle bugs! Later in this chapter, we'll use the `posix_memalign(3)` API—it guarantees allocating memory to a given byte alignment (you specify the number of bytes)! For example, requiring a memory-allocation to be aligned to a page boundary is a fairly common occurrence (Recall, malloc always returns a memory region that is aligned on an 8-byte boundary).

The bottom line: be careful. Read the documentation, think, and decide which API would be appropriate given the circumstances. More on this in the *Further reading* section on the GitHub repository.

# Beyond the basics

In this section, we will dig a bit deeper into dynamic memory management with the `malloc(3)` API family. Understanding these areas, and the content of Chapter 5, *Linux Memory Issues*, and Chapter 6, *Debugging Tools for Memory Issues*, will go a long way in helping developers effectively debug common memory bugs and issues.

## The program break

When a process or thread wants memory, it invokes one of the dynamic memory routines—usually `malloc(3)` or `calloc(3)`; this memory (usually) comes from the **heap segment**. As mentioned earlier, the heap is a dynamic segment – it can grow (toward higher virtual addresses). Obviously though, at any given point in time, the heap has an endpoint or top beyond which memory cannot be taken. This endpoint—the last legally reference-able location on the heap – is called the **program break**.

## Using the sbrk() API

So, how do you know where the current program break is? That's easy – the `sbrk(3)` API, when used with a parameter value of zero, returns the current program break! Let's do a quick lookup:

```
#include <unistd.h>
[...]
    printf("Current program break: %p\n", sbrk(0));
```

You will see some sample output as follows when the preceding line of code runs:

```
$ ./show_curbrk
Current program break: 0x1bb4000
$ ./show_curbrk
Current program break: 0x1e93000
$ ./show_curbrk
Current program break: 0x1677000
$
```

It works, but why does the program break value keep changing (seemingly randomly)? Well, it really *is* random: for security reasons, Linux randomizes the layout of a process's virtual address space (we covered the process VAS layout in `Chapter 2`, *Virtual Memory*). This technique is called **Address Space Layout Randomization (ASLR)**.

Let's do a bit more: we will write a program that, if run without any parameters, merely displays the current program break and exits (like the one we just saw); if passed a parameter – the number of bytes of memory to dynamically allocate – it does so (with `malloc(3)`), then prints the heap address returned as well as the original and current program break. Here, you will only be allowed to request less than 128 KB, for reasons that will be made clear shortly.

Refer to the `ch4/show_curbrk.c`:

```c
int main(int argc, char **argv)
{
    char *heap_ptr;
    size_t num = 2048;

    /* No params, just print the current break and exit */
    if (argc == 1) {
        printf("Current program break: %p\n", sbrk(0));
        exit(EXIT_SUCCESS);
    }

    /* If passed a param - the number of bytes of memory to
     * dynamically allocate - perform a dynamic alloc, then
     * print the heap address, the current break and exit.
     */
    num = strtoul(argv[1], 0, 10);
    if ((errno == ERANGE && num == ULONG_MAX)
         || (errno != 0 && num == 0))
        handle_err(EXIT_FAILURE, "strtoul(%s) failed!\n", argv[1]);
    if (num >= 128 * 1024)
        handle_err(EXIT_FAILURE, "%s: pl pass a value < 128 KB\n",
```

# Dynamic Memory Allocation

```
        argv[0]);

    printf("Original program break: %p ; ", sbrk(0));
    heap_ptr = malloc(num);
    if (!heap_ptr)
        handle_err(EXIT_FAILURE, "malloc failed!");
    printf("malloc(%lu) = %16p ; curr break = %16p\n",
           num, heap_ptr, sbrk(0));
    free(heap_ptr);

    exit(EXIT_SUCCESS);
}
```

Let's try it out:

```
$ make show_curbrk && ./show_curbrk
[...]
Current program break: 0x1247000
$ ./show_curbrk 1024
Original program break: 0x1488000 ; malloc(1024) =        0x1488670 ;
curr break =          0x14a9000
$
```

Interesting (see the following diagram)! With an allocation of 1,024 bytes, the heap pointer that's returned to the start of that memory chunk is `0x1488670`; that's `0x1488670 - 0x1488000 = 0x670 = 1648` bytes from the original break.

Also, the new break value is `0x14a9000`, which is (`0x14a9000 - 0x1488670 = 133520`), approximately 130 KB from the freshly allocated block. Why did the heap grow by so much for a mere 1 KB allocation? Patience; this, and more, will be examined in the next section, *How malloc(3) really behaves*. Meanwhile, refer to the following diagram:

*Chapter 4*

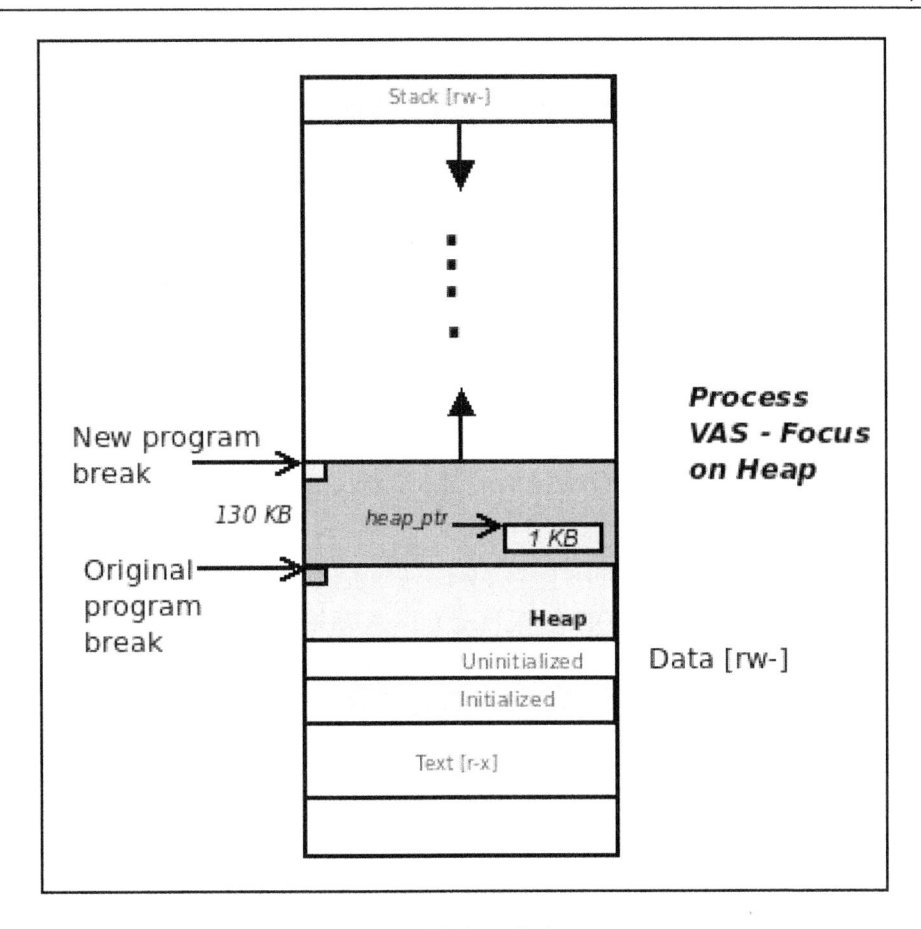

*Heap and the Program Break*

With respect to the preceding diagram:
```
Original program break = 0x1488000
heap_ptr               = 0x1488670
New program break      = 0x14a9000
```

Note that sbrk(2) can be used to increment or decrement the program break (by passing it an integer parameter). At first glance, this might seem like a good way to allocate and deallocate dynamic memory; in reality, it's always better to use the well-documented and portable glibc implementation, the malloc(3) family APIs.

> sbrk is a convenient library wrapper over the brk(2) system call.

## How malloc(3) really behaves

The general consensus it that `malloc(3)` (and `calloc(3)` and `realloc[array](3)`) obtains its memory from the heap segment. This is indeed the case, but digging a bit deeper reveals that it's not *always* the case. The modern glibc `malloc(3)` engine uses some subtle strategies to make the most optimal use of available memory regions and the process VAS—which, especially on today's 32-bit systems, is fast becoming a rather scarce resource.

So, how does it work? The library uses a predefined MMAP_THRESHOLD variable – its value is 128 KB by default – to determine from where memory gets allocated. Let's imagine we are allocating *n* bytes of memory with malloc(n):

- If *n* < MMAP_THRESHOLD, use the heap segment to allocate the requested *n* bytes

- If *n* >= MMAP_THRESHOLD, and if n bytes are not available on the heap's free list, use an arbitrary free region of virtual address space to satisfy the requested *n* bytes allocation

How exactly is the memory allocated in the second case? Ah, `malloc(3)` internally calls `mmap(2)` – the memory map system call. The mmap system call is very versatile. In this case, it is made to reserve a free region of n bytes of the calling process's virtual address space!

> Why use `mmap(2)`? The key reason is that mmap-ed memory can always be freed up (released back to the system) in an independent fashion whenever required; this is certainly not always the case with `free(3)`.

> Of course, there are some downsides: mmap allocations can be expensive because, the memory is page-aligned (and could thus be wasteful), and the kernel zeroes out the memory region (this hurts performance).

> The `mallopt(3)` man page (circa December 2016) also notes that nowadays, glibc uses a dynamic mmap threshold; initially, the value is the usual 128 KB, but if a large memory chunk between the current threshold and DEFAULT_MMAP_THRESHOLD_MAX is freed, the threshold is increased to become the size of the freed block.

# Code example – malloc(3) and the program break

Seeing for ourselves the effect of `malloc(3)` allocations on the heap and process virtual address space is interesting and educational. Check out the output of the following code example (the source is available in this book's Git repository):

```
$ ./malloc_brk_test -h
Usage: ./malloc_brk_test [option | --help]
 option = 0 : show only mem pointers [default]
 option = 1 : opt 0 + show malloc stats as well
 option = 2 : opt 1 + perform larger alloc's (over MMAP_THRESHOLD)
 option = 3 : test segfault 1
 option = 4 : test segfault 2
 -h | --help : show this help screen
$
```

There are several scenarios running in this application; let's examine some of them now.

## Scenario 1 – default options

We run the `malloc_brk_test` program with no parameters, that is, using the defaults:

```
$ ./malloc_brk_test
                              init_brk =      0x1c97000
 #: malloc(        n) =       heap_ptr        cur_brk     delta
                                                          [cur_brk-
init_brk]
 0: malloc(        8) =       0x1c97670       0x1cb8000 [135168]
 1: malloc(     4083) =       0x1c97690       0x1cb8000 [135168]
 2: malloc(        3) =       0x1c98690       0x1cb8000 [135168]
$
```

The process prints out its initial program break value: `0x1c97000`. It then allocates just 8 bytes (via the `malloc(3)` API); under the hood, the glibc allocation engine invokes the *sbrk(2)* system call to grow the heap; the new break is now `0x1cb8000`, an increase of 135,168 bytes = 132 KB from the previous break (clearly seen in the `delta` column in the preceding code)!

*Dynamic Memory Allocation*

Why? Optimization: glibc anticipates that, in the future, the process will require more heap space; instead of the expense of invoking a system call (`sbrk/brk`) each time, it performs one large-ish heap-growing operation. The next two `malloc(3)` APIs (numbers 1 and 2 in the left-most column) prove this is the case: we allocate 4,083 and 3 bytes respectively, and what do you notice? The program break does *not* change – the heap is already large enough to accommodate the requests.

## Scenario 2 – showing malloc statistics

This time, we pass the `1` parameter, asking it to display `malloc(3)` statistics as well (achieved using the `malloc_stats(3)` API):

```
$ ./malloc_brk_test 1
                                     init_brk =   0x184e000
    #: malloc(        n) =           heap_ptr    cur_brk    delta
                                                            [cur_brk-init_brk]
    0: malloc(        8) =           0x184e670   0x186f000  [135168]
Arena 0:
system bytes       =        135168
in use bytes       =          1664
Total (incl. mmap):
system bytes       =        135168
in use bytes       =          1664
max mmap regions   =             0
max mmap bytes     =             0

    1: malloc(     4083) =           0x184e690   0x186f000  [135168]
Arena 0:
system bytes       =        135168
in use bytes       =          5760
Total (incl. mmap):
system bytes       =        135168
in use bytes       =          5760
max mmap regions   =             0
max mmap bytes     =             0

    2: malloc(        3) =           0x184f690   0x186f000  [135168]
Arena 0:
system bytes       =        135168
in use bytes       =          5792
Total (incl. mmap):
system bytes       =        135168
in use bytes       =          5792
max mmap regions   =             0
max mmap bytes     =             0
```

*Chapter 4*

The output is similar, except the program invokes the useful `malloc_stats(3)` API, which queries and prints `malloc(3)` state information to `stderr` (by the way, an arena is an allocation area that's internally maintained by the `malloc(3)` engine). From this output, notice that:

- The available free memory – system bytes – is 132 KB (after performing a tiny 8 byte `malloc(3)`)
- In-use bytes increases with each allocation but system bytes remains the same
- `mmap` regions and `mmap` bytes is zero as no mmap-based allocations have occurred.

## Scenario 3 – large allocations option

This time, we pass the 2 parameter, asking the program to perform larger allocations (greater than `MMAP_THRESHOLD`):

```
$ ./malloc_brk_test 2
                              init_brk =      0x2209000
 #: malloc(       n) =        heap_ptr        cur_brk    delta
                                                         [cur_brk-
init_brk]
[...]

 3: malloc( 136168) =   0x7f57288cd010        0x222a000 [135168]
Arena 0:
system bytes     =       135168
in use bytes     =         5792
Total (incl. mmap):
system bytes     =       274432
in use bytes     =       145056
max mmap regions =            1
max mmap bytes   =       139264

 4: malloc( 1048576) =  0x7f57287c7010        0x222a000 [135168]
Arena 0:
system bytes     =       135168
in use bytes     =         5792
Total (incl. mmap):
system bytes     =      1327104
in use bytes     =      1197728
max mmap regions =            2
max mmap bytes   =      1191936

$
```

*Dynamic Memory Allocation*

(Note that the preceding code we have clipped the output of the first two small allocations and only show the relevant large ones).

Now, we allocate 132 KB (point 3 in the preceding output); some thing to take note of are as follows:

- The allocations (#3 and #4) are for 132 KB and 1 MB – both above the `MMAP_THRESHOLD` (value of 128 KB)
- The (arena 0) heap *in-use bytes* (5,792) has *not* changed at all across these two allocations, indicating that heap memory has *not* been used
- The max mmap regions and max mmap bytes numbers have changed to positive values (from zero), indicating the use of mmap-ed memory

A couple of remaining scenarios will be examined later.

## Where does freed memory go?

`free(3)`, of course, is a library routine – so it stands to reason that when we free up memory, previously allocated by one of the dynamic allocation routines, it does not get freed back to the system, but rather to the process heap (which, of course, is virtual memory).

However, there are at least two cases where this may not occur:

- If the allocation was satisfied internally via *mmap* rather than via the heap segment, it gets immediately freed back to the system
- On modern glibc, if the amount of heap memory being freed is very large, this triggers the return of at least some of the memory chunks back to the OS.

## Advanced features

A few advanced features will now be covered:

- Demand paging
- Locking memory in RAM
- Memory protection
- Allocation with the *alloca(3)*

# Demand-paging

Most of us know that if a process dynamically allocates memory, with `malloc`, say it does `ptr = malloc(8192);`, then, assuming success, the process is now allocated 8 KB of physical RAM. It might come as a surprise, but, on modern OSes such as Linux, this is actually not the case.

So, what is the case? (In this book, we do not delve into kernel-level details. Also, as you might be aware, the granularity of memory at the level of the OS allocator is a *page*, which is typically 4 KB.)

> It's not a good idea to assume anything when writing robust software. So, how can you correctly determine the page size on the OS? Use the `sysconf(3)` API; for example, `printf("page size = %ld\n", **sysconf(_SC_PAGESIZE)**);`, which outputs `page size = 4096`.
>
> Alternatively, use the `getpagesize(2)` system call to retrieve the system page size. (Importantly, see Chapter 19, *Troubleshooting and Best Practices*, covering similar points in the section *A Programmer's Checklist: 7 Rules*).

Realistically, all malloc does is reserve virtual pages of memory from the process VAS.

So, when does the process get the actual physical pages? Ah, as and when the process actually peeks or pokes any byte in a page, in reality when it makes any kind of access on any byte of the page (attempting to read/write/execute it), the process traps into the OS – via a hardware exception called a page fault – and in the OS's fault handler, if all's well, the OS allocates a physical page frame for the virtual page. This highly optimized manner of handing out physical memory to processes is called **demand-paging** – the pages are only physically allocated when they are actually required, on-demand! This is closely related to what OS folks call the memory or VM overcommit feature; yes, it's a feature, not a bug.

*Dynamic Memory Allocation*

> **TIP**
>
> If you want to guarantee that physical page frames are allocated after a virtual allocation you can:
>
> - Do `malloc(3)` followed by `memset(3)` on all the bytes in all pages
> - Just use the `calloc(3)`; it will set the memory to zero, thus faulting it in
>
> On many implementations, the second method – using `calloc(3)` – is faster than the first.

It's really because of demand-paging that we can write an application that malloc's huge amounts of memory and never free's it; it will work as long as the process does not attempt to read, write, or execute any byte in any (virtual) page of the allocated region. Apparently, there are many real-world applications that are quite poorly designed and do exactly this kind of thing – allocate huge amounts of memory via `malloc(3)` just in case we need it. Demand-paging is an OS hedge against wastefully eating up huge amounts of physical memory that hardly gets used in practice.

Of course, you, the astute reader, will realize that to every upside there's probably a downside. In this scenario, this could conceivably happen with several processes simultaneously performing large memory allocations. If all of them allocate large portions of virtual memory and then want to actually claim those pages physically at around the same time, this would put a tremendous amount of memory pressure on the OS! And guess what, the OS makes absolutely no guarantee that it will succeed in servicing everyone. In fact, in the worst case, the Linux OS will run short of physical RAM to the extent that it must invoke a bit of a controversial component – the **Out-of-Memory** (**OOM**) Killer – whose job is to identify the memory-hogging process and kill it and its descendants, thus reclaiming memory and keeping the system alive. Reminds you of the Mafia, huh.

Again, the man page on `malloc(3)` clearly notes the following:

```
By  default, Linux follows an optimistic memory allocation strategy.
This means that when malloc() returns non-NULL there is no guarantee
that the memory really is available.  In case it turns out that the
system is out of memory, one or more processes will be killed by the
OOM  killer.
[...]
```

If interested, dig deeper with the references in the *Further reading* section on the GitHub repository.

## Resident or not?

Now that we clearly understand that the pages allocated by *malloc* and friends are virtual and not guaranteed to be backed by physical frames (at least to start with), imagine we have a pointer to a (virtual) memory region and we know its length. We would now like to know whether the corresponding pages are in RAM, that is, whether they are resident or not.

It turns out there's a system call available that gives precisely this information: mincore(2).

> **TIP**: The mincore(2) system call is pronounced m-in-core, not min-core. *Core* is an old word used to describe physical memory.

Let's take a look at the following code:

```
#include <unistd.h>
#include <sys/mman.h>

int mincore(void *addr, size_t length, unsigned char *vec);
```

Given the starting virtual address and length, mincore(2) populates the third parameter – a vector array. After the call successfully returns, for every byte of the vector array, if the LSB (Least Significant Bit) is set, it implies that the corresponding page *is* resident (in RAM), otherwise it's not (possibly not allocated or in swap).

Usage details are available via the mincore(2) man page: https://linux.die.net/man/2/mincore.

Of course, you should realize that the information returned on page residency is merely a snapshot at that point in time of the state of the memory pages: it could change under us, that is, it is (or could be) very transient in nature.

# Locking memory

We understand that on a virtual memory-based OS, such as Linux, a usermode page can be swapped at any point in time; the Linux kernel memory management code makes these decisions. To the regular application process, this should not matter: any time it attempts to access (read, write, or execute) the page content, the kernel will page it back into RAM, and allow it to use it as though nothing had occurred. This handling is generally called *servicing a page fault* (there is a lot more to it, but for the purpose of this discussion, this is sufficient), and is completely transparent to the usermode application process.

However, there are some situations where memory pages being paged – written from RAM to swap and vice-versa – is undesirable:

- Realtime applications
- Cryptography (security) applications

In real-time applications, the key factor (at least within its critical code paths) is determinism – the iron-clad guarantee that the work will take a certain worst-case amount of time, and no more, no matter the load on the system.

Imagine that the real-time process is executing a critical code path and a data page has to be paged in from the swap partition at that moment – the latency (delay) introduced could ruin the application's characteristics, resulting in dismal failure (or worse). In these cases, we, the developers, need a way to guarantee that said pages of memory can guaranteed to be resident in RAM, thus avoiding any page faulting.

In some types of security applications, they would likely store some secrets in memory (a password, a key); if the memory pages containing these are written out to disk (swap), there is always the possibility that it remains on disk well after the application exits – resulting in what's called information leakage, which is a bug attackers are just waiting to pounce upon! Here, again, the need of the hour is to guarantee that those pages cannot be swapped out.

Enter the mlock(2) (and friends: *mlock2* and *mlockall*) system calls; the express purpose of these APIs is to lock memory pages within the calling process's virtual address space. Let's figure out how to use mlock(2). Here is its signature:

```
int mlock(const void *addr, size_t len);
```

The first parameter, addr, is a pointer to the (virtual) memory region to lock; the second parameter, len, is the number of bytes to lock into RAM. As a trivial example, take look at the following code (here, to keep it easily readable, we don't show error-checking code; in a real application, please do so!):

```
long pgsz = sysconf(_SC_PAGESIZE);
size_t len = 3*pgsz;

void *ptr = malloc(len);

[...]       // initialize the memory, etc

// Lock it!
if (mlock(ptr, len) != 0) {
    // mlock failed, handle it
    return ...;
}

[...]   /* use the memory, confident it is resident in RAM & will stay
           there until unlocked */

munlock(ptr, len);   // it's now unlocked, can be swapped
```

## Limits and privileges

A privileged process, either by running as *root*, or, better yet, by having the CAP_IPC_LOCK capability bit set in order to lock memory (we shall describe process credentials and capabilities in detail in their own chapters - Chapter 7, *Process Credentials*, and Chapter 8, *Process Capabilities*), can lock unlimited amounts of memory.

From Linux 2.6.9 onward, for a non-privileged process, it is limited by the RLIMIT_MEMLOCK soft resource limit (which, typically, is not set very high). Here is an example on an x86_64 Fedora box (as well as Ubuntu):

```
$ prlimit | grep MEMLOCK
MEMLOCK    max locked-in-memory address space    65536    65536 bytes
$
```

## Dynamic Memory Allocation

It's just 64 KB (ditto on an embedded ARM Linux, by default).

> At the time of writing this book, on a recent *Fedora 28* distro running on x86_64, the resource limit for max locked memory seems to have been amped up to 16 MB! The following *prlimit(1)* output shows just this:
>
> ```
> $ prlimit | grep MEMLOCK
> MEMLOCK      max locked-in-memory address space
>  16777216   16777216 bytes
> $
> ```

Hang on a second, though; while using mlock(2), the POSIX standard requires that addr is aligned to a page boundary (that is, if you take the memory start address and divide it by the system page size, the remainder will be zero, that is, (addr % pgsz) == 0. You can use the posix_memalign(3) API to guarantee this; so, we can change our code slightly to accommodate this alignment requirement:

Refer to the following (ch4/mlock_try.c):

```c
[...]
#define CMD_MAX   256
static void disp_locked_mem(void)
{
    char *cmd = malloc(CMD_MAX);
    if (!cmd)
        FATAL("malloc(%zu) failed\n", CMD_MAX);
    snprintf(cmd, CMD_MAX-1, "grep Lck /proc/%d/status", getpid());
    system(cmd);
    free(cmd);
}

static void try_mlock(const char *cpgs)
{
    size_t num_pg = atol(cpgs);
    const long pgsz = sysconf(_SC_PAGESIZE);
    void *ptr= NULL;
    size_t len;

    len = num_pg * pgsz;
    if (len >= LONG_MAX)
        FATAL("too many bytes to alloc (%zu), aborting now\n", len);
/* ptr = malloc(len); */
/* Don't use the malloc; POSIX wants page-aligned memory for mlock */
    posix_memalign(&ptr, pgsz, len);
```

[ 144 ]

```c
    if (!ptr)
        FATAL("posix_memalign(for %zu bytes) failed\n", len);

    /* Lock the memory region! */
    if (mlock(ptr, len)) {
        free(ptr);
        FATAL("mlock failed\n");
    }
    printf("Locked %zu bytes from address %p\n", len, ptr);
    memset(ptr, 'L', len);
    disp_locked_mem();
    sleep(1);

    /* Now unlock it.. */
    if (munlock(ptr, len)) {
        free(ptr);
        FATAL("munlock failed\n");
    }
    printf("unlocked..\n");
    free(ptr);
}

int main(int argc, char **argv)
{
    if (argc < 2) {
        fprintf(stderr, "Usage: %s pages-to-alloc\n", argv[0]);
        exit(EXIT_FAILURE);
    }
    disp_locked_mem();
    try_mlock(argv[1]);
    exit (EXIT_SUCCESS);
}
```

*Dynamic Memory Allocation*

Let's give it a spin:

```
$ ./mlock_try
Usage: ./mlock_try pages-to-alloc
$ ./mlock_try 1
VmLck:          0 kB
Locked 4096 bytes from address 0x1a6e000
VmLck:          4 kB
unlocked..
$ ./mlock_try 32
VmLck:          0 kB
mlock_try.c:try_mlock:79: mlock failed
perror says: Cannot allocate memory
$
$ ./mlock_try 15
VmLck:          0 kB
Locked 61440 bytes from address 0x842000
VmLck:         60 kB
unlocked..
$ sudo ./mlock_try 32
[sudo] password for <user>: xxx
VmLck:          0 kB
Locked 131072 bytes from address 0x7f6b478db000
VmLck:        128 kB
unlocked..
$ prlimit | grep MEMLOCK
MEMLOCK    max locked-in-memory address space    65536    65536
bytes
$
```

> **TIP**
>
> Notice, in the successful cases, the address returned by `posix_memalign(3)`; it's on a page boundary. We can quickly tell by looking at the last three digits (from the right) of the address – if they are all zeroes, it's cleanly divisible by page size and thus on a page boundary. This is because the page size is usually 4,096 bytes, and 4096 decimal = 0x1000 hex!

We request 32 pages; the allocation is successful, but *mlock* fails because 32 pages = 32*4K = 128 KB; the resource limit is just 64 KB for locked memory. However, when we *sudo* it (thus running with root access), it works.

## Locking all pages

*mlock* basically allows us to tell the OS to lock a certain range of memory into RAM. In some real-world cases, though, we cannot predict exactly which pages of memory we will require resident in advance (a real-time application might require various, or all, memory pages to always be resident).

To solve this tricky issue, another system call – *mlockall(2)* – exists; as you can guess, it allows you to lock all process memory pages:

```
int mlockall(int flags);
```

If successful (remember, the same privilege restrictions apply to *mlockall* as to *mlock*), all the process's memory pages – such as text, data segments, library pages, stack, and shared memory segments – are guaranteed to remain resident in RAM until unlocked.

The *flags* argument provides further control to the application developer; it can be bitwise OR of the following:

- MCL_CURRENT
- MCL_FUTURE
- MCL_ONFAULT (Linux 4.4 onward)

Using MCL_CURRENT asks the OS to lock all current pages within the calling process's VAS into memory.

But what if you issue the *mlockall(2)* system call at initialization time, but the real-time process is going to perform an *malloc* of say, 200 kilobytes, 5 minutes from now? We need to guarantee that those 200 KB of memory (which is 50 pages, given a 4 KB page size) is always resident in RAM (otherwise, the real-time application will suffer too great a latency from possible future page faulting). That is the purpose of the MCL_FUTURE flag: it guarantees the memory pages that become part of the calling process's VAS in the future will remain resident in memory until unlocked.

We learned in the *Demand-paging* section that performing *malloc* does nothing more than reserve virtual memory, not physical. As an example, if an (non-real-time) application performs a rather large allocation of a megabyte (that's 512 pages), we understand that only 512 virtual pages are reserved and the physical page frames are not actually allocated – they will get faulted in on-demand. A typical realtime application will therefore need to somehow guarantee that, once faulted in, these 512 pages will remain locked (resident) in RAM. Use the MCL_ONFAULT flag to achieve this.

# Dynamic Memory Allocation

This flag must be used in conjunction with either the `MCL_CURRENT` or `MCL_FUTURE` flag, or both. The idea is that physical memory consumption remains extremely efficient (as no physical allocation is done at the time of *malloc*), and yet, once the application starts to touch the virtual pages (that is, read, write, or execute data or code within the page), the physical page frames get faulted in and they will then be locked. In other words, we do not pre-fault the memory, thus we get the best of both worlds.

The other side of the coin is that, when done, the application can unlock all memory pages by issuing the counterpart API: *munlockall(2)*.

## Memory protection

An application dynamically allocates, say, four pages of memory. By default, this memory is both readable and writable; we refer to these as the *memory protections* on the page.

Wouldn't it be nice if the application developer could dynamically modify memory protections on a per-page basis? For example, keep the first page with default protections, make the second page *read-only*, the third page *read+execute*, and on the fourth page, not allow any kind of access (a guard page, perhaps?).

Well, this feature is precisely what the `mprotect(2)` system call is designed for. Let's delve into how we can exploit it to do all that. Here is its signature:

```
#include <sys/mman.h>
int mprotect(void *addr, size_t len, int prot);
```

It's really quite straightforward: starting at the (virtual) address, `addr`, for `len` bytes (that is, from `addr` up to `addr+len-1`), apply the memory protections specified by the *prot* bitmask. As the granularity of *mprotect* is a page, the first parameter, *addr*, is expected to be page-aligned (on a page boundary; recall that this is exactly what `mlock[all](2)` expects too).

The third parameter, `prot`, is where you specify the actual protections; it is a bitmask and can either be just the `PROT_NONE` bit or the bitwise OR of the remainder:

| Protection bit | Meaning of memory protection |
| --- | --- |
| PROT_NONE | No access allowed on the page |
| PROT_READ | Reads allowed on the page |
| PROT_WRITE | Writes allowed on the page |
| PROT_EXEC | Execute access allowed on the page |

> Within the man page on *mprotect(2)*, there are several other rather arcane protection bits and useful information under the NOTES section. If required (or just curious), read about it here: http://man7.org/linux/man-pages/man2/mprotect.2.html.

## Memory protection – a code example

Let's consider an example program where the process dynamically allocates four pages of memory and wants to set them up so that the memory protections for each page are as shown in the following table:

| Page # | Page 0 | Page 1 | Page 2 | Page 3 |
|---|---|---|---|---|
| Protection bits | rw- | r-- | rwx | --- |

Relevant portions of the code are shown as follows:

First, the *main* function dynamically allocates page-aligned memory (four pages) with the `posix_memalign(3)` API, and then invokes the memory protection and the memory testing functions in turn:

```
[...]
    /* Don't use the malloc; POSIX wants page-aligned memory for
mprotect(2) */
    posix_memalign(&ptr, gPgsz, 4*gPgsz);
    if (!ptr)
        FATAL("posix_memalign(for %zu bytes) failed\n", 4*gPgsz);
    protect_mem(ptr);
    test_mem(ptr, atoi(argv[1]));
[...]
```

Here is the memory protection function:

```
int okornot[4];
static void protect_mem(void *ptr)
{
    int i;
    u64 start_off=0;
    char str_prots[][128] = {"PROT_READ|PROT_WRITE", "PROT_READ",
                             "PROT_WRITE|PROT_EXEC", "PROT_NONE"};
    int prots[4] = {PROT_READ|PROT_WRITE, PROT_READ,
                    PROT_WRITE|PROT_EXEC, PROT_NONE};

    printf("%s():\n", __FUNCTION__);
    memset(okornot, 0, sizeof(okornot));

    /* Loop over each page, setting protections as required */
```

## Dynamic Memory Allocation

```
        for (i=0; i<4; i++) {
            start_off = (u64)ptr+(i*gPgsz);
            printf("page %d: protections: %30s: "
                    "range [0x%llx:0x%llx]\n",
                    i, str_prots[i], start_off, start_off+gPgsz-1);

            if (mprotect((void *)start_off, gPgsz, prots[i]) == -1)
                WARN("mprotect(%s) failed\n", str_prots[i]);
            else
                okornot[i] = 1;
        }
    }
```

After setting up the memory protections, we have the `main()` function invoke the memory testing function, `test_mem`. The second parameter determines whether we will attempt to write on read-only memory (we require this test case for page 1 as it's read-only protected):

```
    static void test_mem(void *ptr, int write_on_ro_mem)
    {
        int byte = random() % gPgsz;
        char *start_off;

        printf("\n----- %s() -----\n", __FUNCTION__);

        /* Page 0 : rw [default] mem protection */
        if (okornot[0] == 1) {
            start_off = (char *)ptr + 0*gPgsz + byte;
            TEST_WRITE(0, start_off, 'a');
            TEST_READ(0, start_off);
        } else
            printf("*** Page 0 : skipping tests as memprot failed...\n");

        /* Page 1 : ro mem protection */
        if (okornot[1] == 1) {
            start_off = (char *)ptr + 1*gPgsz + byte;
            TEST_READ(1, start_off);
            if (write_on_ro_mem == 1) {
                TEST_WRITE(1, start_off, 'b');
            }
        } else
            printf("*** Page 1 : skipping tests as memprot failed...\n");

        /* Page 2 : RWX mem protection */
        if (okornot[2] == 1) {
            start_off = (char *)ptr + 2*gPgsz + byte;
            TEST_READ(2, start_off);
            TEST_WRITE(2, start_off, 'c');
```

```
    } else
        printf("*** Page 2 : skipping tests as memprot failed...\n");

    /* Page 3 : 'NONE' mem protection */
    if (okornot[3] == 1) {
        start_off = (char *)ptr + 3*gPgsz + byte;
        TEST_READ(3, start_off);
        TEST_WRITE(3, start_off, 'd');
    } else
        printf("*** Page 3 : skipping tests as memprot failed...\n");
}
```

Prior to attempting to test it, we check that the page has indeed been protected by the `mprotect` call (via our simple `okornot[]` array). Also, for readability, we build the simple `TEST_READ` and `TEST_WRITE` macros:

```
#define TEST_READ(pgnum, addr) do { \
    printf("page %d: reading: byte @ 0x%llx is ", \
    pgnum, (u64)addr); \
    fflush(stdout); \
    printf(" %x", *addr); \
    printf(" [OK]\n"); \
} while (0)

#define TEST_WRITE(pgnum, addr, byte) do { \
    printf("page %d: writing: byte '%c' to address 0x%llx now ...", \
            pgnum, byte, (u64)addr); \
    fflush(stdout); \
    *addr = byte; \
    printf(" [OK]\n"); \
} while (0)
```

If the process violates any of the memory protections, the OS will summarily kill it via the usual *segfault* mechanism (explained in detail within `Chapter 12`, *Signaling Part II*).

Let's perform some test runs on the `memprot` program; first (for reasons that will become clear soon) we'll try it out on a generic Ubuntu Linux box, then on a Fedora system, and finally on an (emulated) ARM-32 platform!

Case #1.1: The `memprot` program on standard Ubuntu 18.04 LTS with parameter 0 (output reformatted for readability):

```
$ cat /etc/issue
Ubuntu 18.04 LTS \n \l

$ uname -r
```

## Dynamic Memory Allocation

```
    4.15.0-23-generic
$

$ ./memprot
Usage: ./memprot test-write-to-ro-mem [0|1]
$ ./memprot 0
----- protect_mem() -----
page 0: protections: PROT_READ|PROT_WRITE: range
[0x55796ccd5000:0x55796ccd5fff]
page 1: protections: PROT_READ: range [0x55796ccd6000:0x55796ccd6fff]
page 2: protections: PROT_READ|PROT_WRITE|PROT_EXEC: range
[0x55796ccd7000:0x55796ccd7fff]
page 3: protections: PROT_NONE: range [0x55796ccd8000:0x55796ccd8fff]

----- test_mem() -----
page 0: writing: byte 'a' to address 0x55796ccd5567 now ... [OK]
page 0: reading: byte @ 0x55796ccd5567 is 61 [OK]
page 1: reading: byte @ 0x55796ccd6567 is 0 [OK]
page 2: reading: byte @ 0x55796ccd7567 is 0 [OK]
page 2: writing: byte 'c' to address 0x55796ccd7567 now ... [OK]
page 3: reading: byte @ 0x55796ccd8567 is Segmentation fault
$
```

Okay, so the parameter to memprot is 0 or 1; 0 implies that we do not perform a write-to-read-only-memory test, whereas 1 implies we do. Here, we've run it with the 0 parameter.

Some things to notice within the preceding output are as follows:

- The protect_mem() function sets up memory protections on a per-page basis. We have allocated 4 pages, thus we loop 4 times, and on each loop iteration i, perform mprotect(2) on the i-th memory page.
- As you can clearly see in the code, it's been done in this fashion, on each loop iteration
    - Page 0 : rw-: Set page protections to PROT_READ | PROT_WRITE
    - Page 1 : r--: Set page protections to PROT_READ
    - Page 2 : rwx: Set page protections to PROT_READ| PROT_WRITE | PROT_EXEC
    - Page 3 : ---: Set page protections to PROT_NONE, that is, make the page inaccessible

- In the preceding output, the output format displayed after *mprotect* is as follows:

  ```
  page <#>: protections: <PROT_xx|[...]> range
  [<start_addr>:<end_addr>]
  ```
- All goes well; the four pages get new protections as required.
- Next, the `test_mem()` function is invoked, which tests each page's protections (the memory protection of the page is shown within square brackets in the usual [rwx] format):
    - On page 0 [default: rw-]: It writes and reads a random byte within the page
    - On page 1 [r--]: It reads a random byte within the page, and if the user passed the parameter as 1 (not the case here, but it will be in the following case), it attempts to write to a random byte within that page
    - On page 2 [rwx]: As expected, reading and writing a random byte here succeeds
    - On page 3 [---]: It attempts to both read and write a random byte within the page.
        - The very first access – a *read* – fails with a *segfault*; this is expected of course – the page has no permissions whatsoever (we reproduce the output for this case): **page 3: reading: byte @ 0x55796ccd8567 is Segmentation fault**
- To summarize, with the parameter as 0, test cases on pages 0, 1, and 2 succeed; as expected, any access on page 3 causes the OS to kill the process (via the segmentation-violation signal).

*Dynamic Memory Allocation*

Case #1.2: The `memprot` program on standard Ubuntu 18.04 LTS with parameter 1 (output reformatted for readability).

Let's now re-run the program with the parameter set to 1, thus attempting to write to the *read-only* page 1:

```
$ ./memprot 1
----- protect_mem() -----
page 0: protections: PROT_READ|PROT_WRITE: range
[0x564d74f2d000:0x564d74f2dfff]
page 1: protections: PROT_READ: range [0x564d74f2e000:0x564d74f2efff]
page 2: protections: PROT_READ|PROT_WRITE|PROT_EXEC: range
[0x564d74f2f000:0x564d74f2ffff]
page 3: protections: PROT_NONE: range [0x564d74f30000:0x564d74f30fff]

----- test_mem() -----
page 0: writing: byte 'a' to address 0x564d74f2d567 now ... [OK]
page 0: reading: byte @ 0x564d74f2d567 is 61 [OK]
page 1: reading: byte @ 0x564d74f2e567 is 0 [OK]
page 1: writing: byte 'b' to address 0x564d74f2e567 now
...Segmentation fault
$
```

Indeed, as expected, it *segfaults* when it violates the read-only page permissions.

Case #2: The `memprot` program on a standard *Fedora 28* system.

At the time of writing this book, the latest and greatest *Fedora* workstation distribution is ver 28:

```
$ lsb_release -a
LSB Version: :core-4.1-amd64:core-4.1-noarch
Distributor ID: Fedora
Description: Fedora release 28 (Twenty Eight)
Release: 28
Codename: TwentyEight
$ uname -r
4.16.13-300.fc28.x86_64
$
```

We build and run our `memprot` program on this standard *Fedora 28* workstation system (passing 0 as the parameter – implying that we do not attempt writing to the read-only memory page):

```
$ ./memprot 0
----- protect_mem() -----
page 0: protections: PROT_READ|PROT_WRITE: range [0x15d8000:0x15d8fff]
page 1: protections: PROT_READ: range [0x15d9000:0x15d9fff]
page 2: protections: PROT_READ|PROT_WRITE|PROT_EXEC: range
[0x15da000:0x15dafff]
!WARNING! memprot.c:protect_mem:112:
          mprotect(PROT_READ|PROT_WRITE|PROT_EXEC) failed
perror says: Permission denied
page 3: protections: PROT_NONE: range [0x15db000:0x15dbfff]

----- test_mem() -----
page 0: writing: byte 'a' to address 0x15d8567 now ... [OK]
page 0: reading: byte @ 0x15d8567 is 61 [OK]
page 1: reading: byte @ 0x15d9567 is 0 [OK]
*** Page 2 : skipping tests as memprot failed...
page 3: reading: byte @ 0x15db567 is Segmentation fault (core dumped)
$
```

How do we interpret the preceding output? The following is the explanation for the same:

- All goes well for pages 0, 1, and 3: the *mprotect* API succeeds in setting the page's protections exactly as shown

- However, we get a failure (and a *Warning* message) when we attempt the `mprotect(2)` system call on page 2 with the `PROT_READ | PROT_WRITE | PROT_EXEC` attributes. *Why?*

    - The usual OS security is the **Discretionary Access Control (DAC)** layer. Many modern Linux distros, including Fedora, come with a powerful security feature – an additional layer of security within the OS – the **Mandatory Access Control (MAC)** layer. These are implemented on Linux as **Linux Security Modules (LSMs)**. Popular LSMs include the NSA's SELinux (Security-Enhanced Linux), AppArmor, Smack, TOMOYO, and Yama.

[ 155 ]

*Dynamic Memory Allocation*

- Fedora uses SELinux while Ubuntu variants tend to use AppArmor. Whichever the case, it is often these LSMs that can fail userland-issued system calls when they violate a security policy. This is precisely what happened with our mprotect(2) system call on the third page (when the page protections were attempted to be set to [rwx])!
- As a quick proof-of-concept, and to just get it working for now, we temporarily **disable** *SELinux* and retry:

  - **$ getenforce**
    Enforcing
    $ setenforce
    usage: setenforce [ Enforcing | Permissive | 1 | 0 ]
    **$ sudo setenforce 0**
    [sudo] password for <username>: **xxx**
    $ getenforce
    Permissive
    $

*SELinux* is now in permissive mode; retry the application:

```
$ ./memprot 0
----- protect_mem() -----
page 0: protections: PROT_READ|PROT_WRITE: range [0x118e000:0x118efff]
page 1: protections: PROT_READ: range [0x118f000:0x118ffff]
page 2: protections: PROT_READ|PROT_WRITE|PROT_EXEC: range
[0x1190000:0x1190fff]
page 3: protections: PROT_NONE: range [0x1191000:0x1191fff]

----- test_mem() -----
page 0: writing: byte 'a' to address 0x118e567 now ... [OK]
page 0: reading: byte @ 0x118e567 is 61 [OK]
page 1: reading: byte @ 0x118f567 is 0 [OK]
page 2: reading: byte @ 0x1190567 is 0 [OK]
page 2: writing: byte 'c' to address 0x1190567 now ... [OK]
page 3: reading: byte @ 0x1191567 is Segmentation fault (core dumped)
$
```

Now, it works as expected! Don't forget to re-enable the LSM:

```
$ sudo setenforce 1
$ getenforce
Enforcing
$
```

# An Aside – LSM logs, Ftrace

(If you are not interested in this, feel free to skip over this section). The astute reader might wonder: how does one realize that it's the OS security layer (the LSM) that ultimately caused the system call to fail? Broadly, there are two ways: check the given LSM logs, or use the kernel's Ftrace functionality. The first way is simpler, but the second can give us insight at the level of the OS.

## LSM logs

Modern Linux systems use the powerful systemd framework for process-initialization, logging, and more. The logging facility is called the journal and is accessed via the journalctl(1) utility. We use it to verify that it's indeed the SELinux LSM that has caused the issue:

```
$ journalctl --boot | grep memprot
[...]
<timestamp> <host> python3[31861]: SELinux is preventing memprot from using the execheap access on a process.
 If you do not think memprot should need to map heap memory that is both writable and executable.
 If you believe that memprot should be allowed execheap access on processes labeled unconfined_t by default.
 # ausearch -c 'memprot' --raw | audit2allow -M my-memprot
 # semodule -X 300 -i my-memprot.pp
```

It even shows us exactly how we can allow the access.

# Dynamic Memory Allocation

## Ftrace

The Linux kernel has a very powerful built-in tracing mechanism (well, it's one of them) – *Ftrace*. Using `ftrace`, you can verify that it's indeed the *LSM* code that, while honoring its security policy, caused the userspace-issued system call to return failure. I ran a trace (with `ftrace`):

```
22875  3) memprot-29591 | d...+ 10.204 us   | }
22876  3) memprot-29591 | d...              | do_syscall_64() {
22877  3) memprot-29591 | ....              |   SyS_mprotect() {
22878  3) memprot-29591 | ....              |     do_mprotect_pkey() {
22879  3) memprot-29591 | ....              |       down_write_killable() {
22880  3) memprot-29591 | ....              |         _cond_resched() {
22881  3) memprot-29591 | ....   0.034 us   |           rcu_all_qs();
22882  3) memprot-29591 | ....   0.321 us   |         }
22883  3) memprot-29591 | ....   0.616 us   |       }
22884  3) memprot-29591 | ....              |       find_vma() {
22885  3) memprot-29591 | ....   0.107 us   |         vmacache_find();
22886  3) memprot-29591 | ....   0.116 us   |         vmacache_update();
22887  3) memprot-29591 | ....   1.227 us   |       }
22888  3) memprot-29591 | ....              |       security_file_mprotect() {
22889  3) memprot-29591 | ....              |         selinux_file_mprotect() {
22890  3) memprot-29591 | ....              |           avc_has_perm() {
22891  3) memprot-29591 | ....   0.047 us   |             avc_denied();
22892  3) memprot-29591 | ....              |             slow_avc_audit() {
22893  3) memprot-29591 | ....              |               common_lsm_audit() {
```

ftrace output snippet

The `SyS_mprotect` function is what the *mprotect(2)* system call becomes within the kernel; `security_file_mprotect` is the LSM hook function that leads to the the actual SELinux function: `selinux_file_mprotect`; apparently, it fails the access.

Interestingly, Ubuntu 18.04 LTS also uses an LSM – AppArmor. However, it seems that it has not been configured to catch this kind of *write+execute* (heap) page-protection case.

Of course, these topics (LSMs, ftrace) are beyond the scope of this book. To the curious reader (the kind we love), please see more on *LSMs* and *Ftrace* in the *Further reading* section on the GitHub repository.

## An experiment – running the memprot program on an ARM-32

As an interesting experiment, we will cross-compile our preceding *memprot* program for an **ARM system**. I have used a convenient way to do this without real hardware: using the powerful **Free and Open Source Software (FOSS) Quick Emulator (QEMU)** project, to emulate an ARM Versatile Express Cortex-A9 platform!

Cross-compiling the code is indeed simple: notice that there is now a `CROSS_COMPILE` variable in our `Makefile`; it's the cross-compiler prefix – the prefix string identifying the toolchain (common to all tools). It's literally prefixed onto the `CC` (for `gcc`, or `CL` for clang) variable, which is the compiler used to build the target. Unfortunately, going into more detail regarding cross-compiling and root-filesystem build is beyond the scope of this book; for some help, see the *Tip* that follows this example's output. Also, to keep things simple, we will use a direct approach – a separate target for the ARM version within the `Makefile`. Let's check out the relevant portion of the `Makefile`:

```
$ cat Makefile
[...]
CROSS_COMPILE=arm-linux-gnueabihf-
CC=gcc
CCARM=${CROSS_COMPILE}gcc
[...]
common_arm.o: ../common.c ../common.h
    ${CCARM} ${CFLAGS} -c ../common.c -o common_arm.o
memprot_arm: common_arm.o memprot_arm.o
    ${CCARM} ${CFLAGS} -o memprot_arm memprot_arm.c common_arm.o
[...]
```

So, as shown here, we cross-compile the `memprot_arm` program:

```
$ make clean
[...]
$ make memprot_arm
arm-linux-gnueabihf-gcc -Wall -c ../common.c -o common_arm.o
gcc -Wall -c -o memprot_arm.o memprot_arm.c
arm-linux-gnueabihf-gcc -Wall -o memprot_arm memprot_arm.c common_arm.o
$ file ./memprot_arm
./memprot_arm: ELF 32-bit LSB executable, ARM, EABI5 version 1 (SYSV),
dynamically linked, interpreter /lib/ld-linux-armhf.so.3, for
GNU/Linux 3.2.0, BuildID[sha1]=3c720<...>, with debug_info, not
stripped
$
```

Aha, it's generated an ARM executable! We copy this over to our embedded root filesystem, boot the (emulated) ARM board, and try it out:

```
$ qemu-system-arm -m 512 -M vexpress-a9 \
   -kernel <...>/images/zImage \
   -drive file=<...>/images/rfs.img,if=sd,format=raw \
   -append \
    "console=ttyAMA0 rootfstype=ext4 root=/dev/mmcblk0 init=/sbin/init
```

*Dynamic Memory Allocation*

```
"   \
    -nographic -dtb <...>/images/vexpress-v2p-ca9.dtb

[...]
Booting Linux on physical CPU 0x0
Linux version 4.9.1-crk (xxx@yyy) (gcc version 4.8.3 20140320
(prerelease) (Sourcery CodeBench Lite 2014.05-29) ) #16 SMP Wed Jan 24
10:09:17 IST 2018
CPU: ARMv7 Processor [410fc090] revision 0 (ARMv7), cr=10c5387d
CPU: PIPT / VIPT nonaliasing data cache, VIPT nonaliasing instruction
cache

[...]

smsc911x 4e000000.ethernet eth0: SMSC911x/921x identified at
0xa1290000, IRQ: 31
/bin/sh: can't access tty; job control turned off
ARM / $
```

We're on the (emulated) ARM-32 system prompt; let's try running our program:

```
ARM # ./memprot_arm
Usage: ./memprot_arm test-write-to-ro-mem [0|1]
ARM # ./memprot_arm 0
----- protect_mem() -----
page 0: protections: PROT_READ|PROT_WRITE: range [0x24000, 0x24fff]
page 1: protections: PROT_READ: range [0x25000, 0x25fff]
page 2: protections: PROT_READ|PROT_WRITE|PROT_EXEC: range [0x26000,
0x26fff]
page 3: protections: PROT_NONE: range [0x27000, 0x27fff]

----- test_mem() -----
page 0: writing: byte 'a' to address 0x24567 now ... [OK]
page 0: reading: byte @ 0x24567 is 61 [OK]
page 1: reading: byte @ 0x25567 is 0 [OK]
page 2: reading: byte @ 0x26567 is 0 [OK]
page 2: writing: byte 'c' to address 0x26567 now ... [OK]
page 3: reading: byte @ 0x27567 is Segmentation fault (core dumped)
ARM #
```

The reader will notice that, unlike on the *Fedora 28* distro on the x86_64 system we ran this on earlier, the page 2 test case (highlighted in bold) where we attempt to set page 2's memory protections to [rwx] does succeed! Of course, there is no LSM installed.

> **TIP**
> If you would like to try similar experiments, running code on an emulated ARM-32, consider using the **Simple Embedded ARM Linux System (SEALS)** project, again pure open source, to easily build a very simple, yet working, ARM/Linux-embedded system: https://github.com/kaiwan/seals.

Similar memory-protection – setting protection attributes (rwx or none) on a range of memory – can be achieved with the powerful mmap(2) system call (We cover mmap(2) with respect to file I/O in Chapter 18, *Advanced File I/O*).

## Memory protection keys – a brief note

Recent Intel 64-bit processors bring to the table a feature called **Memory Protection Keys (MPK)**. Very briefly, MPK (or *pkeys*, as it's called on Linux) allows userspace to set permissions with page granularity, too. So, if it does the same thing as *mprotect* or *mmap*, what benefit does it bring? See the following:

- It's a hardware feature, so setting a huge range of pages (say, gigabytes of memory) to some particular memory permissions will be much faster than mprotect(2) can manage; this is important for some types of applications
- Applications (in-memory databases, perhaps) could benefit by turning off writes on memory regions until absolutely required, reducing spurious write bugs

How do you exploit MPK? First, be aware that it is currently only implemented on recent Linux kernels and on the x86_64 processor architecture. To make use of it, read up on the man page (section 7) on *pkeys*; it has explanatory notes as well as sample code: http://man7.org/linux/man-pages/man7/pkeys.7.html.

# Using alloca to allocate automatic memory

The glibc library provides an alternate to dynamic memory-allocation with malloc (and friends); the alloca(3) API.

alloca can be thought of as something of a convenience routine: **it allocates memory on the stack** (of the function it is called within). The showcase feature is that free is not required and, the memory is automatically deallocated once the function returns. In fact, free(3) must not be called. This makes sense: memory allocated on the stack is called automatic memory – it will be freed upon that function's return.

# Dynamic Memory Allocation

As usual, there are upsides and downsides – tradeoffs – to using `alloca(3)`:

Here are the `alloca(3)` pros:

- No free is required; this can make programming, readability, and maintainability much simpler. Thus we can avoid the dangerous memory-leakage bug – a significant gain!
- It is considered very fast, with zero internal fragmentation (wastage).
- The primary reason to use it: sometimes, programmers use non-local exits, typically via the `longjmp(3)` and `siglongjmp(3)` APIs. If the programmer uses `malloc(3)` to allocate a memory region and then abruptly leaves the function via a non-local exit, a memory leak will occur. Using *alloca* will prevent this, and the code is easy to implement and understand.

And here are the alloca cons:

- The primary downside of alloca is that there is no guarantee it returns failure when passed a value large enough to cause stack overflow; thus, if this actually does occur at runtime, the process is now in an **undefined behavior** (**UB**) state and will (eventually) crash. In other words, checking alloca for the NULL return, as you do with the `malloc(3)` family, is of no use!
- Portability is not a given.
- Often, alloca is implemented as an inline function; this prevents it from being overridden via a third-party library.

Take a look at the code as follows (`ch4/alloca_try.c`):

```
[...]
static void try_alloca(const char *csz, int do_the_memset)
{
    size_t sz = atol(csz);
    void *aptr;

    aptr = alloca(sz);
    if (!aptr)
        FATAL("alloca(%zu) failed\n", sz);
    if (1 == do_the_memset)
        memset(aptr, 'a', sz);

    /* Must _not_ call free(), just return;
     * the memory is auto-deallocated!
     */
```

[ 162 ]

```
}

int main(int argc, char **argv)
{
  [...]
    if (atoi(argv[2]) == 1)
        try_alloca(argv[1], 1);
    else if (atoi(argv[2]) == 0)
        try_alloca(argv[1], 0);
    else {
        fprintf(stderr, "Usage: %s size-to-alloca
do_the_memset[1|0]\n",
                    argv[0]);
        exit(EXIT_FAILURE);
    }
    exit (EXIT_SUCCESS);
}
```

Let's build it and try it out:

```
$ ./alloca_try
Usage: ./alloca_try size-to-alloca do_the_memset[1|0]
$ ./alloca_try 50000 1
$ ./alloca_try 50000 0
$
```

The first parameter to `alloca_try` is the amount of memory to allocate (in bytes), while the second parameter, if 1, has the `memset` process call on that memory region; if 0, it does not.

In the preceding code snippet, we tried it with an allocation request of 50,000 bytes – it succeeded for both the `memset` cases.

Now, we deliberately pass -1 as the first parameter, which will be treated as an unsigned quantity (thus becoming the enormous value of 0xffffffffffffffff on a 64-bit OS!), which of course should cause `alloca(3)` to fail. Amazingly, it does not report failure; at least it thinks it's okay:

```
$ ./alloca_try -1 0
$ echo $?
0
$ ./alloca_try -1 1
Segmentation fault (core dumped)
$
```

But then, doing `memset` (by passing the second parameter as 1) causes the bug to surface; without it, we'd never know.

To further verify this, try running the program under the control of the library call tracer software, `ltrace`; we pass 1 as the first parameter, forcing the process to invoke `memset` after `alloca(3)`:

```
$ ltrace ./alloca_try -1 1
atoi(0x7ffcd6c3e0c9, 0x7ffcd6c3d868, 0x7ffcd6c3d888, 0)          = 1
atol(0x7ffcd6c3e0c6, 1, 0, 0x1999999999999999)                   = -1
memset(0x7ffcd6c3d730, 'a', -1 <no return ...>
--- SIGSEGV (Segmentation fault) ---
+++ killed by SIGSEGV +++
$
```

Aha! We can see that following memset, the process receives the fatal signal and dies. But why doesn't the `alloca(3)` API show up in `ltrace`? Because it's an inlined function – ahem, one of its downsides.

But watch this; here, we pass 0 as the first parameter, bypassing the call to memset after `alloca(3)`:

```
$ ltrace ./alloca_try -1 0
atoi(0x7fff9495b0c9, 0x7fff94959728, 0x7fff94959748, 0)           = 0
atoi(0x7fff9495b0c9, 0x7fff9495b0c9, 0, 0x1999999999999999)       = 0
atol(0x7fff9495b0c6, 0, 0, 0x1999999999999999)                    = -1
exit(0 <no return ...>
+++ exited (status 0) +++
$
```

It exits normally, as though there were no bug!

Further, you will recall from Chapter 3, *Resource Limits*, we saw that the default stack size for a process is 8 MB. We can test this fact via our `alloca_try` program:

```
$ ./alloca_try 8000000 1
$ ./alloca_try 8400000 1
Segmentation fault (core dumped)
$ ulimit -s
8192
$
```

The moment we go beyond 8 MB, `alloca(3)` allocates too much space, but does not trigger a crash; instead, `memset(3)` causes segfault to occur. Also, ulimit verifies that the stack resource limit is 8,192 KB, that is, 8 MB.

> **TIP**: To conclude, a really, really key point: you can often end up writing software that seems to be correct but is, in fact, not. The only way to gain confidence with the software is to take the trouble to perform 100% code coverage and run test cases against them! It's hard to do, but quality matters. Just do it.

## Summary

This chapter focused upon both the simple and more advanced aspects of dynamic memory management for C application developers on the Linux OS. In the initial section, the basic glibc dynamic memory-management APIs and their correct usage in code was dealt with.

We then moved on to more advanced topics such as the program break (and the `sbrk(3)` API), how `malloc(3)` behaves internally when allocating memory of differing sizes, and the key concept of demand-paging. Then, we delved into the APIs that perform memory locking and memory region protection, and reasons to use them. Finally, we looked at `alloca(3)`, the alternate API. Several code examples were used to solidify the concepts that were learned. The next chapter will cover a really important topic—the variety of memory issues (defects) that can arise on Linux due to poor programming practices with the memory APIs

# Linux Memory Issues
# 5

A simple truism: memory issues exist. The very fact that we program in languages such as C (and C++) implicitly gives rise to literally infinite types of issues! At some point, one realizes (perhaps a bit pessimistically) that programming with care in a managed memory-safe language is ultimately the (only?) realistic way to avoid memory issues altogether.

However, here we are, working with our power tool of choice: the eminent and venerable C programming language! So, what we can do to mitigate, if not eliminate, common memory issues, is the topic of this chapter. Ultimately, the goal is to be truly memory-safe; well, that's easier said than done!

Nevertheless, we shall attempt to have the developer successfully undertake this task by throwing light on the common memory issues they will likely face. In the chapter that follows, we will look into how some powerful memory debug tools can help immensely in this effort.

In this chapter, the developer will learn that although the dynamic memory management APIs (covered in `Chapter 4`, *Dynamic Memory Allocation*) are few, they can—when used carelessly—cause seemingly endless amounts of trouble and bugs!

Specifically, this chapter will throw light on the common memory issues that lead to hard-to-detect bugs in fielded software:

- Incorrect memory-access issues (within this, there are a few types)
- Memory leakage
- Undefined behavior

# Common memory issues

If one were to categorize to fine-granularity memory errors (typically caused via programming in C or C++), one would have a difficult time of it—hundreds of types exist! Instead, let's keep the discussion manageable and check out what would be considered the typical or common memory errors that befall us poor C programmers:

- Incorrect memory accesses
    - Using uninitialized variables
    - Out-of-bounds memory accesses (read/write underflow/overflow bugs)
    - Use-after-free/use-after-return (out-of-scope) bugs
    - Double-free
- Leakage
- **Undefined behavior (UB)**
- Data Races
- Fragmentation (internal implementation) issues
    - Internal
    - External

> All these common memory issues (except fragmentation) are classified as UB; still, we keep UB as a separate entry as we will explore it more deeply. Also, though the word *bug* is colloquially used, one should really (and more correctly) think of it as *defect*.
>
> We do not cover Data Races in this chapter (please hang on until `Chapter 15`, *Multithreading with Pthreads Part II - Synchronization*).

To help test these memory issues, the `membugs` program is a collection of small test cases for each of them.

### Sidebar :: The Clang compiler

LLVM/Clang is an open source compiler for C. We do use the Clang compiler, notably in this and the next chapter, especially for the sanitizer compiler-instrumentation toolset (covered in the next chapter). It remains useful throughout the book (and indeed is used in many of our Makefiles), thus installing Clang on your Linux development system would be a good idea! Again, it is not completely essential and one can stick with the familiar GCC too—provided one is willing to edit the Makefile(s) to switch back to GCC wherever required!

Installing Clang on the Ubuntu 18.04 LTS desktop is easy: `sudo apt install clang`

The Clang documentation can be found at https://clang.llvm.org/docs/index.html.

> **TIP**
>
> When the membugs program is compiled (using both GCC for the normal case as well as the Clang compiler for the sanitizer variants), you will see a lot of compiler warnings being emitted! This is expected; after all, its code is filled with bugs. Relax, and continue reading.
>
> Also, we remind you that the purpose of this chapter is to understand (and classify) typical Linux memory issues; identifying and fixing them using powerful tools is the subject matter of the next chapter. Both are required, so please read on.

Some sample output from the build is shown as follows (output clipped for readability). Right now, we shall not attempt to analyze it; that will happen as we wind through this chapter *(remember, you will need to have Clang installed as well!)*:

```
$ make
gcc -Wall -c ../common.c -o common.o
gcc -Wall -c membugs.c -o membugs.o
membugs.c: In function 'uar':
membugs.c:143:9: warning: function returns address of local variable
[-Wreturn-local-addr]
 return name;
 ^~~~

[...]

gcc -Wall -o membugs membugs.o common.o

[...]
clang -g -ggdb -gdwarf-4 -O0 -Wall -Wextra -fsanitize=address -c
membugs.c -o membugs_dbg_asan.o
membugs.c:143:9: warning: address of stack memory associated with
local variable 'name' returned [-Wreturn-stack-address]
        return name;
               ^~~~

gcc -g -ggdb -gdwarf-4 -O0 -Wall -Wextra -o membugs_dbg membugs_dbg.o
common_dbg.o
[...]
$
```

We also highlight the fact that, in all the test cases we'll run, we use the GCC - generated *membugs* binary executable (not Clang; we shall make use of Clang later with the sanitizer tools).

> **TIP**: During the build, one can capture all the output in to a file like so: `make >build.txt 2>&1`

Run the `membugs` program with the `--help` switch to see all the available test cases:

```
$ ./membugs --help

Usage: ./membugs test_case [ -h | --help]
 test case  1 : uninitialized var test case
 test case  2 : out-of-bounds : write overflow [on compile-time memory]
 test case  3 : out-of-bounds : write overflow [on dynamic memory]
 test case  4 : out-of-bounds : write underflow
 test case  5 : out-of-bounds : read overflow [on compile-time memory]
 test case  6 : out-of-bounds : read overflow [on dynamic memory]
 test case  7 : out-of-bounds : read underflow
 test case  8 : UAF (use-after-free) test case
 test case  9 : UAR (use-after-return) test case
 test case 10 : double-free test case
 test case 11 : memory leak test case 1: simple leak
 test case 12 : memory leak test case 2: leak more (in a loop)
 test case 13 : memory leak test case 3: "lib" API leak
-h | --help : show this help screen
$
```

You will notice that the write and read overflows have two test cases each: one on compile-time memory, and one on dynamically allocated memory. It's important to distinguish the cases, as tools differ in which types of defects they can detect.

## Incorrect memory accesses

Often, bugs and issues in this class are so common as to be blithely overlooked! Beware, they remain very dangerous; take care to find, understand, and fix them.

All classes of overflow and underflow bugs on memory buffers are carefully documented and tracked via the **Common Vulnerabilities and Exposures (CVE)** and the **Common Weakness Enumeration (CWE)** websites. Relevant to what we are discussing, CWE-119 is the *Improper Restriction of Operations within the Bounds of a Memory Buffer* (https://cwe.mitre.org/data/definitions/119.html).

## Accessing and/or using uninitialized variables

To give the reader a sense of the seriousness of these memory issues, we have written a test program, membugs.c. This test program allows the user to test various common memory bugs, which will help them better understand the underlying issues.

Each memory bug test case is given a test case number. So that the reader can easily follow the source code with the explanatory material, we also specify the test case as follows.

### Test case 1: Uninitialized memory access

These are also known as **uninitialized memory reads (UMR)** bugs. A classic case: local (or automatic) variables are, by definition, uninitialized (unlike globals, which are always preset to zero):

```
/* test case 1 : uninitialized var test case */
static void uninit_var()
{
    int x;    /* static mem */

    if (x)
        printf("true case: x=%d\n", x);
    else
        printf("false case\n");
}
```

In the preceding code, it's undefined what will occur at runtime as x is uninitialized and will thus have random content. Now, we run this test case as follows:

```
$ ./membugs 1
true case: x=32604
$ ./membugs 1
true case: x=32611
$ ./membugs 1
true case: x=32627
$ ./membugs 1
true case: x=32709
$
```

Thankfully, modern versions of the compiler (both gcc and clang) will emit a warning about this issue:

```
$ make
[...]
gcc -Wall -c membugs.c -o membugs.o
[...]
membugs.c: In function 'uninit_var':
membugs.c:272:5: warning: 'x' is used uninitialized in this function [-Wuninitialized]
   if (x)
     ^

[...]
clang -g -ggdb -gdwarf-4 -O0 -Wall -Wextra -fsanitize=address -c membugs.c -o membugs_dbg_asan.o
[...]
membugs.c:272:6: warning: variable 'x' is uninitialized when used here [-Wuninitialized]
       if (x)
           ^
membugs.c:270:7: note: initialize the variable 'x' to silence this warning
       int x; /* static mem */
           ^
            = 0
[...]
```

## Out-of-bounds memory accesses

This class is again among the more common—but deadly!—memory-access bugs. They can be classified as different kinds of bugs:

- **Write overflow**: A bug where a write is attempted into a memory buffer after its last legally accessible location
- **Write underflow**: A write is attempted into a memory buffer before its first legally accessible location
- **Read underflow**: A read is attempted on a memory buffer before its first legally accessible location
- **Read overflow**: A read is attempted on a memory buffer after its first legally accessible location

Let's check these out via the source code of our `membugs.c` program.

### Test case 2

Write or buffer overflow on compile-time allocated memory. See the code snippet as follows:

```
/* test case 2 : out-of-bounds : write overflow [on compile-time
memory] */
static void write_overflow_compilemem(void)
{
    int i, arr[5], tmp[8];
    for (i=0; i<=5; i++) {
       arr[i] = 100;  /* Bug: 'arr' overflows on i==5,
                        overwriting part of the 'tmp' variable
                        - a stack overflow! */
    }
}
```

This has caused a stack overflow (also referred to as a stack smashing or **buffer overflow (BOF)**) bug; it's a serious class of vulnerability that attackers have successfully exploited many a time, starting with the Morris Worm virus back in 1988! Check out the resources in the *Further reading* section for more on this vulnerability on the GitHub repository.

Very interestingly, compiling and running this portion of the code on our *Fedora 28* workstation Linux box (by passing the appropriate parameter), shows that there is neither compile-time nor runtime detection of this (and other similar) dangerous bugs by default (more on this later!):

```
$ ./membugs 2
$ ./membugs_dbg 2
$
```

These bugs are also sometimes called off-by-one errors.

There's more, though (as usual); let's do a quick experiment. In the `membugs.c:write_overflow_compilemem()` function, change the number of times we loop from 5 to 50:

```
for (i = 0; i <= 50; i++) {
    arr[i] = 100;
}
```

Rebuild and retry; look at the output now on an *Ubuntu 18.04 LTS* Desktop Linux system (on Fedora too, but with a vanilla kernel):

```
$ ./membugs 2
*** stack smashing detected ***: <unknown> terminated
Aborted
$
```

The fact is, modern compilers use a stack-protector feature to detect stack-overflow bugs and more importantly, attacks. With a large enough value, the overflow was detected; but with the default value, the bug escaped undetected! We stress the importance of using tools (which includes compilers) to detect these hidden bugs in the next chapter.

### Test case 3

Write or BOF on dynamically-allocated memory. See the code snippet as follows:

```
/* test case 3 : out-of-bounds : write overflow [on dynamic memory] */
static void write_overflow_dynmem(void)
{
    char *dest, src[] = "abcd56789";

    dest = malloc(8);
    if (!dest)

        FATAL("malloc failed\n");
```

```
    strcpy(dest, src); /* Bug: write overflow */
    free(dest);
}
```

Again, no compile or runtime detection of the bug occurs:

```
$ ./membugs 3
$ ./membugs 3          << try once more >>
$
```

> Unfortunately, BOF-related bugs and vulnerabilities tend to be quite common in the industry. The root cause is poorly understood, and thus results in poorly written, code; this is where we, as developers, must step up our game!
>
> For real-world examples of security vulnerabilities, please see this table of 52 documented security vulnerabilities (due to various kinds of BOF bugs) on Linux in 2017: https://www.cvedetails.com/vulnerability-list/vendor_id-33/year-2017/opov-1/Linux.html.

## Test case 4

Write Underflow. We dynamically allocate a buffer with `malloc(3)`, decrement the pointer, and then write into that memory location—a write or buffer underflow bug:

```
/* test case 4 : out-of-bounds : write underflow */
static void write_underflow(void)
{
    char *p = malloc(8);
    if (!p)
        FATAL("malloc failed\n");
    p--;
    strncpy(p, "abcd5678", 8); /* Bug: write underflow */
    free(++p);
}
```

In this test case, we don't want the `free(3)` to fail, so we ensure the pointer passed to it is correct. The compiler does not detect any bug here; at runtime though, it does indeed crash, with modern glibc detecting errors (in this case, memory corruption):

```
$ ./membugs 4
double free or corruption (out)
Aborted
$
```

## Test case 5

Read overflow, on compile-time allocated memory. We attempt a read on a compile-time allocated memory buffer, after its last legally accessible location:

```
/* test case 5 : out-of-bounds : read overflow [on compile-time
memory] */
static void read_overflow_compilemem(void)
{
    char arr[5], tmp[8];

    memset(arr, 'a', 5);
    memset(tmp, 't', 8);
    tmp[7] = '\0';

    printf("arr = %s\n", arr); /* Bug: read buffer overflow */
}
```

The way this test case is designed, we have two buffers arranged sequentially in memory. The bug: we deliberately do not null-terminate the first buffer (but do so on the second one), so, the `printf(3)` that will emit on `arr` continues reading into the second buffer, `tmp`. What if the `tmp` buffer contains secrets?

The point, of course is that the compiler cannot catch this seemingly obvious bug. Also, do realize that here we're writing small, simple, easy-to-read test cases; on a real project with a few million lines of code, defects such as this are easy to miss.

Here is the sample output:

```
$ ./membugs 2>&1 | grep -w 5
 option =  5 : out-of-bounds : read overflow [on compile-time memory]
$ ./membugs 5
arr = aaaaattttttt
$
```

Hey, we got to read the secret memory of `tmp`.

In fact, tools such as ASan (Address Sanitizer, seen in the next chapter), classify this bug as a stack buffer overflow.

*Chapter 5*

As an aside, on our *Fedora 28* workstation, we just get junk from the second buffer in this test case:

```
$ ./membugs 5
arr = aaaaa0<5=�
$ ./membugs 5
arr = aaaaa�:��
$
```

This shows us that these bugs can reveal themselves differently, depending on the compiler version, the glibc version, and the machine hardware.

> **TIP**: An always useful testing technique is to try to run your test cases on as many hardware/software variants as possible. Hidden bugs may be exposed! Think of instances such as endianness issues, compiler optimization (padding, packing), and platform-specific alignments.

## Test case 6

Read overflow, on dynamically allocated memory. Again, we attempt a read; this time, on a dynamically allocated memory buffer, after its last legally accessible location:

```c
/* test case 6 : out-of-bounds : read overflow [on dynamic memory] */
static void read_overflow_dynmem(void)
{
    char *arr;

    arr = malloc(5);
    if (!arr)
        FATAL("malloc failed\n",);
    memset(arr, 'a', 5);

    /* Bug 1: Steal secrets via a buffer overread.
     * Ensure the next few bytes are _not_ NULL.
     * Ideally, this should be caught as a bug by the compiler,
     * but isn't! (Tools do; seen later).
     */
    arr[5] = 'S'; arr[6] = 'e'; arr[7] = 'c';
    arr[8] = 'r'; arr[9] = 'e'; arr[10] = 'T';
    printf("arr = %s\n", arr);

    /* Bug 2, 3: more read buffer overflows */
    printf("*(arr+100)=%d\n", *(arr+100));
    printf("*(arr+10000)=%d\n", *(arr+10000));
```

```
        free(arr);
}
```

The test case is pretty much the same as the preceding one (the read overflow on compile-time memory), except that we dynamically allocate the memory buffers, and insert a couple more bugs for fun:

```
$ ./membugs 2>&1 |grep -w 6
 option =   6 : out-of-bounds : read overflow [on dynamic memory]
$ ./membugs 6
arr = aaaaaSecreT
*(arr+100)=0
*(arr+10000)=0
$
```

Hey, Mom, look! We got the secret!

It does not even cause a crash. At first glance, bugs such as this might appear fairly harmless—the truth, though, is that this is a really dangerous bug!

> The well known OpenSSL Heartbleed security bug (CVE-2014-0160) is a great example of exploiting a read overflow, or as it's often called, a buffer over-read, vulnerability.
>
> In a nutshell, the bug allowed a rogue client process to make a seemingly correct request to the OpenSSL server process; in reality, it could request and receive much more memory than it should have been allowed to, because of a buffer over-read vulnerability. In effect, this bug made it possible for attackers to bypass security easily and steal secrets [http://heartbleed.com].
>
> If interested, find more in the *Further reading* section on the GitHub repository.

## Test case 7

Read underflow. We attempt a read on a dynamically allocated memory buffer, before its first legally accessible location:

```
/* test case 7 : out-of-bounds : read underflow */
static void read_underflow(int cond)
{
    char *dest, src[] = "abcd56789", *orig;

    printf("%s(): cond %d\n", __FUNCTION__, cond);
```

```
    dest = malloc(25);
    if (!dest)
        FATAL("malloc failed\n",);
    orig = dest;

    strncpy(dest, src, strlen(src));
    if (cond) {
        *(orig-1) = 'x';
        dest --;
    }
    printf(" dest: %s\n", dest);

    free(orig);
}
```

The test case is designed with a runtime condition; we test it both ways:

```
case 7:
    read_underflow(0);
    read_underflow(1);
    break;
```

If the condition evaluates to true, the buffer pointer is decremented, thus causing a read buffer underflow on the subsequent `printf`:

```
$ ./membugs 7
read_underflow(): cond 0
 dest: abcd56789
read_underflow(): cond 1
 dest: xabcd56789
double free or corruption (out)
Aborted (core dumped)
$
```

Again, glibc comes to our aid by showing us that a double free or corruption has occurred—in this case, it's memory corruption.

## Use-after-free/Use-after-return bugs

**Use-after-free** (UAF) and **use-after-return** (UAR) are dangerous, difficult-to-spot bugs. Check out the following test cases for each of them.

# Test case 8

**Use After Free (UAF).** Operating upon a memory pointer after it has been freed up is obviously a bug, causing UB. The pointer is sometimes called a dangling pointer. Here is a quick test case:

```
/* test case 8 : UAF (use-after-free) test case */
static void uaf(void)
{
    char *arr, *next;
    char name[]="Hands-on Linux Sys Prg";
    int n=512;

    arr = malloc(n);
    if (!arr)
        FATAL("malloc failed\n");
    memset(arr, 'a', n);
    arr[n-1]='\0';
    printf("%s():%d: arr = %p:%.*s\n", __FUNCTION__, __LINE__, arr,
              32, arr);

    next = malloc(n);
    if (!next) {
        free(arr);
        FATAL("malloc failed\n");
    }
    free(arr);
    strncpy(arr, name, strlen(name));   /* Bug: UAF */

    printf("%s():%d: arr = %p:%.*s\n", __FUNCTION__, __LINE__, arr,
              32, arr);
    free(next);
}
```

Again, neither at compile-time nor at runtime is the UAF bug detected, nor does it cause a crash:

```
$ ./membugs 2>&1 |grep -w 8
 option =  8 : UAF (use-after-free) test case
$ ./membugs 8
uaf():158: arr = 0x558012280260:aaaaaaaaaaaaaaaaaaaaaaaaaaaaaaaa
uaf():166: arr = 0x558012280260:Hands-on Linux Sys Prgaaaaaaaaaa
$
```

> **TIP:** Did you notice the neat printf(3) format specifier, %.*s, trick? This format is used to print a string of a specific length (no terminating null required!). First, specify the length in bytes to print, and then the pointer to string.

## Test case 9

**Use After Return (UAR).** Another classic bug, this one involves returning a storage item (or pointer to it) to the calling function. The issue is that the storage is local or automatic, thus implying that once the return is affected, the storage object is now out of scope.

The classic example is shown here: we allocate 32 bytes to a local variable, initialize it, and return it to the caller:

```
/* test case 9 : UAR (use-after-return) test case */
static void * uar(void)
{
    char name[32];
    memset(name, 0, 32);
    strncpy(name, "Hands-on Linux Sys Prg", 22);

    return name;
}
```

This is how the caller invokes the preceding buggy function:

```
[...]
    case 9:
            res = uar();
            printf("res: %s\n", (char *)res);
            break;
[...]
```

Of course, once the return statement in the uar() function takes effect, the name variable is automatically out of scope! Therefore, the pointer to it is invalid, and when run, it fails:

```
$ ./membugs 2>&1 |grep -w 9
 option = 9 : UAR (use-after-return) test case
$ ./membugs 9
res: (null)
$
```

# Linux Memory Issues

Thankfully though, modern GCC (we're using GCC ver 7.3.0) warns us about this common bug:

```
$ make membugs
gcc -Wall -c membugs.c -o membugs.o
membugs.c: In function 'uar':
membugs.c:143:9: warning: function returns address of local variable
[-Wreturn-local-addr]
  return name;
         ^~~~
[...]
```

As mentioned before (but it's always worth repeating), heed and fix all warnings!

Actually, there are times when this bug escapes notice—it looks like it works fine and there's no bug. This is because there is no actual guarantee that the stack memory frame is immediately destroyed upon function return—memory and compiler-optimization might keep the frame around (typically for reuse). Nevertheless, it is a dangerous bug and must be fixed!

> In the next chapter, we'll cover some memory debug tools. As a matter of fact, neither Valgrind nor the Sanitizer tools catch this possibly deadly bug. But, using the ASan toolset appropriately does catch the UAR! Read on.

## Test case 10

Double-free. Once a `malloc` family buffer is freed, one is not allowed to use that pointer at all. Attempting to free the same pointer again (without again allocating it memory via one of the `malloc` family APIs) is a bug: double free. It results in heap corruption; bugs like this are often exploited by attackers to cause **denial-of-service** (**DoS**) attacks or worse (privilege escalation).

Here is a simple test case:

```
/* test case 10 : double-free test case */
static void doublefree(int cond)
{
    char *ptr;
    char name[]="Hands-on Linux Sys Prg";
    int n=512;

    printf("%s(): cond %d\n", __FUNCTION__, cond);
    ptr = malloc(n);
    if (!ptr)
```

```
        FATAL("malloc failed\n");
    strncpy(ptr, name, strlen(name));
    free(ptr);

    if (cond) {
        bogus = malloc(-1UL); /* will fail! */
        if (!bogus) {
            fprintf(stderr, "%s:%s:%d: malloc failed\n",
                    __FILE__, __FUNCTION__, __LINE__);
            free(ptr); /* Bug: double-free */
            exit(EXIT_FAILURE);
        }
    }
}
```

In the preceding test case, we simulate an interesting and quite realistic scenario: a runtime condition (simulated via the `cond` parameter) causes the program to perform a call that, let's say, fails—`malloc(-1UL)` pretty much guarantees that.

Why? Because, on a 64-bit OS, `-1UL = 0xffffffffffffffff = 18446744073709551615 bytes = 16 EB`. That's the entire extent of the virtual address space on 64-bit.

Back to the point: within our malloc error-handling code, an erroneous double-free—of the previously freed `ptr` pointer—occurs, resulting in a double free bug.

The real problem is that often, as developers, we do not write (negative) test cases for error-handling code paths; a defect then escapes undetected into the field:

```
$ ./membugs 10
doublefree(): cond 0
doublefree(): cond 1
membugs.c:doublefree:56: malloc failed
$
```

Interestingly, the compiler does warn us regarding the faulty (read buggy) second malloc (but not regarding the double free!); see the following:

```
$ make
[...]
membugs.c: In function 'doublefree':
membugs.c:125:9: warning: argument 1 value '18446744073709551615'
exceeds maximum object size 9223372036854775807 [-Walloc-size-larger-
than=]
    bogus = malloc(-1UL); /* will fail! */
    ~~~~~~^~~~~~~~~~~~~~
In file included from membugs.c:18:0:
```

*Linux Memory Issues*

```
/usr/include/stdlib.h:539:14: note: in a call to allocation function
'malloc' declared here
 extern void *malloc (size_t __size) __THROW __attribute_malloc__
__wur;
              ^~~~~~
[...]
```

> To help emphasize the importance of detecting and fixing such bugs—and remember, this is just one example— we show as follows some information from the **National Vulnerability Database (NVD)** on double free bugs within the last 3 years (at the time of this writing): `https://nvd.nist.gov/vuln/search/results?adv_search=falseform_type=basicresults_type=overviewsearch_type=last3yearsquery=double+free`

A partial screenshot of the search result performed on the *National Vulnerability Database (NVD)* on double free bugs within the last 3 years (at the time of this writing) follows:

There are **91** matching records.
Displaying matches **1** through **20**.

| Vuln ID | Summary | CVSS Severity |
|---|---|---|
| CVE-2017-18120 | A double-free bug in the read_gif function in gifread.c in gifsicle 1.90 allows a remote attacker to cause a denial-of-service attack or unspecified other impact via a maliciously crafted file, because last_name is mishandled, a different vulnerability than CVE-2017-1000421.<br><br>**Published:** February 02, 2018; 04:29:00 AM -05:00 | (not available) |
| CVE-2018-0101 | A vulnerability in the Secure Sockets Layer (SSL) VPN functionality of the Cisco Adaptive Security Appliance (ASA) Software could allow an unauthenticated, remote attacker to cause a reload of the affected system or to remotely execute code. The vulnerability is due to an attempt to double free a region of memory when the webvpn feature is enabled on the Cisco ASA device. An attacker could exploit this vulnerability by sending | (not available) |

> The complete screenshot has not been shown here.

## Leakage

The golden rule for dynamic memory is to free the memory you allocate.

Memory leakage is the term used to describe the situation where one fails to do so. The programmer thinks that the memory region has indeed been freed up. But it has not—that's the bug. Therefore, this makes the thought-to-be-freed memory region unavailable to the process and system; in effect, it is unusable, even though it should have been usable.

The memory is said to have leaked out. So why can't the programmer just take care of this elsewhere in the code by calling free upon this memory pointer? That's really the crux of the issue: in the typical case, because of the way the code is implemented, it's essentially impossible to regain access to that leaked memory pointer.

A quick test case will demonstrate this.

The `amleaky` function is deliberately written to leak `mem` bytes of memory—its parameter—each time it's invoked.

## Test case 11

Memory leakage - case 1: a (simple) memory leak test case. See the following code snippet:

```
static const size_t BLK_1MB = 1024*1024;
[...]
static void amleaky(size_t mem)
{
    char *ptr;

    ptr = malloc(mem);
    if (!ptr)
        FATAL("malloc(%zu) failed\n", mem);

    /* Do something with the memory region; else, the compiler
     * might just optimize the whole thing away!
     * ... and we won't 'see' the leak.
```

*Linux Memory Issues*

```
        */
     memset(ptr, 0, mem);

     /* Bug: no free, leakage */
}
[...]
/* test case 11 : memory leak test case 1: simple leak */
static void leakage_case1(size_t size)
{
 printf("%s(): will now leak %zu bytes (%ld MB)\n",
     __FUNCTION__, size, size/(1024*1024));
 amleaky(size);
}

[...]

 case 11:
     leakage_case1(32);
     leakage_case1(BLK_1MB);
     break;
[...]
```

As one can clearly see, in the `amleaky` function, the `ptr` memory pointer is a local variable and is thus lost once we return from the buggy function; this makes it impossible to free it later. Also notice—the comment explains it—how we require `memset` to force the compiler to generate code for and use the memory region.

A quick build and execution of the preceding test case will reveal that, again, no obvious compile-time or runtime detection of the leakage occurs:

```
$ ./membugs 2>&1 | grep "memory leak"
 option = 11 : memory leak test case 1: simple leak
 option = 12 : memory leak test case 2: leak more (in a loop)
 option = 13 : memory leak test case 3: lib API leak
$ ./membugs 11
leakage_case1(): will now leak 32 bytes (0 MB)
leakage_case1(): will now leak 1048576 bytes (1 MB)
$
```

# Test case 12

Memory leakage case 2 - leak more (in a loop). Quite often, the buggy leaking code might only be leaking a small amount of memory, a few bytes, by itself. The problem is, what if this leaky function is called in a loop hundreds, or perhaps, thousands of times, during process execution? Now the leakage is significant, and unfortunately, not immediately apparent.

To emulate precisely this and more, we execute two test cases (for Option 12):

- We allocate, and leak, a tiny amount of memory (32 bytes) but in a loop 100,000 times (so, yes, we end up leaking over 3 MB)
- We allocate, and leak, a large amount of memory (1 MB) in a loop 12 times (so, we end up leaking 12 MB).

Here's the relevant code:

```
[...]

/* test case 12 : memory leak test case 2: leak in a loop */
static void leakage_case2(size_t size, unsigned int reps)
{
    unsigned int i, threshold = 3*BLK_1MB;
    double mem_leaked;

    if (reps == 0)
        reps = 1;
    mem_leaked = size * reps;
    printf("%s(): will now leak a total of %.0f bytes (%.2f MB)"
            " [%zu bytes * %u loops]\n",
            __FUNCTION__, mem_leaked, mem_leaked/(1024*1024),
            size, reps);

    if (mem_leaked >= threshold)
        system("free|grep \"^Mem:\"");

    for (i=0; i<reps; i++) {
        if (i%10000 == 0)
            printf("%s():%6d:malloc(%zu)\n", __FUNCTION__, i, size);
        amleaky(size);
    }

    if (mem_leaked >= threshold)
        system("free|grep \"^Mem:\"");
        printf("\n");
}
```

## Linux Memory Issues

```
[...]
  case 12:
  leakage_case2(32, 100000);
  leakage_case2(BLK_1MB, 12);
  break;
[...]
```

The logic ensures that the `printf(3)` within the leaky loop is only displayed on every 10,000 loop iterations.

Also, we would like to see whether memory has indeed leaked. To do so, albeit in an approximate manner, we use the `free` utility:

```
$ free
        total      used       free     shared  buff/cache   available
Mem:  16305508   5906672    348744    1171944    10050092    10248116
Swap:  8000508         0   8000508
$
```

The `free(1)` utility displays, in kilobytes, the current (approximate) amount of memory used, free, and available on the system as a whole. It further divides the used memory between shared, buffered/page-cached; it also displays `Swap` partition statistics. We should also note that this approach of using `free(1)` to detect memory leakage is not considered very accurate; a crude approach at best. The memory reported as in use, free, cached, and so on by the OS can show variations. For our purposes, it's okay.

Our point of interest is the intersection of the `Mem` row and the `free` column; thus, we can see that out of a total available memory of 16 GB (RAM), the amount currently free is approximately 348744 KB ~= 340 MB.

One can quickly try out a one-liner script to display just the region of interest—the `Mem` line:

```
$ free | grep "^Mem:"
Mem:  16305508   5922772    336436    1165960    10046300    10237452
$
```

The third column after `Mem` is the `free` memory (interestingly, it's already reduced from the previous output; that doesn't matter).

Back to the program; we use the `system(3)` library API to run the preceding pipelined shell command within a C program (we'll build our own small emulation of the `system(3)` API in Chapter 10, *Process Creation*):

```
if (mem_leaked >= threshold)
    system("free|grep \"^Mem:\"");
```

The `if` statement ensures that this output only occurs if a threshold of >= 3 MB is leaking.

Here is the output upon execution:

```
$ ./membugs 12
leakage_case2(): will now leak a total of 3200000 bytes (3.05 MB)
   [32 bytes * 100000 loops]
Mem:     16305508      5982408    297708    1149648   10025392   10194628
leakage_case2():        0:malloc(32)
leakage_case2():    10000:malloc(32)
leakage_case2():    20000:malloc(32)
leakage_case2():    30000:malloc(32)
leakage_case2():    40000:malloc(32)
leakage_case2():    50000:malloc(32)
leakage_case2():    60000:malloc(32)
leakage_case2():    70000:malloc(32)
leakage_case2():    80000:malloc(32)
leakage_case2():    90000:malloc(32)
Mem:     16305508      5986996    293120    1149648   10025392   10190040

leakage_case2(): will now leak a total of 12582912 bytes (12.00 MB)
   [1048576 bytes * 12 loops]
Mem:     16305508      5987500    292616    1149648   10025392   10189536
leakage_case2():        0:malloc(1048576)
Mem:     16305508      5999124    280992    1149648   10025392   10177912
$
```

*Linux Memory Issues*

We see the two scenarios executing; check out the values of the `free` column. We shall subtract them to see the memory that's been leaked:

- We allocate, and leak, a tiny amount of memory (32 bytes) but in a loop 100,000 times: `Leaked memory = 297708 - 293120 = 4588 KB ~= 4.5 MB`
- We allocate, and leak, a large amount of memory (1 MB) in a loop 12 times: `Leaked memory = 292616 - 280992 = 11624 KB ~= 11.4 MB`

Of course, do realize that once the process dies, all its memory is freed back to the system. That's why we performed the one-liner script within the process, while it was alive.

## Test case 13

Complex case—wrapper APIs. At times, one can be forgiven for thinking that all programmers are taught: after calling malloc (or calloc, realloc), call free. malloc and free go together! How hard can that be? Why are there are so many sneaky leakage bugs if this is the case?

A key reason that leakage defects occur and are hard to pinpoint is because some APIs—often, third-party library APIs—might internally perform dynamic memory allocation and expect the caller to free the memory. The API will (hopefully) document this important fact; but who (tongue in cheek) reads documentation?

That's really the crux of the issue in real-world software; it is complex and we work on large, complex projects. It is indeed easy to miss the fact that an underlying API allocates memory and the caller is responsible for freeing it. Precisely this occurs quite often.

There's another case: on complex codebases (especially those with spaghetti code), where a lot of deeply nested layers entangle the code, it can get especially hard to perform the required cleanup—including memory-frees—on every possible error case.

> The Linux kernel community offers a clean, though fairly controversial, way to keep cleanup code paths clean and working well, that is, the use of the local go to perform centralized error-handling! It helps indeed. Interested in learning more? Check out section 7, *Centralized exiting of functions* at https://www.kernel.org/doc/Documentation/process/coding-style.rst.

## Test case 13.1

Here is a simple example. Let's emulate this with the following test case code:

```
/*
 * A demo: this function allocates memory internally; the caller
 * is responsible for freeing it!
 */
static void silly_getpath(char **ptr)
{
#include <linux/limits.h>
    *ptr = malloc(PATH_MAX);
    if (!ptr)
        FATAL("malloc failed\n");

    strcpy(*ptr, getenv("PATH"));
    if (!*ptr)
        FATAL("getenv failed\n");
}

/* test case 13 : memory leak test case 3: "lib" API leak */
static void leakage_case3(int cond)
{
    char *mypath=NULL;

    printf("\n## Leakage test: case 3: \"lib\" API"
        ": runtime cond = %d\n", cond);

    /* Use C's illusory 'pass-by-reference' model */
    silly_getpath(&mypath);
    printf("mypath = %s\n", mypath);

    if (cond) /* Bug: if cond==0 then we have a leak! */
        free(mypath);
}
```

We invoke it as:

```
[...]
case 13:
    leakage_case3(0);
    leakage_case3(1);
    break;
```

As usual, no compiler or runtime warnings result. Here is the output (recognize that the first invocation is the buggy case, as `cond` has the value of `0` and thus the `free(3)` will not be called):

```
$ ./membugs 13

## Leakage test: case 3: "lib" API: runtime cond = 0
mypath =
/usr/local/bin:/usr/local/sbin:/usr/bin:/usr/sbin:/sbin:/usr/sbin:/usr
/local/sbin:/home/kai/MentorGraphics/Sourcery_CodeBench_Lite_for_ARM_G
NU_Linux/bin/:/mnt/big/scratchpad/buildroot-2017.08.1/output/host/bin/
:/sbin:/usr/sbin:/usr/local/sbin

## Leakage test: case 3: "lib" API: runtime cond = 1
mypath =
/usr/local/bin:/usr/local/sbin:/usr/bin:/usr/sbin:/sbin:/usr/sbin:/usr
/local/sbin:/home/kai/MentorGraphics/Sourcery_CodeBench_Lite_for_ARM_G
NU_Linux/bin/:/mnt/big/scratchpad/buildroot-2017.08.1/output/host/bin/
:/sbin:/usr/sbin:/usr/local/sbin
$
```

There is no bug apparent by looking at the output—and that is partly what makes these bugs so dangerous!

This case is critical for developers and testers to understand; it warrants checking out a couple of real-world examples.

## Test case 13.2

Example—the *Motif* library. *Motif* is a legacy library, part of the X Window System; it was used (and perhaps still is) to develop GUIs for Unix (and Unix-like) systems.

For the purpose of this example, we will focus on one of its
APIs: `XmStringCreateLocalized(3)`. GUI developers use this function to create what Motif calls a "compound string"—essentially, just a string that holds text in a specific locale (for the purposes of I18N-internationalization). This is its signature:

```
#include <Xm/Xm.h>
XmString XmStringCreateLocalized(char *text);
```

So, let's imagine the developer uses it to generate compound strings (for various purposes; very often, for the labels of a label or push button widget).

So, what's the problem?
Leakage! How? Read the documentation from the man page (https://linux.die.net/man/3/xmstringcreatelocalized) on `XmStringCreateLocalized(3)`:

```
[...]
The function will allocate space to hold the returned compound string.
The application is responsible for managing the allocated space. The
application can recover the allocated space by calling XmStringFree.
[...]
```

Clearly, the developer must not only call `XmStringCreateLocalized(3)` but must also remember to free up the memory internally allocated by it for the compound string by calling `XmStringFree(3)`!

Failing to do so will result in a leak. I have personal experience with this scenario—a buggy application invoked the `XmStringCreateLocalized(3)` and did not call its counterpart, `XmStringFree(3)`. Not only that, this code ran often as it was invoked as part of the body of an outer loop! So, the leakage multiplied.

## Test case 13.3

Example—the Nortel Porting Project. There is a story (refer to the information box as follows) about how developers at Nortel (a large telecom and network equipment multinational corporation in Canada) had a very hard time debugging what turned out to be a memory leakage issue. The crux of it is this: when porting a Unix application to VxWorks, while testing it, they noticed a small 18-byte leak occurring, which would eventually cause the application to crash. Finding the source of the leak was a nightmare— reviewing the code endlessly provided no clues. Finally, the game changer proved to be the use of a leak detection tool (we'll cover this in the coming Chapter 6, *Debugging Tools for Memory Issues*). Within minutes, they uncovered the root cause of the leak: an innocent-looking API, `inet_ntoa(3)` (refer to the information box), which worked in the usual manner on Unix, and as well as in VxWorks. The catch: in the VxWorks implementation, it was allocating memory under the hood—which the caller was responsible for freeing! This fact was documented, but it was a porting project! Once this fact was realized, it was quickly fixed.

> Article: The ten secrets of embedded debugging, Schneider and Fraleigh: https://www.embedded.com/design/prototyping-and-development/4025015/The-ten-secrets-of-embedded-debugging
>
> The man page entry on `inet_ntoa(3)` states: The `inet_ntoa()` function converts the Internet host address in, given in network byte order, to a string in IPv4 dotted-decimal notation. The string is returned in a statically allocated buffer, which subsequent calls will overwrite.

Some observations on programs with leakage bugs:

- The program behaves normally for a long, long while; suddenly, after, say, a month of uptime, it abruptly crashes.
- The root leakage could be very small—a few bytes at a time; but is probably invoked often.
- Attempting to find leakage bugs by carefully matching your instances of `malloc(3)` and `free(3)` does not work; library API wrappers often allocate memory under the hood and expect the caller to free it.
- Leaks often escape unnoticed because they are inherently difficult to spot in large codebases, and once the process dies, the leaked memory is freed back to the system.

Bottom line:

- Do not assume anything
- Read the API documentation carefully
- Use tools (covered in the coming `Chapter 6`, *Debugging Tools for Memory Issues*)

One cannot overstate the importance of using tools to detect memory bugs!

## Undefined behavior

We've covered quite a bit of ground and seen quite a few common memory bugs, which include:

- Incorrect memory accesses
    - Using uninitialized variables
    - Out-of-bounds memory accesses (read/write underflow/overflow bugs)
    - Use-after-free / use-after-return (out-of-scope) bugs
    - Double-free
- Leakage
- Data Races (details follow in a later chapter)

As mentioned earlier, all of these fall into a general categorization—UB. As the phrase implies, the behavior of the process (or thread) is *undefined* once any of these bugs are hit. Even worse, many of them do not display any directly noticeable side effects; but the process is unstable and will—eventually—crash. Leakage bugs, in particular, are major spoilsports in this: the leakage may be around for a long while before a crash actually occurs. Not only that, the trail left behind (that the developer will be breathlessly chasing) might often be a red herring—matters of little consequence, things that have no real bearing on the bug's root cause. All of this, of course, makes debugging UB an experience most of us would prefer to avoid!

The good news is that UB is avoidable, as long as the developer understands the underlying causes of UB (which we have covered in the previous sections), and of course, the ability to use powerful tools to discover, and then fix, these bugs, which is our next topic area.

> For a deeper look at the many, many possible kinds of UB bugs, please check out:*Appendix J.2: Undefined behavior*: a nonnormative, non-exhaustive list of undefined behaviors in C: http://www.open-std.org/jtc1/sc22/wg14/www/docs/n1548.pdf#page=571.
>
> From the in-depth C Programming Language standards—the ISO/IEC 9899:201x Committee Draft dated 02 Dec 2010.
>
> Along similar lines, please see *CWE VIEW: Weaknesses in Software Written in C*: https://cwe.mitre.org/data/definitions/658.html.

## Fragmentation

Fragmentation issues usually refer to problems primarily faced by the internal implementation of the memory allocation engine itself, and not so much by the typical application developer. Fragmentation issues are usually of two types: internal and external.

External fragmentation usually refers to the situation where, after several days of uptime, even if the free memory on the system is, say, 100 MB, the physically contiguous free memory might be less than a megabyte. Thus, with processes taking and releasing various sized memory chunks, memory has become fragmented.

Internal fragmentation usually refers to the wastage of memory caused by using an inefficient allocation strategy; often though, this cannot be helped, since wastage tends to be a side effect of many heap-based allocators. The modern glibc engine uses memory pools, which greatly reduce internal fragmentation.

We shall not attempt to delve into fragmentation issues in this book.

> Suffice it to say that, if in a large project you suspect fragmentation issues, you should try using a tool that displays your process runtime memory map (on Linux, check out /proc/<PID>/maps as a starting point). Interpreting it, you could possibly look at redesigning your application to avoid said fragmentation.

# Miscellaneous

Also, do realize that it's a bug to attempt to use just a pointer to access memory unless the memory has already been allocated. Remember that pointers have no memory; they have to be allocated memory (either statically at compile time or dynamically at runtime).

For example, one writes a C function that uses the parameter as a return value—a common C programming trick (these are often called value-result or in-out parameters):

```
unsigned long *uptr;
[...]
    my_awesome_func(uptr); // bug! value to be returned in 'uptr'
[...]
```

This is a bug; the uptr variable is just a pointer—it has no memory. One way to fix this is as follows:

```
unsigned long *uptr;
[...]
    uptr = malloc(sizeof(unsigned long));
    if (!uptr) {
        [...handle the error...]
    }
    my_awesome_func(uptr); // value returned in 'uptr'
    [...]
    free(uptr);
```

Or, even simpler, why not just use compile-time memory for cases such as this:

```
unsigned long uptr; // compile-time allocated memory
[...]
    my_awesome_func(&uptr); // value returned in 'uptr'
[...]
```

# Summary

In this chapter, we delved into a critical area: the fact that the seemingly simple, dynamic memory management APIs can cause deep and difficult-to-detect bugs in real-world fielded systems.

The common classes of memory bugs, such as **uninitialized memory usage (UMR)**, out-of-bounds accesses (read|write underflow|overflow bugs), and the double free, were covered. Memory leakage is a common and dangerous memory bug—we looked at three different cases of it.

The supplied `membugs` program helps the reader actually see and try out the various memory bugs covered via small test cases. In the next chapter we shall dive into using tools to help identify these dangerous defects.

# 6
# Debugging Tools for Memory Issues

We humans (we assume a human is reading this book and not some form of AI, though, who knows nowadays) are good at many intricate, complex tasks; but, we're also terrible at many mundane ones. That's why we invented computers—with the software to drive them!

Well. We're not really great at spotting details buried deep inside C (or assembly) code—memory bugs are a prime example of cases where we humans can use help. So, guess what: we've invented software tools to help us—they do the mundane, boring job of instrumenting and checking millions and billions of lines of our code and binaries, and are getting really effective at catching our bugs. Of course, when all is said and done, the best tool is still your brain, but nevertheless one might well ask: Who and what will debug the tools that one uses for debugging? The answer, of course, is more tools, and you, the human programmer.

In this chapter, the reader will learn to use two of the best-in-class memory debug tools:

- Valgrind's Memcheck
- Sanitizer tools (ASan)

Useful tables summarizing and comparing their features are provided. Also, glibc's malloc tuning via `mallopt(3)` is seen.

*Debugging Tools for Memory Issues*

> This particular chapter has no source code of it's own; instead, we use the source code from the preceding chapter, `Chapter 5`, *Linux Memory Issues*. Our `membugs` program test cases will be tried and tested under both Valgrind and ASan to see if they can catch the memory bugs that our *memugs* program's test cases work hard to provide. Thus, we definitely suggest you look over the previous chapter, and the `membugs.c` source code, to regain familiarity with the test cases we will be running.

# Tool types

Broadly speaking, within the scope of these areas, there are two kinds of tools:

- Dynamic analysis tools
- Static analysis tools

Dynamic analysis tools work essentially by instrumenting the runtime process. Thus, to gain the most out of them, a lot of attention must be devoted to ensuring that the tools actually run over all possible code paths; done by carefully and painstakingly writing test cases to ensure complete code coverage. This is a key point and will be mentioned again (Importantly, `Chapter 19`, *Troubleshooting and Best Practices*, covers such points). While very powerful, dynamic analysis tools usually result in a significant runtime performance hit and more memory usage.

Static analysis tools, on the other hand, work upon source code; in this sense, they are similar to the compiler. They often go well beyond the typical compiler, aiding the developer in uncovering all kinds of potential bugs. Perhaps the original Unix *lint* program could be considered the precursor to today's powerful static analyzers. Nowadays, very powerful commercial static analyzers (with fancy GUI frontends) exist, and are worth the money and time one spends on them. The downside is that these tools might raise a lot of false positives; the better ones let the programmer perform useful filtering. We won't cover static analyzers in this text (see the *Further reading* section on the GitHub repository, for a list of static analyzers for C/C++).

Now, let's check out some modern-day memory debug tools; they all fall into the dynamic analysis tools class. Do learn how to use them effectively—they're a necessary weapon against all kinds of **Undefined Behavior** (**UB**).

# Valgrind

Valgrind (pronounced as *val-grinned*) is an instrumentation framework for a suite of powerful tools. It is **open source software** (**OSS**), released under the terms of the GNU GPL ver. 2; it was originally developed by Julian Seward. Valgrind is an award-winning suite of tools for memory debugging and profiling. It has evolved to become a framework for creating dynamic analysis tools. In fact, it's really a virtual machine; Valgrind uses a technology called **dynamic binary instrumentation** (DBI) to instrument code. Read more on its homepage: `http://valgrind.org/`.

The tremendous upside of Valgrind is its tool suite—primarily the **Memory Checker** tool ( **Memcheck**). There are several other checker and profiling tools as well, enumerated in the following table (in alphabetical order):

| Valgrind tool name | Purpose |
| --- | --- |
| cachegrind | CPU cache profiler. |
| callgrind | Extension to cachegrind; provides more callgraph info. KCachegrind is a good GUI visualizer for cachegrind/callgrind. |
| drd | Pthreads bug detector. |
| helgrind | Data Race detector for multithreaded applications (mostly Pthreads). |
| massif | Heap profiler (heap usage graphing, max allocations tracking). |
| Memcheck | Memory bugs detector; includes **out-of-bounds** (**OOB**) accesses (read\|write under\|overflow), uninitialized data accesses, UAF, UAR, memory leakage, double free, and overlapping memory region bugs. This is the default tool. |

Note that some of the lesser used tools (such as lackey, nulgrind, none), and some of the experimental tools (exp-bbv, exp-dhat, exp-sgcheck) have not been shown in the table.

Select a tool for Valgrind to run via the `--tool=` option (giving any of the preceding as the parameter). In this book, we focus on Valgrind's Memcheck tool only.

## Using Valgrind's Memcheck tool

Memcheck is Valgrind's default tool; you do not need to pass it explicitly, but can do so with the `valgrind --tool=memcheck <program-to-execute with params>` syntax.

*Debugging Tools for Memory Issues*

As a trivial example, let's run Valgrind on the `df(1)` utility (on an Ubuntu box):

```
$ lsb_release -a
No LSB modules are available.
Distributor ID:    Ubuntu
Description:       Ubuntu 17.10
Release:           17.10
Codename:          artful
$ df --version |head -n1
df (GNU coreutils) 8.26
$ valgrind df
==1577== Memcheck, a memory error detector
==1577== Copyright (C) 2002-2017, and GNU GPL'd, by Julian Seward et al.
==1577== Using Valgrind-3.13.0 and LibVEX; rerun with -h for copyright info
==1577== Command: df
==1577==
Filesystem     1K-blocks     Used Available Use% Mounted on
udev              479724        0    479724   0% /dev
tmpfs             100940    10776     90164  11% /run
/dev/sda1       31863632  8535972  21686036  29% /
tmpfs             504692        0    504692   0% /dev/shm
tmpfs               5120        0      5120   0% /run/lock
tmpfs             504692        0    504692   0% /sys/fs/cgroup
tmpfs             100936        0    100936   0% /run/user/1000
==1577==
==1577== HEAP SUMMARY:
==1577==     in use at exit: 3,577 bytes in 213 blocks
==1577==   total heap usage: 447 allocs, 234 frees, 25,483 bytes allocated
==1577==
==1577== LEAK SUMMARY:
==1577==    definitely lost: 0 bytes in 0 blocks
==1577==    indirectly lost: 0 bytes in 0 blocks
==1577==      possibly lost: 0 bytes in 0 blocks
==1577==    still reachable: 3,577 bytes in 213 blocks
==1577==         suppressed: 0 bytes in 0 blocks
==1577== Rerun with --leak-check=full to see details of leaked memory
==1577==
==1577== For counts of detected and suppressed errors, rerun with: -v
==1577== ERROR SUMMARY: 0 errors from 0 contexts (suppressed: 0 from 0)
$
```

Valgrind literally takes over and runs the `df` process within it, instrumenting all dynamic memory accesses. It then prints its report. In the preceding code, the lines are prefixed with `==1577==`; that's just the PID of the `df` process.

As no runtime memory bugs were found, no output appears (you will see the difference soon when we run our `membugs` program under Valgrind's control). In terms of memory leakage, the report states:

```
definitely lost: 0 bytes in 0 blocks
```

All these are zero values, so it's fine. If the values under `definitely lost` were positive, then this would indeed indicate a memory leakage bug that must be further investigated and fixed. The other labels—`indirectly/possibly lost`, `still reachable`—are often due to complex or indirect memory handling within the code base (in effect, they are usually false positives one can ignore).

The `still reachable` usually signifies that, at process exit, some memory blocks were not explicitly freed by the application (but got implicitly freed when the process died). The following statements show this:

- **In use at exit**: 3,577 bytes in 213 blocks
- **Total heap usage**: 447 allocs, 234 frees, 25,483 bytes

Out of a total of 447 allocs, only 234 frees were done, leaving 447 - 234 = 213 blocks left unfreed.

Okay, now for the interesting bit: let's run our `membugs` program test cases (from the preceding Chapter 5, *Linux Memory Issues*) under Valgrind and see if it catches the memory bugs that the test cases work hard to provide.

We definitely suggest you look over the previous chapter, and the `membugs.c` source code, to regain familiarity with the test cases we will be running.

> The membugs program has a total of 13 test cases; we shall not attempt to display the output of all of them within the book; we leave it as an exercise to the reader to try running the program with all test cases under Valgrind and deciphering its output report.
>
> It would be of interest to most readers to see the summary table at the end of this section, showing the result of running Valgrind on each of the test cases.

### Test case #1: Uninitialized memory access

```
$ ./membugs 1
true: x=32568
$
```

[ 203 ]

## Debugging Tools for Memory Issues

> For readability, we remove parts of the output shown as follows and truncate the program pathname.

Now under Valgrind's control:

```
$ valgrind ./membugs 1
==19549== Memcheck, a memory error detector
==19549== Copyright (C) 2002-2017, and GNU GPL'd, by Julian Seward et al.
==19549== Using Valgrind-3.13.0 and LibVEX; rerun with -h for copyright info
==19549== Command: ./membugs 1
==19549==
==19549== Conditional jump or move depends on uninitialised value(s)
==19549==    at 0x40132C: uninit_var (in <...>/ch3/membugs)
==19549==    by 0x401451: process_args (in <...>/ch3/membugs)
==19549==    by 0x401574: main (in <...>/ch3/membugs)
==19549==

[...]

==19549== Conditional jump or move depends on uninitialised value(s)
==19549==    at 0x4E9101C: vfprintf (in /usr/lib64/libc-2.26.so)
==19549==    by 0x4E99255: printf (in /usr/lib64/libc-2.26.so)
==19549==    by 0x401357: uninit_var (in <...>/ch3/membugs)
==19549==    by 0x401451: process_args (in <...>/ch3/membugs)
==19549==    by 0x401574: main (in <...>/ch3/membugs)
==19549==
false: x=0
==19549==
==19549== HEAP SUMMARY:
==19549==     in use at exit: 0 bytes in 0 blocks
==19549==   total heap usage: 1 allocs, 1 frees, 1,024 bytes allocated
==19549==
==19549== All heap blocks were freed -- no leaks are possible
==19549==
==19549== For counts of detected and suppressed errors, rerun with: -v
==19549== Use --track-origins=yes to see where uninitialised values come from
==19549== ERROR SUMMARY: 6 errors from 6 contexts (suppressed: 0 from 0)
$
```

Clearly, Valgrind has caught the uninitialized memory access bug! The text highlighted in bold clearly reveals the case.

However, notice that though Valgrind can show us the call stack—including the process pathname—it seems to be unable to show us the line number in the source code where the offending bug is present. Hang on, though. We can achieve precisely this by running Valgrind with the debug-enabled version of the program:

```
$ make membugs_dbg
gcc -g -ggdb -gdwarf-4 -O0 -Wall -Wextra -c membugs.c -o membugs_dbg.o

[...]

membugs.c: In function 'uninit_var':
membugs.c:283:5: warning: 'x' is used uninitialized in this function [-Wuninitialized]
  if (x > MAXVAL)
     ^

[...]

gcc -g -ggdb -gdwarf-4 -O0 -Wall -Wextra -c ../common.c -o common_dbg.o
gcc -o membugs_dbg membugs_dbg.o common_dbg.o

[...]
```

> **Common GCC flags used for debugging**
>
> See the `gcc(1)` man page for details. Briefly:
> `-g`: Produce sufficient debugging information such that a tool such as the **GNU Debugger (GDB)** has to debug symbolic information to work with (modern Linux would typically use the DWARF format).
> `-ggdb`: Use the most expressive format possible for the OS.
> `-gdwarf-4`: Debug info is in the DWARF-<version> format (ver. 4 is appropriate).
> `-O0` : Optimization level 0; good for debugging.

In the following code, we retry running Valgrind with the debug-enabled version of our binary executable, `membugs_dbg`:

```
$ valgrind --tool=memcheck ./membugs_dbg 1
==20079== Memcheck, a memory error detector
==20079== Copyright (C) 2002-2017, and GNU GPL'd, by Julian Seward et al.
```

[ 205 ]

*Debugging Tools for Memory Issues*

```
==20079== Using Valgrind-3.13.0 and LibVEX; rerun with -h for
copyright info
==20079== Command: ./membugs_dbg 1
==20079==
==20079== Conditional jump or move depends on uninitialised value(s)
==20079==    at 0x40132C: uninit_var (membugs.c:283)
==20079==    by 0x401451: process_args (membugs.c:326)
==20079==    by 0x401574: main (membugs.c:379)
==20079==
==20079== Conditional jump or move depends on uninitialised value(s)
==20079==    at 0x4E90DAA: vfprintf (in /usr/lib64/libc-2.26.so)
==20079==    by 0x4E99255: printf (in /usr/lib64/libc-2.26.so)
==20079==    by 0x401357: uninit_var (membugs.c:286)
==20079==    by 0x401451: process_args (membugs.c:326)
==20079==    by 0x401574: main (membugs.c:379)
==20079==
==20079== Use of uninitialised value of size 8
==20079==    at 0x4E8CD7B: _itoa_word (in /usr/lib64/libc-2.26.so)
==20079==    by 0x4E9043D: vfprintf (in /usr/lib64/libc-2.26.so)
==20079==    by 0x4E99255: printf (in /usr/lib64/libc-2.26.so)
==20079==    by 0x401357: uninit_var (membugs.c:286)
==20079==    by 0x401451: process_args (membugs.c:326)
==20079==    by 0x401574: main (membugs.c:379)

[...]

==20079==
false: x=0
==20079==
==20079== HEAP SUMMARY:
==20079==     in use at exit: 0 bytes in 0 blocks
==20079==   total heap usage: 1 allocs, 1 frees, 1,024 bytes allocated
==20079==
==20079== All heap blocks were freed -- no leaks are possible
==20079==
==20079== For counts of detected and suppressed errors, rerun with: -v
==20079== Use --track-origins=yes to see where uninitialised values
come from
==20079== ERROR SUMMARY: 6 errors from 6 contexts (suppressed: 0 from
0)
$
```

As usual, read the call stack in a bottom-up fashion and it will make sense!

> **Important**: Please note that, unfortunately, it's quite possible that the precise line numbers shown in the output as follows may not precisely match the line number in the latest version of the source file in the book's GitHub repository.

Here is the the source code (the `nl` utility is used here to show the code with all lines numbered):

```
$  nl --body-numbering=a membugs.c
```

[...]

```
   278     /* option =  1 : uninitialized var test case */
   279     static void uninit_var()
   280     {
   281         int x;
   282
   283         if (x)
   284             printf("true case: x=%d\n", x);
   285         else
   286             printf("false case\n");
   287     }
```

[...]

```
   325             case 1:
   326                 uninit_var();
   327                 break;
```

[...]

```
   377     int main(int argc, char **argv)
   378     {
   379         process_args(argc, argv);
   380         exit(EXIT_SUCCESS);
   381     }
```

We can now see that Valgrind has indeed perfectly captured the buggy case.

**Test case #5:** read overflow on compile-time memory:

```
$ valgrind ./membugs_dbg 5
==23024== Memcheck, a memory error detector
==23024== Copyright (C) 2002-2017, and GNU GPL'd, by Julian Seward et
al.
==23024== Using Valgrind-3.13.0 and LibVEX; rerun with -h for
copyright info
==23024== Command: ./membugs_dbg 5
==23024==
arr = aaaaa◆◆◆◆
==23024==
==23024== HEAP SUMMARY:
==23024==     in use at exit: 0 bytes in 0 blocks
```

## Debugging Tools for Memory Issues

```
==23024==    total heap usage: 1 allocs, 1 frees, 1,024 bytes allocated
==23024==
==23024== All heap blocks were freed -- no leaks are possible
==23024==
==23024== For counts of detected and suppressed errors, rerun with: -v
==23024== ERROR SUMMARY: 0 errors from 0 contexts (suppressed: 0 from
0)
$
```

Would you look at that!? Valgrind fails to catch the read overflow memory bug. Why? It's a limitation: Valgrind can only instrument, and therefore catch, UB (bugs) on dynamically allocated memory. The preceding test case used static compile-time allocated memory.

So, let's try the same test, but this time using dynamically allocated memory; that's precisely what test case #6 is designed to do.

**Test case #6:** read overflow on dynamic memory (for readability, we truncated some of the output):

```
$ ./membugs_dbg 2>&1 |grep 6
 option =  6 : out-of-bounds : read overflow [on dynamic memory]
$ valgrind ./membugs_dbg 6
[...]
==23274== Command: ./membugs_dbg 6
==23274==
==23274== Invalid write of size 1
==23274==    at 0x401127: read_overflow_dynmem (membugs.c:215)
==23274==    by 0x401483: process_args (membugs.c:341)
==23274==    by 0x401574: main (membugs.c:379)
==23274==  Address 0x521f045 is 0 bytes after a block of size 5 alloc'd
==23274==    at 0x4C2FB6B: malloc (vg_replace_malloc.c:299)
==23274==    by 0x4010D9: read_overflow_dynmem (membugs.c:205)
==23274==    by 0x401483: process_args (membugs.c:341)
==23274==    by 0x401574: main (membugs.c:379)
[...]
==23274== Invalid write of size 1
==23274==    at 0x40115E: read_overflow_dynmem (membugs.c:216)
==23274==    by 0x401483: process_args (membugs.c:341)
==23274==    by 0x401574: main (membugs.c:379)
==23274==  Address 0x521f04a is 5 bytes after a block of size 5 alloc'd
==23274==    at 0x4C2FB6B: malloc (vg_replace_malloc.c:299)
==23274==    by 0x4010D9: read_overflow_dynmem (membugs.c:205)
==23274==    by 0x401483: process_args (membugs.c:341)
==23274==    by 0x401574: main (membugs.c:379)
```

```
==23274==
==23274== Invalid read of size 1
==23274==    at 0x4C32B94: strlen (vg_replace_strmem.c:458)
==23274==    by 0x4E91955: vfprintf (in /usr/lib64/libc-2.26.so)
==23274==    by 0x4E99255: printf (in /usr/lib64/libc-2.26.so)
==23274==    by 0x401176: read_overflow_dynmem (membugs.c:217)
==23274==    by 0x401483: process_args (membugs.c:341)
==23274==    by 0x401574: main (membugs.c:379)
==23274==  Address 0x521f045 is 0 bytes after a block of size 5 alloc'd
==23274==    at 0x4C2FB6B: malloc (vg_replace_malloc.c:299)
==23274==    by 0x4010D9: read_overflow_dynmem (membugs.c:205)
==23274==    by 0x401483: process_args (membugs.c:341)
==23274==    by 0x401574: main (membugs.c:379)
[...]
arr = aaaaaSecreT
==23274== Conditional jump or move depends on uninitialised value(s)
==23274==    at 0x4E90DAA: vfprintf (in /usr/lib64/libc-2.26.so)
==23274==    by 0x4E99255: printf (in /usr/lib64/libc-2.26.so)
==23274==    by 0x401195: read_overflow_dynmem (membugs.c:220)
==23274==    by 0x401483: process_args (membugs.c:341)
==23274==    by 0x401574: main (membugs.c:379)
==23274==
==23274== Use of uninitialised value of size 8
==23274==    at 0x4E8CD7B: _itoa_word (in /usr/lib64/libc-2.26.so)
==23274==    by 0x4E9043D: vfprintf (in /usr/lib64/libc-2.26.so)
==23274==    by 0x4E99255: printf (in /usr/lib64/libc-2.26.so)
==23274==    by 0x401195: read_overflow_dynmem (membugs.c:220)
==23274==    by 0x401483: process_args (membugs.c:341)
==23274==    by 0x401574: main (membugs.c:379)
[...]
==23274== ERROR SUMMARY: 31 errors from 17 contexts (suppressed: 0 from 0)
$
```

Well, this time, plenty of errors were caught with precise call stack locations revealing the exact point in the source (as we have compiled with -g).

## Debugging Tools for Memory Issues

### Test case #8: UAF (use-after-free):

```
$ ./membugs_dbg 2>&1 |grep 8
 option =  8 : UAF (use-after-free) test case
$
```

```
$ valgrind ./membugs_dbg 8
==24337== Memcheck, a memory error detector
==24337== Copyright (C) 2002-2017, and GNU GPL'd, by Julian Seward et al.
==24337== Using Valgrind-3.13.0 and LibVEX; rerun with -h for copyright info
==24337== Command: ./membugs_dbg 8
==24337==
uaf():165: arr = 0x521f040:aaaaaaaaaaaaaaaaaaaaaaaaaaaaaaaa
==24337== Invalid write of size 1
==24337==    at 0x4C32E7F: strncpy (vg_replace_strmem.c:549)
==24337==    by 0x400FB5: uaf (membugs.c:173)
==24337==    by 0x4014A6: process_args (membugs.c:348)
==24337==    by 0x401574: main (membugs.c:379)
==24337==  Address 0x521f040 is 0 bytes inside a block of size 512 free'd
==24337==    at 0x4C30D18: free (vg_replace_malloc.c:530)
==24337==    by 0x400F93: uaf (membugs.c:171)
==24337==    by 0x4014A6: process_args (membugs.c:348)
==24337==    by 0x401574: main (membugs.c:379)
==24337==  Block was alloc'd at
==24337==    at 0x4C2FB6B: malloc (vg_replace_malloc.c:299)
==24337==    by 0x400EC5: uaf (membugs.c:159)
==24337==    by 0x4014A6: process_args (membugs.c:348)
==24337==    by 0x401574: main (membugs.c:379)
==24337==
==24337== Invalid read of size 1
==24337==    at 0x4C32B2B: strnlen (vg_replace_strmem.c:425)
==24337==    by 0x4E8FFB2: vfprintf (in /usr/lib64/libc-2.26.so)
==24337==    by 0x4E99255: printf (in /usr/lib64/libc-2.26.so)
==24337==    by 0x400FE2: uaf (membugs.c:174)
==24337==    by 0x4014A6: process_args (membugs.c:348)
==24337==    by 0x401574: main (membugs.c:379)
```

A (partial) screenshot of the action when Valgrind catches the UAF bugs

Valgrind does catch the UAF!

**Test case #8: UAR (use-after-return)**:

```
$ ./membugs_dbg 9
res: (null)
$ valgrind ./membugs_dbg 9
==7594== Memcheck, a memory error detector
==7594== Copyright (C) 2002-2017, and GNU GPL'd, by Julian Seward et al.
==7594== Using Valgrind-3.13.0 and LibVEX; rerun with -h for copyright info
==7594== Command: ./membugs_dbg 9
==7594==
res: (null)
==7594==
==7594== HEAP SUMMARY:
==7594==     in use at exit: 0 bytes in 0 blocks
==7594==   total heap usage: 1 allocs, 1 frees, 1,024 bytes allocated
==7594==
==7594== All heap blocks were freed -- no leaks are possible
==7594==
==7594== For counts of detected and suppressed errors, rerun with: -v
==7594== ERROR SUMMARY: 0 errors from 0 contexts (suppressed: 0 from 0)
$
```

Whoops! Valgrind does not catch the UAR bug!

**Test Case #13:** Memory leak case #3—lib API leak. We run the memory leak test case #3 by selecting 13 as the parameter to *membugs*. It's useful to note that only when run with the `--leak-check=full` option does Valgrind display the origin of the leak (via the displayed call stack):

```
$ valgrind --leak-resolution=high --num-callers=50
--leak-check=full ./membugs_dbg 13
==22849== Memcheck, a memory error detector
==22849== Copyright (C) 2002-2017, and GNU GPL'd, by Julian Seward et al.
==22849== Using Valgrind-3.13.0 and LibVEX; rerun with -h for copyright info
==22849== Command: ./membugs_dbg 13
==22849==

## Leakage test: case 3: "lib" API: runtime cond = 0
mypath =
/usr/local/bin:/usr/local/sbin:/usr/bin:/usr/sbin:/sbin:/usr/sbin:/usr
/local/sbin:/home/kai/MentorGraphics/Sourcery_CodeBench_Lite_for_ARM_G
```

## Debugging Tools for Memory Issues

```
NU_Linux/bin/:/mnt/big/scratchpad/buildroot-2017.08.1/output/host/bin/
:/sbin:/usr/sbin:/usr/local/sbin

## Leakage test: case 3: "lib" API: runtime cond = 1
mypath =
/usr/local/bin:/usr/local/sbin:/usr/bin:/usr/sbin:/sbin:/usr/sbin:/usr
/local/sbin:/home/kai/MentorGraphics/Sourcery_CodeBench_Lite_for_ARM_G
NU_Linux/bin/:/mnt/big/scratchpad/buildroot-2017.08.1/output/host/bin/
:/sbin:/usr/sbin:/usr/local/sbin
==22849==
==22849== HEAP SUMMARY:
==22849==     in use at exit: 4,096 bytes in 1 blocks
==22849==   total heap usage: 3 allocs, 2 frees, 9,216 bytes allocated
==22849==
==22849== 4,096 bytes in 1 blocks are definitely lost in loss record 1 of 1
==22849==    at 0x4C2FB6B: malloc (vg_replace_malloc.c:299)
==22849==    by 0x400A0C: silly_getpath (membugs.c:38)
==22849==    by 0x400AC6: leakage_case3 (membugs.c:59)
==22849==    by 0x40152B: process_args (membugs.c:367)
==22849==    by 0x401574: main (membugs.c:379)
==22849==
==22849== LEAK SUMMARY:
==22849==    definitely lost: 4,096 bytes in 1 blocks
==22849==    indirectly lost: 0 bytes in 0 blocks
==22849==      possibly lost: 0 bytes in 0 blocks
==22849==    still reachable: 0 bytes in 0 blocks
==22849==         suppressed: 0 bytes in 0 blocks
==22849==
==22849== For counts of detected and suppressed errors, rerun with: -v
==22849== ERROR SUMMARY: 1 errors from 1 contexts (suppressed: 0 from 0)
$
```

The Valgrind man page recommends setting `--leak-resolution=high` and `--num-callers=` to 40 or higher.

The man page on `valgrind(1)` covers the many options it provides (such as logging and tool (Memcheck) options); take a look to gain a deeper understanding of this tool's usage.

## Valgrind summary table

With respect to our test cases (incorporated into our `membugs` program), here is Valgrind's report card and memory bugs given as follows:

| Test case # | Test case | Detected by Valgrind? |
| --- | --- | --- |
| 1 | **Uninitialized memory read (UMR)** | Yes |
| 2 | **Out-of-bounds (OOB)**: write overflow [on compile-time memory] | No |
| 3 | OOB: write overflow [on dynamic memory] | Yes |
| 4 | OOB: write underflow [on dynamic memory] | Yes |
| 5 | OOB: read overflow [on compile-time memory] | No |
| 6 | OOB: read overflow [on dynamic memory] | Yes |
| 7 | OOB: read underflow [on dynamic memory] | Yes |
| 8 | UAF, also known as dangling pointer | Yes |
| 9 | UAR, also known as **use-after-scope** (**UAS**) | No |
| 10 | Double free | Yes |
| 11 | Memory leak test case 1: simple leak | Yes |
| 12 | Memory leak test case 1: leak more (in a loop) | Yes |
| 13 | Memory leak test case 1: lib API leak | Yes |

## Valgrind pros and cons : a quick summary

Valgrind pros:

- Catches common memory bugs (UB) on dynamically allocated memory regions
    - Using uninitialized variables
    - Out-of-bounds memory accesses (read/write underflow/overflow bugs)
    - Use-after-free / use-after-return (out-of-scope) bugs
    - Double free
    - Leakage

- No modification to source code required
- No recompile required
- No special compiler flags required

Valgrind cons:

- Performance: target software may run up to 10 to 30 times slower when run under Valgrind.
- Memory footprint: each allocation within the target program requires Valgrind to make a memory allocation as well (making running Valgrind on highly-resource-constrained embedded Linux systems difficult).
- Cannot catch bugs on statically (compile-time) allocated memory regions.
- In order to see the call stack with line-number information, a recompile/build with the -g flag is required.

The fact is, Valgrind remains a powerful weapon in one's armory against bugs. There are many real-world projects that use Valgrind; check out the long list at http://valgrind.org/gallery/users.html.

> There is always more to learn and explore: Valgrind provides a GDB monitor mode allowing you to do advanced debugging on your program via the **GNU debugger** (**GDB**). This is particularly useful for using Valgrind on programs that never terminate (daemons being the classic case).
>
> The third chapter of Valgrind's manual is very helpful in this regard: http://valgrind.org/docs/manual/manual-core-adv.html

## Sanitizer tools

Sanitizers are a suite of open source tools from Google; like other memory debug tools, they tackle the usual common memory bugs and UB issues, including OOB (out-of-bounds accesses: read/write under/over-flow), UAF, UAR, double free, and memory leakage. One of the tools also handles data races in C/C++ code.

A key difference is that the sanitizer tools introduce instrumentation into the code via the compiler. They use a technology called **Compile-time instrumentation** (CTI) as well as shadow memory techniques. As of this writing, ASan is a part of and supports GCC ver 4.8 and LLVM (Clang) ver. 3.1 and above.

# Sanitizer toolset

To use a given tool, compile the program with the flag(s) shown in the Usage column:

| Sanitizer tool (short name) | Purpose | Usage (compiler flags) | Linux platforms [+comments] |
|---|---|---|---|
| **AddressSanitizer (ASan)** | Detecting generic memory errors [heap\|stack\|global buffer over\|under-flow, UAF, UAR, init order bugs] | `-fsanitize=address` | x86, x86_64, ARM, Aarch64, MIPS, MIPS64, PPC64. [Cannot combine with TSan] |
| **Kernel AddressSanitizer (KASAN)** | ASan for Linux kernel-space | `-fsanitize=kernel-address` | x86_64 [kernel ver >=4.0], Aarch64 [kernel ver >= 4.4] |
| **MemorySanitizer (MSan)** | UMR detector | `-fsanitize=memory -fPIE -pie [-fno-omit-frame-pointer]` | Linux x86_64 only |
| **ThreadSanitizer (TSan)** | Data Races detector | `-fsanitize=thread` | Linux x86_64 only. [Cannot combine with ASan or LSan flags] |
| **LeakSanitizer (LSan)** (a subset of ASan) | Memory leakage detector | `-fsanitize=leak` | Linux x86_64 and OS X [cannot combine with TSan] |
| **UndefinedBehaviorSanitizer (UBSan)** | UB detector | `-fsanitize=undefined` | x86, x86_64, ARM, Aarch64, PPC64, MIPS, MIPS64 |

Debugging Tools for Memory Issues

### Additional Documentation

Google maintains a GitHub page with documentation for the sanitizer tools:

- `https://github.com/google/sanitizers`
- `https://github.com/google/sanitizers/wiki`
- `https://github.com/google/sanitizers/wiki/SanitizerCommonFlags`

> There are links leading to each of the tool's individual wiki (documentation) pages. It's recommended you read them in detail when using a tool (for example, each tool might have specific flags and/or environment variables that the user can make use of).

The man page on `gcc(1)` is a rich source of information on the intricacies of the `-fsanitize=` sanitizer tool gcc options. Interestingly, most of the sanitizer tools are supported on the Android (>=4.1) platform as well.

The Clang documentation also documents the use of the sanitizer tools: `https://clang.llvm.org/docs/index.html`.

In this chapter, we focus on using the ASan tool.

## Building programs for use with ASan

As the preceding table shows, we need to compile our target application membugs with the appropriate compiler flag(s). Also, instead of using `gcc` as the compiler, it's recommended we use `clang`.

> `clang` is considered a compiler frontend for several programming languages, including C and C++; the backend is the LLVM compiler infrastructure project. More information on Clang is available on its Wikipedia page.

> You will need to ensure that the Clang package is installed on your Linux box; using your distribution's package manager (`apt-get`, `dnf`, `rpm`) would be the easiest way.

[ 216 ]

This snippet from our Makefile shows how we use `clang` to compile the membugs sanitizer targets:

```
CC=${CROSS_COMPILE}gcc
CL=${CROSS_COMPILE}clang

CFLAGS=-Wall -UDEBUG
CFLAGS_DBG=-g -ggdb -gdwarf-4 -O0 -Wall -Wextra -DDEBUG
CFLAGS_DBG_ASAN=${CFLAGS_DBG} -fsanitize=address
CFLAGS_DBG_MSAN=${CFLAGS_DBG} -fsanitize=memory
CFLAGS_DBG_UB=${CFLAGS_DBG} -fsanitize=undefined

[...]

#--- Sanitizers (use clang): <foo>_dbg_[asan|ub|msan]
membugs_dbg_asan.o: membugs.c
    ${CL} ${CFLAGS_DBG_ASAN} -c membugs.c -o membugs_dbg_asan.o
membugs_dbg_asan: membugs_dbg_asan.o common_dbg_asan.o
    ${CL} ${CFLAGS_DBG_ASAN} -o membugs_dbg_asan membugs_dbg_asan.o common_dbg_asan.o

membugs_dbg_ub.o: membugs.c
    ${CL} ${CFLAGS_DBG_UB} -c membugs.c -o membugs_dbg_ub.o
membugs_dbg_ub: membugs_dbg_ub.o common_dbg_ub.o
    ${CL} ${CFLAGS_DBG_UB} -o membugs_dbg_ub membugs_dbg_ub.o common_dbg_ub.o

membugs_dbg_msan.o: membugs.c
    ${CL} ${CFLAGS_DBG_MSAN} -c membugs.c -o membugs_dbg_msan.o
membugs_dbg_msan: membugs_dbg_msan.o common_dbg_msan.o
    ${CL} ${CFLAGS_DBG_MSAN} -o membugs_dbg_msan membugs_dbg_msan.o common_dbg_msan.o
[...]
```

## Running the test cases with ASan

To refresh our memory, here is the help screen from our membugs program:

```
$ ./membugs_dbg_asan
Usage: ./membugs_dbg_asan option [ -h | --help]
 option =  1 : uninitialized var test case
 option =  2 : out-of-bounds : write overflow [on compile-time memory]
 option =  3 : out-of-bounds : write overflow [on dynamic memory]
 option =  4 : out-of-bounds : write underflow
 option =  5 : out-of-bounds : read overflow [on compile-time memory]
 option =  6 : out-of-bounds : read overflow [on dynamic memory]
 option =  7 : out-of-bounds : read underflow
```

```
option =  8 : UAF (use-after-free) test case
option =  9 : UAR (use-after-return) test case
option = 10 : double-free test case
option = 11 : memory leak test case 1: simple leak
option = 12 : memory leak test case 2: leak more (in a loop)
option = 13 : memory leak test case 3: "lib" API leak
-h | --help : show this help screen
$
```

> The membugs program has a total of 13 test cases; we shall not attempt to display the output of all of them in this book; we leave it as an exercise to the reader to try out building and running the program with all test cases under ASan and deciphering its output report. It would be of interest to readers to see the summary table at the end of this section, showing the result of running ASan on each of the test cases.

**Test case #1:** UMR

Let's try the very first one—the uninitialized variable read test case:

```
$ ./membugs_dbg_asan 1
false case
$
```

It did not catch the bug! Yes, we have hit upon ASan's limitation: AddressSanitizer cannot catch UMR on statically (compile-time) allocated memory. Valgrind did.

Well, that's taken care of by the MSan tool; its specific job is to catch UMR bugs. The documentation states that MSan can only catch UMR on dynamically allocated memory. We found that it even caught a UMR bug on statically allocated memory, which our simple test case uses:

```
$ ./membugs_dbg_msan 1
==3095==WARNING: MemorySanitizer: use-of-uninitialized-value
    #0 0x496eb8 (<...>/ch5/membugs_dbg_msan+0x496eb8)
    #1 0x494425 (<...>/ch5/membugs_dbg_msan+0x494425)
    #2 0x493f2b (<...>/ch5/membugs_dbg_msan+0x493f2b)
    #3 0x7fc32f17ab96 (/lib/x86_64-linux-gnu/libc.so.6+0x21b96)
    #4 0x41a8c9 (<...>/ch5/membugs_dbg_msan+0x41a8c9)

SUMMARY: MemorySanitizer: use-of-uninitialized-value
(<...>/ch5/membugs_dbg_msan+0x496eb8)
Exiting
$
```

It has caught the bug; however, this time, though we have used a debug binary executable, built with the `-g -ggdb` flags, the usual `filename:line_number` information is missing in the stack trace. Actually, a method to obtain this is demonstrated in the next test case.

For now, no matter: this gives us a chance to learn another useful debug technique: `objdump(1)` is one of the toolchain utilities that can greatly help here (we can achieve similar results with tools such as `readelf(1)` or `gdb(1)`). We'll disassemble the binary executable with `objdump(1)` (`-d` switch, and, with source via the `-S` switch), and look within its output for the address where the UMR occurs:

```
SUMMARY: MemorySanitizer: use-of-uninitialized-value
(<...>/ch5/membugs_dbg_msan+0x496eb8)
```

As the output of `objdump` is quite large, we truncate it showing only the relevant portion:

**$ objdump -d -S ./membugs_dbg_msan > tmp**

`<< Now examine the tmp file >>`

**$ cat tmp**

```
./membugs_dbg_msan:     file format elf64-x86-64

Disassembly of section .init:

000000000041a5b0 <_init>:
  41a5b0:  48 83 ec 08      sub    $0x8,%rsp
  41a5b4:  48 8b 05 ad a9 2a 00    mov    0x2aa9ad(%rip),%rax     # 6c4f68 <__gmon_start__>
  41a5bb:  48 85 c0         test   %rax,%rax
  41a5be:  74 02            je     41a5c2 <_init+0x12>

[...]

0000000000496e60 <uninit_var>:
{
  496e60:  55               push   %rbp
  496e61:  48 89 e5         mov    %rsp,%rbp
    int x;  /* static mem */
  496e64:  48 83 ec 10      sub    $0x10,%rsp
[...]
    if (x)
  496e7f:  8b 55 fc         mov    -0x4(%rbp),%edx
  496e82:  8b 31            mov    (%rcx),%esi
  496e84:  89 f7            mov    %esi,%edi
```

*Debugging Tools for Memory Issues*

```
    [...]
    496eaf: e9 00 00 00 00    jmpq  496eb4 <uninit_var+0x54>
    496eb4: e8 a7 56 f8 ff    callq 41c560 <__msan_warning_noreturn>
    496eb9: 8a 45 fb          mov   -0x5(%rbp),%al
    496ebc: a8 01             test  $0x1,%al
[...]
```

The closest match in the `objdump` output to the address provided by MSan as the `0x496eb8` error point is `0x496eb4`. That's fine: just look at the preceding for the first source line of code; it's the following line:

```
    if (x)
```

Perfect. That's exactly where the UMR occurred!

**Test Case #2:** write overflow [on compile-time memory]

We run the `membugs` program, both under Valgrind and ASan, only invoking the `write_overflow_compilemem()` function to test the out-of-bounds write overflow memory errors on a compile-time allocated piece of memory.

**Case 1:** Using Valgrind
Notice how Valgrind does not catch the out-of-bounds memory bug:

```
$ valgrind ./membugs_dbg 2
==8959== Memcheck, a memory error detector
==8959== Copyright (C) 2002-2017, and GNU GPL'd, by Julian Seward et al.
==8959== Using Valgrind-3.13.0 and LibVEX; rerun with -h for copyright info
==8959== Command: ./membugs_dbg 2
==8959==
==8959==
==8959== HEAP SUMMARY:
==8959==     in use at exit: 0 bytes in 0 blocks
==8959==   total heap usage: 0 allocs, 0 frees, 0 bytes allocated
==8959==
==8959== All heap blocks were freed -- no leaks are possible
==8959==
==8959== For counts of detected and suppressed errors, rerun with: -v
==8959== ERROR SUMMARY: 0 errors from 0 contexts (suppressed: 0 from 0)
$
```

This is because Valgrind is limited to working with only dynamically allocated memory; it cannot instrument and work with compile time allocated memory.

**Case 2**: Address Sanitizer

ASan does catch the bug:

```
$ ./membugs_dbg_asan 2
=================================================================
==4125==ERROR: AddressSanitizer: stack-buffer-overflow on address 0x7ffe9f8d8174 at pc 0x00000051271d bp 0x7ffe9f8d8130 sp 0x7
ffe9f8d8128
WRITE of size 4 at 0x7ffe9f8d8174 thread T0
    #0 0x51271c  (/home/seawolf/0tmp/membugs_dbg_asan+0x51271c)
    #1 0x51244e  (/home/seawolf/0tmp/membugs_dbg_asan+0x51244e)
    #2 0x512291  (/home/seawolf/0tmp/membugs_dbg_asan+0x512291)
    #3 0x7fe3408ccb96 (/lib/x86_64-linux-gnu/libc.so.6+0x21b96)
    #4 0x419ea9  (/home/seawolf/0tmp/membugs_dbg_asan+0x419ea9)

Address 0x7ffe9f8d8174 is located in stack of thread T0 at offset 52 in frame
    #0 0x5125ef  (/home/seawolf/0tmp/membugs_dbg_asan+0x5125ef)

  This frame has 1 object(s):
    [32, 52) 'arr' (line 265) <== Memory access at offset 52 overflows this variable
HINT: this may be a false positive if your program uses some custom stack unwind mechanism or swapcontext
      (longjmp and C++ exceptions *are* supported)
SUMMARY: AddressSanitizer: stack-buffer-overflow (/home/seawolf/0tmp/membugs_dbg_asan+0x51271c)
Shadow bytes around the buggy address:
  0x100053f12fd0: 00 00 00 00 00 00 00 00 00 00 00 00 00 00 00 00
  0x100053f12fe0: 00 00 00 00 00 00 00 00 00 00 00 00 00 00 00 00
  0x100053f12ff0: 00 00 00 00 00 00 00 00 00 00 00 00 00 00 00 00
  0x100053f13000: 00 00 00 00 00 00 00 00 00 00 00 00 00 00 00 00
  0x100053f13010: 00 00 00 00 00 00 00 00 00 00 00 00 00 00 00 00
=>0x100053f13020: 00 00 00 00 00 00 00 00 f1 f1 f1 f1 00 00[04]f3
  0x100053f13030: f3 f3 f3 f3 00 00 00 00 00 00 00 00 00 00 00 00
  0x100053f13040: 00 00 00 00 00 00 00 00 00 00 00 00 00 00 00 00
  0x100053f13050: 00 00 00 00 00 00 00 00 00 00 00 00 00 00 00 00
  0x100053f13060: 00 00 00 00 00 00 00 00 00 00 00 00 00 00 00 00
  0x100053f13070: 00 00 00 00 00 00 00 00 00 00 00 00 00 00 00 00
Shadow byte legend (one shadow byte represents 8 application bytes):
  Addressable:           00
```

AddressSanitizer (ASan) catches the OOB write-overflow bug

A similar textual version is shown as follows:

```
$ ./membugs_dbg_asan 2
=================================================================
==25662==ERROR: AddressSanitizer: stack-buffer-overflow on address
0x7fff17e789f4 at pc 0x00000051271d bp 0x7fff17e789b0 sp
0x7fff17e789a8
WRITE of size 4 at 0x7fff17e789f4 thread T0
    #0 0x51271c (<...>/membugs_dbg_asan+0x51271c)
    #1 0x51244e (<...>/membugs_dbg_asan+0x51244e)
    #2 0x512291 (<...>/membugs_dbg_asan+0x512291)
    #3 0x7f7e19b2db96 (/lib/x86_64-linux-gnu/libc.so.6+0x21b96)
    #4 0x419ea9 (<...>/membugs_dbg_asan+0x419ea9)

Address 0x7fff17e789f4 is located in stack of thread T0 at offset 52
in frame
    #0 0x5125ef (/home/seawolf/0tmp/membugs_dbg_asan+0x5125ef)
```

```
[...]
SUMMARY: AddressSanitizer: stack-buffer-overflow
(/home/seawolf/0tmp/membugs_dbg_asan+0x51271c)
[...]
==25662==ABORTING
$
```

Notice, however, that within the stack backtrace, there is no `filename:line#` information. That's disappointing. Can we obtain it?

Yes indeed—the trick lies in ensuring a few things:

- Compile the application with the `-g` switch (to include debug symbolic info; we do this for all the *_dbg versions).
- Besides the Clang compiler, a tool called `llvm-symbolizer` must be installed as well. Once installed, you must figure out its exact location on the disk and add that directory to the path.
- At runtime, the `ASAN_OPTIONS` environment variable must be set to the `symbolize=1` value.

Here, we rerun the buggy case with `llvm-symbolizer` in play:

```
$ export PATH=$PATH:/usr/lib/llvm-6.0/bin/
$ ASAN_OPTIONS=symbolize=1 ./membugs_dbg_asan 2
=================================================================
==25807==ERROR: AddressSanitizer: stack-buffer-overflow on address
0x7ffd63e80cf4 at pc 0x00000051271d bp 0x7ffd63e80cb0 sp
0x7ffd63e80ca8
WRITE of size 4 at 0x7ffd63e80cf4 thread T0
    #0 0x51271c in write_overflow_compilemem
<...>/ch5/membugs.c:268:10
    #1 0x51244e in process_args <...>/ch5/membugs.c:325:4
    #2 0x512291 in main <...>/ch5/membugs.c:375:2
    #3 0x7f9823642b96 in __libc_start_main /build/glibc-
OTsEL5/glibc-2.27/csu/../csu/libc-start.c:310
    #4 0x419ea9 in _start (<...>/membugs_dbg_asan+0x419ea9)
[...]
$
```

Now the `filename:line# information` shows up!

Clearly, ASan can and does instrument compile-time allocated as well as dynamically allocated memory regions, and thus catches both memory-type bugs.

*Chapter 6*

Also, as we saw, it displays a call stack (read it from bottom to top of course). We can see the call chain is:

```
_start --> __libc_start_main --> main --> process_args -->
           write_overflow_compilemem
```

The AddressSanitizer also displays, "Shadow bytes around the buggy address:"; here, we do not attempt to explain the memory-shadowing technique used to catch such bugs; if interested, please see the *Further reading* section on the GitHub repository.

**Test case #3:** write overflow (on dynamic memory)

As expected, ASan catches the bug:

```
$ ./membugs_dbg_asan 3
=================================================================
==25848==ERROR: AddressSanitizer: heap-buffer-overflow on address
0x602000000018 at pc 0x0000004aaedc bp 0x7ffe64dd2cd0 sp
0x7ffe64dd2480
WRITE of size 10 at 0x602000000018 thread T0
    #0 0x4aaedb in __interceptor_strcpy.part.245
(<...>/membugs_dbg_asan+0x4aaedb)
    #1 0x5128fd in write_overflow_dynmem <...>/ch5/membugs.c:258:2
    #2 0x512458 in process_args <...>/ch5/membugs.c:328:4
    #3 0x512291 in main <...>/ch5/membugs.c:375:2
    #4 0x7f93abb88b96 in __libc_start_main /build/glibc-
OTsEL5/glibc-2.27/csu/../csu/libc-start.c:310
    #5 0x419ea9 in _start (<...>/membugs_dbg_asan+0x419ea9)

0x602000000018 is located 0 bytes to the right of 8-byte region
[0x602000000010,0x602000000018) allocated by thread T0 here:
    #0 0x4d9d60 in malloc (<...>/membugs_dbg_asan+0x4d9d60)
    #1 0x512896 in write_overflow_dynmem <...>/ch5/membugs.c:254:9
    #2 0x512458 in process_args <...>/ch5/membugs.c:328:4
    #3 0x512291 in main <...>/ch5/membugs.c:375:2
    #4 0x7f93abb88b96 in __libc_start_main /build/glibc-
OTsEL5/glibc-2.27/csu/../csu/libc-start.c:310
[...]
```

With `llvm-symbolizer` in the path, the `filename:line#` information again shows up.

## Debugging Tools for Memory Issues

Attempting to compile for sanitizer instrumentation (via the -fsanitize= GCC switches) and trying to run the binary executable over Valgrind is not supported; when we try this, Valgrind reports the following:

```
$ valgrind ./membugs_dbg 3
==8917== Memcheck, a memory error detector
==8917== Copyright (C) 2002-2017, and GNU GPL'd, by Julian Seward et al.
==8917== Using Valgrind-3.13.0 and LibVEX; rerun with -h for copyright info
==8917== Command: ./membugs_dbg 3
==8917==
==8917==ASan runtime does not come first in initial library list; you should either link runtime to your application or manually preload it with LD_PRELOAD.
[...]
```

**Test Case #8:** UAF (use-after-free). Take a look at the following code:

```
$ ./membugs_dbg_asan 8
uaf():162: arr = 0x615000000080:aaaaaaaaaaaaaaaaaaaaaaaaaaaaaa
=================================================================
==25883==ERROR: AddressSanitizer: heap-use-after-free on address 0x615000000080 at pc 0x000000444b14 bp 0x7ffde4315390 sp 0x7ffde4314b40
WRITE of size 22 at 0x615000000080 thread T0
    #0 0x444b13 in strncpy (<...>/membugs_dbg_asan+0x444b13)
    #1 0x513529 in uaf <...>/ch5/membugs.c:172:2
    #2 0x512496 in process_args <...>/ch5/membugs.c:344:4
    #3 0x512291 in main <...>/ch5/membugs.c:375:2
    #4 0x7f4ceea9fb96 in __libc_start_main /build/glibc-OTsEL5/glibc-2.27/csu/../csu/libc-start.c:310
    #5 0x419ea9 in _start (<...>/membugs_dbg_asan+0x419ea9)

0x615000000080 is located 0 bytes inside of 512-byte region [0x615000000080,0x615000000280)
freed by thread T0 here:
    #0 0x4d9b90 in __interceptor_free.localalias.0 (<...>/membugs_dbg_asan+0x4d9b90)
    #1 0x513502 in uaf <...>/ch5/membugs.c:171:2
    #2 0x512496 in process_args <...>/ch5/membugs.c:344:4
    #3 0x512291 in main <...>/ch5/membugs.c:375:2
    #4 0x7f4ceea9fb96 in __libc_start_main /build/glibc-OTsEL5/glibc-2.27/csu/../csu/libc-start.c:310

previously allocated by thread T0 here:
    #0 0x4d9d60 in malloc (<...>/membugs_dbg_asan+0x4d9d60)
    #1 0x513336 in uaf <...>/ch5/membugs.c:157:8
```

```
        #2 0x512496 in process_args <...>/ch5/membugs.c:344:4
        #3 0x512291 in main <...>/ch5/membugs.c:375:2
        #4 0x7f4ceea9fb96 in __libc_start_main /build/glibc-
OTsEL5/glibc-2.27/csu/../csu/libc-start.c:310

SUMMARY: AddressSanitizer: heap-use-after-free
(<...>/membugs_dbg_asan+0x444b13) in strncpy
[...]
```

Super. ASan not only reports the UAF bug, it even reports exactly where the buffer was allocated and freed! Powerful stuff.

**Test case #9:** UAR

For the purpose of this example, let's say we compile the membugs program in the usual manner, using gcc. Run the test case:

```
$ ./membugs_dbg 2>&1 | grep -w 9
 option =  9 : UAR (use-after-return) test case
$ ./membugs_dbg_asan 9
res: (null)
$
```

ASan, as such, does not catch this dangerous UAR bug! As we saw earlier, neither does Valgrind. But, the compiler does emit a warning!

Hang on, though: the Sanitizers documentation mentions that ASan can indeed catch this UAR bug, if:

- clang (ver r191186 onward) is used to compile the code (not gcc)
- A special flag, detect_stack_use_after_return is set to 1

So, we recompile the executable via Clang (again, we assume the Clang package is installed). In reality, our Makefile does make use of clang for all the membugs_dbg_* builds. So, ensure we rebuild with Clang as the compiler and retry:

```
$ ASAN_OPTIONS=detect_stack_use_after_return=1 ./membugs_dbg_asan 9
=================================================================
==25925==ERROR: AddressSanitizer: stack-use-after-return on address
0x7f7721a00020 at pc 0x000000445b17 bp 0x7ffdb7c3ba10 sp
0x7ffdb7c3b1c0
READ of size 23 at 0x7f7721a00020 thread T0
    #0 0x445b16 in printf_common(void*, char const*, __va_list_tag*)
(<...>/membugs_dbg_asan+0x445b16)
    #1 0x4465db in vprintf (<...>/membugs_dbg_asan+0x4465db)
    #2 0x4466ae in __interceptor_printf
(<...>/membugs_dbg_asan+0x4466ae)
```

```
    #3 0x5124b9 in process_args <...>/ch5/membugs.c:348:4
    #4 0x512291 in main <...>/ch5/membugs.c:375:2
    #5 0x7f7724e80b96 in __libc_start_main /build/glibc-
OTsEL5/glibc-2.27/csu/../csu/libc-start.c:310
    #6 0x419ea9 in _start
(/home/seawolf/0tmp/membugs_dbg_asan+0x419ea9)

Address 0x7f7721a00020 is located in stack of thread T0 at offset 32
in frame
    #0 0x5135ef in uar <...>/ch5/membugs.c:141

  This frame has 1 object(s):
    [32, 64) 'name' (line 142) <== Memory access at offset 32 is
inside this variable
[...]
```

It does work. As we showed in *Test case #1: UMR*, one can further make use of `objdump(1)` to tease out the exact place where the bug hits. We leave this as an exercise for the reader.

More information on how ASan detects stack UAR can be found at https://github.com/google/sanitizers/wiki/AddressSanitizerUseAfterReturn.

**Test case #10:** double free

The test case for this bug is kind of interesting (refer to the `membugs.c` source); we perform `malloc`, `free` the pointer, then perform another `malloc` with such a large value (`-1UL`, which becomes unsigned and thus too big) that it's guaranteed to fail. In the error-handling code, we (deliberately) free the pointer we already freed earlier, thus generating the double free test case. In simpler pseudocode:

```
ptr = malloc(n);
strncpy(...);
free(ptr);

bogus = malloc(-1UL); /* will fail */
if (!bogus) {
    free(ptr);   /* the Bug! */
    exit(1);
}
```

Importantly, this kind of coding reveals another really crucial lesson: developers often do not pay sufficient attention to error-handling code paths; they may or may not write negative test cases to test them thoroughly. This could result in serious bugs!

Running this via ASan instrumentation does not, at first, have the desired effect: you will see that because of the glaringly enormous `malloc` failure, ASan actually aborts process-execution; hence, it does not detect the real bug we're after—the double free:

```
$ ./membugs_dbg_asan 10
doublefree(): cond 0
doublefree(): cond 1
==25959==WARNING: AddressSanitizer failed to allocate
0xffffffffffffffff bytes
==25959==AddressSanitizer's allocator is terminating the process
instead of returning 0
==25959==If you don't like this behavior set
allocator_may_return_null=1
==25959==AddressSanitizer CHECK failed: /build/llvm-toolchain-6.0-
QjOn7h/llvm-toolchain-6.0-6.0/projects/compiler-
rt/lib/sanitizer_common/sanitizer_allocator.cc:225 "((0)) != (0)"
(0x0, 0x0)
    #0 0x4e2eb5 in __asan::AsanCheckFailed(char const*, int, char
const*, unsigned long long, unsigned long long)
(<...>/membugs_dbg_asan+0x4e2eb5)
    #1 0x500765 in __sanitizer::CheckFailed(char const*, int, char
const*, unsigned long long, unsigned long long)
(<...>/membugs_dbg_asan+0x500765)
    #2 0x4e92a6 in __sanitizer::ReportAllocatorCannotReturnNull()
(<...>/membugs_dbg_asan+0x4e92a6)
    #3 0x4e92e6 in
__sanitizer::ReturnNullOrDieOnFailure::OnBadRequest()
(<...>/membugs_dbg_asan+0x4e92e6)
    #4 0x424e66 in __asan::asan_malloc(unsigned long,
__sanitizer::BufferedStackTrace*) (<...>/membugs_dbg_asan+0x424e66)
    #5 0x4d9d3b in malloc (<...>/membugs_dbg_asan+0x4d9d3b)
    #6 0x513938 in doublefree <...>/ch5/membugs.c:129:11
    #7 0x5124d2 in process_args <...>/ch5/membugs.c:352:4
    #8 0x512291 in main <...>/ch5/membugs.c:375:2
    #9 0x7f8a7deccb96 in __libc_start_main /build/glibc-
OTsEL5/glibc-2.27/csu/../csu/libc-start.c:310
    #10 0x419ea9 in _start
(/home/seawolf/0tmp/membugs_dbg_asan+0x419ea9)

$
```

Yes, but, notice the preceding line of output that says:

```
[...] If you don't like this behavior set allocator_may_return_null=1
[...]
```

## Debugging Tools for Memory Issues

How do we tell ASan this? An environment variable, ASAN_OPTIONS, makes it possible to pass runtime options; looking them up (recall we have provided the documentation links to the sanitizer toolset), we use it like so (one can pass more than one option simultaneously, separating options with a :; for fun, we also turn on the verbosity option, but trim the output):

```
$ ASAN_OPTIONS=verbosity=1:allocator_may_return_null=1
./membugs_dbg_asan 10
==26026==AddressSanitizer: libc interceptors initialized
[...]
SHADOW_OFFSET: 0x7fff8000
==26026==Installed the sigaction for signal 11
==26026==Installed the sigaction for signal 7
==26026==Installed the sigaction for signal 8
==26026==T0: stack [0x7fffdf206000,0x7fffdfa06000) size 0x800000;
local=0x7fffdfa039a8
==26026==AddressSanitizer Init done
doublefree(): cond 0
doublefree(): cond 1
==26026==WARNING: AddressSanitizer failed to allocate
0xffffffffffffffff bytes
membugs.c:doublefree:132: malloc failed
=================================================================
==26026==ERROR: AddressSanitizer: attempting double-free on
0x615000000300 in thread T0:
    #0 0x4d9b90 in __interceptor_free.localalias.0
(<...>/membugs_dbg_asan+0x4d9b90)
    #1 0x5139b0 in doublefree <...>/membugs.c:133:4
    #2 0x5124d2 in process_args <...>/ch5/membugs.c:352:4
    #3 0x512291 in main <...>/ch5/membugs.c:375:2
    #4 0x7fd41e565b96 in __libc_start_main /build/glibc-
OTsEL5/glibc-2.27/csu/../csu/libc-start.c:310
    #5 0x419ea9 in _start
(/home/seawolf/0tmp/membugs_dbg_asan+0x419ea9)

0x615000000300 is located 0 bytes inside of 512-byte region
[0x615000000300,0x615000000500) freed by thread T0 here:
    #0 0x4d9b90 in __interceptor_free.localalias.0
(<...>/membugs_dbg_asan+0x4d9b90)
    #1 0x51391f in doublefree <...>/ch5/membugs.c:126:2
    #2 0x5124d2 in process_args <...>/ch5/membugs.c:352:4
    #3 0x512291 in main <...>/ch5/membugs.c:375:2
    #4 0x7fd41e565b96 in __libc_start_main /build/glibc-
OTsEL5/glibc-2.27/csu/../csu/libc-start.c:310

previously allocated by thread T0 here:
    #0 0x4d9d60 in malloc (<...>/membugs_dbg_asan+0x4d9d60)
```

```
    #1 0x51389d in doublefree <...>/ch5/membugs.c:122:8
    #2 0x5124d2 in process_args <...>/ch5/membugs.c:352:4
    #3 0x512291 in main <...>/ch5/membugs.c:375:2
    #4 0x7fd41e565b96 in __libc_start_main /build/glibc-
OTsEL5/glibc-2.27/csu/../csu/libc-start.c:310

SUMMARY: AddressSanitizer: double-free
(<...>/membugs_dbg_asan+0x4d9b90) in __interceptor_free.localalias.0
==26026==ABORTING
$
```

This time, ASan continues even though it hits an allocation failure, and thus finds the real bug—the double free.

**Test case #11:** memory leak test case 1—simple leak. Refer to the following code:

```
$ ./membugs_dbg_asan 11
leakage_case1(): will now leak 32 bytes (0 MB)
leakage_case1(): will now leak 1048576 bytes (1 MB)

=================================================================
==26054==ERROR: LeakSanitizer: detected memory leaks

Direct leak of 1048576 byte(s) in 1 object(s) allocated from:
    #0 0x4d9d60 in malloc (<...>/membugs_dbg_asan+0x4d9d60)
    #1 0x513e34 in amleaky <...>/ch5/membugs.c:66:8
    #2 0x513a79 in leakage_case1 <...>/ch5/membugs.c:111:2
    #3 0x5124ef in process_args <...>/ch5/membugs.c:356:4
    #4 0x512291 in main <...>/ch5/membugs.c:375:2
    #5 0x7f2dd5884b96 in __libc_start_main /build/glibc-
OTsEL5/glibc-2.27/csu/../csu/libc-start.c:310

Direct leak of 32 byte(s) in 1 object(s) allocated from:
    #0 0x4d9d60 in malloc (<...>/membugs_dbg_asan+0x4d9d60)
    #1 0x513e34 in amleaky <...>/ch5/membugs.c:66:8
    #2 0x513a79 in leakage_case1 <...>/ch5/membugs.c:111:2
    #3 0x5124e3 in process_args <...>/ch5/membugs.c:355:4
    #4 0x512291 in main <...>/ch5/membugs.c:375:2
    #5 0x7f2dd5884b96 in __libc_start_main /build/glibc-
OTsEL5/glibc-2.27/csu/../csu/libc-start.c:310

SUMMARY: AddressSanitizer: 1048608 byte(s) leaked in 2 allocation(s).
$
```

It does find the leak, and pinpoints it. Also notice that LeakSanitizer (LSan) is effectively a subset of ASan.

# Debugging Tools for Memory Issues

**Test case #13:** memory leak test case 3—libAPI leak

Here is a screenshot showcasing the action when ASan (under the hood, LSan) catches the leak:

```
$ ./membugs_dbg_asan 13

## Leakage test: case 3: "lib" API: runtime cond = 0
mypath = /usr/local/sbin:/usr/local/bin:/usr/sbin:/usr/bin:/sbin:/bin:/usr/games:/usr/local
/games:/snap/bin:/sbin:/usr/sbin:/usr/local/sbin:/home/seawolf/kaiwanTECH/usefulsnips:/usr/
lib/llvm-6.0/bin/

## Leakage test: case 3: "lib" API: runtime cond = 1
mypath = /usr/local/sbin:/usr/local/bin:/usr/sbin:/usr/bin:/sbin:/bin:/usr/games:/usr/local
/games:/snap/bin:/sbin:/usr/sbin:/usr/local/sbin:/home/seawolf/kaiwanTECH/usefulsnips:/usr/
lib/llvm-6.0/bin/

=================================================================
==26220==ERROR: LeakSanitizer: detected memory leaks

Direct leak of 4096 byte(s) in 1 object(s) allocated from:
    #0 0x4d9d60 in malloc (/home/seawolf/0tmp/membugs_dbg_asan+0x4d9d60)
    #1 0x513eca in silly_getpath /home/seawolf/kaiwanTECH/book_src/ch5/membugs.c:37:9
    #2 0x513d0d in leakage_case3 /home/seawolf/kaiwanTECH/book_src/ch5/membugs.c:55:2
    #3 0x512522 in process_args /home/seawolf/kaiwanTECH/book_src/ch5/membugs.c:363:4
    #4 0x512291 in main /home/seawolf/kaiwanTECH/book_src/ch5/membugs.c:375:2
    #5 0x7f5f23247b96 in __libc_start_main /build/glibc-OTsEL5/glibc-2.27/csu/../csu/libc-s
tart.c:310

SUMMARY: AddressSanitizer: 4096 byte(s) leaked in 1 allocation(s).
$
```

Well caught!

## AddressSanitizer (ASan) summary table

With respect to our test cases (incorporated into our `membugs` program), here is ASan's report card:

| Test case # | Test case | Detected by Address Sanitizer? |
|---|---|---|
| 1 | UMR | No[1] |
| 2 | OOB (out-of-bounds): write overflow [on compile-time memory] | Yes |
| 3 | OOB (out-of-bounds): write overflow [on dynamic memory] | Yes |
| 4 | OOB (out-of-bounds): write underflow [on dynamic memory] | Yes |

| 5  | OOB (out-of-bounds): read overflow [on compile-time memory] | Yes |
| 6  | OOB (out-of-bounds): read overflow [on dynamic memory] | Yes |
| 7  | OOB (out-of-bounds): read underflow [on dynamic memory] | Yes |
| 8  | UAF (use-after-free) also known as dangling pointer | Yes |
| 9  | UAR also known as UAS (use-after-scope) | Yes[2] |
| 10 | Double free | Yes |
| 11 | Memory leak test case 1: simple leak | Yes |
| 12 | Memory leak test case 1: leak more (in a loop) | Yes |
| 13 | Memory leak test case 1: lib API leak | Yes |

Table 4: AddressSanitizer and Memory Bugs

[1]The **MemorySanitizer** (**MSan**) fulfills exactly this purpose - it does detect UMR. However, there are two things to notice:

- UMR is detected by MSan only on dynamically allocated memory
- Using MSan successfully necessitates using the Clang compiler (it did not work with GCC)

[2]This works with the caveat that the code is compiled with Clang and the `detect_stack_use_after_return=1` flag is passed via `ASAN_OPTIONS`.

## AddressSanitizer pros and cons – a quick summary

ASan pros:

- Catches common memory bugs (UB) on both statically (compile-time) and dynamically allocated memory regions
    - Out-of-bounds (OOB) memory accesses (read/write underflow/overflow bugs)
    - Use-after-free (UAF) bugs
    - Use-after-return (UAR) bugs
    - Double free
    - Leakage

- Performance is far superior to other tools (such as Valgrind); the worst case performance drop seems to be a factor 2x
- No modification to source code required
- Fully supports multithreaded applications

ASan cons:

- ASan cannot detect some types of bugs:
    - UMR (as mentioned earlier, with some caveats, MSan can)
    - Does not detect all UAF bugs
    - IOF (Integer Underflow/Overflow) bugs
- Using a certain tool at a time; cannot always combine multiple sanitizer tools (see the preceding table); this implies that often, separate test cases must be written for ASan, TSan, LSan
- Compiler:
    - Often, the program is required to be recompiled with the LLVM frontend Clang and appropriate compiler flags.
    - In order to see the call stack with line number information, a recompile/build with the -g flag is required.

Here, we've combined the preceding two tables. Refer to the following table, memory bugs - a quick comparison between Valgrind and Address Sanitizer:

| Test case # | Test case | Detected by Valgrind? | Detected by Address Sanitizer? |
|---|---|---|---|
| 1 | UMR | Yes | No[1] |
| 2 | OOB (out-of-bounds): write overflow [on compile-time memory] | No | Yes |
| 3 | OOB (out-of-bounds): write overflow [on dynamic memory] | Yes | Yes |
| 4 | OOB (out-of-bounds): write underflow [on dynamic memory] | Yes | Yes |
| 5 | OOB (out-of-bounds): read overflow [on compile-time memory] | No | Yes |
| 6 | OOB (out-of-bounds): read overflow [on dynamic memory] | Yes | Yes |
| 7 | OOB (out-of-bounds): read underflow [on dynamic memory] | Yes | Yes |
| 8 | UAF (use-after-free) also known as dangling pointer | Yes | Yes |

| 9 | UAR (use-after-return) also known as UAS (use-after-scope) | No | Yes[2] |
| 10 | Double free | Yes | Yes |
| 11 | Memory leak test case 1: simple leak | Yes | Yes |
| 12 | Memory leak test case 1: leak more (in a loop) | Yes | Yes |
| 13 | Memory leak test case 1: lib API leak | Yes | Yes |

[1]MSan fulfills exactly this purpose—it does detect UMR (also see caveats).

It works with the caveats that the code is compiled with Clang and the `detect_stack_use_after_return=1` flag is passed via `ASAN_OPTIONS`.

# Glibc mallopt

Sometimes useful to programmers, glibc provides a means to change the malloc engine's defaults thanks to its ability to pass some specific parameters. The API is `mallopt(3)`:

```
#include <malloc.h>
int mallopt(int param, int value);
```

> Please refer to the man page on `mallopt(3)` for all the gory details (available at `http://man7.org/linux/man-pages/man3/mallopt.3.html`).

As an interesting example, one of the parameters that can be tweaked is `M_MMAP_THRESHOLD`; recall, in the earlier Chapter 5, *Linux Memory Issues*, we covered the fact that on modern glibc, malloc does not always get memory blocks from the heap segment. If the size of the allocation request is above or equal to `MMAP_THRESHOLD`, the request is serviced under the hood via the powerful `mmap(2)` system call (which sets up an arbitrary region of virtual address space of the size requested). The default value of `MMAP_THRESHOLD` is 128 KB; this can be changed via the `M_MMAP_THRESHOLD` parameter using `mallopt(3)`!

Again, this does not imply you should change it; only that you could. The default value is carefully arrived at and probably best suited to most application workloads.

Another useful parameter is `M_CHECK_ACTION`; this parameter determines how glibc reacts when memory errors are detected (say, a write overflow or a double free). Also note that the implementation does *not* detect all types of memory errors (leakage goes unnoticed, for example).

# Debugging Tools for Memory Issues

At runtime, glibc interprets these three **least significant bits** (**LSB**) of the parameter's value to determine how to react:

- **Bit 0**: If set, print a one-line error message to `stderr` providing detailed information regarding the cause; the error-line format is:

```
*** glibc detected *** <program-name>: <function where error was detected> : <error description> : <address>
```

- **Bit 1**: If set, after printing the error message, `abort(3)` is invoked causing the process to terminate. Depending on the version of the library, the stack trace and the relevant portion of the process memory map (via proc) may also be printed.
- **Bit 2**: If set, and if bit 0 set, simplify the error message format.

From glibc ver. 2.3.4, the `M_CHECK_ACTION` default value is 3 (implying binary 011; earlier it was 1).

> **TIP**
> Setting `M_CHECK_ACTION` to a nonzero value can be very useful as it will cause a buggy process to crash at the point the bug is hit, and display useful diagnostics. If it were zero, the process would probably enter an undefined state (UB) and crash at some arbitrary point in the future, making debugging a lot harder.

As a quick reckoner, here are some useful values for `M_CHECK_ACTION` and their meaning:

- 1 (001b): Print a detailed error message but continue execution (process is now in UB!).
- 3 (011b): Print a detailed error message, call stack, memory mappings, and abort execution [default].
- 5 (101b): Print a simple error message and continue execution (process is now in UB!).
- 7 (111b): Print a simple error message, call stack, memory mappings, and abort execution.

The man page on `mallopt(3)` helpfully provides a C program example of using `M_CHECK_ACTION`.

[ 234 ]

# Malloc options via the environment

A useful feature: instead of programmatically using the `mallopt(3)` API, the system allows us to tune some allocation parameters conveniently via environment variables. Most useful, perhaps, from the viewpoint of debug and testing, the `MALLOC_CHECK_` variable is the environment variable corresponding to the `M_CHECK_ACTION` parameter described earlier; thus, we can just set the value, run our application, and see the result for ourselves!

A few examples follow, using our usual membugs application to check out some test cases:

**Test case # 10:** double free with `MALLOC_CHECK_` set:

```
$ MALLOC_CHECK_=1 ./membugs_dbg 10
doublefree(): cond 0
doublefree(): cond 1
membugs.c:doublefree:134: malloc failed
*** Error in `./membugs_dbg': free(): invalid pointer:
0x00005565f9f6b420 ***
$ MALLOC_CHECK_=3 ./membugs_dbg 10
doublefree(): cond 0
doublefree(): cond 1
membugs.c:doublefree:134: malloc failed
*** Error in `./membugs_dbg': free(): invalid pointer:
0x0000562f5da95420 ***
Aborted
$ MALLOC_CHECK_=5 ./membugs_dbg 10
doublefree(): cond 0
doublefree(): cond 1
membugs.c:doublefree:134: malloc failed
$ MALLOC_CHECK_=7 ./membugs_dbg 10
doublefree(): cond 0
doublefree(): cond 1
membugs.c:doublefree:134: malloc failed
$
```

Notice how, with the value of `MALLOC_CHECK_` being 1, the error message, is printed but the process is not aborted; this is what happens when the value of the environment variable is set to 3.

**Test case # 7:** out-of-bounds (read underflow) with `MALLOC_CHECK_` set:

```
$ MALLOC_CHECK_=3 ./membugs_dbg 7
read_underflow(): cond 0
 dest: abcd56789
```

# Debugging Tools for Memory Issues

```
read_underflow(): cond 1
 dest: xabcd56789
*** Error in `./membugs_dbg': free(): invalid pointer:
0x0000562ce36d9420 ***
Aborted
$
```

**Test case # 11:** memory leak test case 1—simple leak with `MALLOC_CHECK_` set:

```
$ MALLOC_CHECK_=3 ./membugs_dbg 11
leakage_case1(): will now leak 32 bytes (0 MB)
leakage_case1(): will now leak 1048576 bytes (1 MB)
$
```

Notice how a leakage bug test case is not detected.

> The preceding examples were executed on an Ubuntu 17.10 x86_64 box; for some reason, interpretation of `MALLOC_CHECK_` on a Fedora 27 box did not seem to work as advertised.

# Some key points

We've covered some powerful memory debug tools and techniques, but at the end of the day, by itself these tools are not enough. Today's developer must keep alert—there are some remaining key points to mention briefly, which will serve to round off this chapter.

## Code coverage while testing

A key point to remember using dynamic analysis tools (we covered using Valgrind's Memcheck tool and ASan/MSan) is that it only really helps the effort if complete code coverage is achieved when running the tool(s) over the test cases!

This point cannot be stressed enough. What use is running a fantastic tool or compiler instrumentation, such as the Sanitizers, over your program if the buggy part of the code does not actually run! The bugs remain dormant, uncaught. As developers and testers, we have to discipline ourselves to write rigorous test cases that actually perform complete code coverage, such that all code—including project code in libraries—is actually tested via these powerful tools.

This is not easy: remember, anything worth doing is worth doing well.

# What is the modern C/C++ developer to do?

In the face of so much UB potential in complex software projects written on C/C++, the concerned developer might well ask, What are we to do?

> Source: `https://blog.regehr.org/archives/1520`. Here is a snippet from the excellent blog article, Undefined Behavior in 2017, by Cuoq and Regehr.
>
> **What is the modern C or C++ developer to do?**
>
> - Be comfortable with the easy UB tools—the ones that can usually be enabled just by adjusting a makefile, such as compiler warnings and ASan and UBSan. Use these early and often, and (crucially) act upon their findings.
> - Be familiar with the hard UB tools—those such as TIS Interpreter that typically require more effort to run—and use them when appropriate.
> - Invest in broad-based testing (track code coverage, use fuzzers) in order to get maximum benefit out of dynamic UB detection tools.
> - Perform UB-aware code reviews: build a culture where we collectively diagnose potentially dangerous patches and get them fixed before they land.
> - Be knowledgeable about what's actually in the C and C++ standards since these are what compiler writers are going by. Avoid repeating tired maxims such as C is a portable assembly language and trust the programmer.

# A mention of the malloc API helpers

There are plenty of `malloc` API helper routines. These can be useful when debugging a difficult scenario; it's a good idea to be aware of what's available.

## Debugging Tools for Memory Issues

On an Ubuntu Linux system, we check with man for a match to the keyword `malloc`:

```
$ man -k malloc
__after_morecore_hook (3) - malloc debugging variables
__free_hook (3)         - malloc debugging variables
__malloc_hook (3)       - malloc debugging variables
__malloc_initialize_hook (3) - malloc debugging variables
__memalign_hook (3)     - malloc debugging variables
__realloc_hook (3)      - malloc debugging variables
malloc (3)              - allocate and free dynamic memory
malloc_get_state (3)    - record and restore state of malloc
implementation
malloc_hook (3)         - malloc debugging variables
malloc_info (3)         - export malloc state to a stream
malloc_set_state (3)    - record and restore state of malloc
implementation
malloc_stats (3)        - print memory allocation statistics
malloc_trim (3)         - release free memory from the top of the heap
malloc_usable_size (3)  - obtain size of block of memory allocated from
heap
mtrace (1)              - interpret the malloc trace log
mtrace (3)              - malloc tracing
muntrace (3)            - malloc tracing
$
```

Quite a few of these `malloc` APIs (reminder: the number three within parentheses,(3), implies it's a library routine) deal with the concept of malloc hooks. The essential idea: one can replace the library `malloc(3)`, `realloc(3)`, `memalign(3)` and `free(3)` APIs with one's own `hook` function, which will be invoked when the application calls the API.

However, we will not be delving further into this area; why not? Recent versions of glibc document the fact that these hook functions are:

- Not MT-Safe (covered in Chapter 16, *Multithreading with Pthreads Part III*)
- Deprecated from glibc ver. 2.24 onward

Finally, it might be obvious, but we would prefer to call this out explicitly: one must realize that using these tools serves a purpose only in testing environments; they are not meant to be used in production! Some studies have revealed security vulnerabilities that can be exploited when running ASan in production; see the *Further reading* section on the GitHub repository.

# Summary

In this chapter, we have attempted to show the reader several key points, tools and techniques; among them:

- Humans will make mistakes; this is especially true with memory unmanaged languages (C, C++).
- There is a real need for powerful memory debug tools on nontrivial codebases.
- We covered two of these best in class dynamic analysis tools in detail:
  - Valgrind's Memcheck
  - Sanitizers (primarily ASan)
- Glibc allows some tuning of malloc via the `mallopt(3)` API, as well as via environment variables.
- Ensuring complete code coverage when building test cases is absolutely crucial to the success of a project.

> The next chapter is related to the essentials aspects of file I/O which is essential for a component reader to know. It introduces you to performing efficient file I/O on the Linux platform. We would request the readers to go through this chapter which is available here: https://www.packtpub.com/sites/default/files/downloads/File_IO_Essentials.pdf. We highly recoomend the readers to read Open at the system call layer, The file descriptor and I/O – the read/write system calls which can help in easy understanding the next chapter that is, `Chapter 7`, *Process Credentials*.

# Process Credentials

In this chapter, and the following one, the reader will learn concepts and practices regarding process credentials and capabilities. Besides being of practical importance to application development in Linux, this chapter, by its very nature, delves deeper into an often overlooked but extremely key aspect: security. The content of this and the following chapter is very much inter-related.

We divide the coverage of this key area into two major parts, each of which is a chapter in this book:

- In this chapter, the traditional-style Unix permissions model is discussed in some detail, and techniques to run programs with root privileges without requiring the root password are shown.
- In `Chapter 8`, *Process Capabilities*, the modern approach, the POSIX capabilities model, is discussed in some detail.

We will attempt to clearly show the reader that, while it is important to learn about the traditional mechanisms and how they operate, it is also important to learn about modern approaches to security. However you look at it, security is of paramount importance, especially these days. The advent of Linux running on all sorts of devices—from tiny IoT and embedded devices to mobile devices, desktops, servers, and super-computing platforms—makes security a key concern for all stakeholders. Hence, the modern capabilities approach should be used when developing software.

In this chapter, we will broadly cover the traditional Unix permissions model, what exactly it is, and how it works to provide security and robustness. A bit of hacking is always fun too!

You will learn about the following:

- The Unix permission model in action
- Real and effective IDs
- Powerful system calls to query and set process credentials

- Hacking attempts (a little bit)
- How `sudo(8)` actually works
- Saved-set IDs
- Important thoughts on security

Along the way, several examples allow you to try out concepts in a hands-on way, to really understand them.

# The traditional Unix permissions model

Right from the early 1970, the Unix OS had, as usual, an elegant and powerful system in place for managing the security of shared objects on the system. These objects included files and directories—perhaps the most commonly thought of ones. Files, directories, and symbolic links are filesystem objects; there are several others, including memory objects (tasks, pipes, shared memory regions, message queues, semaphores, keys, sockets) and pseudo filesystems (proc, sysfs, debugfs, cgroupfs, and so on) and their objects. The point is all these objects are shared in some manner or other, and thus they require a protection mechanism of some sort, to protect them from abuse; this mechanism is called the Unix permission model.

You probably don't want others to read, write, and delete your files; the Unix permission model makes this possible at various granularity levels; again, taking files and directories as a common target, you can set permissions at the level of a directory, or indeed on each file (and directory) within that directory.

To make this clear, let's consider a typical shared object—a file on a disk. Let's create one called `myfile`:

```
$ cat > myfile
This is my file.
It has a few lines of not
terribly exciting content.

A blank line too! WOW.

You get it...
Ok fine, a useful line: we shall keep this file in the book's git
repo.
Bye.
$ ls -l myfile
-rw-rw-r-- 1 seawolf seawolf 186 Feb 17 13:15 myfile
$
```

All output displayed is from an Ubuntu 17.10 x86_64 Linux system; the user is logged in as `seawolf`.

## Permissions at the user level

Earlier we did a quick `ls -l` on the previous `myfile` file; the very first character `-` reveals, of course, that it's a regular file; the next nine characters `rw-rw-r--` are the file permissions. If you remember, these are grouped into three groups—the **Owner** (U), **Group** (G), and **Others** (O) (or Public) permissions, each of which contains three permission bits: **r**, **w**, and **x** (read, write and execute access). This table summarizes this information:

| Access Category | Owner (U) |   |   | Group (G) |   |   | Others (O) |   |   |
|---|---|---|---|---|---|---|---|---|---|
| Permission Bits | r | w | x | r | w | x | r | w | x |
| Example (myfile) | 1 | 1 | 0 | 1 | 1 | 0 | 1 | 0 | 0 |

Interpreting it, we can see that the owner of the file can read and write to it, and so can the group members, but others (those who are not the owner and do not belong to the group the file belongs to) can only perform a read operation on `myfile`. That's security!

So, let's take an example: we attempt to write to the file `myfile`, using the `echo` command:

```
echo "I can append this string" >> myfile
```

Will it work? Well, the answer is, it depends: if the owner or group member of the file (in this example, seawolf) is running the echo(1) process, then the access category will be accordingly set to U or G, and, yes, it will succeed (as U|G does have write access to the file). But if the process's access category is Others or Public, it will fail.

## How the Unix permission model works

A really important point to understand regarding this topic is this: both the shared object that is being worked upon (here, the `myfile` file) and the process that is performing some access (rwx) on the object (here, the echo process) matter. To be more correct, their attributes with respect to permissions matter. The next discussion will help make this clear.

*Process Credentials*

Let's consider this step by step:

1. A user with the login name `seawolf` logs in to the system.
2. On success, the system spawns a shell; the user is now at the shell prompt. (Here, we consider the traditional case of logging into a **command-line interface** (**CLI**) console, not a GUI environment.)

Every user has a record; it's stored in the `/etc/passwd` file. Let's `grep` the file for this user:

```
$ grep seawolf /etc/passwd
seawolf:x:1000:1000:Seawolf,,,:/home/seawolf:/bin/bash
$
```

Generically, just do this: `grep $LOGNAME /etc/passwd`

The `passwd` entry is a row with seven columns that are colon-delimited fields; they are as follows:

```
username:<passwd>:UID:GID:descriptive_name:home_dir:program
```

A few fields require some explanation:

- The second field, `<passwd>`, always shows up as just `x` on modern Linux systems; this is for security. Even the encrypted password is never displayed (hackers can very possibly break it via a brute-force algorithm; it's in a root-only file called `/etc/shadow`).
- The third and fourth fields are the **User IDentifier** (**UID**) and **Group IDentifier** (**GID**) of the user.
- The seventh field is the program to run on successful login; it's usually the shell (as preceding), but it could be anything.

> To programmatically query `/etc/passwd`, check out the `getpwnam[_r](3)`, `getpwent[_r](3)` library layer APIs.

The last point is a key one: the system spawns a shell for the user who logged in. A shell is the **user interface** (UI) between the human user and the system on the CLI environment. After all, it's a process; on Linux, bash is usually the shell we use. The shell you receive when you login is called your login shell. It's important, because its privileges determine the privileges of all processes it launches—in effect, the privileges you have when working on the system are derived from your login shell.

Let's look up our shell process:

```
$ ps
  PID TTY          TIME CMD
13833 pts/5    00:00:00 bash
30500 pts/5    00:00:00 ps
$
```

There it is; our bash process has a **Process Identifier** (PID—a unique integer identifying a process) of 13833. Now, the process has other attributes associated with it; for our current purposes, the key ones are the process **User Identifier** (**UID**) and the process **Group Identifier** (**GID**).

Can one lookup these UID, GID values for a process? Let's try it out with the `id(1)` command:

```
$ id
uid=1000(seawolf) gid=1000(seawolf)
groups=1000(seawolf),4(adm),24(cdrom),27(sudo),[...]
$
```

The `id(1)` command shows us that the process UID is 1000 and the process GID also happens to be 1000. (The username is `seawolf` and this user belongs to several groups.) In the previous example, we have logged in as the user `seawolf`; this fact is reflected by the `id` command. Note that every process we now run from this shell will inherit the privileges of this user account, that is, it will run with the same UID and GID as the login shell!

You might reasonably ask: where does the process get its UID and GID values from? Well, think about it: we logged in as the user `seawolf`, and this account's `/etc/passwd` entry's third and fourth fields are where the process UID and GID come from.

So, every time we run a process from this shell, that process will run with UID 1000 and GID 1000.

We want to understand how exactly the OS checks whether we can perform an operation such as the following:

```
echo "I can append this string" >> myfile
```

So, the key question here is: how exactly, at runtime, when the preceding echo process is attempting to write to the `myfile` file, does the kernel determine whether the write access is allowed. To do this, the OS must determine the following:

- What is the ownership and group membership of the file in question?
- In what access category is the process attempting the access running under (for example, is it U|G|O)?
- For that access category, does the permission bitmask allow access?

To answer the first question: the file's ownership and group membership information (and a lot more regarding the file) is carried as attributes of the key data structure of the filesystem—the **information node (inode)**. The inode data structure is a per-file structure and lives within the kernel (filesystem; it's read into memory when the file is first accessed). User space can of course access this information via system calls. So, the file owner ID is stored in the inode—let's just call it `file_UID`. Similarly, the `file_GID` will also be present in the inode object.

> **TIP**: For the curious reader: you can yourself query any file object's inode by using the powerful `stat(2)` system call. (As usual, look up its man page). In fact, we have used `stat(2)` in Appendix A, *File I/O Essentials*.

## Determining the access category

The second question posed previously: what access category will it run under? is important to answer.

The access category will be either **Owner (U)**, **Group (G)**, or **Other (O)**; they are mutually exclusive. The algorithm used by the OS to determine the access category is something like this:

```
if process_UID == file_UID
then
     access_category = U
else if process_GID == file_GID
then
     access_category = G
else
     access_category = O
fi
```

Actually, it's a bit more complex: a process can belong to several groups simultaneously. So, at permission checking time, the kernel checks all groups; if the process belongs to any one of them, the access category is set to G.

Finally, for that access category, check the permission bitmask (rwx); if the relevant bit is set, the process will be allowed the operation; if not, it won't be.

Let's take a look at the following command:

```
$ ls -l myfile
-rw-rw-r-- 1 seawolf seawolf 186 Feb 17 13:15 myfile
$
```

Another way to clarify—the stat(1) command (which of course is a wrapper over the stat(2) system call) show us the inode content of the file myfile, like this:

```
$ stat myfile
  File: myfile
  Size: 186         Blocks: 8         IO Block: 4096   regular file
Device: 801h/2049d  Inode: 1182119    Links: 1
Access: (0664/-rw-rw-r--)  Uid: ( 1000/ seawolf)   Gid: ( 1000/ seawolf)
Access: 2018-02-17 13:15:52.818556856 +0530
Modify: 2018-02-17 13:15:52.818556856 +0530
Change: 2018-02-17 13:15:52.974558288 +0530
 Birth: -
$
```

Clearly, we are highlighting the file_UID == 1000 and file_GID == 1000.

In our echo example, we find that a few scenarios can play out, depending on who logs in, the group membership(s), and the file's permissions.

So, to understand this properly, let's plant a few scenarios (from now on, we shall just refer to the process UID as the UID and the process GID value as the GID, as opposed to process_UID|GID):

- **User logs in as seawolf**: [UID 1000, GID 1000]
- **User logs in as mewolf**: [UID 2000, GID 1000]
- **User logs in as cato**: [UID 3000, GID 3000]
- **User logs in as groupy**: [UID 4000, GID 3000, GID 2000, GID 1000]

Once logged in, the user attempts this:

```
echo "I can append this string" >> <path/to/>myfile
```

What happens? Which will work (permission allowed) and which won't? Run through the previous scenarios with the previous algorithm, to determine the crucial access category, and you will see; the following table summarizes the cases:

| Case # | Login as | (Process) UID | (Process) GID | Access category (U\|G\|O) | Perm bitmask | Write allowed? |
|---|---|---|---|---|---|---|
| 1 | seawolf | 1000 | 1000 | U | r**w**- | Y |
| 2 | mewolf | 2000 | 1000 | G | r**w**- | Y |
| 3 | cato | 3000 | 3000 | O | r-- | N |
| 4 | groupy | 4000 | 4000,3000, 2000,1000 | G | r**w**- | Y |

The preceding description is still a bit too simplistic, but is a good starting point. In reality, there's a lot more happening under the hood; the following sections shed light on this.

Prior to this, we will take a slight detour: the `chmod(1)` command (which of course becomes the `chmod(2)` system call) is used to set permissions on an object. So, if we do this: `chmod g-w myfile` to remove write permissions from the group category, then the previous table will change (the rows that get G access will now not be allowed to write).

> Here is an interesting observation: processes with the craved-for root access are those that have their `UID = 0`; it's a special value!
>
> Next, to be pedantic, actually the echo command can run in two distinct ways: one, as a process when the binary executable (usually `/bin/echo`) runs, and two, as a built in shell command; in other words, there is no new process, the shell process itself—typically `bash`—runs it.

## Real and effective IDs

We understand from the preceding section that both the shared object that is being worked upon (here, the file myfile) and the process that is performing some access (rwx) on the object (here, the echo process) matter in terms of permissions.

Let's zoom deeper into the process attributes with respect to the permissions model. So far, we have learned that each process is associated with a UID and a GID, thereby allowing the kernel to run its internal algorithms and determine whether access to a resource (or object) should be allowed.

If we look deeper, we find that each process UID is actually not a single integer value, but two values:

- The **Real User ID (RUID)**
- The **Effective User ID (EUID)**

Similarly, the group information is not one integer GID value, rather it's two integers:

- The **Real Group ID (RGID)**
- The **Effective Group ID (EGID)**

So, with respect to privileges, each process has four integer values associated with it: {RUID, EUID, RGID, EGID}; these are called the **process credentials**.

> Pedantically speaking, process credentials also encompass several other process attributes—the process PID, the PPID, PGID, session ID, and the real and effective user and group IDs. In our discussions, for clarity, we restrict their meaning to the last of these—real and effective user and group IDs.

But what exactly do they mean?

Every process has to run under the ownership and group membership of somebody; this somebody is of course the user and group IDs of the person who logs in.

The real IDs are the original values associated with the user who logged in; in effect, they are nothing but the UID:GID pair from the /etc/passwd record for that user. Recall that the id(1) command reveals precisely this information:

```
$ id
uid=1000(seawolf) gid=1000(seawolf) groups=1000(seawolf),4(adm), [...]
$
```

The uid and gid values displayed are obtained from the /etc/passwd record for seawolf. In reality, the uid/gid values become the running process's RUID/RGID values respectively!

[ 249 ]

*Process Credentials*

The real numbers reflect who you originally are—your login account information in the form of integer identifiers. Another way to put it: the real numbers reflect who owns the process.

What about the effective values?

The effective values are to inform the OS as to effectively (at this moment) what privileges (user and group) the process is running under. Here are a couple of key points:

- When performing permission checks, the OS uses the process's effective values, not the real (original) values.
- `EUID = 0` is what the OS actually checks for to determine whether the process has root privilege.

By default it is as follows:

- The EUID = RUID
- The EGID = RGID

This implies that, for the preceding example, the following is true:

```
{RUID, EUID, RGID, EGID} = {1000, 1000, 1000, 1000}
```

Yes. This brings up a question (don't you think?): if the real and effective IDs are the same, then why do we require four numbers at all? Two will do, right?

Well, here's the thing: they usually (by default) are the same, but they can change. Let's see how this can happen.

> Again, here is a pedantic note: on Linux, the permission checking on filesystem operations is predicated on yet another process credential—the filesystem UID (or fsuid; and, analogously, the fsgid). However, it's always the case that the fsuid/fsgid pair shadow the EUID/EGID pair of credentials—thereby, effectively rendering them the same. That's why in our discussion we ignore the `fs[u|g]id` and focus on the usual real and effective user and group IDs.

Before that, though, think about this scenario: a user is logged in, and is on the shell; what are their privileges? Well, just run the `id(1)` program; the output will display the UID and GID, which we now know is actually {RUID, EUID} and the {RGID, EGID} pair with the same values.

For the sake of an easier-to-read example, let's take the liberty of changing the GID value from 1000, to, say, 2000. So, now, if the values are UID=1000 and GID=2000, and the user now runs, shall we say, the vi editor, now the situation is like this, refer to the given table, process credentials - normal case:

| Process credentials / process | RUID | EUID | RGID | EGID |
|---|---|---|---|---|
| bash | 1000 | 1000 | 2000 | 2000 |
| vi | 1000 | 1000 | 2000 | 2000 |

## A puzzle – how can a regular user change their password?

Let's say you're logged in as `seawolf`. For security reasons, you want to update your weak password (`hello123`, whoops!) to a strong secure one. We know that the password is stored in the `/etc/passwd` file. Well, we also saw that on modern Unixes (including Linux of course), for better security it's *shadowed*: it's actually stored in a file called `/etc/shadow`. Let's check it out:

```
$ ls -l /etc/shadow
-rw-r----- 1 root shadow 891 Jun  1  2017 /etc/shadow
$
```

(Remember that we're on an Ubuntu 17.10 x86_64 system; we often point this out, as the exact output might vary on different distributions, and if kernel security mechanisms, such as SELinux, are installed.)

As highlighted, you can see that the file owner is root, the group membership is shadow, and the permission bitmask for UGO is `[rw-][r--][---]`. This means the following:

- The owner (root) can perform read/write operations
- The group (shadow) can perform read-only operations
- The others cannot do anything to the file

You probably also know that the utility you use to change your password is called `passwd(1)` (of course, it's a binary executable program, and is not to be confused with the `/etc/passwd(5)` database).

[ 251 ]

*Process Credentials*

So, think about it, we have a bit of a puzzle here: to change your password, you need write access to `/etc/shadow`, but, clearly, only root has write access to `/etc/shadow`. So, how does it work? (We know it works. You logged in as a regular user, not root. You can change your password using the `passwd(1)` utility—try it out and see.) So, that's a good question.

The clue lies in the binary executable utility itself—`passwd`. Let's check it out; firstly, where's the utility on disk? Refer to the following code:

```
$ which passwd
/usr/bin/passwd
$
```

Let's dig deeper—quote the preceding command and long list it:

```
$ ls -l $(which passwd)
-rwsr-xr-x 1 root root 54224 Aug 21 05:26 /usr/bin/passwd*
$
```

Can you spot anything unusual?

It's the owner execute bit: it's not an `x` as you might expect, but an `s` ! (Really, this is the reason behind the pretty red coloring of the executable name in preceding the long listing.)

It's a special permission bit: for a binary executable file, when there's an `s` in the owner's execute bit, it's referred to as a setuid binary. This means whenever a setuid program is executed, the resultant process's **Effective Userid** (**EUID**) changes (from the default: the original RUID value) to become equal to the owner of the binary executable file; in the previous example, the EUID will become root (as the `/usr/bin/passwd` file is owned by root).

Now we redraw the previous table (Process Credentials - Normal Case) with this new information in hand, with respect to the setuid passwd executable:

| Process credentials / process | RUID | EUID | RGID | EGID |
|---|---|---|---|---|
| bash | 1000 | 1000 | 2000 | 2000 |
| vi | 1000 | 1000 | 2000 | 2000 |
| /usr/bin/passwd | 1000 | 0 | 2000 | 2000 |

Table: process credentials - setuid-root case (third row)

So, this answers how it works: the EUID being the special value 0 (root), the OS now sees the process as being a root process and allows it to write into the /etc/shadow database.

A program such as /usr/bin/passwd, inherits root access by virtue of the setuid bit and the fact that the file owner is root: these kinds of programs are called setuid root binaries (they're also called set-user-ID-root programs).

To quote a frustrated developer's reaction to testers everywhere: *it's not a bug; it's a feature!* Well, it is: the setuid feature is pretty amazing: with no programming whatsoever, you are able to raise the privilege level of a process for a temporary duration.

Think about this. Without this feature, it would be impossible for non-root users (the majority) to change their password. Requesting the system administrator to do this (picture a large organization with a few thousand employees with Linux accounts) would not only have the sysadcontemplate suicide, you would have to provide the sysad with your new password, perhaps not exactly a brilliant security practice.

## The setuid and setgid special permission bits

We can see that setuid program binaries are an important takeaway from the preceding discussion; let's summarize it once more:

- A binary executable file with the owner execute bit set to s is called a **setuid binary**.
- If the owner of said executable file is root, then it's called a **setuid-root binary**.
- When you execute a setuid program, the key point is that the EUID is set to the owner of the binary executable file:
    - Thus, with setuid-root binaries, the process will run as root!
- Of course, once the process dies, you are back to your shell with your regular (default) set of process credentials or privileges.

*Process Credentials*

Conceptually similar to setuid is the notion of the setgid special permission bit:

- A binary executable file with the group execute bit set to `s` is called a setgid binary.
- When you execute a setgid program, the key point is that the EGID is set to the group membership of the binary executable file.
- Of course, once the process dies, you are back to your shell with your regular (default) set of process credentials or privileges.

As mentioned, remember that the `set[u|g]id` special permission bits only have significance on binary executable files, nothing else. For example, attempting to set these bits on a script (bash, Perl, and so on) will have absolutely no effect.

## Setting the setuid and setgid bits with chmod

You have perhaps, by now, thought okay, but how exactly do I set these special permission bits?

This is simple: you use the `chmod(1)` command (or system call); this table shows how chmod can be used to set the `setuid/setgid` permission bits:

| chmod via: | Notation for setuid | Notation for setgid |
|---|---|---|
| symbolic notation | `u+s` | `g+s` |
| octal notation | `4<octal #> (eg. 4755)` | `2<octal #> (eg. 2755)` |

As a trivial example, take a simple `Hello, world` C program and compile it:

```
gcc hello.c -o hello
```

Now we set the setuid bit, then remove it, and set the setgid bit instead (in one operation: via the `u-s,g+s` parameter to chmod), then remove the setgid bit, all the while long-listing the binary executable so that the permissions can be seen:

```
$ ls -l hello
-rwxrwxr-x 1 seawolf seawolf 8336 Feb 17 19:02 hello
$ chmod u+s hello ; ls -l hello
-rwsrwxr-x 1 seawolf seawolf 8336 Feb 17 19:02 hello
$ chmod u-s,g+s hello ; ls -l hello
-rwxrwsr-x 1 seawolf seawolf 8336 Feb 17 19:02 hello
$ chmod g-s hello ; ls -l hello
-rwxrwxr-x 1 seawolf seawolf 8336 Feb 17 19:02 hello
$
```

(As this `Hello, world` program just trivially prints to stdout and nothing more, the setuid/setgid bits have no perceived effect.)

## Hacking attempt 1

Well, well, wasn't that discussion on setuid root interesting! For you, the reader, who's thinking like a hacker (good for you!), why not do this to gain the ultimate prize, a root shell!

- Write a C program to spawn a shell (the `system(3)` library API makes this trivial); we call the code `rootsh_hack1.c`. We want a root shell as the outcome!
- Compile it, get `a.out`. If we run `a.out` now, no big deal; we'll get a shell with the same privileges that we already have. So instead try this:
  - Change permissions with `chmod(1)` to set the `setuid` bit.
  - Change ownership with `chown(1)` of `a.out` to root.
  - Run it: we should now get a root shell.

Wow! Let's try this out!

The code is simple (we don't show the header inclusion here):

```
$ cat rootsh_hack1.c
[...]
int main(int argc, char **argv)
{
    /* Just spawn a shell.
     * If this process runs as root,
     * then, <i>Evil Laugh</i>, we're now root!
     */
    system("/bin/bash");
    exit (EXIT_SUCCESS);
}
```

Now compile and run:

```
$ gcc rootsh_hack1.c -Wall
$ ls -l a.out
-rwxrwxr-x 1 seawolf seawolf 8344 Feb 20 10:15 a.out
$ ./a.out
seawolf@seawolf-mindev:~/book_src/ch7$ id -u
1000
seawolf@seawolf-mindev:~/book_src/ch7$ exit
exit
$
```

[ 255 ]

As expected, when run with no special set[u|g]id permission bits, the a.out process runs with normal privileges, spawning a shell under the same ownership (seawolf)—exactly what the id -u command proves.

Now, we attempt our hack:

```
$ chmod u+s a.out
$ ls -l a.out
-rwsrwxr-x 1 seawolf seawolf 8344 Feb 20 10:15 a.out
$
```

It worked! Well, don't get too excited: we got it to become a setuid binary, but the owner is still seawolf; so it won't make any difference at runtime: the process EUID will become that of the owner of the binary executable—seawolf itself:

```
$ ./a.out
seawolf@seawolf-mindev:~/book_src/ch7$ id -u
1000
seawolf@seawolf-mindev:~/book_src/ch7$ exit
exit
$
```

Hmm. Yes, so what we need to do now is make the owner root:

```
$ chown root a.out
chown: changing ownership of 'a.out': Operation not permitted
$
```

Sorry to burst your bubble, budding hacker: it won't work. This is the security; with chown(1), you can only change ownership of the files (or objects) you own, and, guess what? To your own account only! Only root can use chown to set an object's ownership to anyone else.

This makes sense security-wise. It goes even further; watch this: we'll become root and run chown (by just sudoing it of course):

```
$ sudo chown root a.out
[sudo] password for seawolf: xxx
$ ls -l a.out
-rwxrwxr-x 1 root seawolf 8344 Feb 20 10:15 a.out*
$
```

Did you notice? Even though the chown succeeded, the setuid bit got wiped out! That's security.

[ 256 ]

Okay, let's subvert even that by setting the setuid bit manually on the root-owned a.out (note that this isn't even possible unless we already have root access or the password):

```
$ sudo chmod u+s a.out
$ ls -l a.out
-rwsrwxr-x 1 root seawolf 8344 Feb 20 10:15 a.out
$
```

Ah! Now it is a setuid-root binary executable (indeed, you can't see it here but the color of a.out changed to red). No one's going to stop us! Take a look at this:

```
$ ./a.out
seawolf@seawolf-mindev:~/book_src/ch7$ id -u
1000
seawolf@seawolf-mindev:~/book_src/ch7$ exit
exit
$
```

The spawned shell has a (R)UID of 1000, not 0 What happened?

That's a surprise! Even with root ownership and the setuid bit we do not get a root shell. How come? Because of the security, of course: when run via system(3), modern versions of bash refuse to run as root on startup. This screenshot shows the relevant part of the man page on system(3)—showing the caveat that we're discussing (http://man7.org/linux/man-pages/man3/system.3.html):

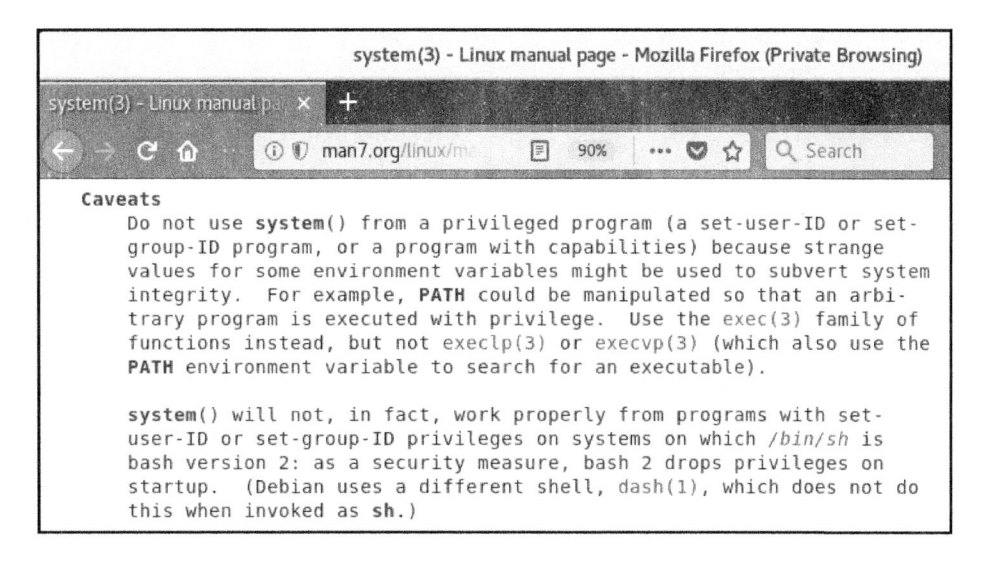

[ 257 ]

The second paragraph sums it up:

> ... as a security measure, bash 2 drops privileges on startup.

## System calls

We understand from our previous discussions that every process alive has a set of four integer values that effectively determine its privileges, the real and effective user and group IDs; they are called the process credentials.

As mentioned earlier, we refer to them as the {RUID, **EUID**, RGID, **EGID**}.

The effective IDs are in bold font, to reiterate the fact that while the real IDs identify the original owner and group, when it comes to actually checking permissions, the kernel uses the effective IDs.

Where are the process credentials stored? The OS keeps this information as part of a rather large process attributes data structure (which is per-process of course); it is in kernel memory space.

> On Unix, this per-process data structure is called the **Process Control Block** (**PCB**); on Linux, it's called the process descriptor or, simply, the task structure.

The point is this: if the data is in kernel address space, the only way to get at it (query or set) is via system calls, of course.

## Querying the process credentials

How do you programmatically (in a C program) query the real and effective UIDs /GIDs? Here are the system calls to do so:

```
#include <unistd.h>
#include <sys/types.h>

uid_t getuid(void);
uid_t geteuid(void);

gid_t getgid(void);
gid_t getegid(void);
```

This is pretty straightforward:

- `getuid(2)` returns the real UID; `geteuid(2)` returns the effective UID
- `getgid(2)` returns the real GID; `getegid(2)` returns the effective GID
- `uid_t` and `gid_t` are glibc typedefs for an unsigned integer

> **TIP**
>
> Here is a neat tip to figure out the typedef for any given data type: you will need to know the header file that contains the definition. Just do this:
>
> ```
> $ echo | gcc -E -xc -include 'sys/types.h' - | grep uid_t
> typedef unsigned int __uid_t;
> typedef __uid_t uid_t;
> $
> ```
>
> Credit: https://stackoverflow.com/questions/2550774/what-is-size-t-in-c.

A question comes up: the preceding system calls do not take any parameters; they return the real or effective [U|G]IDs, yes, but for which process? The answer, of course, is the calling process, the process that issues the system calls.

## Code example

We write a simple C program (`ch7/query_creds.c`); when run, it prints to stdout its process credentials (we show the relevant code):

```
#define SHOW_CREDS() do {                   \
  printf("RUID=%d EUID=%d\n"                \
         "RGID=%d EGID=%d\n",               \
         getuid(), geteuid(),               \
         getgid(), getegid());              \
} while (0)

int main(int argc, char **argv)
{
    SHOW_CREDS();
    if (geteuid() == 0) {
        printf("%s now effectively running as root! ...\n", argv[0]);
        sleep(1);
    }
    exit (EXIT_SUCCESS);
}
```

Build it and try it out:

```
$ ./query_creds
RUID=1000 EUID=1000
RGID=1000 EGID=1000
$ sudo ./query_creds
[sudo] password for seawolf: xxx
RUID=0 EUID=0
RGID=0 EGID=0
./query_creds now effectively running as root! ...
$
```

Note the following:

- On the first run, the four process credential values are the usual ones (1000, in our example). Also, note how by default the EUID = RUID and the EGID = RGID.
- But on the second run we sudo it: once we get the password right, the process runs as root, which of course can be literally seen here: the four process credential values are now all zeros reflecting root authority.

## Sudo – how it works

The sudo(8) utility lets you run a program as another user; without further qualification, that other user is root. Of course, for security, you must correctly enter the root password (or as several distributions allow for desktop computing, the user's own password, if he belongs to a group called sudo).

This brings up a very interesting point: how exactly does the can-do-anything sudo(8) program work? It's simpler than you think! Refer to the following code:

```
$ which sudo
/usr/bin/sudo
$ ls -l $(which sudo)
-rwsr-xr-x 1 root root 145040 Jun 13  2017 /usr/bin/sudo
$
```

We note that the binary executable sudo is really a setuid-root program! So think about it: whenever you run a program with sudo, the sudo process runs with a root privilege straight away—no password, no fuss. But, of course, for security, the user must enter the password; once they enter it correctly, sudo continues execution and executes the command you want it to—as root. If the user fails to enter the password correctly (within three attempts typically), sudo aborts execution.

## What is a saved-set ID?

The so-called saved-set IDs are a convenience feature; the OS is able to save the process's initial effective user id (EUID) value. How does it help? This allows us to switch from the original EUID value the process starts with to, say, an unprivileged normal value (we'll cover how exactly in a moment), and then from the current privileged state back to that saved EUID value (via the `seteuid(2)` system call); thus, the initially saved EUID is called the **saved-set ID**.

In effect, we can on demand switch back and forth between a privileged and unprivileged state for our process!

After we cover a bit more material, an example will help make things clear.

## Setting the process credentials

We know that, from the shell, a convenient way of looking up who we are currently running as is to run the simple `id(1)` command; it displays the real UID and real GID (as well as all supplementary groups we belong to). As we have done earlier, let's try it out while logged in as the user `seawolf`:

```
$ id
uid=1000(seawolf) gid=1000(seawolf)
groups=1000(seawolf),4(adm),24(cdrom),27(sudo), [...]
$
```

Consider again the `sudo(8)` utility; to run a program as another user, not as root, we can use the `-u` or `--user=` switch to `sudo`. For example, let's run the `id(1)` program as the user `mail`:

```
$ sudo -u mail id
[sudo] password for seawolf: xxx
uid=8(mail) gid=8(mail) groups=8(mail)
$
```

As expected, once we provide the correct password, `sudo` runs the `id` program as the mail user, and the output of id now shows us that the (real) user and group IDs are now that of the mail user account! (not seawolf), precisely the effect expected.

But how did `sudo(8)` do this? We understood from the previous section that, when you run sudo (with whatever parameters), it, initially at least, always runs as root. Now the question is, how does it run with the credentials of another user account?

*Process Credentials*

The answer: several system calls exist that let you change the process privileges (the RUID, EUID, RGID, EGID): `setuid(2), seteuid(2), setreuid(2), setresuid(2)` and all their analogs for the GID.

Let's take a quick look at the API signatures:

```
#include <sys/types.h>
#include <unistd.h>

int setuid(uid_t uid);
int setgid(gid_t gid);

int seteuid(uid_t euid);
int setegid(gid_t egid);

int setreuid(uid_t ruid, uid_t euid);
int setregid(gid_t rgid, gid_t egid);
```

The `setuid(2)` system call allows a process to set its EUID to the value passed. If the process has root privileges (later in the next chapter, we shall qualify statements such as this a lot better, when we learn about the POSIX capabilities model), then the RUID and saved-setuid (explained shortly) are also set to this value.

All the `set*gid()` calls are analogous to their UID counterparts.

> On the Linux OS, the seteuid and setegid APIs, though documented as system calls, are actually wrappers over the `setreuid(2)` and `setregid(2)` system calls.

## Hacking attempt 2

Ah, hacking! Well, let's at least attempt to.

We know that EUID 0 is a special value—it means we have root privilege. Think about it—we have a setuid(2) system call. So, even if we're unprivileged, why not just do a quick

`setuid(0);` become privileged, and hack away as root!

Hmm, Linux wouldn't be a very powerful and popular OS if the above hack were to actually work. It won't work, folks: the above system call invocation would fail returning -1; `errno` would be set to `EPERM` and the error message (from `perror(3)` or `strerror(3)`) would be this: Operation not permitted.

Why is this? There's a simple rule within the kernel: an unprivileged process can set its effective IDs to its real IDs—no other value is allowed. In other words, an unprivileged process can set the following:

- Its EUID to its RUID
- Its EGID to its RGID

That's it.

Of course, a (root) privileged process can set its four credentials to any value it chooses. There is no surprise there—this is part and parcel of the power of being root.

> The `seteuid(2)` sets the process effective userid to the value passed; for an unprivileged process, it can only set its EUID to its RUID, the EUID, or the saved setuid.
>
> The `setreuid(2)` sets the real and effective UIDs to the values passed respectively; if -1 is passed, the corresponding value is left untouched. (This can indirectly affect the saved-set value.) The `set[r]egid(2)` calls are identical with respect to the group IDs.

Let's be empirical and try out what we just talked about:

```
$ cat rootsh_hack2.c
[...]
int main(int argc, char **argv)
{
    /* Become root */
    if (setuid(0) == -1)
        WARN("setuid(0) failed!\n");

    /* Now just spawn a shell;
     * <i>Evil Laugh</i>, we're now root!
     */
    system("/bin/bash");
    exit (EXIT_SUCCESS);
}
```

*Process Credentials*

Build and run it. This screenshot shows us a virtual machine seawolf, along with an `ssh`-connected Terminal window in the lower right (where we're logged in as the user seawolf); see the `rootsh_hack2` program running there:

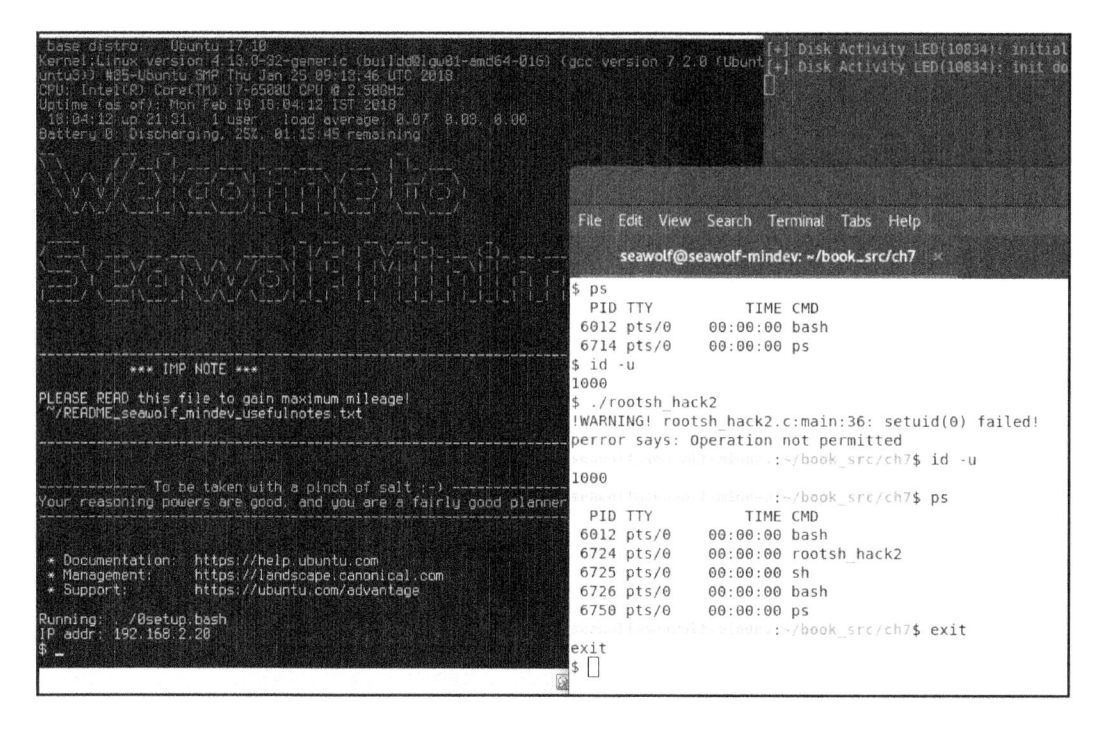

Studying the output of the `ssh` terminal window in the preceding screenshot, we can see the following:

- The original bash process (the shell) has the PID 6012.
- The id command shows that we're running as (a real) UID = 1000 (which is the seawolf user).
- We run `rootsh_hack2`; clearly, the `setuid(0)` fails; the error message is displayed: operation not permitted.
- Nevertheless, it's just a warning message; execution continues, and the process spawns another bash process, in effect, another shell.
- Its PID is 6726 (proving it's unique from the original shell.)

- The id(1) is still 1000, proving we have not really achieved anything significant.
- We exit and are back to our original shell.

But what if we (or worse, a hacker) could trick this process into running as root!? How? By making it a setuid-root executable of course; then we're in trouble:

```
$ ls -l rootsh_hack2
-rwxrwxr-x 1 seawolf seawolf 8864 Feb 19 18:03 rootsh_hack2
$ sudo chown root rootsh_hack2
[sudo] password for seawolf:
$ sudo chmod u+s rootsh_hack2
$ ls -l rootsh_hack2
-rwsrwxr-x 1 root seawolf 8864 Feb 19 18:03 rootsh_hack2
$ ./rootsh_hack2
root@seawolf-mindev:~/book_src/ch7# id -u
0
root@seawolf-mindev:~/book_src/ch7# ps
  PID TTY          TIME CMD
 7049 pts/0    00:00:00 rootsh_hack2
 7050 pts/0    00:00:00 sh
 7051 pts/0    00:00:00 bash
 7080 pts/0    00:00:00 ps
root@seawolf-mindev:~/book_src/ch7# exit
exit
$
```

So, we just simulate being tricked: here we use sudo(8); we enter the password and thus change the binary executable to a setuid-root, a truly dangerous, one. It runs, and it spawns what now turns out to be a root shell (notice, the `id(1)` command proves this fact); we do a `ps` and then `exit`.

It also dawns on us that our previous hacking attempt failed to deliver—the system(3) API refused to elevate privileges when a shell was the parameter to run—which is great security-wise. But, this hacking attempt (#2) proves that you can easily subvert that: just issue a call to `setuid(0)` prior to invoking system (`/bin/bash`), and it succeeds in delivering a root shell—of course, if and only if the process runs as root in the first place: either via the setuid-root approach or by just using sudo(8).

# An aside – a script to identify setuid-root and setgid installed programs

We now begin to understand that `setuid/setgid` programs might be convenient, but from a security viewpoint, they can be potentially dangerous and must be carefully audited. The first step in such an audit is finding out whether and where exactly these binaries exist on the Linux system.

To do so, we write a small shell (bash) script; it will identify and show us the installed `setuid-root` and `setgid` programs on the system (as usual, you can download and try the script from the book's Git repository).

The script performs its work essentially, as shown next (it actually loops over an array of directories; for simplicity, we show a direct example of scanning the `/bin` directory):

```
echo "Scanning /bin ..."
ls -l /bin/ | grep "^-..s" | awk '$3=="root" {print $0}'
```

The output of `ls -l` is piped to `grep(1)`, which uses a regular expression designed to match a string if the first character is a - (a regular file) and if the owner execute bit is s—in other words, a setuid file; the `awk(1)` filter ensures that only if the owner is root do we print the resultant string to stdout.

We run the bash script on two Linux distributions.

On an Ubuntu 17.10 on x86_64:

```
$ ./show_setuidgid.sh
---------------------------------------------------------------
System Information (LSB):
---------------------------------------------------------------
No LSB modules are available.
Distributor ID:    Ubuntu
Description:       Ubuntu 17.10
Release:    17.10
Codename:   artful
kernel: 4.13.0-32-generic
---------------------------------------------------------------
Scanning various directories for (traditional) SETUID-ROOT binaries
...
---------------------------------------------------------------
Scanning /bin              ...
-rwsr-xr-x 1 root root     30800 Aug 11  2016 fusermount
-rwsr-xr-x 1 root root     34888 Aug 14  2017 mount
```

```
-rwsr-xr-x 1 root root    146128 Jun 23  2017 ntfs-3g
-rwsr-xr-x 1 root root     64424 Mar 10  2017 ping
-rwsr-xr-x 1 root root     40168 Aug 21  2017 su
-rwsr-xr-x 1 root root     26696 Aug 14  2017 umount
--------------------------------------------------------------
Scanning /usr/bin         ...
-rwsr-xr-x 1 root root     71792 Aug 21  2017 chfn
-rwsr-xr-x 1 root root     40400 Aug 21  2017 chsh
-rwsr-xr-x 1 root root     75344 Aug 21  2017 gpasswd
-rwsr-xr-x 1 root root     39944 Aug 21  2017 newgrp
-rwsr-xr-x 1 root root     54224 Aug 21  2017 passwd
-rwsr-xr-x 1 root root    145040 Jun 13  2017 sudo
-rwsr-xr-x 1 root root     18448 Mar 10  2017 traceroute6.iputils
--------------------------------------------------------------
Scanning /sbin            ...
--------------------------------------------------------------
Scanning /usr/sbin        ...
--------------------------------------------------------------
Scanning /usr/local/bin   ...
--------------------------------------------------------------
Scanning /usr/local/sbin  ...
--------------------------------------------------------------

Scanning various directories for (traditional) SETGID binaries ...
--------------------------------------------------------------
Scanning /bin             ...
--------------------------------------------------------------
Scanning /usr/bin         ...
-rwxr-sr-x 1 root tty       14400 Jul 27  2017 bsd-write
-rwxr-sr-x 1 root shadow    62304 Aug 21  2017 chage
-rwxr-sr-x 1 root crontab   39352 Aug 21  2017 crontab
-rwxr-sr-x 1 root shadow    22808 Aug 21  2017 expiry
-rwxr-sr-x 1 root mlocate   38992 Apr 28  2017 mlocate
-rwxr-sr-x 1 root ssh      362640 Jan 16 18:58 ssh-agent
-rwxr-sr-x 1 root tty       30792 Aug 14  2017 wall
--------------------------------------------------------------
Scanning /sbin            ...
-rwxr-sr-x 1 root shadow    34816 Apr 22  2017 pam_extrausers_chkpwd
-rwxr-sr-x 1 root shadow    34816 Apr 22  2017 unix_chkpwd
--------------------------------------------------------------
Scanning /usr/sbin        ...
--------------------------------------------------------------
Scanning /usr/local/bin   ...
--------------------------------------------------------------
Scanning /usr/local/sbin  ...
--------------------------------------------------------------
$
```

*Process Credentials*

A system information banner is displayed (so that we can glean system details, mostly obtained using the `lsb_release` utility). Then, the script scans through various system directories printing out all `setuid-root` and `setgid` binaries it finds. Familiar examples, `passwd` and `sudo` are highlighted.

### setgid example – wall

As a great example of `setgid` binaries, take a look at the wall(1) utility, reproduced from the script's output for convenience:

```
-rwxr-sr-x 1 root tty         30792 Aug 14  2017 wall
```

The wall(1) program is used to broadcast any message to all users console (tty) devices (typically the sysad will do this). Now, to write to a `tty` device (recall, folks, Chapter 1, *Linux System Architecture*, and the if it's not a process, it's a file Unix philosophy), what permissions do we require? Let's take the second terminal `tty2` device as an example:

```
$ ls -l /dev/tty2
crw--w---- 1 root tty 4, 2 Feb 19 18:04 /dev/tty2
$
```

We can see that to write to the preceding device we either require root or we must be a member of the `tty` group. Peek again at the wall(1) utility long listing; it's a setgid binary-executable file and the group membership is `tty`; so, when anyone runs it, the wall process runs with an effective group ID (EGID) of `tty`! That solves the problem—no code. No fuss.

Here is a screenshot where wall is used:

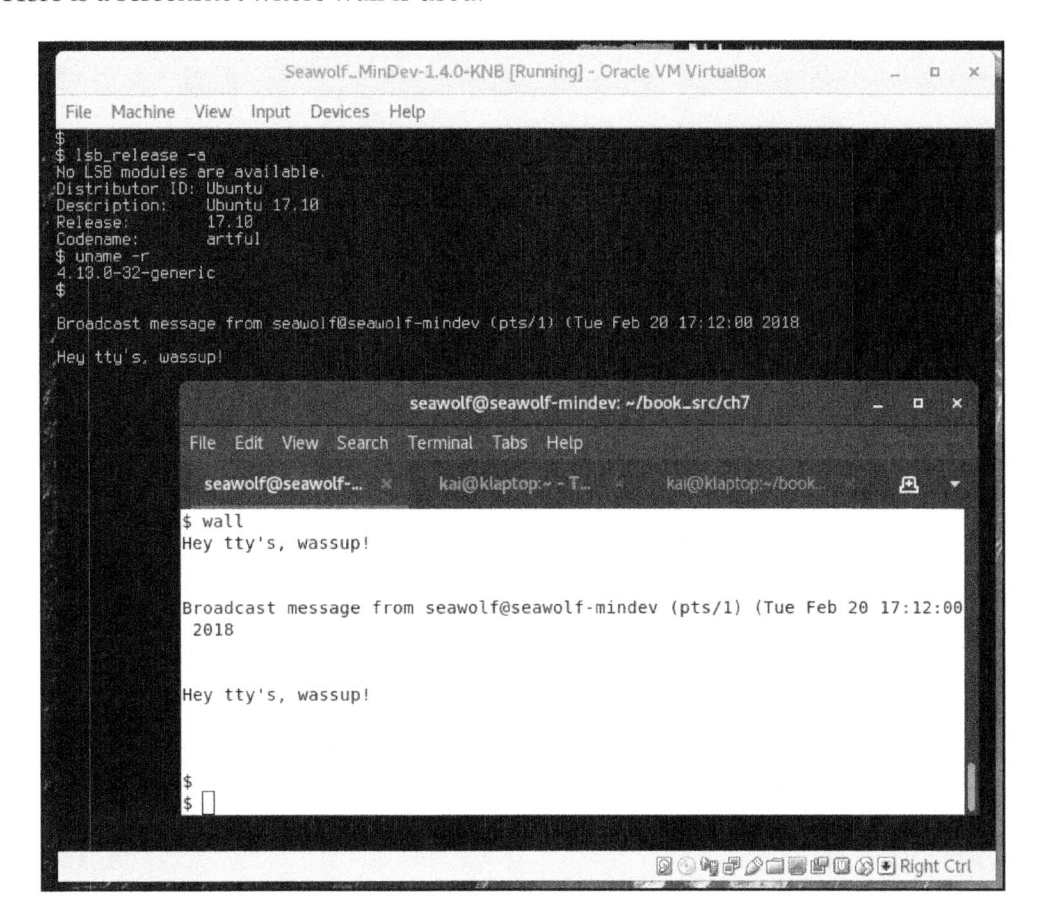

In the foreground, there is an `ssh` connected (to an Ubuntu VM; you can see it in the background) terminal window. It issues the `wall` command as a regular user: because of the `setgid tty`, it works!

Now you can run the earlier script on a Fedora 27 on x86_64:

```
$ ./show_setuidgid.sh 1
----------------------------------------------------------------
System Information (LSB):
----------------------------------------------------------------
LSB Version:       :core-4.1-amd64:core-4.1-noarch
Distributor ID:    Fedora
Description:       Fedora release 27 (Twenty Seven)
Release:    27
```

*Process Credentials*

```
Codename:    TwentySeven
kernel: 4.14.18-300.fc27.x86_64
------------------------------------------------------------------
```
**Scanning various directories for (traditional) SETUID-ROOT binaries ...**
```
------------------------------------------------------------------
Scanning /bin             ...
------------------------------------------------------------------
Scanning /usr/bin         ...
-rwsr-xr-x.   1 root root     52984 Aug  2  2017 at
-rwsr-xr-x.   1 root root     73864 Aug 14  2017 chage
-rws--x--x.   1 root root     27992 Sep 22 14:07 chfn
-rws--x--x.   1 root root     23736 Sep 22 14:07 chsh
-rwsr-xr-x.   1 root root     57608 Aug  3  2017 crontab
-rwsr-xr-x.   1 root root     32040 Aug  7  2017 fusermount
-rwsr-xr-x.   1 root root     31984 Jan 12 20:36 fusermount-
glusterfs
-rwsr-xr-x.   1 root root     78432 Aug 14  2017 gpasswd
```
**-rwsr-xr-x.   1 root root     36056 Sep 22 14:07 mount**
```
-rwsr-xr-x.   1 root root     39000 Aug 14  2017 newgidmap
-rwsr-xr-x.   1 root root     41920 Aug 14  2017 newgrp
-rwsr-xr-x.   1 root root     39000 Aug 14  2017 newuidmap
```
**-rwsr-xr-x.   1 root root     27880 Aug  4  2017 passwd**
```
-rwsr-xr-x.   1 root root     27688 Aug  4  2017 pkexec
-rwsr-xr-x.   1 root root     32136 Sep 22 14:07 su
---s--x--x.   1 root root    151416 Oct  4 18:55 sudo
-rwsr-xr-x.   1 root root     27880 Sep 22 14:07 umount
------------------------------------------------------------------
Scanning /sbin            ...
------------------------------------------------------------------
Scanning /usr/sbin        ...
-rwsr-xr-x. 1 root root    114840 Jan 19 23:25 mount.nfs
-rwsr-xr-x. 1 root root     89600 Aug  4  2017 mtr
-rwsr-xr-x. 1 root root     11256 Aug 21  2017 pam_timestamp_check
-rwsr-xr-x. 1 root root     36280 Aug 21  2017 unix_chkpwd
-rws--x--x. 1 root root     40352 Aug  5  2017 userhelper
-rwsr-xr-x. 1 root root     11312 Jan  2 21:06 usernetctl
------------------------------------------------------------------
Scanning /usr/local/bin  ...
------------------------------------------------------------------
Scanning /usr/local/sbin ...
------------------------------------------------------------------
```
**Scanning various directories for (traditional) SETGID binaries ...**
```
------------------------------------------------------------------
Scanning /bin             ...
------------------------------------------------------------------
Scanning /usr/bin         ...
```

```
-rwxr-sr-x.   1 root   cgred      15640 Aug  3  2017 cgclassify
-rwxr-sr-x.   1 root   cgred      15600 Aug  3  2017 cgexec
-rwx--s--x.   1 root   slocate    40528 Aug  4  2017 locate
-rwxr-sr-x.   1 root   tty        19584 Sep 22 14:07 write
---------------------------------------------------------------
Scanning /sbin           ...
---------------------------------------------------------------
Scanning /usr/sbin       ...
-rwx--s--x. 1 root lock      15544 Aug  4  2017 lockdev
-rwxr-sr-x. 1 root root       7144 Jan  2 21:06 netreport
---------------------------------------------------------------
Scanning /usr/local/bin  ...
---------------------------------------------------------------
Scanning /usr/local/sbin ...
---------------------------------------------------------------
$
```

More setuid-root binaries seem to show up; also, `write(1)` is the equivalent (to `wall(1)`) `setgid tty` utility on Fedora.

## Giving up privileges

From the previous discussion, it seems as if the `set*id()` system calls (`setuid(2)`, `seteuid(2)`, `setreuid(2)`, `setresuid(2)`) are only useful to root, as only with root privileges can we use the system calls to change the process credentials. Well, that's not really the full truth; there's another important case, for non-privileged processes.

Consider this scenario: our program specification requires the initialization code to run with root privileges; the rest of the code does not. Obviously, we don't want to give the end user root access just to run our program. How do we solve this?

Making the program setuid-root would nicely do the trick. As we've seen, a setuid-root process will always run as root; but after the initialization work is done, we can switch back to the unprivileged normal state. How do we do this? Via the `setuid(2)`: recall that setuid for a privileged process sets both the EUID and RUID to the value passed; so we pass it the process's RUID, which we obtain via the getuid:

```
setuid(getuid());    // make process unprivileged
```

This is a useful semantic (often, the `seteuid(getuid())` is all we require). We use this semantic to become our true selves again—quite philosophical, no?

> In **information security** (**infosec**) circles, there is an important principle followed: reduction of the attack surface. Converting a root privileged process to become non-privileged (once its work as root is done) helps toward this goal (to some extent at least).

### Saved-set UID – a quick demo

In the previous section, we've just seen how the useful `seteuid(getuid())` semantic can be used to switch a setuid privileged process to a regular unprivileged state (that's good design and safer). But what if we have this requirement:

```
Time t0: initialization code: must run as root
Time t1: func1(): must *not* run as root
Time t2: func2(): must run as root
Time t3: func3(): must *not* run as root
[...]
```

To achieve the must-run-as-root semantic initially, we can of course create the program to be a setuid-root program. Then, at time t1, we issue the `seteuid(getuid())` giving up root privileges.

But how do we regain root privileges at time t2? Ah, that's where the saved-setuid feature becomes precious. What's more, it's easy to do; here is the pseudo-code to achieve this scenario:

```
t0: we are running with root privilege due to setuid-root binary
    executable being run
 saved_setuid = geteuid()      // save it
t1: seteuid(getuid())          // must *not* run as root
t2: seteuid(saved_setuid)      // switch back to the saved-set, root
t3: seteuid(getuid())          // must *not* run as root
```

We demonstrate the same with an actual C code next. Note that for the demo to work as expected, the user must make the binary executable file into a setuid-root binary by doing this:

```
make savedset_demo
sudo chown root savedset_demo
sudo chmod u+s savedset_demo
```

*Chapter 7*

The following code checks that, at the beginning, the process is indeed running as root; if not, it aborts with a message asking the user to make the binary a setuid-root binary:

```
int main(int argc, char **argv)
{
    uid_t saved_setuid;

    printf("t0: Init:\n");
    SHOW_CREDS();
    if (0 != geteuid())
        FATAL("Not a setuid-root executable,"
            " aborting now ...\n"
            "[TIP: do: sudo chown root %s ;"
            " sudo chmod u+s %s\n"
            " and rerun].\n"
            , argv[0], argv[0], argv[0]);
    printf(" Ok, we're effectively running as root! (EUID==0)\n");

    /* Save the EUID, in effect the "saved set UID", so that
     * we can switch back and forth
     */
    saved_setuid = geteuid();

    printf("t1: Becoming my original self!\n");
    if (seteuid(getuid()) == -1)
        FATAL("seteuid() step 2 failed!\n");
    SHOW_CREDS();

    printf("t2: Switching to privileged state now...\n");
    if (seteuid(saved_setuid) == -1)
        FATAL("seteuid() step 3 failed!\n");
    SHOW_CREDS();
    if (0 == geteuid())
        printf(" Yup, we're root again!\n");

    printf("t3: Switching back to unprivileged state now ...\n");
    if (seteuid(getuid()) == -1)
        FATAL("seteuid() step 4 failed!\n");
    SHOW_CREDS();

    exit (EXIT_SUCCESS);
}
```

Here is a sample run:

```
$ make savedset_demo
gcc -Wall -o savedset_demo savedset_demo.c common.o
#sudo chown root savedset_demo
#sudo chmod u+s savedset_demo
$ ls -l savedset_demo
-rwxrwxr-x 1 seawolf seawolf 13144 Feb 20 09:22 savedset_demo*
$ ./savedset_demo
t0: Init:
RUID=1000 EUID=1000
RGID=1000 EGID=1000
FATAL:savedset_demo.c:main:48: Not a setuid-root executable, aborting
now ...
[TIP: do: sudo chown root ./savedset_demo ; sudo chmod u+s
./savedset_demo
 and rerun].
$
```

The program fails as it detects that it's not running effectively as root in the beginning, implying that it's not a setuid-root binary executable in the first place. So, of course, we must make it a setuid-root binary executable by doing the `sudo chown ...` followed by the `sudo chmod ...`. (Notice how we've kept the code to do so in the Makefile but have commented it out, so that you, the reader, can get some practice).

This screenshot shows that once we do this, it runs as expected, switching back and forth between the privileged and unprivileged states:

```
$ sudo chown root savedset_demo
[sudo] password for seawolf:
$ sudo chmod u+s savedset_demo
$ ls -l savedset_demo
-rwsrwxr-x 1 root seawolf 13144 Feb 20 09:22 savedset_demo*
$ ./savedset_demo
t0: Init:
RUID=1000 EUID=0
RGID=1000 EGID=1000
 Ok, we're effectively running as root! (EUID==0)
t1: Becoming my original self!
RUID=1000 EUID=1000
RGID=1000 EGID=1000
t2: Switching to privileged state now...
RUID=1000 EUID=0
RGID=1000 EGID=1000
 Yup, we're root again!
t3: Switching back to unprivileged state now ...
RUID=1000 EUID=1000
RGID=1000 EGID=1000
$
```

Notice how the really crucial system call to switch back and forth is, after all, the setuid(2); also notice how the EUID changes at different points in time (from 0 at t0, to 1000 at t1, again to 0 at t2 and finally back to 1000 at t3).

> Also note that, to provide interesting examples, we have been mostly using setuid-root binaries. You need not: making the file owner someone else (such as the mail user) would then in effect make it a setuid-mail binary executable, meaning that, when run, the process RUID would be the usual 1000 (seawolf), but the EUID would be that of the mail user's RUID.

## The setres[u|g]id(2) system calls

Here are a couple of wrapper calls—the setresuid(2) and the setresgid(2); their signatures:

```
#define _GNU_SOURCE         /* See feature_test_macros(7) */
#include <unistd.h>

int setresuid(uid_t ruid, uid_t euid, uid_t suid);
int setresgid(gid_t rgid, gid_t egid, gid_t sgid);
```

This pair of system calls is like a superset of the earlier set*id() APIs. With the setresuid(2) system call, a process can set the RUID, EUID, and saved-set-id all at once, with a single system call (the **res** in the system call name stands for **real**, **effective**, and **saved**-set-ID, respectively).

A non-privileged (meaning, non-root) process can only use this system call to set the three IDs to one of the current RUID, the current EUID, or the current saved-set UID, nothing else (the usual security principle at work). Passing -1 implies to leave the corresponding value unchanged. A privileged (root) process can use the call to set the three IDs to any values, of course. (As usual, the setresgid(2) system call is identical except that it sets group credentials).

Some real-world OSS projects indeed use this system call; good examples are the OpenSSH project (the Linux port is called OpenSSH-portable) and the well-known sudo(8) utility.

## Process Credentials

OpenSSH: from its git repository here: https://github.com/openssh/openssh-portable/:

uidswap.c:permanently_drop_suid():

```
void permanently_drop_suid(uid_t uid)
[...]
debug("permanently_drop_suid: %u", (u_int)uid);
if (setresuid(uid, uid, uid) < 0)
    fatal("setresuid %u: %.100s", (u_int)uid, strerror(errno));

[...]

/* Verify UID drop was successful */
    if (getuid() != uid || geteuid() != uid) {
        fatal("%s: euid incorrect uid:%u euid:%u (should be %u)",
            __func__, (u_int)getuid(), (u_int)geteuid(), (u_int)uid);
    }
```

It's interesting to notice the effort taken to ensure that the UID drop was successful—more on this next!

Performing an strace(1) on sudo(8) (notice we have to trace it as root, as attempting to strace a setuid program as a regular user does not work as, while tracing, the setuid bit is deliberately ignored; this output is from an Ubuntu Linux system):

```
$ id mail
uid=8(mail) gid=8(mail) groups=8(mail)
$ sudo strace -e trace=setuid,setreuid,setresuid sudo -u mail id
[...]
setresuid(-1, 0, -1)                    = 0
setresuid(-1, -1, -1)                   = 0
setresuid(-1, 8, -1)                    = 0
setresuid(-1, 0, -1)                    = 0
[...]
```

Clearly, sudo uses the setresuid(2) system call to set permissions, credentials, really, as appropriate (in the preceding example, the process EUID is being set to that of the mail user, the RUID and saved-set-id are being left unchanged).

# Important security notes

Here are a few key points to keep in mind, with regard to security:

- The use of setuid binaries, if poorly designed, is a security risk. Particularly and especially for setuid-root programs, they should be designed and tested to ensure that, while the process is in an elevated privileged state, it never spawns a shell or blindly accepts user commands (which are then internally executed).
- You must check the failure case of any of the `set*id()` system calls (`setuid(2), seteuid(2), setreuid(2), setresuid(2)`).

Consider this pseudo-code:

```
run setuid-root program; EUID = 0
  do required work as root
switch to 'normal' privileges: setuid(getuid())
  do remaining work as non-root
  [...]
```

Think about this: what if the preceding `setuid(getuid())` call failed (for whatever reason) and we did not check? The remaining work would continue to run with root access, very possibly courting disaster! (See the sample code from the OpenSSH-portable Git repo for a real-world example of careful checking.) Let's take a look at the following points:

- The `setuid(2)` system call is deficient in a sense: if the real UID is root, then the saved-set UID is also root; hence, you cannot drop privileges! Obviously, this can be dangerous for setuid-root applications and the like. As an alternative, use the `setreuid(2)` API to have a root process temporarily drop privileges and regain them later (by swapping their RUID and EUID values).
- Even if you have system administrator (root) access, you should never log in as root! You could be (quite easily) tricked into running dangerous programs as root (hackers routinely use this technique to install rootkits onto a system; once successful, do consider your system compromised).
- When a process creates a shared object (say a file), who will own it and what will the group be? In other words, what values will the kernel set in the file's inode metadata structure for UID and GID? The answer is this: the file UID will be the creator process's EUID, and the file GID (group membership) will be the creator process's EGID. This will have a subsequent effect on permissions.

> **TIP:** We recommend that you, the reader, definitely read Chapter 9, *Process Execution*, as well! In it, we show how the traditional permissions model is flawed in many respects, and why and how you should use the superior Linux Capabilities model.

## Summary

In this chapter, the reader has been taken through many important ideas on the design and implementation of the traditional Unix security model. Among other things, we have covered the traditional Unix permission model, the concepts of process real and effective IDs, APIs to query and set them, sudo(8), saved-set IDs.

Again, it bears repeating: we definitely recommend you also read the following Chapter 8, *Process Capabilities*! In it, we show how the traditional permissions model is flawed, and how you should use the superior, modern Linux Capabilities model.

# 8
# Process Capabilities

In two chapter, you will learn concepts and practices regarding process credentials and capabilities. Besides being of practical importance to application development in Linux, this chapter, by its very nature, delves deeper into an often overlooked but extremely important aspect: security.

We have divided the coverage of this key area into two major parts, each of which is a chapter in this book:

- In Chapter 7, *Process Credentials,* the traditional-style Unix permissions model is discussed in some detail, and techniques to run programs with root privileges but without requiring the root password were shown.
- In this Chapter 8, *Process Capabilities,* the *modern* approach, the POSIX capabilities model, is discussed in some detail.

We will attempt to clearly show the reader that, while it is important to learn about the traditional mechanisms and how they operate, this becomes a classic weak link as far as *security* is concerned. However you look at it, security is of paramount importance, especially these days; the advent of Linux running on all sorts of devices—tiny IoT and embedded devices to mobile devices, desktops, servers, and super-computing platforms—makes security a key concern for all stakeholders. Hence, the modern capabilities approach should be used when developing software.

In this chapter, we will cover the *modern approach*—the POSIX capabilities model—in some detail. We will discuss what exactly it is, and how it provides security and robustness. The reader will learn about the following:

- What exactly the modern POSIX Capabilities model is
- Why it is superior to the older (traditional) Unix permissions model
- How to work with capabilities on Linux
- Embedding capabilities into a process or binary executable
- Security tips

Along the way, we will use code examples, which will allow you to try out some of these facilities so that you can gain a better understanding of them.

## The modern POSIX capabilities model

Consider this (fictional) scenario: Vidya is on a project developing a Linux application for Alan and his team. She is working on a component that captures network packets and saves them to a file (for later analysis). The program is called **packcap**. However, to successfully capture the network packets, packcap must run with *root* privileges. Now, Vidya understands that running applications as *root* is not a good security practice; not only that, she knows the customer will not accept the statement: Oh, it didn't work? You must run it logged in as a root or via sudo. Running it via sudo(8) might sound reasonable, but, when you stop to think about it, that implies that every member of Alan's team must be given the *root* password, and this is simply not acceptable.

So, how does she solve the problem? The answer suddenly jumps out at her: Make the *packcap* binary executable a *setuid*-root file; this way, when it's launched, the process will be running with *root* privileges, so there will be no need for a root login/password or sudo. Sounds fantastic.

## Motivation

This—the setuid—root approach—is *exactly* the traditional manner in which problems like the one briefly described above were solved. So, what's changed today (well, over several years now)? In a nutshell: *security concerns over hacking*. The reality is this: All real-world non-trivial programs do have defects (bugs)—hidden, lurking, undiscovered, perhaps, but very much there. The vast scope and complexity of modern real-world software projects make this an unfortunate reality. Certain bugs result in *vulnerabilities* "leaking" into the software product; this is precisely what hackers look to *exploit*. The well-known, yet dreaded, **Buffer Overflow** *(BoF)* attacks are based on software vulnerabilities within several heavily used library APIs! (We highly recommend reading David Wheeler's book *Secure Programming HOWTO - Creating Secure Software*—see the *Further reading* section on the GitHub repository.)

> **At the code level, security issues are bugs; once fixed, the issue disappears.** (See a link to Linux's comments on this in the *Further reading* section on the GitHub repository.)

So what's the point? Simply put the point is this: It's entirely possible that the setuid-root program you deliver to your customer (packcap) has unfortunate and unknown-as-of-now software vulnerabilities embedded within it, which hackers could discover and exploit (yes, there's a whole job description for this—**white-hat hacking** or **pentesting**.)

If the process *hacked into* runs with normal privileges—non-root—at least then the damage is limited to that user account, and it goes no further. But if the process is running with root privilege and the attack succeeds, the hacker might well end up with a *root shell on the system*. The system is now compromised—anything can happen (secrets can be stolen, backdoors and rootkits installed, DoS attacks become trivial.)

It's not only about security, though: by limiting privileges, you gain damage-control benefits as well; bugs and crashes are going to cause limited damage—the situation is far better *contained* than earlier.

# POSIX capabilities

So, going back to our fictional packcap example application, how do we run the process—which requires root, it seems—without root privileges (no root login, setuid-root, or sudo(8) allowed) and yet have it perform its tasks correctly?

Enter the POSIX Capabilities model: In this model, instead of giving a process *blanket access* as a root (or other) user, there is a way to *embed particular capabilities into both the process and/or binary file*. The Linux kernel supports the POSIX capabilities model from very early on—the 2.2 Linux kernels (at the time of writing, we are now in the 4.x kernel series). From a practical viewpoint, the features we describe as follows are available from Linux kernel version 2.6.24 (released January 2008) onward.

This is how it works in a nutshell: Every process—in fact, every *thread*—as part of its OS metadata, contains a bitmask. These are called the *capability bits* or the *capability set*, because *each bit represents a capability*. By carefully setting and clearing bits, the kernel (as well as the user space, if it has the capability) can therefore set *fine granularity permissions* on a per-thread basis (we will cover multithreading in detail in later Chapter 14, *Multithreading with Pthreads Part I - Essentials*, for now, treat the term *thread* as interchangeable with *process*).

> More realistically, and as we shall see next, the kernel maintains *several capability sets (capsets) per thread alive*; each capset consists of an array of two 32-bit unsigned values.

## Process Capabilities

For example, there is a capability bit called `CAP_DAC_OVERRIDE`; it would normally be cleared (0). If set, then the process will bypass all the kernel's file permission checks—for anything: reading, writing, and executing! (This is known as **DAC: Discretionary Access Control**.)

Looking at a few more examples of capability bits would be useful at this point (the full list is available at the *man page* on *capabilities(7)* here: https://linux.die.net/man/7/capabilities). Some snippets follow:

```
[...]
CAP_CHOWN
            Make arbitrary changes to file UIDs and GIDs (see
chown(2)).

CAP_DAC_OVERRIDE
            Bypass file read, write, and execute permission checks.
(DAC is an abbreviation of "discretionary access control".)
[...]

CAP_NET_ADMIN
            Perform various network-related operations:
            * interface configuration;
            * administration of IP firewall, masquerading, and
accounting;
            * modify routing tables;
[...]

CAP_NET_RAW
            * Use RAW and PACKET sockets;
            * bind to any address for transparent proxying.
[...]

CAP_SETUID
            * Make arbitrary manipulations of process UIDs
(setuid(2),
                setreuid(2), setresuid(2), setfsuid(2));

[...]

 CAP_SYS_ADMIN
            Note: this capability is overloaded; see Notes to kernel
            developers, below.

            * Perform a range of system administration operations
                including: quotactl(2), mount(2), umount(2),
swapon(2),
                setdomainname(2);
```

[ 282 ]

```
                    * perform privileged syslog(2) operations (since Linux
    2.6.37,
                      CAP_SYSLOG should be used to permit such operations);
                    * perform VM86_REQUEST_IRQ vm86(2) command;
                    * perform IPC_SET and IPC_RMID operations on arbitrary
                      System V IPC objects;
                    * override RLIMIT_NPROC resource limit;
                    * perform operations on trusted and security Extended
                      Attributes (see xattr(7));
                    * use lookup_dcookie(2);
    << a lot more follows >>
    [...]
```

*In effect, the capabilities model provides fine-grained permissions; a way to slice up the (overly) enormous power of the root user into distinct manageable pieces.*

So, to understand the significant benefit in the context of our fictional packcap example, consider this: With the traditional Unix permissions model, at best, the release binary would be a setuid-root binary executable file; the process would run with root privileges. In the best case, there's no bug, no security issues (or, if there are, they aren't discovered), and all goes well—luckily. But, we don't believe in luck, right?"(In the words of Jack Reacher, Lee Child's protagonist, "Hope for the best, prepare for the worst")." In the worst case, there are exploitable vulnerabilities lurking in the code and there are hackers who will work tirelessly until they find and exploit them. The entire system could be compromised.

On the other hand, with the modern POSIX capabilities model, the packcap binary executable file will *not* require to be setuid at all, never mind setuid-root; the process would run with normal privileges. The work still gets done because we embed the *capability* for precisely that work (in this example, network packet capture) and absolutely nothing else. Even if there are exploitable vulnerabilities lurking in the code, hackers would probably not be as motivated to find and exploit them; the simple reason for this is this is that even if they do manage to gain access (say, an arbitrary code execution bounty), all that can be exploited is the account of the non-privileged users running the process. It's demotivating to the hacker (well, that's a joke, but with truth ingrained within).

Think about it: the Linux capabilities model is one way to implement a well-accepted security practice: *the **Principle of Least Privilege (PoLP):*** Each module in a product (or project) must have access only to the information and resources necessary for its legitimate work, and nothing more.

## Capabilities – some gory details

Linux capabilities are a fairly complex topic. For the purposes of this book, we delve into the subject to the depth necessary for the systems application developer to profit from the discussion. To get the complete details, please check out the man page on capabilities (7) here: http://man7.org/linux/man-pages/man7/capabilities.7.html as well as the kernel documentation on credentials here: https://github.com/torvalds/linux/blob/master/Documentation/security/credentials.rst

## OS support

**Capability bitmask(s)** are often referred to as **capability sets**—we abbreviate this term to **capset**.

To work with the power of the POSIX capabilities model, in the first place, the OS itself must provide "life support" for it; full support implies the following:

- Whenever a process or thread attempts to perform some operation, the kernel is able to check whether the thread is allowed to do so (by checking for the appropriate bit being set in the thread's effective capset—see the next section).
- System calls (and usually wrapper library APIs) must be provided such that a thread can query and set its capsets.
- Linux kernel filesystem code must have a facility such that capabilities can be embedded (or attached) into a binary-executable file (so that when the file "runs", the process acquires those capabilities).

Modern Linux (particularly Kernel Version 2.6.24 onward) supports all three, and thus fully supports the capabilities model.

### Viewing process capabilities via procfs

To understand more details, we need a quick way to "look into" the kernel and retrieve information; the Linux kernel's **proc filesystem** (often abbreviated to **procfs**) provides just this feature (along with more).

> Procfs is a pseudo-filesystem typically mounted on /proc. Exploring procfs to learn more about Linux is a great idea; do check out some links in the *Further reading* section on the GitHub repository.

Here, we shall just focus on the task at hand: to get to the details, procfs exposes a directory called `/proc/self` (which refers to the current process's context, somewhat analogous to the *this* pointer in OOP); under it, a pseudo file named *status* reveals interesting details about the process (or thread) in question. The process's capsets are seen as "Cap*" so we just grep for this pattern. In the next code, we perform this on a regular non-privileged process (*grep* itself via the *self* directory), as well as with a privileged (root) process (*systemd/init PID 1*), to see the differences:

Process/thread capsets: regular process (such as grep):

```
$ grep -i cap /proc/self/status
CapInh:    0000000000000000
CapPrm:    0000000000000000
CapEff:    0000000000000000
CapBnd:    0000003fffffffff
CapAmb:    0000000000000000
```

Process/thread capsets: privileged (root) process (such as systemd/init PID 1):

```
$ grep -i cap /proc/1/status
CapInh:    0000000000000000
CapPrm:    0000003fffffffff
CapEff:    0000003fffffffff
CapBnd:    0000003fffffffff
CapAmb:    0000000000000000
$
```

Enumerated in a table:

| Thread Capability Set (capset) | Typical Value for Non-Privileged Task | Typical Value for Privileged Task |
|---|---|---|
| CapInh (Inherited) | 0x0000000000000000 | 0x0000000000000000 |
| CapPrm (Permitted) | 0x0000000000000000 | 0x0000003fffffffff |
| CapEff (Effective) | 0x0000000000000000 | 0x0000003fffffffff |
| CapBnd (Bounded) | 0x0000003fffffffff | 0x0000003fffffffff |
| CapAmb (Ambient) | 0x0000000000000000 | 0x0000000000000000 |

(This table describes the output from a Fedora 27/Ubuntu 17.10 Linux on x86_64).

Broadly, there are two types of *capability sets*:

- Thread capability sets
- File capability sets

## Thread capability sets

Within thread capsets, there are actually several types per thread.

Linux per-**thread** capability sets:

- **Permitted (Prm):** The overall limiting *superset* of effective capabilities for the thread. If a capability is dropped, it can never be reacquired.
- **Inheritable (Inh):** Inheritance here refers to the absorption of capset attributes across an *exec*. What happens to the capsets when a process executes another process? (Details on the exec are dealt with in a later chapter. For now, suffice it to say that if bash execs vi, then we call bash the predecessor and vi the successor).
  Will the successor process inherit the capsets of the predecessor? Well, yes the *inheritable capset*, that is. From the previous table, we can see that for a non-privileged process, the inherited capset is all zeros, implying that no capabilities are inherited across the exec operation. So, if a process wants to execute another process and that (successor) process must run with elevated privileges, it should use ambient capabilities.
- **Effective (Eff):** These are the capabilities that the kernel actually uses when checking permissions for the given thread.
- **Ambient (Amb):** (From Linux 4.3 onward). These are the capabilities that are inherited across an exec operation. The bits *must* be present (set to 1) in both the permitted and inheritable capsets—only then can it be "ambient". In other words, if a capability is cleared from either a Prm or an Inh, it is also cleared in an Amb.
  If a *set[u|g]id* program or a program with *file capabilities* (as we will see) is executed, the ambient set is cleared. Normally, upon exec, the ambient capset is added to Prm and assigned to Eff (of the successor process).
- **Bounding (Bnd):** This capset is a way *to limit* the capabilities bestowed upon a process during an exec. Its effect:
  - When the process executes another process, the permitted set is the ANDing of the original permitted and bounded capsets: *Prm = Prm* AND *Bnd.* This way, you can limit the successor process's permitted capset.
  - Only if a capability is in the bounding set, can it be added to the inheritable capset.
  - Also, from Linux 2.6.25 onward, the capability bounding set is a per-thread attribute.

Executing a program will have no impact on the capsets unless either of the following is true:

- The successor is a setuid-root or a setgid program
- File capabilities are set on the binary executable that is execed

How can these thread capsets be programmatically queried and changed? Indeed, that's what the *capget(2)* and *capset(2)* system calls are for. However, we would suggest one uses the library-level wrapper APIs *cap_get_proc(3)* and *cap_set_proc(3)* instead.

## File capability sets

At times, we require the ability to "embed" capabilities into a binary-executable file (the discussion regarding the reasons for this is covered in the following section). This will obviously require kernel filesystem support. In early Linux, this system was a kernel-configurable option; from Linux kernel 2.6.33, file capabilities are always compiled into the kernel, and are therefore always present.

File capsets are a powerful security feature—you could say they are the modern equivalent of the older *set[u|g]id* features. To use them in the first place, the OS must support them, and the process (or thread) requires the CAP_FSETCAP capability. Here is the key point: The (previous) thread capsets along with the (coming) file capsets ultimately determine thread capabilities following an *exec* operation.

Here are the Linux file capability sets:

- Permitted (Prm): auto-permitted capabilities
- Inheritable (Inh)
- Effective (Eff): This is a single bit: if set, the new Prm capset gets raised in the Eff set; otherwise, it does not.

Once again, understand the caveat under which the above information has been provided: it's not the complete details. To get them, please check out the man page on capabilities(7) here: https://linux.die.net/man/7/capabilities.

*Process Capabilities*

Here is a screenshot snippet from this man page, showing the algorithm used to determine capabilities during the *exec* operation:

```
Transformation of capabilities during execve()
    During an execve(2), the kernel calculates the new capabilities of the  process
    using the following algorithm:

        P'(ambient)     = (file is privileged) ? 0 : P(ambient)

        P'(permitted)   = (P(inheritable) & F(inheritable)) |
                          (F(permitted) & cap_bset) | P'(ambient)

        P'(effective)   = F(effective) ? P'(permitted) : P'(ambient)

        P'(inheritable) = P(inheritable)    [i.e., unchanged]

    where:

        P          denotes the value of a thread capability set before the execve(2)

        P'         denotes the value of a thread capability set after the execve(2)

        F          denotes a file capability set

        cap_bset   is the value of the capability bounding set (described below).
```

## Embedding capabilities into a program binary

We have understood that the fine granularity of the capabilities model is a major security advantage over the old-style root only or setuid-root approach. So, back to our fictional packcap program: We would like to use *c*apabilities, and not the setuid-root. So, lets say that, upon careful study of the available capabilities, we conclude that we would like the following capabilities to be endowed into our program:

- CAP_NET_ADMIN
- CAP_NET_RAW

Looking up the man page on credentials(7) reveals that the first of them gives a process the ability to perform all required network administrative asks; the second, the ability to use "raw" sockets.

But how exactly does the developer embed these required capabilities into the compiled binary executable file? Ah, that's easily achieved with the getcap(8) and setcap(8) utilities. Obviously, you use getcap(8) to query a given file's capabilities and setcap (8) *to set them upon a given file.*

> "If not already installed, please do install the getcap(8) and setcap(8) utilities on your system (the book's GitHub repo provides a list of madatory and optional software packages)"

The alert reader will notice something fishy here: If you are able to arbitrarily set capabilities upon a binary executable file, then where is the security? (We could just set `CAP_SYS_ADMIN` on the file /bin/bash, and it would now run as the root.) So, the reality is that you can only set capabilities on a file if you already have the `CAP_FSETCAP` capability; from the manual:

```
CAP_SETFCAP  (since Linux 2.6.24)
             Set file capabilities.
```

In effect, practically speaking, you would thus perform the setcap(8) as root via sudo(8); this is because we only get the CAP_SETFCAP capability when running with root privilege.

So, let's do an experiment: We build a simple `hello world` program (`ch8/hello_pause.c`); the only difference is this: We call the `pause(2)` system call after the `printf`; the `pause` has process sleep (forever):

```c
int main(void)
{
    printf("Hello, Linux System Programming, World!\n");
    pause();
    exit(EXIT_SUCCESS);
}
```

We then write another C program to *query* the capabilities on any given process; the code of `ch8/query_pcap.c`:

```c
[...]
#include <sys/capability.h>

int main(int argc, char **argv)
{
    pid_t pid;
    cap_t pcaps;
    char *caps_text=NULL;

    if (argc < 2) {
        fprintf(stderr, "Usage: %s PID\n"
                " PID: process to query capabilities of\n"
                , argv[0]);
        exit(EXIT_FAILURE);
```

[ 289 ]

## Process Capabilities

```
        }
        pid = atoi(argv[1]);

        [...]
        pcaps = cap_get_pid(pid);
        if (!pcaps)
            FATAL("cap_get_pid failed; is process %d valid?\n", pid);

        caps_text = cap_to_text(pcaps, NULL);
        if (!caps_text)
            FATAL("caps_to_text failed\n", argv[1]);

        printf("\nProcess %6d : capabilities are: %s\n", pid, caps_text);
        cap_free(caps_text);
        exit (EXIT_SUCCESS);
}
```

It's simple: the `cap_get_pid(3)` API returns the capability state, essentially the `capsets` of the target process. The only hassle is it's represented via an internal data type called `cap_t`; to read it, we'd have to convert it to human-readable ASCII text; you guessed it, the `cap_to_text (3)`. API has precisely that function. We use it and print the result. (Hey, notice how we must `cap_free(3)` the variable after use; the manual informs us about this.)

Several of these APIs to do with capabilities (broadly the `cap_*` ones), require the `libcap` library to be installed on the system. If not already installed, use your package manager to do so (the correct package is usually called `libcap-dev[el*]`). Obviously, you must link with the `libcap` library (we use the `-lcap` to do so in the Makefile).

Let's try it out:

```
$ ./query_pcap
Usage: ./query_pcap PID
 PID: process to query capabilities of
$ ./query_pcap 1
Process      1 : capabilities are: =
cap_chown,cap_dac_override,cap_dac_read_search,cap_fowner,cap_fsetid,c
ap_kill,cap_setgid,cap_setuid,cap_setpcap,cap_linux_immutable,cap_net_
bind_service,cap_net_broadcast,cap_net_admin,cap_net_raw,cap_ipc_lock,
cap_ipc_owner,cap_sys_module,cap_sys_rawio,cap_sys_chroot,cap_sys_ptra
ce,cap_sys_pacct,cap_sys_admin,cap_sys_boot,cap_sys_nice,cap_sys_resou
rce,cap_sys_time,cap_sys_tty_config,cap_mknod,cap_lease,cap_audit_writ
e,cap_audit_control,cap_setfcap,cap_mac_override,cap_mac_admin,cap_sys
log,cap_wake_alarm,cap_block_suspend,cap_audit_read+ep
$
```

*Chapter 8*

Process PID 1, traditionally (Sys V) *init*, but nowadays `systemd`, runs with *root* privileges; thus, when we use our program to query its capsets (in reality, we get the effective capset returned), we get quite a long capability list! (as expected.)

Next, we build and run the `hello_pause` process in the background; then we query its capabilities:

```
$ make hello_pause
gcc -Wall   -c -o hello_pause.o hello_pause.c
gcc -Wall -o hello_pause hello_pause.c common.o
$ ./hello_pause &
[1] 14303
Hello, Linux System Programming, World!
$ ./query_pcap 14303
Process   14303 : capabilities are: =
$
```

Our `hello_pause` process is of course unprivileged, nor does it have any capabilities embedded within it; thus, as expected, we see it has *no* capabilities.

Now for the interesting part: Firstly, we embed capabilities into our `hello_pause` binary executable file using the `setcap(8)` utility:

```
$ setcap cap_net_admin,cap_net_raw+ep ./hello_pause
unable to set CAP_SETFCAP effective capability: Operation not permitted
$ sudo setcap cap_net_admin,cap_net_raw+ep ./hello_pause
[sudo] password for <xyz>: xxx
$
```

This makes sense: as `root` (technically, now we understand, with CAP_SYS_ADMIN capability), we of course have the CAP_SETFCAP capability, and thus succeed in using `setcap(8)`. Syntactically, we need to specify to `setcap(8)` a capability list followed by an action list; previously, we've specified the `cap_net_admin`, `cap_net_raw` capabilities, and the *add to effective and permitted* as the action list (with the +ep syntax).

Now, we retry our little experiment:

```
$ ./hello_pause &
[2] 14821
Hello, Linux System Programming, World!
$ ./query_pcap 14821
Process   14821 : capabilities are: = cap_net_admin,cap_net_raw+ep
$
```

[ 291 ]

Yes! The *new* `hello_pause` process indeed has the capabilities we wanted it to have.

> What happens if both the traditional setuid-root *and* the modern (file) capabilities are embedded in a binary executable? Well, in that case, when run, *only the capabilities embedded into the file* take effect; the process would have an EUID of 0, but would *not* have full *root* capabilities.

## Capability-dumb binaries

Notice something, though: the `hello_pause` program above *really has no* idea that it actually has these capabilities; in other words, it programmatically has done nothing to query or set POSIX capabilities on itself. Yet, via the file capabilities model (and the setcap(8) utility) we have "injected" capabilities into it. *This type of binary is therefore called a* **capability-dumb binary**.

It's still vastly superior to doing a clumsy setuid-root security-wise, but it could get even "smarter" if the application itself—programmatically—used APIs to query and set capabilities upon itself at runtime. We can think of this kind of app as a **capability-smart binary**.

Often, when porting a legacy setuid-root (or worse, just a *root*) type of application, developers will strip it of the setuid-root bit, knock off *root* ownership from the binary and then convert it into a *capability-dumb* binary by running setcap(8) on it. This is a good first step towards better security (or "hardening").

### Getcap and similar utilities

The `getcap(8)` utility can be used to look up the capabilities embedded in a (binary) *file*. As a quick example lets run `getcap` on the shell program and the ping utility:

```
$ getcap /bin/bash
$ getcap /usr/bin/ping
/usr/bin/ping = cap_net_admin,cap_net_raw+p
$
```

It's clear that bash does not have any file capsets—that's exactly what we expect. Ping, on the other hand, does, so that it can carry out its duties without requiring root privilege.

The `getcap` utility usage is amply demonstrated via a bash script (similar to the one we saw in the previous chapter): `ch8/show_caps.sh`. Run it to see various file capability embedded programs installed on the system (left as a simple exercise for the reader to try out).

Similar in some respects to `getcap(8)`, though a superset of it, is the `capsh(1)` utility—a **capability shell wrapper**; check out its man pages for details.

Also similar to the `query_pcap` program we wrote, is the `getpcaps(1)` utility.

## Wireshark – a case in point

So: the story we cooked up at the beginning of this topic is not entirely fictitious—well, it is, but it has a remarkable real-world parallel: the well known *Wireshark* (previously called Ethereal) network packet sniffer and protocol analyzer application.

On older versions, Wireshark used to run as a `setuid-root` process, to perform packet capture.

Modern versions of Wireshark separate out the packet capture into a program called **dumpcap1**. It does not run as a setuid-root process, it runs with required capability bits embedded into it, giving it just the privileges it requires to do its job—packet capture.

The potential payoff to a hacker now performing a successful attack on it is thus dramatically reduced— instead of gaining *root*, the hacker at best gains the privileges (EUID, EGID) of the user who is running Wireshark and the wireshark group; he does not get root! We use *ls(1)* and *getcap(1)* to see this as follows:

```
$ ls -l /bin/dumpcap
-rwxr-x---. 1 root wireshark 107K Jan 19 19:45 /bin/dumpcap
$ getcap /bin/dumpcap
/bin/dumpcap = cap_net_admin,cap_net_raw+ep
$
```

Notice, in the long listing above, the others (O) access category has no permissions; only a root user and members of Wireshark can execute dumpcap(1). (Do *not* execute it as a root; you will then defeat the whole point: security).

FYI, the actual packet-capture code is in a library called `pcap`—packet capture:

```
# ldd /bin/dumpcap | grep pcap
    libpcap.so.1 => /lib64/libpcap.so.1 (0x00007f9723c66000)
#
```

For your information: A security advisory from Red Hat detailing security issues with wireshark: https://access.redhat.com/errata/RHSA-2012:0509. A snippet from the following proves an important point:

> ... Several flaws were found in Wireshark. If Wireshark read a malformed packet off a network or opened a malicious dump file, it could crash or, possibly, **execute arbitrary code as the user running Wireshark**. (CVE-2011-1590, CVE-2011-4102, CVE-2012-1595) ...

The highlighted text is key: Even if a hacker manages the feat of arbitrary code execution, it will execute with the privileges of the user running Wireshark—not root!

> The details on how exactly to set up *Wireshark* with POSIX capabilities is covered here (under the section entitled *GNU/Linux distributions*: https://wiki.wireshark.org/CaptureSetup/CapturePrivileges.

It should now be amply clear: **dumpcap** is a *capability-dumb* binary; the Wireshark process (or file) itself is not privileged in any manner. Security wins, both ways.

## Setting capabilities programmatically

We've seen how to build a *capability-dumb* binary; now let's figure out how to add or drop process (thread) capabilities at runtime within the program itself.

The other side of the coin from getcap is the setcap of course—we have already worked with the utility on the command line. Now lets work with the relevant APIs.

The thing to understand is this: To work with the process capsets, we require what is called a "capability state" in memory. To get this capability state, we use the `cap_get_proc(3)` API (of course, as mentioned earlier, all these APIs are from the `libcap` library, which we will link into). Once we have a working context, the capability state, we will use the `cap_set_flag(3)` API to set up the transaction:

```
#include <sys/capability.h>
    int cap_set_flag(cap_t cap_p, cap_flag_t flag, int ncap,
                const cap_value_t *caps, cap_flag_value_t value);
```

The first parameter is the capability state we received from the `cap_get_proc()`; the second parameter is the capability set we wish to affect—one of effective, permitted or inherited. The third parameter is the number of capabilities we are manipulating with this one API call. The fourth parameter—this is where we identify the capabilities that we wish to add or drop, but how? We pass a pointer to an *array* of `cap_value_t`. Of course, we must initialize the array; each element holds a capability. The final, fifth parameter `value` can be one of two values: `CAP_SET` to *set* the capability, `CAP_CLEAR` to *drop* it.

Until now, all the work has been within a memory context—the capability state variable; it's not really taken effect upon the process (or thread) capsets. To actually set the capsets upon the process, we use the *cap_set_proc(3)* API:

`int cap_set_proc(cap_t cap_p);`

The parameter to it is the capability state variable that we carefully set up. *Now* the capabilities will be set.

Also realize, unless we run it as *root* (which of course we don't—that's really the whole point), we cannot just raise our capabilities. Hence, within the `Makefile` itself, once the program binary file is built, we perform a `sudo setcap` upon the binary executable file itself (`set_pcap`) enhancing its capabilities; we bestow the `CAP_SETUID` and the `CAP_SYS_ADMIN` capability bits into its permitted and effective capsets.

The next program briefly demonstrates how a process can add or drop capabilities (that are of course *within* it's permitted capset). When run with option 1, it adds the `CAP_SETUID` capability and "proves" it via a simple test function (`test_setuid()`). Here is an interesting bit: Since the binary *file* already has two capabilities embedded within it (we do a `setcap(8)` in the `Makefile`), we actually *need to drop* the `CAP_SYS_ADMIN` capability (from its effective set).

When run with option 2, we want two capabilities—`CAP_SETUID` and `CAP_SYS_ADMIN`; it will work, as these are embedded into the effective and permitted capsets.

Here is the relevant code of `ch8/set_pcap.c`:

```
int main(int argc, char **argv)
{
    int opt, ncap;
    cap_t mycaps;
    cap_value_t caps2set[2];
```

## Process Capabilities

```c
    if (argc < 2)
        usage(argv, EXIT_FAILURE);

    opt = atoi(argv[1]);
    if (opt != 1 && opt != 2)
        usage(argv, EXIT_FAILURE);

    /* Simple signal handling for the pause... */
    [...]

    //--- Set the required capabilities in the Thread Eff capset
    mycaps = cap_get_proc();
    if (!mycaps)
        FATAL("cap_get_proc() for CAP_SETUID failed, aborting...\n");

    if (opt == 1) {
        ncap = 1;
        caps2set[0] = CAP_SETUID;
    } else if (opt == 2) {
        ncap = 2;
        caps2set[1] = CAP_SYS_ADMIN;
    }
    if (cap_set_flag(mycaps, CAP_EFFECTIVE, ncap, caps2set,
            CAP_SET) == -1) {
        cap_free(mycaps);
        FATAL("cap_set_flag() failed, aborting...\n");
    }

/* For option 1, we need to explicitly CLEAR the CAP_SYS_ADMIN
capability; this is because, if we don't, it's still there as it's a
file capability embedded into the binary, thus becoming part of the
process Eff+Prm capsets. Once cleared, it only shows up in the Prm Not
in the Eff capset! */
    if (opt == 1) {
        caps2set[0] = CAP_SYS_ADMIN;
        if (cap_set_flag(mycaps, CAP_EFFECTIVE, 1, caps2set,
                CAP_CLEAR) == -1) {
            cap_free(mycaps);
            FATAL("cap_set_flag(clear CAP_SYS_ADMIN) failed,
aborting...\n");
        }
    }

  /* Have the caps take effect on the process.
   * Without sudo(8) or file capabilities, it fails - as expected.
   * But, we have set the file caps to CAP_SETUID (in the Makefile),
   * thus the process gets that capability in it's effective and
   * permitted capsets (as we do a '+ep'; see below):"
```

```
     *    sudo setcap cap_setuid,cap_sys_admin+ep ./set_pcap
     */
    if (cap_set_proc(mycaps) == -1) {
        cap_free(mycaps);
        FATAL("cap_set_proc(CAP_SETUID/CAP_SYS_ADMIN) failed,
aborting...\n",
                 (opt==1?"CAP_SETUID":"CAP_SETUID,CAP_SYS_ADMIN"));
    }
    [...]

    printf("Pausing #1 ...\n");
    pause();
    test_setuid();
    cap_free(mycaps);

    printf("Now dropping all capabilities and reverting to original
self...\n");
    drop_caps_be_normal();
    test_setuid();

    printf("Pausing #2 ...\n");
    pause();
    printf(".. done, exiting.\n");
    exit (EXIT_SUCCESS);
}
```

Let's build it:

```
$ make set_pcap
gcc -Wall -o set_pcap set_pcap.c common.o -lcap
sudo setcap cap_setuid,cap_sys_admin+ep ./set_pcap
$ getcap ./set_pcap
./set_pcap = cap_setuid,cap_sys_admin+ep
$
```

Notice the setcap(8) has embedded file capabilities into the binary executable set_pcap (which getcap(8) verifies).

Try it out; we'll first run it with option 2:

```
$ ./set_pcap 2 &
[1] 3981
PID   3981 now has CAP_SETUID,CAP_SYS_ADMIN capability.
Pausing #1 ...
$
```

## Process Capabilities

The `pause(2)` system call has put the process to sleep; this is deliberately done so that we can try things out (see the next code). As an aside, to work with this, the program has set up some minimal signal handling; however, this topic will be discussed in detail in subsequent chapters. For now, just understand that the pause (and associated signal handling) allows us to literally "pause" the process, inspect stuff, and once done, send it a signal to continue it:

```
$ ./query_pcap 3981
Process    3981 : capabilities are: = cap_setuid,cap_sys_admin+ep
$ grep -i cap /proc/3981/status
Name:      set_pcap
CapInh:    0000000000000000
CapPrm:    0000000000200080
CapEff:    0000000000200080
CapBnd:    0000003fffffffff
CapAmb:    0000000000000000
$
```

Above, we inspect the process via both our own `query_pcap` program and the proc filesystem. Both the CAP_SETUID and CAP_SYS_ADMIN capabilities are present in both the *Permitted* and *Effective* capsets.

To continue the process, we send it a signal; a simple way—via the `kill(1)` command (details in a later Chapter 11, *Signaling - Part I*). There's quite a bit to see now:

```
$ kill %1
*(boing!)*
test_setuid:
RUID = 1000 EUID = 1000
RUID = 1000 EUID = 0
Now dropping all capabilities and reverting to original self...
test_setuid:
RUID = 1000 EUID = 1000
!WARNING! set_pcap.c:test_setuid:55: seteuid(0) failed...
perror says: Operation not permitted
RUID = 1000 EUID = 1000
Pausing #2 ...
$
```

The funny *(boing!)* is just the process informing us that signal handling has occurred. (Ignore it.) We invoke the `test_setuid()` function, the function code:

```
static void test_setuid(void)
{
    printf("%s:\nRUID = %d EUID = %d\n", __FUNCTION__,
```

[ 298 ]

```
             getuid(), geteuid());
    if (seteuid(0) == -1)
        WARN("seteuid(0) failed...\n");
    printf("RUID = %d EUID = %d\n", getuid(), geteuid());
}
```

We attempt to become *root* (effectively) with the `seteuid(0)` line of code. The output shows us that we have succeeded in doing so as the EUID becomes 0. After this, we call the `drop_caps_be_normal()` function, which "drops" all capabilities *and* reverts us to "our original self", using the earlier-seen `setuid(getuid())` semantic; the function code:

```
static void drop_caps_be_normal(void)
{
    cap_t none;

    /* cap_init() guarantees all caps are cleared */
    if ((none = cap_init()) == NULL)
        FATAL("cap_init() failed, aborting...\n");
    if (cap_set_proc(none) == -1) {
        cap_free(none);
        FATAL("cap_set_proc('none') failed, aborting...\n");
    }
    cap_free(none);

    /* Become your normal true self again! */
    if (setuid(getuid()) < 0)
        FATAL("setuid to lower privileges failed, aborting..\n");
}
```

The program output indeed shows us that the EUID now reverts to non-zero (the RUID of `1000`) and the `seteuid(0)` fails, as expected (now that we've dropped capabilities and root privileges.)

The process then invokes `pause(2)` once more (the "Pausing #2 ..." statement in the output), so that the process remains alive; now we can see this:

```
$ ./query_pcap 3981
Process   3981 : capabilities are: =
$ grep -i cap /proc/3981/status
Name:     set_pcap
CapInh:   0000000000000000
CapPrm:   0000000000000000
CapEff:   0000000000000000
CapBnd:   0000003fffffffff
CapAmb:   0000000000000000
$
```

Indeed, all capabilities have been dropped. (We leave the test case of running the program with option 1 to the reader.)

Here is an interesting point: You might come across the statement `CAP_SYS_ADMIN` is the new root. Really? Let's test it: What if we embed only the `CAP_SYS_ADMIN` capability into the binary file and modify the code to not drop it when running under option 1? At first glance, it would seem that it should not matter—we should still be able to successfully perform the `seteuid(0)` as we're effectively running as root with this capability. But guess what? It doesn't work! Here's the bottom line: This teaches us that while the statement sounds good, it's really not completely true! We still require the `CAP_SETUID` capability to carry out arbitrary usage of the `set*id()` system calls.

We leave it to the reader to write the code for this case and test it as an exercise.

## Miscellaneous

A few remaining miscellaneous, but nevertheless useful, points and tips follow:

### How ls displays different binaries

A screenshot of Fedora 27 (x86_64) showing the pretty colors `ls -l` displays when displaying different binary executable types:

```
$ ls -l /usr/bin/passwd /usr/bin/write /usr/bin/ping /bin/dumpcap
-rwxr-x---. 1 root wireshark 109344 Jan 19 19:45 /bin/dumpcap
-rwsr-xr-x. 1 root root       27880 Aug  4  2017 /usr/bin/passwd
-rwxr-xr-x. 1 root root       62080 Aug  3  2017 /usr/bin/ping
-rwxr-sr-x. 1 root tty        19584 Sep 22 14:07 /usr/bin/write
$
```

What exactly are these binaries? Let's list just that, in the order they're displayed above:

- `dumpcap`: a file capabilities binary executable
- `passwd`: a `setuid-root` binary executable
- `ping`: a file capabilities binary executable
- `write`: a `setgid-tty` binary executable

Note: The precise meaning and coloring can certainly vary across Linux distributions; the output shown is from a Fedora 27 x86_64 system.

## Permission models layering

Now that we have seen details on both models—the traditional UNIX permissions in the previous chapter and the modern POSIX capabilities one in this one, we take a bird's-eye view of the same. The reality of a modern Linux kernel is that the legacy model is actually layered on top of the newer capabilities model; the following table shows this "layering":

| Pros and Cons | Model/Attributes |
|---|---|
| Simpler, less secure | UNIX Permissions<br>Process and File with UID, GID values embedded |
| | Process credentials: {RUID, RGID, EUID, EGID} |
| More complex, more secure | POSIX Capabilities |
| | Thread Capsets, File Capsets |
| | Per Thread: {Inherited, Permitted, Effective, Bounded, Ambient} capsets<br>Binary File: {Inherited, Permitted, Effective} capsets |

A few observations to note due to this layering, as follows:

- At the upper layer: What appears as a single integer, the process UID and GID, is actually two integers under the hood—the real and effective user | group IDs.
- Mid layer: Giving rise to the four process credentials: {RUID, EUID, RGID, EGID}.
- Bottom layer: Which in turn is integrated on modern Linux kernels into the POSIX capabilities model:
    - All kernel subsystems and code now use the capabilities model to control and determine access to an object.
    - Now *root* - the "new" root, really—is predicated on the (overloaded) capability bit `CAP_SYS_ADMIN` being set.
    - the set*id() system calls can be arbitrarily used to set real/effective IDs once the `CAP_SETUID` capability is present:
        - thus, you can make EUID = 0, and so on.

## Security tips

A quick summation of key points regarding security as follows:

- Obviously, with all our discussion, as far as is possible, do not use the now-outdated root mode any longer; this includes the (non) usage of setuid-root programs. Rather, you should use capabilities and assign only the required capabilities to the process:
    - directly or programmatically via the `libcap(3)` APIs ("capability-smart" binaries), or
    - indirectly via the `setcap(8)` file capabilities on the binary ("capability-dumb" binaries).
- If the above has been done via the API route, you should consider dropping capabilities immediately once the need for that capability is done (and raising it only as and when required).
- Containers: a "hot" fairly recent technology (essentially, containers are lightweight virtual machines in a sense), they are quoted as "safe" as they help isolate running code. However, the reality is not so rosy: Container deployment is often done with little or no thought toward security, resulting in highly insecure environments. You can greatly benefit security-wise from the wise use of the POSIX capabilities model. An interesting RHEL blog on how you can ask Docker (a popular container technology product) to drop capabilities and thus greatly increase security is detailed here: `https://rhelblog.redhat.com/2016/10/17/secure-your-containers-with-this-one-weird-trick/`.

## FYI – under the hood, at the level of the Kernel

(The paragraph that follows is just FYI and optional; if interested in deeper details then take a look, or feel free to skip it.)

Within the Linux kernel, all task (process and thread) metadata is kept within a data structure called the *task_struct* (also known as the *process descriptor*). The information on what Linux calls *the security context of a task* is kept within this task structure, embedded inside another data structure called **cred** (short for **credentials**). This structure, *cred*, contains everything we've discussed: The modern POSIX capabilities bitmasks (or capability sets) as well as the traditional-style process privileges: the RUID, EUID, RGID, EGID (as well as the set[u|g]id and fs[u|g]id bits).

The `procfs` method we saw earlier actually looks up the credential information from here. Hackers are obviously interested in accessing the cred structure and being able to modify it on the fly: filling it with zeros in the appropriate places gets them root! Does this sound far-fetched? Check out the *(Some) Linux Kernel Exploits* in the *Further reading* section on the GitHub repository. Unfortunately, it happens more often than anyone would like.

## Summary

In this chapter, the reader has been taken through important ideas on the design and implementation of the modern POSIX capabilities model (on the Linux OS). Among other things, we have covered what POSIX capabilities are, and, crucially, why they are important, especially from the viewpoint of security. The embedding of capabilities into a runtime process or binary executable was also covered.

The whole intent of the discussion, which started in the previous chapter, is to open the application developer's eyes to key security issues that arise when developing code. We hope we have left you, the reader, with a feeling of urgency, and of course the knowledge and tools to deal with security in a modern manner. Today's applications have to not just work; they have to be written with security in mind! or else...

# 9
# Process Execution

Imagine this scenario: while working on a project as a systems programmer (using C on Linux), there is a requirement that, from within the **graphical user interface (GUI)** frontend application, when the end user clicks a certain button, the application must display the content of a system-generated PDF document. We can assume a PDF reader software application is available to us. But, how exactly, will you run it from within your C code?

This chapter will teach you how to perform this important task. Here, we will learn some core Unix/Linux systems programming concepts: How the Unix exec model works, the predecessor/successor terminology, and how to use up to seven exec family APIs to make the whole thing actually work in code. Along the way, of course, code examples are used to clearly illustrate the concepts.

Briefly, the reader will learn about the following key areas:

- The meaning of the exec operation and its semantics
    - Testing the exec operation
    - Using the exec—the wrong and right ways to do so
- Error handling with the exec
- the seven exec family APIs and how to use them in code.

## Technical requirements

One of the exercises in this chapter requires the Poppler package (PDF utils) to be installed; it can be installed as follows:

On Ubuntu: `sudo apt install poppler-utils`

On Fedora: `sudo dnf install poppler-utils-<version#>`

> **TIP:** Regarding the Fedora case: to get the version number, just type the above command, and after typing `poppler-utils-` press the *Tab* key twice; it will autocomplete providing a list of choices. Choose the latest version and press *Enter*.

## Process execution

Here, we study how the Unix/Linux OS, at the level of the system programmer, executes programs. First, we will teach you to understand the important `exec` semantics; once this is clear, you can program it, using the `exec` family of APIs.

### Converting a program to a process

As has been mentioned before, a program is a binary file on a storage medium; by itself, it is a dead object. To run it and thus make it come alive, into a process, we have to execute it. When you run a program from, say, the shell, it does indeed come alive and become a process.

Here is a quick example:

```
$ ps
   PID TTY          TIME CMD
  3396 pts/3    00:00:00 bash
 21272 pts/3    00:00:00 ps
$
```

Looking at the previous code, from the shell (itself a process: bash), we run or execute the `ps(1)` program; `ps` does run; it is now a process; it does its job (here printing out the processes currently alive in this terminal's session), and then politely dies, leaving us back on the shell's prompt.

A moment's reflection will reveal that to have the `ps(1)` program become the `ps` process, some work probably had to be done by the **operating system (OS)**. Indeed, that is the case: The OS executes a program and makes it a running process ultimately via an API, a system call, called the `execve(2)`. For now, though, let's leave the APIs aside and focus on the concept.

# The exec Unix axiom

We learned in `Chapter 2`, *Virtual Memory*, which covered virtual memory, that a process can be visualized as a box (a rectangle), having a **virtual address space** (**VAS**); the VAS consists of homogeneous regions (technically, mappings) called segments. Essentially, a process's VAS is thus made up of several segments—text (code), data segments, library (and other) mappings, and a stack. For your convenience, the diagram representing a process's VAS is reproduced here:

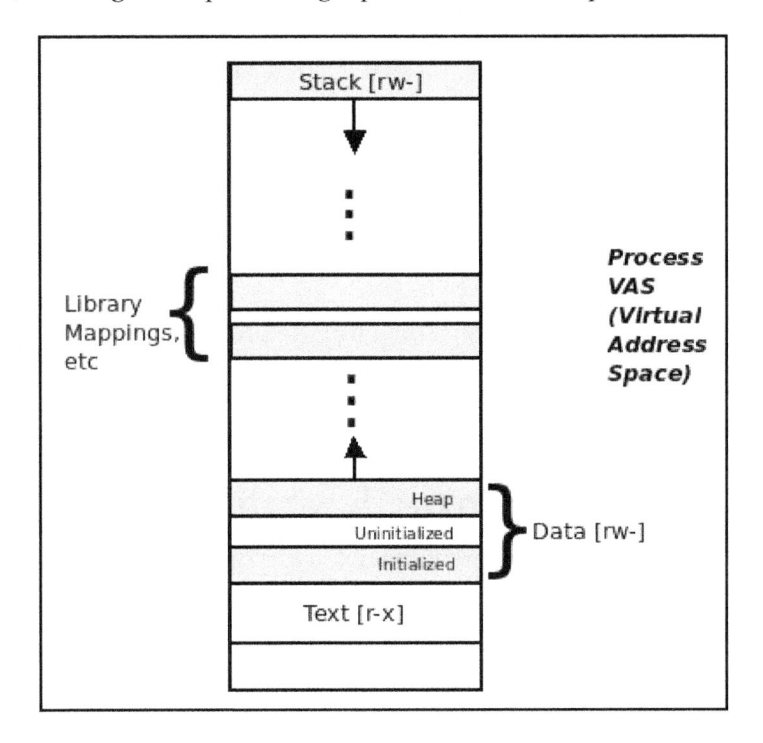

Fig 1 : The process virtual address space (VAS)

> The lower end has a virtual address of 0, and addresses increase as we go up; we have an upward-growing heap and a downward-growing stack.

Every process alive on the machine will have just such a process VAS; thus, it stands to reason, the shell in our preceding small example, bash, has such a process VAS (along with all its other attributes such as **process identifier** (PID), open files, and so on).

[ 307 ]

Process Execution

So, let's imagine that the shell process bash has a **PID** of 3,396. Now, when we run `ps` from the shell, what actually happens?

Well, obviously, as a first step, the shell checks whether `ps` is a built-in command; if so, it runs it; if not, which is the case, it continues on to the second step. Now, the shell parses the `PATH` environment variable, and, say, locates `ps` in `/bin`. The third step, the interesting one!, is where the shell process now executes `/bin/ps` via an API. We shall leave the discussion of the exact API(s) until later; for now, we shall just refer to the possible APIs as the `exec` APIs.

Don't lose the forest for the trees; a key point we now come to is this: The `exec`, when it occurs, causes the calling process (bash) to execute the called **process** (`ps`) by having (among other setups), `ps` overwrite it's **Virtual Address Space (VAS)**. Yes, you read that right—process execution on Unix, and thus Linux, is effected by having one process—the `caller`—get overwritten by the process to execute— the `callee`.

### Terminology

Here is some important terminology to help us: The process that is calling the `exec` (`bash`, in our example), is called the *predecessor*; the process that gets called and executed (`ps` in our example), is called the *successor*.

## Key points during an exec operation

The following sums up important points to note when a predecessor process execs a successor:

- The successor process overwrites (or overlays) the predecessor's virtual address space.
    - In effect, the predecessor's text, data, library, and stack segments are now replaced by that of the successor's.
    - The OS will take care of the size adjustments.
- No new process has been created—the successor now runs in the context of the old predecessor.
    - Several predecessor attributes (including but not limited to the PID and open files) thus get auto-inherited by the successor.
    (The astute reader could then question why, in our previous example, the PID of `ps` is not 3,396 ? Patience, please, we shall have the precise answer on the GitHub repository).

*Chapter 9*

- On a successful exec, there is no possibility of returning to the predecessor; it's gone. Colloquially, performing an exec is like committing suicide for the predecessor: After successful execution, the successor is all that's left; returning to the predecessor is out of the question:

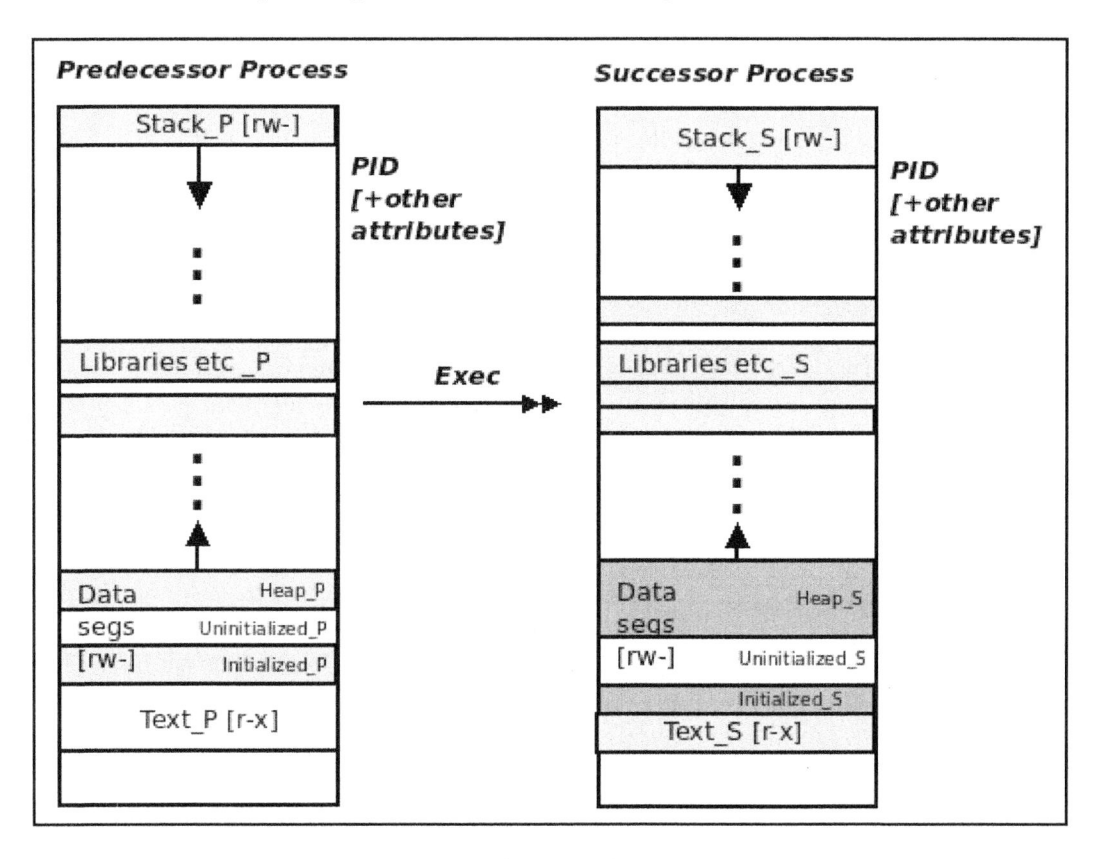

*Fig 2: The exec operation*

## Testing the exec axiom

Can you test this `exec` axiom described above? Sure. Let's try this in three different ways.

*Process Execution*

## Experiment 1 – on the CLI, no frills

Follow the simple steps here:

1. Fire up a shell (a Terminal window, typically, on a GUI-based Linux)
2. In the window, or more precisely, at the shell prompt, type this:

```
$ exec ps
```

What do you notice? Can you explain it?

> Hey, come on, please try it out first, and then read on.
>
> Yes, the terminal window process is the predecessor here; upon an `exec` it's overwritten by the successor process `ps`, which does its work and exits (you probably did not see the output as it disappeared too quickly). `ps` is the successor process, and, of course, we cannot return to the predecessor (the Terminal window)—`ps` has literally replaced its VAS. Thus, the Terminal window effectively disappears.

## Experiment 2 – on the CLI, again

This time, we'll make it easier on you! Follow the given steps:

1. Fire up a shell (a Terminal window, typically, on a GUI-based Linux).
2. In the window, or more precisely, at the shell prompt, run `ps` followed by `bash` —yes, we're spawning a subshell here, followed by `ps` once more. (Check out the next screenshot; notice the PIDs of the original and sub-shell Bash processes - 3,396 and 13,040.).
3. On the sub-shell, `exec` the `ps` command; this `ps` successor process overwrites (or overlays) the process image of the predecessor process—the bash sub-shell.
4. Observe the output: In the `exec ps` command output, the PID of `ps` is the PID of the bash subshell process: 13,040! This suggests that it's running in the context of that process.
5. Also notice we're back to the original bash shell process PID 3,396 now, as, of course, we cannot return to the predecessor:

```
$ ps
  PID TTY          TIME CMD
 3396 pts/3    00:00:00 bash
13030 pts/3    00:00:00 ps
$ bash
$ ps
  PID TTY          TIME CMD
 3396 pts/3    00:00:00 bash
13040 pts/3    00:00:00 bash
13087 pts/3    00:00:00 ps
$ exec ps
  PID TTY          TIME CMD
 3396 pts/3    00:00:00 bash
13040 pts/3    00:00:00 ps
$
```

A third experimental run will follow shortly, once we've got some exec APIs to play with.

## The point of no return

It's important for the systems programmer to understand that, once an exec operation is successful, there is no return to the predecessor process. To illustrate this, consider the rough call graph here:

```
main()
    foo()
        exec(something)
    bar()
```

main() calls foo(), which calls exec(something); once the exec is successful, bar() will never run!

Why not? We cannot reach it in the predecessor's execution path as the entire execution context has now changed—to the context of the successor process (something). The PID remains intact though.

Only if the exec fails will the function bar() get control (as, of course, we would still be in the context of the predecessor).

# Process Execution

As a further fine point, note that it's possible that the `exec()` operation itself succeeds, but the process being executed, something, fails. That's OK; it does not change the semantics; `bar()` will still not execute, as the successor has taken over.

## Family time – the exec family APIs

Now that we have understood the `exec` semantics, it's time we saw how to perform the `exec` operation programmatically. Unix and Linux provide several C APIs, seven in fact, that all ultimately do the same job: They have the predecessor process `exec` the successor.

So, there are seven APIs that all do the same thing? Mostly, yes; hence they are called the `exec` family of APIs.

Lets take a look at them:

```
#include <unistd.h>
extern char **environ;

int execl(const char *path, const char *arg, ...);
int execlp(const char *file, const char *arg, ...);
int execle(const char *path, const char *arg, ...,
           char * const envp[]);
int execv(const char *path, char *const argv[]);
int execvp(const char *file, char *const argv[]);
int execvpe(const char *file, char *const argv[],
            char *const envp[]);
   execvpe(): _GNU_SOURCE
```

Hang on, though we said seven APIs, but the list above has six; indeed: the seventh is special in a sense and not shown above. As usual, have a bit of patience; we will cover it!

The reality is that though each API will ultimately perform the same job, using a particular one helps based on the situation you are in (convenience-wise). Lets not nitpick, and, for now, at least, disregard their differences; instead, let's focus on understanding the first one; the rest will automatically and easily follow.

Take the first API, the `execl(3)`:

```
int execl(const char *path, const char *arg, ...);
```

Does it take two, three, or more parameters? Well, in case you are new to it, the ellipse— . . . — represents a variable argument list or `varargs`, a feature supported by the compiler.

The first parameter is the path name to the application you would like to execute.

From the second parameter onward, the `varargs`, the argument(s) to pass to the successor process are inclusive of `argv[0]`. Think about it, in the simple experiments above, we passed along parameters on the command line via the shell process; in reality, it was really the shell process, the predecessor, that passed arguments required by the successor process. This makes sense: Who else but the predecessor would pass arguments to the successor?

How will the compiler know that you are done passing along arguments? Simple: you must null terminate the argument list: `execl(const char *pathname_to_successor_program, const char *argv0, const char *argv1, ..., const char *argvn, (char *)0);`

Now you can see why it's named the way it is: the `execl` API, of course, performs an exec; the last letter `l` implies long format; each argument of the successor process is passed to it.

To clarify this, let's write a simple example C program; its job is to invoke the `uname` process:

> For readability, only the relevant parts of the code are displayed here; to view and run it, the entire source code is available here: https://github.com/PacktPublishing/Hands-on-System-Programming-with-Linux.

```
int main(int argc, char **argv)
{
    if (argc < 2) {
        [...]
    }
    /* Have us, the predecessor, exec the successor! */
    if (execl("/bin/uname", "uname", argv[1], (char *)0) == -1)
        FATAL("execl failed\n");
    printf("This should never get executed!\n");
    exit (EXIT_SUCCESS);
}
```

Here are a few points to note:

- The first argument to the `execl` API is the path name of the successor.
- The second parameter is the name of the program. Be careful: a fairly typical newbie mistake is to leave it out!
- In this simple case, we only then pass along whatever the user sends as the argument `argv[1]`: `-a` or `-r`; we don't even perform robust error checking to ensure the correct parameter is passed by the user (we leave it as an exercise for you).
- If we just attempt to null-terminate with a single 0, the compiler complains, with a warning such as this (this could differ depending on the `gcc` compiler version you use):
  `warning: missing sentinel in function call [-Wformat=]`.
  To eliminate the warning, you must typecast the 0 with `(char *)` as shown in the code.
- Finally, we use a `printf()` to demonstrate that control will never reach it. Why is this? Well, think about it:
  - Either the `execl` succeeds; thus the successor process (`uname`) takes over.
  - Or the `execl` fails; the `FATAL` macro performs error reporting and terminates the predecessor.

Let's build and try it out:

```
$ ./execl_eg
Usage: ./execl_eg {-a|-r}
 -a : display all uname info
 -r : display only kernel version
$
```

Pass an argument; we show a few examples here:

```
$ ./execl_eg -r
4.13.0-36-generic
$ ./execl_eg -a
Linux seawolf-mindev 4.13.0-36-generic #40-Ubuntu SMP Fri Feb 16
20:07:48 UTC 2018 x86_64 x86_64 x86_64 GNU/Linux
$ ./execl_eg -eww
uname: invalid option -- 'e'
Try 'uname --help' for more information.
$
```

It does work (though, as can be seen from the last case, the `execl_eg` program's argument the error checking isn't great).

> **TIP**: We encourage you to try this simple program out yourself; in fact, experiment a bit: for example, change the first parameter to some unknown (for example, `/bin/oname`) and see what happens.

## The wrong way

Sometimes, to show the right way to do something, it's useful to first see it done the wrong way!

### Error handling and the exec

Some programmer's show off: They don't use an *if* condition to check whether the `exec` API failed; they just write the line of code after an `exec` to be the failure case!

As an example, take the previous program, but change the code to this, the wrong way to do it:

```
execl("/bin/uname", "uname", argv[1], (char *)0);
FATAL("execl failed\n");
```

It works, yes: The only reason control will ever reach the `'FATAL()'` line is if the exec operation failed. This sounds cool, but please, do not code like that. Be professional, follow the rules and good coding style guidelines; you'll be a better programmer and glad for it! (An innocent freshly minted programmer might not even realize that what follows the `execl` above is actually error handling; who could blame him? And he might attempt to put some business logic there!)

### Passing a zero as an argument

Let's say we have a (fictional) requirement: From within our C code, we must execute the program `/projectx/do_this_now` passing along three parameters: -1, 0 and 55. Like so:

`/projectx/do_this_now -1 0 55`

## Process Execution

Recall the syntax of the `exec` API:

```
execl(const char *pathname_to_successor_program, const char
*argv0, const char *argv1, ..., const char *argvn, (char *)0);
```

So, it seems quite trivial; let's do it:

```
execl("/projectx/do_this_now", "do_this_now", -1, 0, 55, (char
*)0);
```

Whoops! The compiler will, or *could*, interpret the second argument to the successor 0 (after the -1) as the NULL terminator, and would therefore not see the following argument 55.

Fixing this is easy; we just have to remember that *each argument to the* successor *process is of data type character pointer*, not integer; the NULL terminator itself is an integer (though to keep the compiler happy we typecast it to (char *)), like so:

```
execl("/projectx/do_this_now", "do_this_now", "-1", "0", "55",
(char *)0);
```

### Specifying the name of the successor

No, we are not debating how to hack who will succeed Queen Elizabeth II to the throne here, sorry. What we are referring to is this: How can you correctly specify the name of the successor process; that is, can we programmatically change it to whatever we like?

At first glance, it looks trivial indeed: The second parameter to the `execl` is the `argv[0]` argument to pass to the successor; in effect, it appears, its name! So, let's try it out: We write a couple of C programs; the first one, the predecessor (`ch9/predcs_name.c`) is passed a name parameter from the user. It then execs another program of ours, `successor_setnm` via the `execl` passing along the user-supplied name as the first parameter (within the API, it sets the successor `argv[0]` parameter to the predecessor's `argv[1]`), like so: `execl("./successor_setnm", argv[1], argv[1], (char *)0);`

Recall the `execl` syntax: `execl(pathname_to_successor_program, argv0, argv1, ..., argvn, 0);`

[ 316 ]

So, the thinking here is: The predecessor has set the successor's `argv[0]` value to `argv[1]`, and thus the successor's name should be the predecessor's `argv[1]`. However, it does not work out; see the output from a sample run:

```
$ ./predcs_name
Usage: ./predcs_name {successor_name} [do-it-right]
$ ./predcs_name UseThisAsName &
[1] 12571
UseThisAsName:parameters received:
argv[0]=UseThisAsName
argv[1]=UseThisAsName
UseThisAsName: attempt to set name to 1st param "UseThisAsName"
[Wrong]
UseThisAsName: pausing now...
$
$ ps
   PID TTY          TIME CMD
  1392 pts/0    00:00:01 Bash
 12571 pts/0    00:00:00 successor_setnm
 12576 pts/0    00:00:00 ps
$
```

We deliberately have the successor process invoke the `pause(2)` system call (it simply causes it to sleep until it receives a signal). This way, we can run it in the background, and then run `ps` to lookup the successor PID and name!

Interesting: We find that, though the name is not what we want in `ps` output (above), it is correct in the `printf`; implying that `argv[0]` has been correctly received and set to the successor.

OK, we must clean up; lets kill off the background process now:

```
$ jobs
[1]+  Running                 ./predcs_name UseThisAsName &
$ kill %1
[1]+  Terminated              ./predcs_name UseThisAsName
$
```

*Process Execution*

So, as is now apparent, what we've done preceding is not enough: To reflect the name we want at the level of the OS, we need an alternate API; one such API is the `prctl(2)` system call (or even the `pthread_setname_np(3)` pthreads API). Without getting into too much detail here, we use it with the `PR_SET_NAME` parameter (as usual, please see the man page on `prctl(2)` for full details). Hence, the correct code using the `prctl(2)` system call (only the relevant code snippet from `successor_setnm.c` is displayed here):

```
[...]
    if (argc == 3) { /* the "do-it-right" case! */
        printf("%s: setting name to \"%s\" via prctl(2)"
            " [Right]\n", argv[0], argv[2]);
        if (prctl(PR_SET_NAME, argv[2], 0, 0, 0) < 0)
            FATAL("prctl failed\n");
    } else { /* wrong way... */
        printf("%s: attempt to implicitly set name to \"%s\""
            " via the argv[0] passed to execl [Wrong]\n",
            argv[0], argv[1]);
    }
[...]

$ ./predcs_name
Usage: ./predcs_name {successor_name} [do-it-right]
$
```

So, we now run it the right way (the logic involves passing along an optional second parameter which will be used to _correctly_ set the successor process name):

```
$ ./predcs_name NotThis ThisNameIsRight &
[1] 12621
ThisNameIsRight:parameters received:
argv[0]=ThisNameIsRight
argv[1]=NotThis
argv[2]=ThisNameIsRight
ThisNameIsRight: setting name to "ThisNameIsRight" via prctl(2)
[Right]
ThisNameIsRight: pausing now...
$ ps
  PID TTY          TIME CMD
 1392 pts/0    00:00:01 Bash
12621 pts/0    00:00:00 ThisNameIsRight
12626 pts/0    00:00:00 ps
$ kill %1
[1]+  Terminated              ./predcs_name NotThis ThisNameIsRight
$
```

This time it works exactly as expected.

# The remaining exec family APIs

Great, we've covered in detail how to and how not to use the first of the exec family of APIs—the execl(3). What about the remainder? Let's check them out; reproduced for the reader's convenience is the list:

```
#include <unistd.h>
extern char **environ;

int execl(const char *path, const char *arg, ...);
int execlp(const char *file, const char *arg, ...);
int execle(const char *path, const char *arg, ...,
           char * const envp[]);
int execv(const char *path, char *const argv[]);
int execvp(const char *file, char *const argv[]);
int execvpe(const char *file, char *const argv[],
            char *const envp[]);
   execvpe(): _GNU_SOURCE
```

As mentioned several times, the execl syntax is this: execl(const char *pathname_to_successor_program, const char *argv0, const char *argv1, ..., const char *argvn, (char *)0);

Recall, it's named execl; the l implies a long format variable argument list: each argument of the successor process is passed to it in turn.

Now let's look at the other APIs in the family.

## The execlp API

The execlp is a slight variation on the execl:

```
int execlp(const char *file, const char *arg, ...);
```

As before, the l in execlp implies a long format variable argument list; the p implies that the environment variable PATH is searched for the program to execute. As you are probably aware, the PATH environment variable consists of a set of colon-delimited (:) directories to search for the program file to run; the first match is the program that is executed.

For example, on our Ubuntu VM (where we are logged in as the user seawolf):

```
$ echo $PATH
/home/seawolf/bin:/home/seawolf/.local/bin:/usr/local/sbin:/usr/local/bin:/usr/sbin:/usr/bin:/sbin:/bin:/usr/games:/usr/local/games
$
```

*Process Execution*

Thus, if you execute a process via the `execlp`, you need not give the absolute or full path name as the first parameter, but just the program name; see how the following two examples differ:

`execl("/bin/uname", "uname", argv[1], (char *)0);`

**`execlp`**`("uname", "uname", argv[1], (char *)0);`

With the `execl`, you have to specify the full path name to `uname`; with the `execlp`, you need not; the library routine will perform the work of looking up the PATH and figuring out the match to `uname`! (It would find the first match in `/bin`).

> **TIP**
> Use the `which` utility to locate a program, in effect finding it's first match in the path. For example:
>
> ```
> $ which uname
> /bin/uname
> $
> ```

This, the fact the `execlp` automatically searches the path, indeed is convenient; note though, this is at the possible cost of security!

> **TIP**
> Hackers write programs called Trojans - essentially, programs that pretend to be something they're not; these are obviously dangerous. If a hacker can place a Trojan version of `uname` in your, say, home directory, and modify the PATH environment variable to search your home directory first, then they could take control when you (think) you are running `uname`.
>
> For security reasons, it's always better to specify the full `pathname` when executing a program (hence, avoid using the `execlp`, `execvp`, and the `execvpe` APIs).

What if the PATH environment variable is undefined? In this case, the APIs default to searching the current working directory (the `cwd`) of the process as well as something called the `confstr` path, which usually defaults to the directory `/bin` followed by `/usr/bin`.

## The execle API

Now for the `execle(3)` API; its signature is:

`int **execle**(const char *path, const char *arg, ...,char * const envp[]);`

As before, the `l` in `execle` implies a long format variable argument list; the `e` implies that we can pass along an array of environment variables to the successor process.

> The process environment consists of a set of `<name>=<value>` variable pairs. The environment is actually unique to each process and is stored within the process stack segment. You can see the entire list via either the `printenv`, `env`, or `set` commands (*set* is a shell built-in). Programmatically, use the `extern char **environ` to gain access to the process's environment.

By default, the successor will inherit the environment of the predecessor process. What if this is not what is required; for example, we would like to execute a process but change the value of, say, the PATH (or perhaps introduce a new environment variable into the mix). To do so, we would have the predecessor process make a copy of the environment, modify it as required (perhaps adding, editing, deleting variables as required), and then pass along the pointer to the new environment to the successor process. That's precisely what the last parameter `char * const envp[]` is meant for.

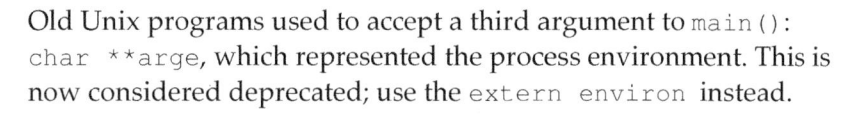

> Old Unix programs used to accept a third argument to `main()`: `char **arge`, which represented the process environment. This is now considered deprecated; use the `extern environ` instead.
>
> There is no mechanism to pass just a few environment variables to the successor process; the whole bunch—in the form of a two-dimensional array of strings (which is itself `NULL`-terminated) must be passed.

## The execv API

The *execv(3)* API's signature is:

`int **execv**(const char *path, char *const argv[]);`

*Process Execution*

As can be seen, the first parameter is the pathname of the successor process. The second parameter is, similar to the environment list above, a two-dimensional array of strings (each of them NULL-terminated) holding all the arguments to pass to the successor, starting from argv[0]. Think about it, it's identical to what we, C programmers, are so used to; this is the signature of the main() function in C:

int main(int argc, char *argv[]);

argc, of course, is the number of parameters received, including the program name itself (held in argv[0]), and argv is a pointer to a two-dimensional array of strings (each of them NULL-terminated) holding all the arguments starting from argv[0].

Hence, we colloquially call this the short format (as opposed to the long format we used earlier - the l style). When you see the v (short for argv), it represents the short format argument-passing style.

Now, the remaining two APIs are simple:

- The execvp(3): short format arguments, and path being searched.
- The execvpe(3): short format arguments, path being searched, and environment list being explicitly passed to the successor. Additionally, this API requires the feature test macro _GNU_SOURCE to be defined (which, incidentally, we do in all this book's source code).

The exec functions with the p in them—the ones that search the PATH—the execlp, execvp, and execvpe, have an additional feature: If the file they are searching for is found but permission to open it is lacking, they will not fail immediately (like the other exec APIs that would fail and set errno to EACCESS); instead, they will continue searching the remainder of the PATH for the file.

## Exec at the OS level

Up until now, we have covered six of the seven *exec family* APIs. Finally, the seventh one is the execve(2). Did you notice? The 2 in brackets conveys that it's a system call (recall the details covered regarding system calls in Chapter 1, *Linux System Architecture*).

The fact is, all the preceding six `exec` APIs are within `glibc`—the library layer; only the `execve(2)` is a system call. You will realize that, ultimately, to have a process be able to execute another program—thus launching or running a successor—will require OS-level support. So, yes, the reality is that all the above six `exec` APIs are merely wrappers; they transform their arguments and invoke the `execve` system call.

This is the signature of the `execve(2)`:

```
int execve(const char *filename, char *const argv[], char *const envp[]);
```

Take a look at the exec family APIs summary table.

## Summary table – exec family of APIs

Here is a table to summarize all seven of the `exec` family APIs:

| Exec API | Arguments: long format (l) | Arguments: short format (v) | PATH searched? (p) | Environment passed? (e) | API layer |
|---|---|---|---|---|---|
| execl   | Y | N | N | N | Lib |
| execlp  | Y | N | Y | N | Lib |
| execle  | Y | N | N | Y | Lib |
| execv   | N | Y | N | N | Lib |
| execvp  | N | Y | Y | N | Lib |
| execvpe | N | Y | Y | Y | Lib |
| execve  | N | Y | N | Y | SysCall |

The exec APIs format: `exec<foo>`, where `<foo>` is differing combinations of `{l,v,p,e}`.

All the listed APIs, on success, as we have learned, do not return at all. Only upon failure, would you see a return value; as per the usual norms, the global variable `errno` will get set to reflect the cause of the error, which can be conveniently looked up via the `perror(3)` or `strerror(3)` APIs (as an example, within the book's provided source code, check out the `FATAL` macro within the `common.h` header file).

*Process Execution*

## Code example

In the introduction to this chapter, we mentioned a requirement: from within a GUI frontend, to display the content of a system-generated PDF document. Lets do this here.

To do so, we would require a PDF reader application; we can assume we have one. Indeed, on many Linux distributions, the evince application is a good PDF reader application, usually preinstalled (true on Ubuntu and Fedora, among others).

Well, here, we shall not bother with a GUI frontend application, we shall use plain old C to write a CLI app that, given a PDF document `pathname`, executes the evince PDF reader application. What PDF document do we display? Ah, that's a surprise! (take a look):

> For readability, only the relevant parts of the code are displayed as follows; to view and run it, the entire source code is available here: https://github.com/PacktPublishing/Hands-on-System-Programming-with-Linux.

```c
const char *pdf_reader_app="/usr/bin/evince";
static int exec_pdf_reader_app(char *pdfdoc)
{
    char * const pdf_argv[] = {"evince", pdfdoc, 0};

    if (execv(pdf_reader_app, pdf_argv) < 0) {
        WARN("execv failed");
        return -1;
    }
    return 0; /* never reached */
}
```

We invoke the preceding function from `main()` as follows:

```c
if (exec_pdf_reader_app(argv[1]) < 0)
    FATAL("exec pdf function failed\n");
```

We build it, then perform a sample run:

```
$ ./pdfrdr_exec
Usage: ./pdfrdr_exec {pathname_of_doc.pdf}
$ ./pdfrdr_exec The_C_Programming_Language_K\&R_2ed.pdf 2>/dev/null
$
```

Here is a screenshot of the action!

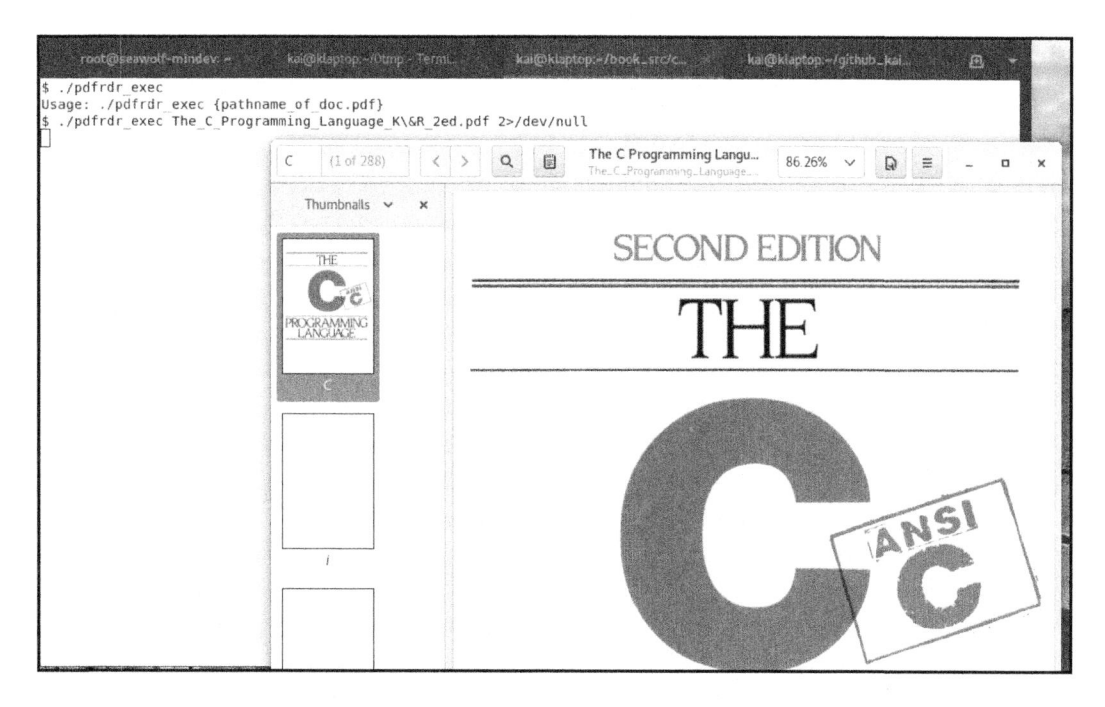

What if we are running Linux on the console only (no GUI)? Then, of course, the preceding app will not work (and evince is unlikely to even be installed). Here is an example of this case:

```
$ ./pdfrdr_exec ~/Seawolf_MinDev_User_Guide.pdf
!WARNING! pdfrdr_exec.c:exec_pdf_reader_app:33: execv failed
perror says: No such file or directory
FATAL:pdfrdr_exec.c:main:48: exec pdf function failed
perror says: No such file or directory
$
```

In this case, why not try modifying the above app to use a CLI PDF toolset instead; one such toolset is from the Poppler project (see the following note). Within it, one of the interesting utilities it provides is `pdftohtml`. Why not use it to generate HTML from a PDF document? We leave it as an exercise for the reader (see the *Questions* section on the GitHub repository).

# Process Execution

> **TIP**: These useful PDF utilities are provided by an open source project called Poppler. You can easily install these PDF utilities, on an Ubuntu box: `sudo apt install poppler-utils`

We can quite easily trace what happens in the `pdfrdr_exec` program; here, we use the `ltrace(1)` to see the library calls issued:

```
$ ltrace ./pdfrdr_exec The_C_Programming_Language_K\&R_2ed.pdf
execv("/usr/bin/evince", 0x7ffcd861fc00 <no return ...>
--- Called exec() ---
g_static_resource_init(0x5575a5aff400, 0x7ffc5970f888, 0x7ffc5970f8a0,
32) = 0
ev_get_locale_dir(2, 0x7ffc5970f888, 0x7ffc5970f8a0, 32)
= 0x7fe1ad083ab9
[...]
```

The key call: the `execv` of course is seen; interestingly, `ltrace` then helpfully tells us that there's no return ... from it. We then see the library APIs of the evince software itself.

What if we use `strace(1)` to see the system calls issued?

```
$ strace ./pdfrdr_exec The_C_Programming_Language_K\&R_2ed.pdf
execve("./pdfrdr_exec", ["./pdfrdr_exec",
"The_C_Programming_Language_K&R_2"...], 0x7fff7f7720f8 /* 56 vars */)
= 0
brk(NULL)                               = 0x16c0000
access("/etc/ld.so.preload", R_OK)      = 0
openat(AT_FDCWD, "/etc/ld.so.preload", O_RDONLY|O_CLOEXEC) = 3
fstat(3, {st_mode=S_IFREG|0644, st_size=0, ...}) = 0
[...]
```

Yes, the very first one is the `execve(2)`, proving that the `execv(3)` library API invokes the `execve(2)` system call. The rest of the output, of course, is the system calls issued by the evince process as it executes.

# Summary

This chapter covered the Unix/Linux `exec` programming model; the key concept of the predecessor and successor processes, and, importantly, how the successor (more-or-less completely) overlays the predecessor. The seven `exec` family APIs were covered, along with several code examples. Error handling, successor name specification, and so on, were covered as well. The systems programmer will now have sufficient knowledge to write C code that correctly executes a given program from within a process.

# 10
# Process Creation

In the previous chapter, we learned how to handle a (fictional) application design and implementation requirement: getting our C program to execute (`exec`) another program altogether. However, the reality is that the discussion remains incomplete; this chapter on process creation will fill in several gaps, and much more.

In this chapter, you will learn about some core Unix/Linux systems programming concepts: the gory details required to correctly program the critical `fork(2)` system call to create a process. Along the journey, Unix aficionado terms such as blocking calls, orphans, and zombies are made clear as well. The material carefully brings out subtle points, turning the average developer into a proficient one. The reader will, in parallel, learn to write C code to implement the preceding key concepts in a Linux systems application. As usual, several code examples are used to clearly illustrate and harden the concepts taught.

The purpose of this chapter is to guide the Linux systems developer into the core system programming worlds of the Unix `fork-exec-wait` semantics and related areas. Briefly, we will focus upon the following areas, helping the reader learn:

- The Unix process creation model
- The whys and the hows of it
- Deeper details, including:
    - How the fork affects memory allocations, open files and so on, and security implications
    - The several forms of the `wait` APIs
    - How these APIs are made use of practically
    - The rules of fork
    - Orphan and zombie processes

# Process creation

Unless a Unix/Linux systems programmer has been living under a rock somewhere, they've certainly heard of, if not directly worked with, the fork(2) system call. Why is it so well known and important? The reason is simple: Unix is a multitasking OS; programmers must exploit the OS's capabilities. To have an application multitask, we need to create multiple tasks or processes; the fork is the Unix way to create a process. In fact, to the typical systems programmer, fork is the only way available to create a process.

> There is another system call to create a process or thread: clone(2). It also creates, well, a custom process. It's not typically used by Linux application developers; library (typically the thread library) developers use it more. In this book, we do not explore clone; for one thing, it's very Linux-specific and non-portable; for another, it's more of a hidden API.
>
> The other way to multitask is by multithreading of course, which will be covered in detail in later chapters.

## How fork works

In theory, the job description of the fork(2) system call can be crystallized down to one simple statement: *create an identical copy of the calling process*. The terminology we shall repeatedly encounter is as follows: the process-calling *fork* is called the **parent** and the newly created, newborn process is called the **child**.

> Please note that, to begin with at least, we shall keep the discussion on how fork works purely conceptual and simple; later, we shall delve deeper and clarify how the OS performs several necessary optimizations.

Fork is a system call; thus, the real work of process creation is carried out by the OS under the hood. Recall from Chapter 2, *Virtual Memory*, that the **virtual address space** (**VAS**) of a process is built out of homogeneous regions called **segments** (or **mappings**). Thus, when a child process is created, the OS will copy the parent's text, data (three of them), library (and other mappings), plus the stack segment to the child.

Hang on though; it does not stop there: There is more, much more, to a process than just its VAS. This includes open files, process credentials, scheduling information, filesystem structures, paging tables, namespaces (PIDs, and so on), audit information, locks, signal handling information, timers, alarms, resource limits, IPC structures, profiling (perf) information, security (LSM) pointers, seccomp, thread stacks and TLS, hardware context (CPU and other registers), and so on.

> Many of the attributes mentioned earlier are well beyond the scope of this book, and we shall not attempt to delve into them. The idea is to show that there is much more to a process than just VAS.

Phew! So, performing a fork involves the kernel copying several things from the parent to the child process. But, think about it: not all attributes are directly inherited by the child from the parent (many are, but certainly not all are). For example, the process PID and PPID (parent PID) is not inherited (can you figure out why?).

As a first-level enumeration, the following process attributes are inherited by the child process upon fork (meaning, it-the new born child-gets a copy of the parent's attributes with the same content):

- The **VAS**:
    - Text
    - Data:
        - Initialized
        - Uninitialized (bss)
        - Heap
    - Library segments
    - Other mappings (for example, shared memory regions, mmap regions, and so on)
    - Stack
- Open files
- Process credentials
- Scheduling information
- Filesystem (VFS) structures
- Paging tables
- Namespaces
- Signal dispositions
- Resource limits

Process Creation

- IPC structures
- Profiling (perf) information
- Security information:
    - Security (LSM) pointers
    - Seccomp
- Thread stacks and TLS
- Hardware context

The following attributes of the parent process are not inherited by the child process upon forking:

- PID, PPID
- Locks
- Pending and blocked signals (cleared for child)
- Timers, alarms (cleared for child)
- Audit information (CPU/time counters are reset for child)
- Semaphore adjustments made via `semop(2)`
- **Asynchronous IO (AIO)** ops and contexts

It's useful to see this in the form of a diagram:

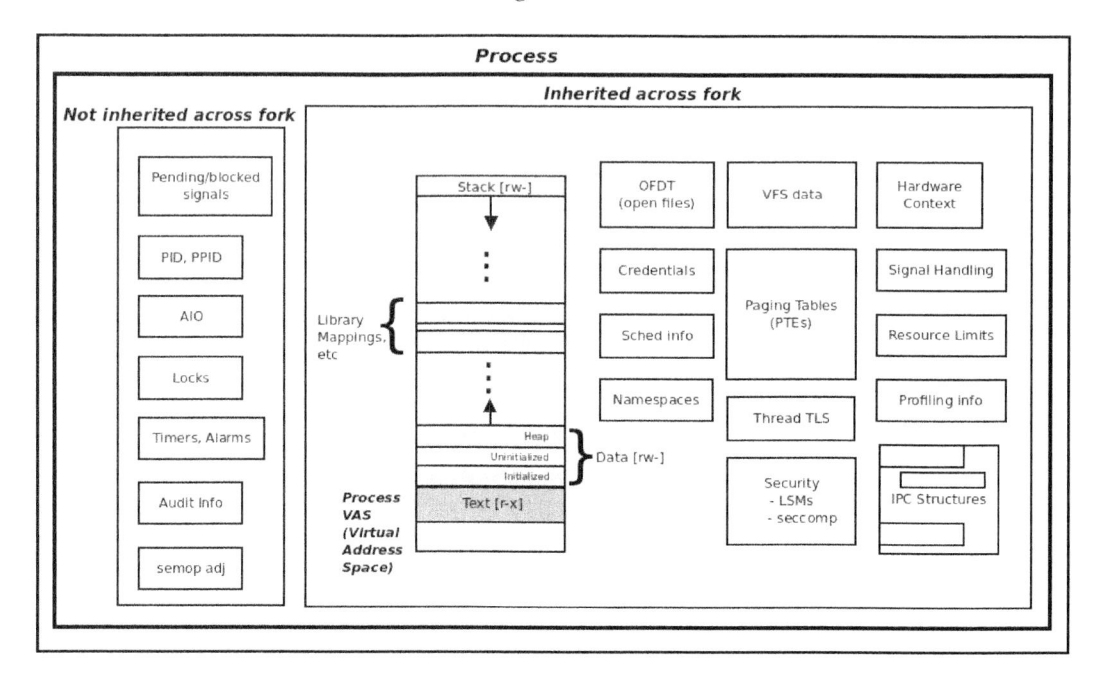

**Process**

*Inherited across fork*

*Not inherited across fork*

| Not inherited across fork | Inherited across fork |
|---|---|
| Pending/blocked signals | Stack [rw-], OFDT (open files), VFS data, Hardware Context |
| PID, PPID | Credentials, Paging Tables (PTEs), Signal Handling |
| AIO | Library Mappings, etc, Sched info, Resource Limits |
| Locks | Namespaces, Thread TLS, Profiling info |
| Timers, Alarms | Heap, Uninitialized, Initialized, Data [rw-] |
| Audit Info | Process VAS (Virtual Address Space), Text [r-x], Security - LSMs - seccomp, IPC Structures |
| semop adj | |

[ 332 ]

*Chapter 10*

As can be seen, fork(2) is indeed a heavyweight operation!

If interested, you can find more detail on the inheritance/non-inheritance characteristics within the man page on fork(2).

## Using the fork system call

The signature of the fork is simplicity itself:

```
pid_t fork(void);
```

This looks trivial, but you know the saying *the devil lies in the details!* Indeed, we shall bring out several subtle, and not-so-subtle, pointers regarding the correct usage of this system call.

To begin to understand how fork works, lets write a simple C program (ch10/fork1.c):

```
int main(int argc, char **argv)
{
    fork();
    printf("Hello, fork.\n");
    exit (EXIT_SUCCESS);
}
```

Build and run it:

```
$ make fork1
gcc -Wall -c ../../common.c -o common.o
gcc -Wall   -c -o fork1.o fork1.c
gcc -Wall -o fork1 fork1.c common.o
$ ./fork1
Hello, fork.
Hello, fork.
$
```

The fork will, on success, have created a new child process.

> A key programming rule: never assume an API succeeds, always check for the failure case !!!

[ 333 ]

*Process Creation*

This cannot be overstressed.

OK, let's modify the code to check for the failure case; any and every system call (with perhaps just two exceptions out of around 380 syscalls) return -1 on failure. Check for it; here is the relevant code snippet (ch10/fork1.c):

```
if (fork() == -1)
    FATAL("fork failed!\n");
printf("Hello, fork.\n");
exit(EXIT_SUCCESS);
```

The output is identical to what we saw previously (of course, since the fork did not fail). So, the printf seems to have been executed twice. Indeed it was: once by the parent process, and once by the new child process. This immediately teaches us something about the way fork works; here, we will attempt to codify these things as the rules of fork. In this book, we shall end up codifying seven rules of fork(2).

# Fork rule #1

**Fork rule #1**: *After a successful fork, execution in both the parent and child process continues at the instruction following the fork.*

Why does it happen this way? Well, think about it: the job of fork is to make a (pretty much) identical copy of the parent in the child; this includes the hardware context (mentioned earlier), which of course includes the **Instruction Pointer** (**IP**) register (sometimes called the **Program Counter** (**PC**)) itself! Hence, the child process too will execute the user mode code at the same location as the parent. As the fork is successful, control will not go the error handling code (the FATAL() macro); instead, it will go to the printf. *The key point is this: this will happen in both the (original) parent and the (new) child process.* Hence the output.

To reinforce the point, we write a third version of this same simple C program (ch10/fork3.c). Here, we just show the printf statement as it's the only line of code that changes (from the ch10/fork3.c):

```
printf("PID %d: Hello, fork.\n", getpid());
```

Build and run it:

```
$ ./fork3
PID 25496: Hello, fork.
PID 25497: Hello, fork.
$
```

[ 334 ]

Ah! Now we can actually see that two processes have run the `printf`! Probably (but not for sure), PID `25496` is the parent process, the other of course is the child. After this, both processes execute the `exit(3)` API, and thus both die.

## Fork rule #2 – the return

Let's take a look at the code we've used so far:

```
if (fork() == -1)
    FATAL("fork failed!\n");
printf("PID %d: Hello, fork.\n", getpid());
exit(EXIT_SUCCESS);
```

OK, we now understand from the first rule that the `printf` will be run twice and in parallel—once by the parent, and once by the child process.

But, think about it: is this really useful? Can a real-world application benefit from this? No. What we are really after, what would be useful, is a division of labor, that is to say, have the child perform some task or tasks, and the parent perform some other task(s), in parallel. That makes the fork attractive and useful.

For example, after the fork, have the child run the code of some function `foo` and the parent run the code of some other function `bar` (of course, these functions can internally invoke any number of other functions as well). Now that would be interesting and useful.

To arrange for this, we would require some means of *distinguishing between the parent and child after the fork*. Again, at first glance, it might appear that querying their PIDs (via the `getpid(2)`) would be the way to do this. Well, you could, but that's a crude way to do so. The proper way to distinguish between the processes is built into the framework itself: It's—guess what—based on the value returned by the fork.

In general, you might quite correctly state that if a function is called once, it returns once. Well, fork is special—when you call a `fork(3)`, it returns twice. How? Think about it, the job of the fork is to create a copy of the parent, the child; once done, both processes must now return to user space from kernel mode; thus fork is called once but returns twice; once in the parent and once in the child process context.

# Process Creation

The key though, is that the kernel guarantees that the return values in parent and child differ; here are the rules regarding the return value of `fork`:

- On success:
    - The return value in the child process is zero (`0`)
    - The return value in the parent process is a positive integer, the PID of the new child
- On failure, `-1` is returned and `errno` is set accordingly (do check!)

So, here we go:

**Fork rule** #2: *To determine whether you are running in the parent or child process, use the fork return value: it's always 0 in the child, and the PID of the child in the parent.*

Here's another detail: look for a moment at the `fork`'s signature:

**pid_t** `fork(void);`

The return value's data type is a `pid_t`, certainly a `typedef`. What is it? Lets find out:

```
$ echo | gcc -E -xc -include 'unistd.h' - | grep "typedef.*pid_t"
typedef int __pid_t;
typedef __pid_t pid_t;
$
```

There we are: it's just an integer, after all. But that's not the point. The point here is that when writing code, do not assume it's integer; just declare the data type as per what the man page specifies; in the case of `fork`, as `pid_t`. This way, even if in future the library developers change `pid_t` to, say, `long`, our code will just require a re-compile. We future-proof our code, keeping it portable.

Now that we understand three fork rules, let's write a small, but better, fork-based application to demonstrate the same. In our demo program, we will write two simple functions `foo` and `bar`; their code is identical, they will emit a print and have the process sleep for the number of seconds passed to them as a parameter. The sleep is to mimic the working of a real program (of course, we can do better, but for now we'll just keep it simple).

[ 336 ]

The `main` function is as follows (as usual, find the full source code on the GitHub repository, `ch10/fork4.c`):

```
int main(int argc, char **argv)
{
    pid_t ret;

    if (argc != 3) {
        fprintf(stderr,
            "Usage: %s {child-alive-sec} {parent-alive-sec}\n",
            argv[0]);
        exit(EXIT_FAILURE);
    }
    /* We leave the validation of the two parameters as a small
     * exercise to the reader :-)
     */

    switch((ret = fork())) {
    case -1 : FATAL("fork failed, aborting!\n");
    case 0 : /* Child */
            printf("Child process, PID %d:\n"
                " return %d from fork()\n"
                    , getpid(), ret);
            foo(atoi(argv[1]));
            printf("Child process (%d) done, exiting ...\n",
                getpid());
            exit(EXIT_SUCCESS);
    default : /* Parent */
            printf("Parent process, PID %d:\n"
                " return %d from fork()\n"
                    , getpid(), ret);
            bar(atoi(argv[2]));
    }
    printf("Parent (%d) will exit now...\n", getpid());
    exit(EXIT_SUCCESS);
}
```

First, here is a number of points to note:

- The return variable has been declared as `pid_t`.
- Rule #1—execution in both the parent and child process continues at the instruction following the fork. Here, the instruction following the fork is not the switch (as is commonly mistaken), but rather the initialization of the variable `ret`! Think about it: it will guarantee that `ret` is initialized twice: once in the parent and once in the child, but to different values.

- Rule #2—to determine whether you are running in the parent or child process, use the fork return value: it's always 0 in the child, and the PID of the child in the parent. Ah, thus we see that the effect of both rules is to make sure that `ret` gets correctly initialized and, therefore, we can switch correctly
- A bit of an aside—the need for input validation. Have a look at the parameters we pass to the `fork4` program as follows:

```
$ ./fork4 -1 -2
Parent process, PID 6797 :: calling bar()...
 fork4.c:bar :: will take a nap for 4294967294s ...
Child process, PID 6798 :: calling foo()...
 fork4.c:foo :: will take a nap for 4294967295s ...
[...]
```

Need we say more (see the output)? This is a defect (a bug). As mentioned in the source code comment, we leave the validation of the two parameters as a small exercise to the reader.

- Instead of an `if` condition, we would prefer to use the switch-case syntax; in your author's opinion, it makes the code more readable and thus better maintainable.
- As we learned in rule 2, fork returns 0 in the child and the PID of the child in the parent; we use this knowledge in the switch-case and we thus effectively, and very readably, distinguish between the child and parent in the code.
- When the child process ID is done, we do not have it call *break*; instead, we have it exit. The reason should be obvious: clarity. Have the child do whatever it requires within its business logic (`foo()`), and then simply have it go away. No fuss; clean code. (If we did use a break, we would require another `if` condition after the `switch` statement; this would be ugly and harder to understand.)
- The parent process falls though the switch-case, it just emits a print, and exits.

Because the functions `foo` and `bar` are identical, we show the code for `foo` only here:

```
static void foo(unsigned int nsec)
{
    printf(" %s:%s :: will take a nap for %us ...\n",
            __FILE__, __FUNCTION__, nsec);
    sleep(nsec);
}
```

OK, let's run it:

```
$ ./fork4
Usage: ./fork4 {child-alive-sec} {parent-alive-sec}
$ ./fork4 3 7
Parent process, PID 8228:
 return 8229 from fork()
 fork4.c:bar :: will take a nap for 7s ...
Child process, PID 8229:
 return 0 from fork()
 fork4.c:foo :: will take a nap for 3s ...
Child process (8229) done, exiting ...
Parent (8228) will exit now...
$
```

As you can see, we chose to keep the child alive for three seconds and the parent alive for seven seconds respectively. Study the output: the return values from fork are as expected.

Now let's run it again but in the background (Also, we give more sleep time, 10 seconds and 20 seconds to the child and parent respectively.) Back on the shell, we shall use `ps(1)` to see the parent and child processes:

```
$ ./fork4 10 20 &
[1] 308
Parent process, PID 308:
 return 312 from fork()
 fork4.c:bar :: will take a nap for 20s ...
Child process, PID 312:
 return 0 from fork()
 fork4.c:foo :: will take a nap for 10s ...
$ ps
  PID TTY          TIME CMD
  308 pts/0    00:00:00 fork4
  312 pts/0    00:00:00 fork4
  314 pts/0    00:00:00 ps
32106 pts/0    00:00:00 bash
$ ps -l
F S   UID   PID  PPID  C PRI  NI ADDR SZ WCHAN  TTY          TIME CMD
0 S  1000   308 32106  0  80   0 -  1111 hrtime pts/0    00:00:00
fork4
1 S  1000   312   308  0  80   0 -  1111 hrtime pts/0    00:00:00
fork4
0 R  1000   319 32106  0  80   0 -  8370 -      pts/0    00:00:00 ps
0 S  1000 32106 32104  0  80   0 -  6003 wait   pts/0    00:00:00 bash
$
$ Child process (312) done, exiting ...          << after 10s >>
```

[ 339 ]

*Process Creation*

```
Parent (308) will exit now...                    << after 20s >>
<Enter>
[1]+  Done                    ./fork4 10 20
$
```

The `ps -l` (l: long listing) reveals more details about each process. (For example, we can see both the PID as well as the PPID.)

In the preceding output, did you notice how the PPID (parent process ID) of the `fork4` parent happens to be the value `32106` and the PID is `308`. Isn't this odd? You usually expect the PPID to be a smaller number than the PID. This is often true, but not always! The reality is that the kernel recycles PIDs from the earliest available value.

**An experiment to simulate work in the child and parent processes**.

Let's do this: We create a copy of the `fork4.c` program, calling it `ch10/fork4_prnum.c`. Then, we modify the code slightly: We eliminate the functions `foo` and `bar`, and, instead of just sleeping, we have the processes simulate some real work by invoking a simple macro `DELAY_LOOP`. (The code is in the header file `common.h`.) The macro prints a given character a given number of times, which we pass as input parameters to `fork4_prnum`. Here is a sample run:

```
$ ./fork4_prnum
Usage: ./fork4_prnum {child-numbytes-to-write} {parent-numbytes-to-
write}
$ ./fork4_prnum 20 100
Parent process, PID 24243:
 return 24244 from fork()
pChild process, PID 24244:
 return 0 from fork()
ccpcpcpcpcpcpcpcpcpcpcpcpcpcpcpcpcpcpcpcpChild process (24244) done,
exiting ...
ppppppppppppppppppppppppppppppppppppppppppppppppppppppppppppppppppppppp
ppppppppppParent (24243) will exit now...
$
```

The `DELAY_LOOP` macro is coded to print the character `p` (for parent) and `c` (for child); the number of times it's printed is passed along as parameters. You can quite literally see the scheduler context switching between the parent and child process! (the interleaved `p`'s and `c`'s demonstrate when each of them has the CPU).

To be pedantic, we should ensure both processes run on exactly one CPU; this can be easily achieved with the `taskset(1)` utility on Linux. We run `taskset` specifying a CPU mask of 0 implying that the job(s) should run only on the CPU 0. (Again, we leave it as a simple look-up exercise for the reader: check out the man page on `taskset(1)`, and learn how to use it:

```
$ taskset -c 0 ./fork4_prnum 20 100
Parent process, PID 24555:
 return 24556 from fork()
pChild process, PID 24556:
 return 0 from fork()
ccppccpcppcpcpccpcpcppcpccpcppcpccppccppChild process (24556) done,
exiting ...
ppppppppppppppppppppppppppppppppppppppppppppppppppppppppppppppppp
ppppppppParent (24555) will exit now...
$
```

We recommend that you actually try out these programs on their system to get a feel for how they work.

## Fork rule #3

**Fork rule #3**: *After a successful fork, both the parent and child process execute code in parallel.*

At first glance, this rule looks pretty much the same as the first rule. But no, what's being stressed here is parallelism. The parent's and child's execution paths run in parallel with each other.

You might wonder how on a single (uni) processor system, this can be? Well, that's right: a fundamental attribute of a modern processor is that exactly one machine instruction can run at any given point in time. So, if we're on a uniprocessor box, it just means that the processes will be time-slicing (or timesharing) on the CPU. So, it's pseudo-parallel; however, the speed of a modern CPU being what it is, a human user will perceive the execution as being in parallel. On a multicore (SMP) system, they would, or could, run truly in parallel. So, the detail regarding a uni-processor is just that: a detail. The key point is that we should visualize both the parent and child as executing code in parallel.

*Process Creation*

So, in the previous code example, this rule tells us that the entire code paths of the parent and child processes will run in parallel; visualizing this parallelism is really the initial difficulty of the fork for folks new to it! To help with precisely that, see the following figures (though we only show the code of the switch-case for brevity): the parent's code path is highlighted in one color (red), and the child's code path in another color (blue):

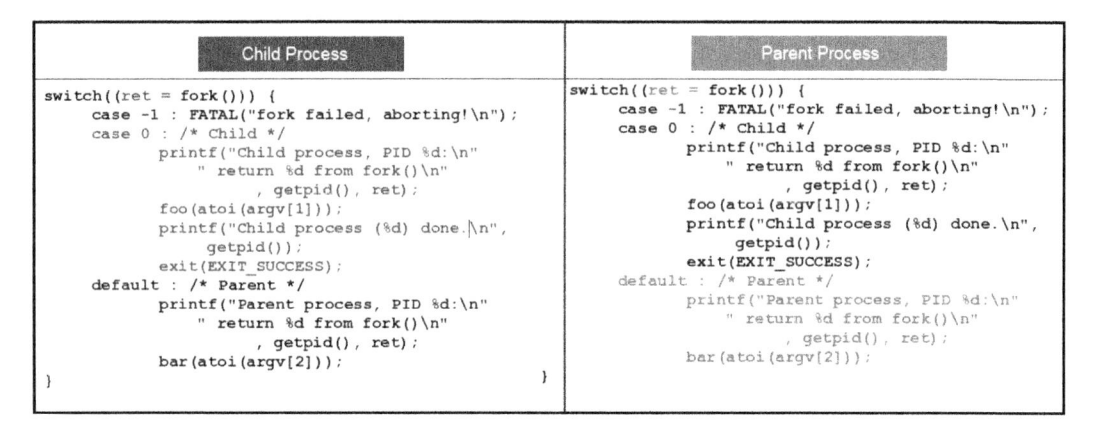

| Child Process | Parent Process |
|---|---|
| ```switch((ret = fork())) {
    case -1 : FATAL("fork failed, aborting!\n");
    case 0 : /* Child */
            printf("Child process, PID %d:\n"
                " return %d from fork()\n"
                    , getpid(), ret);
            foo(atoi(argv[1]));
            printf("Child process (%d) done.\n",
                getpid());
            exit(EXIT_SUCCESS);
    default : /* Parent */
            printf("Parent process, PID %d:\n"
                " return %d from fork()\n"
                    , getpid(), ret);
            bar(atoi(argv[2]));
}``` | ```switch((ret = fork())) {
    case -1 : FATAL("fork failed, aborting!\n");
    case 0 : /* Child */
            printf("Child process, PID %d:\n"
                " return %d from fork()\n"
                    , getpid(), ret);
            foo(atoi(argv[1]));
            printf("Child process (%d) done.\n",
                getpid());
            exit(EXIT_SUCCESS);
    default : /* Parent */
            printf("Parent process, PID %d:\n"
                " return %d from fork()\n"
                    , getpid(), ret);
            bar(atoi(argv[2]));
}``` |

This is the key point: the code in blue and the code in red, the child and parent processes, run in parallel!

```
switch((ret = fork())) {
    case -1 : FATAL("fork failed, aborting!\n");
    case 0 : /* Child */
            printf("Child process, PID %d:\n"
                " return %d from fork()\n"
                    , getpid(), ret);
            foo(atoi(argv[1]));
            printf("Child process (%d) done, exiting ...\n",
                getpid());
            exit(EXIT_SUCCESS);
    default : /* Parent */
            printf("Parent process, PID %d:\n"
                " return %d from fork()\n"
                    , getpid(), ret);
            bar(atoi(argv[2]));
}
```

In the second diagram, the blue and red timeline arrows are used to again depict this parallelism.

## Atomic execution?

While seeing the preceding code flow diagrams, you can be misled into believing that once the process starts executing its code, it continues undisturbed until it finishes. This is certainly not necessarily going to happen; in reality, the process will often get context switched out of and back into the CPU as they run.

This leads us to an important point: *atomic execution*. A piece of code is considered to be atomic IFF (if and only if) it always runs to completion without interruption. Atomicity, especially in userspace, is not guaranteed: often, the process (or thread) execution is interrupted or preempted (sources of interruption/preemption include hardware interrupts, faults, or exceptions, and scheduler context switching). Keeping a code section atomic within the kernel can be arranged, though.

# Fork rule #4 – data

When a parent process forks, we understand that the child is created; it is a copy of the parent. This will include the VAS, and, thus, the data and stack segments. Keeping this fact in mind, check out the following code snippet (ch10/fork5.c):

```
static int g=7;
[...]
int main(int argc, char **argv)
    [...]
    int loc=8;
    switch((ret = fork())) {
    case -1 : FATAL("fork failed, aborting!\n");
    case 0 : /* Child */
        printf("Child process, PID %d:\n", getpid());
        loc ++;
        g --;
        printf( " loc=%d g=%d\n", loc, g);
        printf("Child (%d) done, exiting ...\n", getpid());
        exit(EXIT_SUCCESS);
    default : /* Parent */
#if 1
        sleep(2); /* let the child run first */
#endif
        printf("Parent process, PID %d:\n", getpid());
        loc --;
        g ++;
```

```
                printf( " loc=%d g=%d\n", loc, g);
        }
        printf("Parent (%d) will exit now...\n", getpid());
        exit(EXIT_SUCCESS);
```

The preceding program (ch10/fork5) has an initialized global variable g and an initialized local variable loc. The parent process, after fork, sleeps for two seconds thus more-or-less guaranteeing that the child process runs first (this kind of synchronization is incorrect in production quality code; we shall address this point in detail later in this chapter). Both the child and parent processes work on the global and local variables; the key question here is this: will the data get corrupted?

Let's just run it and see:

```
$ ./fork5
Child process, PID 17271:
 loc=9 g=6
Child (17271) done, exiting ...
Parent process, PID 17270:           << after 2 sec >>
 loc=7 g=8
Parent (17270) will exit now...
$
```

Well, the data variables are not corrupted. Again, the key point here is this: as the child has a copy of the parent's variables, all goes well. They change independently of one another; they do not step on each other's toes. So, consider this:

**Fork rule #4**: *Data is copied across the fork, not shared.*

## Fork rule #5 – racing

Notice the #if 1 and #endif surrounding the sleep(2); statement in the previous code (ch10/fork5.c)? It of course implies that the code will be compiled and thus run.

What if we change the #if 1 to #if 0? It's obvious, the sleep(2); statement is effectively compiled out. Let's do this: rebuild and re-run the fork5 program. What will now happen?

Think about this: fork rule #4 tells us the story. After the fork, we will still have the child and parent processes working on separate copies of the data variables; hence, the values we saw earlier will not change.

However, this time, there is no sleep to crudely synchronize the parent and child; thus, the question arises, will the `printf` for the child or parent code (displaying the variable values) run first? In other words, the question we are really asking is this: in the absence of any kind of synchronization primitive, after the `fork(2)`, which process will get the processor first: parent or child? The short answer is the next rule:

**Fork rule** #5: *After the fork, the order of execution between the parent and child process is indeterminate.*

Indeterminate? Well, this is a fancy way to say *we really have no idea* or *it's unpredictable*. So that is the deal: the systems developer should not try to predict the order of execution. Running the modified `fork5` (`no sleep(2)` statement) now:

```
$ ./fork5
Parent process, PID 18620:
 loc=7 g=8
Parent (18620) will exit now...
Child process, PID 18621:
 loc=9 g=6
Child (18621) done, exiting ...
$
```

Ah, the parent ran first. That does not really mean anything! The parent might run first the next 50,000 times you try it out, but on the 50,001st trial run, the child process may run first. Leave it alone: it's unpredictable.

This leads us to another key point (common in software): We have what's called a **race condition** here. A race is literally what it says: we cannot predict with certainty who will be the winner. In the previous program, we really don't care whether the parent or child process wins the race (runs first): this is called a benign race condition. But often in software design we do actually care; in such cases, we need a way to guarantee the winner. In other words, to defeat the race. This is called synchronization. (As mentioned earlier, we shall address this point in detail later in this chapter.)

## The process and open files

To clearly understand the effect of fork on open files, we need to slightly digress and briefly understand some background information.

Process Creation

> **TIP**: In fact, for those readers very new to performing I/O on files within the Unix paradigm, it will be beneficial to first read through the Appendix A, *File I/O Essentials*, before tackling this section.

A Unix/Linux process, upon startup, will by default be assigned three open files; we've discussed these basic points earlier in the book. For convenience, the three open files are called the stdin, stdout, and stderr of the process; they auto-default to the keyboard, the monitor, and, again, the monitor for stdin, stdout, and stderr respectively. Not only that, real applications will certainly open other files as they perform their tasks. Recall the layered system architecture; if a Linux application opens a file using the fopen(3) library API, it will ultimately boil down to the open(2) system call, which returns a handle to the open file, called a **file descriptor**. (Think about it: consider a Java app running on Linux that opens a file: Ultimately, this time, via the JVM, the work will be done via the same open(2) system call!)

The point here is this: the kernel stores every process's open files within a data structure (in classic Unix terminology, it's called the **Open File Descriptor Table (OFDT)**. We saw earlier in the section that talked about characteristics inherited by the child process upon fork, that open files are indeed inherited by the child. To facilitate this discussion, consider the following pseudo-code snippet:

```
main
...
   foo
       fd = open("myfile", O_RDWR);
       ...
       fork()
           // Child code
           ... work_on_file(fd) ...
           // Parent code
           ... work_on_file(fd) ...
...
```

Here, the file myfile is now available to both processes and can be worked upon via the file descriptor fd! But hang on: it should be clear that working on the same file simultaneously by both child and parent processes could certainly corrupt the file; or if not the file content, at least the application. To perceive this, consider the function work_on_file (pseudo-code):

```
work_on_file(int fd)
{   /* perform I/O */
    lseek(fd, 0, SEEK_SET);
```

```
    read(fd, buf, n);
    lseek(...);
    write(fd, buf2, x);
    ...
}
```

## Fork rule #6 – open files

You can see that without any synchronization, havoc would result! Hence the next fork rule:

**Fork rule #6**: *Open files are (loosely) shared across the fork.*

The upshot of all that is this: the systems programmer must understand that, if the parent process has opened a file (or files), naively working on the file simultaneously (remember fork rule #3!) will likely cause bugs. A key reason is this: although the processes are distinct, the object they work upon, the open file, and, more precisely, its inode, is one distinct object and thus shared. In fact, the file's *seek position* is an attribute of the inode; blindly re-positioning the seek pointer in parent and child without synchronization will pretty much guarantee problems.

There are broadly two choices to keep things running smoothly:

- Have one of the process's close the file
- Synchronize access to the open file

The first of them keeps things simple but is of limited use in real-world applications; they would usually require that the file remains open. Thus, the second choice: how exactly do you synchronize access to the open file?

Again, the details are not covered in this book, but, very briefly, you can synchronize file I/O between processes like so:

- Via the SysV IPC or POSIX semaphore
- Via file locking

The first one works, but crudely. It's not considered the right way. The second solution, using file locking, is definitely the preferred one. (File locking is not covered in detail here, please refer the *Further reading* section for a link to an excellent tutorial on the same on the GitHub repository.)

*Process Creation*

It's also important to realize that when either the parent or child process closes the open file, its access to the open file is closed; the file is still open in the other process. This is really what is meant by the phrase "loosely shared".

As a quick way to demo this issue, we write a simple program ch10/fork_r6_of.c (here, **of** stands for **open file**). We leave it to the reader to go through the source code; an explanation and sample output follows.

First, we have the process open a regular file tst; then, we have the child process do this: seek to offset 10, and write *numlines* (equal to 100) lines of c's. In parallel, we have the parent process do this: seek to offset 10+(80*100), and write *numlines* lines of p's. So when we have finished and we examine the file, we expect that we have 100 lines of cs and 100 lines of ps. But, hey, it does not actually happen that way. Here's the actual run:

```
$ ./fork_r6_of
Parent process, PID 5696:
 in fork_r6_of.c:work_on_file now...
   context: parent process
Child process, PID 5697:
 in fork_r6_of.c:work_on_file now...
   context: child process
Parent (5696) will exit now...
Child (5697) done, exiting ...
$
```

This is the test file's content after the run:

```
$ vi tst
^@^@^@^@^@^@^@^@^@^@ppppppppppppppppppppppppppppppppppppppppppppppppppppppppppppp
ppppppppppppppppppppppppppppp
ccccccccccccccccccccccccccccccccccccccccccccccccccccccccccccccccccccccc
ccccccccc
ppppppppppppppppppppppppppppppppppppppppppppppppppppppppppppppppppppppp
ppppppppp
ccccccccccccccccccccccccccccccccccccccccccccccccccccccccccccccccccccccc
ccccccccc
ppppppppppppppppppppppppppppppppppppppppppppppppppppppppppppppppppppppp
ppppppppp
ccccccccccccccccccccccccccccccccccccccccccccccccccccccccccccccccccccccc
ccccccccc
[...]
:q
$
```

The ps and cs interleave! Yes, indeed, because the processes ran in parallel without any form of synchronization. (By examining the file content, we can literally see how the kernel CPU scheduler context-switched between the parent and the child processes). By not using synchronization, we have set up a race. So how do we set this right? It was mentioned earlier: file locking is really the answer (Note: do not attempt to synchronize with the silly sleep(2) in the parent kind of code we've used; that's just for demonstration; Also, we shall cover the proper way to synchronize the child and parent shortly.)

## Open files and security

A key point again regarding security, for both the exec and fork scenarios.

When you perform an exec operation, the predecessor process's VAS is essentially overwritten by that of the successor process. However, realize that the predecessor process's open files (held within the OS in a per-process structure called the OFDT, mentioned earlier) remain intact and are, in effect, inherited by the successor process. This could pose a serious security threat. Think about it: what if a security-sensitive file being used by the predecessor is not closed and an exec performed? The successor now has access to it via its file descriptor, whether it exploits that knowledge or not.

The same argument holds true for the fork; if a parent process has a security-sensitive file open and then forks, the child too has access to the file (fork rule #6).

To counter exactly this issue, from the Linux 2.6.23 kernel, the open(2) system call, includes a new flag: O_CLOEXEC. When this flag is specified within the open(2), the corresponding file will be closed upon any future exec operation performed by that process. (In earlier kernels, developers had to perform an explicit F_SETFD via fcntl(2) to set the FD_CLOEXEC bit).

When working with fork, the programmer must include logic to close any security-sensitive files in the parent prior to the fork.

## Malloc and the fork

A common mistake that programmers might stumble upon or make, is this: consider a successful memory allocation done in a process, with say, `p = malloc(2048)`. Assume that the variable `p` is global. Some time later, the process forks. The developer now wants the parent process to communicate some information to the child; so, she says, lets just write into the shared buffer `p`, and the job will be done. No, it does not work! Let's elaborate: the malloced buffer is visible to both processes, but not in the way they think. The mistaken assumption is that the malloced buffer is shared between the parent and child process; it is not shared, it's copied to the child's VAS. Please recall fork rule #4: Data is not shared; it's copied across the fork.

We must test this case; have a look at the following code snippet (source file: `ch10/fork_malloc_test.c`):

> For readability, only the relevant parts of the code are displayed here; to view and run it, the entire source code is available here: https://github.com/PacktPublishing/Hands-on-System-Programming-with-Linux.

```
const int memsz=2048;
static char *gptr;
[...]
main(int argc, char **argv)
{
    gptr = malloc(memsz);
    [...]
    printf("Init: malloc gptr=%p\n", gptr);
    [...]
    switch ((ret = fork())) {
    case -1: [...]
    case 0:         /* Child */
        printf("\nChild process, PID %d:\n", getpid());
        memset(gptr, 'c', memsz);
        disp_few(gptr);
        [...]
        printf("Child (%d) done, exiting ...\n", getpid());
        exit(EXIT_SUCCESS);
    default:        /* Parent */
#if 1
        sleep(2);   /* let the child run first */
#endif
        printf("\nParent process, PID %d:\n", getpid());
        memset(gptr, 'p', memsz);
        disp_few(gptr);
        [...]
```

```
        }
        free(gptr);
    [...]
```

The `disp_few` function to display a few (16) bytes of the memory buffer is simple:

```
    static inline void disp_few(char *p)
    {
        int i;
        printf(" malloc gptr=%p\n ", p);
        for (i=0; i<16; i++)
            printf("%c", *(p+i));
        printf("\n");
    }
```

We build and run it:

```
    $ ./fork_malloc_test
    Init: malloc gptr=0x1802260

    Child process, PID 13782:
     malloc gptr=0x1802260
     cccccccccccccccc
    Child (13782) done, exiting ...

    Parent process, PID 13781:
     malloc gptr=0x1802260
     PPPPPPPPPPPPPPPP
    Parent (13781) will exit now...
    $
```

Immediately, the first thing to notice is this: the pointer to the memory buffer (0x1802260) in both the parent and child process is the same leading one to the conclusion that it's the same memory buffer being pointed at. Well, it's not; it's an easy mistake to make. Check out the *content* of the malloced buffer in the parent and child; it's ps in the parent and cs in the child; if it were really the very same buffer, the content would be identical. So, then, what is going on?

As mentioned several times now, data is copied across the fork, not shared (our fork rule #4). OK, but then how come the address is the same? There are two reasons:

- The address is a virtual address (not a physical address, as we should well know from the discussions in Chapter 2, *Virtual Memory*)
- It is actually the same virtual address; modern OSes such as Linux do not, immediately on fork, make a copy of the data and stack segments; they use an optimized semantic called **copy-on-write** (**COW**).

*Process Creation*

## COW in a nutshell

This requires a bit of explanation. Until now, to keep the discussion conceptually simple, we have said that upon fork, the kernel copies all the parent's VAS segments (plus all the other inherited process attributes) to the new child process. This is an exaggeration; the reality is, attempting to do this would make the `fork(2)` untenable in practice as it would require too much RAM and too much time. (As it is, even with several optimizations, the fork is still considered heavyweight.)

Let's digress: one of the optimizations, upon fork is that the kernel does not copy the text (code) segment into the child; it merely shares the parent's text segment (virtual) pages with the child process. This works well, as text is in any case only readable and executable (r-x); thus, as it can never change, why make a copy?

But what about the data and stack segments? Their pages are read-write (rw-) after all so how can the OS just share them with the child? Ah, that's where the COW semantics come in handy. To understand COW, consider a single virtual page that has been marked as COW by the OS. It essentially means this: As long as both processes (parent and child) treat the page as read-only, they can share it; no copy is necessary. But the moment one of them modifies (even a byte in) the page, the OS intervenes and creates a copy of the page, which is then handed off to the process that performed the write.

So, if we have a global variable `g=5` and `fork(2)`, the page containing g is marked COW by the OS; the parent and child share it, until either writes to g. At that point, the OS creates a copy of the page containing the (updated) variable and hands it to the writer. Thus, the granularity of COW is a page.

As a matter of fact, COW is aggressively enforced by Linux to optimize to the maximum extent possible. Its not just the data and stack segments, most of the other inheritable process attributes we discussed earlier are actually not copied to the child, they are COW-shared, effectively making Linux's fork extremely efficient.

Additional insight into these important points can be gained by noticing the same effect, the COW optimization, carried out on the data variables (globals and locals) as well; just run our test case program with any parameter and it internally runs a small test case on two variables: a global and a local:

```
$ ./fork_malloc_test anyparameter
Init: malloc gptr=0xabb260
Init: loc=8, g=5

Child process, PID 17285:
 malloc gptr=0xabb260
```

```
 cccccccccccccccc
 loc=9, g=4
 &loc=0x7ffc8f324014, &g=0x602084
Child (17285) done, exiting ...

Parent process, PID 17284:
 malloc gptr=0xabb260
 ppppppppppppppppp
 loc=7, g=6
 &loc=0x7ffc8f324014, &g=0x602084
Parent (17284) will exit now...
$
```

Notice the addresses of the global g and the local loc are the same in the parent and child processes. But why? COW will have been performed as they have been written. Yes, but think: it's all virtual addressing; the physical addresses will actually differ under the hood.

You sometimes gets the feeling that modern OSes go out of their way to confuse and confound the poor systems programmer! The two important points we made earlier seem to contradict each other:

- Fork rule #4: Data is copied across the fork, not shared
- Data/stack (and a lot else) is not actually copied upon fork, but rather COW-shared

How do we resolve this situation? It's easy, actually: The first (our fork rule #4) is the correct way to think when working with the fork; the second statement is what really happens under the hood at the OS layer. It's about optimization, that is all.

Here is a suggestion: When wearing the hat of an application developer, do not get overly concerned with the underlying OS's COW optimization details; it's more important to understand the intention rather than the optimization. Thus, as far as the Linux application developer using fork(2) is concerned, the key conceptual point that remains is fork rule #4: data is copied across the fork, not shared.

## Waiting and our simpsh project

Lets set ourselves an interesting learning exercise: a small project. We want to implement, using C on the Linux OS of course, a very simple shell of our own. Lets call it our simpsh—simple shell—project.

*Process Creation*

> Note: simpsh is a very small, minimally functioning shell. It works with only single-word commands. It does not support features such as redirection, piping, shell built-ins, and so on. It's meant to be a learning exercise.

The specification, for now at least is this: Display a prompt (say >>), accept a user command at the prompt, and execute it. This is the stopping condition: if the user enters `quit`, terminate (similar to typing `logout`, `exit`, or `Ctrl + D` on an actual shell process).

It seems pretty straightforward: In our C program you get into a loop, display the required prompt, accept the user input (let's use the `fgets(3)` to do this) into a `cmd` variable, and then use one of the exec family APIs (a simple `execl(3)` sounds promising) to execute it.

Well, yes, except, how could you forget, the predecessor process is effectively lost after the exec operation succeeds! Our shell will be lost once we exec anything (just like our earlier experiment 1: on the CLI and experiment 2—demonstrated).

For example, if with the previous naive approach, we attempt to execute `ps(1)` with our shell simpsh, it would look like this:

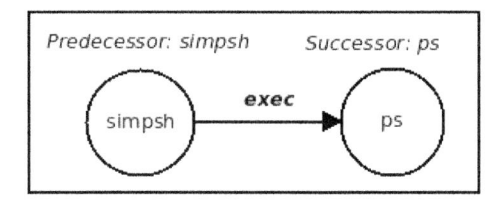

*Predecessor: simpsh*     *Successor: ps*

simpsh  →(exec)→  ps

## The Unix fork-exec semantic

So, that does not work. What we need, really, is a way for our simple shell simpsh to remain alive and well *after* the exec operation, but how can we achieve that?

The fork is the answer! Here's what we'll do: after the user supplies input (a command), we have our shell fork. We now have two identical shells alive: the original parent (let's say it has PID x) and the brand new child shell (PID y). The child shell is used as the sacrificial lamb: We have it exec the user command. So, yes, the child is the predecessor process that is impossible to return to; but that's OK as we have the parent shell process alive and well!

This well-known technique is called the *fork-exec* semantic. It combines what several other OSes call a spawn into two discrete operations: a process creation (fork), and a process execution (exec). Once again, the brilliant Unix design is shown off:

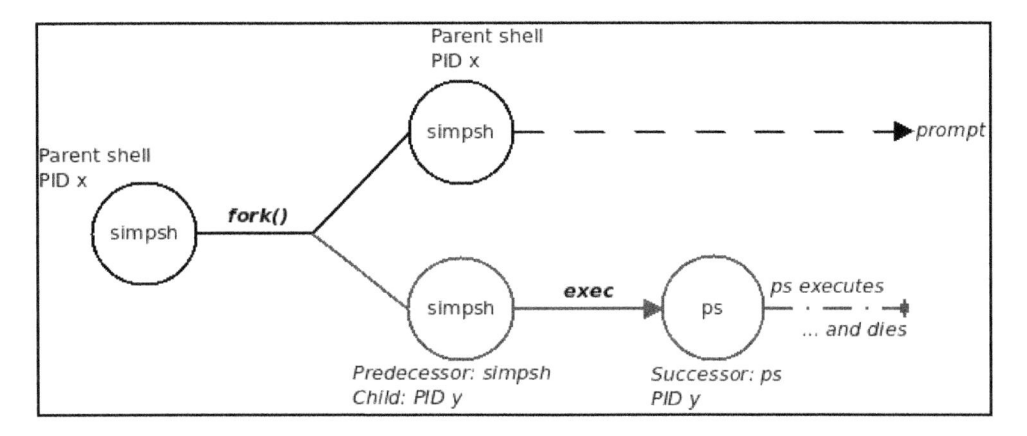

In the preceding diagram, visualize the timeline as the (horizontal) **x**-axis. Also, we use the color blue to show the child's execution path.

Once the parent shell detects that the execed child has completed, it displays the shell prompt again.

## The need to wait

The fork-exec is really interesting, but hang on a second: While the child process performs an `exec` on the user command, and the successor is running (indicated by the dot-dash blue line in the preceding diagram), what should the parent process do? Obviously, it should wait, but for how long? Should we have it sleep? Well, no, as sleep takes the number of seconds to sleep as its argument. We do not know in advance how long the successor will take (it could be milliseconds, it could be months). The correct thing to do is this: have the parent process wait until the child (now the successor) dies.

This is precisely what the `wait(2)` API is designed to do. When the parent process issues the `wait(2)` API, it is put to sleep; the moment its child dies, it's woken up!

## Performing the wait

The `wait(2)` API is a classic example of a blocking call: The calling process is put into a sleep state until the event it is waiting (or blocking) upon occurs. When the event does occur, it is woken up and continues to run.

So, think about it: a process forks; the parent process then issues the `wait(2)` API, and the event it is blocking upon is the death of the child! The child continues to run, of course; when the child does die, the kernel wakes up, or unblocks, the parent; it now continues to execute its code. Here is the signature of `wait(2)`:

```
#include <sys/types.h>
#include <sys/wait.h>
pid_t wait(int *wstatus);
```

For now, we shall ignore the to `wait(2)`; we shall just pass NULL (or 0) (of course, we shall cover it shortly).

## Defeating the race after fork

Recall the example code we saw earlier in chapter `ch10/fork5.c`. In this program, we artificially, and crudely, waited for the child process by introducing a `sleep(2);` statement in the parent's code:

```
[...]
   default: /* Parent */
#if 1
   sleep(2); /* let the child run first */
#endif
   printf("Parent process, PID %d:\n", getpid());
[...]
```

This is not good enough: What if the child process takes longer than two seconds to complete its work? If it takes just a few milliseconds, then we unnecessarily waste time.

This is how we resolve the race: Who will run first, the parent or the child? Clearly, fork rule #5 tells us that it's indeterminate. But, in real-world code, we need a way to guarantee that one of them indeed runs first—say, the child process. With the wait API, we now we have a proper solution! We change the preceding code snippet to this:

```
[...]
   default: /* Parent */
   wait(0);    /* ensure the child runs first */
```

```
    printf("Parent process, PID %d:\n", getpid());
[...]
```

Think about how this works: After the fork, it's a race: If the child process does run first, then no harm is done. However, at some point in the near future, the parent process will get the CPU; that's fine as all it does is block upon the child by calling wait. If the parent does run first after the fork, the same thing occurs: it blocks upon the child by calling wait. We have effectively defeated the race! By issuing the wait as the first thing done in the parent process after fork, we effectively guarantee that the child runs first.

## Putting it together – our simpsh project

So, now that we have all the bits and pieces in place—namely, the fork-exec semantic and the `wait` API—we can see how our simple shell should be designed.

In the C program, get into a loop, display the required prompt, accept user input (let's use the `fgets(3)` to do this—why? Please read the upcoming tip) into a `cmd` variable, and then fork. In the child code (use fork rule #2 to distinguish between the parent and child), use one of the many exec family APIs (a simple `execlp(3)` sounds promising here) to execute the user supplied command. In parallel (recall fork rule #3), have the parent process invoke the wait API; the parent now sleeps until the child dies. Now loop around again and repeat the whole thing until the user types `'quit'` to quit. Everyone's happy!

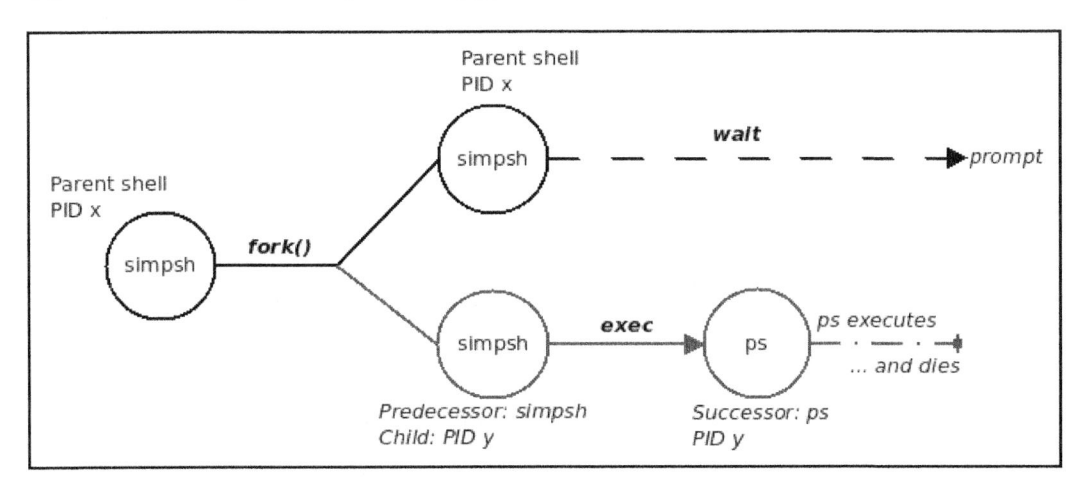

In effect, we now have a `fork-exec-wait` semantic that is exploited!

> fgets(3): For security reasons, do not use the traditionally taught APIs such as gets(3) or scanf(3) to receive user input; they are poorly implemented, and they do not provide any bounds-checking capabilities. The fgets(3) does; thus, using it, or getline(3), is far superior security-wise. (Again, as mentioned earlier in this book, hackers exploit these vulnerabilities in commonly used APIs to perform stack-smashing, or other types of attacks.)

Of course, our simpsh shell is rather limited in scope: it only works with single-word commands (such as ps, ls, vi, w, and so on). Read the code and think about why this is the case.

Here we go (source code: ch10/simpsh_v1.c):

> For readability, only the relevant parts of the code are displayed here; to view and run it, the entire source code is available here: https://github.com/PacktPublishing/Hands-on-System-Programming-with-Linux.

```
static void do_simpsh(void)
{
[...]
while (1) {
    if (!getcmd(cmd)) {
        free(cmd);
        FATAL("getcmd() failed\n");
    }
    /* Stopping condition */
    if(!strncmp(cmd, "quit", 4))
        break;
[...]
```

As you can see, we enter the loop, accept the user's command via the getcmd function we wrote (the fgets is issued within it), and then check whether the user has typed quit, in which case we exit.

The real work, the fork-exec-wait semantic, happens here, within the loop:

```
[...]
/* Wield the powerful fork-exec-wait semantic ! */
switch ((ret = fork())) {
case -1:
    free(cmd);
    FATAL("fork failed, aborting!\n");
case 0: /* Child */
```

```
            VPRINT
            (" Child process (%7d) exec-ing cmd \"%s\" now..\n",
                getpid(), cmd);
            if (execlp(cmd, cmd, (char *)0) == -1) {
                WARN("child: execlp failed\n");
                free(cmd);
                exit(EXIT_FAILURE);
            }
            /* should never reach here */
            exit(EXIT_FAILURE); // just to avoid gcc warnings
    default: /* Parent */
            VPRINT("Parent process (%7d) issuing the wait...\n",
                getpid());
            /* sync: child runs first, parent waits for child's death */
            if (wait(0) < 0)
                FATAL("wait failed, aborting..\n");
        } // switch
    } // while(1)
```

(The logic pertaining to argument passing—displaying the help screen, verbose switch, the actual fgets, the calloc/free, and so on, is not explicitly shown; please refer to the source file simpsh_v1.c).

Let's give it a try:

```
$ ./simpsh_v1 --help
Usage: ./simpsh_v1 [-v]|[--help]
 -v : verbose mode
 --help : display this help screen.
$ ./simpsh_v1 -v
>> ps
  Parent process ( 1637) issuing the wait...
  Child process ( 1638) exec-ing cmd "ps" now..
 PID TTY TIME CMD
 1078 pts/0 00:00:00 bash
 1637 pts/0 00:00:00 simpsh_v1
 1638 pts/0 00:00:00 ps
>> uname
  Parent process ( 1637) issuing the wait...
  Child process ( 1639) exec-ing cmd "uname" now..
Linux
>> uname -a
  Parent process ( 1637) issuing the wait...
  Child process ( 1640) exec-ing cmd "uname -a" now..
!WARNING! simpsh_v1.c:do_simpsh:90: child: execlp failed
perror says: No such file or directory
>> www
  Parent process ( 1648) issuing the wait...
```

*Process Creation*

```
      Child process ( 1650) exec-ing cmd "www" now..
    !WARNING! simpsh_v1.c:do_simpsh:90: child: execlp failed
    perror says: No such file or directory
    >> quit
      Parent process ( 1637) exiting...
    $
```

We run the program in verbose mode; you can see the shell prompt string >> as well as every verbose print; they are prefixed with [v]:. Notice how it works for single word commands; the moment we pass something unknown or with more than one word (for example www and uname -a ), the execlp(3) fails; we catch the failure and emit a warning message; the program continues until the user quits.

Here is another quick experiment: We can use our simpsh_v1 program to spawn another shell (/bin/sh):

```
    $ ./simpsh_v1 -v
    >> sh
    [v]: Parent process ( 12945) issuing the wait...
    [v]: Child process ( 12950) exec-ing cmd "sh" now..
    $ ps
     PID TTY      TIME CMD
     576 pts/3 00:00:00 git-credential-
    3127 pts/3 00:00:01 bash
    12945 pts/3 00:00:00 simpsh_v1
    12950 pts/3 00:00:00 sh                        << the newly spawned sh
    >>
    12954 pts/3 00:00:00 ps
    31896 pts/3 00:00:40 gitg
    $ exit
    exit
    >> ps
    [v]: Parent process ( 12945) issuing the wait...
    [v]: Child process ( 12960) exec-ing cmd "ps" now..
     PID TTY      TIME CMD
     576 pts/3 00:00:00 git-credential-
    3127 pts/3 00:00:01 bash
    12945 pts/3 00:00:00 simpsh_v1
    12960 pts/3 00:00:00 ps
    31896 pts/3 00:00:40 gitg
    >>
```

It works as expected (hey, you could even experiment with spawning the same process simpsh_v1). So, there we are, a first very simple but functioning shell.

Why exactly do commands that are more than one word long fail? The answer lies in how we're executing the successor, using the `execlp(3)` API. Recall, for execlp, we are to pass the program name (the PATH will be auto-searched of course) and all arguments, starting with `argv[0]`. Well, in our simple implementation, we just don't pass anything more than the first argument `argv[0]`; that's why.

So, how do we make it work with commands with any number of arguments? Well, it really involves some amount of string-processing work: We will have to tokenize the arguments into individual strings, initializing an `argv` array of pointers to them, and using that `argv` via the `execv[pe]` API. We leave it as a slightly more challenging exercise to the reader! (Tip: the C library provides APIs for tokenizing strings; `strtok(3)`, `strtok_r(3)`; look them up).

> In effect, our simpsh project is a simplistic implementation of the `system(3)` library API. Note that from a security viewpoint, it's always recommended to use field-proven and tested APIs like `system(3)` rather than a home-grown `fork-exec-wait` piece of code. Here, of course, we code it for learning purposes.

## The wait API – details

In our simpsh program, we did use the `wait(2)` API, but have not really delved into details:

```
pid_t wait(int *wstatus);
```

The thing to understand is this: `wait(2)` is a blocking call; it causes the calling process to block until a child process dies.

To be technically correct, the `wait(2)` (and associated APIs that we shall see later) actually block upon the child process(es) undergoing a state change; well, the state change is the child's death, right? Yes, but it's really important to understand that it's not just that: the possible state changes are as follows:

- The child process terminates as follows:
    - Normally (by falling off `main`, or calling `[_]exit()`)
    - Abnormally (killed by a signal).
- The child was sent a signal that stopped it (usually `SIGSTOP` or `SIGTSTP`).
- Having been stopped, it was delivered a signal that continued (resumed) it (usually `SIGCONT`; we shall cover signaling in detail in the next chapter).

The generic `wait(2)` system call, though, blocks upon the death (termination) of the child, not any of the other signal-related state changes mentioned earlier. (Can that be done? Yes, indeed, we cover the `waitpid(2)` system call later in this chapter).

The parameter to wait, is a pointer to an integer `wstatus`. In reality, it is treated as more of a return rather than a parameter to pass along; this is a pretty common C programming technique: Treat a parameter as a return value. System calls on Linux often use it; this technique is often referred to as a value-result or an in-out parameter. Think about this: We pass the address of the variable; the API internally, having the address, can update it (poke it).

The next thing regarding the parameter `wstatus` is this: The integer is treated as a bitmask, not as an absolute value. This, again, is a common C optimization trick that programmers employ: We can fit several pieces of information into an integer by treating it as a bitmask. So, how do you interpret this returned bitmask? For portability reasons, the C library provides predefined macros that help us interpret the bitmask (these are in `<sys/wait.h>` usually). The macros work in pairs: The first macro returns a Boolean value; if it returns true, look up the second macro's result; if it returns false, disregard the second macro completely.

A digression: a process can die in one of two ways: normally or abnormally. Normal termination implies that the process died voluntarily; it just fell off `main()` or called `exit(3)` or `_exit(2)` passing the exit status as an argument (the convention for exit status: zero implies success, non-zero implies failure and is treated as the failure code). On the other hand, abnormal termination implies that the process died involuntarily—it was killed, typically via a signal.

Here are the wait macro pairs and their meaning:

| First macro | Second macro | Meaning |
| --- | --- | --- |
| WIFEXITED | WEXITSTATUS | Child died normally: WIFEXITED is true; then, WEXITSTATUS—exit status of child. Child died abnormally: WIFEXITED is false |
| WIFSIGNALED | WTERMSIG | Child died due to signal: WIFSIGNALED is true; then, WTERMSIG is the signal that killed it. |
|  | WCOREDUMP | True if, upon death, the child produced a core dump. |
| WIFSTOPPED | WSTOPSIG | True if child was stopped by signal; then, WSTOPSIG is the signal that stopped it. |
| WIFCONTINUED | - | True if child was stopped and later resumed (continued) by a signal (SIGCONT). |

*Chapter 10*

(In the row containing WCOREDUMP, the indentation is intended to mean that you can tell that WCOREDUMP is only meaningful if WIFSIGNALED is true).

What about the actual return value itself of wait(2)? Clearly, -1 indicates failure (and of course the kernel will set errno to reflect the cause of the failure); else, on success, it's the PID of the process that died, thus unblocking the parent's wait.

To try out the things we have just learned, we make a copy of the simpsh_v1 program and call it ch10/simpsh_v2.c. Again, we only show the relevant snippets here; the complete source code files are on the book's GitHub repository:

```
[...]
  default: /* Parent */
      VPRINT("Parent process (%7d) issuing the wait...\n",
          getpid());
      /* sync: child runs first, parent waits for child's death */
      if ((cpid = wait(&wstat)) < 0) {
          free(cmd);
          FATAL("wait failed, aborting..\n");
      }
      if (gVerbose)
          interpret_wait(cpid, wstat);
  } // switch
} // while(1)
[...]
```

As you can see, we now capture the return value of wait (2) (the PID of the child that changed state), and if we are running in verbose mode, we call our own function interpret_wait; it will provide output detailing what status change exactly occurred; here it is:

```
static void interpret_wait(pid_t child, int wstatus)
{
    VPRINT("Child (%7d) status changed:\n", child);
    if (WIFEXITED(wstatus))
        VPRINT(" normal termination: exit status: %d\n",
            WEXITSTATUS(wstatus));
    if (WIFSIGNALED(wstatus)) {
        VPRINT(" abnormal termination: killer signal: %d",
                WTERMSIG(wstatus));
        if (WCOREDUMP(wstatus))
            VPRINT(" : core dumped\n");
        else
            VPRINT("\n");
    }
```

[ 363 ]

```
        if (WIFSTOPPED(wstatus))
            VPRINT(" stopped: stop signal: %d\n",
                WSTOPSIG(wstatus));
        if (WIFCONTINUED(wstatus))
            VPRINT(" (was stopped), resumed (SIGCONT)\n");
}
```

The VPRINT macro is simple; it results in a printf(3) if the process is in verbose mode. We try the program (version 2) out:

```
$ ./simpsh_v2 -v
>> ps
 Parent process ( 2095) issuing the wait...
 Child process ( 2096) exec-ing cmd "ps" now..
PID TTY TIME CMD
1078 pts/0 00:00:00 bash
2095 pts/0 00:00:00 simpsh_v2
2096 pts/0 00:00:00 ps
 Child ( 2096) status changed:
 normal termination: exit status: 0
>> quit
 Parent process ( 2095) exiting...
$
```

As you can see, we run it in verbose mode; we can see that the child process ps(1) had a status change: It died normally, with an exit status of zero, indicating success.

> Interesting: this is how bash knows whether the process that just ran succeeded or not; it plugs in the exit status—fetched via an API similar to wait—into the variable ? (which you can access using $?.)

## The scenarios of wait

Until now, we've covered the generic wait(2) API; however, we have only really discussed one possible scenario regarding the wait; there are several more. Let's check them out.

## Wait scenario #1

It's the simple case (one we've already come across): a process forks, creating one child process. The parent subsequently issues the *wait* API; it now blocks on a status change in it's child process; recall, the possible status changes the child can possibly go through are these:

- State transition from running (R): dead; that is to say, the child terminates (normally/abnormally)
- State transition from running/asleep (R|S|D) to stopped state (T); that is to say, it receives a signal causing it be stopped
- State transition from stopped state (T) to ready-to-run (R); that is to say, from a stopped state to a ready-to-run state

(The state transitions and the letters representing the process state are covered in `Chapter 17`, *CPU Scheduling on Linux*, on scheduling). Whichever may occur, the fact is that the parent is unblocked and continues to execute its code path; the `wait(2)` API returns (along with which we receive the PID of the child that died or was signaled), as well as the detailed status bitmask.

## Wait scenario #2

Consider this scenario: A process forks (creates) two children; let's call the parent process P and the children C1 and C2. Recall fork rule #3—the parent and the children processes will all continue to run in parallel. Now, P calls `wait`; what will happen?

This is the answer: process P will remain blocked until one of the children dies (or stops), but which one? Any one; whichever one changes state first. So how will the systems programmer know which process dies or stopped? That's easy: The return value is the PID of the process that died or stopped.

In other words, we devise a corollary: a wait blocks on a single child process; to block on n children requires n waits.

An interesting exercise would be to construct the preceding scenario in code; ensure that the parent process indeed waits upon both children (this very exercise is mentioned as `fork2c` on the GitHub repository).

*Process Creation*

> **TIP:** To have a parent wait upon all possible children, invoke the `wait` API as the condition of a while loop; as long as waitable children exist, it will block and return positive; the moment there are no waitable children, the `wait` returns `-1`; check for that as the condition to break out of the loop. Note though, that there are scenarios requiring a non-blocking wait to be set up; we shall cover these as well.

## Fork bombs and creating more than one child

Say we want to write code to create three children; would this, the code shown as follows, do it?

```
main()
{
    [...]
    fork();
    fork();
    fork();
    [...]
}
```

Of course not! (try it and see).

Recall fork rule #1: Execution in both the parent and child process continues at the instruction following the fork. Thus, as you can see, after the first fork, both the parent and child run the second fork (so we'll now have a total of four processes), and then all four will run the third fork (giving us a total of eight processes), and so on (havoc!).

If fork is called in this uncontrolled manner—it ends up creating $2^3 = 8$ children! In other words, it's exponential; n forks implies $2^n$ children will be created in a runaway sprint.

Imagine what damage can be done with this code:

```
int main(void)
{
    while(1)
        fork();
}
```

It's quite rightly called a fork bomb!—a type of **denial-of-service** (**DoS**) attack.

Interestingly, because of modern Unixes (including Linux of course) having COW-based copying semantics, the memory overhead incurred may not be that large. Of course, it still consumes huge amounts of CPU; also, a simple calloc within the while loop would cause memory to be eaten up as well.

> By the way, carefully tuned resource limits (we studied this in an earlier chapter in detail) can help mitigate the fork bomb (and similar) DoS attack risks. Even better, would be careful tuning via cgroups for resource bandwidth control. Here is the fork bomb wikipedia link: https://en.wikipedia.org/wiki/Fork_bomb.

OK, so, `fork(); fork();` is not the way to create two children. (Try out the exercise `Smallbomb` on the GitHub repository.)

How do you do so correctly? It's straightforward: take into account the parent and child's execution paths, distinguish between them (fork rule #2), and just have the parent create a second child process. This code snippet demonstrates the same:

```
static void createChild(int sleep_time)
{
    pid_t n;
    switch (n = fork()) {
    case -1:
        perror("fork");
        exit(1);
    case 0: // Child
        printf("Child 2 PID %d sleeping for %ds...\n", getpid(),
            sleep_time);
        sleep(sleep_time);
        exit(0);
    default: ; // Parent returns..
    }
}
int main(void)
{
[...]
switch (n = fork()) {  // create first child
 case -1:
    perror("fork");
    exit(1);
 case 0: // Child
    printf("Child 1 PID %d sleeping for %ds...\n", getpid(),
        c1_slptm);
    sleep(c1_slptm);
    exit(0);
 default: // Parent
```

```
        createChild(c2_slptm); // create second child
        /* Wait until all children die (typically) */
        while ((cpid = wait(&stat)) != -1) {
            printf("Child %d changed state\n", cpid);
        }
    }
```

## Wait scenario #3

What if a process has no children, never had any children (a bachelor chap), and it issues the `wait(2)` API? At first glance, this seems to be a problem case, as perhaps it could cause deadlock; but, no, the kernel is smarter than that. The kernel code of `wait` checks, and upon finding that the calling process has no children (dead or alive or stopped or whatever), it simply *fails* the *wait*. (FYI, `errno` gets set to `ECHILD` implying the process had no unwaited-for children).

Again, recall one of our golden rules: *never assume anything; always check for the failure case*. Importantly, our `Chapter 19`, *Troubleshooting and Best Practices*, covers such points.

There is one more `wait` scenario; however, we need to cover more information first.

## Variations on the wait – APIs

There are a couple of additional system calls to perform the job of *waiting upon the child(ren) process(es)*; we cover them next.

### The waitpid(2)

Consider that we have a process with three children; it is required that the parent waits (blocks) upon the termination of a particular child process. If we use the generic `wait` API, we have seen that it will get unblocked upon the state change of any of the children. The answer to this conundrum: the `waitpid(2)` system call:

```
pid_t waitpid(pid_t pid, int *wstatus, int options);
```

The first parameter `pid` is set to the PID of the child to wait upon. However, other values are possible; if `-1` is passed, it generically waits for any `waitable` child process. (There are other more arcane cases; we refer you to the man page for them). In other words, issuing this is equivalent to a generic `wait(&stat);` API call:

```
    waitpid(-1, &stat, 0);
```

The second parameter is the usual status integer bitmask that we saw in detail with the `wait` API.

The third parameter is called `options`; previously, we set it to zero, implying no special behavior. What other values can it take? Well, you can pass just zero or the bitwise OR of the following (it's also a bitmask):

| Options parameter value | Meaning |
| --- | --- |
| 0 | Default, same as `wait(2)` |
| WNOHANG | Only block upon live children; if there are none, return immediately |
| WUNTRACED | Also unblock when a child process stops (and does not necessarily terminate) |
| WCONTINUED | Also unblock when a stopped child process is resumed (via the `SIGCONT` signal being delivered to it) |

At first, the WNOHANG option might sound strange; how can you block upon anything but a live child? Well, with a little patience, we shall soon resolve this peculiarity.

To test the `waitpid(2)`, we again make a copy of our `simpsh_v2.c` and call it `ch10/simpsh_v3.c`; the only meaningful difference in the code is that we now use the `waitpid(2)` instead of the generic `wait` API, passing along options as required; from `ch10/simpsh_v3.c`:

```
[...]
default: /* Parent */
    VPRINT("Parent process (%7d) issuing the waitpid...\n",
        getpid());
    /* sync: child runs first, parent waits
     * for child's death.
     * This time we use waitpid(2), and will therefore also get
     * unblocked on a child stopping or resuming!
     */
    if ((cpid = waitpid(-1, &wstat,
                WUNTRACED|WCONTINUED)) < 0) {
        free(cmd);
        FATAL("wait failed, aborting..\n");
    }
    if (gVerbose)
        interpret_wait(cpid, wstat);
[...]
```

*Process Creation*

Now we run it:

```
$ ./simpsh_v3 -v
>> read
  Parent process ( 15040) issuing the waitpid...
  Child process ( 15058) exec-ing cmd "read" now..
```

We issue the `read` (a bash built-in) command, as it itself is a blocking call, so we know that the child process `read` will be alive and asleep. In another terminal window, we look up the PIDs of our `simpsh_v3` process and of the command we ran from within it (the `read`):

```
$ pgrep simpsh
15040
$ pstree -A -h 15040 -p
simpsh_v3(15040)---read(15058)
$
```

(The useful `pstree(1)` utility shows us the process tree's parent-child hierarchy. Look up it's man page for details).

Now we send SIGTSTP (the terminal stop signal) to the `read` process; it gets stopped:

```
$ kill -SIGTSTP 15058
```

Getting stopped is a status change that we are looking for! Recall, our waiting code now is this:

```
waitpid(-1, &wstat, WUNTRACED|WCONTINUED))
```

Thus, the moment the child stops the WUNTRACED option takes effect, and in the original terminal window we see this:

```
  Child ( 15058) status changed:
    stopped: stop signal: 20
>>
```

We now continue the child by sending it the signal SIGCONT:

```
$ kill -SIGCONT 15058
$
```

[ 370 ]

As our (parent) `waitpid(2)` is also using the `WIFCONTINUED` option, in the original Terminal window, we see this (though it does require the user to press the *Enter* key it seems):

```
Child ( 15058) status changed:
  (was stopped), resumed (SIGCONT)
```

We have so much more control over the child(ren). (Young parents, please note!)

The `fork-exec-wait` Unix framework is powerful indeed.

## The waitid (2)

For further fine tuning and control, there is the `waitid(2)` system call as well (from Linux 2.6.9):

```
int waitid(idtype_t idtype, id_t id, siginfo_t *infop, int options);
```

The first two parameters will in effect specify the children to wait upon:

| waitid(2): 1st parameter: idtype | Second parameter: id |
| --- | --- |
| P_PID | Set to the PID of the child to wait (block) upon |
| P_PGID | Wait upon any child whose process group ID (PGID) matches this number |
| P_ALL | Wait upon any child (this parameter is ignored) |

The fourth `options` parameter is similar to how it was used with the `waitpid(2)`, but not identical; there are some additional options that can be passed along; again, it's a bitmask, not an absolute value: the `WNOHANG` and `WCONTINUED` options have the same meaning as with the `waitpid(2)` system call.

Additionally, the following options can be bitwise-ORed:

- `WEXITED`: Block upon children that have (already) terminated (again, we shall soon make clear why this even exists)
- `WSTOPPED`: Block upon children that will enter the stopped state (similar to the `WUNTRACED` option)
- `WNOWAIT`: Block upon children, but once unblocked, leave them in a waitable state so that they can be waited-upon again with a later wait* API.

*Process Creation*

The third parameter is a (large) data structure of type `siginfo_t`; (we shall cover details in Chapter 11, *Signaling - Part I*). On return of `waitid(2)`, this will get populated by the kernel. Various fields get set by the OS, among them, the PID of the child that changed state (`si_pid`), `si_signo` set to `SIGCHLD`, `si_status`, `si_code`. We intend to cover these in a later chapter (for now, please refer to the man page).

> There are BSD variations of `wait` APIs too: the `wait3` and the `wait4`. However, these are nowadays considered outdated; use the `waitpid(2)` or `waitid(2)` APIs instead.

## The actual system call

We have seen several APIs that perform the work of having the parent process `wait` until the child changes state (dies, or stops, or resumes after stop):

- `wait`
- `waitpid`
- `waitid`
- `wait3`
- `wait4`

Interestingly, and similar to the situation with the exec family APIs, the Linux implementation is such that most of the preceding APIs are library (`glibc`) wrappers: The fact is that, on the Linux OS, of all the preceding APIs, `wait4(2)` is the actual system call API.

Performing an `strace(1)` on a program that uses one of the `wait` APIs proves the point (we `strace` our `simpsh_v1` program, which calls `wait`):

```
$ strace -e trace=process -o strc.txt ./simpsh_v1
>> ps
 PID TTY          TIME CMD
14874 pts/6    00:00:00 bash
27248 pts/6    00:00:00 strace
27250 pts/6    00:00:00 simpsh_v1
27251 pts/6    00:00:00 ps
>> quit
$
```

[ 372 ]

This is the output of strace:

```
execve("./simpsh_v1", ["./simpsh_v1"], 0x7fff79a424e0 /* 56 vars */) =
0
arch_prctl(ARCH_SET_FS, 0x7f47641fa4c0) = 0
clone(child_stack=NULL,
 flags=CLONE_CHILD_CLEARTID|CLONE_CHILD_SETTID|SIGCHLD,
 child_tidptr=0x7f47641fa790) = 27251
wait4(-1, NULL, 0, NULL) = 27251
[...]
```

While discussing performing an strace, another interesting question does arise: if you strace an application that calls fork(2), after the fork API, will strace trace the execution path of the child process as well? By default, no, but just pass along the -f option, and it will!

The man page on strace(1) says this:

```
-f          Trace child processes as they are created by currently
traced processes as a result of the fork(2), vfork(2) and clone(2)
system calls. ...
```

In a similar vein, systems programmers are probably aware of the tremendously powerful GNU debugger—GDB. If one is debugging a multiprocess application with gdb(1), how can one request GDB which process's execution path to follow after encountering a fork in the instruction stream? The setting is called follow-fork-mode: in gdb; here, we show an example of setting the mode to child:

**(gdb) show follow-fork-mode**
Debugger response to a program call of fork or vfork is "parent".
**(gdb) set follow-fork-mode child**
(gdb)

> **With respect to GDB**: Debugging multi-process applications with GDB: Using the GDB attach <PID> command is useful to attach to another process (say, the child). GDB also provides a powerful catch command; see help catch in GDB for more details.

## A note on the vfork

Decades ago, the BSD Unix developers came up with an efficient special case system call— the vfork(2). The idea at the time, was to perform some optimizations where you performed a fork and almost immediately an exec in the child (the fork-exec, in other words). As we know, using the fork-exec is quite a common and useful semantic (the shell and network servers use it heavily). When the vfork is called instead of the fork, the kernel does not go through the heavy copying operations usually required; it optimizes things.

The bottom line is this: At the time, vfork(2) was useful on Unix; but today's Linux fork(2) is as optimized as can be, rendering the vfork to the back door. It's still there, for perhaps two reasons:

- Compatibility—to aid the porting of BSD apps to Linux
- It is apparently useful on some arcane special Linuxes that run on MMU-less processors ( like uClinux)

On today's regular Linux platforms, it is not recommended to use the vfork(2); just stick to the fork(2).

## More Unix weirdness

From fork rule #3, we understand that the parent and child processes run in parallel. What if one of them terminate? Will the other die too? Well, no, of course not; they are independent entities. However, there are side effects.

## Orphans

Consider this scenario: A process forks, the parent and child are alive and running their individual code paths in parallel. Let's say the parent's PID is 100 and the child's is 102, implying the child's PPID is 100 of course.

The parent process, for whatever reason, dies. The child continues on without any trouble, except for a side effect: The moment the parent (PID 100) dies, the child's PPID (100) is now invalid! Thus, the kernel intervenes, setting the child's PPID to the overall mothership—the ancestor of all user space tasks, the root of the process tree—the init, or on recent Linux, the systemd, process! It's PID is, by venerable Unix convention, always the number 1.

Terminology: the child that lost its immediate parent is now said to be re-parented by systemd (or init), and its PPID will thus be 1; this child is now an orphan.

> **TIP**: There is a possibility that the overall ancestor process (init or systemd) does *not* have PID 1, and thus the orphan's PPID may not be 1; this can occur, for example, on Linux containers or custom namespaces.

We notice that the child's PPID value abruptly changed; thus, the systems programmer must ensure that they do *not* depend on the PPID value being the same (which can always be queried via the `getppid(2)` system call) for any reason!

## Zombies

The orphaned process does not pose any problem; there is another scenario with the distinct possibility of a nasty problem arising out of it.

Consider this scenario: a process forks, the parent and child are alive and running their individual code paths in parallel. Let's say the parent's PID is 100 and the child's is 102, implying the child's PPID is 100 of course.

Now we delve into a further level of detail: the parent process is supposed to wait upon the termination of its children (via any of the available `wait*(2)` APIs of course); what if it does not? Ah, this is really the bad case.

Imagine this scenario: the child process terminates, but the parent is not waiting (blocking) upon it; thus it continues to execute its code. The kernel, however, is not pleased: The Unix rule is that the parent process must block upon its children! As the parent isn't, the kernel cannot afford to completely clean up the just-dead child; it does release the entire VAS freeing up all the memory, it does flush and close all open files, as well as other data structures, but it does not clear the child's entry in the kernel's process table. Thus, the dead child still has a perfectly valid PID and some miscellaneous information (it's exit status, exit bitmask, and so on). The kernel keeps these details as this is the Unix way: the parent must wait upon its children and reap them, that is, fetch their termination status information, when they die. How does the parent process reap the child(ren)? Simple: by performing the wait!

So, think about it: The child has died; the parent has not bothered to *wait* for it; the kernel has cleaned up, to some extent, the child process. But it technically exists, as it's half dead and half alive; it's what we call a ***zombie process***. In fact, this is a process state on Unix: Z for zombie (you can see this in the output of `ps -l`; additionally, the process is marked as *defunct*).

# Process Creation

So why not just kill off the zombie(s)? Well, they're already dead; we cannot kill them. The reader might then query, well, so what? let them be. OK, there are two reasons that zombies cause real headaches on production systems:

- They take up a precious PID
- The amount of kernel memory taken up by the zombie is not insignificant (and essentially is a waste)

So, the bottom line is this: a couple of zombies might be OK, but dozens and hundreds, and more, are certainly not. You could reach a point where the system is so clogged with zombies that no other process can run—the `fork(2)` fails with `errno` set to `EAGAIN` (try again later) as no PIDs are available! It's a dangerous situation.

The Linux kernel developers had the insight to provide a quick fix: if you notice zombies on the system, you can, at least temporarily, get rid of them by killing their parent process! (Once the parent is dead, of what use is it to have the zombies? The point was, they remained so that the parent could reap them by doing a wait). Note that this is merely a bandage, not a solution; the solution is to fix the code (see the following rule).

This is a key point; in fact, what we call the wait scenario #4: the wait gets unblocked with children that already terminated, in effect, the zombies. In other words, you not only should, you must, wait upon all children; otherwise, zombies will occur (Note that the zombie is a valid process state on the Unix/Linux OS; every process, on the 'way' to death will pass through the **zombie** (Z) state. For most it's transient; it should not remain in this state for any significant length of time).

## Fork rule #7

All of this neatly brings us to our next rule of fork.

**Fork rule** #7: *The parent process must wait (block) upon the termination (death) of every child, directly or indirectly.*

The fact is that, just like the `malloc-free`, the `fork-wait` go together. There will be situations in real-world projects where it might look impossible for us to force the parent process to block on the wait after the fork; we shall address how these seemingly difficult situations can be easily addressed (that's why we refer to an indirect method as well; hint: it's to do with signaling, the topic of the next chapter).

# The rules of fork – a summary

For your convenience, this table summarizes the fork rules we have encoded in this chapter:

| Rule | The rule of fork |
|---|---|
| 1 | After a successful fork, execution in both the parent and child process continues at the instruction following the fork |
| 2 | To determine whether you are running in the parent or child process, use the fork return value: it's always 0 in the child, and the PID of the child in the parent |
| 3 | After a successful fork, both the parent and child process execute code in parallel |
| 4 | Data is copied across the fork, not shared |
| 5 | After the fork, the order of execution between the parent and child process is indeterminate |
| 6 | Open files are (loosely) shared across the fork |
| 7 | The parent process must wait (block) upon the termination (death) of every child, directly or indirectly |

# Summary

A core area of Unix/Linux systems programming is learning how to correctly handle the all-important fork(2) system call, to create a new process on the system. Using the fork(2) correctly takes a lot of deep insights. This chapter helped the systems developer by providing several key rules of fork. The concepts learned—the rules, working with data, open files, security issues, and so on—were revealed via several code examples. A lot of details on how to wait for your children processes correctly were discussed. What exactly are orphans and zombie processes, and why and how we should avoid zombies was dealt with too.

# 11
# Signaling - Part I

Signals are a crucial mechanism for the Linux system developer to understand and exploit. We cover this rather large topic over two chapters in this book, this chapter and the next one.

In this chapter, the reader is introduced to what signals are, why they are useful to the systems developer, and, most importantly of course, how exactly the developer is to handle and thus exploit the signalling mechanism.

We will continue this exploration in the next chapter.

In this chapter, the reader will learn the following:

- What exactly signals are.
- Why they are useful.
- The available signals.
- How exactly you can handle signals in an application, which really involves many things—blocking or unblocking signals, writing safe handlers, getting rid of pesky zombies once and for all, working with apps where the signal volume is high, and more.

# Why signals?

At times, the systems programmer requires the OS to provide an asynchronous facility—some way of letting you know that a certain event or condition has occurred. Signals provide that very feature on the Unix/Linux OSes. A process can trap or subscribe to a signal; when this occurs, the process will asynchronously be notified of the fact by the OS, and will then run the code of a function in response: a signal handler.

Take the following example cases:

- A CPU-intensive process is busy working on a scientific or mathematical calculation (for easy understanding, let's say it's generating primes); recall (from `Chapter 3`, *Resource Limits*) that there is an upper limit on CPU usage and that it's been set to a particular value. What if it's breached? The process will be killed by default. Can we prevent this?
- The developer wants to perform a common task: set up a timer and have it expire in, say, 1.5 seconds from now. How will the OS inform the process that the timer has expired?
- On some Sys V Unixes (typically running on enterprise-class servers), what if a sudden power failure occurs? An event is broadcast to all processes (that have expressed an interest in, or subscribed to the event) informing them of the same: they could flush their buffers, and save their data.
- A process has an inadvertent defect (a bug); it makes an invalid memory access. The memory subsystem (well, technically, the MMU and the OS) determines it must be killed. How exactly will it be killed?
- Linux's asynchronous IO (AIO) framework, and many other such scenarios.

All of these example scenarios are serviced by the same mechanism: signals.

# The signal mechanism in brief

A signal can be defined as an asynchronous event that is delivered to a target process. Signals are delivered to the target process either by another process or the OS (the kernel) itself.

At the code level, a signal is merely an integer value; more correctly, it is a bit in a bitmask. It's important to understand that, although the signal may seem like an interrupt, it is not an interrupt. An interrupt is a hardware feature; a signal is purely a software mechanism.

OK, let's try a simple exercise: run a process, putting it in an infinite loop, and then manually send it a signal via the keyboard. Find the code in (ch11/sig1.c):

```
int main(void)
{
    unsigned long int i=1;
    while(1) {
        printf("Looping, iteration #%02ld ...\n", i++);
        (void)sleep(1);
    }
    exit (EXIT_SUCCESS);
}
```

> **TIP**: Why is the `sleep(1);` code typecast to `(void)`? This is our way of informing the compiler (and possibly any static analysis tool) that we are not concerned about its return value. Well, the fact is we should be; there will be more on this later.

It's working is quite obvious: let's build and run it, and, after the third loop iteration, we press the *Ctrl + C* key combination on the keyboard.

```
$ ./sig1
Looping, iteration #01 ...
Looping, iteration #02 ...
Looping, iteration #03 ...
^C
$
```

Yes, as expected, the process terminates. But how exactly did this happen?

Here is the answer in brief: signalling. More verbosely, this is what occurs (it's still kept simple, though): when the user presses the *Ctrl + C* key combination (shown as `^C` in the output), the kernel's `tty` layer code processes this input, cooks the input key combination into, and delivers a signal to the foreground process on the shell.

But, hang on a second. Remember, a signal is just an integer value. So, which integer? Which signal? The *Ctrl + C* key combination is mapped to the the SIGINT signal, integer value 2, thus causing it to be delivered to the process. (The next section begins to explain the different signals; for now, let's not get too stressed out about it).

*Signaling - Part I*

So, OK, the `SIGINT` signal, value 2, was delivered to our `sig1` process. But then what? Here, again, is a key point: every signal is associated with a function to run when it is delivered; this function is called the **signal handler**. If we do not change it, the default signal function runs. Well, that brings up the question: Since we have not written any default (or other) signal-handling code, then who has provided this default signal handler function? The short answer is this: the OS (the kernel) handles all cases in which a process receives a signal for which the app has not installed any handler; in other words, for the default case.

The action performed by the signal handler function or the underlying kernel code determines what will happen to the target process when the signal arrives. So, now we can understand better: the action carried out by the default signal handler (kernel code, really) for the `SIGINT` signal is to terminate the process, in effect, causing the receiving process to die.

We show this in the form of a diagram as follows:

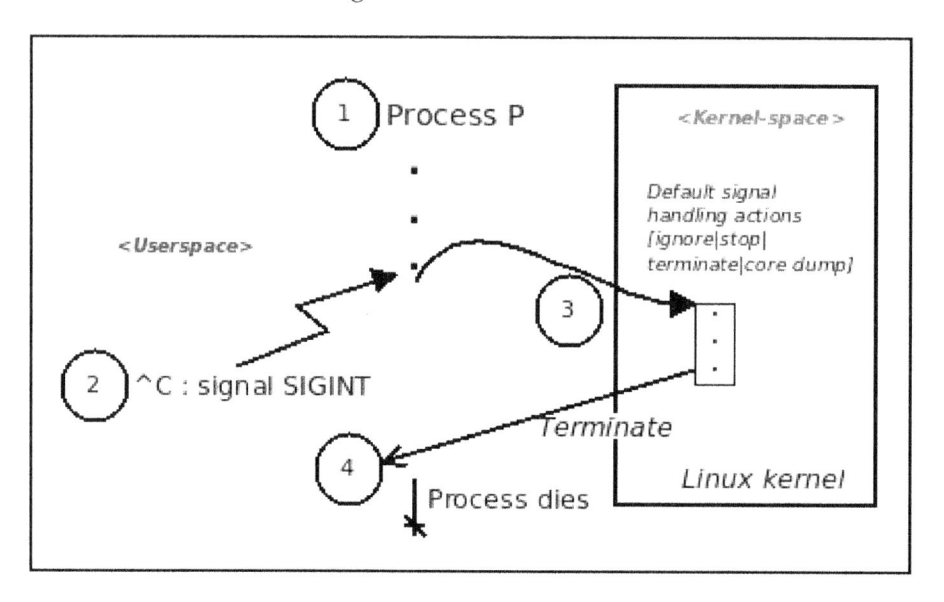

Signal delivered via keyboard, default handler causes process to die

From this diagram, we can see the following steps:

1. A process, **P** comes alive and runs its code.
2. The user presses ^C, in effect causing the `SIGINT` signal to be sent to the process.

[ 382 ]

3. As we have not set up any signal handler, the default signal handling action for this signal, which is part of the OS, is invoked.
4. This default signal handling code within the OS causes the process to die.

FYI, for the default case—that is, all cases where the application developer has not installed a specific signal-handling routine (we will learn how exactly to install our own signal handlers shortly)—what exactly does the OS code that handles these cases do? Depending on the signal being processed, the OS will perform one of these five possible actions (see the following table for details):

- Ignore the signal
- Stop the process
- Continue the (previously stopped) process
- Terminate the process
- Terminate the process and emit a core dump

The really interesting and powerful thing is this: the programmer has the ability to change–to re-vector the signal handling to their own function(s)! In effect, we can trap or catch signals by using certain APIs. Once we do so, when the signal occurs, control will not go to the default signal- handling (OS) code, but, rather, to the function we want it to. In this manner, the programmer can take charge and work with the powerful signalling mechanism.

Of course, there is much more to it: the devil does indeed lie in the details! Read on.

## Available signals

The Unix/Linux OS provides a set of 64 signals in total. They are broadly divided into two types: the standard or Unix signals and the real-time signals. We shall find that while they do share common attributes, there are some important differences as well; here, we shall investigate the Unix (or standard) signals and later, the latter.

The generic communication interface for signalling from userspace, besides the keyboard key combinations (such as *Ctrl* + *C*), is the `kill(1)` utility (and, consequently, the `kill(2)` system call).

> Besides the kill, there are several other APIs that deliver a signal; we shall flesh out more on this in a later section of this chapter.

*Signaling - Part I*

Running the `kill(1)` utility with the `-l` or list option lists the available signals on the platform:

```
$ kill -l
 1) SIGHUP    2) SIGINT    3) SIGQUIT   4) SIGILL    5) SIGTRAP
 6) SIGABRT   7) SIGBUS    8) SIGFPE    9) SIGKILL  10) SIGUSR1
11) SIGSEGV  12) SIGUSR2  13) SIGPIPE  14) SIGALRM  15) SIGTERM
16) SIGSTKFLT 17) SIGCHLD 18) SIGCONT  19) SIGSTOP  20) SIGTSTP
21) SIGTTIN  22) SIGTTOU  23) SIGURG   24) SIGXCPU  25) SIGXFSZ
26) SIGVTALRM 27) SIGPROF 28) SIGWINCH 29) SIGIO    30) SIGPWR
31) SIGSYS    34) SIGRTMIN 35) SIGRTMIN+1 36) SIGRTMIN+2 37) SIGRTMIN+3
38) SIGRTMIN+4 39) SIGRTMIN+5 40) SIGRTMIN+6 41) SIGRTMIN+7 42) SIGRTMIN+8
43) SIGRTMIN+9 44) SIGRTMIN+10 45) SIGRTMIN+11 46) SIGRTMIN+12
47) SIGRTMIN+13 48) SIGRTMIN+14 49) SIGRTMIN+15 50) SIGRTMAX-14
51) SIGRTMAX-13 52) SIGRTMAX-12 53) SIGRTMAX-11 54) SIGRTMAX-10
55) SIGRTMAX-9 56) SIGRTMAX-8 57) SIGRTMAX-7 58) SIGRTMAX-6 59) SIGRTMAX-5
60) SIGRTMAX-4 61) SIGRTMAX-3 62) SIGRTMAX-2 63) SIGRTMAX-1
64) SIGRTMAX
$
```

Perhaps the moniker `kill(1)` is a misnomer: the kill utility just sends a signal to a given process (or job). Thus (per your author at least), the name `sendsig` might have been a better choice for the utility.

> An FAQ: where are the signals numbered `32` and `33`?
> They are internally used by the Linux Pthreads implementation (called NPTL), and are hence unavailable to app developers.

## The standard or Unix signals

As can be seen from the output of kill, all supported signals on the platform are shown; the first 31 of these (on your typical Linux box) are called the standard or Unix signals. Unlike the real-time signals that follow, each standard/Unix signal has a very specific name, and, as you might guess, purpose.

(Worry not; we shall discuss the real-time signals, numbers 34 to 64, in the next chapter).

The table you will see shortly, essentially reproduced from the man page on signal(7), summarizes the standard (Unix) signals in the following column order: the signal's symbolic name, integer value(s), the default action taken upon delivery to a process, and a comment describing the signal.

The default action column has the following types: the default action of the signal handler is to:

- **Terminate**: Terminate the process.
- **Term&Core**: Terminate the process and emit a core dump. (A core dump is, essentially, a snapshot of the process's dynamic segments, the data and stack segments, at the time when the (fatal) signal was delivered). This terminate and core dump action occurs when the kernel sends a fatal signal to a process. The implication is that the process has done something illegal (buggy); an exception is the SIGQUIT signal: we get a core dump when SIGQUIT is delivered to a process.
- **Ignore**: Ignore the signal.
- **Stop**: Process enters the stopped (frozen/suspended) state (represented by T in the output of ps -l).
- **Continue**: Continue execution of a previously stopped process.

Refer to the table Standard or Unix signals:

| Signal | Integer value | Default action | Comment |
|---|---|---|---|
| SIGHUP | 1 | Terminate | Hang up detected on controlling terminal or death of controlling process |
| SIGINT | 2 | Terminate | Interrupt from keyboard : ^C |
| SIGQUIT | 3 | Term&Core | Quit from keyboard : ^\ |
| SIGILL | 4 | Term&Core | Illegal Instruction |
| SIGABRT | 6 | Term&Core | Abort signal from abort(3) |
| SIGFPE | 8 | Term&Core | Floating-point exception |
| SIGKILL | 9 | Terminate | (Hard) kill signal |
| SIGSEGV | 11 | Term&Core | Invalid memory reference |
| SIGPIPE | 13 | Terminate | Broken pipe: write to pipe with no readers; see pipe(7) |
| SIGALRM | 14 | Terminate | Timer signal from alarm(2) |
| SIGTERM | 15 | Terminate | Termination signal (soft kill) |
| SIGUSR1 | 30,10,16 | Terminate | User-defined signal 1 |
| SIGUSR2 | 31,12,17 | Terminate | User-defined signal 2 |
| SIGCHLD | 20,17,18 | Ignore | Child stopped or terminated |
| SIGCONT | 19,18,25 | Continue | Continue if stopped |
| SIGSTOP | 17,19,23 | Stop | Stop process |
| SIGTSTP | 18,20,24 | Stop | Stop typed at terminal : ^Z |

*Signaling - Part I*

| | | | |
|---|---|---|---|
| SIGTTIN | 21,21,26 | Stop | Terminal input for background process |
| SIGTTOU | 22,22,27 | Stop | Terminal output for background process |

> At times, the second column, the signal's integer value, has three numbers. Well, it's like this: the numbers are architecture-(meaning CPU) dependent; the middle column represents the value for the x86 architecture.
>
> Always use the symbolic name of the signal in code (such as `SIGSEGV`), including scripts, and never the number (such as `11`). You can see that the numeric value changes with the CPU, which could lead to non-portable buggy code!

> What if the system admin needs to urgently kill a process? Yes, its quite possible that, while logged into an interactive shell, time is very precious and an extra couple of seconds may make a difference. In such cases, typing kill `-9` is better than kill `-SIGKILL`, or even kill `-KILL`. (The previous point is with regard to writing source code).
>
> Passing the signal number to kill `-l` causes it to print the signal's symbolic name (albeit in a shorthand notation). For example:
> ```
> $ kill -l 11
> SEGV
> $
> ```

The preceding table (and, as a matter of fact the following table as well) reveal that, with two exceptions, all the signals have a special purpose. Scanning the comment column reveals it. The exceptions are `SIGUSR1` and `SIGUSR2` these are general purpose signals; their use is left entirely to the imagination of the application designers.

Further, the man page informs us that the following signals (shown in this table) are newer and included in the `SUSv2` and `POSIX.1-2001` standards:

| Signal | Integer Value | Default Action | Comment |
|---|---|---|---|
| SIGBUS | 10,7,10 | Term&Core | Bus error (bad memory access) |
| SIGPOLL | | Terminate | Pollable event (Sys V). Synonym for SIGIO |
| SIGPROF | 27,27,29 | Terminate | Profiling timer expired |
| SIGSYS | 12,31,12 | Term&Core | Bad system call (SVr4); see also seccomp(2) |
| SIGTRAP | 5 | Term&Core | Trace/breakpoint trap |
| SIGURG | 16,23,21 | Ignore | Urgent condition on socket (4.2BSD) |

| | | | |
|---|---|---|---|
| SIGVTALRM | 26,26,28 | Terminate | Virtual alarm clock (4.2BSD) |
| SIGXCPU | 24,24,30 | Term&Core | CPU time limit exceeded (4.2BSD); see prlimit(2) |
| SIGXFSZ | 25,25,31 | Term&Core | File size limit exceeded (4.2BSD); see prlimit(2) |

Newer standard or Unix signals

A few remaining (not so common) signals are further mentioned by the same man page (signal(7)). Take a look if you are interested.

It's important to note that, out of all the signals mentioned, only two of them cannot be caught, ignored or blocked: the SIGKILL and the SIGSTOP. This is because the OS must guarantee a way to kill and/or stop a process.

# Handling signals

In this section, we shall discuss in detail how exactly signals are handled by the application developer programmatically (using C code, of course).

Glance back at *Figure 1*. You can see how the OS performs default signal handling, which runs when an uncaught signal is delivered to the process. This seems good, until we realize that, pretty often, the default action is to simply kill (or terminate) the process. What if the application demands we do something else? Or, what if, realistically, the application does crash, instead of just abruptly dying (and perhaps leaving important files and other metadata in an inconsistent state). Perhaps we can put the program into a sane state by performing some required cleanup, flushing buffers, closing open files, logging the state/debug information, and so on, informing the user of the sorry state of affairs (with a nice dialog box perhaps), and *then* have the process die, gracefully and peacefully, if you will.

The ability to catch or trap a signal is the key to achieving these goals. As mentioned earlier, to re-vector the flow of control such that it's not the default signal-handling kernel code, but our custom signal handling code that executes when the signal arrives.

So, how do we achieve this? By using APIs to register interest in and thus handle signals. Broadly, there are three available APIs to catch or trap a signal:

- `sigaction(2)` system call
- `signal(2)` system call
- `sigvec(3)` library API

Well, of these three APIs, the `sigvec` is nowadays considered deprecated. Also, unless the work is really simplistic, you are urged to forgo the `signal(2)` API in favor of the `sigaction` API. Effectively, the powerful way to handle signals is via the `sigaction(2)` system call; it is the one we shall discuss in depth.

## Using the sigaction system call to trap signals

The `sigaction(2)` system call is the right way to trap or catch signals; it's powerful, POSIX compliant, and can be used to hone your application's signal-handling superbly.

At a high level, the `sigaction` system call is used to register a signal handler for a given signal. If the signal's handler function was `foo`, we can use `sigaction` to change its signal handler to `bar`. As usual, there is a lot more we can specify as well, which has a powerful impact upon signal handling, and we shall come to all that shortly. Here is the signature:

```
#include <signal.h>
int sigaction(int signum, const struct sigaction *act,
              struct sigaction *oldact);
```

> Feature Test Macro Requirements for `glibc` (see `feature_test_macros(7)`): sigaction(): _POSIX_C_SOURCE siginfo_t: _POSIX_C_SOURCE >= 199309L

The man page on `sigaction(2)` informs us (via the Feature Test Macro Requirements section; see further on for a few details) that using `sigaction` requires the definition of the `_POSIX_C_SOURCE` macro; this is almost always the case with modern code on Linux. Further, usage of the `siginfo_t` data structure (explained later in this chapter) requires you to have POSIX version `199309L` or later. (The format is YYYYMM; hence, that's the POSIX standard draft as of September 1993; again, this would certainly be the case on any reasonably modern Linux platform).

## Sidebar – the feature test macros

A quick digression: feature test macros are a `glibc` feature; they allow a developer to specify, at compile time, the exact feature set by defining these macros in the source. The manual (man) pages always specify (as required), the feature test macros required to be present to support a certain API or feature.

With regard to these feature test macros, on both the Ubuntu (17.10) and Fedora (27) Linux distributions, we have tested the source code of this book upon, the value of `_POSIX_C_SOURCE` is `200809L`. The macro is defined in the header file `<features.h>`, which is itself included in the header `<unistd.h>`.

A simple test program to print a few feature test macros is provided within the book's GitHub source tree here: `https://github.com/PacktPublishing/Hands-on-System-Programming-with-Linux/tree/master/misc`. Why not give it a try on your Linux platform?

> More on feature test macros from the `glibc` documentation: `http://www.gnu.org/software/libc/manual/html_node/Feature-Test-Macros.html`.

## The sigaction structure

The `sigaction(2)` system call takes three parameters, of which the second and third are of the same data type.

The first parameter `int signum` is the signal to trap. This straight away reveals an important point: signals are meant to be trapped one at a time—you can only trap one signal with a single call to `sigaction`. Do not attempt to be overly clever and do things such as pass a bitmask of signals (bitwise-ORed) together; that's a bug. Of course, you can always call `sigaction` multiple times or in a loop.

The data type of the second and third parameters is a pointer to a structure called, again, `sigaction`. The `sigaction` structure definition is as follows (from the header `/usr/include/bits/sigaction.h`):

```
/* Structure describing the action to be taken when a signal arrives.
 */
struct sigaction
  {
    /* Signal handler. */
#ifdef __USE_POSIX199309
```

## Signaling - Part I

```
        union
          {
            /* Used if SA_SIGINFO is not set. */
            __sighandler_t sa_handler;
            /* Used if SA_SIGINFO is set. */
            void (*sa_sigaction) (int, siginfo_t *, void *);
          }
        __sigaction_handler;
# define sa_handler __sigaction_handler.sa_handler
# define sa_sigaction __sigaction_handler.sa_sigaction
#else
        __sighandler_t sa_handler;
#endif

        /* Additional set of signals to be blocked. */
        __sigset_t sa_mask;

        /* Special flags. */
        int sa_flags;

        /* Restore handler. */
        void (*sa_restorer) (void);
    };
```

The first member, a function pointer, refers to the signal handler function itself. On modern Linux distributions, the __USE_POSIX199309 macro will indeed be defined; hence, as can be seen, the signal handler value is a union of two elements, implying that at runtime, exactly one of them will be used. The previous comments make it clear: by default, the sa_handler prototype function is used; however, if the flag SA_SIGINFO is passed along (in the third member sa_flags), then the sa_sigaction styled function is used. We shall make this clear with sample code soon.

The C library specifies __sighandler_t as: typedef void (*__sighandler_t) (int);

As mentioned previously, it's a pointer to a function that will receive one parameter: an integer value (yes, you guessed it: the signal that is delivered).

Before going deeper into the data structure, it would be instructive to write and try out a simple C program that handles a couple of signals, using defaults for most of the previously mentioned sigaction structure members.

The source code of the main() function of ch11/sig2.c:

```
int main(void)
{
 unsigned long int i = 1;
 struct sigaction act;

 /* Init sigaction to defaults via the memset,
  * setup 'siggy' as the signal handler function,
  * trap just the SIGINT and SIGQUIT signals.
  */
 memset(&act, 0, sizeof(act));
 act.sa_handler = siggy;
 if (sigaction(SIGINT, &act, 0) < 0)
     FATAL("sigaction on SIGINT failed");
 if (sigaction(SIGQUIT, &act, 0) < 0)
     FATAL("sigaction on SIGQUIT failed");

 while (1) {
     printf("Looping, iteration #%02ld ...\n", i++);
     (void)sleep(1);
 } [...]
```

We deliberately memset(3) the sigaction structure to all zeros, to initialize it (initializing is always good coding practice in any case!). Then, we initialize the signal handler to our own signal-handling function siggy.

Notice how, to trap two signals, we require two sigaction(2) system calls. The second parameter, the pointer to struct sigaction, is to be populated by the programmer and is considered to be the new settings for the signal. The third parameter is, again, a pointer to struct sigaction; it, however, is a value-result type: if non-NULL and allocated, the kernel will populate it with the previous settings of the signal. This is a useful feature: what if the design requires you to perform a save and restore of some signal dispositions. Here, as a simple case, we just set the third parameter to NULL, implying that we are not interested in the previous signal state.

We then enter the same (as sig1.c) infinite loop... Our simple signal handler function siggy is shown here:

```
static void siggy(int signum)
{
  const char *str1 = "*** siggy: handled SIGINT ***\n";
  const char *str2 = "*** siggy: handled SIGQUIT ***\n";

  switch (signum) {
  case SIGINT:
```

*Signaling - Part I*

```
    if (write(STDOUT_FILENO, str1, strlen(str1)) < 0)
        WARN("write str1 failed!");
    return;
  case SIGQUIT:
    if (write(STDOUT_FILENO, str2, strlen(str2)) < 0)
        WARN("write str2 failed!");
    return;
  }
}
```

The signal handler receives one integer value as its parameter: the signal that caused control to reach here. Hence, we can multiplex on multiple signals: set up a common signal handler and perform a simple switch-case to handle each specific signal.

The signal handling function's return type is `void`, of course. Ask yourself: Where will it return? It's an unknown. Remember, signals can arrive asynchronously; we have no idea when exactly the handler will run.

Let's try it out:

```
$ make sig2
gcc -Wall -c ../common.c -o common.o
gcc -Wall -c -o sig2.o sig2.c
gcc -Wall -o sig2 sig2.c common.o
$ ./sig2
Looping, iteration #01 ...
Looping, iteration #02 ...
Looping, iteration #03 ...
^C*** siggy: handled SIGINT ***
Looping, iteration #04 ...
Looping, iteration #05 ...
^\*** siggy: handled SIGQUIT ***
Looping, iteration #06 ...
Looping, iteration #07 ...
^C*** siggy: handled SIGINT ***
Looping, iteration #08 ...
Looping, iteration #09 ...
^\*** siggy: handled SIGQUIT ***
Looping, iteration #10 ...
Looping, iteration #11 ...
^Z
[1]+  Stopped                 ./sig2
$ kill %1
[1]+  Terminated              ./sig2
$
```

Chapter 11

You can see that this time, the SIGINT (via keyboard ^C) and the SIGQUIT (via keyboard ^\ key combination) signals are being handled by the application.

So, how do we terminate the app? Well, one way is to open another terminal window and kill the app via the kill utility. For now, though, we use another method: we send the SIGTSTP signal to the process (via keyboard ^Z key combination) to put it into the stopped state; we get back the shell. Now, we simply kill it via kill(1). ([1] is the process's job number; you can use the jobs command to see all current jobs on the session).

We show this in the form of a diagram as follows:

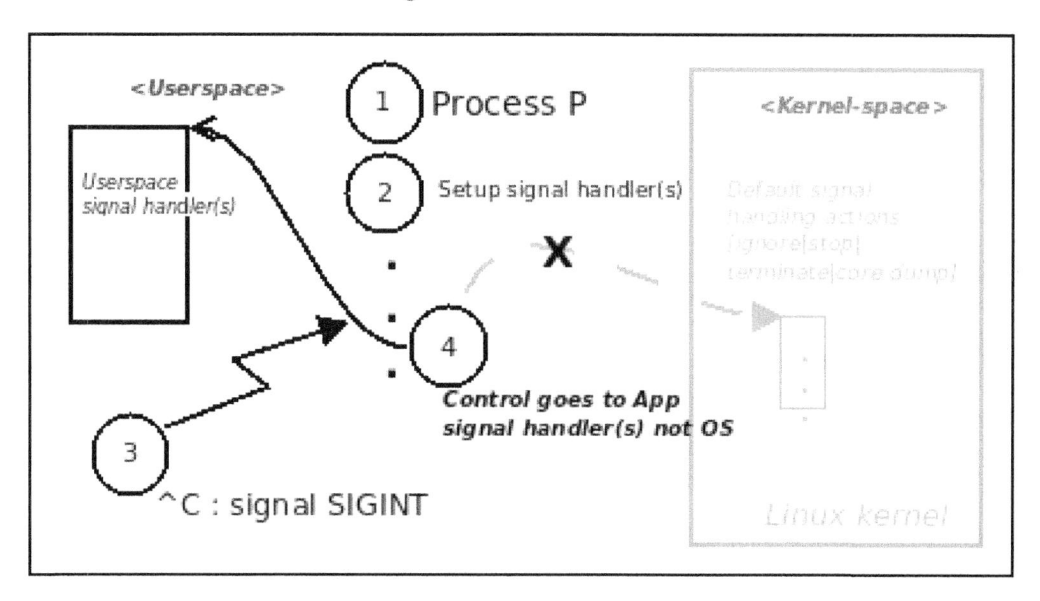

Figure 2: Handling a Signal

Clearly, as demonstrated by our simple sig2 application and *Figure 2*, once a signal is trapped (via the sigaction(2) (or the signal) system call), when it is delivered to the process, control is now re-vectored to the new application-specific signal handler function, and not to the default OS signal-handling code.

In the program sig2, all looks good, except that you, the careful reader, may have noticed a bit of a puzzle: in the siggy signal handler function's code, why not just use a simple printf(3) to emit a message. Why the write(2) system call? Actually, there's a really good reason behind this. This, and more, is coming up.

[ 393 ]

*Signaling - Part I*

> **TIP**: Trap all required signals as early as possible, in the application's initialization. This is because signals can arrive at any moment; the sooner we are ready to handle them, the better.

## Masking signals

While a process is running, what if it wants to block (or mask) certain signals? This is indeed possible via the API interface; in fact, the second member of the `sigaction(2)` structure is the signal mask, the mask of signals to block from delivery to the process while the signal handler function is running. A mask typically implies a bitwise-or of signals:

```
...
/* Additional set of signals to be blocked. */
    __sigset_t sa_mask;
...
```

Do notice the previous comment; it implies some signal is already being blocked. Yes, indeed; let's say a process traps a signal n via the `sigaction` system call. At some later point that signal n is delivered to it; while our process handles the signal—that is, runs the code of its signal handler—that signal n is blocked from delivery to the process. For how long is it blocked? Until we return from the signal handler. In other words, the OS auto-blocks the signal currently being handled. This usually is precisely what we want, and it works to our advantage.

### Signal masking with the sigprocmask API

What if we want to block (or mask) some other signals during execution. For example, while processing a critical region of code? The system call `sigprocmask(2)` is designed for this purpose: `int sigprocmask(int how, const sigset_t *set, sigset_t *oldset);`

The signal sets are essentially bitmasks of the signals in question. The set is the new set of signals to mask, while `oldset` is actually a return value (the value-result type of parameter), or the previous (or current) value of the signal mask.
The `how` parameter determines the behavior and can take these values:

- `SIG_BLOCK` : Additionally, block (mask) the signals specified in the signal set set (along with the signals already masked)
- `SIG_UNBLOCK` : Unblock (unmask) the signals specified in the signal set set

- `SIG_SETMASK` : The signals specified in the signal set set are masked, overwriting the previous values

## Querying the signal mask

So, we understand that you can set the process's signal mask at the time of `sigaction(2)` (via the `sa_mask` member), or via the `sigprocmask(2)` system call (as mentioned previously). But how exactly can you query the state of the process signal mask at any arbitrary point in time?

Well, again, via the `sigprocmask(2)` system call. But, logically, this API sets a mask, right? This is the trick: if the first parameter set is set to `NULL`, then the second parameter is effectively ignored, while in the third parameter `oldset`, the current signal mask value is populated, and thus we can query the signal mask without altering it.

The `ch11/query_mask` program demonstrates this, the code is built upon our previous example `sig2.c`. Hence, we do not need to show the entire source; we just show the relevant code, in `main()`:

```
[...]
/* Init sigaction:
 * setup 'my_handler' as the signal handler function,
 * trap just the SIGINT and SIGQUIT signals.
 */
memset(&act, 0, sizeof(act));
act.sa_handler = my_handler;
/* This is interesting: we fill the signal mask, implying that
 * _all_ signals are masked (blocked) while the signal handler
 * runs! */
sigfillset(&act.sa_mask);

if (sigaction(SIGINT, &act, 0) < 0)
    FATAL("sigaction on SIGINT failed");
if (sigaction(SIGQUIT, &act, 0) < 0)
    FATAL("sigaction on SIGQUIT failed");
[...]
```

As you can see, this time we use the `sigfillset(3)` (one of the useful POSIX signal set operations or `sigsetops(3)` operators) to populate the signal mask with all 1's, implying that, while the signal handler code is running, all signals will be masked (blocked).

## Signaling - Part I

Here is the relevant portion of the signal handler code:

```
static void my_handler(int signum)
{
    const char *str1 = "*** my_handler: handled SIGINT ***\n";
    const char *str2 = "*** my_handler: handled SIGQUIT ***\n";
    show_blocked_signals();
    switch (signum) {
    [...]
```

Ah! Here, the intelligence is within the `show_blocked_signals` function; we have this function in our common code source file: `../common.c`. Here's the function:

```
/*
 * Signaling: Prints (to stdout) all signal integer values that are
 * currently in the Blocked (masked) state.
 */
int show_blocked_signals(void)
{
    sigset_t oldset;
    int i, none=1;

    /* sigprocmask:
     * int sigprocmask(int how, const sigset_t *set, sigset_t
*oldset);
     * if 'set' is NULL, the 'how' is ignored, but the
     * 'oldset' sigmask value is populated; thus we can query the
     * signal mask without altering it.
     */
    sigemptyset(&oldset);
    if (sigprocmask(SIG_UNBLOCK, 0, &oldset) < 0)
        return -1;

    printf("\n[SigBlk: ");
    for (i=1; i<=64; i++) {
        if (sigismember(&oldset, i)) {
            none=0;
            printf("%d ", i);
        }
    }
    if (none)
        printf("-none-]\n");
    else
        printf("]\n");
    fflush(stdout);
    return 0;
}
```

*Chapter 11*

The key here is this: the `sigprocmask(2)` is used with a NULL second parameter (the mask to set); hence, as stated earlier, the how parameter is ignored and the value-result third parameter `oldset` will hold the current process signal mask.

We can query each signal bit in the bitmask using, again, the `sigsetops: sigismember(3)` convenience method. Now all that's left to do is iterate over each bit in the mask and print the signal number, if the bit is set, or ignore it if it is cleared.

Here's the output of a test run:

```
$ make query_mask
gcc -Wall -c ../common.c -o common.o
gcc -Wall -c -o query_mask.o query_mask.c
gcc -Wall -o query_mask query_mask.c common.o
$ ./query_mask
Looping, iteration #01 ...
Looping, iteration #02 ...
Looping, iteration #03 ...
^C
[SigBlk: 1 2 3 4 5 6 7 8 10 11 12 13 14 15 16 17 18 20 21 22 23 24 25
26 27 28 29 30 31 34 35 36 37 38 39 40 41 42 43 44 45 46 47 48 49 50
51 52 53 54 55 56 57 58 59 60 61 62 63 64 ]
*** my_handler: handled SIGINT ***
Looping, iteration #04 ...
Looping, iteration #05 ...
^\
[SigBlk: 1 2 3 4 5 6 7 8 10 11 12 13 14 15 16 17 18 20 21 22 23 24 25
26 27 28 29 30 31 34 35 36 37 38 39 40 41 42 43 44 45 46 47 48 49 50
51 52 53 54 55 56 57 58 59 60 61 62 63 64 ]
*** my_handler: handled SIGQUIT ***
Looping, iteration #06 ...
Looping, iteration #07 ...
^Z
[2]+  Stopped                 ./query_mask
$ kill %2
[2]+  Terminated              ./query_mask
$
```

Notice how the blocked signals are printed out. Hey, can you spot the missing signals?

> `SIGKILL(#9)` and `SIGSTOP(#19)` cannot be masked; also, signals 32 and 33 are internally reserved for and used by the `Pthreads` implementation.

[ 397 ]

## Sidebar – signal handling within the OS – polling not interrupts

Here, we do not intend to delve deep into the Linux kernel internal details of signal handling; rather, we'd like to make clear a common misconception hinted at earlier: handling signals is not at all like hardware interrupt handling. Signals are not interrupts, nor faults or exceptions; all of these— interrupts, traps, exceptions, faults—are raised by the PIC/MMU/CPU hardware on a computer. Signals are purely a software feature.

Delivering a signal to a process implies setting some members in the task structure of the task (in kernel memory), the so-called `TIF_SIGPENDING` bit, and the particular bit(s) representing the signal(s) in the task's `sigpending` set; this way, the kernel knows whether, and which, signals are pending delivery to the process.

The reality is that at opportune points in time (which occur regularly), the kernel code checks whether a signal(s) is pending delivery, and, if so, delivers it, running or consuming the signal handler(s) of the process (in userland context). Signal handling is thus considered to be more of a polling mechanism rather than an interrupt one.

## Reentrant safety and signalling

There is an important-to-understand issue during signal handling, when working with reentrant-unsafe (also called async-signal-unsafe) functions within a signal handler.

Of course, to understand this issue, you must first understand what exactly a reentrant function is, and, subsequently, what is meant by reentrant-safe or async-signal-safe functions.

### Reentrant functions

A reentrant function is one that can be reentered while an ongoing invocation is still running. It's simpler than it sounds; check out this pseudo-code snippet:

```
signal_handler(sig)
{
    my_foo();
    < ... >
}
```

```
my_foo()
{
    char mybuf[MAX];
    <...>
}

do_the_work_mate()
{
    my_foo();
    <...>
}
```

Now imagine this sequence of activity:

- The function `my_foo()` is invoked by the business logic function `do_the_work_mate()`; it operates on the local buffer `mybuf`

- While this is still running, a signal is dispatched to this process

- The signal handler code preempts whatever was executing at the moment it occurred and runs

    - It reinvokes the function `my_foo()`

So, there we see it: the function `my_foo()` is reentered. By itself, that's OK; the important question here is: is it safe?

Recall (from our coverage in Chapter 2, *Virtual Memory*) that the process stack is used to hold function call frames and, hence, any local variables. Here, the reentrant function `my_foo()` only uses a local variable. It's been invoked twice; each invocation will be a separate call frame on the process stack. The key point: each invocation of `my_foo()` works on a copy of the local variable `mybuf`; thus, it is safe. Hence, it's documented as being `reentrant-safe`. In the signal-handling context, it's called being `async-signal-safe`: invoking the function from within a signal handler while a previous invocation is still running is safe.

OK, let's add a twist to the previous pseudo-code: change the function `my_foo()`'s local variable `mybuf` to become a global (or static) variable. Now think about what happens when it's reentered; this time, distinct stack call frames cannot save us. As `mybuf` is global, there exists only one copy of it, which will be in an inconsistent state from the first function invocation (by `do_the_work_mate()`). When the second invocation of `my_foo()` occurs, we will work on this inconsistent global `mybuf`, thus corrupting it. Hence, clearly, this is unsafe.

### Async-signal-safe functions

As a general rule, functions that use only local variables are reentrant-safe; any usage of a global or a static data renders them unsafe. This is a key point: you can only call those functions in a signal handler that are documented as being reentrant-safe or signal-async-safe.

The man page on `signal-safety(7)` http://man7.org/linux/man-pages/man7/signal-safety.7.html provides details for this.

> On Ubuntu, the man page with this name (`signal-safety(7)`) was installed in recent versions only; it does work on Ubuntu 18.04.

Among them, it publishes a list of (alphabetically ordered) functions that the `POSIX.1` standard requires an implementation to guarantee are implemented as being async-signal-safe, (See man page version 4.12, dated 2017-03-13)

So the bottom line is this: from within a signal handler, you can only invoke the following:

- C library functions or system calls that are in the signal-safety(7) man page (do look it up)
- Within a third-party library, functions explicitly documented as being async-signal-safe
- Your own library or other functions that have been explicitly written to be async-signal-safe

Also, don't forget that your signal handler function itself must be reentrant-safe. Do not access application global or static variables within it.

## Alternate ways to be safe within a signal handler

What if we must access some global state within our signal handler routine? There do exist some alternate ways of making it signal-safe:

- At the point you must access these variables, ensure that all signals are blocked (or masked), and, once done, restore the signal state (unmask).

- Perform some kind of locking on shared data while accessing it.
    - In multiprocess applications (the case we are talking about here), (binary) semaphores can be used as a locking mechanism to protect shared data across processes.
    - In multithreaded applications, the use of an appropriate locking mechanism (mutex locks, perhaps; we shall, of course, cover this in a later chapter in detail).
- If your requirement is to just operate upon global integers (a common case for signal handling!), use a special data type (the `sig_atomic_t`). Seen later on.

The reality is that the first approach, blocking signals when required, is difficult to achieve in practice on complex projects (although you certainly can arrange for all signals to be masked while handling a signal by setting the signal mask to all 1s, as demonstrated in the previous section, *Querying the signal mask*).

The second approach, locking, is realistic though performance-sensitive for multiprocess and multithreaded applications.

Here and now, while discussing signalling, we shall cover the third approach. Another reason for this is because working on (querying and/or setting) an integer within a signal handler is a very common case.

> Within the code we show in this book, there is the occasional use of async-signal-unsafe functions being used within a signal handler (usually one of the `[f|s|v]printf(3)` family). We stress that this has been done purely for demonstration purposes only; please do not give into temptation and use async-signal-unsafe functions in production code!

## Signal-safe atomic integers

Visualize a multiprocess application. A process, A, must complete a certain quantum of work (let's say it must complete running a function `foo()`) and let another process, B, know that it has done so (in other words, we want synchronization between the two processes; see the next info box as well).

## Signaling - Part I

A simple way to achieve this is as follows: have process A send a signal (say `SIGUSR1`) to process B when it has reached the required point. In turn, process B traps `SIGUSR1`, and when it does arrive, in its signal handler, it sets a global buffer to an appropriate message string to let the rest of the application know that we have reached this point.

In the following tables, visualize the timeline going vertically ($y$ axis) downward.

Pseudo-code—the wrong way:

| Process A | Process B |
|---|---|
| Do work | Set up signal handler for `SIGUSR1` |
| Work on `foo()` | `char gMsg[32];    // global`<br>Do work |
| `foo()` done; send `SIGUSR1` to process B | |
| | `signal_handler()` function entered asynchronously |
| | `strncpy(gMsg, "chkpointA", 32);` |
| [...] | [...] |

This looks fine, except that, please notice that, this global update on the message buffer `gMsg` is not guaranteed to be atomic. It's entirely possible that attempting to do so will result in a race—a condition in which we cannot predict with any certainty what the final result of the global variable will be. It's exactly this kind of data race that is the perfect breeding ground for a class of difficult-to-see-and-solve racy bugs. You must avoid them by using proper programming practices.

The solution: Switch from using a global buffer to a global integer-like variable of data type `sig_atomic_t`, and, importantly, mark it as `volatile` (so that the compiler disables optimizations around it).

Pseudo-code – the right way:

| Process A | Process B |
|---|---|
| Do work | Set up signal handler for `SIGUSR1` |
| Work on `foo()` | `volatile sig_atomic_t gFlag=0;`<br>Do work |
| `foo()` done; send `SIGUSR1` to process B | |
| | `signal_handler()` function entered asynchronously |
| | `gFlag = 1;` |
| [...] | [...] |

This time it will work just fine, without any race. (Writing the complete working code of the previous program is suggested as an exercise to readers).

> It's important to realize that the usage of `sig_atomic_t` makes an (integer) variable only async-signal safe, not thread-safe. (Thread safety will be covered in detail in later Chapter 14, *Multithreading with Pthreads Part I - Essentials*).
>
> True process synchronization should be performed using an IPC mechanism appropriate for the purpose. Signals do serve as a primitive IPC mechanism; depending on your project, other IPC mechanisms (sockets, message queues, shared memory, pipes, and semaphores) might well be a better way to do so, though.

According to Carnegie Mellon University's Software Engineering Institute (CMU SEI) CERT C Coding Standard:

SIG31-C: Do not access shared objects in signal handlers (https://wiki.sei.cmu.edu/confluence/display/c/SIG31-C.+Do+not+access+shared+objects+in+signal+handlers)

The type `sig_atomic_t` is the integer type of an object that can be accessed as an atomic entity even in the presence of asynchronous interrupts.

*Signaling - Part I*

Additional note:

It's worth checking out the code examples provided within the last link as well. Also, within the same context, the CMU SEI's CERT C Coding Standard, the following points are noted, regarding the correct way to perform signal handling:

- SIG30-C. Call only asynchronous-safe functions within signal handlers.
- SIG31-C: Do not access shared objects in signal handlers.
- SIG34-C. Do not call signal() from within interruptible signal handlers.
- SIG35-C. Do not return from a computational exception signal handler.

The last bullet point is perhaps better phrased by the POSIX.1 committee:

The behavior of a process is undefined after it returns normally from a signal-catching function for a SIGBUS, SIGFPE, SIGILL, or SIGSEGV signal that was not generated by kill(2), sigqueue(3), or raise(2).

In other words, once your process receives any of the previously mentioned fatal signals from the OS, it can perform cleanup within it's signal handler, but then it must terminate. (Allow us this joke: the hero exclaiming "Not today, Death!", is all well and good in the movies, but when SIGBUS, SIGFPE, SIGILL, or SIGSEGV come calling, it's time to clean up and gracefully die!). As a matter of fact, we delve into this aspect in a lot of detail within the next chapter.

# Powerful sigaction flags

From the previous section The sigaction structure, recall that one of the members of the sigaction structure is as follows:

```
/* Special flags. */
    int sa_flags;
```

These special flags are very powerful. With them, the developer can precisely specify signal semantics that would otherwise be hard or impossible to obtain. The default value of zero implies no special behavior.

We shall first enumerate the `sa_flags` possible values in this table and then proceed to work with them:

| sa_flag | Behavior or semantic it provides (from the man page on `sigaction(2)`). |
|---|---|
| SA_NOCLDSTOP | If `signum` is SIGCHLD, do not generate SIGCHLD when children stop or stopped children continue. |
| SA_NOCLDWAIT | (Linux 2.6 and later) If `signum` is SIGCHLD, do not transform children into zombies when they terminate. |
| SA_RESTART | Provide behavior compatible with BSD signal semantics by making certain system calls restartable across signals. |
| SA_RESETHAND | Restore the signal action to the default upon entry to the signal handler. |
| SA_NODEFER | Do not prevent the signal from being received from within its own signal handler. |
| SA_ONSTACK | Call the signal handler on an alternate signal stack provided by `sigaltstack(2)`. If an alternate stack is not available, the default (process) stack will be used. |
| SA_SIGINFO | The signal handler takes three arguments, not one. In this case, `sa_sigaction` should be set instead of `sa_handler`. |

Keep in mind that `sa_flags` is an integer value interpreted by the OS as a bitmask; bitwise-ORing several flags together to imply their combined behavior is indeed common practice.

## Zombies not invited

Let's get started with the flag `SA_NOCLDWAIT`. First, a quick digression:

As we learned in Chapter 10, *Process Creation*, a process can fork, resulting in an act of creation: a new child process is born! From that chapter, it is now relevant to recall our Fork **Rule #7**: The parent process must wait (block) upon the termination (death) of every child, directly or indirectly.

The parent process can wait (block) upon the child's termination via the wait system call API set. As we learned earlier, this is essential: if the child dies and the parent has not waited upon it, the child becomes a zombie—an undesirable state to be in, at best. At worst, it can terribly clog system resources.

*Signaling - Part I*

However, blocking upon the death of the child (or children) via the wait API(s) causes the parent to become synchronous; it blocks, and thus, in a sense, it defeats the whole purpose of multiprocessing, to be parallelized. Can we not be asynchronously notified when our children die? This way, the parent can continue to perform processing, running in parallel with its children.

Ah! Signals to the rescue: the OS will deliver the SIGCHLD signal to the parent process whenever any of its children terminate or enter the stopped state.

Pay attention to the last detail: the SIGCHLD will be delivered even if a child process stops (and is thus not dead). What if we do not want that? In other words, we only want the signal sent to us when our children die. That is precisely what the SA_NOCLDSTOP flag performs: no child death on stop. So, if you do not want to get spoofed by the stopping of the children into thinking they're dead, use this flag. (This also applies when a stopped child is subsequently continued, via the SIGCONT).

## No zombies! – the classic way

The previous discussion should also make you realize that, hey, we now have a neat asynchronous way in which to get rid of any pesky zombies: trap the SIGCHLD, and in its signal handler, issue the wait call (using any of the wait APIs covered in Chapter 9, *Process Execution*), preferably with the WNOHANG option parameter such that we perform a non-blocking wait; thus, we do not block upon any live children and just succeed in clearing any zombies.

Here is the classic Unix way to clear zombies:

```
static void child_dies(int signum)
{
    while((pid = wait3(0, WNOHANG, 0)) != -1);
}
```

Delving into depth here would be of academic interest only on modern Linux (modern Linux, in your author's opinion, being the 2.6.0 Linux kernel and beyond, which, by the way, was released on December 18, 2003).

## No zombies! – the modern way

So, with modern Linux, avoiding zombies became vastly easier: just trap the SIGCHLD signal using sigaction(2), specifying the SA_NOCLDWAIT bit in the signal flags bitmask. That's it: zombie worries banished forever! On the Linux platform, the SIGCHLD signal is still delivered to the parent process—you can use it to keep track of children, or whatever accounting purposes you may dream up.

By the way, the POSIX.1 standard also specifies another way to get rid of the pesky zombie: just ignore the SIGCHLD signal (with the SIG_IGN). Well, you can use this approach, with the caveat that then you will never know when a child does indeed die (or stop).

So, useful stuff: let's put our new knowledge to the test: we rig up a small multiprocess application that generates zombies, but also clears them in the modern way as follows (ch11/zombies_clear_linux26.c):

> For readability, only the relevant parts of the code are displayed; to view and run it, the entire source code is available here: https://github.com/PacktPublishing/Hands-on-System-Programming-with-Linux.

```c
int main(int argc, char **argv)
{
    struct sigaction act;
    int opt=0;

    if (argc != 2)
        usage(argv[0]);

    opt = atoi(argv[1]);
    if (opt != 1 && opt != 2)
        usage(argv[0]);

    memset(&act, 0, sizeof(act));
    if (opt == 1) {
        act.sa_handler = child_dies;
        /* 2.6 Linux: prevent zombie on termination of child(ren)! */
        act.sa_flags = SA_NOCLDWAIT;
    }
    if (opt == 2)
        act.sa_handler = SIG_IGN;
    act.sa_flags |= SA_RESTART | SA_NOCLDSTOP; /* no SIGCHLD on stop of child(ren) */

    if (sigaction(SIGCHLD, &act, 0) == -1)
```

## Signaling - Part I

```
        FATAL("sigaction failed");
    printf("parent: %d\n", getpid());
    switch (fork()) {
    case -1:
        FATAL("fork failed");
    case 0: // Child
        printf("child: %d\n", getpid());
        DELAY_LOOP('c', 25);
        exit(0);
    default: // Parent
        while (1)
            pause();
    }
    exit(0);
}
```

(For now, ignore the SA_RESTART flag in the code; we shall explain it shortly). Here is the signal handler for SIGCHLD:

```
#define DEBUG
//#undef DEBUG
/* SIGCHLD handler */
static void child_dies(int signum)
{
#ifdef DEBUG
    printf("\n*** Child dies! ***\n");
#endif
}
```

Notice how we only emit a printf(3) within the signal handler when in debug mode (as it's async-signal unsafe).

Let's try it out:

```
$ ./zombies_clear_linux26
Usage: ./zombies_clear_linux26 {option-to-prevent-zombies}
 1 : (2.6 Linux) using the SA_NOCLDWAIT flag with sigaction(2)
 2 : just ignore the signal SIGCHLD
$
```

OK, first we try it with option 1; that is, using the SA_NOCLDWAIT flag:

```
$ ./zombies_clear_linux26 1 &
[1] 10239
parent: 10239
child: 10241
c $ cccccccccccccccccccccccc
*** Child dies! ***
```

[ 408 ]

```
$ ps
  PID TTY          TIME CMD
 9490 pts/1    00:00:00 bash
10239 pts/1    00:00:00 zombies_clear_1
10249 pts/1    00:00:00 ps
$
```

Importantly, checking with `ps(1)` reveals there is no zombie.
Now run it with option 2:

```
$ ./zombies_clear_linux26 2
parent: 10354
child: 10355
cccccccccccccccccccccccc
^C
$
```

Notice that the `*** Child dies! ***` message (that we did get in the previous run) does not appear, proving that we never enter the signal handler for SIGCHLD. Of course not; we ignored the signal. While that does prevent the zombie, it also prevents us from knowing that a child has died.

# The SA_NOCLDSTOP flag

Regarding the SIGCHLD signal, there is an important point to realize: The default behavior is that, whether a process dies or stops, or a stopped child continues execution (typically via the SIGCONT signal being sent to it), the kernel posts the SIGCHLD signal to its parent.

Perhaps this is useful. The parent is informed of all these events—the child's death, stop-page, or continuation. On the other hand, perhaps we do not want to be spoofed into thinking that our child process has died, when in reality it has just been stopped (or continued).

For such cases, use the SA_NOCLDSTOP flag; it literally means no SIGCHLD on child stop (or resume). Now you will only get the SIGCHLD upon child death.

# Interrupted system calls and how to fix them with the SA_RESTART

Traditional (older) Unix OSes suffered from an issue regarding the handling of signals while processing blocking system calls.

### Blocking APIs

> An API is said to be blocking when, on issuing the API, the calling process (or thread) is put into a sleep state. Why is this? This is because the underlying OS or device driver understands that the event that the caller needs to wait upon has not yet occurred; thus, it must wait for it. Once the event (or condition) arises, the OS or driver wakes up the process; the process now continues to execute its code path.
>
> Examples of blocking APIs are common: read, write, select, wait (and its variants), accept, and so on.

Take a moment to visualize this scenario:

- A process traps a signal (say, SIGCHLD).
- The process, at some later point, issues a blocking system call (say, the accept(2) system call).
- While it's in the sleep state, the signal is delivered to it.

The following pseudo code illustrates the same:

```
[...]
sigaction(SIGCHLD, &sigact, 0);
[...]
sd = accept( <...> );
[...]
```

> By the way, the accept(2) system call is how a network server process blocks (waits) upon a client connecting to it.

What should happen, now that the signal is delivered? The correct behavior is this: the process should wake up, handle the signal (run the code of its signal handler), and go to sleep once again, continuing to block upon the event it was waiting upon.

On older Unixes (your author has come across this on an old SunOS 4.x), the signal is delivered, the signal handler code runs, but after that the blocking system call fails, returning -1. The errno variable is set to EINTR, which translates to an interrupted system call.

This is considered a bug, of course. The poor Unix application developer had to resort to some temporary fixes, often resorting to wrapping each and every system call (foo in this example) in a loop, like so:

```
while ((foo() == -1) && (errno == EINTR));
```

This is not easily maintainable.

The POSIX committee subsequently fixed this, requiring an implementation to provide a signal flag SA_RESTART. When this flag is used, the kernel will auto-restart any blocking system calls that happen to get interrupted by a signal or signals.

So, just use the useful SA_RESTART flag within your sigaction(2) when registering your signal handler(s), and this issue will disappear.

> In general, using the SA_RESTART flag when programming the sigaction(2) would be a good idea. Not always, though; the Chapter 13, *Timers*, shows us use cases in which we deliberately keep away from this flag.

## The once only SA_RESETHAND flag

The SA_RESETHAND signal flag is a bit peculiar. On older Unix platforms, there existed a bug that went like this: a signal is trapped (via the signal(2) function), the signal is dispatched, and then the process handles the signal. But, immediately on entering the signal handler, the kernel now resets the signal action to the original OS default handling code. So, the second time the signal arrives, the default handler code runs, often killing the process in the bargain. (Again, Unix developers sometimes had to resort to some bad racy code to try to fix this).

Thus, the signal would effectively be delivered only once. On today's modern Linux systems, a signal handler remains as it is; it is not reset by default to the original handler. Unless, of course, you want this once-only behavior, in this case, use the SA_RESETHAND flag (you would imagine that it's not terribly popular). Also, SA_ONESHOT is an older deprecated name for the same flag.

## To defer or not? Working with SA_NODEFER

Lets recall how signals are handled by default:

- A process traps a signal n.
- Signal n is delivered to the process (either by another process or the OS).
- The signal handler is dispatched; that is, it runs in response to the signal.
    - Signal n is now auto-masked; that is, blocked from delivery to the process.
    - Signal handling is completed.
    - Signal n is now auto-unmasked, that is, enabled for delivery to the process.

This is reasonable: while handling a particular signal, that signal is masked. This is the default behavior.

However, what if you are writing, say, an embedded real-time application, where the signal delivery implies some real-world event has occurred and the application must respond to this immediately (as soon as possible). In cases such as this, we would perhaps want to disable the auto-masking of signals, thus allowing the signal handler to be reentered the moment it arrives. Precisely this can be achieved by using the SA_NODEFER signal flag.

> The English word defer means to delay or postpone; to put off until later.

This is the default behavior, which you can change when the flag is specified.

### Signal behavior when masked

To understand this better, let's take a fictional example: say we trap a signal n, and the execution time for our signal handler for signal n is 55 ms (milliseconds). Also, visualize a scenario in which, via a timer (for a while at least), signal n is delivered to the process continually at 10-ms intervals. Now let's examine what would happen in the default case and the case in which we use the SA_NODEFER flag.

## Case 1 : Default : SA_NODEFER bit cleared

Here, we are *not* using the SA_NODEFER signal flag. So, when the first instance of signal n arrives, our process jumps into the signal-handling code (which will take 55 ms to complete). However, the second signal will arrive just 10 ms into the signal handling code. But, hang on, it's auto-masked! Hence, we will not process it. In fact, a simple calculation will show that up to five instances of signal n will reach our process in the 55-ms signal handling time frame:

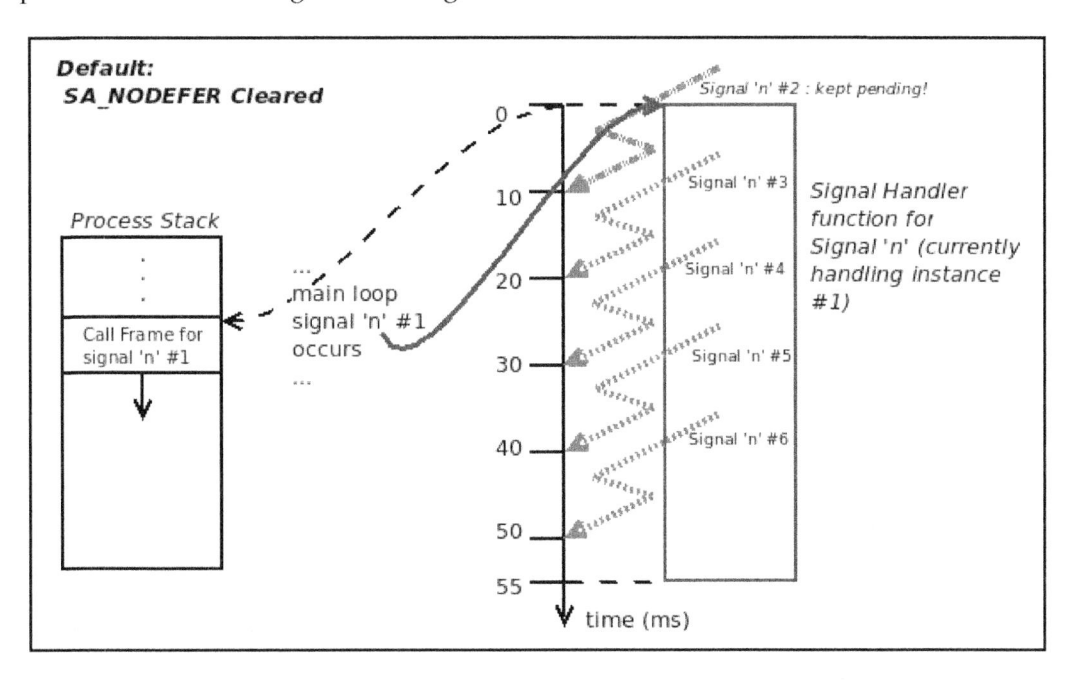

Figure 3: Default behavior: SA_NODEFER bit cleared: no queue, one signal instance pending delivery, no real impact on stack

So, what exactly happens? Will these five signals be queued up for delivery once the handler completes? Ah! This is an important point: standard or Unix signals are not queued. However, the kernel does understand that one or more signals are pending delivery to the process; hence, once signal handling is done, exactly one instance of the pending signal is delivered (and the pending signal mask is subsequently cleared).

*Signaling - Part I*

Thus, in our example, even though five signals were pending delivery, the signal handler will get invoked only once. In other words, no signals were queued, but one signal instance was served. This is how signalling works by default.

*Figure 3* shows this situation: the dashed signal arrows represent signals that were delivered after entering the signal handler; hence, just one instance is kept pending. Notice the process stack: the signal instance #1 of signal n (obviously) gets a call frame on the stack when the signal handler is invoked, nothing more.

Question: What if the situation is as shown, but another signal, signal m, is delivered?

Answer: If signal m has been caught and is currently unmasked, it will be processed immediately; in other words, it will preempt everything, and its handler will run. Of course, the context is saved by the OS such that whatever got preempted can be later continued once context is restored. This has us conclude the following:

- Signals are peers; they have no priority associated with them.

- For standard signals, if several instances of the same integer value are delivered, and that signal is currently masked (blocked), then only one instance is kept pending; there is no queuing.

## Case 2 : SA_NODEFER bit set

Now let's reconsider the very same scenario, only this time we use the SA_NODEFER signal flag. So, when the first instance of signal n arrives, our process jumps into the signal-handling code (which will take 55 ms to complete). As before, the second signal will arrive just 10 ms into the signal-handling code, but hang on, this time it is not masked; it is not deferred. Thus, we will reenter the signal handler function immediately. Then, 20 ms later (after the signal handler was first entered by signal n instance #1), the third signal instance arrives. Again, we will reenter the signal handler function. Yes, this will happen five times.

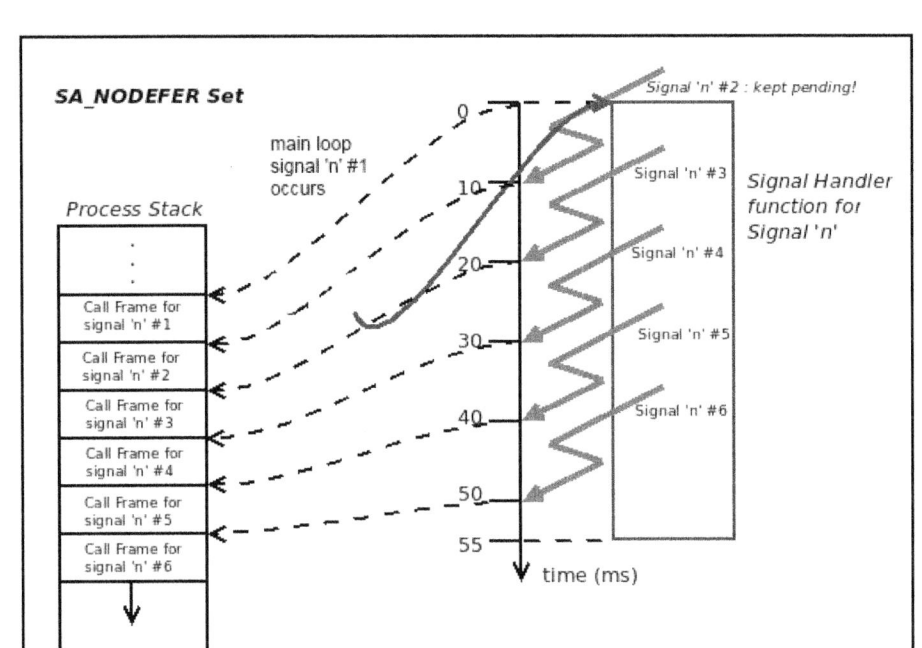

Figure 4 shows us this scenario:

Figure 4: SA_NODEFER bit set: no queue: all signal instances processed upon delivery, stack intensive

This looks good, but please realize the following:

- The signal handler code itself must be written to be reentrant-safe (no global or static variable usage; only call async-signal safe functions within it), as it is being continually reentered in this scenario.
- Stack usage: every time the signal handler is reentered, do realize that an additional call frame has been allocated (pushed) on to the process stack.

The second point bears thinking about: what if so many signals arrive (while handling previous invocations) that we overload and, indeed, overflow the stack? Well, disaster. Stack overflow is a bad bug; no exception handling is practically possible (we cannot, with any degree of confidence, catch or trap into a stack overflow issue).

Signaling - Part I

A interesting code example ch11/defer_or_not.c follows to demonstrate both of these cases:

> For readability, only key parts of the code are displayed; to view the complete source code, build and run it; the entire tree is available for cloning from the book's GitHub repo here: https://github.com/PacktPublishing/Hands-on-System-Programming-with-Linux

```
static volatile sig_atomic_t s=0, t=0;
[...]
int main(int argc, char **argv)
{
 int flags=0;
 struct sigaction act;
[...]
 flags = SA_RESTART;
 if (atoi(argv[1]) == 2) {
     flags |= SA_NODEFER;
     printf("Running with the SA_NODEFER signal flag Set\n");
 } else {
     printf("Running with the SA_NODEFER signal flag Cleared
[default]\n");
 }

 memset(&act, 0, sizeof(act));
 act.sa_handler = sighdlr;
 act.sa_flags = flags;
 if (sigaction(SIGUSR1, &act, 0) == -1)
     FATAL("sigaction failed\n");
 fprintf(stderr, "\nProcess awaiting signals ...\n");

 while (1)
     (void)pause();
 exit(EXIT_SUCCESS);
}
```

Here is the signal handler function:

```
/*
 * Strictly speaking, should not use fprintf here as it's not
 * async-signal safe; indeed, it sometimes does not work well!
 */
static void sighdlr(int signum)
{
  int saved;
  fprintf(stderr, "\nsighdlr: signal %d,", signum);
  switch (signum) {
```

```
    case SIGUSR1:
      s ++; t ++;
      if (s >= MAX)
           s = 1;
      saved = s;
      fprintf(stderr, " s=%d ; total=%d; stack %p :", s, t, stack());
      DELAY_LOOP(saved+48, 5); /* +48 to get the equivalent ASCII value
*/
      fprintf(stderr, "*");
      break;
    default:;
    }
}
```

We deliberately let the signal-handling code take a fairly long time (via our use of the `DELAY_LOOP` macro) so that we can simulate the case in which the same signal is delivered multiple times while it is being handled. In a real-world application, always strive to keep your signal handling as brief as is possible.

The inline-assembly stack() function is an interesting way to get a register's value. Read the following comment to see how it works:

```
/*
 * stack(): return the current value of the stack pointer register.
 * The trick/hack: on x86 CPU's, the ABI tells us that the return
 * value is always in the accumulator (EAX/RAX); so we just initialize
 * it to the stack pointer (using inline assembly)!
 */
void *stack(void)
{
 if (__WORDSIZE == 32) {
     __asm__("movl %esp, %eax");
 } else if (__WORDSIZE == 64) {
     __asm__("movq %rsp, %rax");
 }
 /* Accumulator holds the return value */
}
```

> The processor ABI - Application Binary Interface—documentation is an important area for the serious systems developer to be conversant with; check out more on this in the *Further reading* section on the GitHub repository.

*Signaling - Part I*

To properly test this application, we write a small shell script `bombard_sig.sh`, which literally bombards the given process with the (same) signal (we use SIGUSR1 here). The user is expected to pass the process PID and the number of signal instances to send as parameters; if the second parameter is given as -1, the script continually bombards the process. Here is the key code of the script:

```
SIG=SIGUSR1
[...]
NUMSIGS=$2
n=1
if [ ${NUMSIGS} -eq -1 ] ; then
  echo "Sending signal ${SIG} continually to process ${1} ..."
  while [ true ] ; do
    kill -${SIG} $1
    sleep 10e-03    # 10 ms
  done
else
  echo "Sending ${NUMSIGS} instances of signal ${SIG} to process ${1} ..."
  while [ ${n} -le ${NUMSIGS} ] ; do
    kill -${SIG} $1
    sleep 10e-03    # 10 ms
    let n=n+1
  done
fi
```

## Running of case 1 – SA_NODEFER bit cleared [default]

Next, we execute the test case wherein the `SA_NODEFER` flag is cleared; this is the default behavior:

```
$ ./defer_or_not
Usage: ./defer_or_not {option}
option=1 : don't use (clear) SA_NODEFER flag (default sigaction style)
option=2 : use (set) SA_NODEFER flag (will process signal immd)
$ ./defer_or_not 1
PID 3016: running with the SA_NODEFER signal flag Cleared [default]
Process awaiting signals ...
```

Now, in another terminal window, we run the shell script:

```
$ ./bombard_sig.sh $(pgrep defer_or_not) 12
```

[ 418 ]

> **TIP**
> The `pgrep` figures out the PID of the `defer_or_not` process: useful! Just ensure the following:
> (a) Only one instance of the process you are sending signals to is alive, or `pgrep` returns multiple PIDs and the script fails.
> (b) The name passed to pgrep is 15 characters or less.

As soon as the script runs, firing off (12) signals to the process, this output appears:

```
sighdlr: signal 10, s=1 ; total=1; stack 0x7ffc8d021a70 :11111*
sighdlr: signal 10, s=2 ; total=2; stack 0x7ffc8d021a70 :22222*
```

Studying the preceding output, we notice as follows:

- `SIGUSR1` is caught and its signal handler runs; it emits a stream of numbers (incremented on each signal instance).
  - To do so correctly, we use a couple of `volatile sig_atomic_t` globals (one for the value to print in the `DELAY_LOOP` macro and one to keep track of the total number of signals delivered to the process).
- The asterisk character * at the end of the digits implies that, by the time you see it, the signal handler has completed execution.
- Though 12 instances of the `SIGUSR1` signal were delivered, the process was handling the first signal instance when the remaining 11 signals arrived; hence, only one was kept pending and processed after the handler completed. Of course, on different systems, it can always happen that you see more than one signal instance being handled.
- Finally, notice that we print the stack pointer value at every signal handler invocation; it's a user-space virtual address, of course (recall our discussions in `Chapter 2`, *Virtual Memory*); more importantly, it's identical, implying that the very same stack frame was reused for the signal handler function (this often happens).

## Running of case 2 – SA_NODEFER bit set

Next, we execute the test case, wherein the `SA_NODEFER` flag is set (first ensure you have killed off any old instances of the `defer_or_not` process):

```
$ ./defer_or_not 2
PID 3215: running with the SA_NODEFER signal flag Set
Process awaiting signals ...
```

*Signaling - Part I*

Now, in another Terminal window, we run the shell script:

```
$ ./bombard_sig.sh $(pgrep defer_or_not) 12
```

As soon as the script runs, firing off (12) signals to the process, the output is as follows:

```
sighdlr: signal 10, s=1 ; total=1; stack 0x7ffe9e17a0b0 :
sighdlr: signal 10, s=2 ; total=2; stack 0x7ffe9e1799b0 :2
sighdlr: signal 10, s=3 ; total=3; stack 0x7ffe9e1792b0 :3
sighdlr: signal 10, s=4 ; total=4; stack 0x7ffe9e178bb0 :4
sighdlr: signal 10, s=5 ; total=5; stack 0x7ffe9e1784b0 :5
sighdlr: signal 10, s=6 ; total=6; stack 0x7ffe9e177db0 :6
sighdlr: signal 10, s=7 ; total=7; stack 0x7ffe9e1776b0 :7
sighdlr: signal 10, s=8 ; total=8; stack 0x7ffe9e176fb0 :8
sighdlr: signal 10, s=9 ; total=9; stack 0x7ffe9e1768b0 :9
sighdlr: signal 10, s=1 ; total=10; stack 0x7ffe9e1761b0 :1
sighdlr: signal 10, s=2 ; total=11; stack 0x7ffe9e175ab0
:22222*1111*9999*8888*7777*6666*5555*4444*3333*2222*11111*
sighdlr: signal 10, s=3 ; total=12; stack 0x7ffe9e17adb0 :33333*
```

This time, notice these things:

- SIGUSR1 is caught and its signal handler runs; it emits a stream of numbers (incremented on each signal instance).
    - To do so correctly, we use a volatile sig_atomic_t global (one for the value to print in the DELAY_LOOP and one to keep track of the total number of signals delivered to the process).
- The asterisk character *at the end of the digits implies that, by the time you see it, the signal handler has completed execution; notice that this time, the * does not appear until much later.
- Twelve instances of the signal SIGUSR1 are delivered one after the other: this time, each instance preempts the previous one (setting up a new call frame on the process stack; notice the unique stack pointer addresses).
- Notice how, after all signal instances have been handled, control is restored to the original context; we literally can see the stack unwind.
- Finally, look carefully at the stack pointer values; they are progressively decreasing. This, of course, is because on the x86[_64] CPU (as is the case on most modern CPUs), a downward-growing stack is the way it works.

Do try out the program for yourself and see. It is interesting and powerful, but, remember, this is at the cost of being very stack intensive!

How expensive is it (in terms of stack memory usage)? We can actually calculate the size of each stack (call) frame; take any two differing instances and subtract the lower from the higher. For example, let's take the preceding case s=6 and s=5 : s=5: 0x7ffe9e1784b0    s=6:  0x7ffe9e177db0

So, call frame size = 0x7ffe9e1784b0 - 0x7ffe9e177db0 = 0x700 = 1792 bytes.

Here, for this particular application use case, each signal-handling call frame takes up to 1,792 bytes of memory.

Let's consider a worst-case scenario now: With an embedded real-time application, what if we receive, say, 5,000 signals very rapidly, while a previous instance is running (and of course the SA_NODEFER flag is set): We shall then end up creating 5,000 additional call frames on the process stack, which will cost approximately 5,000 x 1,792 = 8,960,000 = ~ 8.5 MB!

Why not actually test this case? (The value of being empirical - trying things out rather than just assuming them, is critical. See Chapter 19, *Troubleshooting and Best Practices*, as well). We do so as follows:

```
$ ./defer_or_not 2
PID 7815: running with the SA_NODEFER signal flag Set
Process awaiting signals ...
```

In another Terminal window, run the bombard_sig.sh script, asking it to generate 5,000 signal instances. Refer to the following command:

```
$ ./bombard_sig.sh $(pgrep defer_or_not) 5000
Sending 5000 instances of signal SIGUSR1 to process 7815 ...
```

This is the output in the first Terminal window:

```
<...>
sighdlr: signal 10, s=1 ; total=1;  stack 0x7ffe519b3130 :1
sighdlr: signal 10, s=2 ; total=2;  stack 0x7ffe519b2a30 :2
sighdlr: signal 10, s=3 ; total=3;  stack 0x7ffe519b2330 :3
sighdlr: signal 10, s=4 ; total=4;  stack 0x7ffe519b1c30 :4
sighdlr: signal 10, s=5 ; total=5;  stack 0x7ffe519b1530 :5
sighdlr: signal 10, s=6 ; total=6;  stack 0x7ffe519b0e30 :6
sighdlr: signal 10, s=7 ; total=7;  stack 0x7ffe519b0730 :7
sighdlr: signal 10, s=8 ; total=8;  stack 0x7ffe519b0030 :8
sighdlr: signal 10, s=9 ; total=9;  stack 0x7ffe519af930 :9
sighdlr: signal 10, s=1 ; total=10; stack 0x7ffe519af230 :1
sighdlr: signal 10, s=2 ; total=11; stack 0x7ffe519aeb30 :2
```

*Signaling - Part I*

```
--snip--
sighdlr: signal 10, s=8 ; total=2933; stack 0x7ffe513a2d30 :8
sighdlr: signal 10, s=9 ; total=2934; stack 0x7ffe513a2630 :9
sighdlr: signal 10, s=1 ; total=2935; stack 0x7ffe513a1f30 :1
sighdlr: signal 10, s=2 ; total=2936; stack 0x7ffe513a1830 :2
sighdlr: signal 10, s=3 ; total=2937; stack 0x7ffe513a1130
:Segmentation fault
$
```

It crashes, of course, when it runs out of stack space.(Again, the results may vary on different systems; if you do not experience a crash, via stack overflow, with these numbers, try increasing the number of signals sent via the script and see...).

As we learned in Chapter 3, *Resource Limits*, the typical process stack resource limit is 8 MB; thus, here we are in real danger of overflowing the stack, which will result in a fatal and sudden crash, of course. So, be careful! If you intend to use the SA_NODEFER flag, take the trouble to stress test your application under heavy workloads and see if more of the stack is being used than is safe.

## Using an alternate signal stack

Notice how our previous test case, sending 5,000 SIGUSR1 signals to the defer_or_not application running with SA_NODEFER set, caused it to crash with a segmentation fault (often abbreviated as segfault). The OS sent the signal SIGSEGV (segmentation violation) to the process when it made an invalid memory reference; in other words, a bug related to a memory access. Trapping the SIGSEGV could be very valuable; we can gain information concerning how and why the application crashed (in fact, we shall do precisely this in the next chapter).

However, think carefully: in the last test case (the 5,000 signals... one), the reason the process crashed is that its stack overflowed. Thus, the OS delivered the signal SIGSEGV; we want to trap this signal and handle it. But there's no space on the stack, so how can the signal handler function itself get invoked? This is a problem.

An interesting solution exists: we can allocate (virtual) memory space for, and set up a separate alternate stack to be used for signal handling only. How? Via the sigaltstack(2) system call. It's used for these kind of circumstances: you need to handle a SIGSEGV, but you're out of stack space. Think about our previous real-time high-volume signal-handling application: we could perhaps redesign it such that we allocate a lot more space for a separate signal stack, so that it works in practice.

# Implementation to handle high-volume signals with an alternate signal stack

Here's an attempt at precisely that: the code for ch11/altstack.c and a run-time test. Also, we have added a neat feature (to the previous version: the defer_or_not program): sending the process SIGUSR2 signal will have it print out the first and the most recent stack pointer address. It will also calculate and display the delta—in effect, the amount of stack memory used so far by the application.

Changes from ch11/defer_or_not.c:

- We also trap the signals.
    - SIGUSR2: to display the first and the most-recent stack pointer addresses and the delta between them.
    - SIGSEGV: this is important in real-world applications. Trapping the segfault allows us to take control if the process crashes (here, probably due to stack overflow here) and perhaps display (or in real apps, write to a log) relevant information, perform cleanup, and then call abort(3) to exit. Realize that, after all, we must exit: the process is in an undefined state once this signal arrives from the OS. (Note that more detail on handling the SIGSEGV is covered in the next chapter).
- To avoid too much noise in the output, we replace the DELAY_LOOP macro with a silent version of the same.

> For readability, only key parts of the code are displayed; to view the complete source code, build, and then run it, the entire tree is available for cloning from GitHub here: https://github.com/PacktPublishing/Hands-on-System-Programming-with-Linux.

In ch11/altstack.c:main():

```
<...>
altstacksz = atoi(argv[1])*1024;
setup_altsigstack(altstacksz);
<...>
```

The setup_altsigstack() functions code is as follows:

```
static void setup_altsigstack(size_t stack_sz)
{
    stack_t ss;
```

```
        printf("Alt signal stack size = %zu\n", stack_sz);
        ss.ss_sp = malloc(stack_sz);
        if (!ss.ss_sp)
            FATAL("malloc(%zu) for alt sig stack failed\n", stack_sz);
        ss.ss_size = stack_sz;
        ss.ss_flags = 0;
        if (sigaltstack(&ss, NULL) == -1)
            FATAL("sigaltstack for size %zu failed!\n", stack_sz);
}
```

The signal handling code is as follows:

```
static volatile sig_atomic_t s=0, t=0;
static volatile unsigned long stk_start=0, stk=0;

static void sighdlr(int signum)
{
    if (t == 0)
        stk_start = (unsigned long)stack();
    switch (signum) {
    case SIGUSR1:
        stk = (unsigned long)stack();
        s ++; t ++;
        if (s >= MAX)
            s = 1;
        fprintf(stderr, " s=%d ; total=%d; stack %p\n", s, t, stack());
        /* Spend some time inside the signal handler ... */
        DELAY_LOOP_SILENT(5);
        break;
    case SIGUSR2:
        fprintf(stderr, "*** signal %d:: stack@: t0=%lx last=%lx : delta=%ld ***\n", signum, stk_start, stk, (stk_start-stk));
        break;
    case SIGSEGV:
        fprintf(stderr, "*** signal %d:: stack@: t0=%lx last=%lx : delta=%ld ***\n", signum, stk_start, stk, (stk_start-stk));
        abort();
    }
}
```

Let's perform some tests and run them considering the following cases.

## Case 1 – very small (100 KB) alternate signal stack

We deliberately allocate a very small amount of space for the alternate signal stack—just 100 kilobytes. Needless to say, it overflows quickly and segfaults; our handler for SIGSEGV runs, printing out some stats:

```
$ ./altstack 100
Alt signal stack size = 102400
Running: signal SIGUSR1 flags: SA_NODEFER | SA_ONSTACK | SA_RESTART
Process awaiting signals ...
```

In another Terminal window, run the shell script:

```
$ ./bombard_sig.sh $(pgrep altstack) 120
Sending 120 instances of signal SIGUSR1 to process 12811 ...
```

Now, the output in the original window:

```
<...>
 s=1 ; total=1; stack 0xa20ff0
 s=2 ; total=2; stack 0xa208f0
 s=3 ; total=3; stack 0xa201f0

--snip--

 s=1 ; total=49; stack 0xa0bff0
 s=2 ; total=50; stack 0xa0b8f0
 s=3 ; total=51; stack 0xa0b1f0
*** signal 11:: stack@: t0=a20ff0 last=a0aaf0 : delta=91392 ***
Aborted
$
```

As can be seen, according to our metrics, the total alternate signal stack usage was 91,392 bytes, close to 100 KB, at the time it was overflowed.

The shell script terminates with the expected:

```
<...>
./bombard_sig.sh: line 30: kill: (12811) - No such process
bombard_sig.sh: kill failed, loop count=53
$
```

## Case 2 : A large (16 MB) alternate signal stack

This time, we deliberately allocate a generous amount of space for the alternate signal stack—16 megabytes. It can now handle a few thousand continuous signals. But, of course, at some point it will also overflow:

```
$ ./altstack 16384
Alt signal stack size = 16777216
Running: signal SIGUSR1 flags: SA_NODEFER | SA_ONSTACK | SA_RESTART
Process awaiting signals ...
```

In another Terminal window, run the shell script:

```
$ ./bombard_sig.sh $(pgrep altstack) 12000
Sending 12000 instances of signal SIGUSR1 to process 13325 ...
```

Now the output in the original window:

```
<...>
 s=1 ; total=1; stack 0x7fd7339239b0
 s=2 ; total=2; stack 0x7fd7339232b0
 s=3 ; total=3; stack 0x7fd733922bb0

--snip--

 s=2 ; total=9354; stack 0x7fd732927ab0
 s=3 ; total=9355; stack 0x7fd7329273b0
*** signal 11:: stack@: t0=7fd7339239b0 last=7fd732926cb0 :
delta=16764160 ***
Aborted
$
```

The shell script terminates with the expected:

```
./bombard_sig.sh: line 30: kill: (13325) - No such process
bombard_sig.sh: kill failed, loop count=9357
$
```

This time, it managed to process around nine thousand signals before it ran out of stack. The total alternate signal stack usage was a huge 16,764,160 bytes, or close to 16 MB, at the time it was overflowed.

# Different approaches to handling signals at high volume

In conclusion, if you have a scenario in which a high volume of multiple signals of the same type (as well as other signals) are delivered at a rapid pace to the process, we run the risk of losing (or dropping) signals if we use the usual methods. As we have seen, we can successfully handle all signals in several ways, each with their own approaches to signal-handling at high volume—pros and cons as shown in the following table:

| Method | Pros | Cons/Limitations |
|---|---|---|
| Use `sigfillset(3)` just prior to calling `sigaction(2)` to ensure that while the signal is being handled, all other signals are blocked. | Simple and straightforward approach. | Can lead to significant (unacceptable) delays in handling and/or dropping of signals. |
| Setting the `SA_NODEFER` signal flag and handling all signals as they arrive. | Simple and straightforward approach. | On load, heavy stack usage, danger of stack overflow. |
| Use an alternate signal stack, set the `SA_NODEFER` signal flag, and handle all signals as they arrive. | Can specify alternate stack size as required. | More work to setup; must carefully test under load to determine (max) stack size to use. |
| Use real-time signals (covered in the following chapter). | The OS queues pending signals automatically, low stack usage, signal prioritization possible. | System-wide limit on the maximum number that can be queued (can be tuned as root). |

# Summary

In this chapter, the reader has initially been introduced to the notion of signalling on the Linux OS, what signals are, why they are useful, and, then, in a lot of detail, how to effectively handle signals within your application.

Of course, there being even more to it, the following chapter continues this important discussion. See you there.

# 12
# Signaling - Part II

As mentioned in the previous chapter, signals are a crucial mechanism for the Linux system developer to understand and exploit. The previous chapter covered several areas: an introduction, why signaling is useful to the systems developer, and, most importantly, how exactly the developer is to handle and thus exploit the signaling mechanism.

This chapter continues this exploration. Here, we will drill down into the inner details of process crash handling with signaling, how to recognize and avoid common issues when dealing with signals, working with real-time signals, sending signals, and finally, alternative means of performing signal handling.

In this chapter, the reader will learn the following:

- Gracefully handling process crashes, and collecting valuable diagnostics at that point
- Handling common gotchas to do with signaling—errno races, the correct way to sleep (yes, you read that right!)
- Handling powerful real-time signals
- Sending signals to other processes, and performing IPC via signals
- Alternative signal-handling techniques

# Gracefully handling process crashes

A bug in the application that caused a crash at runtime? My God, how is this possible?

Unfortunately, to the well-heeled software veteran, though, this is not a big surprise. Bugs exist; they can hide really well, for years, sometimes; one day, they come out and—bang!—the process crashes.

Here, our intention is not to discuss debugging techniques or tools (let's save that for another book perhaps, shall we?); instead, it's this key point: if our application process does crash, can we do something? Certainly: in the previous chapter, we have learned in detail how we can trap signals. Why not design our application such that we trap the typical fatal signals—the SIGBUS, SIGFPE, SIGILL, and SIGSEGV—and, in their signal handler(s), perform useful tasks such as these:

- Perform critical application cleanup—for example, free up memory regions, flush and close open files, and so on
- Write relevant details to a log file (the signal that caused the crash, the signal's origin, reason, CPU register values, and so on)
- Inform the end user that, hey, too bad, we crashed
- Kindly allow us to collect crash details, and we'll do better next time, we promise!

This not only gives us valuable information that can help you debug the root cause of the crash, but also has the application die gracefully.

# Detailing information with the SA_SIGINFO

Let's recall the very first member of the `sigaction` structure we saw in the previous, Chapter 11, *Signaling - Part I*, *The sigaction structure* section; it's a function pointer, and it specifies the signal handler:

```
struct sigaction
  {
    /* Signal handler. */
#ifdef __USE_POSIX199309
    union
      {
        /* Used if SA_SIGINFO is not set. */
        __sighandler_t sa_handler;
        /* Used if SA_SIGINFO is set. */
```

```
            void (*sa_sigaction) (int, siginfo_t *, void *);
        }
        __sigaction_handler;
# define sa_handler __sigaction_handler.sa_handler
# define sa_sigaction __sigaction_handler.sa_sigaction
#else
        __sighandler_t sa_handler;
#endif

--snip--
    };
```

The preceding highlighted code highlights the fact that as it's in a union, the signal handler can be either one of the following:

- sa_handler : when the SA_SIGINFO flag is cleared
- sa_sigaction : when the SA_SIGINFO flag is set

So far, we have used the sa_handler style prototype for the signal handler:

void (*sa_handler)(int);

It receives just one parameter: the integer value of the signal that occurred.

If you set the SA_SIGINFO flag (while issuing the sigaction(2) system call of course), the signal handler function prototype now becomes this: void (*sa_sigaction)(int, siginfo_t *, void *);

The parameters are as follows:

- The integer value of the signal that occurred
- A pointer to a structure of type siginfo_t (a typedef, obviously)
- An internal-use-only (undocumented) pointer called the **ucontext**

The second parameter is where the power lies!

## The siginfo_t structure

When you use the SA_SIGINFO signal flag and a trapped signal occurs, the kernel populates a data structure: the siginfo_t structure.

*Signaling - Part II*

The `siginfo_t` structure definition (slightly simplified; there is some #if wrapping around the first few members which we need not worry about here) is shown next(It's in the header `/usr/include/x86_64-linux-gnu/bits/types/siginfo_t.h` on Ubuntu and `/usr/include/bits/types/siginfo_t.h` on a Fedora box):

```
typedef struct {
    int si_signo; /* Signal number. */
    int si_code;
    int si_errno; /* If non-zero, an errno value associated with
            this signal, as defined in <errno.h>. */

    union
    {
        int _pad[__SI_PAD_SIZE];
    /* kill(). */
      struct
      {
          __pid_t si_pid; /* Sending process ID. */
          __uid_t si_uid; /* Real user ID of sending process. */
      } _kill;

    /* POSIX.1b timers. */
      struct
      {
          int si_tid; /* Timer ID. */
          int si_overrun; /* Overrun count. */
          __sigval_t si_sigval; /* Signal value. */
      } _timer;

    /* POSIX.1b signals. */
      struct
      {
          __pid_t si_pid; /* Sending process ID. */
          __uid_t si_uid; /* Real user ID of sending process. */
          __sigval_t si_sigval; /* Signal value. */
      } _rt;

    /* SIGCHLD. */
      struct
      {
          __pid_t si_pid; /* Which child. */
          __uid_t si_uid; /* Real user ID of sending process. */
          int si_status; /* Exit value or signal. */
          __SI_CLOCK_T si_utime;
          __SI_CLOCK_T si_stime;
      } _sigchld;
```

```
        /* SIGILL, SIGFPE, SIGSEGV, SIGBUS. */
      struct
      {
        void *si_addr; /* Faulting insn/memory ref. */
        __SI_SIGFAULT_ADDL
        short int si_addr_lsb; /* Valid LSB of the reported
address. */
        union
        {
          /* used when si_code=SEGV_BNDERR */
          struct
          {
            void *_lower;
            void *_upper;
          } _addr_bnd;
          /* used when si_code=SEGV_PKUERR */
          __uint32_t _pkey;
        } _bounds;
      } _sigfault;

        /* SIGPOLL. */
      struct
      {
          long int si_band; /* Band event for SIGPOLL. */
          int si_fd;
      } _sigpoll;

        /* SIGSYS. */
#if __SI_HAVE_SIGSYS
      struct
      {
          void *_call_addr; /* Calling user insn. */
          int _syscall; /* Triggering system call number. */
          unsigned int _arch; /* AUDIT_ARCH_* of syscall. */
      } _sigsys;
#endif
    } _sifields;
} siginfo_t ;
```

*Signaling - Part II*

The first three members are integers:

- `si_signo` : signal number—the signal that was delivered to the process
- `si_code` : signal origin; an enum; typical values are as follows:
    SI_QUEUE    : Sent by `sigqueue(3)`
    SI_USER     : Sent by `kill(2)`
    SI_KERNEL   : Sent by kernel
    SI_SIGIO    : Sent by queued SIGIO
    SI_ASYNCIO  : Sent by AIO completion
    SI_MESGQ    : Sent by real time message queue state change
    SI_TIMER    : Sent by timer expiration
- `si_errno` : (if non-zero) the errno value

Here's the really interesting part: the fourth member of the structure is a union (`_sifields`) of seven structures. We understand that a union implies that any one member will be instantiated at runtime: it will be one of the seven structures depending on which signal is received!

Take a look at the union within the `siginfo_t` structure previously shown; the comments within the union quite clearly point out which signal(s) will cause which data structure to be instantiated at runtime.

For example, we see within the union that this structure will be populated when the SIGCHLD signal is received (that is, when a child process dies, stops, or continues):

```
/* SIGCHLD. */
struct
{
    __pid_t si_pid; /* Which child. */
    __uid_t si_uid; /* Real user ID of sending process. */
    int si_status; /* Exit value or signal. */
    __SI_CLOCK_T si_utime;
    __SI_CLOCK_T si_stime;
} _sigchld;
```

The information is with respect to the child process; hence, we receive the PID and real UID of the process that died (or was stopped or continued, unless the SA_NOCLDWAIT flag was used, of course). Further, we receive the integer bitmask `si_status` telling us how exactly the child died (and so on). Also, some audit information, `si_utime` and `si_stime`, the time spent by the child process in user and kernel space respectively.

[ 434 ]

Recall from our detailed discussion in Chapter 10, *Process Creation*, *The wait API - Details* section, that we could obtain the child termination status information via (any of) the wait APIs. Well, here, we can see, it's simpler: use the SA_SIGINFO flag, trap the SIGCHLD signal, and, in the handler function, just look up the relevant values from the union!

> **TIP**: The man page on sigaction(2) describes the siginfo_t structure members in depth, providing detailed information. Do read through it.

## Getting system-level details when a process crashes

A wealth of information can be gleaned from the kernel when a process dies via the SIGSEGV: memory bugs or defects, a common case, as we have discussed in the Chapters 4, *Dynamic Memory Allocation*, Chapter 5, *Linux Memory Issues*, and Chapter 6, *Debugging Tools for Memory Issues*. (This section also applies to the fatal signals SIGBUS, SIGILL, and SIGFPE. Incidentally, SIGFPE occurs not just upon a divide-by-zero error but in any kind of arithmetic-related exception).

The man page on sigaction(2) reveals the following:

```
...
The following values can be placed in si_code for a SIGSEGV signal:

SEGV_MAPERR
    Address not mapped to object.
SEGV_ACCERR
    Invalid permissions for mapped object.
SEGV_BNDERR (since Linux 3.19)
    Failed address bound checks.
SEGV_PKUERR (since Linux 4.6)
    Access was denied by memory protection keys. See pkeys(7). The
    protection key which applied to this access is available via
 si_pkey.
...
```

The SEGV_MAPERR means that the address the process is attempting to access (for read, write, or execute) is invalid; there is either no **Page Table Entry** (**PTE**) entry available for it, or it refuses to map to any valid address.

*Signaling - Part II*

The `SEGV_ACCERR` is easy to understand: the attempted access (read, write, or execute) cannot be performed, as permission is lacking (for example, attempting to write to a read-only memory page).

Peculiarly, the `SEGV_BNDERR` and `SEGV_PKUERR` macros fail to compile; we shall not attempt to use them here.

> The glibc library provides the helper routines `psignal(3)` and `psiginfo(3)`; passed an informational string, they print it, appending a : and then the actual signal that occurred and information on the cause of the signal being delivered and the faulting address (looked up from the siginfo_t structure) respectively. We use the `psiginfo(3)` in our example code as follows.

### Trapping and extracting information from a crash

Next, we will see a test program `ch12/handle_segv.c`, with deliberate bugs, to help us understand the use cases possible. All this will result in the `SIGSEGV` signal being generated by the OS. How the application developer handles this signal is important: we demonstrate how you can use it to gather important details, such as the address of the memory location upon whose access the crash took place and the value of all registers at that point in time. These details often provide useful clues into the root cause of the memory bug.

To help understand how we are constructing this program, run it without any parameters:

```
$ ./handle_segv
Usage: ./handle_segv u|k r|w
u => user mode
k => kernel mode
 r => read attempt
 w => write attempt
$
```

As can be seen, we can thus perform four kinds of invalid memory accesses: in effect, four bug cases:

- Invalid user [u] mode read [r]
- Invalid user [u] mode write [w]
- Invalid kernel [k] mode read [r]
- Invalid kernel [k] mode write [w]

Some typedefs and macros we use are as follows:

```
typedef unsigned int u32;
typedef long unsigned int u64;

#define ADDR_FMT "%lx"
#if __x86_64__  /* 64-bit; __x86_64__ works for gcc */
 #define ADDR_TYPE u64
 static u64 invalid_uaddr = 0xdeadfaceL;
 static u64 invalid_kaddr = 0xffff0b9ffacedeadL;
#else
 #define ADDR_TYPE u32
 static u32 invalid_uaddr = 0xfacedeadL;
 static u32 invalid_kaddr = 0xdeadfaceL;
#endif
```

The main function is shown as follows:

```
int main(int argc, char **argv)
{
 struct sigaction act;
 if (argc != 3) {
    usage(argv[0]);
    exit(1);
 }

 memset(&act, 0, sizeof(act));
 act.sa_sigaction = myfault;
 act.sa_flags = SA_RESTART | SA_SIGINFO;
 sigemptyset(&act.sa_mask);
 if (sigaction(SIGSEGV, &act, 0) == -1)
    FATAL("sigaction SIGSEGV failed\n");

if ((tolower(argv[1][0]) == 'u') && tolower(argv[2][0] == 'r')) {
   ADDR_TYPE *uptr = (ADDR_TYPE *) invalid_uaddr;
   printf("Attempting to read contents of arbitrary usermode va uptr = 0x"
           ADDR_FMT ":\n", (ADDR_TYPE) uptr);
   printf("*uptr = 0x" ADDR_FMT "\n", *uptr); // just reading

 } else if ((tolower(argv[1][0]) == 'u') && tolower(argv[2][0] ==
'w')) {
    ADDR_TYPE *uptr = (ADDR_TYPE *) & main;
    printf
    ("Attempting to write into arbitrary usermode va uptr (&main
actually) = 0x" ADDR_FMT ":\n", (ADDR_TYPE) uptr);
    *uptr = 0x2A; // writing
```

[ 437 ]

## Signaling - Part II

```
   } else if ((tolower(argv[1][0]) == 'k') && tolower(argv[2][0] ==
'r')) {
      ADDR_TYPE *kptr = (ADDR_TYPE *) invalid_kaddr;
      printf
   ("Attempting to read contents of arbitrary kernel va kptr = 0x"
ADDR_FMT ":\n", (ADDR_TYPE) kptr);
      printf("*kptr = 0x" ADDR_FMT "\n", *kptr); // just reading

   } else if ((tolower(argv[1][0]) == 'k') && tolower(argv[2][0] ==
'w')) {
      ADDR_TYPE *kptr = (ADDR_TYPE *) invalid_kaddr;
      printf
   ("Attempting to write into arbitrary kernel va kptr = 0x" ADDR_FMT
":\n",
         (ADDR_TYPE) kptr);
      *kptr = 0x2A; // writing
   } else
      usage(argv[0]);
   exit(0);
}
```

va = virtual address.

Here is the key part: the signal handler for the SIGSEGV:

```
static void myfault(int signum, siginfo_t * si, void *ucontext)
{
  fprintf(stderr,
     "%s:\n------------------ FATAL signal --------------------------
\n",
     APPNAME);
    fprintf(stderr," %s: received signal %d. errno=%d\n"
" Cause/Origin: (si_code=%d): ",
         __func__, signum, si->si_errno, si->si_code);

  switch (si->si_code) {
      /* Possible values si_code can have for SIGSEGV */
  case SEGV_MAPERR:
      fprintf(stderr,"SEGV_MAPERR: address not mapped to object\n");
      break;
  case SEGV_ACCERR:
      fprintf(stderr,"SEGV_ACCERR: invalid permissions for mapped
object\n");
      break;
  /* SEGV_BNDERR and SEGV_PKUERR result in compile failure? */

  /* Other possibilities for si_code; here just to show them... */
  case SI_USER:
```

```
            fprintf(stderr,"user\n");
            break;
        case SI_KERNEL:
            fprintf(stderr,"kernel\n");
            break;

--snip--

        default:
            fprintf(stderr,"-none-\n");
        }
<...>
        /*
         * Placeholders for real-world apps:
         * crashed_write_to_log();
         * crashed_perform_cleanup();
         * crashed_inform_enduser();
         *
         * Now have the kernel generate the core dump by:
         *  Reset the SIGSEGV to (kernel) default, and,
         *  Re-raise it!
         */
        signal(SIGSEGV, SIG_DFL);
        raise(SIGSEGV);
    }
```

There is much to observe here:

- We print out the signal number and origin value

- We interpret the signal origin value (via the switch-case)

    - Particularly for SIGSEGV, the SEGV_MAPERR, and SEGV_ACCERR

Here comes the interesting bit: the following code prints out the faulting instruction or address! Not only that, we devise a means by which we can print out most of the CPU registers as well via our `dump_regs` function. As mentioned earlier, we also make use of the helper routine `psiginfo(3)` as follows:

```
    fprintf(stderr," Faulting instr or address = 0x" ADDR_FMT "\n",
        (ADDR_TYPE) si->si_addr);
    fprintf(stderr, "--- Register Dump [x86_64] ---\n");
    dump_regs(ucontext);
    fprintf(stderr,
        "-------------------------------------------------------
```

## Signaling - Part II

```
\n");
psiginfo(si, "psiginfo helper");
fprintf(stderr,
    "-----------------------------------------------------------
\n");
```

We then just keep some dummy stubs for the functionality you probably want in a real-world application, when handling a fatal signal such as this (here, we do not actually write any code, as it's of course very application-specific):

```
/*
 * Placeholders for real-world apps:
 * crashed_write_to_log();
 * crashed_perform_cleanup();
 * crashed_inform_enduser();
 */
```

Finally, calling abort(3) so that the process terminates (as it's now in an undefined state and cannot continue) is one way to finish. However, think for a second: if we abort() now, the process dies without the kernel getting a chance to generate a core dump. (As mentioned, a core dump is essentially a snapshot of the process's dynamic memory segments at the time of the crash; it's very useful for developers to debug and determine the root cause of the crash). So, having the kernel generate a core dump would indeed be useful. How can we arrange for this? Its quite simple really: we need to do the following:

- Reset the SIGSEGV signal's handler to the (kernel) default
- Have the signal (re)raised on the process

This code fragment achieves just this:

```
[...]
 * Now have the kernel generate the core dump by:
 * Reset the SIGSEGV to glibc default, and,
 * Re-raise it!
 */
signal(SIGSEGV, SIG_DFL);
raise(SIGSEGV);
```

As it's a simple case, we just use the simpler signal(2) API to revert the signal's action to the default. Then, again, we use the library API raise(3) to raise a given signal on the calling process. (The error-checking code has been left out for easy readability.)

## Register dumping

As mentioned, the `dump_regs` function prints out CPU register values; here are a few things to note regarding this:

- It's very CPU-specific (the example case shown as follows works only for the x86_64 CPUs).
- To actually gain access to the CPU registers, we make use of the undocumented third parameter to the signal handler function (note: when used with `SA_SIGINFO`), the so-called user context pointer. It is possible to interpret it (as we demonstrate here), but, of course, as it's not officially visible via the glibc system call (or other) interfaces, you cannot rely on this functionality. Use with caution (and a lot of testing).

Having said that, let's check out the code:

```
/* arch - x86[_64] - specific! */
static inline void dump_regs(void *ucontext)
{
#define FMT "%016llx"
ucontext_t *uctx = (ucontext_t *)ucontext;

fprintf(stderr,
" RAX = 0x" FMT " RBX = 0x" FMT " RCX = 0x" FMT "\n"
" RDX = 0x" FMT " RSI = 0x" FMT " RDI = 0x" FMT "\n"
" RBP = 0x" FMT " R8  = 0x" FMT "  R9  = 0x" FMT "\n"

" R10 = 0x" FMT " R11 = 0x" FMT " R12 = 0x" FMT "\n"
" R13 = 0x" FMT " R14 = 0x" FMT " R15 = 0x" FMT "\n"
" RSP = 0x" FMT "\n"

"\n RIP = 0x" FMT " EFLAGS = 0x" FMT "\n"
" TRAP# = %02lld ERROR = %02lld\n"
/* CR[0,1,3,4] unavailable */
" CR2 = 0x" FMT "\n"
, uctx->uc_mcontext.gregs[REG_RAX]
, uctx->uc_mcontext.gregs[REG_RBX]
, uctx->uc_mcontext.gregs[REG_RCX]
, uctx->uc_mcontext.gregs[REG_RDX]
, uctx->uc_mcontext.gregs[REG_RSI]
, uctx->uc_mcontext.gregs[REG_RDI]
, uctx->uc_mcontext.gregs[REG_RBP]
, uctx->uc_mcontext.gregs[REG_R8]
, uctx->uc_mcontext.gregs[REG_R9]
, uctx->uc_mcontext.gregs[REG_R10]
, uctx->uc_mcontext.gregs[REG_R11]
, uctx->uc_mcontext.gregs[REG_R12]
```

## Signaling - Part II

```
        , uctx->uc_mcontext.gregs[REG_R13]
        , uctx->uc_mcontext.gregs[REG_R14]
        , uctx->uc_mcontext.gregs[REG_R15]
        , uctx->uc_mcontext.gregs[REG_RSP]
        , uctx->uc_mcontext.gregs[REG_RIP]
        , uctx->uc_mcontext.gregs[REG_EFL]
        , uctx->uc_mcontext.gregs[REG_TRAPNO]
        , uctx->uc_mcontext.gregs[REG_ERR]
        , uctx->uc_mcontext.gregs[REG_CR2]
        );
}
```

Now, let's run two of the test cases:

```
Test Case: Userspace, Invalid Read
$ ./handle_segv u r
Attempting to read contents of arbitrary usermode va uptr =
0xdeadface:
handle_segv:
------------------ FATAL signal --------------------------
 myfault: received signal 11. errno=0
 Cause/Origin: (si_code=1): SEGV_MAPERR: address not mapped to object
 Faulting instr or address = 0xdeadface
 --- Register Dump [x86_64] ---
RAX = 0x00000000deadface RBX = 0x0000000000000000 RCX =
0x0000000000000000
RDX = 0x0000000000000000 RSI = 0x0000000001e7b260 RDI =
0x0000000000000000
RBP = 0x00007ffc8d842110 R8  = 0x0000000000000008 R9  =
0x0000000000000000
R10 = 0x0000000000000000 R11 = 0x0000000000000246 R12 =
0x0000000000400850
R13 = 0x00007ffc8d8421f0 R14 = 0x0000000000000000 R15 =
0x0000000000000000
RSP = 0x00007ffc8d842040
RIP = 0x0000000000400e84 EFLAGS = 0x0000000000010202
TRAP# = 14 ERROR = 04
CR2 = 0x00000000deadface
------------------------------------------------------------
psiginfo helper: Segmentation fault (Address not mapped to object
[0xdeadface])
------------------------------------------------------------
Segmentation fault (core dumped)
$
```

Here are some things to note:

- The origin value is SEGV_MAPERR: yes, the arbitrary userspace virtual address we attempted to read (0xdeadface) is not present (or mapped), hence the segfault!
- The faulting address is revealed as the invalid arbitrary userspace virtual address we attempted to read (0xdeadface):
    - An aside: an important value—the faulting instruction or address—is actually the value saved in the x86's **control register 2** (**CR2**), as can be seen.
    - The TRAP number shows up as 14; trap 14 on an x86[_64] is the Page Fault. The reality is: when the process attempted to read the invalid virtual address (0xdeadface), the bad access resulted in the x86[_64] MMU raising a bad page fault exception, which in turn led to the OS fault handler code running and killing the process via the SIGSEGV.
- The CPU registers are dumped as well.

> The curious reader will perhaps wonder what exactly each register is used for. This is an area beyond this book's scope; nevertheless, the reader can find useful information by seeking out the CPU OEM's **Application Binary Interface** (**ABI**) documentation; among many things, it specifies register usage for function calling, return, parameter passing, and so on. Check out the *Further reading* section on the GitHub repository for more on ABI docs.

- The psiginfo(3) takes effect as well, printing out the cause of the signal and the faulting address
- The message Segmentation fault (core dumped) tells us that our strategy worked: we reset the signal handling for the SIGSEGV to the default one and re-raised the signal, causing the OS (kernel) to generate a core dump. The resulting core file (generated on a Fedora 28 x86_64 box) shows up as shown below:

```
$ ls -l corefile*
-rw-------. 1 kai kai 389120 Jun 24 14:23
'corefile:host=<hostname>:gPID=2413:gTID=2413:ruid=1000:sig=11:exe=<!<
path>!<to>!<executable>!ch13!handle_segv.2413'
$
```

*Signaling - Part II*

Here are a couple of points to mention:

- The detailed analysis and interpretation of a core dump is beyond the scope of this book. Using GDB to analyze a core dump is easy; a little googling will yield results.
- The name given to the core file varies; modern Fedora distribution set the name to be very descriptive (as you can see); in reality, the core filename is controlled via a kernel tunable in the proc filesystem. See the man page on `core(5)` for details.

We run the kernel-space, invalid write test case for our `handle_segv` program as follows:

```
Test Case: Kernel-space, Invalid Write
$ ./handle_segv k w
Attempting to write into arbitrary kernel va kptr =
0xffff0b9ffacedead:
handle_segv:
------------------ FATAL signal ---------------------------
 myfault: received signal 11. errno=0
 Cause/Origin: (si_code=128): kernel
 Faulting instr or address = 0x0
 --- Register Dump [x86_64] ---
RAX = 0xffff0b9ffacedead RBX = 0x0000000000000000 RCX =
0x0000000000000000
RDX = 0x0000000000000000 RSI = 0x00000000023be260 RDI =
0x0000000000000000
RBP = 0x00007ffcb5b5ff60 R8  = 0x0000000000000010 R9  =
0x0000000000000000
R10 = 0x0000000000000000 R11 = 0x0000000000000246 R12 =
0x0000000000400850
R13 = 0x00007ffcb5b60040 R14 = 0x0000000000000000 R15 =
0x0000000000000000
RSP = 0x00007ffcb5b5fe90

RIP = 0x0000000000400ffc EFLAGS = 0x0000000000010206
TRAP# = 13 ERROR = 00
CR2 = 0x0000000000000000
----------------------------------------------------------
psiginfo helper: Segmentation fault (Signal sent by the kernel
[(nil)])
----------------------------------------------------------
Segmentation fault (core dumped)
$
```

[ 444 ]

Note that, this time, the trap value is 13; on the x86[_64] MMU, that's the **General Protection Fault (GPF)**. Again, this bad access resulted in the x86[_64] MMU raising a GPF exception, which in turn led to the OS fault handler code running and killing the process via the SIGSEGV. The trap being a GPF is a clue: we have violated a protection rule; recall from Chapter 1, *Linux System Architecture*: a process (or thread) running in a higher, more privileged level can always access memory at a lower privilege level but not vice versa of course. Here, the process at ring three attempted to access memory at ring zero; hence, the MMU raised the GPF exception and the OS killed it (via the SIGSEGV).

This time, unfortunately, the CR2 value and thus the faulting address is 0x0 (in the case where the crash occurs in kernel-space). However, we still get valuable details in other registers (the instruction and stack pointer values, and so on, as we shall see next).

## Finding the crash location in source code

The RIP (Instruction Pointer; EIP on IA-32, PC on the ARM) is useful: using its value and some utilities, we can pretty much pinpoint the location in code when the process crashed. How? There are several ways; some of them are as follows:

- Use the toolchain utility objdump (with the -d -S switches)
- An easier way is to use gdb(1) (see the following)
- With the addr2line(1) utility

With GDB:

Load up gdb(1) with the debug version (compiled with the -g switch) of the program, and then use the list command as shown here:

```
$ gdb -q ./handle_segv_dbg
Reading symbols from ./handle_segv_dbg...done.
(gdb) list *0x0000000000400ffc
<< 0x0000000000400ffc is the RIP value >>
0x400ffc is in main (handle_segv.c:212).
207 } else if ((tolower(argv[1][0]) == 'k') && tolower(argv[2][0] ==
'w')) {
208 ADDR_TYPE *kptr = (ADDR_TYPE *) invalid_kaddr; // arbitrary kernel
virtual addr
209 printf
210 ("Attempting to write into arbitrary kernel va kptr = 0x" ADDR_FMT
":\n",
211 (ADDR_TYPE) kptr);
212 *kptr = 0x2A; // writing
```

*Signaling - Part II*

```
213 } else
214 usage(argv[0]);
215 exit(0);
216 }
(gdb)
```

The `list * <address>` command literally pinpoints the code that caused the crash, reproduced here for clarity:

```
(gdb) l *0x0000000000400ffc
0x400ffc is in main (handle_segv.c:212).
```

Line 212 is as follows:

```
212: *kptr = 0x2A; // writing
```

This is exactly right.

With `addr2line`:

The `addr2line(1)` utility provides a similar feature; again, run it against the built-for-debug (compiled with `-g`) version of the binary executable file via it's `-e` switch:

```
$ addr2line -e ./handle_segv_dbg 0x0000000000400ffc
<...>/handle_segv.c:212
$
```

Also, think about it: our previous `ch12/altstack.c` program can, and will, suffer a segmentation fault when its alternate signal stack is overflowed; we leave it as an exercise to the reader to write a `SIGSEGV` handler similar to the one shown here to properly handle the case.

> **TIP:** Finally, though, we have shown that handling the segfault, the SIGSEGV, can be very beneficial to figuring out the cause of a crash; the simple fact remains that once this signal is generated upon a process, the process is considered to be in an undefined, in effect, unstable, state. Thus, there is no guarantee that whatever work we perform in its signal handler will actually go through as intended. Thus, keeping the signal handling code to a minimum would be recommended.

# Signaling – caveats and gotchas

Signals, being asynchronous events, can cause errors and bugs in subtle ways that are not immediately apparent to the casual reviewer (or programmer, for that matter). Some kinds of functionality or behavior are directly or indirectly affected by the arrival of one or more signal; you need to be alert to possible subtle races and similar conditions.

One important area in this that we have already covered is as follows: inside a signal handler, you can only invoke functions that are documented as being (or have been designed to be) async-signal safe. Other areas too deserve some contemplation; read on.

## Handling errno gracefully

A race with the uninitialized global integer `errno` can occur in programs using system calls and signals.

## What does errno do?

Remember the errno global; it's an uninitialized global integer in the process's uninitialized data segment (process layout was covered in Chapter 2, *Virtual Memory*).

What is errno for? Whenever a system call fails, it returns -1 to userspace. But why did it fail? Ah, the error diagnostic, the reason it failed, is returned to userspace like this: glibc, in conjunction with the kernel, pokes the global errno with a positive integer value. This value is actually an index into a two-dimensional array of English error messages (which is NULL-terminated); it's called `_sys_errlist`. So, looking up `_sys_errlist`[errno] reveals the English error message: the reason the system call failed.

Instead of the developer performing all the work, convenience routines such as `perror(3)`, `strerror(3)`, and `error(3)` are designed to emit error messages by looking up `_sys_errlist[errno]`. Programmers very often use routines such as this in the system call error- handling code (in fact, we do: check out our code for the macros `WARN` and `FATAL`—they call the `handle_err` function, which in turn invokes `perror(3)` as part of its processing).

*Signaling - Part II*

> Here is a useful-to-look-up item—the list of all possible `errno` values resides in the header file `/usr/include/asm-generic/errno-base.h`.

## The errno race

Consider this situation:

1. A process sets up a signal handler for several signals:
   - Let's say the signal handler for `SIGUSR1` is called `handle_sigusr`.
2. Now the process is running a part of its code, a function `foo`:
   - foo issues a system call, say the `open(2)`
   - The system call fails returning -1
     - errno gets set to the positive integer 13 reflecting the error permission denied (errno macro EACCES).
   - The system call's error-handling code calls `perror(3)` to emit the English error message.

All this seems innocent enough, yes. However, now let's consider signals in the mix; check out the following scenario:

- <...>
   - foo issues a system call, say the `open(2)`.
   - The system call fails returning -1.
     - errno gets set to the positive integer 13 reflecting the error permission denied (errno macro EACCES).
- The signal `SIGUSR1` is delivered at this instant to the process.
   - Control is switched to the signal handler routine, `handle_sigusr`.
     - The code here issues another system call, say, `stat(2)`.

[ 448 ]

- The stat(2) system call fails returning -1.
  - errno now gets set to the positive integer 9 reflecting the error bad file number (errno macro EBADF).
- The signal handler returns.
- The system call's error-handling code calls perror(3) to emit the English error message.

As can be seen, the value of errno gets overwritten from the value 13 to the value 9 because of the sequence of events. The result is that the application developer (along with everyone else on the project) is now confounded by the weird error reporting (the error bad file number is possibly reported twice!). Races—the bane of programmers!

## Fixing the errno race

The fix for the previous race is actually quite simple.

Whenever you have a signal handler with code within it that could possibly cause the errno value to change, save errno upon function entry and restore it just before returning from the handler.

Gain access to the errno variable simply by including its header file. Here is a quick example code snippet of a signal handler that does this:

```
<...>
include <errno.h>
<...>

static void handle_sigusr(int signum)
{
    int myerrno = errno;
    <... do the handling ...>
    <... syscalls, etc ...>
    errno = myerror;
}
```

## Sleeping correctly

Yes, even sleeping requires sufficient knowledge to perform correctly!
Often, your process has to enter a sleep state. We have all probably learned to use the sleep(3) API to do so:

```
#include <unistd.h>
unsigned int sleep(unsigned int seconds);
```

As a simple example, let's say that the process must work this way (pseudo code follows):

```
<...>
func_a();
sleep(10);
func_b();
<...>
```

It's quite clear: the process must sleep for 10 seconds; the code shown should work. Is there a problem?

Well, yes, signals: what if the process enters the sleep, but three seconds into the sleep a signal arrives? The default behavior (meaning, unless signals are masked) is to handle the signal, and you would imagine, go back to sleep for the remaining time (seven seconds). But, no, that's not what happens: the sleep is aborted! The astute reader might argue that it's possible to fix this behavior (a blocking system call interrupted by signals) by using the SA_RESTART flag; indeed, it sounds reasonable, but the reality is that even using the flag does not help (the sleep has to be manually restarted).

Further, it's important to realize that the sleep(3) API documents that its return value is the amount of time remaining to sleep; so unless sleep(3) returns 0, the sleep is not done! The developer is actually expected to invoke sleep(3) in a loop, until the return value is 0.

> What does making a process (or thread) "go to sleep" really mean? The key point is this: a process (or thread) that's asleep cannot run on the CPU while in that state; it is not even a candidate for the OS scheduler (technically, the transition from state Running->sleeping is a dequeue from a run queue and an enqueue on to a wait queue within the OS, and vice versa). More on this in Chapter 17, *CPU Scheduling on Linux*.

So, we conclude that just using a `sleep(3)` in the code is not that great an idea because of the following:

- The sleep, once interrupted by signal delivery, must be manually restarted.
- The granularity of `sleep(3)` is very coarse: a second. (A second is a very, very long time for a modern microprocessor! Many real-world applications rely on at least millisecond-to-microsecond-level granularity.)

So, what is the solution?

## The nanosleep system call

Linux provides a system call, `nanosleep(2)`, that in theory can provide nanosecond-level granularity, that is, a sleep of a single nanosecond. (Well, in practice, the granularity will also depend on the resolution of the hardware timer chip on the board.) This is the prototype of this API:

```
#include <time.h>
int nanosleep(const struct timespec *req, struct timespec *rem);
```

The system call has two parameters both are pointers to structure of data type `struct timespec`; this structure definition is as follows:

```
struct timespec {
    time_t tv_sec;  /* seconds */
    long tv_nsec;   /* nanoseconds */
};
```

Obviously, this allows you to specify the sleep time in seconds and nanoseconds; the first parameter `req` is the required time (s.ns), the second parameter `rem` is the remaining time to sleep. See, the OS helps us out here: if the sleep is interrupted by a signal (any signal that is non-fatal), the `nanosleep` system call fails returning -1, and errno is set to the value `EINTR` (Interrupted system call). Not only that, the OS calculates and returns (into this second pointer, a value-result type of parameter), the amount of time remaining to sleep accurate to the nanosecond. This way, we detect the case, set `req` to `rem`, and manually reissue the `nanosleep(2)` to have the sleep continue until it's fully done.

## Signaling - Part II

To demonstrate, we show a small application next (source code: ch12/sleeping_beauty.c); the user can invoke either the usual sleep(3) method of sleeping, or use the highly superior nanosleep(2) API such that the sleep time is accurate:

```
static void sig_handler(int signum)
{
    fprintf(stderr, "**Signal %d interruption!**\n", signum);
}

int main(int argc, char **argv)
{
    struct sigaction act;
    int nsec = 10, ret;
    struct timespec req, rem;

    if (argc == 1) {
        fprintf(stderr, "Usage: %s option=[0|1]\n"
            "0 : uses the sleep(3) function\n"
            "1 : uses the nanosleep(2) syscall\n", argv[0]);
        exit(EXIT_FAILURE);
    }
    /* setup signals: trap SIGINT and SIGQUIT */
    memset(&act, 0, sizeof(act));
    act.sa_handler = sig_handler;
    sigemptyset(&act.sa_mask);
    act.sa_flags = SA_RESTART;
    if (sigaction(SIGINT, &act, 0) || sigaction(SIGQUIT, &act, 0))
        FATAL("sigaction failure\n");

    if (atoi(argv[1]) == 0) {           /* sleep */
        printf("sleep for %d s now...\n", nsec);
        ret = sleep(nsec);
        printf("sleep returned %u\n", ret);
    } else if (atoi(argv[1]) == 1) { /* nanosleep */
        req.tv_sec = nsec;
        req.tv_nsec = 0;
        while ((nanosleep(&req, &rem) == -1) && (errno == EINTR)) {
            printf("nanosleep interrupted: rem time: %07lu.%07lu\n",
                rem.tv_sec, rem.tv_nsec);
            req = rem;
        }
    }
    exit(EXIT_SUCCESS);
}
```

Note the following from the previous code:

- Passing 0 as the parameter has us invoke the usual sleep(3).
    - We deliberately code without using a loop here, as this is how most programmers call sleep(3) (and thus we can see the pitfalls).
- Passing 1 as the parameter has us invoke the powerful nanosleep(2) API; we initialize the required time to be 10 seconds (same as in the previous case).
    - But, this time, we call the nanosleep(2) in a loop, checking for the signal interruption case errno == EINTR, and if so,
    - We set req to rem and call it again!
    - (For fun, we print the time remaining s.ns):

```
$ ./sleeping_beauty
Usage: ./sleeping_beauty option=[0|1]
0 : uses the sleep(3) function
1 : uses the nanosleep(2) syscall
$
```

Let's try both cases: first, the usual sleep(3) method:

```
$ ./sleeping_beauty 0
sleep for 10 s now...
^C**Signal 2 interruption!**
sleep returned 7
$
```

A few seconds into the sleep, we press ^C; the signal arrives, but the sleep is aborted (as shown, an additional seven seconds of the sleep remain, which the code here simply ignores)!

Now for the good case: sleeping via the nanosleep(2):

```
$ ./sleeping_beauty 1
^C**Signal 2 interruption!**
nanosleep interrupted: rem time: 0000007.249192148
^\**Signal 3 interruption!**
nanosleep interrupted: rem time: 0000006.301391001
^C**Signal 2 interruption!**
nanosleep interrupted: rem time: 0000004.993030983
^\**Signal 3 interruption!**
nanosleep interrupted: rem time: 0000004.283608684
^C**Signal 2 interruption!**
nanosleep interrupted: rem time: 0000003.23244174
```

*Signaling - Part II*

```
^\**Signal 3 interruption!**
nanosleep interrupted: rem time: 0000001.525725162
^C**Signal 2 interruption!**
nanosleep interrupted: rem time: 0000000.906662154
^\**Signal 3 interruption!**
nanosleep interrupted: rem time: 0000000.192637791
$
```

This time, our dear `sleeping_beauty` runs (sleeps?) to completion even in the presence of continuous interruption via multiple signals. You should notice, though, this fact: there is going to be some overhead, yes. The only guarantee made by the OS is that the sleep continues for at least as long as required, possibly a bit longer.

Note: although using the `nanosleep(2)` results in a highly superior implementation to the usual `sleep(3)` API, the fact is that even the `nanosleep` is subject to (what could become significant) time overruns when the code is within a loop and a sufficiently large number of signals interrupts our loop many, many times (as could occur in our previous example). In cases such as this, we can end up oversleeping quite a bit. To fix this, the POSIX standard, and Linux, provide an even better `clock_nanosleep(2)` system call: using it with a real-time clock and a flag value of `TIMER_ABSTIME` takes care of the oversleeping issue. Also note that though Linux's `sleep(3)` API is internally implemented via `nanosleep(2)`, the sleep semantics remain as described; it's the app developer's responsibility to call the sleep code in a loop, checking for return value and the failure case.

## Real-time signals

Recall the output of the `kill -l` (l for list) command; the platform's supported signals are displayed—numeric integer and symbolic name, both. The first 31 signals are the standard or Unix signals (seen in Chapter 11, *Signaling - Part I*, *The standard or Unix signals* section); we have been working with them quite a bit now.

Signal numbers 34 to 64 all start with SIGRT—SIGRTMIN to SIGRTMAX—they are called the **real time** signals:

```
$ kill -l |grep "SIGRT"
31) SIGSYS      34) SIGRTMIN     35) SIGRTMIN+1  36) SIGRTMIN+2  37) SIGRTMIN+3
38) SIGRTMIN+4  39) SIGRTMIN+5   40) SIGRTMIN+6  41) SIGRTMIN+7  42) SIGRTMIN+8
43) SIGRTMIN+9  44) SIGRTMIN+10  45) SIGRTMIN+11 46) SIGRTMIN+12 47) SIGRTMIN+13
48) SIGRTMIN+14 49) SIGRTMIN+15  50) SIGRTMAX-14 51) SIGRTMAX-13 52)
```

```
       SIGRTMAX-12
53) SIGRTMAX-11  54) SIGRTMAX-10  55) SIGRTMAX-9  56) SIGRTMAX-8  57)
SIGRTMAX-7
58) SIGRTMAX-6   59) SIGRTMAX-5   60) SIGRTMAX-4  61) SIGRTMAX-3  62)
SIGRTMAX-2
63) SIGRTMAX-1   64) SIGRTMAX
$
```

(The first one, SIGSYS seen here is not a real time signal; it shows up because it's in the same line as the other SIGRT's and so grep(1) prints it.)

## Differences from standard signals

So, how do the so-called real time signals differ from the regular standard signals; the following table reveals this:

| Characteristic | Standard signals | Real time signals |
|---|---|---|
| Numbering | 1 - 31 [1] | 34 - 64 [2] |
| Standard first defined in | POSIX.1-1990 (it's old) | POSIX 1003.1b : real time Extensions to POSIX (2001) |
| Meaning assigned | Individual signals have a particular meaning (and are named accordingly); the exception is SIGUSR[1|2] | Individual RT signals have no particular meaning; their meaning is app-defined |
| Behavior when blocked and multiple instances of same signal continuously delivered | Out of n instances of the same signal, n-1 are lost; only 1 instance is kept pending and delivered to the target process when unblocked | All instances of RT signals are queued and delivered to the target process by the OS when unblocked (there is a system-wide upper limit [3]) |
| Signal priority | The same: all standard signals are peers | FCFS unless pending; if pending, then signals delivered from lowest to highest numbered realtime signal [4] |
| Inter Process Communication (IPC) | Crude IPC; you can use SIGUSR[1|2] to communicate, but no data can be passed | Better: via the sigqueue(3), a single data item, an integer or pointer value, can be sent to a peer process (which can retrieve it) |

Differences between standard and realtime signals

[1] Signal number 0? Does not exist, used to check for process existence (seen later).

[2] An FAQ: whatever happened to realtime signal numbers 32 and 33? The answer: they are reserved for use by the pthreads implementation, and thus unavailable to the application developer.

[3] The system-wide upper limit is a resource limit and can thus be queried or set via the `prlimit(1)` utility (or the `prlimit(2)` system call):

```
$ prlimit |grep SIGPENDING
SIGPENDING max number of pending signals 63229     63229 signals
$
```

(Recall from Chapter 3, *Resource Limits*, that the first number is the soft limit, the second is the hard limit).

[4] RT signal priority: multiple instances of realtime signals are processed in exactly the order they were delivered (in other words, **First Come First Served** (**FCFC**). However, if these multiple real time signals are pending delivery to the process, that is, they are currently blocked, then they are processed in priority order, rather non-intuitively, `SIGRTMIN` being the highest priority signal and `SIGRTMAX` being the lowest.

## Real time signals and priority

The POSIX standard, and the Linux documentation, states that when multiple real time signals of different types are pending delivery to a process (that is the process is blocking them); then, at some point, when the process's signal mask is unblocked (thereby allowing the signals to be delivered), the signals are indeed delivered in priority order: lowest signal number to highest signal number.

Let's test this: we write a program that traps and blocks upon the delivery of three real time signals: {`SIGRTMAX-5`, `SIGRTMAX`, `SIGRTMIN+5`}. (Have a look at the output of `kill -l`; their integer values are {59, 64, 39} respectively.)

Importantly, our program will, at the time of `sigaction(2)`, use the `sigfillset(3)` convenience method to populate the signal mask member of struct sigaction with all 1s, thereby ensuring that all signals are blocked (masked) while the signal handler code is running.

Consider the following:

- The process (code: ch12/rtsigs_waiter.c) traps the RT signals (with sigaction)
  {SIGRTMAX-5, SIGRTMAX, SIGRTMIN+5} : integer values {59, 64, 39} respectively.
- Then, we have a shell script (bombard_sigrt.sh) send these three real time signals continually (or for the number requested) in batches of three, in the following order:
  {SIGRTMAX-5, SIGRTMAX, SIGRTMIN+5} : integer values {59, 64, 39} respectively.
- The first of the RT signals (# 59) causes the process to enter the signal handler routine; recall, we have specified (at the time of sigaction(2)) that all signals are blocked (masked) while the signal handler code runs.
  - We deliberately use our DELAY_LOOP_SILENT macro to keep the signal handler running for a while.
- Accordingly, the RT signals delivered by the script cannot interrupt the handler (they are blocked), so the OS queues them up.
- Once the signal handler completes and returns, the next RT signal in the queue is delivered to the process.
  - In priority order, they are delivered least to highest, like so:
    {SIGRTMIN+5, SIGRTMAX-5, SIGRTMAX} : integer values {39, 59, 64}.

The next run verifies this behavior on Linux:

> We do not show the source code here; to view the complete source code, build it, and run it, the entire tree is available for cloning from GitHub here: https://github.com/PacktPublishing/Hands-on-System-Programming-with-Linux/blob/master/ch12/rtsigs_waiter.c and https://github.com/PacktPublishing/Hands-on-System-Programming-with-Linux/blob/master/ch12/bombard_sigrt.sh.

```
$ ./rtsigs_waiter
Trapping the three realtime signals
Process awaiting signals ...
```

*Signaling - Part II*

In another Terminal window we run the bombard script:

```
$ ./bombard_sigrt.sh
Usage: bombard_sigrt.sh PID-of-process num-RT-signals-batches-to-send
 (-1 to continously bombard the process with signals).
$
$ ./bombard_sigrt.sh $(pgrep rtsigs_waiter) 3
Sending 3 instances each of RT signal batch
 {SIGRTMAX-5, SIGRTMAX, SIGRTMIN+5} to process 3642 ...
 i.e. signal #s {59, 64, 39}
SIGRTMAX-5 SIGRTMAX SIGRTMIN+5 SIGRTMAX-5 SIGRTMAX SIGRTMIN+5
SIGRTMAX-5 SIGRTMAX SIGRTMIN+5
$
```

In the original Terminal window where the rtsigs_waiter process is running, we now see this:

```
sighdlr: signal 59, s=1 ; total=1; stack 0x7ffd2f9c6100 :*
sighdlr: signal 39, s=2 ; total=2; stack 0x7ffd2f9c6100 :*
sighdlr: signal 39, s=3 ; total=3; stack 0x7ffd2f9c6100 :*
sighdlr: signal 39, s=4 ; total=4; stack 0x7ffd2f9c6100 :*
sighdlr: signal 59, s=5 ; total=5; stack 0x7ffd2f9c6100 :*
sighdlr: signal 59, s=6 ; total=6; stack 0x7ffd2f9c6100 :*
sighdlr: signal 64, s=7 ; total=7; stack 0x7ffd2f9c6100 :*
sighdlr: signal 64, s=8 ; total=8; stack 0x7ffd2f9c6100 :*
sighdlr: signal 64, s=9 ; total=9; stack 0x7ffd2f9c6100 :*
```

Note the following:

- The first RT signal sent by the script is the SIGRTMAX-5 (value 59); hence, it enters the signal handler and is processed.
    - While the signal handler is running, all signals are blocked.
- The script continues to pump out the remaining RT signals (see its output), while they are masked.
- Thus, they are queued by the OS and delivered once the handler completes in priority order: lowest to highest numbered RT signal, that is, the priority order is from SIGRTMIN (highest) to SIGRTMAX (lowest).
- As they are queued, no signals are lost.

Here is a screenshot demonstrating the same, for a larger number of RT signals:

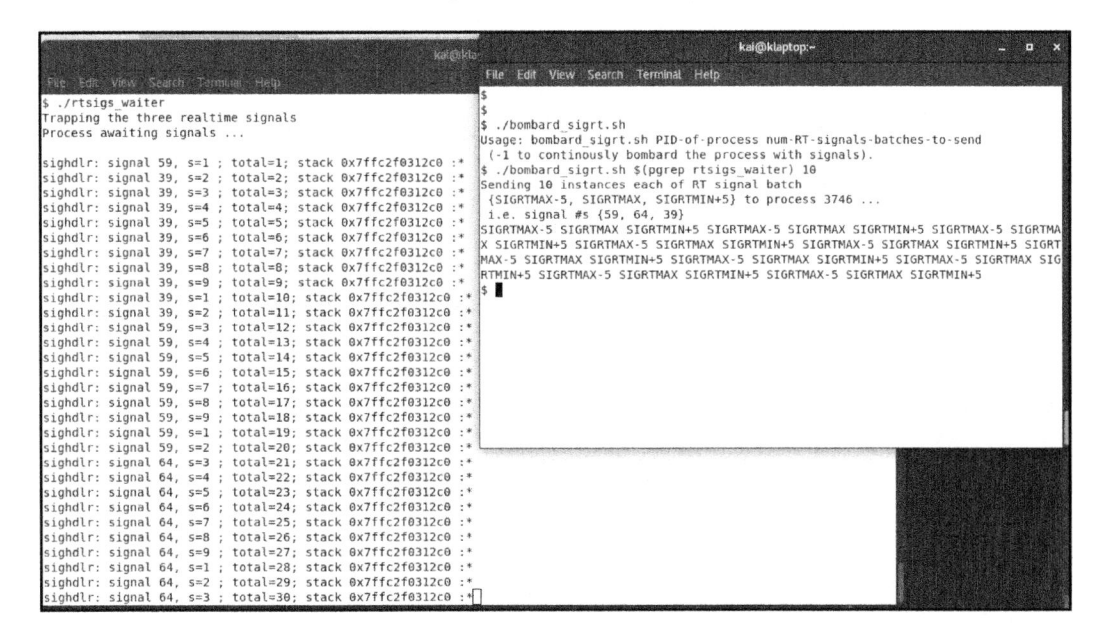

[screenshot of two terminal windows showing rtsigs_waiter output and bombard_sigrt.sh usage]

Passing 10 to the script (see the right hand window) has it deliver 3x10: 30 RT signals in 10 batches of {SIGRTMIN+5, SIGRTMAX-5, SIGRTMAX}). Note, in the left hand window, how (except for the first instance of course) they are (queued and) processed in priority order, lowest to highest—first, all the 39s {SIGRTMIN+5}, then all the 59s {SIGRTMAX-5}, and finally the lowest priority 64s {SIGRTMAX} RT signals.

The script sends signals to the process by issuing the kill(1) command; it will be explained in detail later in this chapter.

To conclude, real time signals are processed as follows:

- If unblocked, they are processed one after the other in FCFS order.
- If blocked, they are queued and delivered in priority order—the lowest RT signal being the highest priority and the the highest RT signal being the lowest priority.

As always, you, the reader, are strongly encouraged to check out the code and try out these experiments yourself.

# Sending signals

We have typically seen cases where the kernel sends signals to a process; there is no reason a process cannot send a signal (or several) to another process. In this section, we delve into the details of sending signals to processes from a process, and ideas related to the same.

You might wonder, even if you could send a signal to another process, how would it be useful? Well, think about it: signal-sending could be used as an **interprocess communication** (**IPC**) mechanism, for one. Also, it's a way of checking for a process's existence! There are other useful cases, such as sending yourself a signal. Let's explore these further.

## Just kill 'em

How do we send a signal to another process: the short answer, via the kill(2) system call. The kill API can deliver a signal, any signal, to a process given its PID; the function signature from the man page on kill(2):

```
#include <sys/types.h>
#include <signal.h>

int kill(pid_t pid, int sig);
```

Note it's very generic—you can send pretty much any signal to any process (it might perhaps have been better named as sendsig, but, of course, that's not as exciting a name as kill).

The user command kill(1) is, of course, a wrapper over the kill(2) system call.

Quite obviously, from the previous API, you can infer that the signal sig is sent to the process that has the PID value pid. Hang on, though, there are several special cases to consider as well; see the following table:

| kill PID value | Meaning |
| --- | --- |
| > 0 | The signal is sent to the process with numeric PID equal to this value (the usual case). |
| 0 | The signal is sent to all processes within the process group [1] of the caller. |
| -1 | The signal is sent to all processes for which the caller has permission to send (see next), except the overall ancestor process, PID 1 (traditionally init, nowadays systemd). [2] |
| < -1 | The signal is sent to all processes within the process group one having ID, pid. |

[ 460 ]

[1] Process group: Every process will be a member of a process group (each pgrp will have its own unique ID, equal to the PID of the first member, called the process group leader. Use `ps j` to look up process group details; also, the system calls `get|set]pgid(2)`, `[get|set]pgrp(2)`, are available.

If you run a chain of processes via pipes (for example, `ps aux |tail |sort -k6n`) and, once it's running, type ^C on the keyboard, then we understand the signal SIGINT is generated via the kernel's tty layer; but to which process? All the processes currently running as part of the preceding pipeline form the foreground process group. The significance with regard to signaling: any signals generated via the keyboard (such as ^C, ^\, ^Z), is delivered to all processes belonging in the foreground process group. (Thus all three will receive the signal. Check the *Further reading* section for a link to more information on process groups on the GitHub repository.)

[2] On Linux, `kill(-1, sig)` does not send `sig` to the calling process itself.

## Killing yourself with a raise

Dramatic as it sounds, here we point out a simple wrapper API: the *raise(3)* library call. Here is its signature:

```
include <signal.h>
int raise(int sig);
```

It's really very simple: given a signal number, the raise API raises, sends, the given signal to the calling process (or thread). If the signal in question is caught, the raise will return only once the signal handler has completed.

Recall that we have used this API in our `handle_segv.c` program earlier in this chapter: we used it to ensure that, for the signal SIGSEGV, after our own handling is done, we re-raise the same signal on ourselves, thereby ensuring that the core dump occurs.

(Well, philosophically, though, there's only so much that getting that raise will do for your happiness quotient.)

## Agent 00 – permission to kill

In Ian Fleming's books, James Bond is a double-oh agent (007): a secret agent with permission to kill!

*Signaling - Part II*

Well, like Bond, we too can kill; um, a process, of course, that is, send it a signal. It's nowhere as dramatic and exciting as Bond, but, hey, we can! Well, IFF (if and only if) we have the permission to do so.

The required permission: the sending process must either:

- Have root privileges—Under the modern capabilities model (recall Chapter 8, *Process Capabilities*), the requirement becomes that a process has the CAP_KILL capability bit set; from the man page on capabilities(7): CAP_KILL : Bypass permission checks for sending signals (see kill(2)).
- Own the target process, which implies that the sender's EUID (effective UID) or RUID (real UID) and the target's EUID or RUID, respectively, should match.

The man page on kill(2) specifies in more detail some corner cases on Linux regarding permissions to send signals; take a look if interested.

So, tempting as it sounds, just performing a loop like (pseudo-code follows) will not necessarily work for all processes alive, mostly because of a lack of permissions of course:

```
for i from 1 to PID_MAX
    kill(i, SIGKILL)
```

Even if you were to run code such as the one shown previously as root, the system will disallow abruptly terminating key processes such as systemd (or init). (Why not try it—it's a suggested exercise anyway. Of course, trying stuff like this is asking for trouble; we suggest you try this a test VM.)

## Are you there?

Checking for a process's very existence, is it alive now?, can be crucial to an application. For example, an application function receives the PID of a process as a parameter. Before it actually does something with the process via the provided PID (perhaps send it a signal), it would be a good idea to verify that the process is indeed valid (what if it's dead or the PID invalid?).

The kill(2) system call helps us in this regard: the second parameter to kill is the signal to send; using the value 0 (recall there is no signal numbered 0) validates the first parameter: the PID. How exactly? If the kill(2) returns failure, either the PID is invalid or we do not have permission to send the process (or process group) a signal.

The following pseudo-code demonstrates this:

```
static int app_func_A(int work, pid_t target)
{
    [...]
    if (kill(target, 0) < 0)
        <handle it>
        return -1;
    [...it's fine; do the work on 'target'...]
}
```

## Signaling as IPC

We learned that a fundamental side effect of the virtual memory architecture that modern OSes (such as Linux) use is that a process can only access memory within its own **virtual address space** (**VAS**); and that too only the valid mapped memory.

Practically speaking, this implies a process cannot read from or write into the VAS of any other process. Yes; but then, how do you communicate with other processes? This scenario is critical in many multi-process applications.

The short answer: IPC mechanisms. The Linux OS has several; here, we make use of one of them: signaling.

## Crude IPC

Think about it, it's quite simple: processes A and B are part of a multi-process application. Now process A wants to inform process B that it has completed some work; upon receiving this information, we expect process B to acknowledge the same.

We can devise a simple IPC scheme via signaling as follows:

- Process A is performing its work.
- Process B is performing its work (they run in parallel of course).
- Process A reaches a milestone; it informs process B of this by sending it SIGUSR1 (via the kill(2)).
- Having trapped the signal, process B enters its signal handler and verifies things as required.

*Signaling - Part II*

- It acknowledges the message by sending process A, say, SIGUSR2 (via the kill(2)).
- Having trapped the signal, process A enters its signal handler, understands that the ack has been received from B, and life continues.

(The reader can try this as a small exercise.)

However, we should realize an important detail: IPC implies the ability to send data to another process. Above, however, we have not been able to transmit or receive any data; just the fact that we can communicate via signals (well, you could argue that the signal number itself is data; true, in a limited sense). So we think of this as a crude IPC mechanism.

## Better IPC – sending a data item

This leads us to the next interesting fact: it is possible to send a data quantum—a piece of data—via signals. To see how, let's revisit the powerful struct siginfo_t we studied earlier in this chapter. To have the signal handler receive the pointer to it, recall that we use the SA_SIGINFO flag when calling sigaction(2).

Recall the fact that, within struct siginfo_t, the first three members are simple integers, the fourth member is a union of structures, there are seven of them—only one of which will get instantiated at runtime; the one that does depends on which signal is being handled!

To help us recall, here's the initial portion of struct siginfo_t:

```
typedef struct {
    int si_signo; /* Signal number. */
    int si_code;
    int si_errno; /* If non-zero, an errno value associated with
            this signal, as defined in <errno.h>. */
    union
    {
        int _pad[__SI_PAD_SIZE];
        /* kill(). */
        struct
        {
            __pid_t si_pid; /* Sending process ID. */
            __uid_t si_uid; /* Real user ID of sending process. */
        } _kill;

        [...]
```

[ 464 ]

Within the union of structures, the structure of interest to us right now is the one that deals with real time signals—this one:

```
[...]
/* POSIX.1b signals. */
    struct
    {
        __pid_t si_pid; /* Sending process ID. */
        __uid_t si_uid; /* Real user ID of sending process. */
        __sigval_t si_sigval; /* Signal value. */
    } _rt;
[...]
```

So, it's quite straightforward: if we trap some real time signals and use SA_SIGINFO, we shall be able to retrieve the pointer to this structure; the first two members reveal the PID and RUID of the sending process. That itself is valuable information!

The third member though, the sigval_t, is the key (in /usr/include/asm-generic/siginfo.h on Ubuntu and in /usr/include/bits/types/__sigval_t.h on Fedora):

```
union __sigval
{
    int __sival_int;
    void *__sival_ptr;
};
typedef union __sigval __sigval_t;
```

Note that the sigval_t is itself a union of two members: an integer and a pointer! We know that a union can only have one of its members instantiated at runtime; so the deal here is: the sender process populates one of the preceding members with data and then sends a real time signal to the receiver process. The receiver can extract the data quantum sent by appropriately de-referencing the preceding union. This way, one is able to send data across processes; the data is effectively piggy-backed on a real time signal! Quite cool.

But think: we can use only one of the members to piggy-back our data, either the integer int sival_int or the void * sival_ptr pointer. Which should one use? It's instructive to recall what we learned in Chapter 10, *Process Creation* on process creation: every address within a process is a virtual address; that is, my virtual address X is likely not pointing to the same physical memory as your virtual address X. In other words, attempting to communicate data via a pointer, which is after all nothing but a virtual address, might now work as well as expected. (If you are unsure about this, might we suggest rereading the *malloc and The fork* sections in Chapter 10, *Process Creation*.)

*Signaling - Part II*

In conclusion, using an integer to hold and communicate data to our peer process would usually be a better idea. In fact, C programmers know how to extract, literally, every last bit from memory; you can always treat the integer as a bitmask and communicate even more information!

Additionally, the C library provides a helper routine to quite easily send a signal with data embedded within, the `sigqueue(3)` API. Its signature:

```
#include <signal.h>
int sigqueue(pid_t pid, int sig, const union sigval value);
```

The first two parameters are obvious: the process to send the signal `sig` to; the third parameter value is the union discussed.

Lets try this out; we write a small producer-consumer type of application. We run the consumer process in the background; it polls, waiting for the producer to send it some data. (As you might guess, polling is not ideal; in the multithreading topics, we shall cover superior methods; for now, we shall just simplistically poll.) When the receiver detects data has been sent to it, it displays all relevant details.

First, a sample run: to begin, we run the consumer (receiver) process (`ch12/sigq_ipc/sigq_recv.c`) in the background:

```
$ ./sigq_recv &
[1] 13818
./sigq_recv: Hey, consumer here [13818]! Awaiting data from producer
(will poll every 3s ...)
$
```

Next, we run the producer (`ch12/sigq_ipc/sigq_sender.c`), sending a data item to the consumer:

```
$ ./sigq_sender
Usage: ./sigq_sender pid-to-send-to value-to-send[int]
$ ./sigq_sender $(pgrep sigq_recv) 42
Producer [13823]: sent signal 34 to PID 13818 with data item 42
$ nanosleep interrupted: rem time: 0000002.705461411
```

The consumer processes the signal, understands that data has arrived, and in the next polling cycle prints out the details:

```
Consumer [13818] received data @ Tue Jun 5 10:20:33 2018
:
signal # : 34
Producer: PID : 1000
          UID : 1000              data item : 42
```

[ 466 ]

> For readability, only key parts of the source code are displayed next; to view the complete source code, build it and run it, the entire tree is available for cloning from GitHub here: https://github.com/PacktPublishing/Hands-on-System-Programming-with-Linux.

Here's the receiver: ch12/sigq_ipc/sigq_recv.c:main() function:

```
#define SIG_COMM    SIGRTMIN
#define SLP_SEC     3

[...]
static volatile sig_atomic_t data_recvd=0;
[...]
int main(int argc, char **argv)
{
 struct sigaction act;

 act.sa_sigaction = read_msg;
 sigfillset(&act.sa_mask); /* disallow all while handling */
 act.sa_flags = SA_SIGINFO | SA_RESTART;
 if (sigaction(SIG_COMM, &act, 0) == -1)
     FATAL("sigaction failure");

 printf("%s: Hey, consumer here [%d]! Awaiting data from producer\n"
         "(will poll every %ds ...)\n",
         argv[0], getpid(), SLP_SEC);

/* Poll ... not the best way, but just for this demo... */
 while(1) {
    r_sleep(SLP_SEC);
    if (data_recvd) {
        display_recv_data();
        data_recvd = 0;
    }
 }
 exit(EXIT_SUCCESS);
}
```

We poll upon the arrival of the real time signal, sleeping in a loop for three seconds on each loop iteration; polling is really not the best way to code; for now, we just keep things simple and do so (in the Chapters 14, *Multithreading with Pthreads Part I - Essentials* and Chapter 15, *Multithreading with Pthreads Part II - Synchronization*, we shall cover other efficient means of synchronizing on a data value).

*Signaling - Part II*

As explained in the section *Sleeping correctly*, we prefer to use our own wrapper over nanosleep(2), our r_sleep() function, keeping the sleep safe.

In the meantime, a part of the sender code:
ch12/sigq_ipc/sigq_sender.c: send_peer():

```
static int send_peer(pid_t target, int sig, int val)
{
 union sigval sv;

 if (kill(target, 0) < 0)
     return -1;

 sv.sival_int = val;
 if (sigqueue(target, sig, sv) == -1)
     return -2;
 return 0;
}
```

This function performs the work of checking that the target process is indeed alive, and if so, sending it the real time signal via the useful sigqueue(3) library API. A key point: we wrap or embed the data to be sent inside the sigval union, as an integer value.

Back to the receiver: when it does receive the real time signal, its designated signal handler code, read_msg(), runs:

```
[...]
typedef struct {
   time_t timestamp;
   int signum;
   pid_t sender_pid;
   uid_t sender_uid;
   int data;
} rcv_data_t;
static rcv_data_t recv_data;

[...]

/*
 * read_msg
 * Signal handler for SIG_COMM.
 * The signal's receipt implies a producer has sent us data;
 * read and place the details in the rcv_data_t structure.
 * For reentrant-safety, all signals are masked while this handler
 runs.
```

```
 */
static void read_msg(int signum, siginfo_t *si, void *ctx)
{
 time_t tm;

 if (time(&tm) < 0)
     WARN("time(2) failed\n");

 recv_data.timestamp = tm;
 recv_data.signum = signum;
 recv_data.sender_pid = si->si_pid;
 recv_data.sender_uid = si->si_uid;
 recv_data.data = si->si_value.sival_int;

 data_recvd = 1;
}
```

We update a structure to hold the data (and metadata), allowing us to conveniently print it whenever required.

## Sidebar – LTTng

As a very interesting aside, wouldn't it be wonderful if one could actually trace the flow of the sender and receiver processes as they execute? Well, Linux provides several tools to do precisely this. Among the more sophisticated ones is a software called **Linux Tracing Toolkit next generation (LTTng)**.

LTTng is really powerful; once set up, it has the ability to trace both kernel and user space (although tracing user space involves the application developers explicitly instrumenting their code). Well, your author used LTTng to perform a trace of the system (kernel-space) while the previous processes ran; LTTng did its job, capturing trace data (in a format called CTF).

Then, the superb *Trace Compass* GUI application was used to display and interpret the trace session in a meaningful manner; the following screenshot shows an example; you can see the point at which the sender sent the signal to the receiver process via the `sigqueue(3)` library API, which, as you can see, translated to the `rt_sigqueueinfo(2)` system call (its entry point inside the kernel shows up as the `syscall_entry_rt_sigqueueinfo` event as follows).

*Signaling - Part II*

Next, the receiver process (`sigq_trc_recv` here) received (and then processed) the signal:

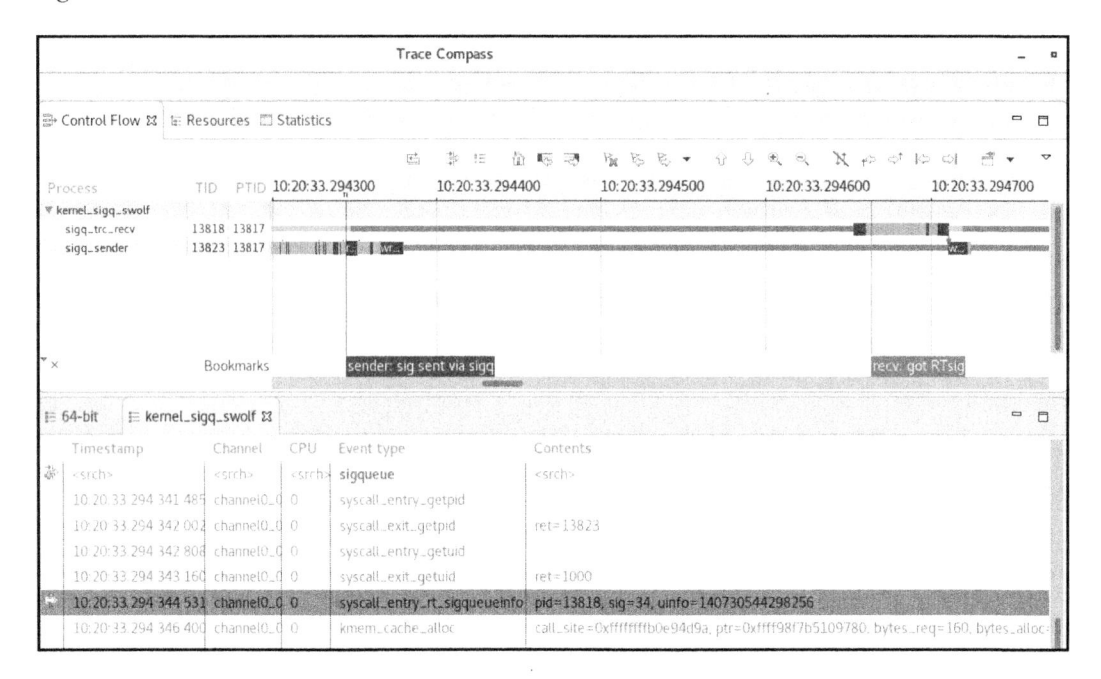

[Screenshot of Trace Compass showing Control Flow view with processes kernel_sigq_swolf, sigq_trc_recv (TID 13818, PTID 13817), and sigq_sender (TID 13823, PTID 13817), along with event trace entries including sigqueue, syscall_entry_getpid, syscall_exit_getpid (ret=13823), syscall_entry_getuid, syscall_exit_getuid (ret=1000), syscall_entry_rt_sigqueueinfo (pid=13818, sig=34, uinfo=140730544298256), and kmem_cache_alloc.]

(As a fun thing to do: calculate the time delta between the real time signal being sent and the signal being received, bookmarked in purple and red color, respectively. It's approximately 300 ms (microseconds).)

The details of LTTng is not within the scope of this book's coverage; please see the *Further reading* section on the GitHub repository.

For completeness, we note the following APIs to send signals as well:

- `pthread_kill(3)` : an API to send a signal to a particular thread within the same process
- `tgkill(2)` : an API to send a signal to a particular thread within a given thread group
- `tkill(2)` : a deprecated predecessor to tgkill

Let's ignore these for now; these APIs become more relevant in the context of multithreading in later Chapter 14, *Multithreading with Pthreads Part I - Essentials*, in the book.

# Alternative signal-handling techniques

So far, in the previous chapter as well as this one on signaling, we have seen and learned to use several techniques with regard to asynchronously trapping and working with signals. The essential idea is this: the process is busy performing its work, running its business logic; a signal suddenly arrives; nevertheless, the process must handle it. We saw in quite some detail how one leverages the powerful `sigaction(2)` system call to do so.

Now, we look at signal handling in a different manner: synchronously handling signals, that is, how to have the process (or thread) wait for (block upon) signals and handle them as they arrive.

The chapters to come on multithreading will provide some use cases of the same.

# Synchronously waiting for signals

At first glance, and the traditional manner in which signaling is taught, it appears that as signals are asynchronous in nature, why would one ever attempt to synchronously block upon signals delivered? Well, the reality is: performing robust signal handling in large projects is a difficult thing to do correctly and consistently. A lot of the complexity stems from the issue of signal-async safety; we are not allowed to use just any API within a signal handler; only a relatively small subset of APIs is considered async-signal-safe and is viable to use. This raises significant hurdles in large programs, and of course, at times, programmers inadvertently cause defects (bugs) (that too, ones that are difficult to catch during testing).

These signal-handling difficulties pretty much vanish when one eliminates the whole asynchronous signal handler with signal-safety requirements design. How? By synchronously blocking upon signals and, when the signal(s) arrive, handling them then and there.

Thus, the goal in this section is to teach the budding systems programmer these important concepts (and their APIs); learning to use these can significantly decrease oddities and bugs.

A number of useful mechanisms exist on the Linux OS to perform synchronous signal handling; let's start with the simple yet useful `pause(2)` system call.

## Pause, please

The pause is a very good example of a blocking call; when a process calls this API, it blocks, that is, it goes to sleep waiting for an event; the event: the arrival of any signal to it. The moment a signal arrives, the pause is unblocked and execution continues. Of course, delivery of a fatal signal will cause the unsuspecting process to die:

```
include <unistd.h>
 int pause(void);
```

Throughout, we have said that checking system calls for their failure case -1 is considered very important: a best practice to always follow. The pause(2) throws up an interesting exception case: it seems to be the one system call that always returns -1 and errno is set to the value EINTR Interrupted system call (the interruption being the signal of course).

For this reason, we often code the pause as follows:

```
(void)pause();
```

The typecast to void is to inform tools such as the compiler and static analyzers that we don't really care about the return value from pause.

## Waiting forever or until a signal arrives

Often, one would like to wait forever, or until a signal arrives. One way to do so is the very simple, but very bad, terribly expensive spin on the CPU code such as this:

```
while (1);
```

Ugh! That's just ugly: please do not write code like that!

Slightly better, but still quite off, is this:

```
while (1)
    sleep(1);
```

The pause can be used to effectively and efficiently set up a useful wait forever or until I receive any signal semantic, as follows:

```
while (1)
    (void)pause();
```

This semantic is very useful for this wait forever or until I receive any signal situation, as it's inexpensive (hardly any CPU usage as the pause(2) has the caller immediately go to sleep), and get unblocked only when a signal arrives. Then, the whole scenario repeats (due to the infinite loop of course).

## Synchronously blocking for signals via the sigwait* APIs

Next, we briefly visit a set of related functions, the sigwait* APIs; they are as follows:

- sigwait(3)
- sigwaitinfo(2)
- sigtimedwait(2)

All of these APIs allow a process (or thread) to block (wait) upon the delivery of one or more signal.

### The sigwait library API

Let's start with the sigwait(3):

```
include <signal.h>
  int sigwait(const sigset_t *set, int *sig);
```

The sigwait(3) library API allows a process (or thread) to block, wait, until any signal in the signal-set set is pending delivery to it. The moment a signal arrives, the sigwait is unblocked; the particular signal that arrived, its integer value, is placed in the value-result second parameter sig. Under the hood, the sigwait removes the signal just delivered from the process (or thread) pending mask.

Thus, the sigwait(3) is advantageous to the pause(2) by virtue of the following:

- You can wait upon the delivery of particular signals to the process
- When one of those signals is delivered, its value is known

The return value from sigwait(3) is 0 on success and a positive value on error (note that it being a library API, errno remains unaffected). (Internally, the sigwait(3) is implemented via the sigtimedwait(2) API.)

*Signaling - Part II*

However, things are not always as simple as they appear at first glance. The reality is that there are a couple of important points to consider:

- A risky situation called a race can be set up if the signals one intends waiting upon are not first blocked by the calling process. (Technically, this is as there is a window of opportunity between a signal being delivered to the process and the sigwait call initializing). Once running, though, the sigwait will atomically unblock the signals, allowing them to be delivered upon the caller process.
- What if a signal (one within the signal set we define), is also trapped (caught) via either the sigaction(2) or signal(2) API, AND via the sigwait(3) API? In such a scenario, the POSIX standard states that it is up to the implementation to decide how to handle the delivered signal; Linux seems to favor handling the signal via the sigwait(3). (This makes sense: if a process issues the sigwait API, the process blocks on signals. If a signal does become pending (meaning, it has just been delivered) on the process, then the sigwait API sucks in or consumes the signal: it is now no longer pending delivery on the process, and thus cannot be caught via signal handlers set up via the sigaction(2) or signal(3) APIs.)

To test this, we write a small application ch12/sigwt/sigwt.c as well as a shell script ch12/sigwt/bombard.sh to shower all signals upon it. (The reader will find the code within the book's GitHub repository, as always; this time, we leave it as an exercise to the reader to study the source, and experiment with it.) A couple of sample runs follow:

In one Terminal window, we run our sigwt program as follows:

```
$ ./sigwt
Usage: ./sigwt 0|1
 0 => block All signals and sigwait for them
 1 => block all signals except the SIGFPE and SIGSEGV and sigwait
  (further, we setup an async handler for the SIGFPE, not the SIGSEGV)
$ ./sigwt 0
./sigwt: All signals blocked (and only SIGFPE caught w/ sigaction)
[SigBlk: 1 2 3 4 5 6 7 8 10 11 12 13 14 15 16 17 18 20 21 22 23 24 25
26 27 28 29 30 31 34 35 36 37 38 39 40 41 42 43 44 45 46 47 48 49 50
51 52 53 54 55 56 57 58 59 60 61 62 63 64 ]
./sigwt: waiting upon signals now ...
```

Note how we have first blocked all signals (via the `sigprocmask(2)`; we invoke our generic `common.c:show_blocked_signals()` function to display all currently blocked signals in the process signal mask; as expected, all are blocked, with the obvious exception of signal numbers 9, 19, 32, and 33 (why?)). Recall that, once running, the `sigwait(3)` will atomically unblock the signals, allowing them to be delivered upon the caller.

In another Terminal window, run the shell script; the script's job is simple: it sends (via `kill(1)`) every signal—from 1 to 64, except for `SIGKILL` (9), `SIGSTOP` (19), 32, and 33—the two RT signals reserved for use by the pthreads framework:

```
$ ./bombard.sh $(pgrep sigwt) 1
Sending 1 instances each of ALL signals to process 2705
1 2 3 4 5 6 7 8 10 11 12 13 14 15 16 17 18 20 21 22 23 24 25 26 27 28
29 30 31 34 35 36 37 38 39 40 41 42 43 44 45 46 47 48 49 50 51 52 53
54 55 56 57 58 59 60 61 62 63 64
$
```

In the original window, we observe the output:

```
Received signal# 1
Received signal# 2
Received signal# 3
Received signal# 4
Received signal# 5
Received signal# 6
Received signal# 7
Received signal# 8
Received signal# 10
Received signal# 11
[...]
Received signal# 17
Received signal# 18
Received signal# 20
Received signal# 21
[...]
Received signal# 31
Received signal# 34
Received signal# 35
Received signal# 36
Received signal# 37
[...]
Received signal# 64
```

*Signaling - Part II*

All delivered signals were processed via the sigwait! Including the SIGFPE (# 8) and the SIGSEGV (# 11). This is as they were synchronously sent by another process (the shell script) and not by the kernel.

A quick `pkill(1)` kills off the sigwt process (as if one needs reminding: SIGKILL and SIGSTOP cannot be masked):

```
pkill -SIGKILL sigwt
```

Now for the next test case, running it with option 1:

```
$ ./sigwt
Usage: ./sigwt 0|1
 0 => block All signals and sigwait for them
 1 => block all signals except the SIGFPE and SIGSEGV and sigwait
 (further, we setup an async handler for the SIGFPE, not the SIGSEGV)
$ ./sigwt 1
./sigwt: removing SIGFPE and SIGSEGV from the signal mask...
./sigwt: all signals except SIGFPE and SIGSEGV blocked
[SigBlk: 1 2 3 4 5 6 7 10 12 13 14 15 16 17 18 20 21 22 23 24 25 26 27
28 29 30 31 34 35 36 37 38 39 40 41 42 43 44 45 46 47 48 49 50 51 52
53 54 55 56 57 58 59 60 61 62 63 64 ]
./sigwt: waiting upon signals now ...
```

Note how signal numbers 8 (SIGFPE) and 11 (SIGSEGV) are not among the rest that are now blocked (besides the usual suspects, 9, 19, 32, 33). Recall that, once running, the `sigwait(3)` will atomically unblock the signals, allowing them to be delivered upon the caller.

In another Terminal window, run the shell script:

```
$ ./bombard.sh $(pgrep sigwt) 1
Sending 1 instances each of ALL signals to process 13759
1 2 3 4 5 6 7 8 10 11 ./bombard.sh: line 16: kill: (13759) - No such
process
bombard.sh: "kill -12 13759" failed, loop count=1
$
```

In the original window, we observe the output:

```
Received signal# 1
Received signal# 2
Received signal# 3
Received signal# 4
Received signal# 5
Received signal# 6
Received signal# 7
```

[ 476 ]

```
*** siggy: handled SIGFPE (8) ***
Received signal# 10
Segmentation fault (core dumped)
$
```

As we trapped the `SIGFPE` (via `sigaction(2)`), it was handled; however, the uncaught `SIGSEGV` of course causes the process to die abnormally. Not very pleasant at all.

A little tinkering with the code reveals an interesting aspect; the original code snippet is this:

```
[...]
if (atoi(argv[1]) == 1) {
    /* IMP: unblocking signals here removes them from the influence of
     * the sigwait* APIs; this is *required* for correctly handling
     * fatal signals from the kernel.
     */
    printf("%s: removing SIGFPE and SIGSEGV from the signal
mask...\n",         argv[0]);
    sigdelset(&set, SIGFPE);
#if 1
    sigdelset(&set, SIGSEGV);
#endif
[...]
```

What if we effectively block the `SIGSEGV` by changing the preceding `#if 1` to `#if 0`? Let's do so, rebuild, and retry:

```
[...]
Received signal# 1
Received signal# 2
Received signal# 3
Received signal# 4
Received signal# 5
Received signal# 6
Received signal# 7
*** siggy: handled SIGFPE (8) ***
Received signal# 10
Received signal# 11
Received signal# 12
[...]
```

This time the SIGSEGV is processed via the sigwait! Yes, indeed; but only because it was artificially generated by a process, and not sent by the OS.

*Signaling - Part II*

So, as usual, there's more to it: how exactly signal handling happens is determined by the following:

- Whether or not the process blocks the signal prior to calling sigmask (or variants)
- With regard to fatal signals (such as SIGILL, SIGFPE, SIGSEGV, SIGBUS, and so on), how the signal is generated matters: artificially, via just a process (kill(2)) or actually generated via the kernel (due to a bug of some sort)
- We find the following:
    - If the signal is blocked by the process before invoking the sigwait, then, if the signal is delivered artificially via kill(2) (or variants), the sigwait will get unblocked upon delivery of the signal and the application developer can handle the signal.
    - However, if the fatal signal is delivered via the OS due to a bug, then, whether or not the process blocks it, the default action takes place, abruptly (and disgracefully) killing the process! This is probably not what one wants; thus, we conclude that it's better to trap fatal signals like the preceding via the usual asynchronous sigaction(2) style and not via the sigwait (or variants thereof).

## The sigwaitinfo and the sigtimedwait system calls

The sigwaitinfo(2) system call is similar to sigwait: provided with a set of signals to watch out for, the function puts the caller to sleep until any one of those signals (in set) are pending. Here are their prototypes:

```
#include <signal.h>
int sigwaitinfo(const sigset_t *set, siginfo_t *info);
int sigtimedwait(const sigset_t *set, siginfo_t *info,
    const struct timespec *timeout);
```

In terms of a return, the sigwait API was able to provide us with the signal number of the signal that got delivered to the calling process. However, recall that there is a much more powerful feature of the sigaction(2) API—the ability to return valuable diagnostic and other information within the siginfo_t data structure. Well, that's precisely what the sigwaitinfo(2) system call provides! (We covered the siginfo_t structure and what you can interpret from it earlier in the section detailing information with the SA_SIGINFO.)

[ 478 ]

And the `sigtimedwait(2)`? Well, it's quite apparent; it's identical to the `sigwaitinfo(2)` API, except that there is an additional parameter—a timeout value. Hence, the function will block the caller either until one of the signals in set is pending, or the timeout expires (whichever occurs first). The timeout is specified via a simple `timespec` structure, which allows one to provide the time in seconds and nanoseconds:

```
struct timespec {
    long tv_sec; /* seconds */
    long tv_nsec; /* nanoseconds */
}
```

If the structure is memset to zero, the `sigtimedwait(2)` returns immediately, either with information returned about a signal that was pending, or an error value. Both the `sigwaitinfo(2)` and the `sigtimedwait(2)` APIs return the actual signal number on success and `-1` on failure, with `errno` set appropriately.

> **TIP**
> An important point to note (it has been mentioned previously, but it's key): neither the `sigwait`, `sigwaitinfo`, or `sigtimedwait` APIs can wait for synchronously generated signals from the kernel; typically the ones that indicate a failure of some sort, like the `SIGFPE` and the `SIGSEGV`. These can only be caught in the normal asynchronous fashion—via `signal(2)` or `sigaction(2)`. For such cases, as we have repeatedly shown, the `sigaction(2)` system call would be the superior choice.

## The signalfd(2) API

The reader will recall that, in Chapter 1, *Linux System Architecture*, in the section entitled, *The Unix philosophy in a nutshell*, we drove home the point that a cornerstone of the Unix philosophy is this:

On Unix, everything is a process; if it's not a process, it's a file.

Experienced Unix and Linux developers are very used to the idea (abstraction, really) of treating stuff as if it were a file; this includes devices, pipes, and sockets. Why not signals?

*Signaling - Part II*

That's precisely the idea behind the `signalfd(2)` system call; with `signalfd`, you can create a file descriptor and associate it with a signal set. Now, the application programmer is free to monitor signals using a variety of familiar file-based APIs—among them the `read(2)`, `select(2)` and `poll(2)` (and its variations), and the `close(2)`.

Also, similar to the `sigwait*` family of APIs we covered, `signalfd` is another way to have a process (or thread) synchronously block upon signals.

How do you make use of the `signalfd(2)` API? Its signature is as follows:

```
#include <sys/signalfd.h>
int signalfd(int fd, const sigset_t *mask, int flags);
```

The first parameter, `fd`, is either an existing signal descriptor, or the value -1. When -1 is passed, the system call creates a new signal file descriptor (we should obviously call it in this manner at first). The second parameter mask is the signal `mask`—the set of signals that this signal descriptor will be associated with. As before with the sigwait* APIs, one is expected to block these signals (via the `sigprocmask(2)`).

It's important to understand that the `signalfd(2)` system call, by itself, is not a blocking call. The blocking behavior comes into play only on invocation of a file-related API, such as `read(2)`, `select(2)`, or `poll(2)`. Only then is the caller put into a sleep state. The moment one of the signals in the set is delivered to the calling process (or is already pending on it), the file-related API returns.

The third parameter to `signalfd(2)` is a `flags` value—a means to change the default behavior. It's only from Linux kernel version 2.6.27 onwards that the flags work well; the possible values are as follows:

- SFD_NONBLOCK : use non-blocking I/O semantics on the signal descriptor (equivalent to the `fcntl(2)` O_NONBLOCK).
- SFD_CLOEXEC : if the process ever execs another process (via the exec family APIs), ensure that the signal descriptor is closed (this is good for security as otherwise, all the predecessor process' open files are inherited across the exec operation to the successor; equivalent to the `open(2)` FD_CLOEXEC).

In terms of return value, the signalfd(2) API returns the newly created signal descriptor on success; of course, this is if the first parameter was -1. If not, then it should be an already existing signal descriptor; then, this value is returned on success. On failure, as usual, -1 is returned and the errno variable reflects the diagnostic.

Here, we shall limit the discussion of using the signalfd(2) to reading signal information via the familiar read(2) system call; this time, on the signal descriptor returned by the signalfd API.

The way the read(2) works in a nutshell (read(2) was covered in detail in Appendix A, *File I/O Essentials*): we specify a file (in this case, signal) descriptor to read from as the first parameter, the buffer to place the just-read data as the second parameter, and the maximum number of bytes to read as the third parameter:

```
ssize_t read(int fd, void *buf, size_t count);
```

> **TIP**
> These are the common typdefs:
> size_t is essentially an unsigned long (integer)
> ssize_t is essentially a signed long (integer)

The second parameter here is special: a pointer to (one or more) structures of type signalfd_siginfo. The struct signalfd_siginfo is quite analogous to the siginfo_t we saw in some detail in the earlier section, *The siginfo_t structure*. Detailed information regarding the signal that arrived will be populated here.

> We leave it to the interested reader to glean the details of the signalfd_siginfo data structure from the man page on signalfd(2) here: https://linux.die.net/man/2/signalfd. The page also contains a small example program.

The third parameter to read, the size, must in this case be at least sizeof(signalfd_siginfo) bytes.

## Summary

In this chapter, the reader has been taken through some advanced details with regard to signaling: how to handle crashing processes via appropriate fatal signal trapping, and once in the handler, getting key details including CPU registers, and so on. This was done by learning to interpret the powerful `siginfo_t` data structure. Further, handling races when working with the `errno` variable, and learning how to sleep correctly was covered.

Real time signals and their differences from regular Unix signals was covered; then, there was a section regarding the different means of sending signals to other processes. Finally, we looked at signal handling by synchronously blocking upon a given set of signals (using various APIs).

In the next `Chapter 13`, *Timers*, we shall make use of the knowledge we gained here (and in the preceding) `Chapter 11`, *Signaling - Part I*, and learn how to set up and use timers effectively.

# 13
# Timers

Timers give us the ability to set up an artifact where the OS lets us know once the specified time has expired—is a ubiquitous application (and, indeed, kernel) feature. Of course, the timer is usually only useful if it is running in parallel with the application logic; this asynchronous notification behavior is achieved by different means, very often by having the kernel send the relevant process a signal.

In this chapter, we shall explore the available interfaces on Linux for setting up and working with timers. These interfaces fall into two broad categories—the older APIs (`alarm(2)`, `[get|set]itimer(2)`), and the shiny, newer POSIX APIs (`timer_create(2)`, `timer_[set|get]time(2)`, and so on). Of course, as signals are quite heavily employed along with timers, we make use of the signal interfaces as well.

We would also like to point out that, due to the intrinsic dynamic nature of timers, statically seeing the output of our sample programs in the book will not suffice; as usual, we definitely urge the reader to clone the book's GitHub repository and try out the code themselves.

In this chapter, the reader will learn to use the various timer interfaces (APIs) exposed by the Linux kernel. We begin with the older ones, which, though they have limitations are still very much used in system software, as the need arises. A simple **command-line interface** (**CLI**)- only digital clock program is written and analyzed using these APIs. Then we move the reader on to the more recent and powerful POSIX Timer API set. Two very interesting sample programs—a "how quickly can you react" game and a run-walk interval timer application—are shown and studied. We close with a brief mention of using timer APIs via the file abstraction, and what a watchdog timer is.

# Older interfaces

As previously mentioned, the older interfaces include the following:

- The `alarm(2)` system call
- The interval timer `[get|set]itimer(2)` system call APIs

Let's begin with the first of them.

## The good ol' alarm clock

The `alarm(2)` system call allows a process to set up a simple timeout mechanism; its signature is as follows:

```
#include <unistd.h>
unsigned int alarm(unsigned int seconds);
```

It is, indeed, quite self-explanatory. Let's take a simple example: A process wants to set up a timer that will expire in three seconds from now, so `alarm(3)` is essentially the code to use to do this.

What exactly happens in the aforementioned code? Three seconds after the alarm system call is issued—that is, after the timer has been armed—the kernel will send the signal `SIGALRM` to the process.

> The default action of `SIGALRM` (signal # 14 on x86) is to terminate the process.

Thus, we expect the developer to catch the signal (via the `sigaction(2)` system call would be best, as discussed in depth in the preceding `Chapter 11`, *Signaling - Part I*, and `Chapter 12`, *Signaling - II* ).

If the parameter input to alarm is 0, any pending `alarm(2)` will be canceled (Actually, this will happen in any case when the alarm API is invoked.)

Notice that the alarm API, unusually for a system call, returns an unsigned integer (thus -1 cannot be returned, which is the usual failure case). Instead, it returns the number of seconds to any previous programmed timeout, or zero if none was pending.

A simple program (ch13/alarm1.c) demonstrating the basic usage of alarm(2) follows; the parameter specifies the number of seconds to time out in.

> For readability, only the key parts of the source code are displayed in the following; to view the complete source code, build it, and run it, the entire tree is available for cloning from GitHub here: https://github.com/PacktPublishing/Hands-on-System-Programming-with-Linux.

The signal trapping and timer arming code is shown as follows:

```
[...]
/* Init sigaction to defaults via the memset,
 * setup 'sig_handler' as the signal handler function,
 * trap just the SIGALRM signal.
 */
memset(&act, 0, sizeof(act));
act.sa_handler = sig_handler;
if (sigaction(SIGALRM, &act, 0) < 0)
    FATAL("sigaction on SIGALRM failed");

alarm(n);
printf("A timeout for %ds has been armed...\n", n);
pause(); /* wait for the signal ... */
```

What happens once the SIGALRM signal is dispatched to the process by the kernel; that is, once the timer times out? The signal handler runs, of course. Here it is:

```
static void sig_handler(int signum)
{
    const char *str = " *** Timeout! [SIGALRM received] ***\n";
    if (signum != SIGALRM)
        return;
    if (write(STDOUT_FILENO, str, strlen(str)) < 0)
        WARN("write str failed!");
}
```

Here's a quick build and test run:

```
$ make alarm1
gcc -Wall -UDEBUG -c ../common.c -o common.o
gcc -Wall -UDEBUG -c alarm1.c -o alarm1.o
gcc -Wall -UDEBUG -o alarm1 alarm1.o common.o
$ ./alarm1
Usage: ./alarm1 seconds-to-timeout(>0)
$ ./alarm1 3
A timeout for 3s has been armed...
    *** Timeout! [SIGALRM received] ***         << 3 seconds later!
>>
$
```

We now enhance the previous code (ch13/alarm1.c) to have the timeout continually repeat (the source file is ch13/alarm2_rep.c); the relevant code snippet (which has changed from the previous code) is as follows:

```
[...]
alarm(n);
printf("A timeout for %ds has been armed...\n", n);
/* (Manually) re-invoke the alarm every 'n' seconds */
while (1) {
    pause(); /* wait for the signal ... */
    alarm(n);
    printf(" Timeout for %ds has been (re)armed...\n", n);
}
[...]
```

Though it does not apply here, realize that calling alarm(2) automatically cancels any previously pending timeout. A quick trial run is as follows:

```
$ ./alarm2_rep 1
A timeout for 1s has been armed...
 *** Timeout! [SIGALRM received] ***
 Timeout for 1s has been (re)armed...
 *** Timeout! [SIGALRM received] ***
 Timeout for 1s has been (re)armed...
 *** Timeout! [SIGALRM received] ***
 Timeout for 1s has been (re)armed...
 *** Timeout! [SIGALRM received] ***
 Timeout for 1s has been (re)armed...
^C
$
```

The alarm now repeats (every second in the above example run). Also notice how we just kill the process with a keyboard *Ctrl + C* (delivering the `SIGINT`, which, as we haven't trapped it, just terminates the foreground process.

## Alarm API – the downer

Now that we have looked at using the (simplistic) `alarm(2)` API, it's important to realize that it has several downsides:

- A very coarse granularity timeout (a minimum of one second, which is a very long time on a modern processor!)
- Running more than a single timeout in parallel is not possible
- It's not possible to query or modify the timeout value at a later point—attempting to do so will cancel it
- Mixing the following APIs can result in problems/conflicts (in the following, the latter API may be internally implemented using the former)
    - `alarm(2)` and `setitimer(2)`
    - `alarm(2)` and `sleep(3)`
- It's always possible that the timeout occurs later than expected (overrun)

As we progress through this chapter, we will find more powerful functions that can overcome most of these issues. (Well, to be fair, the poor `alarm(2)` does have an upside: for simplistic purposes, it's really quick and easy to use!)

## Interval timers

The interval timer APIs allow a process to set up and query a timer that can be programmed to auto-recur at a fixed time interval. The relevant system calls are these:

```
#include <sys/time.h>
int getitimer(int which, struct itimerval *curr_value);
int setitimer(int which, const struct itimerval *new_value,
              struct itimerval *old_value);
```

Quite obviously, the `setitimer(2)` is used to set up a new timer; the `getitimer(2)` can be used to query it, and returns the time remaining.

The first parameter to both is `which`—it specifies the type of timer to use. Linux allows us to use three types of interval timer:

- `ITIMER_REAL`: Use this timer type to count down in real-time, which is also called wall clock time. Upon timer expiry, the kernel sends the signal `SIGALRM` to the calling process.
- `ITIMER_VIRTUAL`: Use this timer type to count down in virtual time; that is, the timer only counts down when the calling process (all threads) is running in user space on the CPU. Upon timer expiry, the kernel sends the signal `SIGVTALRM` to the calling process.
- `ITIMER_PROF`: Use this timer type to count down in virtual time too; this time, the timer counts down when the calling process (all threads) is running in both user-space and/or kernel space on the CPU. Upon timer expiry, the kernel sends the signal `SIGPROF` to the calling process.

Thus, to have a timer that should expire when a certain amount of time has expired, use the first one; one can use the remaining two types to profile a process's CPU usage. Only one timer of each of the preceding types can be used at a time (more on this is to follow).

The next parameter to examine is the `itimerval` data structure (and its internal `timeval` structure members; both are defined in the `time.h` header):

```
struct itimerval {
    struct timeval it_interval;    /* Interval for periodic timer */
    struct timeval it_value;       /* Time until next expiration */
};

struct timeval {
    time_t      tv_sec;            /* seconds */
    suseconds_t tv_usec;           /* microseconds */
};
```

(FYI, both the internal `time_t` and the `suseconds_t` typedefs translate to a long (integer) value.)

As we can see, this—the second parameter to setitimer(2), which is a pointer to struct itimerval called new_value—is where we specify the new timer's expiration times, such as:

- In the it_value structure member, place the initial timeout value. This value decreases as the timer runs down, and, at some point, will hit zero; at this point, the appropriate signal corresponding to the timer type will be delivered to the calling process.
- Subsequent to the previous step, the it_interval structure member is checked. If it is non-zero, this value will be copied into the it_value structure, causing the timer to effectively auto-reset and run again for that amount of time; in other words, this is how the API fulfills the interval timer role.

Also, clearly, the time expiry is expressed in seconds:microseconds.

For example, if we wanted a repeating (interval) timeout every second, we need to initialize the structures as follows:

```
struct itimerval mytimer;
memset(&mytimer, 0, sizeof(struct itimerval));
mytimer.it_value.tv_sec = 1;
mytimer.it_interval.tv_sec = 1;
setitimer(ITIMER_REAL, &mytimer, 0);
```

(Error checking code is not shown in the previous code for clarity.) Precisely this is done in the simple digital clock demo program that follows.

A few special cases exist:

- To cancel (or disarm) a timer, set both fields of the it_timer structure to zero and invoke the setitimer(2) API.
- To create a single-shot timer—that is, one that expires exactly once—initialize both fields of the it_interval structure to zero, and then invoke the setitimer(2) API.
- If the third parameter to setitimer(2) is non-NULL, the previous timer value is returned here (as if the getitmer(2) API were invoked).

As is usual, the pair of system calls returns 0 on success and -1 on failure (with errno set appropriately).

As there is one signal generated upon expiry of each type of timer, one can only have one instance of each timer type running concurrently within a given process. If we try and set up multiple timers of the same type (for example, ITIMER_REAL), it's always possible that multiple instances of the same signal (in this example, SIGALRM) will be delivered to the process—and to the same handler routine—simultaneously. As we learned in Chapter 11, *Signaling - Part I*, and Chapter 12, *Signaling - Part II*, regular Unix signals cannot be queued, and signal instances might thus be dropped. In effect, it is best (and safest) to work concurrently with one of each type of timer in a given process.

The following table contrasts the simple alarm(2) system call API that we saw earlier with the more powerful [set|get]itimer(2) interval timer APIs that we have just seen:

| Feature | Simple timer [alarm(2)] | Interval timers [setitimer(2), getitimer(2)] |
|---|---|---|
| Granularity (resolution) | Very coarse; 1 second | Fine granularity; in theory, 1 microsecond (in practice, typically milliseconds prior to 2.6.16 HRT[1]) |
| Query time remaining | Not possible | Yes, with getitimer(2) |
| Modify timeout | Not possible | Yes |
| Cancel timeout | Yes | Yes |
| Auto-repeating | No, but it can be set up manually | Yes |
| Multiple timers | Not possible | Yes, but at most three—one of each type (real, virtual, and profiling)—per process |

Table 1 : A quick comparison of the simple alarm(2) API and interval timers

**[1] High-resolution timers (HRT)**; implemented in Linux 2.6.16 onward. See a link to a detailed paper on this in the *Further reading* section on the GitHub repository.

What is knowledge without application? Let's try out the interval timer API.

# A simple CLI digital clock

We humans are quite used to seeing a clock tick away, one second at a time. Why not write a quick C program that mimics a (very simplistic command-line) digital clock that must show us the correct date and time every single second! (Well, personally, I prefer seeing the old-fashioned analog clocks, but, hey, this book does not go into the closely held secret mantras to perform graphical drawing with X11.)

How we achieve this is quite simple, really: we set up an interval timer that times out every one second. The program (ch13/intv_clksimple.c) which demonstrates the basic usage of the quite powerful setitimer(2) API follows.

> For readability, only key parts of the source code are displayed in the following; to view the complete source code, build it, and run it, the entire tree is available for cloning from GitHub here: https://github.com/PacktPublishing/Hands-on-System-Programming-with-Linux.

The signal trapping and set up of the single-second interval timer is shown as follows:

```
static volatile sig_atomic_t opt;
[...]
int main(int argc, char **argv)
{
    struct sigaction act;
    struct itimerval mytimer;
[...]
    memset(&act, 0, sizeof(act));
    act.sa_handler = ticktock;
    sigfillset(&act.sa_mask); /* disallow all signals while handling */
    /*
     * We deliberately do *not* use the SA_RESTART flag;
     * if we do so, it's possible that any blocking syscall gets
     * auto-restarted. In a timeout context, we don't want that
     * to happen - we *expect* a signal to interrupt our blocking
     * syscall (in this case, the pause(2)).
     * act.sa_flags = SA_RESTART;
     */
    if (sigaction(SIGALRM, &act, 0) < 0)
        FATAL("sigaction on SIGALRM failed");
    /* Setup a single second (repeating) interval timer */
    memset(&mytimer, 0, sizeof(struct itimerval));
    mytimer.it_value.tv_sec = 1;
    mytimer.it_interval.tv_sec = 1;
    if (setitimer(ITIMER_REAL, &mytimer, 0) < 0)
```

```
            FATAL("setitimer failed\n");
    while (1)
        (void)pause();
```

Notice the self-explanatory comment on why we typically do not use the SA_RESTART flag when working with signals that deliver timeouts.

Setting up the interval timer is easy: we initialize the itimerval structure such that we set the seconds members—of the internal timeval structures—to 1 (we just leave the microseconds as zero), and issue the setitimer(2) system call. The timer is armed—it starts counting down. When a second has elapsed, the kernel will deliver the signal SIGALRM to the process (as the timer type is ITIMER_REAL). The signal handler routine ticktock will perform the task of obtaining and printing out the current timestamp (see its code as follows). The interval component being set to 1, the timer will automatically and repeatedly fire every single second.

```
    static void ticktock(int signum)
    {
        char tmstamp[128];
        struct timespec tm;
        int myerrno = errno;

        /* Query the timestamp ; both clock_gettime(2) and
         * ctime_r(3) are reentrant-and-signal-safe */
        if (clock_gettime(CLOCK_REALTIME, &tm) < 0)
            FATAL("clock_gettime failed\n");
        if (ctime_r(&tm.tv_sec, &tmstamp[0]) == NULL)
            FATAL("ctime_r failed\n");

        if (opt == 0) {
            if (write(STDOUT_FILENO, tmstamp, strlen(tmstamp)) < 0)
                FATAL("write failed\n");
        } else if (opt == 1) {
          /* WARNING! Using the printf / fflush here in a signal handler
is         * unsafe! We do so for the purposes of this demo app only; do
not
           * use in production.
           */
            tmstamp[strlen(tmstamp) - 1] = '\0';
            printf("\r%s", tmstamp);
            fflush(stdout);
        }
        errno = myerrno;
    }
```

The previous signal handler routine gets invoked once a second, every second (as, of course, the kernel delivers the signal SIGALRM to the process upon timer expiry). The job of this routine is clear: it must query and print the current date-time; that is, the timestamp.

## Obtaining the current time

Querying the current time is, at first glance, straightforward. Many programmers use the following API sequence to achieve it:

```
time(2)
localtime(3)
strftime(3)
```

We do not. Why is this? Recall our discussion on the async-signal-safe (reentrant) functions in the first of Chapters 11, *Signaling - Part I*, (within the section *Reentrant Safety and Signaling*). Of the aforementioned three APIs, only the time(2) API is considered signal-safe; the other two are not (that is, they should not be used within a signal handler). The relevant man page (signal-safety(7)) confirms this.

Hence, we use documented async-signal-safe APIs-the time(2), clock_gettime(2) and ctime_r(3)—to perform the role of obtaining the timestamp safely. A quick peek at them follows.

The clock_gettime(2) system call's signature is this:

```
int clock_gettime(clockid_t clk_id, struct timespec *tp);
```

The first parameter is the clock source or clock type to use; the fact is that the Linux OS (and glibc) supports many different built-in types of clocks; among them are the following:

- CLOCK_REALTIME: A system-wide wall-clock clock (in real-time); use this to query the timestamp.
- CLOCK_MONOTONIC: Monotonic clocks count in one direction (up, obviously; travelling backwards through time is a feature still being worked upon by mad (or are they?) scientists). It usually counts the time elapsed since the system boot.
- CLOCK_BOOTTIME (from Linux 2.6.39): This is pretty much the same as CLOCK_MONOTONIC, except that it takes into account time the system has been suspended.

- CLOCK_PROCESS_CPUTIME_ID: A measure of CPU time spent on CPU by all threads of a given process (via PID; use the clock_getcpuclockid(3) API to query it).
- CLOCK_THREAD_CPUTIME_ID: A measure of CPU time spent on CPU by a specific thread (use the pthread_getcpuclockid(3) API to query it).

There are more; please refer the man page on clock_gettime(2) for details. For our current purposes, CLOCK_REALTIME is the one we will go with.

The second parameter to clock_gettime(2) is a value-result style one; in effect, this is a return value. Upon a successful return, it will hold the timestamp in the timeval structure; the structure is defined in the time.h header, and holds the current timestamp in seconds and nanoseconds:

```
struct timespec {
    time_t tv_sec;  /* seconds */
    long tv_nsec;   /* nanoseconds */
};
```

We shall be quite satisfied with the value in seconds.

But how exactly is this value in seconds and nanoseconds interpreted? It's actually very common in the Unix universe: Unix systems store time as the number of seconds elapsed since January 1, 1970 midnight (00:00)—think of it as Unix's birth! This time value is called time since the Epoch or Unix time. Okay, so it's going to be a rather large number of seconds today, right? So how does one express it in a human-readable format? We're glad you asked, as that's precisely the job of the ctime_r(3) API:

```
char *ctime_r(const time_t *timep, char *buf);
```

The first parameter will be (a pointer to) the time_t member we got returned from the clock_gettime(2) API; again, the second parameter is a value result-style return—on successful completion, it will hold the human-readable timestamp! Note that it's the application programmer's job to allocate memory for the buffer buf (and subsequently free it as required). In our code, we just use a statically allocated local buffer. (Of course, we perform error checking on all APIs.)

Finally, depending on the opt value (passed by the user), we either use the (safe) write(2) system call or the (unsafe!) printf(3)/fflush(3) APIs to print out the current time.

> **TIP**
> The code `printf("\r%s", tmstamp);` has the `printf(3)` using the `\r` format—this is the carriage return, which effectively brings the cursor back to the beginning of the same line. This gives the appearance of a clock constantly updating. This is nice, except for the fact that using `printf(3)` itself is signal-unsafe!

## Trial runs

Here is a trial run, first with the signal-safe `write(2)` method:

```
$ ./intv_clksimple
Usage: ./intv_clksimple {0|1}
 0 : the Correct way (using write(2) in the signal handler)
 1 : the *Wrong* way (using printf(3) in the signal handler) *@your
risk*
$ ./intv_clksimple 0
Thu Jun 28 17:52:38 2018
Thu Jun 28 17:52:39 2018
Thu Jun 28 17:52:40 2018
Thu Jun 28 17:52:41 2018
Thu Jun 28 17:52:42 2018
^C
$
```

And now, here's one with the signal-unsafe `printf(3)`/`fflush(3)` method:

```
$ ./intv_clksimple 1
 *WARNING* [Using printf in signal handler]
Thu Jun 28 17:54:53 2018^C
$
```

It looks nicer, what with the timestamp being continually refreshed on the same line, but is unsafe. This book cannot show you, dear reader, the pleasant effect of the carriage return- style `printf("\r...")`. Do try it out on your Linux system to see this for yourself.

We understand that using the `printf(3)` and `fflush(3)` APIs within a signal handler is bad programming practice—they are not async-signal safe.

But what if the low-level design specification demands that we use exactly these APIs? Well, there's always a way: why not redesign the program to use one of the synchronous blocking APIs to wait upon and catch signal(s) wherever appropriate (Remember, when trapping fatal signals such as `SIGILL`, `SIGFPE`, `SIGSEGV`, and `SIGBUS`, it's recommended to use the usual async `sigaction(2)` API): the `sigwait(3)`, `sigwaitinfo(2)`, `sigtimedwait(2)` or even the `signalfd(2)` API (that we covered in Chapter 12, *Signaling - Part II*, section *Synchronously blocking for signals via the sigwait\* APIs*). We leave this as an exercise for the reader.

## A word on using the profiling timers

We have explored, in some detail, the usage of the `ITIMER_REAL` timer type—which counts down in real-time. What about using the other two—the `ITIMER_VIRTUAL` and `ITIMER_PROF`—timers? Well, the code styling is very similar; there's nothing new there. The catch that a developer who is new to this faces is this: the signal(s) may never seem to arrive at all!

Let's take a simple code snippet using the `ITIMER_VIRTUAL` timer:

```
static void profalrm(int signum)
{
    /* In production, do Not use signal-unsafe APIs like this! */
    printf("In %s:%d sig=%d\n", __func__, __LINE__, signum);
}

[...]

// in main() ...

struct sigaction act;
struct itimerval t1;

memset(&act, 0, sizeof(act));
act.sa_handler = profalrm;
sigfillset(&act.sa_mask); /* disallow all signals while handling */
if (sigaction(SIGPROF, &act, 0) < 0)
    FATAL("sigaction on SIGALRM failed");
```

```
[...]
memset(&t1, 0, sizeof(struct itimerval));
t1.it_value.tv_sec = 1;
t1.it_interval.tv_sec = 1;
if (setitimer(ITIMER_PROF, &t1, 0) < 0)
    FATAL("setitimer failed\n");

while (1)
    (void)pause();
```

When run, no output appears—the timer is seemingly not working.

That's really not the case—it is working, but the catch is this: the process merely sleeps via the pause(2). While sleeping, its not running on CPU; hence, the kernel has hardly decremented the (aforementioned, second-by-second) interval timer at all! Remember, both the ITIMER_VIRTUAL and ITIMER_PROF timers only decrement (or count down), when the process is on CPU. Thus, the one-second timer never actually expires, and the SIGPROF signal is never sent.

So, now, the way to solve the previous issue becomes obvious: let's introduce some CPU processing into the program and reduce the timeout value. Our trusty DELAY_LOOP_SILENT macro (see source file common.h) has the process spin over some silly logic—the point being that it becomes CPU-intensive. Also, we have reduced the timer expiry to be expire for every 10 ms the process spends on the CPU:

```
[...]
memset(&t1, 0, sizeof(struct itimerval));
t1.it_value.tv_sec = 0;
t1.it_value.tv_usec = 10000;         // 10,000 us = 10 ms
t1.it_interval.tv_sec = 0;
t1.it_interval.tv_usec = 10000;      // 10,000 us = 10 ms
if (setitimer(ITIMER_PROF, &t1, 0) < 0)
    FATAL("setitimer failed\n");

while (1) {
    DELAY_LOOP_SILENT(20);
    (void)pause();
}
```

This time, upon running, we see this:

```
In profalrm:34 sig=27
In profalrm:34 sig=27
In profalrm:34 sig=27
In profalrm:34 sig=27
In profalrm:34 sig=27
...
```

The profiling timer is indeed working.

# The newer POSIX (interval) timers mechanism

Earlier in this chapter, we saw in *Table 1 : A quick comparison of the simple alarm(2) API and interval timers*, that, although the interval timer `[get|set]itimer(2)` APIs are superior to the simplistic `alarm(2)` API, they still lack important modern features. The modern POSIX (interval) timer mechanism addresses several shortcomings, some of which are as follows:

- The resolution is improved a thousand-fold with the addition of nanosecond granularity timers (with the addition of an arch-independent HRT mechanism, which is integrated into 2.6.16 Linux kernel onward).
- A generic `sigevent(7)` mechanism—which is a way to handle asynchronous events such as timer expiry (our use case), AIO request completion, delivery of a message, and so on—to handle timer expiry. We are now not forced to tie timer expiry to the signaling mechanism.
- Importantly, a process (or thread) can now set up and manage any number of timers.
- Well, ultimately, there's always an upper limit: in this case, it's the resource limit `RLIMIT_SIGPENDING`. (More technically, the fact is that the OS allocates a queued real-time signal for every timer created, which is thus the limit.)

These points are fleshed out as follows, so read on.

# Typical application workflow

The design approach (and APIs used) to set up and use a modern POSIX timer follows; the sequence is typically in the order shown here:

- Signal(s) setup.
    - Assuming the notification mechanism being used is a signal, first trap the signal(s) via `sigaction(2)`.
- Create and initialize the timer(s).
    - Decide on the clock type (or source) to use to measure the elapsed time.
    - Decide on the timer-expiry event-notification mechanism to be used by your application—typically, whether to use (the usual) signals or a (newly spawned) thread.
    - The aforementioned decisions are implemented via the `timer_create(2)` system call; thereby it allows one to create a timer, and, of course, we can create multiple timers by invoking it multiple times.
- Arm (or disarm) a particular timer using `timer_settime(2)`. To arm a timer means to effectively start it running—counting down; disarming a timer is the opposite—stopping it in its tracks.
- To query the time remaining (to expiration) in a particular timer (and its interval setting) use `timer_gettime(2)`.
- Check the overrun count of a given timer using `timer_getoverrun(2)`.
- Delete (and obviously disarm) a timer using `timer_delete(2)`.

## Creating and using a POSIX (interval) timer

As seen previously, we use the powerful `timer_create(2)` system call to create a timer for the calling process (or thread, for that matter):

```
#include <signal.h>
#include <time.h>
int timer_create(clockid_t clockid, struct sigevent *sevp,
            timer_t *timerid);
Link with -lrt.
```

## Timers

> We have to link with the **real time** (**rt**) library to make use of this API. The `librt` library implements the POSIX.1b Realtime Extensions to POSIX interfaces. Find a link to the `librt` man page in the *Further Reading* section on the GitHub repository.

The first parameter passed to `timer_create(2)` informs the OS of the clock source to be used; we avoid repetition of the matter and refer the reader to the section *Obtaining the current time* covered earlier in the chapter, in which we enumerated several of the commonly used clock sources in Linux. (Also, as noted there, one can refer to the man page on `clock_gettime(2)` for additional details.)

The second parameter passed to `timer_create(2)` is interesting: it provides a generic way to specify the timer-expiry event-notification mechanism to be used by your application! To understand this, let's take a look at the `sigevent` structure:

```
#include <signal.h>

union sigval {       /* Data passed with notification */
    int sival_int;       /* Integer value */
    void *sival_ptr;     /* Pointer value */
};

struct sigevent {
    int sigev_notify;          /* Notification method */
    int sigev_signo;           /* Notification signal */
    union sigval sigev_value;  /* Data passed with notification */
    void (*sigev_notify_function) (union sigval);
    /* Function used for thread notification (SIGEV_THREAD) */
    void *sigev_notify_attributes; /* Attributes for notification
    thread(SIGEV_THREAD) */
    pid_t sigev_notify_thread_id;
         /* ID of thread to signal (SIGEV_THREAD_ID) */
};
```

(Recall that we have already come across and used the `union sigval` mechanism to pass along a value to a signal handler in Chapter 11, *Signaling - Part I*, and Chapter 12, *Signaling - Part II*.)

Valid values for the `sigev_notify` member are enumerated in the following:

| Notification method<br>`:sigevent.sigev_notify` | Meaning |
| --- | --- |
| SIGEV_NONE | Nothing done upon event arrival—a null notification |
| SIGEV_SIGNAL | Notification by sending the process the signal specified in the `sigev_signo` member |
| SIGEV_THREAD | Notification by invoking (actually, spawning) a (new) thread whose function is `sigev_notify_function`, the parameter passed to it is `sigev_value`, and if `sigev_notify_attributes` is non-NULL it should be a `pthread_attr_t` structure for the new thread. (Readers, note that we shall cover multithreading in detail in subsequent chapters.) |
| SIGEV_THREAD_ID | Linux-specific and used to specify a kernel thread that will run upon timer expiry; realistically, only threading libraries make use of this functionality. |

Table 2 : Using the sigevent(7) mechanism

In the first case, SIGEV_NONE, the timer can always be manually checked for expiry via the `timer_gettime(2)` API.

The more interesting and common case is the second one, SIGEV_SIGNAL. Here, a signal is delivered to the process whose timer has expired; the process's `sigaction(2)` handler's `siginfo_t` data structure is populated appropriately; for our use case—that of using a POSIX timer—this is as follows:

- `si_code` (or signal origin field) is set to the value SI_TIMER to denote that a POSIX timer has expired (look up the other possibilities within the man page on `sigaction`)
- `si_signo` is set to the signal number (`sigev_signo`)
- `si_value` will be the value set in the union `sigev_value`

For our purposes (in this chapter, at least), we shall only consider the case of setting the `sigevent` notification type to the value SIGEV_SIGNAL (and thus setting the signal to deliver in the `sigev_signo` member).

# Timers

The third parameter passed to `timer_create(2)`, `timer_t *timerid`, is a (now common) value result-style one; it is, in effect, the return ID of the newly created POSIX timer! Of course, the system call returns -1 on failure (and `errno` is set accordingly), and 0 on success. The `timerid` is the handle to the timer—we shall typically pass it as a parameter in the subsequent POSIX timer APIs to specify a particular timer to act upon.

## The arms race – arming and disarming a POSIX timer

As mentioned previously, we use the `timer_settime(2)` system call to either arm (start) or disarm (stop) a timer:

```
#include <time.h>
int timer_settime(timer_t timerid, int flags,
                  const struct itimerspec *new_value,
                  struct itimerspec *old_value);
Link with -lrt.
```

As one can have multiple concurrent POSIX timers running simultaneously, thus we need to specify exactly which timer we are referring to; this is done via the first parameter `timer_id`, which is the timer's ID, and the effective return of the previously seen `timer_create(2)` system call.

The important data structure employed here is the `itimerspec`; its definition is as follows:

```
struct timespec {
    time_t tv_sec;   /* Seconds */
    long   tv_nsec;  /* Nanoseconds */
};

struct itimerspec {
    struct timespec it_interval; /* Timer interval */
    struct timespec it_value;    /* Initial expiration */
};
```

[ 502 ]

So, it should be quite clear: within the third parameter, a pointer to
the `itimerspec` structure called, `new_value`:

- We can specify the time to the (theoretical) resolution to a single nanosecond! Note that the time is measured with respect to the clock source that was specified by the `timer_create(2)` API.
  - This reminds us, one can always query the clock resolution with the `clock_getres(2)` API.
- With respect to initializing the `it_value` (`timespec` structure):
  - Set it to a non-zero value to specify the initial timer-expiry value.
  - Set it to zero to specify that we are disarming (stopping) the timer.
  - What if this structure is holding a positive value already? Then it's overwritten, and the timer is re-armed with the new values.
- Not only that, but, by initializing the `it_interval` (`timespec` structure) to a non-zero value, we will set up a repeating - interval - timer (hence the name POSIX interval timer); the time interval being the value it is initialized to. The timer will continue to fire indefinitely, or until it's disarmed or deleted. If, instead, this structure is zeroed out, the timer becomes a one-shot timer (firing just once when the time specified in the it_value member elapses).

In general, set the `flags` value to 0—the man page on `timer_settime(2)` specifies an additional flag that could be used. Finally, the fourth parameter `old_value` (again, a pointer to struct `itimerspec`) works as follows:

- If 0, it is simply ignored.
- If non-zero, it is a means to query the time remaining to the expiry of the given timer.
- The time to expiry will be returned in the `old_value->it_value` member (in seconds and nanoseconds), and the interval it was set will be returned in the `old_value->it_interval` member.

As expected, the return value on success is 0 and is -1 on failure (with `errno` being set appropriately).

## Querying the timer

A given POSIX timer can be queried at any point to fetch the time remaining to timer expiry via the `timer_gettime(2)` system call API; its signature is as follows:

```
#include <time.h>
int timer_gettime(timer_t timerid, struct itimerspec *curr_value);
```

Quite obviously, the first parameter passed to `timer_gettime(2)` is the ID of the particular timer to query, and the second parameter passed is the value result-style return—the time to expiry is returned in it (within the structure of type `itimerspec`).

As we know from preceding, the struct `itimerval` itself consists of two data structures of type `timespec`; the time remaining to timer expiry will be placed in the `curr_value->it_value` member. If this value is 0, it implies that the timer has been stopped (disarmed). If the value placed in the `curr_value->it_interval` member is positive, it indicates the interval at which the timer will repeatedly fire (after the first timeout); if 0, it implies the timer is a single-shot one (with no repeating timeouts).

## Example code snippet showing the workflow

In the following, we display code snippets from our sample program `ch13/react.c` (see more on this rather interesting reaction time game app in the following section), which clearly illustrates the sequence of steps previously described.

- Signal(s) set up:
    - Assuming the notification mechanism being used is a signal, first trap the signal(s) via `sigaction(2)` as follows:

```
struct sigaction act;
[...]
// Trap SIGRTMIN : delivered on (interval) timer expiry
memset(&act, 0, sizeof(act));
act.sa_flags = SA_SIGINFO | SA_RESTART;
act.sa_sigaction = timer_handler;
if (sigaction(SIGRTMIN, &act, NULL) == -1)
    FATAL("sigaction SIGRTMIN failed\n");
```

- Create and initialize the timer(s):
    - Decide on the clock type (or source) to use to measure the elapsed time:
        - We use the real-time clock CLOCK_REALTIME the system-wide wall clock time, as our timer source.
    - Decide on the timer-expiry event-notification mechanism to be used by your application—typically, whether to use (the usual) signals or a (newly spawned) thread.
        - We use signaling as the timer-expiry event-notification mechanism.
    - The aforementioned decisions are implemented via the timer_create(2) system call, which allows one to create a timer; of course, we can create multiple timers by invoking it multiple times:

```
struct sigevent sev;
[...]
/* Create and init the timer */
sev.sigev_notify = SIGEV_SIGNAL;
sev.sigev_signo = SIGRTMIN;
sev.sigev_value.sival_ptr = &timerid;
if (timer_create(CLOCK_REALTIME, &sev, &timerid) == -1)
    FATAL("timer_create failed\n");
```

- Arm (or disarm) a particular timer using the timer_settime(2) API. To arm a timer means to effectively start it running, or counting down; disarming a timer is the opposite—stopping it in its tracks:

```
static struct itimerspec itv;    // global
[...]
static void arm_timer(timer_t tmrid, struct itimerspec *itmspec)
{
    VPRINT("Arming timer now\n");
    if (timer_settime(tmrid, 0, itmspec, NULL) == -1)
        FATAL("timer_settime failed\n");
    jumped_the_gun = 0;
}
[...]
printf("Initializing timer to generate SIGRTMIN every %ld ms\n",
 freq_ms);
memset(&itv, 0, sizeof(struct itimerspec));
itv.it_value.tv_sec = (freq_ms * 1000000) / 1000000000;
```

# Timers

```
        itv.it_value.tv_nsec = (freq_ms * 1000000) % 1000000000;
        itv.it_interval.tv_sec = (freq_ms * 1000000) / 1000000000;
        itv.it_interval.tv_nsec = (freq_ms * 1000000) % 1000000000;
        [...]
        arm_timer(timerid, &itv);
```

- To query the time remaining (to expiration) in a particular timer (and its interval setting), use `timer_gettime(2)`

This is not performed in this particular application.

- Check the overrun count of a given timer using `timer_getoverrun(2)`

An explanation of what this API does, and why we might need it, is provided in the following section, *Figuring the overrun*.

```
    /*
     * The realtime signal (SIGRTMIN) - timer expiry - handler.
     * WARNING! Using the printf in a signal handler is unsafe!
     * We do so for the purposes of this demo app only; do Not
     * use in production.
     */
    static void timer_handler(int sig, siginfo_t * si, void *uc)
    {
      char buf[] = ".";

      c++;
      if (verbose) {
          write(2, buf, 1);
    #define SHOW_OVERRUN 1
    #if (SHOW_OVERRUN == 1)
          {
              int ovrun = timer_getoverrun(timerid);
              if (ovrun == -1)
                  WARN("timer_getoverrun");
              else {
                  if (ovrun)
                      printf(" overrun=%d [@count=%d]\n", ovrun, c);
              }
          }
    #endif
      }
    }
```

[ 506 ]

- Delete (and obviously disarm) a timer using `timer_delete(2)`

This is not performed in this particular application (as the process exit will, of course, delete all timers associated with the process.)

As the man page on `timer_create(2)` informs us, a few more points to note on POSIX (interval) timers are as follows:

- Upon `fork(2)`, all timers get auto-disarmed; in other words, timers are not going to continue towards expiry in the child process.
- Upon `execve(2)`, all timers are deleted and will thus not be visible in the successor process.
- Something useful of note is that (from the Linux 3.10 kernel onward) the proc filesystem can be used to query the timer(s) a process owns; just lookup cat the pseudo-`file` `/proc/<pid>/timers` to see them (if they exist).
- From the Linux 4.10 kernel onward, POSIX timers are a kernel-configurable option (at kernel build time, they are enabled by default).

As we have repeatedly mentioned, the man pages are a very precious and useful resource that is available to developers; again, the man page on `timer_create(2)` (https://linux.die.net/man/2/timer_create) provides a nice example program; we urge the reader to refer to the man page, read it, build it and try the program out.

## Figuring the overrun

Let's say we use signaling as the event-notification mechanism to tell us that a POSIX timer has expired, and let's say that the timer-expiry period is a very small amount of time (say, a few tens of microseconds); for example, 100 microseconds. This implies that every 100 microseconds the signal will be delivered to the target process!

In these circumstances, it's quite reasonable to expect that the process, being delivered the same ever-repeating signal at such a high rate, cannot possibly handle it. We also know from our knowledge on signaling that, in cases precisely like this, using a real-time signal would be far superior to using a regular Unix signal, as the OS has the ability to queue real-time signals but not regular signals—they (regular signals) will be dropped and only a single instance preserved.

*Timers*

So, we shall use a real-time signal (say, `SIGRTMIN`) to denote timer expiry; however, with a really tiny timer expiry (for example, as we said, 100 microseconds), even this technique will not suffice! The process will certainly be overrun by the rapid delivery of the same signal. For precisely these situations, one can retrieve the actual number of overruns that occurred between the timer expiry and the actual signal processing. How do we do this? There are two ways:

- One is via the signal handler's `siginfo_t->_timer->si_overrun` member (implying we specified the `SA_SIGINFO` flag when trapping the signal with sigaction)—this is the overrun count.
- However, this method is Linux-specific (and non-portable). A simpler, portable method of obtaining the overrun count is by using the `timer_getoverrun(2)` system call. The downside here being that system calls have far more overhead than a memory lookup; as in life, when there's an upside, there's also a downside.

## POSIX interval timers – example programs

Programming is ultimately learned and understanding is deeply internalized by doing, not simply seeing or reading. Let's take our own advice and cut a couple of decent code examples, to illustrate using the POSIX (interval) timer APIs. (Of course, dear reader, it implies you do the same!)

The first sample program is a small CLI game of "how quickly can you react"? The second sample program is a simple implementation of a run-walk timer. Read on for the gory details.

## The reaction – time game

We all understand that modern computers are fast! Of course, that's a very relative statement. How fast, exactly? That's an interesting question.

### How fast is fast?

In `Chapter 2`, *Virtual Memory*, in the section on the memory pyramid, we saw *Table 2: Memory Hierarchy Numbers*. Here, a representative look at the numbers was done—the typical access speeds for different kinds of memory technologies (for both the embedded and server space) are enumerated in the table.

*Chapter 13*

A quick recap gives us the following in terms of typical memory (and network) access speeds. Of course, these numbers are only indicative, and the very latest hardware might well have superior performance characteristics; here, the concept is what's being focused upon:

| CPU registers | CPU caches | RAM | Flash | Disk | Network roundtrip |
|---|---|---|---|---|---|
| 300 - 500 ps | 0.5 ns (L1) to 20 ns (L3) | 50–100 ns | 25–50 us | 5–10 ms | >= 100s of ms |

Table 3 : Hardware memory speed summary table

Most of these latency values are so tiny that we, as humans, cannot actually visualize them (see the information box on *average human reaction times* further on). So, that brings up the question. What minimally tiny numbers can we humans even hope to quite correctly visualize and relate to? The short answer is a few hundred milliseconds.

Why do we make such a statement? Well, if a computer program told you to react quick as you can and press a certain keyboard key combination immediately upon seeing a message, how long would it take? So, what we're really attempting to test here is the human reaction time to a visual stimulus. Ah, that's what we can empirically answer by writing this precise program: a reaction timer!

> Do note that this simple visual stimulus reaction test is not considered to be scientific; we completely ignore important delay-inducing mechanisms such as the computer-system hardware and software itself. So don't beat yourself up on the results you get when you try it out!

## Our react game – how it works

So, at a high level, here's the step-by-step plan for the program (the actual code is shown in the following section; we suggest you first read this and then check out the code):

- Create and initialize a simple alarm; program it to expire at a random time—anywhere between 1 and 5 seconds from the program's start
- The moment the alarm expires, do the following:
    - Arm a POSIX (interval) timer (to the frequency specified in the first parameter).
    - Display a message requesting the user to press *Ctrl + C* on the keyboard
    - Take a timestamp (let's call it `tm_start`).

- When the user actually presses ^C (*Ctrl + C*; which we will know, simply, by trapping SIGINT via `sigaction(2)`), again, take a timestamp (let's call it `tm_end`.
- Calculate the user's reaction time (as `tm_end` - `tm_start`) and display it.

(Notice how the previous steps follow the *Typical application workflow* we described earlier in this chapter.)

Additionally, we ask the user to specify the interval timer's interval in milliseconds (the first parameter), and an optional verbose option as the second parameter.

Breaking it down further (in more detail), the initialization code performs the following:

- Traps signals via `sigaction(2)`:
    - SIGRTMIN: We shall use signal notification to specify the timer expiration; this is the signal generated upon our POSIX interval timer's expiry.
    - SIGINT: The signal generated when the user reacts by pressing the ^C keyboard key combination.
    - SIGALRM: The signal generated when our initial random alarm expires
- Set up the POSIX interval timer:
    - Initialize the `sigevent` structure.
    - Create the timer (with a real-time clock source) with `timer_create(2)`.
    - Initialize the `itimerspec` structure to the frequency value specified by the user (in ms)

Then:

- Displays a message to the user:

    ```
    We shall start a timer anywhere between 1 and 5 seconds of
    starting this app.

    GET READY ...
      [ when the "QUICK! Press ^C" message appears, press ^C
    quickly as you can ]
    ```

- At any random time between 1 and 5 seconds the alarm expires
- We enter the SIGALRM handler function
  - It displays the *** QUICK! Press ^C !!! *** message
  - It calls timer_settime(2) to arm the timer
  - It takes the tm_start timestamp (with the clock_gettime(2) API)
  - The POSIX interval timer now runs; it expires every freq_ms milliseconds (the value provided by the user); when running in verbose mode, we display a . for each timer expiry
- The user, at some point, near or far, reacts and presses *Ctrl + C(^C)*; in the code for the signal handler for SIGINT, we do the following:
  - Take the tm_end timestamp (with the clock_gettime(2) API)
  - Calculate the delta (the reaction time!) via tm_end - tm_start, and display it
- Exit.

## React – trial runs

It is best to see the program in action; of course, the reader would do well (and enjoy this exercise a whole lot more!) to actually build and try it out for himself/herself:

```
$ ./react
Usage: ./react <freq-in-millisec> [verbose-mode:[0]|1]
  default: verbosity is off
   f.e.: ./react 100    => timeout every 100 ms, verbosity Off
       : ./react   5 1 => timeout every   5 ms, verbosity On

How fast can you react!?
Once you run this app with the freq-in-millisec parameter,
we shall start a timer anywhere between 1 and 5 seconds of
your starting it. Watch the screen carefully; the moment
the message "QUICK! Press ^C" appears, press ^C (Ctrl+c
simultaneously)!
Your reaction time is displayed... Have fun!

$
```

# Timers

We first run it with a 10 millisecond frequency and without verbosity:

```
$ ./react 10
Initializing timer to generate SIGRTMIN every 10 ms
[Verbose: N]
We shall start a timer anytime between 1 and 5 seconds from now...

GET READY ...
 [ when the "QUICK! Press ^C" message appears, press ^C quickly as you
can ]
```

After a random interval of between 1 and 5 seconds, this message appears and the user must react:

```
*** QUICK! Press ^C !!! ***
^C
*** PRESSED ***
 Your reaction time is precisely 0.404794198 s.ns [~= 405 ms,
count=40]
$
```

Next, with a 10 millisecond frequency and verbose mode on:

```
$ ./react 10 1
Initializing timer to generate SIGRTMIN every 10 ms
timer struct ::
 it_value.tv_sec = 0 it_value.tv_nsec = 10000000
 it_interval.tv_sec = 0 it_interval.tv_nsec = 10000000
[SigBlk: -none-]
[Verbose: Y]
We shall start a timer anytime between 1 and 5 seconds from now...

GET READY ...
 [ when the "QUICK! Press ^C" message appears, press ^C quickly as you
can ]
```

After a random interval of between 1 and 5 seconds, this message appears and the user must react:

```
react.c:arm_timer:161: Arming timer now

*** QUICK! Press ^C !!! *
```

Now the period character, ., appears rapidly, appearing once for every single expiry of our POSIX interval timer; that is, once every 10 ms in this run.

```
.................................^C
*** PRESSED ***
 Your reaction time is precisely 0.379339662 s.ns [~= 379 ms, count=37]
$
```

In our previous sample runs, the user took 405 ms and 379 ms to react; as we mentioned, it's in the hundreds of milliseconds range. Take the challenge—how much better can you do?

> Research findings indicate the following numbers for average human reaction times:
>
> | Stimulus | Visual | Auditory | Touch |
> |---|---|---|---|
> | Average human reaction time | 250 ms | 170 ms | 150 ms |
>
> Source: https://backyardbrains.com/experiments/reactiontime.
>
> We have become used to using phrases such as "in the blink of an eye" to mean really quickly. Interestingly, how long does it actually take to blink an eye? Research indicates that it takes an average of 300 to 400 ms!

## The react game – code view

Some key functionality aspects are shown as follows; first is the code that sets up the signal handler for SIGRTMIN and creates the POSIX interval (ch13/react.c):

> For readability, only key parts of the source code are displayed in the following; to view the complete source code, build it, and run it, the entire tree is available for cloning from GitHub, here: https://github.com/PacktPublishing/Hands-on-System-Programming-with-Linux.

```
static int init(void)
{
  struct sigevent sev;
  struct rlimit rlim;
  struct sigaction act;
```

## Timers

```c
    // Trap SIGRTMIN : delivered on (interval) timer expiry
    memset(&act, 0, sizeof(act));
    act.sa_flags = SA_SIGINFO | SA_RESTART;
    act.sa_sigaction = timer_handler;
    if (sigaction(SIGRTMIN, &act, NULL) == -1)
      FATAL("sigaction SIGRTMIN failed\n");

[...]

/* Create and init the timer */
    sev.sigev_notify = SIGEV_SIGNAL;
    sev.sigev_signo = SIGRTMIN;
    sev.sigev_value.sival_ptr = &timerid;
    if (timer_create(CLOCK_REALTIME, &sev, &timerid) == -1)
      FATAL("timer_create failed\n");

    printf("Initializing timer to generate SIGRTMIN every %ld ms\n",
        freq_ms);
    memset(&itv, 0, sizeof(struct itimerspec));
    itv.it_value.tv_sec = (freq_ms * 1000000) / 1000000000;
    itv.it_value.tv_nsec = (freq_ms * 1000000) % 1000000000;
    itv.it_interval.tv_sec = (freq_ms * 1000000) / 1000000000;
    itv.it_interval.tv_nsec = (freq_ms * 1000000) % 1000000000;
[...]
```

The surprise start is implemented as follows:

```c
/* random_start
 * The element of surprise: fire off an 'alarm' - resulting in SIGALRM being
 * delivered to us - in a random number between [min..max] seconds.
 */
static void random_start(int min, int max)
{
    unsigned int nr;

    alarm(0);
    srandom(time(0));
    nr = (random() % max) + min;

#define CHEAT_MODE     0
#if (CHEAT_MODE == 1)
    printf("Ok Cheater :-) get ready; press ^C in %ds ...\n", nr);
#endif
    alarm(nr);
}
```

It's invoked as follows:

```
#define MIN_START_SEC 1
#define MAX_START_SEC 5
[...]
random_start(MIN_START_SEC, MAX_START_SEC);
```

The signal handler (the function `startoff`) and associated logic for the alarm (for SIGALRM) is as follows:

```
static void arm_timer(timer_t tmrid, struct itimerspec *itmspec)
{
  VPRINT("Arming timer now\n");
  if (timer_settime(tmrid, 0, itmspec, NULL) == -1)
      FATAL("timer_settime failed\n");
  jumped_the_gun = 0;
}

/*
 * startoff
 * The signal handler for SIGALRM; arrival here implies the app has
 * "started" - we shall arm the interval timer here, it will start
 * running immediately. Take a timestamp now.
 */
static void startoff(int sig)
{
  char press_msg[] = "\n*** QUICK! Press ^C !!! ***\n";

  arm_timer(timerid, &itv);
  write(STDERR_FILENO, press_msg, strlen(press_msg));

  //--- timestamp it: start time
  if (clock_gettime(CLOCK_REALTIME, &tm_start) < 0)
      FATAL("clock_gettime (tm_start) failed\n");
}
```

*Timers*

Remember, while the user is lolling around, our POSIX interval timer continues to set and reset itself at the frequency specified by the user (as the first parameter passed, which we save in the variable `freq_ms`); so, every `freq_ms` milliseconds, our process will receive the signal `SIGRTMIN`. Here's its signal handler routine:

```
static volatile sig_atomic_t gTimerRepeats = 0, c = 0, first_time = 1,
    jumped_the_gun = 1;
[...]
static void timer_handler(int sig, siginfo_t * si, void *uc)
{
  char buf[] = ".";

  c++;
  if (verbose) {
      write(2, buf, 1);
#define SHOW_OVERRUN 1
#if (SHOW_OVERRUN == 1)
      {
          int ovrun = timer_getoverrun(timerid);
          if (ovrun == -1)
              WARN("timer_getoverrun");
          else {
              if (ovrun)
                  printf(" overrun=%d [@count=%d]\n", ovrun, c);
          }
      }
#endif
  }
}
```

When the user does (finally!) press ^C, the signal handler for SIGINT (the function `userpress`) is invoked:

```
static void userpress(int sig)
{
  struct timespec res;

  // timestamp it: end time
  if (clock_gettime(CLOCK_REALTIME, &tm_end) < 0)
    FATAL("clock_gettime (tm_end) failed\n");

  [...]
     printf("\n*** PRESSED ***\n");
     /* Calculate the delta; subtracting one struct timespec
      * from another takes a little work. A retrofit ver of
      * the 'timerspecsub' macro has been incorporated into
      * our ../common.h header to do this.
```

```
             */
            timerspecsub(&tm_end, &tm_start, &res);
            printf
                (" Your reaction time is precisely %ld.%ld s.ns"
                " [~= %3.0f ms, count=%d]\n",
                res.tv_sec, res.tv_nsec,
                res.tv_sec * 1000 +
                    round((double)res.tv_nsec / 1000000), c);
        }
      [...]
      c = 0;
      if (!gTimerRepeats)
         exit(EXIT_SUCCESS);
   }
```

## The run:walk interval timer application

This book's author is a self-confessed recreational runner. In my humble opinion, runners/joggers, especially when starting out (and frequently, even experienced ones), can benefit from a consistently followed run:walk pattern (the unit is minutes, typically).

The idea behind this is that running continuously is hard, especially for beginners. Often, coaches have the newbie runner follow a useful run:walk strategy; run for some given amount of time, then take a walk break for a given time period, then repeat—run again, walk again—indefinitely, or until your target distance (or time) goal is met.

For example, when a beginner runs distances of, say, 5 km or 10 km, (s)he might follow a consistent 5:2 run:walk pattern; that is, run for 5 minutes, walk for 2 minutes, keep repeating this, until the run is done. (Ultra-runners, on the other hand, might prefer something akin to a 25:5 strategy.)

Why not write a run:walk timer application to help out both our budding and serious runners.

We shall do just that. First, though, from the viewpoint of understanding this program better, let's imagine the program is written and working—we shall give it a spin.

*Timers*

## A few trial runs

When we simply run the program without passing any parameters, the help screen is displayed:

```
$ ./runwalk_timer
Usage: ./runwalk_timer Run-for[sec] Walk-for[sec] [verbosity-level=0|[1]|2]
 Verbosity Level :: 0 = OFF [1 = LOW] 2 = HIGH
$
```

As can be seen, the program expects a minimum of two parameters:

- The time to run (in seconds) [required]
- The time to walk (in seconds) [required]
- The verbosity level [optional]

The optional third parameter, the verbosity level, allows the user to request more or less information as the program executes (always a useful way to instrument, and thus help debug, programs). We provide three possible verbosity levels:

- `OFF`: Nothing besides the required matter is displayed (pass the third parameter 0)
- `LOW`: The same as for level OFF, plus we use the period character . to show the elapse of time—every second, a . is printed to `stdout` [default]
- `HIGH`: The same as for level OFF, plus we show the internal data structure values, time to timer expiry, and so on (pass the third parameter 2)

Let's first try running at the default verbosity level (LOW), with the following spec:

- Run for 5 seconds
- Walk for 2 seconds

Okay, okay, we know, you're fitter than that—you can run:walk for longer than 5s:2s. Forgive us, but here's the thing: for the purpose of the demo, we do not really want to wait until 5 minutes and then another 2 minutes have elapsed, just to see if it works, right? (When you're using this app on your run, then please convert minutes to seconds and go for it!).

Enough said; let's fire up the run:walk POSIX timer for a 5:2 run:walk interval:

```
$ ./runwalk_timer 5 2
************ Run Walk Timer ************
               Ver 1.0
```

```
Get moving... Run for 5 seconds
.....           << each "." represents 1 second of elapsed time >>
*** Bzzzz!!! WALK! *** for 2 seconds
..
*** Bzzzz!!! RUN! *** for 5 seconds
.....
*** Bzzzz!!! WALK! *** for 2 seconds
..
*** Bzzzz!!! RUN! *** for 5 seconds
....^C
+++ Good job, bye! +++
$
```

Yes, it works; we break it off by typing ^C (*Ctrl + C*).

The preceding trial run was at the default verbosity level of LOW; now let's rerun it with the same 5:2 run:walk interval, but with the verbosity level set to HIGH by passing 2 as the third parameter:

```
$ ./runwalk_timer 5 2 2
************ Run Walk Timer ************
              Ver 1.0

Get moving... Run for 5 seconds
trun= 5 twalk= 2; app ctx ptr = 0x7ffce9c55270
runwalk: 4.999s
runwalk: 3.999s              << query on time remaining >>
runwalk: 2.999s
runwalk: 1.999s
runwalk: 0.999s
its_time: signal 34. runwalk ptr: 0x7ffce9c55270 Type: Run. Overrun: 0

*** Bzzzz!!! WALK! *** for 2 seconds
runwalk: 1.999s
runwalk: 0.999s
its_time: signal 34. runwalk ptr: 0x7ffce9c55270 Type: Walk. Overrun:
0

*** Bzzzz!!! RUN! *** for 5 seconds
runwalk: 4.999s
runwalk: 3.999s
runwalk: 2.999s
runwalk: 1.999s
runwalk: 0.999s
its_time: signal 34. runwalk ptr: 0x7ffce9c55270 Type: Run. Overrun: 0

*** Bzzzz!!! WALK! *** for 2 seconds
runwalk: 1.999s
```

# Timers

```
runwalk: 0.999s
its_time: signal 34. runwalk ptr: 0x7ffce9c55270 Type: Walk. Overrun:
0

*** Bzzzz!!! RUN! *** for 5 seconds
runwalk: 4.999s
runwalk: 3.999s
runwalk: 2.999s
^C
+++ Good job, bye! +++
$
```

The details are revealed; every second, the time remaining on our POSIX timer's expiry is shown (to the resolution of a millisecond). When the timer does expire, the OS delivers the real-time signal SIGRTMIN to the process; we enter the signal handler its_time, then we print out the signal information obtained from the struct siginfo_t pointer. We receive the signal number (34) and the pointer within the union si->si_value, which is the pointer to our application context data structure, so that we can access it without the use of globals (more on this later). (Of course, as noted several times, it's unsafe to use printf(3) and variants in a signal handler as they are signal-async-unsafe. We have done it here just as a demo; do not code like this for production use. A Bzzzz!!! message represents the buzz of the timer going off, of course; the program instructs the user to proceed with RUN! or WALK!, accordingly, and the number of seconds to do it for. The whole process repeats indefinitely.

## The low – level design and code

This simple program will allow you to set up the number of seconds to run and to walk. It will time out accordingly.

In this application, we use a simple one-shot POSIX timer to do the job. We set the timer to use signal notification as the timer expiry notification mechanism. We set up a signal handler for a RT signal (SIGRTMIN). Next, we initially set the POSIX timer to expire after the run period, then, when the signal does arrive in the signal handler, we reset (re-arm) the timer to expire after the walk period seconds. This essentially repeats forever, or until the user aborts the program by pressing ^C.

> For readability, only key parts of the source code are displayed in the following; to view the complete source code, build it, and run it, the entire tree is available for cloning from GitHub, here: https://github.com/PacktPublishing/Hands-on-System-Programming-with-Linux.

Many real-world applications (indeed, any software) often requires several pieces of information—the state or application context—to be available to all functions at any given point in time; in other words, to be global. Ordinarily, one would just declare them as global (static) variables and proceed. We have a suggestion: why not encapsulate all of them into a single data structure? In fact, why not make it our own by typedef-ing a structure. Then we can allocate memory to it, initialize it, and just pass around its pointer in a manner that does not require it to be global. That would be efficient and elegant.

```
// Our app context data structure
typedef struct {
  int trun, twalk;
  int type;
  struct itimerspec *itmrspec;
  timer_t timerid;
} sRunWalk;
```

In our app, to keep things simple, we just statically allocate memory to (further, notice that it's a local variable, not global):

```
int main(int argc, char **argv)
{
  struct sigaction act;
  sRunWalk runwalk;
  struct itimerspec runwalk_curval;
  [...]
```

The initialization work is carried out here:

```
/*------------------ Our POSIX Timer setup
 * Setup a 'one-shot' POSIX Timer; initially set it to expire upon
 * 'run time' seconds elapsing.
 */
static void runwalk_timer_init_and_arm(sRunWalk * ps)
{
  struct sigaction act;
  struct sigevent runwalk_evp;

  assert(ps);
```

*Timers*

```
    act.sa_sigaction = its_time;
    act.sa_flags = SA_SIGINFO;
    sigfillset(&act.sa_mask);
    if (sigaction(SIGRTMIN, &act, 0) < 0)
        FATAL("sigaction: SIGRTMIN");
    memset(ps->itmrspec, 0, sizeof(sRunWalk));
    ps->type = RUN;
    ps->itmrspec->it_value.tv_sec = ps->trun;

    runwalk_evp.sigev_notify = SIGEV_SIGNAL;
    runwalk_evp.sigev_signo = SIGRTMIN;
    // Pass along the app context structure pointer
    runwalk_evp.sigev_value.sival_ptr = ps;

    // Create the runwalk 'one-shot' timer
    if (timer_create(CLOCK_REALTIME, &runwalk_evp, &ps->timerid) < 0)
        FATAL("timer_create");

    // Arm timer; will exire in ps->trun seconds, triggering the RT
 signal
    if (timer_settime(ps->timerid, 0, ps->itmrspec, NULL) < 0)
        FATAL("timer_settime failed");
}
[...]
runwalk_timer_init_and_arm(&runwalk);
[...]
```

In the preceding code, we do the following:

- Trap the real-time signal (SIGRTMIN) (delivered upon timer expiry).
- Initialize our app context run:walk data structure:
    - In particular, we set the type to run and the timeout value (seconds) to the time passed by the user in the first parameter.
- The timer-expiry event-notification mechanism is selected as signaling via the sigev_notify member of our sigevent structure.
    - It is useful to set the data passed along via the sigev_value.sival_ptr member as the pointer to our app context; this way, we can always gain access to it within the signal handler (eliminating the need to keep it global).
- Create the POSIX timer with the real-time clock source, and set it's ID to the timerid member of our app context runwalk structure
    - Arm—or start—the timer. (Recall, it's been initialized to expire in run seconds.)

In our preceding trial run, the run is set for 5 seconds, so, 5 seconds from the start, we shall asynchronously enter the signal handler for SIGRTMIN, its_time, as shown here:

```
static void its_time(int signum, siginfo_t *si, void *uctx)
{
    // Gain access to our app context
    volatile sRunWalk *ps = (sRunWalk *)si->si_value.sival_ptr;

    assert(ps);
    if (verbose == HIGH)
        printf("%s: signal %d. runwalk ptr: %p"
               " Type: %s. Overrun: %d\n",
               __func__, signum,
               ps,
               ps->type == WALK ? "Walk" : "Run",
               timer_getoverrun(ps->timerid)
        );

    memset(ps->itmrspec, 0, sizeof(sRunWalk));
    if (ps->type == WALK) {
        BUZZ(" RUN!");
        ps->itmrspec->it_value.tv_sec = ps->trun;
        printf(" for %4d seconds\n", ps->trun);
    }
    else {
        BUZZ(" WALK!");
        ps->itmrspec->it_value.tv_sec = ps->twalk;
        printf(" for %4d seconds\n", ps->twalk);
    }
    ps->type = !ps->type; // toggle the type

    // Reset: re-arm the one-shot timer
    if (timer_settime(ps->timerid, 0, ps->itmrspec, NULL) < 0)
        FATAL("timer_settime failed");
}
```

In the signal handling code, we do the following:

- (As mentioned previously) gain access to our app context data structure (by typecasting the si->si_value.sival_ptr to our (sRunWalk *) data type).
- In HIGH verbose mode, we display more details (again, do not use printf(3) in production).

*Timers*

- Then, if the just-expired timer was the RUN one, we call our buzzer function BUZZ with the WALK message parameter, and, importantly:
    - Re-initialize the timeout value (seconds) to the duration for WALK (the second parameter passed by the user).
    - Toggle the type from RUN to WALK.
    - Re-arm the timer via the timer_settime(2) API.
- And vice versa when transiting from the just-expired WALK to RUN mode.

This way, the process runs forever (or until the user terminates it via ^C), continually timing out for the next run:walk interval.

## Timer lookup via proc

One more thing: interestingly, the Linux kernel allows us to peek deep inside the OS; this is (typically) achieved via the powerful Linux proc filesystem. In our current context, proc allows us to look up all the timers that a given process has. How is this done? By reading the pseudo-file /proc/<PID>/timers. Check it out. The screenshot below illustrates this being performed on the runwalk_timer process:

```
$
$
$ ./runwalk_timer 5 2
************ Run Walk Timer ************
                Ver 1.0

Get moving... Run for 5 seconds
.....
*** Bzzzz!!!   WALK! ***       for   2  seconds
..
*** Bzzzz!!!   RUN!  ***       for   5  seconds
.....
*** Bzzzz!!!   WALK! ***       for   2  seconds
..
*** Bzzzz!!!   RUN!  ***       for   5  seconds
.....
*** Bzzzz!!!   WALK! ***       for   2  seconds
..
*** Bzzzz!!!   RUN!  ***       for   5  seconds
.....
*** Bzzzz!!!   WALK! ***       for   2  seconds
..
*** Bzzzz!!!   RUN!  ***       for   5  seconds
```

```
$
$
$
$ cat /proc/$(pgrep runwalk_timer)/timers
ID: 0
signal: 34/00007ffd52d4b920
notify: signal/pid.24975
ClockID: 0
$
$
```

The terminal window on the left is where the `runwalk_timer` application runs; while it's running, in the terminal window on the right, we lookup the proc filesystem's pseudo-file `/proc/<PID>/timers`. The output clearly reveals the following:

- There's just one (POSIX) timer within the process (ID 0).
- The timer-expiry event-notification mechanism is signaling, because we can see that `notify:signal/pid.<PID>` and signal: 34 are associated with this timer (signal: 34 is `SIGRTMIN`; use `kill -l 34` to verify this).
- The clock source associated with this timer is `ClockID 0`; that is, the real-time clock.

# A quick mention

To round off this chapter, we present a quick look at two interesting technologies: timers via the file abstraction model and watchdog timers. These sections are not covered in detail; we leave it to the interested reader to dig further.

# Timers via file descriptors

Do you recall a key philosophy of the Unix (and, thus, Linux) design that we covered in Chapter 1, *Linux System Architecture*, of this book? That is, everything is a process; if it's not a process, it's a file. The file abstraction is heavily used on Linux; here, too, with timers, we find that there is a way to represent and use timers via the file abstraction.

How is this done? The `timerfd_*` APIs provide the required abstraction. In this book, we shall not attempt to delve into the intricate details; rather, we would like the reader to become aware that one can use the file abstraction—reading a timer via the read(2) system call—if required.

# Timers

The following table quickly outlines the `timerfd_*` API set:

| API | Purpose | Equivalent to the POSIX timer API |
|---|---|---|
| `timerfd_create(2)` | Create a POSIX timer; the return value on success is the file descriptor associated with this timer. | `timer_create(2)` |
| `timerfd_settime(2)` | (Dis)arm a timer referred to by the first parameter `fd`. | `timer_settime(2)` |
| `timerfd_gettime(2)` | On successful completion, returns both the time to expiry and interval of the timer referred to by the first parameter `fd`. | `timer_gettime(2)` |

Table 4 : The timerfd_* APIs

```
include <sys/timerfd.h>

int timerfd_create(int clockid, int flags);

int timerfd_settime(int fd, int flags,
  const struct itimerspec *new_value, struct itimerspec *old_value);

int timerfd_gettime(int fd, struct itimerspec *curr_value);
```

The real advantage to using file descriptors to represent various objects is that one can use a uniform, powerful set of APIs to operate upon them. In this particular case, we can monitor our file-based timer(s) via the `read(2)`, `poll(2)`, `select(2)`, `epoll(7)`, and similar APIs.

What if the process that created the fd-based timer forks or execs? Upon a `fork(2)`, the child process will inherit a copy of the file descriptor pertaining to any timer created in the parent via the `timerfd_create(2)` API. Effectively, it shares the same timer as the parent process.

Upon an `execve(2)`, the timer(s) remain valid in the successor process and will continue expiring upon timeout; unless, upon creation, the TFD_CLOEXEC flag was specified.

More detail (along with an example) can be found in the man page here: https://linux.die.net/man/2/timerfd_create.

# A quick note on watchdog timers

A watchdog is essentially a timer-based mechanism that is used to periodically detect if the system is in a healthy state, and if it is deemed not to be, to reboot it.

This is achieved by setting up a (kernel) timer (with, say, a 60-second timeout). If all is well, a watchdog daemon process will consistently disarm the timer before it expires, and subsequently re-enable (arm) it; this is known as *petting the dog*. If the daemon does not disarm the watchdog timer (due to something having gone badly wrong), the watchdog is annoyed and reboots the system.

> A daemon is a system background process; more on daemons in `Appendix B`, *Daemon Processes*.

A pure software watchdog implementation will not be protected against kernel bugs and faults; a hardware watchdog (which latches into the board-reset circuitry) will always be able to reboot the system as and when required.

Watchdog timers are very often used in embedded systems, especially deeply embedded ones (or those unreachable by a human for whatever reason); in a worst-case scenario, it can reboot, and hopefully move along with its designated tasks again. A famous example of a watchdog timer causing reboots is the Pathfinder robot, NASA sent to the Martian surface back in 1997 (yes, the one that encountered the priority inversion concurrency bug while on Mars. We shall explore this a little in `Chapter 15`, *Multithreading with Pthreads Part II - Synchronization*, on multithreading and concurrency). And, yes, that's the very same Pathfinder robot that is given a role in the superb movie The Martian! More on this in the *Further reading* section on the GitHub repository.

# Summary

In this chapter, the reader has been taken through the various interfaces exposed by Linux with regard to creating and using timers. Setting up and managing timeouts is an essential component of many, if not most, systems applications. The older interfaces—the venerable `alarm(2)` API, followed by the `[s|g]etitimer(2)` system calls—were shown with example code. Then, we delved into the newer and better POSIX timers, including the advantages provided by them, and how to use them in a practical fashion. This was greatly aided with the help of two fairly elaborate sample programs—the react game and the run:walk timer application. Finally, the reader was introduced to the notion of using timers via file abstractions, and to the watchdog timer.

The next chapter is where we begin our long three-chapter journey on understanding and using the powerful multithreading framework on Linux.

# 14
# Multithreading with Pthreads Part I - Essentials

Have you downloaded a large file using a download-accelerator type of application? Have you played an online game? A flight simulator program? Used word processing, web browsers, Java apps, and so on? (The temptation to put in a smiley emoji here is high!)

It's quite likely that you have used at least some of these; so what? All of these disparate applications have something in common: it's highly likely that they are all designed for multithreading, meaning that their implementation uses multiple threads that run in parallel with each other. Multithreading has indeed become almost a way of life for the modern programmer.

Explaining a topic as large as multithreading is itself a big task; hence we are dividing the coverage into three separate chapters. This one is the first of them.

This chapter is itself logically divided into two broad parts: in the first, we carefully consider and understand the concepts behind the threading model—the what and why of multithreading. What exactly is a thread, why do we want threads, and a quick take on how multithreading has evolved on the Linux platform.

In the second part, we focus on the thread management APIs—the how (to some extent) of multithreading on Linux. The API set required to create and manage threads is discussed, with, of course, a lot of practical code to be seen and tried out.

At the outset of this topic, we must also clearly point out the fact that in this book we are only concerned with multithreading in the context of software programming; particularly, the **POSIX threads** (**pthreads**) implementation and specifically, pthreads on the Linux platform. We do not attempt to deal with various other multithreaded frameworks and implementations that have sprung up (such as MPI, OpenMP, OpenCL, and so on) or hardware threading (hyperthreading, GPUs with CUDA, and so on).

In this chapter, you will learn about programming with multiple threads on the Linux platform, specifically, getting started with the pthreads programming model or framework. This chapter is broadly divided into two parts:

- In the first, key multithreading concepts—the what and the why of multithreading —are covered, laying the groundwork for the second part (and indeed the two subsequent chapters on multithreading).
- The second part covers the essential pthreads APIs required to build a functional multithreaded application on Linux (it deliberately does not cover all aspects, through; the next two chapters will build on this one).

# Multithreading concepts

In this section, we'll learn about the what and why of multithreading on the Linux platform. We will begin by answering the FAQ, "what exactly is a thread?".

## What exactly is a thread?

In the good (or bad?) old days, Unix programmers had a straightforward software model (which got inherited pretty much exactly by other OSes and vendors): there is a process that lives in a **virtual address space** (**VAS**); the VAS essentially consists of homogeneous regions (essentially collections of virtual pages) called segments: text, data, other mappings (libraries), and stack. The text is really the executable—in fact, the machine—code that is fed to the processor. We have certainly covered all of this earlier in this book (you can brush up on these basics in Chapter 2, *Virtual Memory*).

A thread is an independent execution (or flow) path within a process. The life and scope of a thread, in the familiar procedural programming paradigm we typically work with, is simply a function.

So, in the traditional model we mentioned previously, we have a single thread of execution; that thread, in the C programming paradigm, is the `main()` function! Think about it: the `main()` thread is where execution begins (well, at least from the app developer's viewpoint) and ends. This model is (now) called the single threaded software model. As opposed to what? The multithreaded one, of course. So, there we have it: it is possible to have more than one thread alive and executing concurrently (in parallel) with other independent threads within the same process.

But, hang on, can't processes generate parallelism too and have multiple copies of themselves working on different aspects of the application? Yes, of course: we have covered the `fork(2)` system call in all its considerable glory (and implications) in `Chapter 10`, *Process Creation*. This is known as the multiprocessing model. So, if we have multiprocessing – where several processes run in parallel and, hey, they get the work done—the million dollar question becomes: "why multithreading at all?" (Kindly deposit a million dollars and we shall provide the answer.) There are several good reasons; check out the upcoming sections (especially *Motivation – why threads?*; we do suggest that first-time readers follow the sequence as laid out in this book) for more detail.

## Resource sharing

In `Chapter 10`, *Process Creation*, we repeatedly pointed out that although the fork(2) system call is very powerful and useful, it's considered to be a heavyweight operation; performing the fork takes a lot of CPU cycles (and thus time) and is expensive in terms of memory (RAM), too. Computer scientists were looking for a way to lighten this; the result, as you have guessed, is the thread.

Hang on, though: for the convenience of the reader, we reproduce a diagram—*The Linux process – inheritance and non-inheritance across the fork()*—from `Chapter 10, Process Creation`:

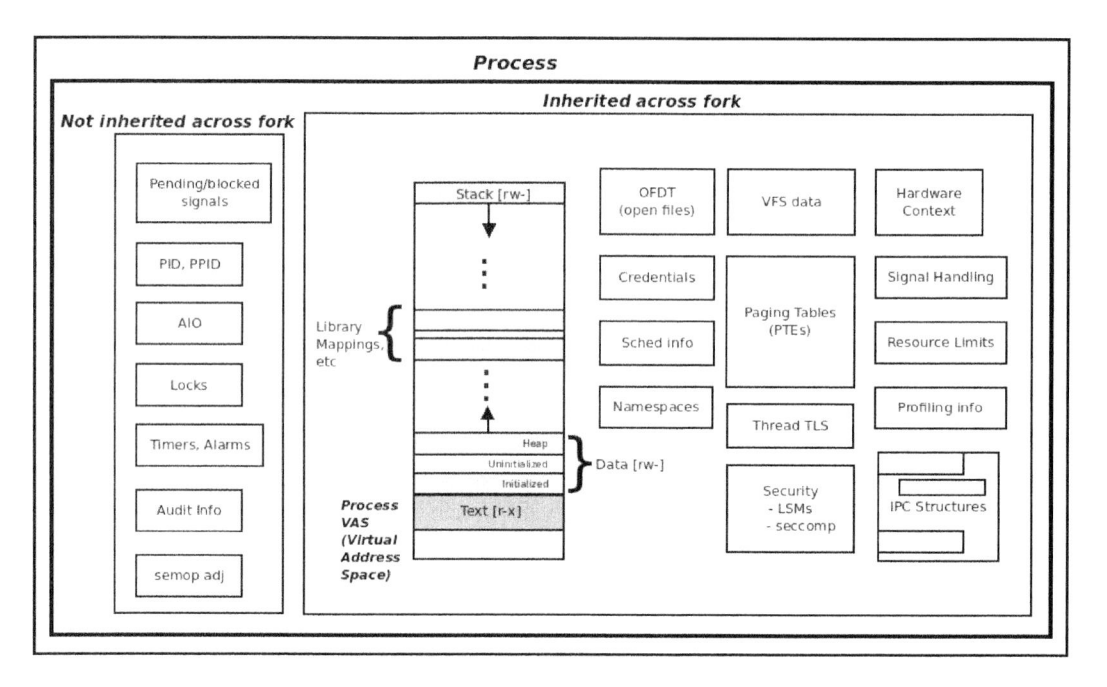

Figure 1: The Linux process – inheritance and non-inheritance across the fork()

This diagram is important because it shows us why the fork is a heavy weight operation: every time you invoke the fork(2) system call,, the complete VAS of the parent process and all the data structures on the right inherited across fork side of the diagram have to be copied into the newly born child process. That is indeed a lot of work and memory usage! (Okay, we're exaggerating a bit: as mentioned in Chapter 10, *Process Creation*, modern OSes, especially Linux, do take a lot of pains to optimize the fork. Nevertheless, it's heavy. Check out our example 1 demo program that follows—the creation and destruction of a process is much slower (and takes much more RAM) than the creation and destruction of a thread.

The reality is this: when a process creates a thread, the thread shares (almost) everything with all other threads of the same process—all of the preceding VAS, thus the segments, and all the data structures—except for a stack.

Every thread has its own private stack segment. Where does it reside? Obviously, within the VAS of the creating process; where exactly it resides is really inconsequential to us (recall that it's all virtual memory, in any case, not physical). The question that's a lot more relevant and important to the app developer is how large the thread stack will be. The short answer: the same as usual (typically 8 MB on the Linux platform), but we shall get to the nitty-gritty details later in this chapter. Just think of it this way: the stack of main() always resides at the very top of the (user mode) virtual address space; the stacks of the remaining threads in the process can reside anywhere in this space. Realistically, they typically reside in the virtual memory space between the heap and the stack (of main).

# Multithreading with Pthreads Part I - Essentials

The following diagram helps us understand the memory layout of a multithreaded process on Linux; in the upper portion of the diagram is the process before `pthread_create(3)`; the lower portion shows the process after the thread has been successfully created:

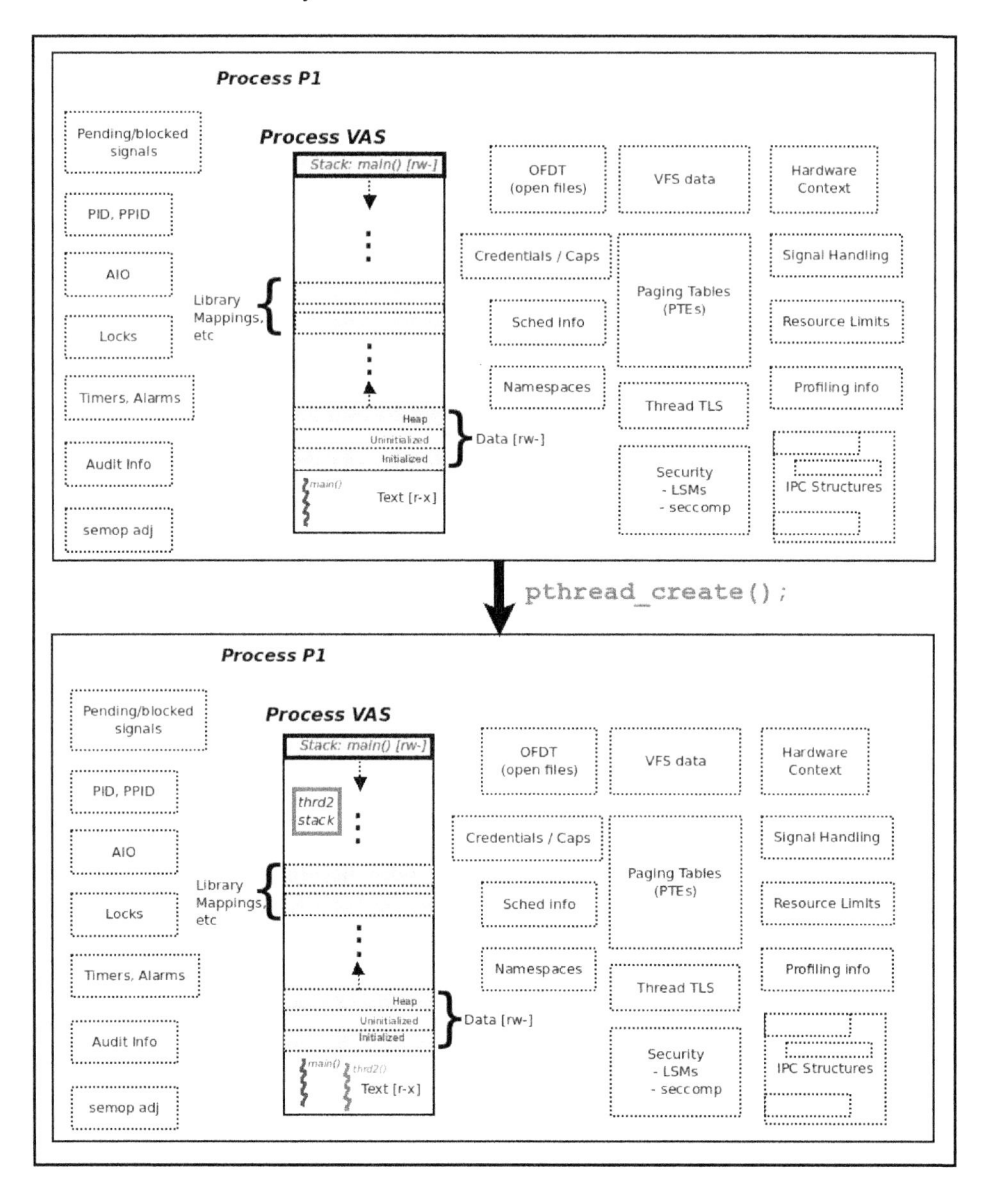

Fig 2 : The thread – everything except the stack is shared across pthread_create()

The blue squiggle in the process text segment represents the `main()` thread; its stack is also clearly seen. We use the dashed lines to indicate that all these memory objects (both user and kernel space) are shared across `pthread_create(3)`. As can clearly be seen, the only new objects after `pthread_create(3)` are the new thread itself (**thrd2**; shown as a red squiggle in the process text segment) and a new stack for the just born thread **thrd2** (in red). Contrast this diagram with *Fig 1*; when we fork(2), pretty much everything has to be copied into the newly born child process.

> From what we have described so far, the only difference between a process and a thread is that of resource sharing—processes do not share, they copy; threads do share everything, except for the stack. Dig a little deeper and you will realize that both software and hardware state have to be maintained on a per thread basis. The Linux OS does exactly that: it maintains a per-thread task structure within the OS; the task structure contains all the process/thread attributes, including software and hardware context (CPU register values and so on) information.
>
> Again, digging a little deeper, we realize that the OS does maintain a distinct copy of the following attributes per thread: the stack segment (and thus the stack pointer), possible alternate signal stack (covered in the `Chapter 11`, *Signaling - Part I*), both regular signal and real-time signal masks, thread ID, scheduling policy and priority, capability bits, CPU affinity mask, and the errno value (don't worry—several of these will be explained along the way).

## Multiprocess versus multithreaded

To help clearly understand why and how threads can provide a performance benefit, let's perform a few experiments! (the importance of being empirical - experimenting, trying things out - is a critical feature; our `Chapter 19`, *Troubleshooting and Best Practices*, covers more on such points). First, we take two simple example programs: one, a program that compares the creation and destruction of processes versus threads, and two, a program that performs matrix multiplication in two ways—one via the traditional single threaded process model, and two, via the multithreaded model.

So, what we are really comparing here is the performance in terms of execution time between using the multiprocess versus multithreaded model. We will have the reader note that, right here and now, we will not be taking pains to detail and explain the thread code right now for two reasons; one, it's besides the point, and two, until we have covered the thread APIs in some detail, it will not really make sense to do so. (So in effect, dear reader, we ask that you ignore the thread code for now; just follow along, and build and reproduce what we do here; the code and APIs will become clear to you as you learn more.)

## Example 1 – creation/destruction – process/thread

The process model: Here's what we do: in a loop (that executes a total of 60,000 times!), create and destroy a process by calling `fork(2)` and subsequently exiting. (We take care of details such as clearing any possible zombie by waiting in the parent for the child to die before proceeding in the loop.) The relevant code is as follows (ch14/speed_multiprcs_vs_multithrd_simple/create_destroy/fork_test.c):

> For readability, only the relevant parts of the code are displayed in the following code; to view and run it, the entire source code can be found here: https://github.com/PacktPublishing/Hands-on-System-Programming-with-Linux.

```
...
#define NFORKS 60000
void do_nothing()
{
  unsigned long f = 0xb00da;
}
int main(void)
{
  int pid, j, status;

  for (j = 0; j < NFORKS; j++) {
        switch (pid = fork()) {
        case -1:
              FATAL("fork failed! [%d]\n", pid);
        case 0: // Child process
              do_nothing();
              exit(EXIT_SUCCESS);
        default: // Parent process
              waitpid(pid, &status, 0);
        }
  }
```

```
    exit(EXIT_SUCCESS);
}
```

We run it prefixed with the `time(1)` utility, which gives us a rough idea of the time taken by the program on the processor; the time spent shows up as three components: `real` (total wall-clock time spent), `user` (time spent in user space), and `sys` (time spent in kernel space):

```
$ time ./fork_test

real    0m10.993s
user    0m7.436s
sys     0m2.969s
$
```

Obviously, the precise values you get on your Linux box can, and likely will, vary. And, no, `user` + `sys` does not add up exactly to real, either.

## The multithreading model

Again, here's what we do: it's key to understand that the code used here (`ch14/speed_multiprcs_vs_multithrd_simple/create_destroy/pthread_test.c`), is equivalent in all respects to the previous code except that here we work with threads and not processes: in a loop (that executes a total of 60,000 times!), create and destroy a thread by calling `pthread_create(3)` and subsequently `pthread_exit(3)`. (We take care of details such as waiting in the calling thread for the sibling thread to terminate by invoking `pthread_join(3)`.) As mentioned earlier, let's skip the code/API details for now and just see the execution:

```
$ time ./pthread_test

real    0m3.584s
user    0m0.379s
sys     0m2.704s
$
```

Wow, the threaded code has run approximately 3x faster than the process model code! The conclusion is obvious: creating and destroying a thread is much faster than creating and destroying a process.

> A technical side note: For the more curious geeks: why exactly is the `fork(2)` so much slower than `pthread_create(3)`? Those familiar with OS development will understand that Linux makes heavy use of the performance-enhancing **copy-on-write(COW)** memory techniques within its internal implementation of `fork(2)`. Thus, it begs the question, if COW is heavily used, then what is slowing the fork down? The short answer: page table creation and setup cannot be COW-ed; it takes a while to do. When creating threads of the same process, this work (page table setup) is completely skipped.
>
> Even so, Linux's fork is pretty much considered to be the fastest of any comparable OS today.

As an aside, a far more accurate way to measure the time spent—and performance characteristics in general—is by using the well-known `perf(1)` utility (note that in this book, we do not intend to cover `perf` in any detail whatsoever; if interested, please look up the *Further reading* section on the GitHub repository for some links to perf-related materials):

```
$ perf stat ./fork_test

 Performance counter stats for './fork_test':

       9054.969497  task-clock (msec)        #    0.773 CPUs utilized
            61,245  context-switches         #    0.007 M/sec
               202  cpu-migrations           #    0.022 K/sec
         15,00,063  page-faults              #    0.166 M/sec
   <not supported>  cycles
   <not supported>  instructions
   <not supported>  branches
   <not supported>  branch-misses

      11.714134973 seconds time elapsed

$
```

As can be seen in the preceding code, on a virtual machine, current versions of `perf` cannot show all the counters; this does not impede us in any way here as all we're really after is the final time it took to execute—which is shown in the last line of `perf` output.

The following code shows `perf(1)` for the multithreaded app:

```
$ perf stat ./pthread_test

Performance counter stats for './pthread_test':

      2377.866371 task-clock (msec)       # 0.587 CPUs utilized
           60,887 context-switches        # 0.026 M/sec
              117 cpu-migrations          # 0.049 K/sec
               69 page-faults             # 0.029 K/sec
   <not supported> cycles
   <not supported> instructions
   <not supported> branches
   <not supported> branch-misses

       4.052964938 seconds time elapsed
$
```

> For interested readers, we have also provided a wrapper script (ch14/speed_multiprcs_vs_multithrd_simple/create_destroy/perf_runs.sh), allowing the user to perform a record and report session with `perf(1)`.

## Example 2 – matrix multiplication – process/thread

A well-known exercise is to write a program to compute the (dot) product of two given matrices. Essentially, we would like to perform the following:

```
matrix C = matrix A * matrix B
```

Again, we emphasize the fact that here, we are not really concerned with the details of the algorithm (and code); what concerns us here is how, at a design level the matrix multiplication is performed. We propose (and write the corresponding code for) two ways:

- Sequentially, via the single threaded model
- In parallel, via the multithreaded model

> Note: None of this—the algorithm or code—is purported to be original or ground-breaking in any manner; these are well-known programs.

In the first model, one thread—`main()`, of course—will run and perform the computation; the program can be found here: `ch14/speed_multiprcs_vs_multithrd_simple/matrixmul/prcs_matrixmul.c`.

In the second, we will create at least as many threads as there are CPU cores on the target system to take full advantage of the hardware (this aspect is dealt with in a later section of this chapter called *How many threads can you create?*); each thread will perform a part of the computation, in parallel with the other threads. The program can be found here: `ch14/speed_multiprcs_vs_multithrd_simple/matrixmul/thrd_matrixmul.c`.

In the multithreaded version, for now, we just hardcode the number of CPU cores in our code to four as it matches one of our native Linux test systems.

To truly appreciate how the process(es) and/or threads of our applications actually consume CPU bandwidth, let's use the interesting `gnome-system-monitor` GUI application to see resource consumption graphically! (To run it, assuming it's installed, just type `$ gnome-system-monitor &` on the shell).

> **TIP**
> We remind you that all software and hardware requirements have been enumerated in some detail in the software-hardware list material available on this book's GitHub repository.

We will perform the experiment as follows:

1. Run the apps on a native Linux box with four CPU cores:

*Chapter 14*

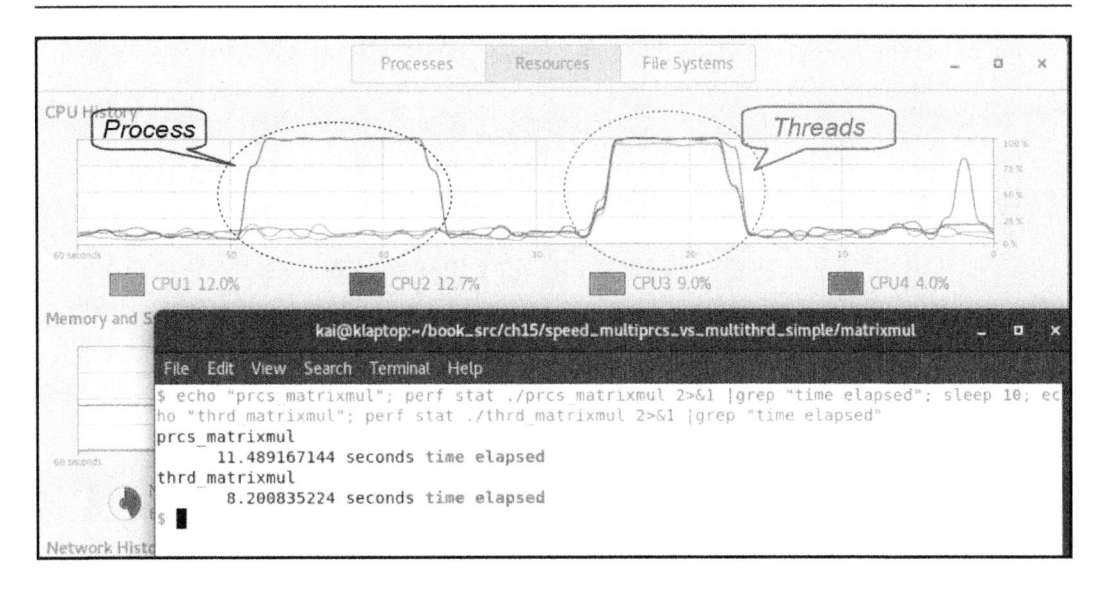

```
kai@klaptop:~/book_src/ch15/speed_multiprcs_vs_multithrd_simple/matrixmul
File  Edit  View  Search  Terminal  Help
$ echo "prcs matrixmul"; perf stat ./prcs matrixmul 2>&1 |grep "time elapsed"; sleep 10; ec
ho "thrd matrixmul"; perf stat ./thrd_matrixmul 2>&1 |grep "time elapsed"
prcs_matrixmul
      11.489167144 seconds time elapsed
thrd_matrixmul
       8.200835224 seconds time elapsed
$
```

Look carefully at the preceding (annotated) screenshot (zoom in if you are reading the electronic version); we will notice several items of interest:

- In the foreground is the terminal window app where we run the prcs_matrixmul and the thrd_matrixmul applications:
    - We use perf(1) to accurately measure the time taken and deliberately filter out all output except for the final number of seconds elapsed during execution.
- In the background, you can see the gnome-system-monitor GUI app running.
- The (native Linux) system—the particular one that we have tested this on—has four CPU cores:
- One way to find the number of CPU cores on your system is by using the following code: getconf -a | grep _NPROCESSORS_ONLN | awk '{print $2}'
  (you can update the NCORES macro in the source code thrd_matrixmul.c to reflect this value)
- The prcs_matrixmul app runs first; while it runs, it consumes 100% CPU bandwidth on exactly one CPU core out of the four available (it happens to be CPU core #2)
- Notice how, on the middle-to-left of the **CPU History** meter, the red line representing **CPU2** shoots up to a 100% (highlighted with a purple ellipse and labeled **Process**)!

[ 541 ]

- At the time the screenshot was actually taken (OS on the X-axis timeline; it moves from right to left), the CPUs are back to normal levels.
- Next (after a gap of 10 seconds in this particular run), the `thrd_matrixmul` app runs; and herein lies the key point: While it runs, it consumes 100% CPU bandwidth on all four CPU cores!
- Notice at how, approximately just after the 15s marking (read it from right-to-left) on the X-axis timeline, all four CPU cores shoot to 100% – that's during the execution of `thrd_matrixmul` (highlighted with a red ellipsis and labeled **Threads**).

What does this tell us? Something really important: the underlying Linux OS CPU scheduler will try and take advantage of the hardware and, if possible, schedule our four application threads to run in parallel on the four CPUs available! Hence, we get higher throughput, higher performance, and more bang for our buck.

> Understandably, you might at this point wonder about and have a lot of questions on how Linux performs CPU (thread) scheduling; worry not, but please have some patience—we shall explore CPU scheduling in some detail in `Chapter 17`, *CPU Scheduling on Linux*.

2. Restricted to exactly one CPU:

The `taskset(1)` utility allows one to run a process on a specified set of processor core(s). (This ability to associate a process with a given CPU(s) is called CPU affinity. We shall come back to this in the chapter on scheduling.) Using `taskset` in its basic form is easy: `taskset -c <cpu-mask> <app-to-run-on-given-cpus>`

As you can see from the following screenshot, we contrast performing a run of the `thrd_matrixmul` app on all four CPU cores on the system (in the usual way) with running it on exactly one CPU by specifying the CPU mask via `taskset(1)`; the screenshot again clearly reveals how, on the former run, all four CPUs are pressed into action by the OS (and it takes a total of 8.084s), whereas on the latter run only a single CPU (it shows up as **CPU3** in green) is employed to execute its code (resulting in a total time of 11.189s):

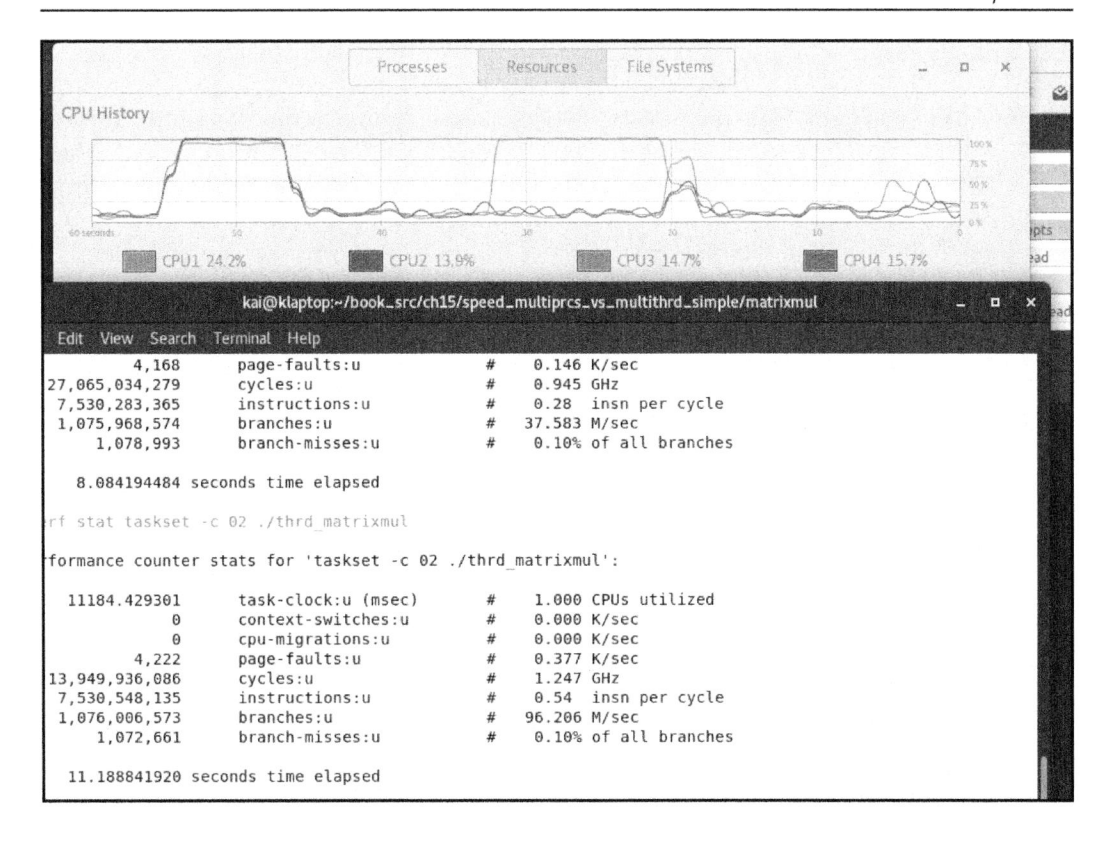

```
                    4,168      page-faults:u               #     0.146 K/sec
           27,065,034,279      cycles:u                    #     0.945 GHz
            7,530,283,365      instructions:u              #     0.28  insn per cycle
            1,075,968,574      branches:u                  #    37.583 M/sec
                1,078,993      branch-misses:u             #     0.10% of all branches

              8.084194484 seconds time elapsed

rf stat taskset -c 02 ./thrd_matrixmul

formance counter stats for 'taskset -c 02 ./thrd_matrixmul':

              11184.429301    task-clock:u (msec)          #     1.000 CPUs utilized
                        0    context-switches:u            #     0.000 K/sec
                        0    cpu-migrations:u              #     0.000 K/sec
                    4,222    page-faults:u                 #     0.377 K/sec
           13,949,936,086    cycles:u                      #     1.247 GHz
            7,530,548,135    instructions:u                #     0.54  insn per cycle
            1,076,006,573    branches:u                    #    96.206 M/sec
                1,072,661    branch-misses:u               #     0.10% of all branches

             11.188841920 seconds time elapsed
```

Seeing what we have just learned in this section, you might leap to the conclusion, "hey, we've found the answer: let's just always use multithreading." But, of course, experience tells us that there is no silver bullet. The reality is that although threading does indeed offer some real advantages, as with everything in life, there are also downsides to it. We shall postpone more discussion on the pros and cons in Chapter 16, *Multithreading with Pthreads Part III*; do keep this in mind, though.

For now, let's do one more experiment to clearly illustrate the fact that not just multithreading, but multiprocessing—the use of fork to spawn multiple processes—is very helpful as well to gain higher throughput.

## Example 3 – kernel build

So, one last experiment (for this section): we will build (cross-compile) a Linux kernel ver. 4.17 for the ARM Versatile Express platform (with its default configuration). The details of the kernel build and so on are out of scope of this book, but that's all right: the key point here is that the kernel build is definitely a CPU and RAM intensive operation. Not only that, the modern `make(1)` utility is multiprocess capable! One can tell `make` the number of jobs—processes, really—to internally spawn (fork) via its `-jn` option switch, where `n` is the number of jobs (threads). We use a heuristic (a rule of thumb) to determine this:

```
n = number-of-CPU-cores * 2
```

(multiply by 1.5 on very high-end systems with a lot of cores.)

Knowing this, check out the experiments that follow.

### On a VM with 1 GB RAM, two CPU cores and parallelized make -j4

We configure the guest VM to have two processors, and proceed with the parallelized build (by specifying `make -j4` ):

```
$ cd <linux-4.17-kernel-src-dir>
$ perf stat make V=0 -j4 ARCH=arm CROSS_COMPILE=arm-linux-gnueabihf-all
scripts/kconfig/conf --syncconfig Kconfig
  CHK     include/config/kernel.release
  SYSHDR  arch/arm/include/generated/uapi/asm/unistd-oabi.h
  SYSHDR  arch/arm/include/generated/uapi/asm/unistd-common.h
  WRAP    arch/arm/include/generated/uapi/asm/bitsperlong.h
  WRAP    arch/arm/include/generated/uapi/asm/bpf_perf_event.h
  WRAP    arch/arm/include/generated/uapi/asm/errno.h

[...]                    << lots of output >>

  CC      arch/arm/boot/compressed/string.o
  AS      arch/arm/boot/compressed/hyp-stub.o
  AS      arch/arm/boot/compressed/lib1funcs.o
  AS      arch/arm/boot/compressed/ashldi3.o
  AS      arch/arm/boot/compressed/bswapsdi2.o
  AS      arch/arm/boot/compressed/piggy.o
  LD      arch/arm/boot/compressed/vmlinux
  OBJCOPY arch/arm/boot/zImage
  Kernel: arch/arm/boot/zImage is ready

 Performance counter stats for 'make V=0 -j4 ARCH=arm
```

```
       CROSS_COMPILE=arm-linux-gnueabihf- all':

          1174027.949123 task-clock (msec)    # 1.717 CPUs utilized
               3,80,189 context-switches      # 0.324 K/sec
                  7,921 cpu-migrations        # 0.007 K/sec
             2,13,51,434 page-faults          # 0.018 M/sec
          <not supported> cycles
          <not supported> instructions
          <not supported> branches
          <not supported> branch-misses

            683.798578130 seconds time elapsed
       $ ls -lh <...>/linux-4.17/arch/arm/boot/zImage
       -rwxr-xr-x 1 seawolf seawolf 4.0M Aug 13 13:10   <...>/zImage*
       $ ls -lh <...>/linux-4.17/vmlinux
       -rwxr-xr-x 1 seawolf seawolf 103M Aug 13 13:10   <...>/vmlinux*
       $
```

The build took a total time of approximately 684 seconds (11.5 min). Just so you know, the compressed kernel image for ARM—the one we boot with—is the file called zImage; the uncompressed kernel image (used only for debug purposes) is the vmlinux file.

While it was running, doing a quick ps -LA during the build indeed reveals its multiprocess—not multithreaded—nature:

```
$ ps -LA
[...]
11204 11204 pts/0   00:00:00 make
11227 11227 pts/0   00:00:00 sh
11228 11228 pts/0   00:00:00 arm-linux-gnuea
11229 11229 pts/0   00:00:01 cc1
11242 11242 pts/0   00:00:00 sh
11243 11243 pts/0   00:00:00 arm-linux-gnuea
11244 11244 pts/0   00:00:00 cc1
11249 11249 pts/0   00:00:00 sh
11250 11250 pts/0   00:00:00 arm-linux-gnuea
11251 11251 pts/0   00:00:00 cc1
11255 11255 pts/0   00:00:00 sh
11256 11256 pts/0   00:00:00 arm-linux-gnuea
11257 11257 pts/0   00:00:00 cc1
[...]
$
```

## On a VM with 1 GB RAM, one CPU core and sequential make -j1

We configure the guest VM to have only one processor, clean up the build directory, and proceed once more, but this time with a sequential build (by specifying make -j1):

```
$ cd <linux-4.17-kernel-src-dir>
$ perf stat make V=0 -j1 ARCH=arm CROSS_COMPILE=arm-linux-gnueabihf- all
scripts/kconfig/conf --syncconfig Kconfig
  SYSHDR  arch/arm/include/generated/uapi/asm/unistd-common.h
  SYSHDR  arch/arm/include/generated/uapi/asm/unistd-oabi.h
  SYSHDR  arch/arm/include/generated/uapi/asm/unistd-eabi.h
  CHK     include/config/kernel.release
  UPD     include/config/kernel.release
  WRAP    arch/arm/include/generated/uapi/asm/bitsperlong.h

[...]                       << lots of output >>

  CC      crypto/hmac.mod.o
  LD [M]  crypto/hmac.ko
  CC      crypto/jitterentropy_rng.mod.o
  LD [M]  crypto/jitterentropy_rng.ko
  CC      crypto/sha256_generic.mod.o
  LD [M]  crypto/sha256_generic.ko
  CC      drivers/video/backlight/lcd.mod.o
  LD [M]  drivers/video/backlight/lcd.ko

 Performance counter stats for 'make V=0 -j1 ARCH=arm CROSS_COMPILE=arm-linux-gnueabihf- all':

    1031535.713905 task-clock (msec) # 0.837 CPUs utilized
          1,78,172 context-switches  # 0.173 K/sec
                 0 cpu-migrations    # 0.000 K/sec
        2,13,29,573 page-faults      # 0.021 M/sec
   <not supported> cycles
   <not supported> instructions
   <not supported> branches
   <not supported> branch-misses

    1232.146348757 seconds time elapsed
$
```

The build took a total time of approximately 1232 seconds (20.5 min), which is nearly twice as long as the previous build!

You might be asking this question: so, if the build with one process took around 20 minutes and the same build with multiple processes took approximately half the time, why use multithreading at all? Multiprocessing seems to be as good!

No, please think: our very first example regarding process versus thread creation/destruction taught us that spawning (and terminating) processes is much slower than doing the same with threads. That is still a key advantage that many applications exploit. After all, threads are far more efficient than processes in terms of creation and destruction.

In a dynamic, unpredictable environment, where we do not know in advance how much work will be required, the use of multithreading to be able to quickly create worker threads (and quickly have them terminated) is very important. Think of the famous Apache web server: it's multithreaded by default (via its `mpm_worker` module in order to quickly serve client requests). In a similar fashion, the modern NGINX web server uses thread pools (more on this for those interested can be found in the *Further reading* section on the GitHub repository).

# Motivation – why threads?

Threading does indeed offer a number of useful advantages; here, we attempt to enumerate some of the more important ones. We think of this in terms of motivation for the application architect to make use of multithreading because of potential advantages to be gained. We divide this discussion into two areas: design and performance.

## Design motivation

In terms of design, we take into account the following:

### Taking advantage of potential parallelism

Many real-world applications will benefit from designing them in such a manner that the work can be split into distinct units, and these units or work parcels can run in parallel—concurrently—with each other. At the implementation level, we can use threads to implement the work parcels.

As an example, a download accelerator program exploits the network by having several threads perform network I/O. Each thread is assigned work to download only a portion of the file; they all run in parallel, effectively gaining more network bandwidth than a single thread could, and when done, the destination file is stitched together.

Many such examples abound; recognizing the potential for parallelism is an important part of the architect's job.

## Logical separation

The threading model intuitively lends itself to letting the designer logically separate work. For example, a GUI frontend application might have a few threads managing the GUI state, waiting for and reacting to user input, and so on. Other threads could be used to handle the app's business logic. Not mixing the **user interface** (UI) with the business logic is a key element of good design.

## Overlapping CPU with I/O

This point is similar in fashion to the previous one—the logical separation of tasks. In the context of what we're discussing, CPU refers to software that is CPU-intensive or CPU-bound (the canonical example being the `while (1);` piece of C code); I/O refers to software that is in a blocked state—we say that it is waiting on I/O, meaning that it is waiting on some other operation to complete (perhaps a file or network read, or any blocking API, in fact) before it can move forward; this is referred to as I/O bound.

So, think of it this way: let's say we have a series of tasks to perform (with no dependencies between them): task A, task B, task C, and task D.

Let's also say that task A and task C are highly CPU-bound, whereas task B and task D are more I/O-bound. If we use the traditional single threaded approach, then of course each task has to be carried out in sequence; so, the process ends up waiting—for perhaps a long while—for tasks B and D, thus delaying task C. If, on the other hand, we use a multithreaded approach, we can separate the tasks as individual threads. Thus, even while the threads for tasks B and D are blocked on I/O, the threads for task A and C continue to make progress.

This is called overlapping CPU with I/O. Decoupling (and separating out) tasks when there is no dependency between them, by using threads, is a design approach that is usually worth pursuing. It leads to better application responsiveness.

## Manager-worker model

Threads quite easily lend themselves to the familiar manager-worker model; a manager thread (often `main()`) creates worker threads on demand (or pools them); when work arises, a worker thread handles it. Think of busy web servers.

## IPC becoming simple(r)

Performing IPC between processes takes a learning curve, experience, and just a lot of work. With threads belonging to a process, IPC—communication—between them is as simple as writing and reading global memory (well, to be honest, it's not that simple, as we shall learn when we reach the topics on concurrency and synchronization in the next chapter; it's still less work conceptually and literally than processing IPC).

# Performance motivation

As the two examples in the previous section quite clearly showed us, using multithreading can raise application performance significantly; some of the reasons for this are mentioned here.

## Creation and destruction

Preceding example 1 clearly showed us that the time taken for the creation and destruction of a thread is far less than that of a process. Many applications require that you do this almost constantly. (We shall see that creating and destroying threads is programmatically much simpler to do than doing the same with processes.)

## Automatically taking advantage of modern hardware

Preceding example 2 clearly illustrated this point: when running a multithreaded app on modern multicore hardware (high-end enterprise class servers can have in excess of 700 CPU cores!), the underlying OS will take care of optimally scheduling threads onto available CPU cores; the app developers need not concern themselves with this. Effectively, the Linux kernel will try and ensure perfect SMP scalability whenever possible, which will result in higher throughput and, ultimately, speed gains. (Again, dear reader, we're being optimistic here: the reality is that with heavy parallelism and CPU cores also comes the heavy downsides of concurrency concerns; we shall discuss all of this in more detail in upcoming chapters.)

## Resource sharing

We have already covered this very point in the *Resource sharing* section earlier in the beginning portion of this chapter (re-read it, if required). The bottom line is this: thread creation is comparatively cheap as opposed to process creation (the same goes for destruction). Also, the memory footprint of a thread as opposed to a process is much lower. Thus, resource sharing, and the associated performance advantages, are obtained.

## Context switching

Context switching is an unfortunate reality on the OS—it's meta-work that must be done every time the OS switches from running one process to running another process (we have voluntary and involuntary context switches). The actual amount of time it takes to context switch is highly dependent on the hardware system and the software quality of the OS; typically, though, it's in the region of tens of microseconds for x86-based hardware systems. That sounds quite tiny: to get an idea of why this is considered important (and indeed wasteful), look at the output of running `vmstat 3` on an average Linux desktop computer (`vmstat(1)` is a famous utility; used this way, it gives us a nice 10,000-foot view of system activity; hey, also try out its modern successor, `dstat(1)`):

```
$ vmstat 3
procs -------memory---------- --swap-- --io-- -system-- ------cpu---
--
 r  b   swpd   free   buff  cache   si   so    bi    bo   in    cs us sy id wa
st
 0  0 287332 664156 719032 6168428  1    2   231   141    73    22 23 16 60  1
 0
 0  0 287332 659440 719056 6170132  0    0     0   124  2878  2353  5  5 89  1
 0
 1  0 287332 660388 719064 6168484  0    0     0   104  2862  2224  4  5 90  0
 0
 0  0 287332 662116 719072 6170276  0    0     0   427  2922  2257  4  6 90  1
 0
 0  0 287332 662056 719080 6170220  0    0     0    12  2358  1984  4  5 91  0
 0
 0  0 287332 660876 719096 6170544  0    0     0    88  2971  2293  5  6 89  1
 0
 0  0 287332 660908 719104 6170520  0    0     0    24  2982  2530  5  6 89  0
 0
[...]
```

(Please look up the man page on `vmstat(1)` for a detailed explanation of all fields). Preceding under the `system` heading, we have two columns: `in` and `cs` (hardware) interrupts and context switches, respectively, that have occurred in the last one second. Just look at the numbers (ignore the first output line, though)! It's fairly high. This is why it really does matter to system designers.

Context switching between the threads of the same process takes a lot less work (and thus time) than between processes (or threads belonging to different processes). This makes sense: a good amount of the kernel code can be effectively short-circuited when the overall process remains the same. Thus, this becomes another advantage of using threads.

# A brief history of threading

Threads—a sequential flow of control—have been around for a long while now; only, they went under the name of processes (reports put this at the time of the Berkeley Timesharing System, 1965). Then, by the early 1970s, along came Unix, which cemented the process as the combination of a VAS and a sequential flow of control. As mentioned earlier, this is now called the single threaded model, as of course only a single thread of control—the main function—existed.

Then, in May 1993, Sun Solaris 2.2 came out with UI threads, and a thread library called *libthread*, which exposed the UI API set; in effect, modern threads. Competing Unix vendors quickly came up with their own proprietary multithreaded solutions (with runtime libraries exposing APIs)—Digital with DECthreads (which was later absorbed by Compaq Tru64 Unix and subsequently HP-UX), IBM with AIX, Silicon Graphics with IRIX, and so on—each with their own proprietary solution.

# POSIX threads

Proprietary solutions poses a major problem to the big customer who owns heterogeneous hardware and software from several of these vendors; being proprietary, it is difficult to get the differing libraries and API sets to talk to each other. It's the usual problem—a lack of interoperability. The good news: in 1995, the IEEE formed a separate POSIX committee—IEEE 1003.1c—the **POSIX threads (pthreads)** committee, to evolve a standardized solution for an API for multithreading.

> POSIX: Apparently, the original name of the IEEE body is **Portable Operating System Interface for Computing Environments** (**POSICE**). Richard M. Stallman (RMS) suggested shortening the name to **Portable Operating System Interface for uniX** (**POSIX**), and that name has stuck.

So, the bottom line is that pthreads is an API standard; formally, IEEE 1003.1c-1995. The upshot of all of this is that all Unix and Unix-like OS vendors gradually built implementations supporting pthreads; so, today (in theory, at least), you can write a pthreads multithreaded application and it will run unmodified on any pthreads-compliant platform (in practice, expect a bit of porting effort).

## Pthreads and Linux

Of course, Linux wanted to be compliant with the POSIX threads standard; but who would actually build an implementation (remember, the standard is merely a draft specification document; it's not code)? Back in 1996, Xavier Leroy stepped up and built Linux's first pthreads implementation—a threading library called Linux threads. All considered, it was a good effort, but was not fully compatible with the (then brand new) pthreads standard.

An early effort at resolving problems was called **Next Generation Posix Threads** (**NGPT**). At around the same time, Red Hat threw in a team to work on this area as well; they called the project **Native Posix Threading Library** (**NPTL**). In the best traditions of open source culture, the NGPT developers worked together with their counterparts at NPTL and began merging the best features of NGPT into NPTL. NGPT development was abandoned sometime in 2003; by then, the realistic implementation of pthreads on Linux—which remains to this day—is NPTL.

> **More technically**: NPTL was entrenched as the superior threading API interface, even as features were integrated into the 2.6 Linux kernel (December 2003 onward), which helped greatly improve threading performance.
>
> NPTL implements the 1:1 threading model; this model provides true multithreading (user and kernel state) and is also known as the native threads model. Here, we do not intend to delve into these internal details; a link has been provided for interested readers in the *Further reading* section on the GitHub repository.

One can look up the threading implementation (since glibc 2.3.2) with the following code (on a Fedora 28 system):

```
$ getconf GNU_LIBPTHREAD_VERSION
NPTL 2.27
$
```

Clearly, it's NPTL.

# Thread management – the essential pthread APIs

In this—the second major portion of this first chapter on multithreading—we shall now focus on the mechanics: using the pthreads API, how exactly does the programmer create and manage threads in an effective fashion? We will explore the essential pthreads API interfaces to fulfill this key purpose; this knowledge is the building block for writing functional and performance-friendly pthreads applications.

We will take you through the thread life cycle in terms of API sets—creating, terminating, joining upon (waiting for), and in general, managing the threads of a process. We will also cover thread stack management.

This, of course, implies that we have a pthreads runtime library installed on the Linux system. On modern Linux distributions, this will certainly be the case; it's only if you are using a rather exotic embedded Linux that you will have to verify this. The name of the pthreads library on the Linux platform is libpthread.

A couple of key points regarding the pthread APIs are as follows:

- All pthread APIs require the `<pthread.h>` header file to be included in the source.
- The API often uses the object-oriented concepts of data hiding and data abstraction; many data types are internal typedefs; this design is deliberate: we want portable code. Thus, the programmer must not assume types and must work with the provided helper methods where applicable to access and/or query data types. (Of course, the code itself is the usual procedural C; nevertheless, many concepts are modeled around object orientation. Interestingly, the Linux kernel also follows this approach.)

## Thread creation

The pthreads API for creating a thread is `pthread_create(3)`; its signature is as follows:

```
#include <pthread.h>
int pthread_create(pthread_t *thread, const pthread_attr_t *attr,
                   void *(*start_routine) (void *), void *arg);
```

When compiling pthread applications, it's very important to specify the `-pthread` `gcc` option switch (it enables required macros for using the libpthread library(more on this to follow).

`pthread_create` is the API to invoke to create a new thread within the calling process. On success, the new thread will be running concurrently (in parallel) with other threads that may be alive in that process at that point in time; but what code will it be running? It will start by running the code of the `start_routine` function (the third parameter to this API: a pointer to the function). Of course, this `thread` function can subsequently make any number of function calls.

The new thread's thread ID will be stored in the opaque data item `thread`—the first parameter (it's a value-result style parameter). Its data type, `pthread_t` is deliberately opaque; we must not assume that it's an integer (or any such thing). We shall soon come across when and how we use the thread ID.

Notice that the third parameter, the function pointer—the routine run by the new thread—itself receives a void* parameter—a generic pointer. This is a common and helpful programming technique, enabling us to pass absolutely any value(s) to the newly created thread. (This kind of parameter is often referred to as client data or tag in the literature.) How do we pass it? Via the fourth parameter to `pthread_create(3)`, `arg`.

The second parameter to `pthread_create(3)` is a thread attribute structure; here, the programmer should pass the attributes of the thread being created (we shall discuss some of them shortly). There is a shortcut: passing NULL here implies that the library should use the default attributes when creating a thread. However, the defaults on a certain Unix might differ substantially from those on a different Unix or Linux; writing portable code implies one does not assume any defaults, but rather explicitly initializes a thread with attributes that are correct for the application. Thus, our recommendation would definitely be to not pass NULL, but to explicitly initialize a `pthread_attr_t` structure and pass it along (the code examples that follow will illustrate this).

Finally, the return value to `pthread_create(3)` is 0 on success and non-zero on failure; `errno` is set to a few values as appropriate (we refer you to the man page on `pthread_create(3)` for these details).

When a new thread is created, it inherits certain attributes from its creating thread; these include the following:

- The creating thread's capability sets (recall our discussion in Chapter 8, *Process Capabilities*); this is Linux-specific
- The creating thread's CPU affinity mask; this is Linux-specific
- The signal mask

Any pending signals and pending timers (alarms) in the new thread are cleared. CPU execution times will be reset as well for the new thread.

> Just so you know, on the Linux libpthreads implementation, `pthread_create(3)` calls the `clone(2)` system call, which, within the kernel, actually creates the thread.
> Interestingly, modern glibc's fork implementation also invokes the `clone(2)` system call. Flags passed to `clone(2)` determine how resource sharing is done.

It's about time that we did some coding! We will write a really simple (and actually quite buggy!) `hello, world.` for pthreads application (`ch14/pthreads1.c`):

```
[...]
#include <pthread.h>
#include "../common.h"
#define NTHREADS 3

void * worker(void *data)
{
        long datum = (long)data;
        printf("Worker thread #%ld says: hello, world.\n", datum);
        printf(" #%ld: work done, exiting now\n", datum);
}

int main(void)
{
        long i;
        int ret;
        pthread_t tid;

        for (i = 0; i < NTHREADS; i++) {
                ret = pthread_create(&tid, NULL, worker, (void *)i);
```

```
                if (ret)
                        FATAL("pthread_create() failed! [%d]\n", ret);
        }
        exit(EXIT_SUCCESS);
}
```

As you can see, we loop three times, and on each loop iteration we create a thread. Notice the third parameter to the `pthread_create(3)`—a function pointer (just providing the name of the function is sufficient; the compiler will figure the rest); this is the the thread's work routine. Here, it's the function `worker`. We also pass the fourth parameter to `pthread_create`—recall that's it's the client data, any data you would like to pass to the newly created thread; here, we pass the loop index `i` (of course, we appropriately typecast it so that the compiler won't complain).

In the `worker` function, worker, we gain access to the client data (received as the formal parameter `data`) by again type-casting the `void *` back to its original type, `long`:

`long datum = (long)data;`

We then merely emit a couple of printf's to show that, yes, we are here indeed. Notice how all the worker threads run the same code—the `worker` function. This is entirely acceptable; recall that code (text) is read-execute in terms of page permissions; running text in parallel is not only all right, but it's often desirable (providing high throughput).

To build it, we have provided the Makefile; note, though, that all the pthreads APIs aren't linked in by default, like glibc. No, they are, of course, in libpthread, which we shall have to both explicitly compile (to our source files) and link in to our binary executable via the `-pthread` directive. The following snippet from the Makefile shows this being done:

```
CC := gcc
CFLAGS=-O2 -Wall -UDEBUG -pthread
LINKIN := -pthread

#--- Target :: pthreads1
pthreads1.o: pthreads1.c
    ${CC} ${CFLAGS} -c pthreads1.c -o pthreads1.o
pthreads1: common.o pthreads1.o
    ${CC} -o pthreads1 pthreads1.o common.o ${LINKIN}
```

Building it now works, but—and please note this carefully—the program does not work well at all! In the following code, we perform some test runs by looping around ./pthreads1:

```
$ for i in $(seq 1 5); do echo "trial run #$i:" ; ./pthreads1; done
trial run #1:
Worker thread #0 says: hello, world.
Worker thread #0 says: hello, world.
trial run #2:
Worker thread #0 says: hello, world.
Worker thread #0 says: hello, world.
 #0: work done, exiting now
trial run #3:
Worker thread #1 says: hello, world.
Worker thread #1 says: hello, world.
 #1: work done, exiting now
trial run #4:
trial run #5:
$
```

As you can see the `hello, world.` message only appears intermittently and not at all in trial runs 4 and 5 (of course, the output you see when you try this out can certainly vary due to timing issues).

Why is it like this? Simple: we have inadvertently set up a buggy situation—a race! Where exactly? Look at the code again, carefully: what does the `main()` function do once the loop is done? It calls `exit(3)`; thus the entire process terminates, not just the main thread! And who is to say that the worker threads completed their work before this occurred? Ah—that, ladies and gentlemen, is your classic race.

So, how do we fix it? For now, we shall just perform a couple of quick fixes; the proper way to avoid racy code is via synchronization; this is a big topic and deserves a chapter by itself (as you shall see). Okay, first, let's fix the problem of the main thread prematurely exiting.

## Termination

The `exit(3)` library API causes the calling process—along with all of its threads – to terminate. If you would like a single thread to terminate, have it invoke the `pthread_exit(3)` API instead:

```
#include <pthread.h>
  void pthread_exit(void *retval);
```

# Multithreading with Pthreads Part I - Essentials

This parameter specifies the exit status of the calling thread; for the time being, we ignore it and just pass NULL (we shall examine using this parameter shortly).

So, back to our racy app (ch14/pthreads1.c); let's make a second, better version (ch14/pthreads2.c). The problem, really, with our first version was the race—the main thread calls exit(3), causing the entire process to die, probably before the worker threads got a chance to complete their work. So, let's fix this by having main() call pthread_exit(3)! Also, why not have our thread worker function terminate properly by explicitly invoking the pthread_exit(3) as well?

The following are the modified code snippets for the worker() and main() functions (ch14/pthreads2.c):

```
void * worker(void *data)
{
      long datum = (long)data;
      printf("Worker thread #%ld running ...\n", datum);
      printf("#%ld: work done, exiting now\n", datum);
      pthread_exit(NULL);
}
[...]
  for (i = 0; i < NTHREADS; i++) {
       ret = pthread_create(&tid, NULL, worker, (void *)i);
       if (ret)
             FATAL("pthread_create() failed! [%d]\n", ret);
  }
#if 1
      pthread_exit(NULL);
#else
      exit(EXIT_SUCCESS);
#endif
[...]
```

Let's try out the preceding program:

```
$ ./pthreads2
Worker thread #0 running ...
#0: work done, exiting now
Worker thread #1 running ...
#1: work done, exiting now
Worker thread #2 running ...
#2: work done, exiting now
$
```

That's much better!

# The return of the ghost

There is still a hidden problem. Let's do some more experimentation: let's write a third version of this program (let's call it ch14/pthreads3.c). In it, we say, what if the worker threads take longer to perform their work (than they are currently taking)? We can easily simulate this with a simple sleep(3) function, which is going to be introduced into the worker routine:

```
[...]
void * worker(void *data)
{
        long datum = (long)data;
        printf("Worker thread #%ld running ...\n", datum);
        sleep(3);
        printf("#%ld: work done, exiting now\n", datum);
        pthread_exit(NULL);
}
[...]
```

Let's try it out:

```
$ ./pthreads3
Worker thread #0 running ...
Worker thread #1 running ...
Worker thread #2 running ...

[... All three threads sleep for 3s ...]

#1: work done, exiting now
#0: work done, exiting now
#2: work done, exiting now
$
```

Well? It looks just fine. Is it really? There's just one more quick and minor modification that has to be done; increase the sleep time from 3 seconds to, say, 30 seconds, and rebuild and retry (the only reason we do this is to give the end user a chance to type a `ps(1)` command, as shown in the following screenshot, before the app dies). Now, run it in the background , and take a closer look!

```
$
$
$ ./pthreads3 &
[1] 3906
$ Worker thread #0 running ...
Worker thread #1 running ...
Worker thread #2 running ...

$ ps -LA|grep pthreads3
  3906  3906 pts/0    00:00:00 pthreads3 <defunct>
  3906  3907 pts/0    00:00:00 pthreads3
  3906  3908 pts/0    00:00:00 pthreads3
  3906  3909 pts/0    00:00:00 pthreads3
$ #2: work done, exiting now
#1: work done, exiting now
#0: work done, exiting now
```

Check out the preceding screenshot: we run the `pthreads3` app in the background; the app (well, the main thread of the app) creates an additional three threads. The threads merely block by going to sleep for thirty seconds each. As we ran the process in the background, we get control on the shell process; now we run `ps(1)` with the -LA option switches. From the man page on `ps(1)`:

- -A: Select all processes; identical to -e
- -L: Show threads, possibly with LWP and NLWP columns

All right! (GNU) `ps(1)` can even show us every thread alive by making use of the `-L` option switch (try out `ps H` too). With the `-L` switch, the first column in the output of `ps` is the PID of the process (quite familiar to us); the second column is the thread **Light Weight Process (LWP)**; in effect, this is the PID of the individual thread as seen by the kernel. Interesting. Not just that, look at the numbers carefully: where the PID and LWP match, it's the `main()` thread of the process; where the PID and LWP differ, it tells us that this is a child, or more correctly just a peer thread, belonging to the process; the LWP is the thread PID as seen by the OS. So, in our sample run, we have the process PID of 3906, along with four threads: the first one is the `main()` thread (as its PID == its LWP value), while the remaining three have the same PID—proving they belong to the same overall process, but their individual thread PIDs (their LWPs) are unique – 3907, 3908, and 3909!

The problem we have been referring to, though, is that in the first line—which represents the main thread—of the `ps` output is that the process name is followed by the phrase `<defunct>` (on the extreme right). The alert reader will remember that defunct is another term for zombie! Yes indeed, the infamous zombie has returned to haunt us.

The main thread, by invoking `pthread_exit(3)` (recall the code of main in `ch14/pthreads3.c`), has exited before the other threads in the process; the Linux kernel thus marks it as a zombie. As we learned in Chapter 10, *Process Creation*, zombies are undesirable entities; we really do not want a zombie hanging around (wasting resources). So, the question, of course, is how do we prevent the main thread from becoming a zombie? The answer is straightforward: do not allow the main thread to terminate before the other threads in the application; in other words, the recommendation is to always keep `main()` alive, waiting for all the other threads to die, before it itself terminates (and thus the process terminates). How? Read on.

Again, it goes without saying (but we shall say it!): the process remains alive as long as at least one thread within it remains alive.

As a quick aside, when will the worker threads run with respect to each other and main? In other words, is it guaranteed that the first thread created will run first, followed by the second thread, then the third, and so on?

The short answer: no, there is no such guarantee. Especially on modern **Symmetric Multiprocessor** (**SMP**) hardware and a modern multiprocess-and-multithreaded-capable OS such as Linux, the actual order at runtime is indeterminate (which is a fancy way of saying it can't be known). In reality, it's up to the OS scheduler to make these decisions (that is, in the absence of real-time scheduling policies and thread priorities; we shall tackle these topics later in this book).

Another trial run of our `./pthreads2` sample program reveals this very case:

```
$ ./pthreads2
Worker thread #0 running ...
#0: work done, exiting now
Worker thread #2 running ...
#2: work done, exiting now
Worker thread #1 running ...
#1: work done, exiting now
$
```

Can you see what happened? The order shown in the preceding code is: `thread #0`, followed by `thread #2`, followed by `thread #1`! It's unpredictable. Do not assume any specific order of execution when designing your multithreaded applications. (We shall cover synchronization in a later chapter, which teaches us how to achieve the order we require.)

## So many ways to die

How can a thread terminate? It turns out there are several ways:

- Explicitly, by invoking `pthread_exit(3)`.
- Implicitly, by returning from the thread function; the return value is implicitly passed (as though via `pthread_exit` parameter).
- Implicitly, by falling off the thread function; that is, hitting the close brace `}`; note however that this is not recommended (a later discussion will show you why)
- Any thread invoking the `exit(3)` API will, of course, cause the entire process, along with all threads in it, to die.
- The thread gets canceled (which we will cover later).

# How many threads is too many?

So, by now, we know how to create an application process with a few threads executing within it. We will repeat a code snippet from our very first demo program, `ch14/pthreads1.c`, as follows:

```
#include <pthread.h>
#define NTHREADS 3
[...]

int main(void)
{
  [...]
  for (i = 0; i < NTHREADS; i++) {
        ret = pthread_create(&tid, NULL, worker, (void *)i);
        if (ret)
              FATAL("pthread_create() failed! [%d]\n", ret);
  }
  [...]
```

Clearly, the process—well, we really mean the main thread of the process (or application)—goes in a loop, and each loop iteration creates a thread. So, when it's done, we will have three threads in addition to the main thread, which is a total of four threads, alive in the process.

This is obvious. The point here is this: creating threads is so much simpler than creating (child) processes with the `fork(2)`; with fork, we had to carefully code it, getting the child to run its code while the parent continues with its code path (recall the switch-case construct; take another quick look at our `ch10/fork4.c` code example, if you wish to). With `pthread_create(3)`, things have become easy for the application programmer – just call the API in a loop—and voila! You get as many threads as you like! In the preceding code snippet, imagine tweaking it, changing the value of NTHREADS from 3 to 300; and just like that, the process will produce 300 threads. What if we made NTHREADS 3,000? Or 30,000!?

Thinking about this brings up a couple of pertinent questions: one, how many threads can you actually create? And two, how many threads should you create? Please, read on.

## How many threads can you create?

If you think about it, there must be some artificial constraint upon the number of threads that the underlying OS will allow an application to create; otherwise, system resources would get exhausted pretty quickly. In fact, this is not really something new; our whole discussion in Chapter 3, *Resource Limits*, was really about similar things.

With regard to threads (and processes), there are two (direct) limits that impact the number of threads that can exist at any given point in time:

- Per process resource limits: You will recall from our Chapter 3, *Resource Limits*, that there are two utilities to look up the currently defined resource limits: ulimit(1) and prlimit(1), the latter being the modern interface. Let's take a quick look at the resource limit for max user processes; also realize that although the word processes is used, you should actually think of these as threads:

    ```
    $ ulimit -u
    63223
    $
    ```

    Similarly, prlimit() shows us the following:

    ```
    $ prlimit --nproc
    RESOURCE DESCRIPTION                SOFT    HARD    UNITS
    NPROC    max number of processes    63223   63223   processes
    $
    ```

    > **TIP**
    > Here, we have shown you how to query the limit via the CLI; to see how to change it—both interactively and programmatically with API interfaces – refer to Chapter 3, *Resource Limits*.

- System-wide limits: The Linux OS maintains a system-wide (not per-process) limit on the total number of threads that can be alive at any given point in time. This value is exposed to the user space via the proc filesystem:

    ```
    $ cat /proc/sys/kernel/threads-max
    126446
    $
    ```

So, the thing to understand is that if either of the preceding two limits are breached, `pthread_create(3)` (and similarly, the `fork(2)`) will fail (typically setting `errno` to the value `EAGAIN` try again; the OS saying, in effect, "I cannot do this for you right now, please try again later").

Can you change these values? Yes, of course, but with the usual caveat—you require root (super user) access to do so. (Again, we have discussed these points in detail with respect to in Chapter 3, *Resource Limits*) Regarding the system-wide limit, you can indeed change it as the root. But, hang on, blindly changing system parameters like this without an understanding of the impact is a sure way to lose grip on a system! So, let's start by asking ourselves this: the OS sets the `threads-max` limit at boot time; what does it base the value on?

The short answer: it's directly proportional to the amount of RAM on the system. This makes sense: ultimately, memory is the key limiting resource with regard to creating threads and processes.

> In more detail for our dear OS-level geek readers: kernel code at boot time sets the `/proc/sys/kernel/threads-max` value so that thread (task) structures within the OS can take a maximum of one-eighth of available RAM. (The threads-max minimum value is 20; the maximum value is the constant `FUTEX_TID_MASK` `0x3fffffff`.)
> Also, by default, the per-process resource limit for the maximum number of threads is half of the system limit.

As seen from the preceding code, the value we obtained was 126,446; this was done on a native Linux laptop with 16 GB of RAM. Running the same commands on a guest VM with 1 GB of RAM yields the following results:

```
$ cat /proc/sys/kernel/threads-max
7420
$ prlimit --nproc
RESOURCE DESCRIPTION              SOFT  HARD  UNITS
NPROC    max number of processes  3710  3710  processes
$
```

Setting the `threads-max` kernel tunable to too high a value – beyond `FUTEX_TID_MASK` – will cause it to be brought down to that value (but, of course, that is almost certainly too large in any case). But even within limits, you can stray too far, causing the system to become vulnerable (to **denial-of-service** (**DoS**) attacks, perhaps!). On an embedded Linux system, lowering the limit might actually help by constraining the system.

## Code example – creating any number of threads

So, let's put it to the test: we will write a simple extension of our previous program, this time allowing the user to specify the number of threads to attempt to create within the process as the parameter (ch14/cr8_so_many_threads.c). The main function is as follows:

```
int main(int argc, char **argv)
{
  long i;
  int ret;
  pthread_t tid;
  long numthrds=0;

  if (argc != 2) {
      fprintf(stderr, "Usage: %s number-of-threads-to-create\n",
argv[0]);
      exit(EXIT_FAILURE);
  }
  numthrds = atol(argv[1]);
  if (numthrds <= 0) {
      fprintf(stderr, "Usage: %s number-of-threads-to-create\n",
argv[0]);
      exit(EXIT_FAILURE);
  }

  for (i = 0; i < numthrds; i++) {
      ret = pthread_create(&tid, NULL, worker, (void *)i);
      if (ret)
          FATAL("pthread_create() failed! [%d]\n", ret);
  }
  pthread_exit(NULL);
}
```

It's quite simple: we convert the string value the user passed as the first parameter to a numeric one with numthrds; we then have main loop numthrds times, invoking pthread_create(3) and thus creating a brand new thread upon each loop iteration! Once created, what do the new threads do? It's clear – they execute the code of the worker function. Let's take a look:

```
void * worker(void *data)
{
    long datum = (long)data;
    printf("Worker thread #%5ld: pausing now...\n", datum);
    (void)pause();
```

```
            printf(" #%5ld: work done, exiting now\n", datum);
            pthread_exit(NULL);
}
```

Again, this is very simple: the worker threads just emit a `printf(3)`—which is useful because they print out their thread number—it's just the loop index of course. Then, they go to sleep via the `pause(2)` system call. (This system call is useful: it's a perfect blocking call; it puts the calling thread to sleep until a signal arrives.)

All right, let's try it out:

```
$ ./cr8_so_many_threads
Usage: ./cr8_so_many_threads number-of-threads-to-create
$ ./cr8_so_many_threads 300
Worker thread #    0: pausing now...
Worker thread #    1: pausing now...
Worker thread #    2: pausing now...
Worker thread #    3: pausing now...
Worker thread #    5: pausing now...
Worker thread #    6: pausing now...
Worker thread #    4: pausing now...
Worker thread #    7: pausing now...
Worker thread #   10: pausing now...
Worker thread #   11: pausing now...
Worker thread #    9: pausing now...
Worker thread #    8: pausing now...

[...]

Worker thread #  271: pausing now...
Worker thread #  299: pausing now...
Worker thread #  285: pausing now...
Worker thread #  284: pausing now...
Worker thread #  273: pausing now...
Worker thread #  287: pausing now...
[...]
^C
$
```

It works (notice that we've truncated the output as there would be far too much to show in this book). Notice how the order in which the threads come alive and execute (emitting their `printf`) is random. We can see that the last thread we created is the one highlighted in bold—thread # `299` (0 to 299 is 300 threads).

Now, let's run it again, but this time ask it to create an impossibly large number of threads (we are currently trying this out on a guest VM with 1 GB of RAM):

```
$ prlimit --nproc ; ulimit -u
RESOURCE DESCRIPTION              SOFT HARD UNITS
NPROC    max number of processes  3710 3710 processes
3710
$ ./cr8_so_many_threads 40000
Worker thread # 0: pausing now...
Worker thread # 1: pausing now...
Worker thread # 2: pausing now...
Worker thread # 4: pausing now...

[...]

Worker thread # 2139: pausing now...
Worker thread # 2113: pausing now...
Worker thread # 2112: pausing now...
FATAL:cr8_so_many_threads.c:main:52: pthread_create() #2204 failed !
[11]
   kernel says: Resource temporarily unavailable
$
```

> Obviously, again, the results that you will see will depend on your system; we encourage the reader to try it out on different systems. Also, it's possible that the actual failure message may have appeared somewhere higher up in your Terminal window; scroll up to find it!

> The name of the thread, as shown by `ps(1)`, and so on, can be set via the `pthread_setname_np(3)` API; note that the `np` suffix implies that the API is non-portable (Linux-only).

## How many threads should one create?

The number of threads you create really does depend on the nature of the application. For our discussion here, we will consider which the application tends to be – CPU versus IO bound.

Earlier in this chapter (specifically within the sections on *Design Motivation* and *Overlapping CPU with I/O*), we mentioned the fact that a thread, in terms of its execution behavior, falls somewhere on a continuum, somewhere between two extremes: one extreme being a completely CPU-bound task and the other extreme being a completely I/O-bound task. The continuum may be visualized like this:

```
◄─────────────────────────────────────────────────►
100%                                           100%
CPU-bound                                   IO-bound
```

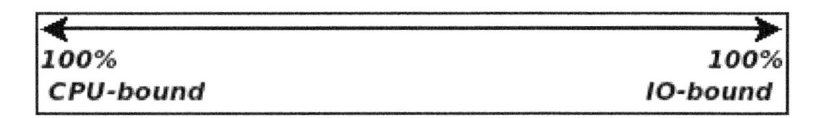

Fig 3: The CPU-bound/IO-bound continuum

A thread that is a 100% CPU-bound will be continually hammering away on the CPU; a 100% I/O-bound thread is one that is always in a blocking (or wait) state, never executing on CPU. Both extremes are unrealistic in real applications; however, it's quite easy to visualize the domains where they tend to have one of these. For example, domains that involve heavy mathematical processing (scientific models, vector graphics such as flash animations in a web browser, matrix multiplication, and so on), (un)compression utilities, multimedia codecs, and so on will certainly tend to be more CPU-bound. On the other hand, many (but not all) applications that us humans interact with on a daily basis (think of your email client, web browser, word processing, and so on) tend to wait for the human to do something; in effect, they tend to be I/O-bound.

Therefore—a bit simplistically, but nevertheless—this serves as a useful design rule of thumb: if the application being designed is I/O-bound in nature, then creating even a large-ish number of threads that just wait for work is all right; this is because they will be asleep the majority of the time, thus not placing any strain on the CPU(s) (of course, create too many threads and they do strain memory.)

On the other hand, if the application is determined to be highly CPU-bound, then creating a large number of threads will stress the system (and end up causing thrashing – a phenomenon wherein the meta-work takes longer than the actual work!). Thus, for CPU-bound workloads, the thumb rule is this:

```
max number of threads = number of CPU cores * factor;
  where factor = 1.5 or 2.
```

> **TIP**: Note, though, that there do exist CPU cores that do not provide any **hyperthreading** (HT) features; on cores like this, factor should just remain 1.

Actually, our discussion has been quite simplistic: many real-world applications (think of powerful web servers such as Apache and NGINX) will dynamically create and adjust the number of threads required based on the exact circumstances, configuration presets, and present workload. Nevertheless, the preceding discussion serves as a starting point so that you can start thinking about design for multithreaded applications.

## Thread attributes

In our initial discussion on *Thread Creation* earlier in this chapter, we saw the `pthread_create(3)` API; the second parameter is a pointer to the thread attribute structure: `const pthread_attr_t *attr`. We mentioned there that passing NULL here, in effect, has the library create a thread with default attributes. While that is indeed the case, the problem is that, for truly portable applications, this is not good enough. Why? Because the default thread attributes actually differ quite widely from implementation to implementation. The right way-specify the thread attributes explicitly at thread creation time.

Firstly, of course, we need to learn what attributes a pthread has. The following table enumerates this:

| Attribute | Meaning | APIs: `pthread_attr_[...](3)` | Values Possible | *Linux Default* |
| --- | --- | --- | --- | --- |
| Detach state | Create threads as joinable or detached | `pthread_attr_ [get\|set]detachstate` | PTHREAD_CREATE_JOINABLE PTHREAD_CREATE_DETACHED | PTHREAD_CREATE_JOINABLE |
| Scheduling/contention scope | Set of threads against which we compete for resources (CPU) | `pthread_attr_ [get\|set]scope` | PTHREAD_SCOPE_SYSTEM PTHREAD_SCOPE_PROCESS | PTHREAD_SCOPE_SYSTEM |
| Scheduling/inheritance | Determines whether scheduling attributes are inherited implicitly from calling a thread or explicitly from the attr structure | `pthread_attr_ [get\|set]inheritsched` | PTHREAD_INHERIT_SCHED PTHREAD_EXPLICIT_SCHED | PTHREAD_INHERIT_SCHED |
| Scheduling/policy | Determines the scheduling policy of the thread being created | `pthread_attr_ [get\|set]schedpolicy` | SCHED_FIFO SCHED_RR SCHED_OTHER | SCHED_OTHER |
| Scheduling/priority | Determines the scheduling priority of the thread being created | `pthread_attr_ [get\|set]schedparam` | struct sched_param holds int sched_priority | 0 (non real-time) |

| Stack/guard region | A guard region for the thread's stack | pthread_attr_ [get\|set]guardsize | Stack guard region size in bytes | 1 page |
|---|---|---|---|---|
| Stack/location, size | Query or set the thread's stack location and size | pthread_attr_ [get\|set]stack pthread_attr_ [get\|set]stackaddr pthread_attr_ [get\|set]stacksize | Stack address and/or stack size, in bytes | Thread Stack Location: left to the OS Thread Stack Size: 8 MB |

As you can see, clearly understanding what exactly many of these attributes signify requires further information. Please be patient as we proceed through this chapter (and, in fact, this book), as several of these attributes and their meanings will become abundantly clear ( details on scheduling will be shown in Chapter 17, *CPU Scheduling on Linux*).

## Code example – querying the default thread attributes

For now, a useful experiment would be to query the default attributes of a newly born thread whose attribute structure is specified as NULL (default).
How? pthread_default_getattr_np(3) will do the trick (note though, that again, the _np suffix implies that it's a Linux-only, non-portable API):

```
#define _GNU_SOURCE /* See feature_test_macros(7) */
#include <pthread.h>
int pthread_getattr_default_np(pthread_attr_t *attr);
```

Interestingly, as this function depends on the _GNU_SOURCE macro being defined, we must first define the macro (early in the source); otherwise, the compile triggers warnings and possibly fails. (In our code, we thus use #include "../common.h" first as our *common.h* header defines the _GNU_SOURCE macro.)

Our code example can be found here, within this book's GitHub repository: ch14/disp_defattr_pthread.c.

In the following code, we display a trial run on a Fedora x86_64 box running the 4.17.12 Linux kernel:

```
$ ./disp_defattr_pthread
Linux Default Thread Attributes:
Detach State : PTHREAD_CREATE_JOINABLE
Scheduling
  Scope       : PTHREAD_SCOPE_SYSTEM
  Inheritance : PTHREAD_INHERIT_SCHED
```

```
    Policy        : SCHED_OTHER
    Priority      : 0
 Thread Stack
    Guard Size :      4096 bytes
    Stack Size : 8388608 bytes
$
```

> For readability, only key parts of the source code are displayed; to view the complete source code, build and run it, the entire tree is available for cloning from GitHub here: https://github.com/PacktPublishing/Hands-on-System-Programming-with-Linux.

The key function here is shown in the following code (ch14/disp_defattr_pthread.c); we first query and display the thread attribute structure's "detached state" (these terms will be explained in detail shortly):

```
static void display_thrd_attr(pthread_attr_t *attr)
{
  int detachst=0;
  int sched_scope=0, sched_inh=0, sched_policy=0;
  struct sched_param sch_param;
  size_t guardsz=0, stacksz=0;
  void *stackaddr;

  // Query and display the 'Detached State'
  if (pthread_attr_getdetachstate(attr, &detachst))
      WARN("pthread_attr_getdetachstate() failed.\n");
  printf("Detach State : %s\n",
    (detachst == PTHREAD_CREATE_JOINABLE) ? "PTHREAD_CREATE_JOINABLE"
:
    (detachst == PTHREAD_CREATE_DETACHED) ? "PTHREAD_CREATE_DETACHED"
:
    "<unknown>");
```

Next, various scheduling attributes are queried and displayed (some details covered later in Chapter 17, *CPU Scheduling on Linux*):

```
//--- Scheduling Attributes
  printf("Scheduling \n");
  // Query and display the 'Scheduling Scope'
  if (pthread_attr_getscope(attr, &sched_scope))
      WARN("pthread_attr_getscope() failed.\n");
  printf(" Scope : %s\n",
    (sched_scope == PTHREAD_SCOPE_SYSTEM) ? "PTHREAD_SCOPE_SYSTEM" :
    (sched_scope == PTHREAD_SCOPE_PROCESS) ? "PTHREAD_SCOPE_PROCESS" :
    "<unknown>");
```

```
    // Query and display the 'Scheduling Inheritance'
    if (pthread_attr_getinheritsched(attr, &sched_inh))
        WARN("pthread_attr_getinheritsched() failed.\n");
    printf(" Inheritance : %s\n",
      (sched_inh == PTHREAD_INHERIT_SCHED) ? "PTHREAD_INHERIT_SCHED" :
      (sched_inh == PTHREAD_EXPLICIT_SCHED) ? "PTHREAD_EXPLICIT_SCHED" :
      "<unknown>");

    // Query and display the 'Scheduling Policy'
    if (pthread_attr_getschedpolicy(attr, &sched_policy))
        WARN("pthread_attr_getschedpolicy() failed.\n");
    printf(" Policy : %s\n",
            (sched_policy == SCHED_FIFO)   ? "SCHED_FIFO" :
            (sched_policy == SCHED_RR)     ? "SCHED_RR" :
            (sched_policy == SCHED_OTHER)  ? "SCHED_OTHER" :
             "<unknown>");

    // Query and display the 'Scheduling Priority'
    if (pthread_attr_getschedparam(attr, &sch_param))
        WARN("pthread_attr_getschedparam() failed.\n");
    printf(" Priority : %d\n", sch_param.sched_priority);
```

Finally, the thread stack attributes are queried and displayed:

```
    //--- Thread Stack Attributes
    printf("Thread Stack \n");
    // Query and display the 'Guard Size'
    if (pthread_attr_getguardsize(attr, &guardsz))
        WARN("pthread_attr_getguardsize() failed.\n");
    printf(" Guard Size : %9zu bytes\n", guardsz);

    /* Query and display the 'Stack Size':
     * 'stack location' will be meaningless now as there is no
     * actual thread created yet!
     */
    if (pthread_attr_getstack(attr, &stackaddr, &stacksz))
        WARN("pthread_attr_getstack() failed.\n");
    printf(" Stack Size : %9zu bytes\n", stacksz);
}
```

> **TIP**
> In the preceding code, we put in
> the `pthread_getattr_default_np(3)` API to query the default thread attributes. Its counterpart,
> the `pthread_setattr_default_np(3)` API, allows you to specify what exactly the default thread attributes should be when creating a thread, and the second parameter to `pthread_create(3)` is passed as NULL. Do see its man page for details.

There is an alternate way to write a similar program: why not create a thread with a NULL attribute structure—thus making it default attributes—and then issue the `pthread_getattr_np(3)` API to query and display the actual thread attributes? We leave this as an exercise to the reader (in fact, the man page on `pthread_attr_init(3)` supplies just such a program).

## Joining

Imagine an application where a thread (typically, main) has spawned off several other worker threads. Each worker thread has a specific job to do; once done, it terminates (via `pthread_exit(3)`). How will the creator thread know when a worker thread is done (terminated)? Ah, that is precisely where joining comes in. With the join, the creator thread can wait for, or block upon, the death (termination) of another thread within the process!

Does this not sound very much like the `wait(2)` system call that a parent process issues to wait for the death of a child? True, but as we shall see shortly, it's certainly not identical.

Also, importantly, the return value from the thread that terminated is passed along to the thread that issued the join upon it. This way, it comes to know whether the worker succeeded in its task or not (and if not, the failure value can be examined to pinpoint the cause of failure):

```
#include <pthread.h>
int pthread_join(pthread_t thread, void **retval);
```

The first parameter to pthread_join(3), thread, is the ID of the thread to wait for. The moment it terminates, the calling thread will receive, in the second parameter (yes, it's a value-result style parameter), the return value from the thread that terminated—which, of course is the value passed via its pthread_exit(3) call.

Thus, the join is very helpful; using this construct, you can ensure that a thread can block upon the termination of any given thread. Specifically, in the case of the main thread, we often use this mechanism to ensure that main waits for all other application threads to terminate before it itself terminates (thus preventing the zombie we saw earlier). This is considered the right approach.

Recall that in the earlier section, *The return of the ghost*, we clearly saw how the main thread, dying before its counterparts, becomes an inadvertent zombie (the ch14/pthreads3.c program). A quick example, built upon this previous code, will help clarify things. So, let's enhance that program – we shall now call it ch14/pthreads_joiner1.c – so that we have the main thread wait for all other threads to die by invoking the pthread_join(3) API on each of the worker threads, and only then itself terminate:

```c
int main(void)
{
  long i;
  int ret, stat=0;
  pthread_t tid[NTHREADS];
  pthread_attr_t attr;

  /* Init the thread attribute structure to defaults */
  pthread_attr_init(&attr);
  /* Create all threads as joinable */
  pthread_attr_setdetachstate(&attr, PTHREAD_CREATE_JOINABLE);

  // Thread creation loop
  for (i = 0; i < NTHREADS; i++) {
      printf("main: creating thread #%ld ...\n", i);
      ret = pthread_create(&tid[i], &attr, worker, (void *)i);
      if (ret)
          FATAL("pthread_create() failed! [%d]\n", ret);
  }
  pthread_attr_destroy(&attr);
```

There are a few things to notice here:

- To perform the join subsequently, we require each thread's ID; hence, we declare an array of pthread_t (the tid variable). Each element will store the corresponding thread's ID value.
- Thread attributes:
    - Until now, we have not explicitly initialized and made use of a thread attribute structure when creating threads. Here, we rectify this shortcoming. pthread_attr_init(3) is used to initialize (to defaults) an attribute structure.
    - Furthermore, we explicitly make the threads joinable by setting up this attribute within the structure (via the pthread_attr_setdetachstate(3) API).
    - Once the threads are created, we must destroy the thread attribute structure (via the pthread_attr_destroy(3) API).

It is key to understand that only threads that have their detach state set as joinable can be joined upon. Interestingly, a joinable thread can later be set to the detached state (by calling the pthread_detach(3) API upon it); there is no converse routine.

The code continues; we now show you the thread worker function:

```
void * worker(void *data)
{
        long datum = (long)data;
        int slptm=8;

        printf(" worker #%ld: will sleep for %ds now ...\n", datum,
slptm);
        sleep(slptm);
        printf(" worker #%ld: work (eyeroll) done, exiting now\n",
datum);

        /* Terminate with success: status value 0.
         * The join will pick this up. */
        pthread_exit((void *)0);
}
```

Easy: we just have the so-called worker threads sleep for 8 seconds and then die; the `pthread_exit(3)`, this time, passes the return status 0 as a parameter. In the following code snippet, we continue the code of main:

```
    // Thread join loop
    for (i = 0; i < NTHREADS; i++) {
        printf("main: joining (waiting) upon thread #%ld ...\n", i);
        ret = pthread_join(tid[i], (void **)&stat);
        if (ret)
            WARN("pthread_join() failed! [%d]\n", ret);
        else
            printf("Thread #%ld successfully joined; it terminated with"
                "status=%d\n", i, stat);
    }
    printf("\nmain: now dying... <Dramatic!> Farewell!\n");
    pthread_exit(NULL);
}
```

Here's the key part: in a loop, the main thread blocks (waits) upon the death of each worker thread via the `pthread_join(3)` API; the second (value-result style) parameter, in effect, returns the status of the thread that just terminated. The usual zero-upon-success convention is followed, thus allowing the main thread to figure out whether the worker threads completed their work successfully or not.

Let's build and run it:

```
$ make pthreads_joiner1
gcc -O2 -Wall -UDEBUG -c ../common.c -o common.o
gcc -O2 -Wall -UDEBUG -c pthreads_joiner1.c -o pthreads_joiner1.o
gcc -o pthreads_joiner1 pthreads_joiner1.o common.o -lpthread
$ ./pthreads_joiner1
main: creating thread #0 ...
main: creating thread #1 ...
 worker #0: will sleep for 8s now ...
main: creating thread #2 ...
 worker #1: will sleep for 8s now ...
main: joining (waiting) upon thread #0 ...
 worker #2: will sleep for 8s now ...

<< ... worker threads sleep for 8s ... >>

 worker #0: work (eyeroll) done, exiting now
 worker #1: work (eyeroll) done, exiting now
 worker #2: work (eyeroll) done, exiting now
Thread #0 successfully joined; it terminated with status=0
main: joining (waiting) upon thread #1 ...
Thread #1 successfully joined; it terminated with status=0
```

# Multithreading with Pthreads Part I - Essentials

```
main: joining (waiting) upon thread #2 ...
Thread #2 successfully joined; it terminated with status=0

main: now dying... <Dramatic!> Farewell!
$
```

As the worker threads die, they are picked up, or joined, by the main thread via `pthread_join`; not only that, their termination status—return value—can be examined.

Okay, we'll make a copy of the preceding program and call it `ch14/pthreads_joiner2.c`. The only change we make is instead of having each worker thread sleep for an identical 8 seconds, we'll make the sleep time dynamic. We will change the code; for instance, this line would be changed: `sleep(slptm);`

The new line would read as follows: `sleep(slptm-datum);`

Here, `datum` is the value passed to the thread—the loop index. This way, we find that the worker threads sleep as follows:

- Worker thread #0 sleeps for (8-0) = 8 seconds
- Worker thread #1 sleeps for (8-1) = 7 seconds
- Worker thread #2 sleeps for (8-2) = 6 seconds

Obviously, worker thread #2 will terminate first; so what? Well, think about it: in the meantime, the main thread is looping around `pthread_join`, but in the order of thread #0, thread #1, thread #2. Now, thread #0 will die last and thread #2 will die first. Will this be an issue?

Let's try it out and see:

```
$ ./pthreads_joiner2
main: creating thread #0 ...
main: creating thread #1 ...
main: creating thread #2 ...
main: joining (waiting) upon thread #0 ...
 worker #0: will sleep for 8s now ...
 worker #1: will sleep for 7s now ...
 worker #2: will sleep for 6s now ...

<< ... worker threads sleep for 8s, 7s and 6s resp ... >>

 worker #2: work (eyeroll) done, exiting now
 worker #1: work (eyeroll) done, exiting now
 worker #0: work (eyeroll) done, exiting now
Thread #0 successfully joined; it terminated with status=0
```

[ 578 ]

```
main: joining (waiting) upon thread #1 ...
Thread #1 successfully joined; it terminated with status=0
main: joining (waiting) upon thread #2 ...
Thread #2 successfully joined; it terminated with status=0

main: now dying... <Dramatic!> Farewell!
$
```

What do we notice? In spite of worker thread #2 dying first, worker thread #0 gets joined first because, in the code, that is the thread we wait for first!

## The thread model join and the process model wait

By now, you should have begun to realize that although the `pthread_join(3)` and `wait(2)` (and family) APIs seem to be very similar, they are certainly not equivalent; several differences between them exist and are enumerated in the following table:

| Situation | Thread: `pthread_join(3)` | Process: `wait[pid](2)` |
|---|---|---|
| Condition | A thread being waited for must have its detached state attribute set as joinable, not detached. | None; any child process can (and in fact must) be waited upon (recall our *fork rule #7*) |
| Hierarchy | None: any thread can join on any other thread; there is no requirement of a parent-child relationship. In fact, we do not consider threads to live within a strict parent-child hierarchy as processes do; all threads are peers. | A strict parent-child hierarchy exists; only a parent can wait for a child process. |
| Order | With threads, one is forced to join (wait) upon the particular thread specified as the parameter to `pthread_join(3)`. In other words, if there are, say, three threads running and main issues the join within an ascending ordered loop, then it must wait for the death or thread #1, then thread #2, and then thread #3. If thread #2 terminates earlier, there is no help for it. | With wait, a process can wait upon the death (or stoppage) of any child, or specify a particular child process to wait for with waitpid. |

| | | |
|---|---|---|
| Signaling | No signal is sent upon a thread's death. | Upon a process's death, the kernel sends the SIGCHLD signal to the parent process. |

A few other points to note regarding pthread_join(3) are as follows:

- You require the thread ID of a thread in order to join upon it; this is deliberately done so that we can, in effect, only join the threads of our application process. Attempting to join on other threads (like a third-party library thread) would be poor design.
- What if the thread we are waiting for (to die) has already died? Then pthread_join(3) just returns immediately.
- What if a thread tries to join upon itself? This results in failure (with errno set to EDEADLK).
- Attempting to have several threads join upon one thread results in undefined behavior; avoid this.
- If a thread attempting to join on another thread is cancelled (covered later), the target thread remains as it was (joinable).

## Checking for life, timing out

Sometimes, we might have a situation wherein we want to check whether a particular thread is still alive or not; one way to do so is via the pthread_tryjoin_np(3) API:

```
#define _GNU_SOURCE /* See feature_test_macros(7) */
#include <pthread.h>

int pthread_tryjoin_np(pthread_t thread, void **retval);
int pthread_timedjoin_np(pthread_t thread, void **retval,
                         const struct timespec *abstime);
```

The first parameter to pthread_tryjoin_np(3) is the thread we are attempting to join to; (the second parameter, as usual, is the target thread's termination status). Notice the try phrase within the API – this typically specifies that the call is non-blocking; in other words, we perform a non-blocking join on the target thread. If the target thread is alive, then instead of waiting for it to die, the API returns immediately with an error: errno will be set to EBUSY (and the man page tells us that this implies the thread had not yet terminated at the time of the call).

What if we would like to wait (block) upon a target thread's death, but not forever? In other words, we would like to wait for a given maximum time period. This can be achieved via the pthread_timedjoin_np(3) API; the first two parameters are the usual ones (the same as with pthread_join), while the third parameter specifies the timeout in terms of the absolute time (or what is often called Unix time – the number of seconds (and nanoseconds) elapsed since midnight 1 January 1970—the Epoch!).

As covered in Chapter 13, *Timers*, the timespec data structure is of the following format:

```
struct timespec {
    time_t tv_sec;  /* seconds */
    long tv_nsec;   /* nanoseconds */
};
```

That's easy; but how do we specify the time as UNIX time (or time since the Epoch)? We refer the reader to the man page on pthread_timedjoin_np(3), which gives a simple example of the same (also, we ask you try this API out as an exercise).

> Another thing I noticed when using the pthread_timedjoin_np(3) API: it's possible that the join times out and then proceeds to, say, release some resources – like performing free(3) on a heap buffer—while the worker thread is still alive and using it. This is a bug, of course; it also goes to show that you must carefully think out and test the design; usually, using a blocking join on all worker threads, thus ensuring they have all terminated before freeing up resources, is the right approach.

> Again, we remind you that the _np suffix to the APIs implies that they are non-portable (Linux-only).

## Join or not?

A thread that is explicitly set to the detached state cannot be joined upon; so, what happens when it dies? Its resources are disposed of by the library.

A thread that is explicitly set to the joinable state (or if joinable is the default state) must be joined upon; failure to do so results in a kind of resource leakage. So, be careful: if you have created threads to be joinable, then you must ensure that the join is performed.

Performing a join on other app threads by the main thread is usually considered a best practice, since it prevents the zombie thread behavior we saw earlier. Also, it's usually important for the creator thread to come to know whether its workers successfully performed their job or not, and if not, why not. The join makes all of this possible.

However, it is possible that your application does not want to wait around for some worker threads; in this case, ensure that you create them as detached.

## Parameter passing

Recall the signature of the `pthread_create(3)` API:

```
int pthread_create(pthread_t *thread, const pthread_attr_t *attr,
                   void *(*start_routine) (void *), void *arg);
```

The third parameter is the thread function—in effect, the life and scope of the newly born thread. It receives a single parameter of type `void *`; this parameter to the new born thread is passed via the fourth parameter to `pthread_create`: `void *arg`.

As mentioned earlier, its data type is a generic pointer, precisely so that we can, in effect, pass along any data type as a parameter, and then in the thread routine, appropriately typecast and use it. Until now, we have come across simple use cases of the same – typically, passing along an integer value as the parameter. In our very first simple multithreaded app – `ch14/pthreads1.c` – in our main function, we did the following:

```
long i;
int ret;
pthread_t tid;

for (i = 0; i < NTHREADS; i++) {
    ret = pthread_create(&tid, NULL, worker, (void *)i);
    ...
}
```

And, in the thread routine worker, we performed a simple typecast-and-use:

```
void * worker(void *data)
{
    long datum = (long)data;
...
```

That's easy, but it does raise a fairly obvious question: in the pthread_create(3) API, as there seems to be just one placeholder for the arg (the parameter) how can you pass along more than one data item – several parameters, in effect – to the thread routine?

## Passing a structure as a parameter

The preceding heading gives it away: we pass a data structure. But how, exactly? Allocate memory to a pointer to the data structure, initialize it, and pass the pointer typecast as void *. (In fact, this is a very common approach that C programmers use.) In the thread routine, as usual, typecast and use it.

To bring clarity, we will try this out ( ch14/param_passing/struct_as_param.c):

> For readability, only key parts of the source code are displayed; to view the complete source code, build, and run it, the entire tree is available for cloning from GitHub here: https://github.com/PacktPublishing/Hands-on-System-Programming-with-Linux.

```
/* Our data structure that we intend to pass as a parameter to the
threads. City Airport information. */
typedef struct {
    char IATA_code[IATA_MAXSZ];
            /* http://www.nationsonline.org/oneworld/IATA_Codes/ */
    char city[CITY_MAXSZ];     /* city name */
    float latitude, longitude; /* coordinates of the city airport */
    unsigned int altitude;     /* metres */
  /* todo: add # runways, runway direction, radio beacons freq, etc
etc */
    unsigned long reserved;    /* for future use */
} Airport;
/* yes! the {lat,long,alt} tuple is accurate :-) */
static const Airport city_airports[3] = {
    { "BLR", "Bangalore International", 13.1986, 77.7066, 904, 0 },
    { "BNE", "Brisbane International", 27.3942, 153.1218, 4, 0 },
    { "BRU", "Brussels National", 50.9010, 4.4856, 58, 0 },
};
```

## Multithreading with Pthreads Part I - Essentials

As an example, we build our very own airport info data structure, airport, and then set up an array (`city_airports`), initializing a few members of it.

In the main function, we declare an array of pointers to the airport structure; we know that a pointer by itself has no memory, so in the thread creation loop, we allocate memory to each pointer and then initialize it to an airport (via a simple memcpy(3)):

```
    Airport * plocdata[NTHREADS];
...
    // Thread creation loop
    for (i = 0; i < NTHREADS; i++) {
        printf("main: creating thread #%ld ...\n", i);

        /* Allocate and initialize data structure to be passed to the
         * thread as a parameter */
        plocdata[i] = calloc(1, sizeof(Airport));
        if (!plocdata[i])
            FATAL("calloc [%d] failed\n", i);
        memcpy(plocdata[i], &city_airports[i], sizeof(Airport));

        ret = pthread_create(&tid[i], &attr, worker, (void
*)plocdata[i]);
        if (ret)
            FATAL("pthread_create() index %d failed! [%d]\n", i, ret);
    }
```

Okay, so we already know that the preceding code is not really optimal; we could have just passed the `city_airports[i]` structure pointer as the parameter to the thread. For the sake of a pedantic example, making use of our just allocated `plocdata[i]` structures, we memcpy one structure into another.

Then, in the pthread_create(3) call, we pass the pointer to our data structure as the fourth parameter. This will become the argument to the thread; in the thread routine, we declare an arg pointer of the same data type and equate it to the typecast data pointer we receive:

```
    void * worker(void *data)
    {
      Airport * arg = (Airport *)data;
      int slptm=8;

      printf( "\n----------- Airports Details ---------------\n"
        " IATA code : %.*s %32s\n"
        " Latitude, Longitude, Altitude : %9.4f %9.4f %9um\n"
        , IATA_MAXSZ, arg->IATA_code,
```

[ 584 ]

```
        arg->city,
        arg->latitude, arg->longitude, arg->altitude);
...
```

We can then proceed to use `arg` as a pointer to Airport; in the preceding demo code, we merely print out the values in the structure. We encourage the reader to build and run this code.

> **TIP**: Did you notice the `%.*s` C printf format specifier trick in the preceding code? This is done when we want to print a string that is not necessarily NULL-terminated; the `%.*s` format specifier allows one to specify the size followed by the string pointer. The string will be printed to only size bytes.

## Thread parameters – what not to do

The really key thing to keep in mind when passing a parameter to a thread routine is that you must guarantee that the parameter passed along is thread-safe; essentially, that it does not get modified in any manner while a thread (or threads) are using it.

(Thread safety is a crucial aspect of working with threads; we shall revisit this point often in upcoming chapters, too).

To help understand the possible issues clearly, let's take a couple of typical examples. In the first one, we shall (attempt to) pass the loop index as the parameter to the newly born thread such as, in main (code: `ch14/pthreads1_wrong.c`):

```
    printf("main: &i=%p\n", &i);
    for (i = 0; i < NTHREADS; i++) {
        printf("Creating thread #%ld now ...\n", i);
        ret = pthread_create(&tid, NULL, worker, (void *)&i);
        ...
    }
```

Did you notice!? We have passed the parameter as `&i`. So? Dereferencing it correctly in the thread routine should still work, right:

```
void * worker(void *data)
{
    long data_addr = (long)data;
    long index = *(long *)data_addr;
    printf("Worker thread: data_addr=%p value=%ld\n",
            (void *)data_addr, index);
    pthread_exit((void *)0);
}
```

## Multithreading with Pthreads Part I - Essentials

Looks okay – let's give it a try!

```
$ ./pthreads1_wrong
main: &i=0x7ffebe160f00
Creating thread #0 now ...
Creating thread #1 now ...
Worker thread: data_addr=0x7ffebe160f00 value=1
Creating thread #2 now ...
Worker thread: data_addr=0x7ffebe160f00 value=2
Worker thread: data_addr=0x7ffebe160f00 value=3
$
```

Well, it works. But hang on, try it a few more times—timing coincidences can fool you into thinking that all's well when it's really not:

```
$ ./pthreads1_wrong
main: &i=0x7fff4475e0d0
Creating thread #0 now ...
Creating thread #1 now ...
Creating thread #2 now ...
Worker thread: data_addr=0x7fff4475e0d0 value=2
Worker thread: data_addr=0x7fff4475e0d0 value=2
Worker thread: data_addr=0x7fff4475e0d0 value=3
$
```

There's a bug! The index value has evaluated to the value 2 twice; why? Think carefully: we have passed the loop index by reference – as the pointer to the loop variable. Thread 1 comes alive, and looks up its value – so does thread 2, as does thread 3. But wait: isn't it possible that we have a race here? Isn't it possible that by the time thread 1 runs and looks up the value of the loop variable it has already changed underneath it (because, don't forget, the loop is running in main)? That, of course, is precisely what happened in the preceding code.

In other words, passing the variable by address is unsafe because its value could change while it is being read (by the worker threads) as it being simultaneously written to (by main); hence, it's not thread-safe and therefore will be buggy (racy).

The solution is actually really simple: do not pass the loop index by address; just pass it as a literal value:

```
for (i = 0; i < NTHREADS; i++) {
    printf("Creating thread #%ld now ...\n", i);
    ret = pthread_create(&tid, NULL, worker, (void *)i);
    ...
}
```

Now, each worker thread receives a copy of the loop index, thus eliminating any race, thus making it safe.

Now, don't jump to the conclusion that, hey, okay, so we should never pass a pointer (an address) as a parameter. Of course you can! Just ensure that it's thread-safe – that its value cannot change underneath it while being manipulated by main and the other application threads.

Refer back to the ch14/struct_as_param.c code we demonstrated in the previous section; we very much pass the thread parameter as a pointer to a structure. Look closely: each pointer was separately allocated (via calloc(3)) in the main thread creation loop. Thus, each worker thread received its own copy of the structure; hence, all is safe and it works well.

An interesting exercise (that we leave to the reader) is to deliberately insert a defect into the struct_as_param application by using exactly one allocated structure (not three) and passing it to each of the worker threads. This time, it will be racy and will (eventually) fail.

# Thread stacks

We understand that whenever a thread is created, it acquires a new, freshly allocated piece of memory for its stack. This leads to the understanding that (obviously, but we shall state it nevertheless) all local variables declared within a thread function will remain private to that thread; this is because they will reside in that thread's stack. (Refer back to *Fig 2* in this chapter – the new stack of the newly created thread is shown in red). Also, whenever a context switch occurs, the **Stack Pointer** (**SP**) register is updated to point to the current thread's stack.

## Get and set thread stack size

Knowing, and being able to change, the size of thread stacks does matter (do see the link provided in the *Further reading* section on the GitHub repository, which mentions a real-world experience on how setting up a stack that's too small for a certain platform caused random and really hard-to-debug failures).

So, what is the default thread stack size? The answer has already been provided; recall the disp_defattr_pthread program we ran earlier in this chapter (in the *Code example – querying the default thread attributes* section): it shows us that the default thread stack size on the (modern NPTL) Linux platform is 8 MB.

The pthreads API set provides a few routines to set and query the thread stack size. One way is as follows:

```
#include <pthread.h>
int pthread_attr_setstacksize(pthread_attr_t *attr, size_t stacksize);
int pthread_attr_getstacksize(const pthread_attr_t *attr,
                              size_t *stacksize);
```

As we have already used `pthread_attr_getstacksize(3)` in the earlier `disp_defattr_pthread` program, we shall refrain from showing its usage once more over here. Setting the thread size is easily done with the complementary `pthread_attr_setstacksize(3)` API – the second parameter is the required size (in bytes). Note, though, that both of these APIs have the phrase _attr_ in them, implying that the stack size is actually set or queried from the thread attribute structure and not a live thread itself. This leads us to understand that we can only set or query the stack size at the time of creation of the thread by setting up the attribute structure (which is, of course, subsequently passed as the second parameter to `pthread_create(3)`). Once a thread is created, its stack size cannot be changed. The exception to this rule is the stack of the main thread.

## Stack location

Where in memory (technically, where in the VAS of the given process) does the thread stack actually reside? The following points help us in this regard:

- The stack of the main thread is always situated at the very top of the process VAS.
- The stacks of all other threads in the process are located somewhere between the process heap segment and the stack of main; the precise location is not known in advance to the app developer; in any case, we should not need to know.
- This is not directly related, but important: recall from Chapter 2, *Virtual Memory*, that, for most processors, the stack(s) conform to the stack-grows-down semantic; that is, the direction of growth of the stack segment is toward lower virtual addresses.

Though we should not need to, is there a way to specify the location of the thread stack? Well, yes, if you insist: the pthread_attr_[get|set]stack(3) APIs can be used for this purpose, as well as to set and/or query the thread stack's size:

```
#include <pthread.h>
int pthread_attr_setstack(pthread_attr_t *attr,
                  void *stackaddr, size_t stacksize);
int pthread_attr_getstack(const pthread_attr_t *attr,
                  void **stackaddr, size_t *stacksize);
```

Although you can use pthread_attr_setstack to set the stack location, it's recommended that this be left to the OS. Also, if you do use it, it's again recommended that both the stack location, stackaddr, and the stack size, stacksize, be a multiple of the system page size (and that the location is aligned to a page boundary). Aligning the thread stack to a page boundary can be easily achieved via the posix_memalign(3) API (we have covered example usage of this API in Chapter 4, *Dynamic Memory Allocation*).

Be careful: if you are specifying the stack location within the thread attribute structure, and creating threads in a loop (as is the normal fashion), you must ensure that each thread receives a unique stack location (this is often done by allocating the stack memory via the aforementioned posix_memalign(3) and then passing its return value as the stack location). Also, of course, the memory pages that will be used for the thread stack(s) must have both read-write permission (recall mprotect(2) from Chapter 4, *Dynamic Memory Allocation*).

After all is said and done, the mechanics of setting and querying the thread stack is straightforward; the really key point is this: (stress) test your application to ensure that the provided thread stack memory is sufficient. As we saw in the Chapters 11, *Signaling - Part I*, overflowing the stack is a serious defect and will cause undefined behavior.

## Stack guards

This neatly brings us to the next point: is there a way to have the application know that stack memory is in danger of being, or rather, has been, overflowed?
Indeed: stack guards. Guard memory is a region of one or more virtual memory pages that has been deliberately placed, and with appropriate permissions, to ensure that any attempt to access that memory results in failure (or a warning of some sort; for example, a signal handler for SIGSEGV could provide just such a semantic - with the caveat that once we've received the SIGSEGV, we are in an undefined state and must terminate; but at least we'll know and can fix the stack size!):

```
#include <pthread.h>
int pthread_attr_setguardsize(pthread_attr_t *attr, size_t guardsize);
int pthread_attr_getguardsize(const pthread_attr_t *attr,
                              size_t *guardsize);
```

The guard region is an additional memory region allocated at the end of the thread stack for the number of bytes specified. The default (guard) size is the system page size. Note, again, that the guard size is an attribute of the thread and can thus only be specified at thread creation time (and not later). We will run the (code: ch14/stack_test.c) app like so:

```
$ ./stack_test
Usage: ./stack_test size-of-thread-stack-in-KB
$ ./stack_test 2560
Default thread stack size       : 8388608 bytes
Thread stack size now set to    : 2621440 bytes
Default thread stack guard size :    4096 bytes

main: creating thread #0 ...
main: creating thread #1 ...
main: creating thread #2 ...
 worker #0:
main: joining (waiting) upon thread #0 ...
 worker #1:

 *** In danger(): here, sizeof long is 8
 worker #2:
Thread #0 successfully joined; it terminated with status=1
main: joining (waiting) upon thread #1 ...
dummy(): parameter val = 115709118
Thread #1 successfully joined; it terminated with status=0
main: joining (waiting) upon thread #2 ...
Thread #2 successfully joined; it terminated with status=1
main: now dying... <Dramatic!> Farewell!
$
```

In the preceding code, we specify 2,560 KB (2.5 MB) as the thread stack size. Though this is far less than the default (8 MB), it turns out to be enough (for x86_64 at least, a quick back-of-the-envelope calculation shows that, for the given program parameters, we shall require a minimum of 1,960 KB to be allocated for each thread stack).

In the following code, we run it again, but this time specify the thread stack size as a mere 256 KB:

```
$ ./stack_test 256
Default thread stack size       : 8388608 bytes
Thread stack size now set to    :  262144 bytes
Default thread stack guard size :    4096 bytes

main: creating thread #0 ...
main: creating thread #1 ...
 worker #0:
main: creating thread #2 ...
 worker #1:
main: joining (waiting) upon thread #0 ...
Segmentation fault (core dumped)
$
```

And, as expected, it segfaults.

> **TIP**
> Examining the core dump with GDB will reveal a lot of clues regarding why the segfault occurred – including, very importantly, the state of the thread stacks (in effect, the stack `backtrace(s)`), at the time of the crash. This, however, goes beyond the scope of this book.
> We definitely encourage you to learn about using a powerful debugger such as GDB (see the *Further reading* section on the GitHub repository as well).

Also (on our test system at least), the kernel emits a message into the kernel log regarding this crash; one way to look up the kernel log messages is via the convenience utility `dmesg(1)`. The following output is from an Ubuntu 18.04 box:

```
$ dmesg
[...]
kern :info : [<timestamp>] stack_test_dbg[27414]: segfault at
7f5ad1733000 ip 0000000000400e68 sp 00007f5ad164aa20 error 6 in
stack_test_dbg[400000+2000]
$
```

[ 591 ]

The code for the preceding application can be found here: ch14/stack_test.c:

> For readability, only key parts of the source code are displayed; to view the complete source code, build it, and run it, the entire tree is available for cloning from GitHub here: https://github.com/PacktPublishing/Hands-on-System-Programming-with-Linux.

```
int main(int argc, char **argv)
{
[...]
  stack_set = atoi(argv[1]) * 1024;
[...]
  /* Init the thread attribute structure to defaults */
  pthread_attr_init(&attr);
[...]
  /* Set thread stack size */
  ret = pthread_attr_setstacksize(&attr, stack_set);
  if (ret)
      FATAL("pthread_attr_setstack(%u) failed! [%d]\n", TSTACK, ret);
  printf("Thread stack size now set to : %10u bytes\n", stack_set);
[...]
```

In main, we show the thread stack size attribute being initialized to the parameter passed by the user (in KB). The code then goes on to create three worker threads and then joins (waits) on them.

In the thread worker routine, we have only thread #2 performing some actual work—you guessed it, stack-intensive work. The code for this is as follows:

```
void * worker(void *data)
{
  long datum = (long)data;

  printf(" worker #%ld:\n", datum);
  if (datum != 1)
      pthread_exit((void *)1);
  danger();
...
```

The danger function, of course, is the one where this dangerous, potentially stack-overflowing work is carried out:

```
static void danger(void)
{
#define NEL    500
  long heavylocal[NEL][NEL], alpha=0;
  int i, j;
```

```
    long int k=0;

    srandom(time(0));

    printf("\n *** In %s(): here, sizeof long is %ld\n",
        __func__, sizeof(long));
    /* Turns out to be 8 on an x86_64; so the 2d-array takes up
     * 500 * 500 * 8 = 2,000,000 ~= 2 MB.
     * So thread stack space of less than 2 MB should result in a
segfault.
     * (On a test box, any value < 1960 KB = 2,007,040 bytes,
     * resulted in segfault).
     */

    /* The compiler is quite intelligent; it will optimize away the
     * heavylocal 2d array unless we actually use it! So lets do some
     * thing with it...
     */
    for (i=0; i<NEL; i++) {
        k = random() % 1000;
        for (j=0; j<NEL-1; j++)
            heavylocal[i][j] = k;
        /*printf("hl[%d][%d]=%ld\n", i, j, (long)heavylocal[i][j]);*/
    }

    for (i=0; i<NEL; i++)
        for (j=0; j<NEL; j++)
            alpha += heavylocal[i][j];
    dummy(alpha);
}
```

The preceding function uses large amounts of (thread) stack space since we have declared a local variable called `heavylocal` – a 2D-array of NEL*NEL elements (NEL=500). On an x86_64 with a long data type occupying 8 bytes, this works out to approximately 2 MB of space! Thus, specifying the thread stack size as any less than 2 MB should result in a stack overflow (the stack guard memory region will in fact detect this) and therefore result in a segmentation violation (or segfault); this is precisely what happened (as you can see in our trial run).

Interestingly, if we merely declare the local variable but do not actually make use of it, modern compilers will just optimize the code out; hence, in the code, we strive to make some (silly) use of the `heavylocal` variable.

A few additional points on the stack guard memory region, to round off this discussion, are as follows:

- If an application has used `pthread_attr_setstack(3)`, it implies that it is managing thread stack memory itself, and any guard size attribute will be ignored.
- The guard region must be aligned to a page boundary.
- If the size of the guard memory region is less than a page, the actual (internal) size will be rounded to a page; `pthread_attr_getguardsize(3)` returns the theoretical size.
- The man page on `pthread_attr_[get|set]guardsize(3)` does provide additional information, including possible glibc bugs within the implementation.

# Summary

This chapter forms the first of three on the large topic of writing multithreaded applications on the Linux platform. Here, we have covered two key areas: the first was in regards to the all-important concepts regarding what exactly is a thread, and we contrast it to the process model (which we studied in `Chapter 9`, *Process Execution* and `Chapter 10`, *Process Creation*). Why you would prefer a multithreaded design was covered in some detail, and included three examples. In this way, the motivation to use a multithreaded design approach was being brought out.

The second part of this chapter focused on the actual pthread APIs (and their related concepts), how we create a thread—how many can and how many should be created was addressed as well. Thread termination basics, thread attributes, passing along a parameter to the newly created thread, what is joining and how to perform it, and finally, details on how we can manipulate the thread stack (and stack guard) size was covered. Many example programs were shown to help solidify the concepts that were taught.

In the next chapter, we shall focus squarely on another critical aspect of writing powerful and safe multithreaded software – the issues of concurrency, races, critical sections, deadlock (and it's avoidance) and atomicity; how we deal with these using the mutex lock (and it's variants), as well as the condition variable.

# 15
# Multithreading with Pthreads Part II - Synchronization

One of the key reasons that multithreading is powerful and makes a big impact performance-wise is that it lends itself to the notion of parallelism or concurrency; from what we learned in the previous `Chapter 14`, *Multithreading with Pthreads Part I - Essentials*, we understand that multiple threads of a process can (and indeed do) execute in parallel. On large multicore systems (multicore is pretty much the norm now, even in embedded systems), the effect is magnified.

However, as experience teaches us, there's always a trade-off. With parallelism comes the ugly potential for races and the subsequent defects. Not only that, situations like this typically become extremely hard to debug, and therefore, fix.

In this chapter, we shall attempt to:

- Make the reader aware as to where and what exactly these concurrency (race) defects are
- How to avoid them with good design and coding practices in multithreaded applications

Again, this chapter divides itself into two broad areas:

- In the first part, we clearly explain the problem(s), such as how atomicity matters and deadlock issues.
- in the latter part of this chapter, we present the locking (and other) mechanisms that the pthreads API set makes available to the application developer to help tackle and avoid these issues altogether.

# The racing problem

First and foremost, let's attempt to understand what and where exactly the problem we are trying to resolve is. In the previous chapter, we learned that all threads of a process share everything except for the stack; each thread has its own private stack memory space.

Look carefully again at `Chapter 14`, *Multithreading with Pthreads Part I-Essentials: Fig 2*, (leaving out the kernel stuff); the virtual address space—the text and data segments, but not the stack segment—are shared between all threads of a process. The data segment, of course, is where global and static variables reside.

At the risk of overstating these facts, this implies that all the threads of a given process truly (if not poss, then make COW also normal font not **Copy On Write** (**COW**)) share the following:

- The text segment
- The data segments—initialized data, uninitialized data (earlier referred to as the BSS), and the heap segment
- Pretty much all the kernel-level objects and data maintained for the process by the OS (again, refer to `Chapter 14`, *Multithreading with Pthreads Part I-Essentials : Fig 2*)

A really important point to understand is that sharing the text segment is not a problem at all. Why? Text is code; the machine code—the opcodes and operands that make up what we call the machine language — reside in these memory pages. Recall from `Chapter 2`, *Virtual Memory*, that all pages of text (code) have the same permissions: **read-execute** (**r-x**). This is important, since multiple threads executing text (code) in parallel is not only fine—it's encouraged! This is what parallelism is all about, after all. Think about it; if we only read and execute code, we do not modify it in any manner whatsoever; therefore, it's completely safe, even when being executed in parallel.

On the other hand, data pages have permissions of **read-write** (**rw**). This implies that a thread, A, working on a page of data in parallel—concurrently with another thread, B,—is inherently dangerous. Why? It's fairly intuitive: they can end up clobbering the memory values within the page. (One can imagine both threads writing to, for example, a global linked list simultaneously.) The key point is that shared writable memory has to be protected against concurrent access so that data integrity is preserved at all times.

To really understand why we care so much about these issues, please read on.

# Concurrency and atomicity

Concurrent execution implies that multiple threads can run truly in parallel on multiple CPU cores. When this happens on text (code), it's good; we get higher throughput. However, the moment we run concurrently while working on shared writable data, we will have a problem with data integrity. This is because text is read-only (and executable), whereas data is read-write.

What we would really like, of course, is to be greedy and have the best of both worlds: execute code concurrently via multiple threads, but the moment we must work on shared data, stop the concurrency (parallelism), and have just one thread run through the data section sequentially until it's done, then resume parallel execution.

## The pedagogical bank account example

A classic (pedagogical) example is that of the faulty bank account software application. Imagine that Kaloor (needless to say, fictional names and figures have been employed here), a freelance sculptor, has an account with his bank; his current balance is $12,000.00. Two transactions, deposits of $3,000 and $8,000, which are payments for work he has successfully completed, are issued simultaneously. It does not take a genius to see that (assuming that there are no other transactions), very soon, his account balance should reflect an amount of $23,000.00.

For the purpose of this example, let's visualize that the banking software application is a multithreaded process; to keep things very simple, we consider that a thread is spawned off to handle a transaction. The server system that the software runs upon is a powerful multicore machine—it has, say, 12 CPU cores. This, of course, implies that threads can run in parallel on different cores simultaneously.

So, let's visualize that for each of Kaloor's transactions we have a thread running to perform it—thread A and thread B. Thread A (running on, say, CPU #0) works upon the first deposit of $3,000 and thread B (running on, say, CPU #1) works upon the (almost immediate) second deposit of $8,000.

## Multithreading with Pthreads Part II - Synchronization

We consider two cases here:

- The case where, by chance, the transactions go through successfully. The following diagram clearly shows this case:

| Time | Thread A on CPU 0 | Thread B on CPU 1 | Balance |
|---|---|---|---|
| t0 |  |  | 12000 |
| t1 | read bal |  | 12000 |
| t2 |  | read bal | 12000 |
| t3 | deposit 3000 |  | 12000 |
| t4 |  | deposit 8000 | 12000 |
| t5 | update bal = 12000+3000 |  | 15000 |
| t6 |  | update bal = 15000+8000 | **23000** |

Figure 1: The bank account: correct, by chance

- The case where, again by chance, the transactions do not go through successfully. The following diagram shows this case:

| Time | Thread A on CPU 0 | Thread B on CPU 1 | Balance |
|---|---|---|---|
| t0 |  |  | 12000 |
| t1 | read bal |  | 12000 |
| t2 |  | read bal | 12000 |
| t3 | deposit 3000 |  | 12000 |
| t4 |  | deposit 8000 | 12000 |
| t5 | update bal = 12000+3000 | update bal = 12000+8000 | 15000 |
| t6 |  |  | 20000 |

Figure 2: The bank account: incorrect, by chance

The problem area is highlighted in the preceding tables: It's quite clear that thread B has performed an invalid read on the balance—it has read a stale value of $12,000 (the value as of time **t4**) instead of fetching the actual current value of $15,000—resulting in an effective loss of $3,000 for poor Kaloor.

How did this happen? In a nutshell, a race condition has caused the problem. To understand the race, look carefully at the preceding table and visualize the activity:

- The variable representing the current balance in the account; balance is global:
    - It is residing in the data segment
    - It is shared by all threads of the process
- **At time t3, thread A on CPU #0**: A deposit of $3,000 is made; the `balance` is still $12,000 (not updated yet)
- **At time t4, thread B on CPU #1**: A deposit of $8,000 is made; the balance is still $12,000 (not updated yet)
- **At time t5**:
    - Thread A on CPU #0: update the balance
    - Simultaneously, but on the other core:
        - Thread B on CPU #1: update the balance
        - By chance, what if thread B ran on CPU #1 a few microseconds before thread A on CPU #0 could update the balance variable!?
        - Then, thread B reads the balance as $12,000 ($3,000 short!) This is called a dirty read and is at the heart of the problem. This very situation is called a race; a race being a situation in which the outcome is undefined and unpredictable. In most cases, this will be a problem (as it is here); in some rare cases where it does not matter, it's referred to as a benign race.

The fact to be emphasized is that the operation of depositing funds and updating the balance (or the converse, withdrawing funds and updating the balance) has to be guaranteed to be atomic. They cannot race, as that would be a defect (a bug).

The phrase atomic operation (or atomicity) in a software programming context implies that the operation, once begun, will run to completion without interruption.

*Multithreading with Pthreads Part II - Synchronization*

## Critical sections

How do we fix the preceding race? It's quite straightforward, really: we have to ensure that, as stated earlier, the banking operations—deposits, withdrawals, and so on—are guaranteed to do two things:

- Be the only thread running the code at that point in time
- Be atomic — run to completion, without interruption

Once this is achieved, the shared data will be safe from corruption. The section of code that must run in the fashion described previously is called a critical section.

In our fictional banking application, the threads running the code to perform a banking operation (a deposit or a withdrawal) must do so in a critical section, shown as follows:

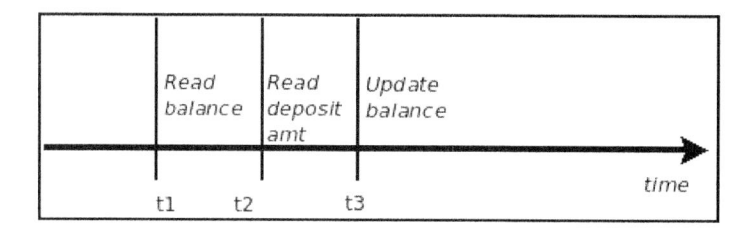

Figure 3: The critical section

So, now, let's say that the banking application is corrected to take these facts into account; the vertical timeline execution path of thread A and thread B would now be as follows:

| Time | Thread A on CPU 0 | Thread B on CPU 1 | Balance | |
|---|---|---|---|---|
| t0 | | | 12000 | |
| t1 | read bal | | 12000 | |
| t2 | deposit 3000 | | 12000 | Critical Section |
| t3 | update bal = 12000+3000 | | 15000 | |
| t4 | | read bal | 15000 | |
| t5 | | deposit 8000 | 15000 | Critical Section |
| t6 | | update bal = 15000+8000 | 23000 | |

Fig 4: Correct banking application—critical section

[ 600 ]

Here, both thread A and thread B, once they begin their (deposit) operations, run it alone and to completion (without interruption); hence, sequentially and atomically.

To sum this up:

- A critical section is code that must:
    - Run without interference from other threads in the process (as it works upon some shared resource such as global data)
    - Run atomically (to completion, without interruption)
- If the code of the critical section can run in parallel with other threads, this is a defect (a bug), called a race
- To prevent races, we have to guarantee that the code of the critical section runs alone and atomically
- To do so, we must synchronize critical sections

Now, the question is: how do we synchronize a critical section? Read on.

# Locking concepts

There are several forms of synchronization in software; one of the commonly encountered ones, and indeed one that we shall be working with quite a bit, is called **locking**. A lock, in programming terms, and as seen by the application developer, is ultimately a data structure instantiated as a variable.

When one requires a critical section, just encapsulate the code of the critical section between a lock and a corresponding unlock operation. (For now, don't worry about the code-level API details; we shall cover that later. Here, we are just focusing on getting the concepts right.)

Let's represent the critical section, along with the synchronization mechanism—a lock— using a diagram (a superset of the preceding *Figure 3*):

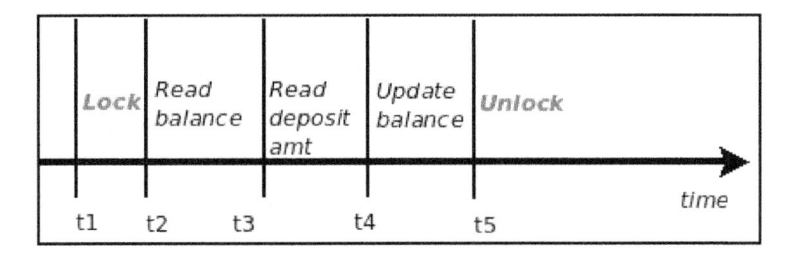

Fig 5: Critical section with locking

The basic premise of a lock is as follows:

- Only one thread can hold or own a lock at any given point in time; that thread is the owner of the lock.
- Upon the unlock, when more than one thread attempts to get or take the lock, the kernel will guarantee that exactly one thread will get the lock.
- The thread that gets the lock is called the winner (or the lock owner); the threads that tried for but did not get the lock are called the losers.

So, visualize this: say that we have three threads, A, B, and C, running in parallel on different CPU cores, all attempting to take a lock. The guarantee of the lock is that exactly one thread gets it—let's say that thread C wins, taking the lock (thus thread C is the winner or owner of the lock); threads A and B are the losers. What happens after that?

- The winner thread sees the lock operation as a non-blocking call; it continues into the critical section (probably working on some shared writable resource, such as global data).
- The loser threads see the lock operation as a blocking call; they now block (wait), but on what exactly? (Recall that a blocking call is one in which we wait upon an event occurring and get unblocked once it occurs.) Well, the unlock operation, of course!
- The winner thread, upon (atomically) completing the critical section, performs the unlock operation.
- Either thread A or B will now get the lock, and the whole sequence repeats.

In a more generic manner, we can now understand it as: if N threads are in competition for a lock, the guarantee of the lock operation (by the OS) is that exactly one thread—the winner—will get the lock. So, we shall have one winner and N-1 losers. The winner thread proceeds into the code of the critical section; in the interim, all the N-1 loser threads wait (block) upon the unlock operation. At some point in the future (hopefully soon), the winner performs the unlock; this re-triggers the whole sequence again: the N-1 losers again compete for the lock; we shall have one winner and N-2 losers; the winner thread proceeds into the code of the critical section. In the interim, all the N-2 loser threads wait (block) upon the unlock operation and so on, until all the loser threads have become winners and have hence run the code of the critical section.

# Is it atomic?

The preceding discussion on the necessity for atomic execution of a critical section might make you, the programmer, apprehensive: perhaps you are wondering, how does one recognize a critical section? Well, that's easy: if you have the potential for parallelism (multiple threads can run through the code path in parallel) and the code path is working on some shared resource (usually global or static data), then you have a critical section, implying that you will protect it via locking.

> A quick thumb rule: in the majority of cases, multiple threads will be running through code paths. Thus, in a general sense, the mere presence of some writable shared resource of any sort—a global, a static, an IPC shared-memory region, (even) a data item representing a hardware register in a device driver— makes the code path into a critical section. The rule is this: just protect it.

The fictional bank account example we saw in the previous section makes it amply clear that we had a critical section which required protection (via locking). However, one does come across cases in which it is perhaps not as apparent whether we indeed require locking. Take this example: we have a global integer g in a multithreaded C application program; at some point, we increment its value, such as: g ++;

It looks simple, but wait! It's a writeable shared resource—global data; multiple threads might run through this code in parallel, thus rendering it a critical section which requires protection (via a lock). Yes? Or no?

On the face of it, a simple increment (or decrement) operation might appear to be atomic (recall that atomic runs to completion without interruption) in and of itself, thus requiring no special protection via locks or any other form of synchronization. But is this really the case?

Before we go any further, there is (yet) another key fact to be aware of which is, the only thing guaranteed to be atomic on a modern microprocessor in a single machine language instruction. After every machine instruction completes, the control unit on the CPU checks whether it has to service anything else, typically a hardware interrupt or (software) exception condition; if so, it sets the program counter (IP or PC) to that address and branches off; if not, execution continues sequentially with the PC register being appropriately incremented.

So, think carefully about this: whether or not an increment operation g++ is atomic or not really depends on two factors:

- The **Instruction Set Architecture** (**ISA**) of the microprocessor being used (in simpler terms, it depends on the CPU itself)
- How the C compiler for that processor generates code

If the compiler generates a single machine language instruction for the g++ C code, then execution will indeed be atomic. But will it? Let's find out! (the importance of being empirical - experimenting, trying things out—is a critical feature; our Chapter 19, *Troubleshooting and Best Practices*, covers more on such points).

A very interesting website, https://godbolt.org (screenshots will follow), allows one to see how various compilers compile a given piece of high-level language code (at the time of writing this book, it supports 14 languages, including C and C++, and various compilers, including, of course, gcc(1) and clang(1). Interestingly, with the language drop-down set to **C++**, one can also compile via gcc for ARM!).

Let's begin by visiting this website and then doing the following:

1. Select C as the language via the drop-down
2. Select, in the right window pane, the compiler as **x86_64 gcc 8.2**
3. In the left window pane, key in the following program:

```
int g=41;
int main(void)
{
    g ++;
}
```

Chapter 15

The following is the output:

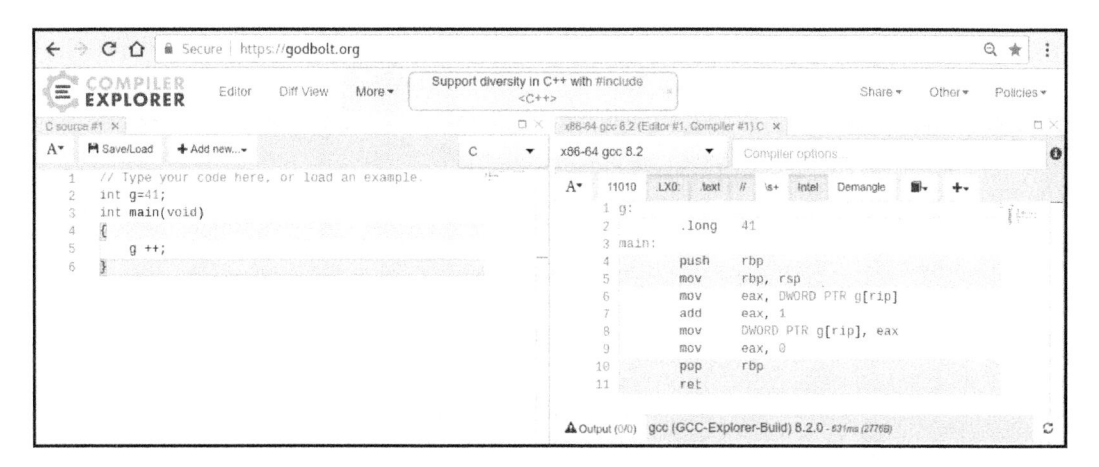

Figure 6: g++ increment via gcc 8.2 on x86_64, no optimization

Look at the right window pane—one can see the assembly language generated by the compiler (which, of course, will subsequently become machine code corresponding to the processor ISA). So? Note that the g++ C high-level language statement is highlighted in a pale yellow color in its left window pane; the same color is used in the right window to highlight the corresponding assembly. What does one, quite glaringly, notice? The single line of C code, g++; , has become four assembly language instructions. Thus, by virtue of our preceding learning, this code cannot be considered to be atomic in and of itself (but we can certainly force it to be atomic by using a lock).

[ 605 ]

# Multithreading with Pthreads Part II - Synchronization

The next experiment: leave everything the same, except notice that in the right window pane there is a text widget into which you are allowed to type in option switches to pass on to the compiler; we type -O2, implying that we would like the compiler to use optimization level 2 (a fairly high optimization level). Now, for the output:

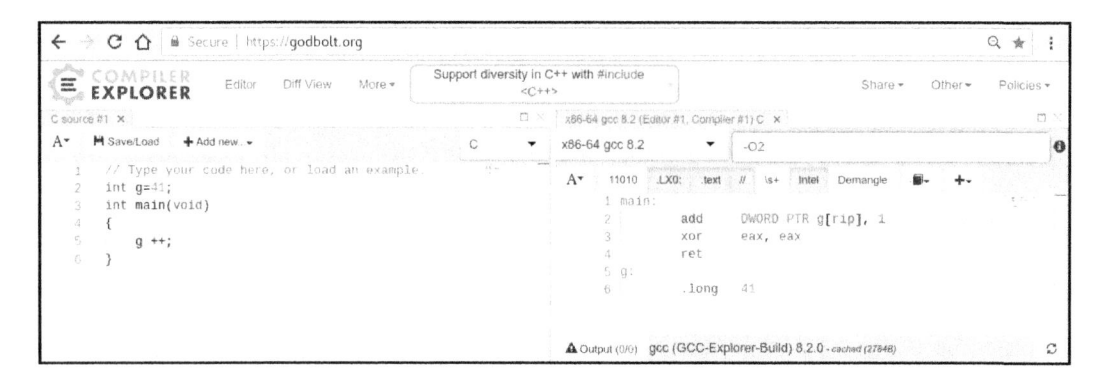

Figure 7: g++ increment via gcc 8.2 on x86_64, optimization level 2

The g++ C code now boils down to just one assembly instruction, thus indeed becoming atomic.

With the ARM compiler, and no optimization, g++ translates to several lines of assembly— clearly, non-atomic:

Fig 8: g++ increment via gcc 7.2.1 on ARM, no optimization

Our conclusion? It is usually important for applications that the code we write remains portable across (CPU) architectures. In the preceding example, we clearly find that the code generated by the compiler for the simple g++ operation is sometimes atomic and sometimes not. (It will depend on several factors: the CPU's ISA, the compiler, and the optimization level -On that it's compiled at, and so on.) Hence, the only safe conclusion one can make is this: be safe, and wherever there exists a critical section, protect it (with locks, or other means).

## Dirty reads

Many programmers new to these topics make a fatal assumption, and think something like this: Okay, I understand that when modifying a shared resource—like a global data structure — I will be required to treat the code as a critical section and protect it with locking, but, my code is only iterating over a global linked list; it's only reading it and never writing to it and hence, this is not a critical section and does not require protection (I'll even get brownie points for high performance).

Burst the bubble, please! It is a critical section. Why? Visualize this: while your code is iterating over the global linked list (only reading it), precisely because you have not taken a lock or synchronized in some other manner, another writer thread can very well be writing to the data structure while you are reading it. Think about it: this is a recipe for disaster; it's entirely possible that your code will end up reading stale or half-written inconsistent data. This is called a *dirty read*, and it can happen when you do not protect the critical section. In fact, this is precisely the defect in our fictional banking application example.

Once again, we (re)stress these facts:

- If the code is accessing a writable shared resource of any sort and there is the potential for parallelism, then it's a critical section. Protect it.
- Some side effects of this include the following:
    - If your code does have parallelism but works only on local variables, there is no issue and it's not a critical section. (Remember: each thread has its own private stack, and so using local variables without explicit protection is fine.)
    - If a global variable is marked as `const`, then of course it's fine—it's read-only, in any case.

(Note though, that the const keyword in C does not actually guarantee that the value is indeed constant (as one typically understands it)! It just means that the variable is read-only, but the data it refers to can still be changed if another pointer has access to it from underneath using a macro instead might help).

Using locks correctly has a learning curve, perhaps a bit steeper than other programming constructs; this is because, one has to first learn to recognize critical sections, and therefore the need for locks (covered in the previous section), then learn and use good design locking guidelines, and third, understand and avoid nasty deadlocks!

# Locking guidelines

In this section, we will present a small but important set of heuristics or guidelines for the developer to keep in mind while designing and implementing multithreaded code that makes use of locks. These may or may not apply in a given situation; with experience, one learns to apply the right guidelines at the appropriate times.

Without further ado, here they are:

- **Keep locking granularity fine enough**: lock data, not code.
- **Simplicity is key**: Complex locking scenarios involving multiple locks and threads lead to not just performance issues (the extreme case being deadlock), but also to other defects. Keeping the design as simple as it can be is always good practice.
- **Prevent Starvation**: Holding a lock for an arbitrarily long amount of time leads to the loser threads starving; one has to design—and indeed test—to ensure that, as a rule of thumb, every critical section (the code between the lock and the unlock operations) completes as soon as possible. Good design ensures that there is no possibility of a critical section of code taking far too long; using a timeout in conjunction with the lock is one way to alleviate this issue (more on this later).
- It's really important to also understand that locking creates bottlenecks. Good physical analogies for locking are as follows:
    - A funnel: Think of the stem of the funnel as the critical section—it's only wide enough to allow one thread to go through at a time (the winner); the loser threads remain blocked in the mouth of the funnel
    - A single toll booth on a multi-lane busy highway

Thus, avoiding long critical sections is key:

- Build synchronization into the design, and avoid the temptation that goes something like, okay, I'll first write the code and then come back and look at locking. It typically does not go well; locking is a complex business as it is; trying to postpone its correct design and implementation only aggravates the issue.

Let's examine the first of these points in a bit more detail.

## Locking granularity

While working on an application, let's say there are several places which require data protection via locking—in other words, several critical sections:

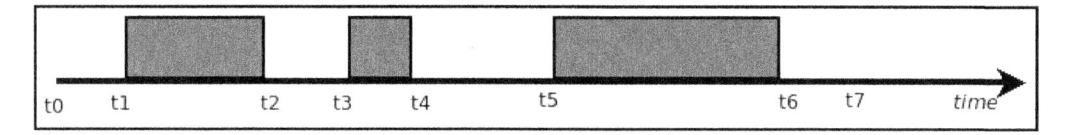

Fig 9: Timeline with several critical sections

We have shown the critical sections (the places that, as we have learned, require synchronization—locking) with the solid red rectangles on the timeline. The developer might well realize, why not simplify this? Just take a single lock at time **t1** and unlock it at time **t6**:

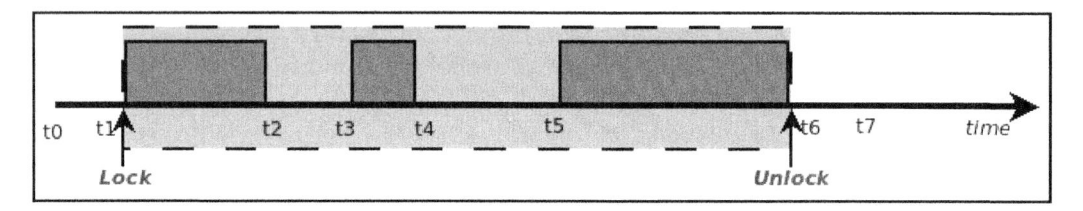

Figure 10: Coarse granularity locking

This will work in protecting all the critical sections. But this is at the cost of performance. Think about it; each time a thread runs through the preceding code path, it must take the lock, perform the work, and then unlock. That's fine, but what about parallelism? It's effectively defeated; the code from **t1** to **t6** is now serialized. This kind of over-amplified locking-of-all-critical-sections-with-one-big-fat-lock is called coarse granularity locking.

Recall our earlier discussion: code (text) is never an issue—there is no need at all to lock here; just lock the places where writable shared data of any sort is being accessed. These are the critical sections! This gives rise to fine granularity locking—we only take the lock at the point in time where a critical section begins and unlock where it ends; the following diagram reflects this:

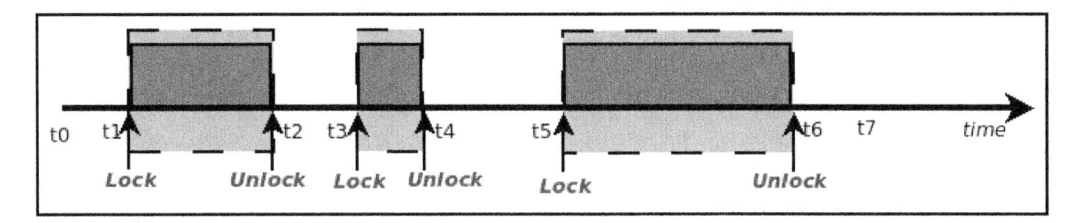

Figure 11: Fine granularity locking

As we stated previously, a good rule of thumb to keep in mind is to lock data, not code.

> **TIP**
> Is super-fine granularity locking always best? Perhaps not; locking is a complex business. Practical work has shown that, sometimes, holding a lock while even working on code (pure text—the code between the critical sections), is okay. It is a balancing act; the developer must ideally use experience and trial-and-error to judge locking granularity and efficiency, constantly testing and re-evaluating the code paths for robustness and performance as one goes along.

Straying too far in either direction might be a mistake; too coarse a locking granularity yields poor performance, but too fine a granularity can too.

# Deadlock and its avoidance

A deadlock is the undesirable situation wherein it is impossible for the threads in question to make further progress. The typical symptom of deadlock is that the application (or device driver or whatever software it is) appears to hang.

# Common deadlock types

Thinking about a couple of typical deadlock scenarios will help the reader understand it better. Recall that the basic premise of a lock is that there can only be one winner (the thread that obtained the lock) and N-1 losers. Another key point is that only the winner thread can perform the unlock operation—no other thread can do so.

## Self deadlock (relock)

Knowing the aforementioned information, visualize this scenario: there is one lock (we just call it L1) and three threads in competition for it (let's just call them threads A, B, and C); let's say thread B is the winner. That's fine, but what happens if thread B, within its critical section, again attempts to take the same lock, L1? Well, think about it: lock L1 is currently in the locked state, thus forcing thread B to block (wait) upon it getting unlocked. However, no thread but thread B itself can possibly perform the unlock operation, so thread B will end up waiting forever! There we have it: deadlock. This type of deadlock is termed the self deadlock, or the relock error.

One might argue, and indeed the case does exist, can't a lock be taken recursively? Yes, as we shall see later that this can be done within the pthreads API. However, good design often argues against using recursive locks; indeed, the Linux kernel does not allow it.

## The ABBA deadlock

A more complex form of deadlock can emerge in a scenario which involves nested locking: two or more competing threads and two or more locks. Here, let's take the simplest case: a scenario with two threads (A and B) working with two locks (L1 and L2).

Let's say that this is what unfolds over the vertical timeline, as the following table reveals:

| Time | Thread A | Thread B |
|---|---|---|
| t1 | Attempt to take lock L1 | Attempt to take lock L2 |
| t2 | Gets lock L1 | Gets lock L2 |
| t3 | <--- In critical section of L1 ---> | <--- In critical section of L2 ---> |
| t4 | Attempt to take lock L2 | Attempt to take lock L1 |
| t5 | Block on L2 being unlocked | Block on L1 being unlocked |
|  | <waits forever: deadlock> | <waits forever: deadlock> |

It's quite clear that each thread waits for the other to unlock the lock it wants; thus, each thread waits forever, guaranteeing a deadlock. This kind of deadlock is often called the deadly embrace or the ABBA deadlock.

## Avoiding deadlock

Avoiding deadlock is obviously something we would want to ensure. In addition to the points covered in the *Locking guidelines* section, there is one more key point, which is that the order in which multiple locks are taken matters; keeping the lock ordering consistent throughout will provide protection against deadlocks.

To understand why, let's re-look at the ABBA deadlock scenario we just covered (refer to the preceding table). Look at the table again: notice that thread A takes lock L1 and then attempts to take lock L2, while thread B does the opposite. We shall now represent this scenario, but with a key caveat: lock ordering! This time, we shall have a lock ordering rule; it could be as simple as this: first, take lock L1, and then take lock L2:

lock L1 --> lock L2

With this lock ordering in mind, we find the scenario could play out as follows:

| Time | Thread A | Thread B |
| --- | --- | --- |
| t1 | Attempt to take lock L1 | Attempt to take lock L1 |
| t2 |  | Gets lock L1 |
| t3 | <Waits for L1 to be unlocked> | <--- In critical section of L1 ---> |
| t4 |  | Unlock L1 |
| t5 | Gets lock L1 |  |
| t6 | <--- In critical section of L1 ---> | Attempt to take lock L2 |
| t7 | Unlock L1 | Gets locks L2 |
| t8 | Attempt to take lock L2 | <--- In critical section of L2 |
| t9 | <Waits for L2 to be unlocked> | ---> |
| t10 |  | Unlock L2 |
| t11 | Gets lock L2 | <Continues with other work> |
| t12 | <--- In critical section of L2 ---> | ... |
| t13 | Unlock L2 | ... |

The key point here is that both threads attempt to take locks in a given order; first L1, and then L2. In the preceding table, we can visualize a case in which thread B obtains the locks first, forcing thread A to wait. This is completely fine and expected; no deadlock occurring is the whole point.

The precise ordering itself does not really matter; what does matter is the fact that the designers and developers document the lock ordering to be followed and stick to it.

> The lock ordering semantics, and indeed developer comments regarding this key point, can be often found within the source tree of the Linux kernel (ver 4.19, as of this writing). Here's one example: `virt/kvm/kvm_main.c`
>
> ```
> ...
> /*
>  * Ordering of locks:
>  *
>  * kvm->lock --> kvm->slots_lock --> kvm->irq_lock
>  */
> ...
> ```

So, looking back at our first table, we can now clearly see that the deadlock occurred because the lock ordering rule was violated: thread B took lock L2 before taking lock L1!

# Using the pthread APIs for synchronization

Now that we have covered the required theoretical background information, let's move on with the actual practice: for the remainder of this chapter, we shall focus on how to use the pthreads API to perform synchronization, thus avoiding races.

We have learned that to protect writable shared data of any kind in a critical section, we require locking. The pthreads API provides the mutex lock for exactly this use case; we intend to hold the lock for a short while only—the duration of the critical section.

There are scenarios, though, in which we require a different kind of synchronization—we require to synchronize based on a certain data element's value; the pthreads API provides the **condition variable** (**CV**) for this use case.

Let's cover these in turn.

# The mutex lock

The word **mutex** is really an abbreviation for **mutual exclusion**; to the mutual exclusion of all other (loser) threads, one thread—the winner—holds (or owns) the mutex lock. Only when it is unlocked can another thread take the lock.

> An FAQ: What really is the difference between the semaphore and the mutex lock? Firstly, the semaphore can be used in two ways—one, as a counter (with the counting semaphore object), and two (relevant to us here), essentially as a mutex lock—the binary semaphore.
> Between the binary semaphore and the mutex lock, there exists two primary differences: one, the semaphore is meant to be used to synchronize between processes and not the threads internal to a single process (it is indeed a well-known IPC facility); the mutex lock is meant to synchronize between the threads of a given (single) process. (Having said that, it is possible to create a process-shared mutex, but it's never the default).
> Two, the SysV IPC implementation of the semaphore provides the possibility of having the kernel unlock the semaphore (via the semop(2) SEM_UNDO flag) if the owner process is abruptly killed (always possible via signal #9); no such possibility even exists for the mutex—the winner must unlock it (we shall cover how the developer can ensure this later).

Let's get started with a simple example of initializing, using, and destroying a mutex lock. In this program, we shall create three threads and merely increment three global integers, once each within the worker routine of the threads.

> For readability, only key parts of the source code are displayed; to view the complete source code, build, and run it. The entire tree is available for cloning from GitHub here: https://github.com/PacktPublishing/Hands-on-System-Programming-with-Linux.

Code: ch15/mutex1.c:
```
    static long g1=10, g2=12, g3=14;    /* our globals */
    pthread_mutex_t mylock;     /* lock to protect our globals */
```

In order to use a mutex lock, one must first initialize it to the unlocked state; this can be done as follows:

```
if ((ret = pthread_mutex_init(&mylock, NULL)))
    FATAL("pthread_mutex_init() failed! [%d]\n", ret);
```

Alternatively, we could perform the initialization as a declaration, such as:

```
pthread_mutex_t mylock = PTHREAD_MUTEX_INITIALIZER;
```

In fact, there are a few mutex attributes that can be specified for the mutex lock (via the pthread_mutexattr_init(3) API); we shall get to this later in this chapter. For now, the attributes will be the system defaults.

Also, once we are done, we must destroy the mutex lock(s):

```
if ((ret = pthread_mutex_destroy(&mylock)))
    FATAL("pthread_mutex_destroy() failed! [%d]\n", ret);
```

As usual, we then create the (three) worker threads in a loop (we do not show this code here as it is repetitious). Here is the thread's worker routine:

```
void * worker(void *data)
{
    long datum = (long)data + 1;
    if (locking)
        pthread_mutex_lock(&mylock);

    /*--- Critical Section begins */
    g1 ++; g2 ++; g3 ++;
    printf("[Thread #%ld] %2ld %2ld %2ld\n", datum, g1, g2, g3);
    /*--- Critical Section ends */

    if (locking)
        pthread_mutex_unlock(&mylock);

    /* Terminate with success: status value 0.
     * The join will pick this up. */
    pthread_exit((void *)0);
}
```

Because the data we are working on with each thread is a writable shared (it's in the data segment!) resource, we recognize that this is a critical section!

Thus, we must protect it—here, we do so with a mutex lock. So, just prior to entering the critical section, we first take the mutex lock and then work on the global data, and then unlock our lock, rendering the operation safe against races. (Notice that in the preceding code we only perform the locking and unlocking if the variable called `locking` is true; this is a deliberate way to test our code. In production, of course, please do away with the if condition and just perform the locking!) The attentive reader will also notice that we have kept the critical section quite short—it only encapsulates the global update and subsequent `printf(3)`, nothing more. (This is important for good performance; recall what we learned in the earlier section on *Locking granularity*.)

As mentioned previously, we deliberately provide an option to the user to avoid using locking altogether—this of course will, or rather, could, result in buggy behavior. Let's try it out:

```
$ ./mutex1
Usage: ./mutex1 lock-or-not
 0 : do Not lock (buggy!)
 1 : do lock (correct)
$ ./mutex1 1
At start:     g1 g2 g3
              10 12 14
[Thread #1] 11 13 15
[Thread #2] 12 14 16
[Thread #3] 13 15 17
$
```

It does work as expected. Even if we pass the parameter as zero—thus turning locking off— the program does (usually) seem to work correctly:

```
$ ./mutex1 0
At start:     g1 g2 g3
              10 12 14
[Thread #1] 11 13 15
[Thread #2] 12 14 16
[Thread #3] 13 15 17
$
```

## Multithreading with Pthreads Part II - Synchronization

Why? Ah, this is important to understand: recall what we learned in the earlier section Is it atomic? With a simple integer increment and compiler optimization set to a high level (-O2 in fact, here), it's quite possible that the integer increments are atomic and thus do not really require locking. However, this may not always be the case, especially when we do something more complex than mere increments or decrements on an integer variable. (Think about reading/writing a large global linked list, and so on)! The bottom line: we must always recognize critical section(s) and ensure that we protect them.

## Seeing the race

To demonstrate exactly this issue (actually seeing the data race), we will write another demo program. In this one, we will calculate the factorial of a given number (a quick reminder: 3! = 3 x 2 x 1 = 6; recall from your school days—the notation N! means factorial of N). Here's the relevant code:

> For readability, only key parts of the source code are displayed; to view the complete source code, build, and run it. The entire tree is available for cloning from GitHub here: https://github.com/PacktPublishing/Hands-on-System-Programming-with-Linux.

Code: ch15/facto.c:

In main(), we initialize our mutex lock (and create two worker threads; we do not show the code to create the threads, destroy them, as well as the mutex):

```
    printf( "Locking mode : %s\n"
            "Verbose mode : %s\n",
            (gLocking == 1?"ON":"OFF"),
            (gVerbose == 1?"ON":"OFF"));

    if (gLocking) {
        if ((ret = pthread_mutex_init(&mylock, NULL)))
            FATAL("pthread_mutex_init() failed! [%d]\n", ret);
    }
    ...
```

The thread's worker routine is as follows:

```
void * worker(void *data)
{
    long datum = (long)data + 1;
    int N=0;
...
    if (gLocking)
        pthread_mutex_lock(&mylock);

    /*--- Critical Section begins! */
    factorize(N);
    printf("[Thread #%ld] (factorial) %d ! = %20lld\n",
      datum, N, gFactorial);
    /*--- Critical Section ends */

    if (gLocking)
        pthread_mutex_unlock(&mylock);
...
```

Recognizing the critical section, we take (and subsequently unlock) our mutex lock. The code of the `factorize` function is as follows:

```
/*
 * This is the function that calculates the factorial of the given
parameter.
Stress it, making it susceptible to the data race, by turning verbose
mode On; then, it will take more time to execute, and likely end up
"racing" on the value of the global gFactorial. */
static void factorize(int num)
{
    int i;
    gFactorial = 1;
    if (num <= 0)
        return;
    for (i=1; i<=num; i++) {
        gFactorial *= i;
        VPRINT(" i=%2d fact=%20lld\n", i, gFactorial);
    }
}
```

## Multithreading with Pthreads Part II - Synchronization

Read the preceding comment carefully; it's key to this demo. Let's try it out:

```
$ ./facto
Usage: ./facto lock-or-not [verbose=[0]|1]
Locking mode:
 0 : do Not lock (buggy!)
 1 : do lock (correct)
(TIP: turn locking OFF and verbose mode ON to see the issue!)
$ ./facto 1
Locking mode : ON
Verbose mode : OFF
[Thread #2] (factorial) 12 ! =        479001600
[Thread #1] (factorial) 10 ! =          3628800
$
```

The results are correct (verify this for yourself). Now we rerun it with locking off and verbose mode on:

```
$ ./facto 0 1
Locking mode : OFF
Verbose mode : ON
facto.c:factorize:50: i= 1 fact=                 1
facto.c:factorize:50: i= 2 fact=                 2
facto.c:factorize:50: i= 3 fact=                 6
facto.c:factorize:50: i= 4 fact=                24
facto.c:factorize:50: i= 5 fact=               120
facto.c:factorize:50: i= 6 fact=               720
facto.c:factorize:50: i= 7 fact=              5040
facto.c:factorize:50: i= 8 fact=             40320
facto.c:factorize:50: i= 9 fact=            362880
facto.c:factorize:50: i=10 fact=           3628800
[Thread #1] (factorial) 10 ! =             3628800
facto.c:factorize:50: i= 1 fact=                     1
facto.c:factorize:50: i= 2 fact=           7257600    <-- Dirty Read!
facto.c:factorize:50: i= 3 fact=          21772800
facto.c:factorize:50: i= 4 fact=          87091200
facto.c:factorize:50: i= 5 fact=         435456000
facto.c:factorize:50: i= 6 fact=        2612736000
facto.c:factorize:50: i= 7 fact=       18289152000
facto.c:factorize:50: i= 8 fact=      146313216000
facto.c:factorize:50: i= 9 fact=     1316818944000
facto.c:factorize:50: i=10 fact=    13168189440000
facto.c:factorize:50: i=11 fact=   144850083840000
facto.c:factorize:50: i=12 fact=  1738201006080000
[Thread #2] (factorial) 12 ! =     1738201006080000
$
```

Aha! In this case, `10!` works, but `12!` is wrong! We can literally see from the preceding output that a dirty read has occurred (at the i==2 iteration of the calculation for 12!), causing the defect. Well, of course: we did not protect the critical section here (locking was turned off); it's really no wonder that it went wrong.

What we would like to stress, again, is that these races are delicate timing coincidences; in a buggy implementation, your test cases might still succeed, but of course that does not guarantee anything (it will likely fail in the field, as Murphy's Law tells us!). (An unfortunate truth is that testing can reveal the presence of errors but not their absence. Importantly, `Chapter 19`, *Troubleshooting and Best Practices*, covers such points).

> **TIP**: The reader will realize that, as these data races are delicate timing coincidences, they may or may not occur exactly as shown here on your test systems. Retrying the app a few times may help reproduce these scenarios.

We leave it to the reader to try out the use case with locking mode on and verbose mode on; it should work, of course.

## Mutex attributes

A mutex lock can have several attributes associated with it. Furthermore, we enumerate several of them.

### Mutex types

A mutex can be one of four types, the default usually—but not always (it depends upon the implementation)—being the normal mutex. The type of mutex used affects the behavior of the lock and unlock. The types are: PTHREAD_MUTEX_NORMAL, PTHREAD_MUTEX_ERRORCHECK, PTHREAD_MUTEX_RECURSIVE, and PTHREAD_MUTEX_DEFAULT.

The system man page on `pthread_mutex_lock(3)` describes the behavior depending on the mutex type with a table; for the reader's convenience, we have reproduced the same here.

If a thread attempts to relock a mutex that it has already locked, pthread_mutex_lock(3) shall behave as described in the relock column of the following table. If a thread attempts to unlock a mutex that it has not locked or a mutex which is unlocked, pthread_mutex_unlock(3) shall behave as described in the **Unlock When Not Owner** column of the following table:

| Mutex Type | Robustness | Relock | Unlock When Not Owner |
|---|---|---|---|
| NORMAL | non-robust | deadlock | undefined behavior |
| NORMAL | robust | deadlock | error returned |
| ERRORCHECK | either | error returned | error returned |
| RECURSIVE | either | recursive (see below) | error returned |
| DEFAULT | non-robust | undefined behavior† | undefined behavior† |
| DEFAULT | robust | undefined behavior† | error returned |

If the mutex type is PTHREAD_MUTEX_DEFAULT, the behavior of pthread_mutex_lock(3) may correspond to one of the three other standard mutex types, as described in the preceding table. If it does not correspond to one of those three, the behavior is undefined for the cases marked †.

The relock column directly corresponds to what we described earlier in this chapter as the self-deadlock scenario, such as, what effect attempting to re-lock an already-locked lock (poetic wording, perhaps?) will have. Clearly, except for the recursive and error check mutex case, the end result is either undefined (which means that anything can happen!) or a deadlock indeed.

Similarly, attempting to unlock a mutex by any thread except the owner either results in an undefined behavior or an error.

One might wonder: why does the locking API behave differently—in terms of error return or failures—depending on the type of the mutex? Why not just have one standard behavior for all types and thus simplify the situation? Well, it's the usual trade-off between simplicity and performance: the way it's implemented allows, for example, a well-written, programmatically proven correct real-time embedded application to forgo extra error checking and thus gain speed (which is especially important on critical code paths). On the other hand, in a development or debug environment, the developer might choose to allow extra checking to catch defects before shipping. (The man page on `pthread_mutex_destroy(3)` has a section entitled *Tradeoff Between Error Checks and Performance Supported* that describes this aspect in some detail.)

The pair of APIs to `get` and `set` a mutex's type attribute (the first column in the preceding table) are quite straightforward:

```
include <pthread.h>
int pthread_mutexattr_gettype(const pthread_mutexattr_t *restrict
attr,    int *restrict type);
int pthread_mutexattr_settype(pthread_mutexattr_t *attr, int type);
```

## The robust mutex attribute

Glancing at the preceding table, one spies the robustness column; what does it mean? Recall that only the owner thread of a mutex lock can possibly unlock the mutex; now, we ask, what if, by some chance, the owner thread dies? (Well, firstly, good design will ensure this never happens; secondly, even if it does, there are ways to protect against thread cancellation, a topic we will cover in the next chapter.) On the face of it, there is no help for it; any other threads waiting on the lock will now just deadlock (effectively, they will just hang). This behavior is in fact the default; it's also the behavior that's set up by the robust attribute known as PTHREAD_MUTEX_STALLED. To the (possible) rescue in such a situation, there does exist another value for the robust mutex attribute: PTHREAD_MUTEX_ROBUST. One can always query and set these attributes upon the mutex via the following pair of APIs:

```
#include <pthread.h>
int pthread_mutexattr_getrobust(const pthread_mutexattr_t *attr,
    int *robustness);
int pthread_mutexattr_setrobust(const pthread_mutexattr_t *attr,
    int robustness);
```

[ 623 ]

If this attribute (the value PTHREAD_MUTEX_ROBUST) is set upon the mutex lock, then if the owner thread dies while holding the mutex, a subsequent `pthread_mutex_lock(3)` upon the lock will succeed, returning the value EOWNERDEAD. Hang on, though! Even though the call returns a (so-called) successful return, it's important to understand that the lock in question is now considered to be in an inconsistent state and has to be reset into a consistent state via the `pthread_mutex_consistent(3)` API:

```
int pthread_mutex_consistent(pthread_mutex_t *mutex);
```

A return value of zero here indicates success; the mutex is now back in a consistent (stable) state and can be used normally (use it, and at some point, you must of course unlock it).

To sum this up, to use the robust attribute mutex, use the following:

- Initialize the mutex lock:
  ```
  pthread_mutexattr_t attr;
  pthread_mutexattr_init(&attr);
  ```
    - Set the robust attribute on it:
      ```
      pthread_mutexattr_setrobust(&attr, PTHREAD_MUTEX_ROBUST);
      ```
- Owner thread
    - Lock it: `pthread_mutex_lock(&mylock)`
    - Now, assume that the thread owner abruptly dies (while holding the mutex lock)
- Another thread (perhaps main) can assume ownership:
    - First, detect the case:
        - ```
          ret = pthread_mutex_lock(&mylock);
          if (ret == EOWNERDEAD) {
          ```
    - Then, make it consistent:
      ```
      pthread_mutex_consistent(&mylock)
      ```
    - Use it (or just unlock it)
    - Unlock it: `pthread_mutex_unlock(&mylock)`
      ```

Instead of duplicating the wheel, we point the reader to a simple, readable example of using the robust mutex attribute feature described previously. Find it within the man page of `pthread_mutexattr_setrobust(3)`.

> Under the hood, the Linux pthreads mutex lock is implemented via the `futex(2)` system call (and thus by the OS). The futex (fast user mutex) provides a fast, robust, atomic-only instructions locking implementation. Links with more details can be found in the *Further reading* section on the GitHub repository.

## IPC, threads, and the process-shared mutex

Visualize a large application that consists of several independent multithreaded processes. Now, if the processes want to communicate with each other (and they often will want to), how can this be achieved? The answer, of course, is **Inter-process Communication** (IPC)—mechanisms that exist for this very purpose. Broadly speaking, there are several IPC mechanisms available on the typical Unix/Linux platforms; these include shared memory (as well as the `mmap(2)`), message queues, semaphores (typically for synchronization), named (FIFO) and unnamed pipes, sockets (Unix and internet domain), and, to some extent, signals.

> Unfortunately, due to space constraints, we do not cover process IPC mechanisms in this book; we urge the interested reader to look into the links (and books) provided on IPC in the *Further reading* section on the GitHub repository.

The thing to stress here is that all of these IPC mechanisms are meant for communication between VM-isolated processes. So, our discussion here being focused on multithreading, how do the threads within a given process communicate with each other? Well, that's quite simple, really: just as one can set up and use a shared memory region to effectively and efficiently communicate between processes (writing and reading into that region, synchronizing access via a semaphore), threads can simply and effectively use a global memory buffer (or any appropriate data structure) as a medium within which to communicate with each other, and, of course, synchronize access to the global memory region via a mutex lock.

Interestingly, it is possible to use a mutex lock as a synchronization primitive between threads belonging to different processes. This is achieved by setting up the mutex attribute called pshared, or process-shared. The pair of APIs to get and set the pshared mutex attribute are as follows:

```
int pthread_mutexattr_getpshared(const pthread_mutexattr_t *attr,
    int *pshared);
int pthread_mutexattr_setpshared(pthread_mutexattr_t *attr,
    int pshared);
```

The second parameter, pshared, can be set to one of the following:

- **PTHREAD_PROCESS_PRIVATE** : The default; here, the mutex is only visible to threads within the process in which the mutex has been created.
- **PTHREAD_PROCESS_SHARED**: Here, the mutex is visible to any threads that have access to the memory region in which the mutex is created, including threads of different processes.

But how does one actually ensure that the memory region in which the mutex exists is shared between processes (without which it will not be possible for the processes in question to use the mutex)? Well, it's really back to basics: we must make use of one of the IPC mechanisms we mentioned—shared memory turns out to be the right one to use. So, we have the application set up a shared memory region (via either the traditional SysV IPC shmget(2) or the newer POSIX IPC shm_open(2) system calls), and have our process-shared mutex lock instantiated in this shared memory.

So, let's tie all this together with a simple application: we will write an application that creates two shared memory regions:

- One, a small shared memory region to act as a shared space for a process-shared mutex lock and an once-only initialization control (more on this in a minute)
- Two, a shared memory region to act as a simple buffer to store IPC messages

We will initialize a mutex with the process-shared attribute so that it can be used between threads of differing processes to synchronize access; here, we fork and have a thread of the original parent process and the newly born child process compete for the mutex lock. Once they (sequentially) obtain it, they write a message into the second shared memory segment. At the end of the app, we destroy the resources and display the shared memory buffer (as a simple proof-of-concept).

Chapter 15

Let's just try out our app (ch15/pshared_mutex_demo.c):

> We have added some blank lines in the following code for readability.

```
$ ./pshared_mutex_demo
./pshared_mutex_demo:15317: shmem segment successfully created /
accessed. ID=38928405
./pshared_mutex_demo:15317: Attached successfully to shmem segment at
0x7f45e9d50000
./pshared_mutex_demo:15317: shmem segment successfully created /
accessed. ID=38961174
./pshared_mutex_demo:15317: Attached successfully to shmem segment at
0x7f45e9d4f000

[pthread_once(): calls init_mutex(): from PID 15317]

Worker thread #0 [15317] running ...
 [thrd 0]: attempting to take the shared mutex lock...
 [thrd 0]: got the (shared) lock!
#0: work done, exiting now

 Child[15319]: attempting to taking the shared mutex lock...
 Child[15319]: got the (shared) lock!

main: joining (waiting) upon thread #0 ...
Thread #0 successfully joined; it terminated with status=0

Shared Memory 'comm' buffer:
00000000 63 63 63 63 63 00 63 68 69 6c 64 20 31 35 33 31  ccccc.child 1531
00000016 39 20 68 65 72 65 21 0a 00 74 74 74 74 74 00 74  9 here!..ttttt.t
00000032 68 72 65 61 64 20 31 35 33 31 37 20 68 65 72 65  hread 15317 here
00000048 21 0a 00 00 00 00 00 00 00 00 00 00 00 00 00 00  !...............
00000064 00 00 00 00 00 00 00 00 00 00 00 00 00 00 00 00  ................
00000080 00 00 00 00 00 00 00 00 00 00 00 00 00 00 00 00  ................
00000096 00 00 00 00 00 00 00 00 00 00 00 00 00 00 00 00  ................
00000112 00 00 00 00 00 00 00 00 00 00 00 00 00 00 00 00  ................
```

[ 627 ]

# Multithreading with Pthreads Part II - Synchronization

In the real world, things are not quite as simple as this; there does exist an additional synchronization issue to think about: how can one ensure that the mutex lock is initialized correctly and atomically (by only one process or thread), and, only initialized once, should other threads attempt to use it? In our demo program, we have used the `pthread_once(3)` API to achieve guaranteed once-only initialization of the mutex object (but have ignored the have-threads-wait-and-only-use-it-once-initialized issue). issue). (An interesting Q&A on Stack Overflow highlights this very concern; take a look: https://stackoverflow.com/questions/42628949/using-pthread-mutex-shared-between-processes-correctly#.) However, the reality is that the `pthread_once(3)` API is meant to be used between the threads of a process. Also, POSIX requires that the initialization of the `once_control` is done statically; here, we have performed it at run time, so it's not perfect.

In the main function, we set up and initialize the (IPC) shared memory segments; we urge the reader to carefully go through the source code (reading all the comments) and try it out for themselves as well:

> For readability, only key parts of the source code are displayed; to view the complete source code, build, and run it. The entire tree is available for cloning from GitHub here: https://github.com/PacktPublishing/Hands-on-System-Programming-with-Linux.

```
...

  /* Setup a shared memory region for the process-shared mutex lock.
   * A bit of complexity due to the fact that we use the space within
for:
   * a) memory for 1 process-shared mutex
   * b) 32 bytes of padding (not strictly required)
   * c) memory for 1 pthread_once_t variable.
   * We need the last one for performing guaranteed once-only
   * initialization of the mutex object.
   */
  shmaddr = shmem_setup(&gshm_id, argv[0], 0,
            (NUM_PSMUTEX*sizeof(pthread_mutex_t) + 32 +
                sizeof(pthread_once_t)));
  if (!shmaddr)
      FATAL("shmem setup 1 failed\n");

  /* Associate the shared memory segment with the mutex and
   * the pthread_once_t variable. */
  shmtx = (pthread_mutex_t *)shmaddr;
  mutex_init_once = (pthread_once_t *)shmaddr +
                      (NUM_PSMUTEX*sizeof(pthread_mutex_t)) + 32;
  *mutex_init_once = PTHREAD_ONCE_INIT; /* see below comment on
```

```
pthread_once */

    /* Setup a second shared memory region to be used as a comm buffer
*/
    gshmbuf = shmem_setup(&gshmbuf_id, argv[0], 0, GBUFSIZE);
    if (!gshmbuf)
        FATAL("shmem setup 2 failed\n");
    memset(gshmbuf, 0, GBUFSIZE);

    /* Initialize the mutex; here, we come across a relevant issue: this
     * mutex object is already instantiated in a shared memory region
that
     * other processes might well have access to. So who will initialize
     * the mutex? (it must be done only once).
     * Enter the pthread_once(3) API: it guarantees that, given a
     * 'once_control' variable (1st param), the 2nd param - a function
     * pointer, that function will be called exactly once.
     * However: the reality is that the pthread_once is meant to be used
     * between the threads of a process. Also, POSIX requires that the
     * initialization of the 'once_control' is done statically; here, we
     * have performed it at runtime...
     */
    pthread_once(mutex_init_once, init_mutex);
...
```

The init_mutex function which initializes the mutex with the process-shared attribute is shown as follows:

```
static void init_mutex(void)
{
    int ret=0;

    printf("[pthread_once(): calls %s(): from PID %d]\n",
        __func__, getpid());
    ret = pthread_mutexattr_init(&mtx_attr);
    if (ret)
        FATAL("pthread_mutexattr_init failed [%d]\n", ret);

    ret = pthread_mutexattr_setpshared(&mtx_attr,
PTHREAD_PROCESS_SHARED);
    if (ret)
        FATAL("pthread_mutexattr_setpshared failed [%d]\n", ret);
    ret = pthread_mutex_init(shmtx, &mtx_attr);
    if (ret)
        FATAL("pthread_mutex_init failed [%d]\n", ret);
}
```

The code of the worker thread—the worker routine—is shown in the following code. Here, we need to operate upon the second shared memory segment, implying of course that this is a critical section. Hence, we take the process-shared lock, perform the work, and subsequently unlock the mutex:

```
void * worker(void *data)
{
  long datum = (long)data;
  printf("Worker thread #%ld [%d] running ...\n", datum, getpid());
  sleep(1);
  printf(" [thrd %ld]: attempting to take the shared mutex lock...\n",
datum);

  LOCK_MTX(shmtx);
  /*--- critical section begins */
  printf(" [thrd %ld]: got the (shared) lock!\n", datum);
  /* Lets write into the shmem buffer; first, a 5-byte 'signature',
     followed by a message. */
  memset(&gshmbuf[0]+25, 't', 5);
  snprintf(&gshmbuf[0]+31, 32, "thread %d here!\n", getpid());
  /*--- critical section ends */
  UNLOCK_MTX(shmtx);

  printf("#%ld: work done, exiting now\n", datum);
  pthread_exit(NULL);
}
```

Notice that the lock and unlock operations are carried out by macros; here they are:

```
#define LOCK_MTX(mtx)   do {                                      \
  int ret=0;                                                       \
  if ((ret = pthread_mutex_lock(mtx)))                             \
    FATAL("pthread_mutex_lock failed! [%d]\n", ret);              \
} while(0)

#define UNLOCK_MTX(mtx) do {                                      \
  int ret=0;                                                       \
  if ((ret = pthread_mutex_unlock(mtx)))                           \
    FATAL("pthread_mutex_unlock failed! [%d]\n", ret);            \
} while(0)
```

We leave it to the reader to look at the code where we fork and have the newly born child process essentially do the same thing as the preceding worker thread—operate upon the (same) second shared memory segment; being a critical section, it too attempts to take the process-shared lock, and once it gets it, performs the work, and subsequently unlocks the mutex.

> Unless there is some compelling reason not to do so, when setting up IPC between processes, we suggest that you use one (or some) of the numerous IPC mechanisms that have been explicitly designed for this very purpose. Using the process-shared mutex as a synchronization mechanism between the threads of two or more processes is possible, but ask yourself if it is really required.
>
> Having said that, there are some advantages to using a mutex over the traditional (binary) semaphore object; these include the fact that the mutex is always associated with an owner thread, and only the owner can operate upon it (preventing some illegal or defective scenarios), and that mutexes can be set up to use nested (recursive) locking, and deal with the priority inversion problem effectively (via the inheritance protocol and/or priority ceiling attributes).

# Priority inversion, watchdogs, and Mars

An **Real Time Operating System** (**RTOS**) often has time-critical multithreaded applications running on it. Very simplistically, but nevertheless true, the primary rule for the RTOS scheduler to decide which thread to run next is the highest priority runnable thread must be the thread that is running. (By the way, we shall cover CPU scheduling with regard to the Linux OS in `Chapter 17`, *CPU Scheduling on Linux*; don't worry about the details for now.)

## Priority inversion

Let's visualize an application that contains three threads; one of them is a high priority thread (let's calls it thread A with priority 90), the other is a low priority thread (let's calls it thread B with priority 10) and finally a medium priority thread, C. (The priority range for the SCHED_FIFO scheduling policy is 1 to 99, with 99 being the highest possible priority; more on this in a later chapter.) So, we can imagine that we have these three threads within a process at differing priorities:

- Thread A: high priority, 90
- Thread B: low priority, 10
- Thread C: medium priority, 45

# Multithreading with Pthreads Part II - Synchronization

Furthermore, let's consider that we have some shared resource, X, which is coveted by threads A and B; this, of course, constitutes a critical section, and thus, we will need to synchronize access to it for correctness. We shall use a mutex lock to do so.

The normal case might well work like this (let's ignore thread C for now): thread B is on the CPU running some code; thread A is working on something else on another CPU core. Neither thread is in the critical section; thus, the mutex is in the unlocked state.

Now (at time **t1**), thread B hits the code of the critical section and takes the mutex lock, thus becoming the owner. It now runs the code within the critical section (working on X). In parallel, what if—at time **t2**— thread A too happens to hit the critical section and thus attempts to take the mutex lock? Well, we know that it's already locked, and thus thread A will have to wait (block) upon the unlock that will be performed (hopefully, soon) by thread B. Once thread B unlocks the mutex (at time **t3**), thread A takes it (at time **t4**; we consider that the delay **t4-t3** is very tiny), and life (quite happily) continues. This seems fine:

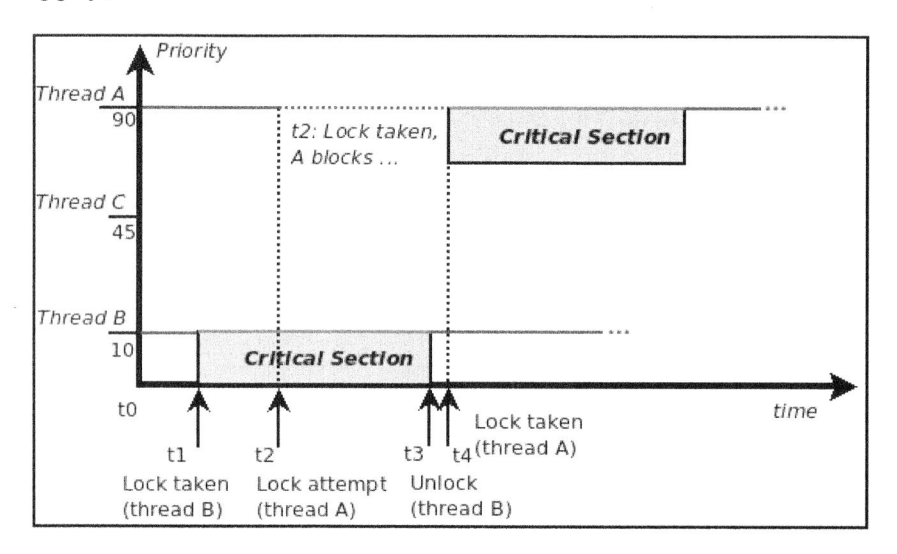

Fig 12: Mutex locking: the normal good case

However, a potential bad case exists as well! Read on.

## Watchdog timer in brief

A watchdog is a mechanism which is used to periodically detect that the system is in a healthy state, and, if it is deemed not to be, to reboot it. This is achieved by setting up a (kernel) timer (to say, a 60 second timeout). If all's well, a watchdog daemon process (a daemon is nothing but a system background process) will consistently cancel the timer (before it expires, of course) and subsequently re-enable it; this is known as **petting the dog**. If the daemon does not (due to something having gone badly wrong), the watchdog is annoyed and reboots the system! A pure software watchdog implementation will not be protected against kernel bugs and faults; a hardware watchdog (which latches into the board reset circuitry) will always be able to reboot the system as and when required.

Often, the high priority threads of embedded applications are designed to have very real deadlines within which they must complete some work; otherwise, the system is considered to have failed. One wonders, what if at run time the OS itself—due to an unfortunate bug— simply crashes or hangs (panics)? The application thread(s) then cannot continue; we need a way to detect and get out of this mess. Embedded designers often make use of **watchdog timer** (**WDT**) hardware circuitry (and an associated device driver) to achieve precisely this. If the system or a critical thread does not meet its deadline (fails to pet the dog), the system is rebooted.

So, back to our scenarios. Let's say we have a deadline for the high priority thread A of 100 ms; repeat the preceding locking scenario in your mind, but with this difference (refer to *Fig 13:* as well):

- **Thread B** (the low priority thread), obtains the mutex lock at time **t1**.
- **Thread A** also requests the mutex lock at time **t2** (but has to wait upon the unlock by thread B).
- Before thread B can complete the critical section, another medium priority thread C (running on the same CPU core and at priority 45) wakes up! It will immediately preempt thread B as its priority is higher (recall that the highest priority runnable thread must be the thread that is running).
- Now, until thread C gets off the CPU, thread B cannot complete the critical section, and therefore cannot perform the unlock.
- This, in turn, can significantly delay thread A, which is blocking upon the yet-to-happen unlock by thread B:
    - However, thread B has been preempted by thread C, hence it cannot perform the unlock.

## Multithreading with Pthreads Part II - Synchronization

- What if the time to unlock exceeds the deadline for thread A (at time **t4**)?
  - Then the watchdog timer will expire, forcing a system reboot:

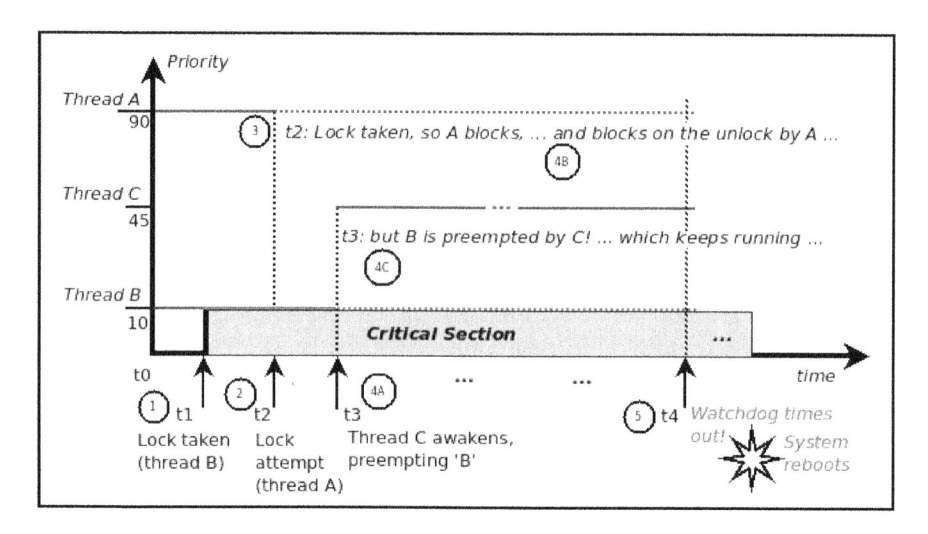

Fig 13: Priority inversion

Interesting, and unfortunate; did you notice that the highest priority thread (A) was in effect forced to wait upon the lowest priority thread (B) on the system? This phenomenon is in fact a documented software risk, formally called priority inversion.

Not only that, consider what might happen if several medium priority threads woke up while thread B was in its critical section (and thus holding the lock)? The potential time wait for thread A can now become very large; such situations are known as unbounded priority inversion.

*Chapter 15*

## The Mars Pathfinder mission in brief

Very interestingly, this precise scenario priority inversion played out quite dramatically in a literally out of this world setting: on the surface of Mars! NASA successfully landed a robot spacecraft (the Pathfinder Lander) on the Martian surface on July 4, 1997; it then proceeded to unload and deploy a smaller robot—the Sojourner Rover—onto the surface. However, controllers found that the lander ran into problems—every so often it would reboot. Detailed analysis of the live telemetry feed ultimately revealed the underlying issue—it was the software, which had hit a priority inversion issue! To their immense credit, NASA's **Jet Propulsion Laboratory** (**JPL**) team, along with engineers from Wind River, the company that supplied a custom VxWorks RTOS to NASA, diagnosed and debugged the situation from Earth, determined the root cause defect as a priority inversion issue, fixed it, uploaded the new firmware to the rover, and it all worked:

Figure 14: Photo from the Mars Pathfinder Lander

The news spread (in a viral fashion) when an MS engineer, Mike Jones, at an IEEE Real-Time Symposium, wrote an interesting email about what occurred with NASA's Pathfinder mission; this was ultimately, and in detail, responded to by the team leader of NASA's JPL, Glenn Reeves, with a now quite famous article entitled *What Really Happened on Mars?*. Many interesting insights were captured in this and subsequent articles written on the topic. In my opinion, all software engineers would do themselves a favor by reading these! (Do look up the links provided in the *Further reading* section on the GitHub repository under Mars Pathfinder and Priority Inversion.)

Glenn Reeves stresses a few important lessons learned and the reasons why they were able to reproduce and fix the issue, and one of them is this: We strongly believe in the test what you fly and fly what you test philosophy. In effect, because of the design decisions to keep relevant detailed diagnostic and debug information in trace/log ring buffers, which could be dumped at will (and sent to Earth), they were able to debug the root issue at hand.

## Priority inheritance – avoiding priority inversion

Okay, great; but how does one fix such an issue as priority inversion? Interestingly, this is a known risk, and the design of the mutex includes a built-in solution. Two mutex attributes exist with regard to helping address the priority inversion issue—**priority inheritance** (**PI**) and priority ceiling.

PI is an interesting solution. Think about it, the key issue is the way in which the OS schedules threads. In an OS (and especially on an RTOS), the scheduling of a real-time thread—deciding who runs—is essentially directly proportional to the priority of the competing threads: the higher your priority, the better the chance you will run. So, let's take a quick relook at our preceding scenario example. Recall that we have these three threads at differing priorities:

- Thread A: high priority, 90
- Thread B: low priority, 10
- Thread C: medium priority, 45

The priority inversion occurred when thread B held the mutex lock for a long while, thus forcing thread A to block on the unlock for perhaps far too long (over the deadline). So, think about this: what if, the moment thread B grabs the mutex lock, we increase its priority to that of the highest priority thread on the system which is also waiting on the same mutex lock. Then, of course, thread B will get priority 90 and thus cannot be preempted (by thread C or any other thread for that matter)! This ensures that it completes its critical section quickly and unlocks the mutex; the moment it unlocks it, it goes back to its original priority. This solves the problem; this approach is termed PI.

The pthreads API set provides a pair of APIs to query and set the protocol mutex attribute, upon which you can make use of PI:

```
int pthread_mutexattr_getprotocol(const pthread_mutexattr_t
    *restrict attr, int *restrict protocol);
int pthread_mutexattr_setprotocol(pthread_mutexattr_t *attr,
    int protocol);
```

The value that the protocol parameter can take is one of the following: PTHREAD_PRIO_INHERIT, PTHREAD_PRIO_NONE, or PTHREAD_PRIO_PROTECT (the default being PTHREAD_PRIO_NONE). When a mutex has one of the INHERIT or PROTECT protocols, its owner thread is affected in terms of scheduling priority.

A thread that holds the lock (owns it) on any mutexes initialized with the PTHREAD_PRIO_INHERIT protocol will inherit the highest priority (and therefore execute at that priority) of any thread that is blocked upon (waiting) on any of these mutexes (robust or non-robust) that also uses this protocol.

A thread that holds the lock (owns it) on any mutexes initialized with the PTHREAD_PRIO_PROTECT protocol will inherit the highest priority ceiling (and therefore execute at that priority) of any thread that also uses this protocol, regardless of whether or not they are currently blocking upon (waiting) on any of these mutexes (robust or non-robust).

If a thread uses mutexes initialized with differing protocols, it will execute at the highest priority defined among them.

On the Pathfinder mission, the RTOS used was the well-known VxWorks by Wind River. The mutex (or semaphores) certainly had the PI attribute; it's just that the JPL software team missed turning on the PI attribute of a mutex lock, resulting in the priority inversion issue! (Actually, the software team was well aware of it and used it in several places, but not the one place that struck — Murphy's Law at work!)

Furthermore, the developer can make use of priority ceiling—this is the minimum priority at which the owner thread will execute the code of the critical section. Thus, being able to specify this, one can ensure that it's at a sufficiently high value to guarantee that the owner thread does not get preempted while in the critical section. The pthreads `pthread_mutexattr_getprioceiling(3)` and `pthread_mutexattr_setprioceiling(3)` API's can be used to query and set the priority ceiling attribute of a mutex. (It must fall within the valid SCHED_FIFO priority range, typically 1 to 99 on the Linux platform).

> Again, in practice, there are some challenges in using priority inheritance and ceiling attributes, which are, mostly, performance overheads:
> - Heavier task/context switching can result
> - Priority propagation can add overhead
> - With many threads and many locks, there is performance overhead, as well the potential for deadlock climbs

## Summary of mutex attribute usage

In effect, if you would like to thoroughly test and debug your application and don't really care about performance (right now, at least), then set up your mutex as follows:

- Set the robust attribute on it (allowing one to catch the owner-dies-without-unlocking case): `pthread_mutexattr_setrobust(&attr, PTHREAD_MUTEX_ROBUST)`
- Set the type to error checking (allowing one to catch the self-deadlock / relock case): `pthread_mutexattr_settype(&attr, PTHREAD_MUTEX_ERRORCHECK)`

On the other hand, a well-designed and proven application that requires you to squeeze out performance would use the normal (default) mutex type and attributes. The preceding cases will not be caught (and will instead result in undefined behavior), but then, they should never occur!

If one requires a recursive lock, (obviously) set the mutex type to PTHREAD_MUTEX_RECURSIVE. With the recursive mutex, it's important to realize that if the mutex lock is performed n times, it must also be unlocked n times in order for it be considered to be truly in the unlocked state (and therefore lockable again).

In a multiprocess and multithreaded application, if there is a need to use a mutex lock between threads of different processes, this can be achieved via the process-shared attribute of the mutex object. Note that, in this case, the memory that contains the mutex must itself be shared between the processes (we usually use a shared memory segment).

The PI and the priority ceiling attributes allow the developer to safeguard the application against a well-understood software risk: priority inversion.

# Mutex locking – additional variants

This section helps one understand additional—slightly different semantics—to mutex locking. We will cover the timeout mutex variant, the "busy-waiting" use case, and the reader-writer lock.

## Timing out on a mutex lock attempt

In the earlier section, *Locking guidelines*, under the label prevent starvation, we understood that holding a mutex lock for a long-ish time leads to performance issues; noticeably, the loser threads will starve. A way to ward off this issue (although, of course, fixing the underlying root cause of any starvation is the important thing to do!) is to have the loser threads wait upon the mutex lock for only a certain amount of time; if it takes longer to be unlocked, forget it. This is precisely the functionality that the pthread_mutex_timedlock(3) API provides:

```
#include <pthread.h>
#include <time.h>
int pthread_mutex_timedlock(pthread_mutex_t *restrict mutex,
        const struct timespec *restrict abstime);
```

It's quite obvious: all locking semantics remains the same as they do for the usual pthread_mutex_lock(3), except that if the time spent blocking (waiting) upon the lock exceeds the second parameter—the time specified as an absolute value, where the API returns failure—the value returned will be ETIMEDOUT. (We have already programmed timeouts in detail in Chapter 13, *Timers*.)

Note, though, that other error return values are possible (for example, EOWNERDEAD for a robust mutex in which the previous owner terminates, EDEADLK for a deadlock being detected on an error-checking mutex, and so on.). Please refer to the man page on pthread_mutex_timedlock(3) for details.

## Busy-waiting (non-blocking variant) for the lock

We understand how a mutex lock works normally: if a lock is already locked, then attempting to take the lock will cause that thread to block (wait upon) the unlock occurring. What if one wants a design which goes something like this: if the lock is locked, don't make me wait; I'll do some other work and retry? This semantic is often referred to as busy-waiting or non-blocking, and is provided by the trylock variant. As the name suggests, we try for the lock and if we get it, great; if not, it's okay—we do not force the thread to wait. The lock might be taken by any thread within the process (or even outside if it's a process-shared mutex) including the same thread—if it's marked as recursive. But hold on; if the mutex lock is indeed a recursive lock, then taking it will succeed immediately and the call will return straight away.

The API for this is as follows:

```
int pthread_mutex_trylock(pthread_mutex_t *mutex);
```

While this busy-waiting semantic is useful on occasion—specifically, it is used to detect and prevent certain types of deadlock—be careful when using it. Think about it: for a lightly contented lock (one which is not being used often, in which the thread attempting to take the lock will very likely get it straight away), using this busy-wait semantic might be useful. But for a heavily contented lock (a lock on a hot code path, taken and released often), this can actually hurt one's chances of obtaining the lock! Why? Because you are not willing to wait for it. (Funny how software mimics life sometimes, yes?)

## The reader-writer mutex lock

Visualize a multithreaded application with some ten worker threads; let's say that, most of the time (say 90% of the time), eight of the workers are busy scanning a global linked list (or similar data structure). Now, of course, since it's global, we know that it's a critical section; failing to protect it with a mutex can easily result in a dirty read bug. But, this is at a major performance cost: as each worker thread wants to search the list, it is forced to wait upon the unlock event from the owner.

Computer scientists have come up with quite an innovate alternative for situations like this (also referred to as the reader-writer problem), wherein the data accesses are such that for the majority of time (shared) data is only being read and not written to. We use a special variant of the mutex lock called the reader-writer lock:

```
int pthread_rwlock_rdlock(pthread_rwlock_t *rwlock);
int pthread_rwlock_tryrdlock(pthread_rwlock_t *rwlock);
int pthread_rwlock_wrlock(pthread_rwlock_t *rwlock);
```

Notice that it's a new type of lock altogether: the `pthread_wrlock_t`.

If a thread obtains a read lock for itself, the key point is this: the implementation now trusts that this thread will only read and never write; thus, no actual locking is done and the API will just return success! This way, readers actually run in parallel, thus keeping performance high; there is no safety issue or race, as they guarantee they will only read.

However, the moment a thread wishes to write data, it must obtain a write lock: when this happens, normal locking semantics apply. The writer thread must now wait for all readers to perform the unlock, and then the writer gets the write lock and proceeds. While it's within the critical section, no thread—reader nor writer—will be able to intervene; they will have to, as is usual, block (wait) upon the writer's unlock. Thus, both scenarios are now optimized.

The usual suspects—the APIs—for setting up the reader-writer mutex lock attributes exist (in alphabetical order):

- `pthread_rwlockattr_destroy(3P)`
- `pthread_rwlockattr_getpshared(3P)`
- `pthread_rwlockattr_setkind_np(3P)`
- `pthread_rwlockattr_getkind_np(3P)`
- `pthread_rwlockattr_init(3P)`
- `pthread_rwlockattr_setpshared(3P)`

Note that the APIs suffixed with `_np` imply they are non-portable, and Linux-only.

Similarly, the reader-writer locking APIs follow the usual pattern—the timeout and try variants are present as well:

- `pthread_rwlock_destroy(3P)`
- `pthread_rwlock_init(3P)`
- `pthread_rwlock_timedrdlock(3P)`
- `pthread_rwlock_tryrdlock(3P)`
- `pthread_rwlock_unlock(3P)`
- `pthread_rwlock_rdlock(3P)`

- `pthread_rwlock_timedwrlock(3P)`
- `pthread_rwlock_trywrlock(3P)`
- `pthread_rwlock_wrlock(3P)`

We expect the programmer to set up in a normal manner—initialize the rwlock attribute object, initialize the rwlock itself (with `pthread_rwlock_init(3P)`), destroy the attribute structure once done with it, and then perform the actual locking as required.

Note, though, that when using reader-writer locks, the application should be carefully tested for performance; it has been noted to be a slower implementation than the usual mutex lock. Also, there is the additional worry that, under load, the reader-writer locking semantics might result in writer starvation. Think: if readers keep coming up, the writer thread might have to wait for a long time before it gets the lock.

Apparently, with the reader-writer lock, the opposite dynamic can also occur: the readers could be starved. Interestingly, Linux provides a non-portable API, allowing the programmer to specify which kind of starvation to prevent—reader or writer—with the default being that the writers starve. The API to invoke to set this up is `pthread_rwlockattr_setkind_np(3)`. This allows some degree of tuning based on your specific workload. (However, the implementation apparently still suffers from a bug wherein, in effect, writer starvation remains the reality. We do not attempt to go into this further; the reader is referred to the man page if further aid is required.)

Nevertheless, the reader-writer lock variant is often useful; think of applications that need to often scan some key-value map data structure and perform a table lookup of some sort. (For example, an OS often has network code paths that often look up the routing table but rarely update it.) The invariant is that the global shared data in question is often read from but rarely written to.

## The spinlock variant

A bit of repetition here: we already understand how a mutex lock works normally; if a lock is already locked, then attempting to take the lock will cause that thread to block (wait upon) the unlock occurring. Let's dig a little deeper; how exactly do the loser threads block—wait upon — the unlock of the mutex? The answer is that, for the mutex lock, they do so by sleeping (being scheduled off CPU by the OS). This, in fact, is one of the defining properties of the mutex lock.

On the other hand, there exists a different kind of lock altogether—the spinlock (very commonly used within the Linux kernel) whose behavior is quite the opposite: it works by having the loser threads wait upon the unlock operation by spinning (polling)—well, the reality is that the actual spinlock implementation is a lot more refined and efficient than it's made to sound here; this discussion is well beyond the scope of this book, though. At first glance, polling seems to be a poor way to have the loser threads wait on the unlock; the reason it works well with the spinlock is that the time taken within the critical section is guaranteed to be very small (technically, less than the time required to perform two context switches), thus making the spinlock much more efficient to use than the mutex when the critical section tiny.

Though the pthreads implementation does provide the spinlock, one should be clear on these points:

- The spinlock is only meant to be used by extreme performance real-time threads that employ a real-time OS scheduling policy (SCHED_FIFO, and possibly SCHED_RR; we discuss these in Chapter 17, *CPU Scheduling on Linux*).
- The default scheduling policy on the Linux platform is never a real-time one; it's the non-real-time SCHED_OTHER policy, which is well-suited to non-deterministic applications; using the mutex lock is the way to go.
- Using spinlocks in user space is not considered the right design approach; moreover, the code will be a lot more susceptible to deadlock and (unbounded) priority inversion scenarios.

For the preceding reasons, we refrain from delving into the following pthreads spinlock APIs:

- `pthread_spin_init(3)`
- `pthread_spin_lock(3)`
- `pthread_spin_trylock(3)`
- `pthread_spin_unlock(3)`
- `pthread_spin_destroy(3)`

If required, do look them up within their respective manual pages (but also be doubly careful if employing them!).

# A few more mutex usage guidelines

In addition to the tips and guidelines that were provided earlier (refer to the *Locking Guidelines* section), think upon this as well:

- How many locks should one use?
- With many lock instances, how to know which lock variable to use and when?
- Test whether a mutex is locked or not.

Let's take these points up one by one.

In small applications (like the kind shown here), perhaps using just a single lock to protect critical sections is enough; it has the advantage of keeping things simple (which is a big deal). However, in a large project, using just one lock to perform locking on every critical section one might encounter has the potential to become a major performance breaker! Think about why exactly this is: the moment that one mutex lock is hit anywhere in the code, all parallelism stops, and the code runs in a serialized fashion; if this happens often enough, performance will rapidly degrade.

> Interestingly, the Linux kernel, for years, had a major performance headache precisely because of one lock that was being used throughout large cross sections of the codebase—so much so, that it was nicknamed the **big kernel lock** (**BKL**) (a giant lock). It was finally gotten rid of only in the 2.6.39 version of the Linux kernel (see the *Further reading* section on the GitHub repository for a link to more on the BKL).

So, while there is no rule to decide exactly how many locks one should use, the heuristic is to think about the simplicity versus performance trade off. As a tip, in large production-quality projects (like the Linux kernel), we often use a single lock to protect a single datum— a data object; typically, this is a data structure. This would ensure that the global data is protected while accessed, but only by the code paths that actually access it and not every code path, thus ensuring both data safety as well as parallelism (performance).

Okay, great. Now, if we do follow this guideline, what if we end up with a few hundred locks!? (Yes, this is entirely possible in large projects that have a few hundred global data structures.) Now, we have another practical problem: the developer must ensure that they use the correct lock to protect a given data structure (of what use is using lock X meant for data structure X while accessing data structure Y? That would be a serious defect). So, a practical issue is how do I know for sure which data structure is protected by which lock or, another way to state it: how (how do I know for sure which lock variable protects which data structure?) The naive solution is to name each lock appropriately, perhaps something like `lock_<DataStructureName>`. Hmm, not as simple as it appears!

> Informal polls have revealed that, often, one of the hardest things a programmer does is variable naming! (See the *Further reading* section on the GitHub repository for a link to this.)

So, here's a tip: embed the lock that protects a given data structure inside the data structure itself; in other words, make it a member of the data structure it protects! (Again, the Linux kernel often uses this approach.)

## Is the mutex locked?

In certain situations, the developer might be tempted to ask: given a mutex, can I find out if it's in the locked or unlocked state? Perhaps the reasoning is: if locked, let's unlock it.

There is a way to test this: with the `pthread_mutex_trylock(3)` API. If it returns `EBUSY`, it implies that the mutex is currently locked (otherwise, it should return 0, implying it's unlocked). But wait! There is an inherent race condition here; just think about this:

```
if (pthread_mutex_trylock(&mylock) != EBUSY)) {    <-- time t1
    // it's unlocked                                <-- time t2
}
// it's locked
```

By the time we reach time t2, there is no guarantee that another thread has not, by now, locked the mutex in question! So, this approach is incorrect. (The only realistic way to do this kind of synchronization is to abandon doing this via mutex locks and use condition variables instead; that's what we cover in the next section.)

*Multithreading with Pthreads Part II - Synchronization*

This concludes our (rather long) coverage on mutex locking. Before we are done, we would like to point out another point of interest: we stated earlier that being atomic implies being able to run the critical code section to completion without interruption. But the reality is that our modern systems do interrupt us with (alarming) regularity—hardware interrupts and exceptions being the norm! Thus, one should realize that:

- In user space, with it being impossible to mask hardware interrupts, processes and threads will get interrupted at any point in time due to them. Thus, it's essentially impossible to be truly atomic with user space code. (But so what if we're interrupted by hardware interrupts/faults/exceptions? They will perform their work and hand control back to us, all very quickly. It's highly unlikely we race, sharing global writable data with these code entities).
- In kernel space, though, we run with OS privilege, actually making it possible to mask even hardware interrupts, and thus allowing us to run in a truly atomic fashion (how do you think the well-known Linux kernel spinlock works?).

Now that we have covered the typical APIs used for locking, we encourage the reader to, one, work on trying out examples in a hands-on manner; and two, revisit the sections covered earlier in sections, *Locking guidelines* and *Deadlock*.

## Condition variables

A CV is an inter-thread event notification mechanism. Where we use the mutex lock to synchronize (serialize) access to a critical section, thus protecting it, we use condition variables to facilitate efficient communication—in terms of synchronizing based on the value of a data item—between the threads of a process. The following discussion will make this clearer.

Often, in multithreaded application design and implementation, one is faced with this type of situation: a thread, B, is performing some work and another thread, A, is awaiting the completion of that work. Only when thread B completes the work should thread A continue; how can we efficiently implement this in code?

## No CV – the naive approach

One might recall that the exit status of a thread (via `pthread_exit(3)`) is passed back to the thread that calls `pthread_join(3)`; could we make use of this feature? Well, no: for one thing, it's not necessarily the case that thread B will terminate once the designated work is complete (it might only be a milestone and not all of the job it has to perform), and two, even if it does terminate, perhaps some other thread besides the one invoking `pthread_join(3)` might need to know.

Okay; why not have thread A poll upon the completion by the simple technique of having thread B set a global integer (call it `gWorkDone`) to 1 when the work is complete (and having thread A poll on it, of course), perhaps something like the following in pseudocode:

| Time | Thread B | Thread A |
|---|---|---|
| t0 | Initialize: `gWorkDone = 0` | < common > |
| t1 | Perform the work ... | `while (!gWorkDone) ;` |
| t2 | ... | ... |
| t3 | Work done; `gWorkDone = 1` | ... |
| t4 |  | Detected; break out of the loop and continue |

It might work, but it doesn't. Why not?:

- One, polling on a variable for unbounded periods of time is very expensive in CPU terms (and is just bad design).
- Two, notice that we are operating upon a shared writable global variable without protecting it; this is exactly the way to introduce data races, and thus bugs, into the application.

Hence, the approach shown in the preceding table is considered to be a naive, inefficient, and even possibly buggy (racy).

## Using the condition variable

The correct approach is to use a CV. A condition variable is a way for threads to synchronize upon the value of data in an efficient manner. It achieves the same end result as the naive polling approach does, but in a far more efficient and, even more importantly, correct manner.

# Multithreading with Pthreads Part II - Synchronization

Check out the following table:

| Time | Thread B | Thread A |
|---|---|---|
| t0 | Initialize: gWorkDone = 0 ; init the {CV, mutex} pair | < common > |
| t1 | | Wait upon signal from thread B : lock the associated mutex; `pthread_cond_wait()` |
| t2 | Perform the work ... | < ... blocking ... > |
| t3 | Work done; lock the associated mutex; signal thread A : `pthread_cond_signal()`; unlock the associated mutex | ... |
| t4 | | Unblocked; check to see that the work is really done, and if so, unlock the associated mutex, and continue... |

Though the preceding table shows us the sequence of steps, some explanation is required. In the naive approach, we saw that one of the (serious) shortcomings is the fact that the global shared data variable was being manipulated without protection! The condition variable solves this by requiring that a condition variable be always associated with a mutex lock; we can think of it as a **{CV, mutex} pair**.

The idea is simple: every time we intend to use the global predicate that tells us whether or not the work has been completed (`gWorkDone`, in our example), we lock the mutex, read/write the global, unlock the mutex, thus—importantly!—protecting it.

The beauty of the CV is that we do not require polling at all: the thread awaiting work completion uses `pthread_cond_wait(3)` to block (wait) upon that event occurring, and the thread that has completed work "signals" its counterpart via the `pthread_cond_signal(3)` API:

```
int pthread_cond_wait(pthread_cond_t *restrict cond,
                      pthread_mutex_t *restrict mutex);
int pthread_cond_signal(pthread_cond_t *cond);
```

> **TIP**: Though we use the word signal here, this has nothing to do with Unix/Linux signals and signaling that we covered in earlier Chapters 11, *Signaling - Part I*, and Chapter 12, *Signaling - II*.

[ 648 ]

(Notice how the {CV, mutex} pair go together). Of course, just as with threads, we must first initialize the CV and its associated mutex lock; the CV is initialized either statically via:

pthread_cond_t cond = PTHREAD_COND_INITIALIZER;

Or dynamically (at runtime) via the following API:

```
int pthread_cond_init(pthread_cond_t *restrict cond,
                      const pthread_condattr_t *restrict attr);
```

If specific, non-default attributes of the CV are to be set up, one can do so via the `pthread_condattr_set*(3P)` APIs, or just set the CV to default by first invoking the `pthread_condattr_init(3P)` API and passing the initialized CV attribute object as the second parameter to `pthread_cond_init(3P)`:

```
int pthread_condattr_init(pthread_condattr_t *attr);
```

Conversely, when done, use the following APIs to destroy the CV attribute object and the CV itself:

```
int pthread_condattr_destroy(pthread_condattr_t *attr);
int pthread_cond_destroy(pthread_cond_t *cond);
```

## A simple CV usage demo application

Too many inits/destroys? Looking at the following simple code (`ch15/cv_simple.c`) will clarify their usage; we write a small program to demonstrate the usage of a condition variable and its associated mutex lock. Here, we create two threads, A and B. We then have thread B perform some work and thread A synchronize upon completion of that work by using the {CV, mutex} pair:

> For readability, only key parts of the source code are displayed; to view the complete source code, build and run it. The entire tree is available for cloning from GitHub here: https://github.com/PacktPublishing/Hands-on-System-Programming-with-Linux.

```
...
#define LOCK_MTX(mtx)  do { \
  int ret=0; \
  if ((ret = pthread_mutex_lock(mtx))) \
    FATAL("pthread_mutex_lock failed! [%d]\n", ret); \
} while(0)

#define UNLOCK_MTX(mtx)  do { \
  int ret=0; \
```

## Multithreading with Pthreads Part II - Synchronization

```
       if ((ret = pthread_mutex_unlock(mtx))) \
           FATAL("pthread_mutex_unlock failed! [%d]\n", ret); \
    } while(0)

   static int gWorkDone=0;
   /* The {cv,mutex} pair */
   static pthread_cond_t mycv;
   static pthread_mutex_t mycv_mutex = PTHREAD_MUTEX_INITIALIZER;
```

In the preceding code, we again show the macros that implement the mutex lock and unlock, the global predicate (Boolean) variable `gWorkDone`, and of course, the {CV, mutex} pair of variables.

In the following code, in main, we initialize the CV attribute object and the CV itself:

```
    // Init a condition variable attribute object
       if ((ret = pthread_condattr_init(&cvattr)))
           FATAL("pthread_condattr_init failed [%d].\n", ret);
    // Init a {cv,mutex} pair: condition variable & it's associated
    mutex
       if ((ret = pthread_cond_init(&mycv, &cvattr)))
           FATAL("pthread_cond_init failed [%d].\n", ret);
    // the mutex lock has been statically initialized above.
```

The worker threads A and B are created and start their work (we do not repeat the code showing thread creation here). Here, you will find the worker routine for thread A— it must wait until thread B completes the work. We use the {CV, mutex} pair to easily and efficiently achieve this.

The library does, however, require the application to guarantee that prior to invoking the `pthread_cond_wait(3P)` API, the associated mutex lock is taken (locked); otherwise, this will result in undefined behavior (or an actual failure when the mutex type is `PTHREAD_MUTEX_ERRORCHECK` or a robust mutex). Once the thread is blocking upon the CV, the mutex lock is auto-released.

Also, if a signal is delivered while the thread is blocked upon the wait condition, it shall be processed and the wait will be resumed; it could also cause a return value of zero for a spurious wake up (more on this in a minute):

```
    static void * workerA(void *msg)
    {
      int ret=0;

      LOCK_MTX(&mycv_mutex);
      while (1) {
          printf(" [thread A] : now waiting on the CV for thread B to
```

```
                        finish...\n");
        ret = pthread_cond_wait(&mycv, &mycv_mutex);
        // Blocking: associated mutex auto-released ...
        if (ret)
            FATAL("pthread_cond_wait() in thread A failed! [%d]\n",
ret);
        // Unblocked: associated mutex auto-acquired upon release from
the condition wait...
        printf(" [thread A] : recheck the predicate (is the work really
"
               "done or is it a spurious wakeup?)\n");
        if (gWorkDone)
            break;
        printf(" [thread A] : SPURIOUS WAKEUP detected !!! "
                "(going back to CV waiting)\n");
    }
    UNLOCK_MTX(&mycv_mutex);
    printf(" [thread A] : (cv wait done) thread B has completed it's
work...\n");
    pthread_exit((void *)0);
}
```

It's very important to understand this: merely returning from the `pthread_cond_wait(3P)` does not necessarily imply that the condition we were waiting (blocking) upon — in this case, thread B completing the work—actually occurred! In software, receiving a spurious wakeup (a false wakeup due to some other event — perhaps a signal) can occur; robust software will literally recheck the condition in a loop to determine that the reason we were awoken is the right one—in our case here, that the work has indeed been completed. This is why we run in an infinite loop and, once unblocked from `pthread_cond_wait(3P)`, check whether the global integer `gWorkDone` is actually having the value we expect (1, in this case, signifying completion of the work).

All right, but think about this too: even reading a shared global becomes a critical section (otherwise a dirty read could result); hence, we need to take the mutex before doing so. Ah, this is where the {CV, mutex} pair idea has a built-in automatic mechanism that really helps us out—the moment we call `pthread_cond_wait(3P)`, the associated mutex lock is automatically and atomically released (unlocked), and then we block upon the condition variable signal. The moment the other thread (B, here) signals us (on the same CV, obviously), we are unblocked from `pthread_cond_wait(3P)` and the associated mutex lock is automatically and atomically locked, allowing us to recheck the global (or whatever). So, we do our work and then unlock it.

Here's the code for the worker routine for thread B, which performs some sample work and then signals thread A:

```
static void * workerB(void *msg)
{
  int ret=0;

  printf(" [thread B] : perform the 'work' now (first sleep(1) :-)) ...\n");
  sleep(1);
  DELAY_LOOP('b', 72);
  gWorkDone = 1;

  printf("\n [thread B] : work done, signal thread A to continue ...\n");
  /* It's not strictly required to lock/unlock the associated mutex
   * while signalling; we do it here to be pedantically correct (and
   * to shut helgrind up).
   */
  LOCK_MTX(&mycv_mutex);
  ret = pthread_cond_signal(&mycv);
  if (ret)
      FATAL("pthread_cond_signal() in thread B failed! [%d]\n", ret);
  UNLOCK_MTX(&mycv_mutex);
  pthread_exit((void *)0);
}
```

Notice the comment detailing why we again take the mutex lock just prior to the signal. Okay, let's try it out (we suggest you build and run the debug version as then, the delay loop shows up correctly):

```
$ ./cv_simple_dbg
 [thread A] : now waiting on the CV for thread B to finish...
 [thread B] : perform the 'work' now (first sleep(1) :-)) ...
bbbbbbbbbbbbbbbbbbbbbbbbbbbbbbbbbbbbbbbbbbbbbbbbbbbbbbbbbbbbbbbbbbbbbbbb
bb
 [thread B] : work done, signal thread A to continue ...
 [thread A] : recheck the predicate (is the work really done or is it a spurious wakeup?)
 [thread A] : (cv wait done) thread B has completed it's work...
$
```

[ 652 ]

The API also provides a timeout variant of the blocking call:

```
int pthread_cond_timedwait(pthread_cond_t *restrict cond,
    pthread_mutex_t *restrict mutex, const struct timespec *restrict
abstime);
```

The semantics are identical to that of pthread_cond_wait, except that the API returns (with a failure value of ETIMEDOUT) if the time specified in the third parameter, abstime, has (already) passed. The clock used to measure the time that's elapsed is an attribute of the CV and can be set via the pthread_condattr_setclock(3P) API.

(Both pthread_cond_wait and the pthread_cond_timedwait are cancellation points; this topic is dealt with in the next chapter.)

## CV broadcast wakeup

As we saw previously, the pthread_cond_signal(3P) API is used to unblock a thread that is blocked upon a particular CV. A variant of this API is as follows:

```
int pthread_cond_broadcast(pthread_cond_t *cond);
```

This API allows you to unblock multiple threads that are blocking on the same CV. So, for example, what if we have three threads blocking on the same CV; when the application calls the pthread_cond_broadcast(3P), which thread will run first? Well, this is like asking, when threads are created, which one will run first (recall these discussions from the previous chapter). The answer, of course, is that, in the absence of particular scheduling policies, it is indeterminate. The same answer holds for the question when applied to the CV unblock and run on CPU.

To continue, once the waiting threads are unblocked, recall that the associated mutex will be taken, but of course only one of the unblocked threads will get it first. Again, this depends on scheduling policy and priority. With all defaults, it remains indeterminate which thread gets it first. In any case, in the absence of real-time characteristics, this should not matter to the application (if the application is real-time, then read our Chapter 17, *CPU Scheduling on Linux*, and setting up real-time scheduling policies and priorities first on each application thread).

## Multithreading with Pthreads Part II - Synchronization

Also, the manual page on these APIs clearly states that although the threads invoking the preceding APIs (`pthread_cond_signal` and the `pthread_cond_broadcast`) do not require that you hold the associated mutex lock when doing so (recall, we always have a {CV, mutex} pair), pedantically correct semantics demand that they do hold the mutex, perform the signal or broadcast, and then unlock the mutex (our example app, `ch15/cv_simple.c`, does follow this guideline).

To round off this discussion on CVs, here are a few tips:

- Do not use the condition variable approach from within a signal handler; the code is not considered to be async signal-safe (recall our earlier Chapter 11, *Signaling - Part I*, and Chapter 12, *Signaling - Part II*).
- Using the well-known Valgrind suite (recall that we covered Valgrind's Memcheck tool in Chapter 6, *Debugging Tools for Memory Issues*), specifically the tool named helgrind, is useful (sometimes) to detect synchronization errors (data races) in pthreads multithreaded applications. The usage is simple:
  `$ valgrind --tool=helgrind [-v] <app_name> [app-params ...]`:
    - helgrind, though, like many tools of this type, can quite often raise many false positives. For example, we find that eliminating `printf(3)` in the `cv_simple` application we wrote previously removes plenty of (false positive) errors and warnings from helgrind!
    - Prior to invoking the `pthread_cond_signal` and/or the `pthread_cond_broadcast` APIs, if the associated mutex lock is not first acquired (it's not required), helgrind complains.

Do try helgrind out (again, the *Further reading* section on the GitHub repository has a link to its (really good) documentation).

# Summary

We began this chapter by focusing on the key concepts of concurrency, atomicity, and the need to recognize critical sections and protect them. Locking is a typical way to achieve this; the pthreads API set provides the powerful mutex lock to do so. However, using locks, especially on large projects, is fraught with hidden problems and dangers—we discussed useful *Locking guidelines, Deadlock and its avoidance*.

This chapter then went on to guide the reader in the usage of the pthreads mutex lock. A lot of ground was covered here, including various mutex attributes, the importance of recognizing and avoiding the priority inversion issue, and variations on the mutex lock. Finally, we covered the need for and usage of the condition variable (CV) and how it can be used to efficiently facilitate inter-thread event notification.

The next chapter is the final one in this trilogy of chapters on multithreading; in it, we shall focus on the important issues of thread safety (and thread-safe APIs), thread cancellation and cleanup, mixing signals with MT, a few FAQs and tips, and look at the pros and cons of the multiprocess vs the multithreaded model.

# 16
# Multithreading with Pthreads Part III

Having covered, in `Chapters 14`, *Multithreading with Pthreads Part I - Essentials*, and `Chapter 15`, *Multithreading with Pthreads Part II - Synchronization*, a lot of the whys and hows of writing powerful **multithreaded** (**MT**) applications, this chapter focuses on teaching the reader several key safety aspects of MT programming.

It sheds some light on many key safety aspects of developing safe and robust MT applications; here, the reader will learn about thread safety, why it is required, and how to make a function thread-safe. While running, it's possible to have one thread kill another thread; this is achieved via the thread-cancelation mechanism—going hand in hand with cancelation, how does one ensure that prior to terminating a thread, one ensures that it first releases any resources it is still holding (such as locks and dynamic memory)? Thread cleanup handlers are covered to show this.

Finally, this chapter delves into how to safely mix multithreading and signaling, some pros and cons of multiprocess versus multithreaded, as well as some tips and FAQs.

## Thread safety

A key, and unfortunately often not a clearly apparent, issue when developing multithreaded applications is that of thread safety. A *thread-safe*, or, as the man pages like to specify it, MT-Safe, function or API is one that can be safely executed in parallel by multiple threads with no adverse issue.

## Multithreading with Pthreads Part III

To understand what this thread-safety issue actually is, let's go back to one of the programs we saw in Appendix A, *File I/O Essentials;* you can find the source code within the book's GitHub repository: https://github.com/PacktPublishing/Hands-on-System-Programming-with-Linux/blob/master/A_fileio/iobuf.c. In this program, we used fopen(3) to open a file in append mode and then performed some I/O (reads/writes) upon it; we duplicate a small paragraph of that chapter here:

- We fopen(3) a stream (in append mode: a) to our destination, just a regular file in the /tmp directory (it will be created if it does not exist)
- Then, in a loop, for a number of iterations provided by the user as a parameter, we will do the following:
    - Read several (512) bytes from the source stream (they will be random values) via the fread(3) stdio library API
    - Write those values to our destination stream via the fwrite(3) stdio library API (checking for EOF and/or error conditions)

Here's a snippet of the code, mainly the testit function performs the actual I/O; refer to: https://github.com/PacktPublishing/Hands-on-System-Programming-with-Linux/blob/master/A_fileio/iobuf.c:

```
static char *gbuf = NULL;

static void testit(FILE * wrstrm, FILE * rdstrm, int numio)
{
  int i, syscalls = NREAD*numio/getpagesize();
  size_t fnr=0;

  if (syscalls <= 0)
      syscalls = 1;
  VPRINT("numio=%d total rdwr=%u expected # rw syscalls=%d\n",
              numio, NREAD*numio, NREAD*numio/getpagesize());

  for (i = 0; i < numio; i++) {
     fnr = fread(gbuf, 1, NREAD, rdstrm);
     if (!fnr)
         FATAL("fread on /dev/urandom failed\n");

     if (!fwrite(gbuf, 1, fnr, wrstrm)) {
         free(gbuf);
         if (feof(wrstrm))
             return;
         if (ferror(wrstrm))
             FATAL("fwrite on our file failed\n");
```

```
        }
    }
}
```

Notice the first line of code, it's really important to our discussion; the memory buffer used to hold the source and destination data is a global (static) variable, `gbuf`.

Here's where it's allocated in the `main()` function of the app:

```
...
    gbuf = malloc(NREAD);
    if (!gbuf)
        FATAL("malloc %zu failed!\n", NREAD);
...
```

So what? In Appendix A, *File I/O Essentials*, we worked with the implicit assumption that the process is single-threaded; so long as this assumption remains true, the program will work well. But think carefully about this; the moment we want to port this program to become multithreaded-capable, the code is not good enough. Why? It should be quite clear: if multiple threads simultaneously execute the code of the `testit` function (which is exactly the expectation), the presence of the global shared writable memory variable, `gbuf`, tells us that we will have critical sections in the code path. As we learned in detail in Chapter 15, *Multithreading with Pthreads Part II - Synchronization*, every critical section must be either eliminated or protected to prevent data races.

In the preceding code fragment, we happily invoke both `fread(3)` and `fwrite(3)` on this global buffer without any protection whatsoever. Just visualize multiple threads that run through this code path simultaneously; the result is havoc.

So, now we can see it and conclude that the `testit` function is not thread-safe (at the very least, the programmer must document this fact, preventing others from using the code in a multithreaded application!).

Worse imagine that the preceding thread-unsafe function we developed is merged into a shared library (often referred to as a shared object file on Unix/Linux); any (multithreaded) application that links into this library will have access to this function. If multiple threads of such an application ever invoke it, we have a potential race—a bug, a defect! Not just that, such defects are the really hard-to-spot and hard-to-understand ones, causing issues and perhaps all kinds of temporary bandage fixes (which only make the situation worse and the customer even less confident in the software). Disasters are caused in seemingly innocent ways indeed.

Our conclusion on this is either render the function thread-safe, or clearly document it as being thread-unsafe (and only use it, if at all, in a single-threaded context).

## Making code thread-safe

Obviously, we would prefer to make the `testit` function thread-safe. Now the question becomes, how exactly can we do that? Well, again, it's quite straightforward: there are two approaches (more than two, actually, but we'll get to that later).

If we can eliminate any and all global shared writable data in the code path, we will have no critical sections and no problem; in other words, it will become thread-safe. So, one way to achieve this is to ensure that the function uses only local (automatic) variables. The function is now reentrant safe. Before proceeding further, it's important to understand some key points regarding reentrant and thread safety.

## Reentrant-safe versus thread-safe

How exactly is reentrant-safe different from thread-safe? Confusion does prevail. Here's a concise take: reentrant safety is an older issue prior to the advent of multitasking and multithreading OSes, the implication being that only one thread of concern is executing. For a function to be reentrant-safe, it should be able to be correctly re-invoked from another context while the previous context has not yet completed execution (think of a signal handler re-invoking a given function while it is already executing). The key requirement: it should use only local variables or have the ability to save and restore the global it uses such that it's safe. (These ideas have been dealt with in `Chapter 11`, *Signaling - Part I*, in the *Reentrant safety and signaling* section. As we mentioned in that chapter, a signal handler should only call functions that are guaranteed to be reentrant safe; in the signal-handling context, these functions are referred to as being async-signal-safe.)

On the other hand, thread safety is a much more recent issue—we are referring to modern OSes that are multithreaded-capable. A function that is thread-safe can be invoked in parallel from multiple threads (running on multiple CPU cores perhaps) simultaneously, without breaking it. The shared writable data is the thing that matters as code is in any case only readable can executable and thus completely safe to execute in parallel.

Making a function thread-safe via the use of a mutex lock (these discussions follow in some detail with examples) is indeed possible but introduces performance issues. There are better ways to make a function thread-safe: refactoring it, or using TLS or TSD—we'll cover these in the *Thread safety via TLS* and *Thread safety via TSD* section.

In short, reentrant safety is concerned with one thread re-invoking a function while an active invocation still exists; thread safety is concerned with multiple threads—concurrent code—executing the same function in parallel. (An excellent Stack Overflow post describes this in more detail; please refer to the *Further reading* section on the GitHub repository.)

Now, back to our earlier discussions. In theory, using only local variables sounds good (and, for small utility functions, we should design it that way), but the reality is that there are complex projects that evolve in such a manner that using global shared writable data objects within functions becomes something that cannot always be avoided. In such circumstances, from what we learned in the previous `Chapter 15`, *Multithreading with Pthreads Part II - Synchronization*, on synchronization, we know the answer: identify and protect the critical sections using a mutex lock.

Yes, that would work, but at a significant cost to performance. Remember, locks defeat parallelism and serialize the code flow, creating bottlenecks. Achieving thread safety without using a mutex lock is what actually constitutes a truly reentrant-safe function. Such code would indeed be a useful thing, and it can be done; there are two powerful techniques to achieve this, called TLS and TSD. A little patience please, we shall cover how to use these in the section: *Thread safety via TLS* and *Thread safety via TSD*.

> A point to emphasize: the designer and programmer must guarantee that all code that can be executed by multiple threads at any point in time is designed, implemented, tested, and documented to be thread-safe. This is one of the key challenges to meet when designing and implementing multithreaded applications.

On the other hand, if one can guarantee that a function will always only be executed by a single thread (an example is an early initialization routine called from main() before threads are created), then obviously there is no need to guarantee that it's thread-safe.

# Summary table – approaches to making functions thread-safe

Let's summarize the preceding points in the form of a table that tells us how to achieve the all-important goal of thread-safety for all our functions:

| Approach to make a function thread-safe | Comments |
| --- | --- |
| Use only local variables | Naive; hard to achieve in practice. |
| Use global and/or static variables and protect critical sections with mutex locks | Viable but can significantly impact performance [1] |
| Refactor the function, making it reentrant-safe-eliminate the use of static variables in a function by using more parameters as required | Useful approach—several old `foo` glibc functions refactored to `foo_r`. |
| **Thread local storage** (TLS) | Ensures thread safety by having one copy of the variable per thread; toolchain and OS-version-dependent. Very powerful and easy to use. |
| **Thread-specific data** (TSD) | Same goal: make data thread-safe –older implementation, more work to use. |

Table 1: Approaches to making functions thread-safe

[1] Though we say that using the mutex can significantly impact performance, the mutex performance is, in the normal case, really very high (largely due to its internal implementation on Linux via the futex–fast user mutex).

Let's check out these approaches in more detail.

The first one, using only local variables, being a fairly naive approach, will probably only work well with small programs; we shall leave it at that.

# Thread safety via mutex locks

Given that a function does use global and/or static variables, and the decision is to continue to use them (the second approach we mention in *Table 1*), obviously the places in the code where they are used constitute critical sections. As Chapter 15, *Multithreading with Pthreads Part II - Synchronization*, has shown in detail, we must *protect* these critical sections; here, we use the pthreads mutex lock to do so.

For readability, only key parts of the source code are displayed here; to view the complete source code, build and run it, the entire tree is available for cloning from GitHub: https://github.com/PacktPublishing/Hands-on-System-Programming-with-Linux.

We apply this approach the addition of a pthread mutex lock to our sample function (we rename it appropriately; find the full source code here: ch16/mt_iobuf_mtx.c) in the following snippet:

```
static void testit_mt_mtx(FILE * wrstrm, FILE * rdstrm, int numio,
                                int thrdnum)
{
...
   for (i = 0; i < numio; i++) {
       LOCK_MTX(&mylock);
       fnr = fread(gbuf, 1, NREAD, rdstrm);
       UNLOCK_MTX(&mylock);
       if (!fnr)
           FATAL("fread on /dev/urandom failed\n");

       LOCK_MTX(&mylock);
       if (!fwrite(gbuf, 1, fnr, wrstrm)) {
           free(gbuf);
           UNLOCK_MTX(&mylock);
           if (feof(wrstrm))
               return;
           if (ferror(wrstrm))
               FATAL("fwrite on our file failed\n");
       }
       UNLOCK_MTX(&mylock);
   }
}
```

Here, we use the same macros to perform the mutex lock and unlock as we did in (To avoid repetition, we do not show the code to initialize the mutex lock, please refer to Chapter 15, *Multithreading with Pthreads Part II - Synchronization*, for these details. Also we added an additional thrdnum parameter to the function, so as to be able to print out the thread number that's currently running through it.)

The key point: at the critical sections—the places in the code where we access (read or write) the shared writable global variable, gbuf—we take the mutex lock, perform the access (in our case, at the fread(3) and fwrite(3)), and unlock the mutex.

Now, even when multiple threads run through the preceding function, there will be no data-integrity issue. Yes, it will work, but at a significant performance cost; as stated earlier, each critical section (the code between a lock and the corresponding unlock) will be serialized. Hence, locking can form bottlenecks in the code path, especially if, as in our example, the `numio` parameter is a large number, then the for loop will execute for a while. Similarly, bottlenecks will result if the function is a busy one and is invoked often. (a quick check with `perf(1)` revealed that the single-threaded version took 379 ms to perform a 100,000 I/Os and the multithreaded version with locking took 790 ms for the same number of I/Os.)

We have covered this, but let's quickly test ourselves: why did we not protect the places in the code that use the variables such as `fnr` and `syscalls`? The answer is because it's a local variable; more to the point, every thread will get its own copy of a local variable when it executes the preceding function, because every thread has its own private stack—and local variables are instantiated on the stack.

To make the program work, we have had to refactor how the preceding function is actually set up as the thread-worker routine; we find we need to pass various parameters to each thread using a custom data structure, and then have a small `wrapper` function—`wrapper_testit_mt_mtx()`—invoke the actual I/O function; we leave it to the reader to check out the source in detail.

Let's run it:

```
$ ./mt_iobuf_mtx 10000
./mt_iobuf_mtx: using default stdio IO RW buffers of size 4096 bytes;
# IOs=10000
mt_iobuf_mtx.c:testit_mt_mtx:62: [Thread #0]: numio=10000    total
rdwr=5120000    expected # rw syscalls=1250
mt_iobuf_mtx.c:testit_mt_mtx:66: gbuf = 0x23e2670
mt_iobuf_mtx.c:testit_mt_mtx:62: [Thread #1]: numio=10000    total
rdwr=5120000    expected # rw syscalls=1250
mt_iobuf_mtx.c:testit_mt_mtx:66: gbuf = 0x23e2670
 Thread #0 successfully joined; it terminated with status=0
 Thread #1 successfully joined; it terminated with status=0
$
```

This reveals the full picture; clearly, the I/O buffer being used, gbuf, is the same for both threads (look at the addresses printed out), hence the need to lock it.

As an aside, within the standard-file streaming APIs, there exists (non-standard) *_unlocked APIs, such as `fread_unlocked(3)` and `fwrite_unlocked(3)`. These are the same as their regular counterparts, except that they are explicitly marked to be MT-unsafe in the documentation. It's not advisable to use them.

> **TIP**: By the way, open files are a shared resource between the threads of a process; the developer must take this into account as well. Performing IO simultaneously with multiple threads on the same underlying file object can cause corruption, unless file-locking techniques are used. Here, in this specific case, we are explicitly using a mutex lock to protect critical sections – which happen to be at the precise points where we perform file I/O, so explicit file-locking becomes unnecessary.

## Thread safety via function refactoring

As we saw in the preceding example, we need the mutex lock because the gbuf global buffer was being used by all application threads as their I/O buffer. So, think on this: what if we can allocate an I/O buffer that's local to each thread? That would indeed solve the issue! How exactly, will be shown with the following code.

But first, now that you are familiar with the previous example (where we used the mutex lock), study the output of the refactored program:

```
$ ./mt_iobuf_rfct 10000
./mt_iobuf_rfct: using default stdio IO RW buffers of size 4096 bytes;
# IOs=10000
mt_iobuf_rfct.c:testit_mt_refactored:51: [Thread #0]: numio=10000
total rdwr=5120000   expected # rw syscalls=1250
 iobuf = 0x7f283c000b20
mt_iobuf_rfct.c:testit_mt_refactored:51: [Thread #1]: numio=10000
total rdwr=5120000   expected # rw syscalls=1250
 iobuf = 0x7f2834000b20
 Thread #0 successfully joined; it terminated with status=0
 Thread #1 successfully joined; it terminated with status=0
$
```

The key realization: the I/O buffer used here, `iobuf`, is unique for each thread (just look at the addresses printed out)! Thus, this eliminates the critical sections in the I/O function and the need to use a mutex. In effect, the function is using only local variables and is thus both reentrant and thread-safe.

## Multithreading with Pthreads Part III

> For readability, only key parts of the source code are displayed here. To view the complete source code, build and run it; the entire tree is available for cloning from GitHub: `https://github.com/PacktPublishing/Hands-on-System-Programming-with-Linux`.

The following code snippets clearly reveal how this is set up (the full source code: `ch16/mt_iobuf_rfct.c`):

```
struct stToThread {
    FILE *wrstrm, *rdstrm;
    int thrdnum, numio;
    char *iobuf;
};
static struct stToThread *ToThread[NTHREADS];
static void * wrapper_testit_mt_refactored(void *msg)
{
  struct stToThread *pstToThread = (struct stToThread *)msg;
  assert (pstToThread);

  /* Allocate the per-thread IO buffer here, thus avoiding the global
   * heap buffer completely! */
  pstToThread->iobuf = malloc(NREAD);
  ...
  testit_mt_refactored(pstToThread->wrstrm, pstToThread->rdstrm,
          pstToThread->numio, pstToThread->thrdnum,
          pstToThread->iobuf);

  free(pstToThread->iobuf);
  pthread_exit((void *)0);
}
```

As can be seen, we refactor by adding an additional buffer pointer member to our custom `stToThread` structure. The important part: in the thread-wrapper function, we then allocate it memory and pass the pointer it to our thread routine. We add an additional parameter to our thread I/O routine for this very purpose:

```
static void testit_mt_refactored(FILE * wrstrm, FILE * rdstrm, int numio, int thrdnum, char *iobuf)
{
...
  for (i = 0; i < numio; i++) {
      fnr = fread(iobuf, 1, NREAD, rdstrm);
      if (!fnr)
          FATAL("fread on /dev/urandom failed\n");
      if (!fwrite(iobuf, 1, fnr, wrstrm)) {
          ...
  }
```

Now, in the preceding I/O loop, we operate upon the per-thread `iobuf` buffer, thus there is no critical section, no need for locking.

## The standard C library and thread safety

A significant amount of the standard C library (glibc), code is not thread-safe. What? one asks. But, hey, a lot of this code was written back in the 1970s and 1980s, when multithreading did not exist (for Unix, at least); thus, one can hardly blame them for not designing it to be thread-safe!

### List of APIs not required to be thread-safe

The standard C library, glibc, has many older functions that, in the words of the Open Group manual, need not be thread-safe (or are not required to be thread-safe). All functions defined by this volume of POSIX.1-2017 shall be thread-safe, except that the following functions need not be thread-safe. What does that actually mean? Simple: these APIs are not thread-safe. So, be careful—do not use them in MT applications. The complete list can be found at: http://pubs.opengroup.org/onlinepubs/9699919799/functions/V2_chap02.html#tag_15_09_01.

> Of course, the preceding list is only valid as of POSIX.1-2017 and is bound to get outdated. The reader must be aware of this recurring issue, and the need to constantly update information like this.

Also, they are mostly library-layer (glibc) APIs. Of all the preceding APIs, only one of them—`readdir(2)`-is a system call; that too is considered deprecated (we are to use its glibc wrapper, `readdir(3)`). As a rule of thumb, all system calls are written to be thread-safe.

> An interesting aside: PHP, a popular web-scripting language, is not considered thread-safe; hence, web servers that serve PHP pages do so using the traditional multiprocess model and not a faster multithreaded framework (for example, Apache uses its internal `mpm_prefork` module—which is single-threaded – to deal with PHP pages).

So, seeing what we have just discussed, does one conclude that glibc is no longer viable to develop thread-safe MT apps? No sir, work has been done to convert (refactor, really) many of the preceding APIs to render them thread-safe. Read on.

## Refactoring glibc APIs from foo to foo_r

Of course, today, with MT applications being the de facto reality, what do we do? The glibc maintainers understand these issues, and have used precisely the refactoring techniques – passing additional parameters to avoid the usage of global and/or static variables (like we did previous with our ch16/mt_iobuf_rfct.c code), including using parameters as return values—to refactor standard glibc functions to become thread-safe. The glibc naming convention is if the older function is named foo, the refactored, usually reentrant- and thread-safe, version is named foo_r.

To help lend clarity to this discussion, let's take an example of a glibc API that has both the older foo and the newer foo_r functionality. The ctime(3) API is often used by application developers; given a Unix-time timestamp, it converts it into a human-readable date-timestamp (ASCII text). (Recall that we have used the ctime API in Chapter 13, *Timers*.) Let's recall, directly from Chaptr 13, *Timers*, that Unix systems store time as the number of seconds elapsed since January 1, 1970, midnight (00:00) – think of it as Unix's birth! This time value is called time since the Epoch or Unix time. OK, but it's going to be a rather large number of seconds today, right? So how does one express it in a human-readable format? Glad you asked; that's precisely the job of the ctime(3) and the ctime_r(3) APIs.

The signature of the ctime(3) API is as follows:

```
include <time.h>
char *ctime(const time_t *timep);
```

Do you spot the issue here for multithreaded applications? The return value is the time represented in plain ASCII text; it is stored by ctime(3) in a static (thus, shared) data variable. If multiple threads execute the ctime(3) more or less simultaneously (and that, my friend, is exactly what can, and indeed does, happen on modern multicore systems!), there is always the risk that we perform dirty reads or writes on the shared data. Simply because it is not protected; simply because when the ctime(3) was first designed and implemented, only a single thread would ever run it at a given point in time. Which is not the case today, of course. In other words, ctime(3) is marked in the man page as being MT-Unsafe, that is, it is not thread-safe. Thus, calling ctime(3) from an MT application is wrong—you run the risk of having a race, a bug, or a defect at some point.

The good glibc folks have literally re-implemented (refactored) ctime(3) to become reentrant and thread-safe; the newer API is christened ctime_r(3). Here is a quote from its man page: the reentrant version ctime_r() does the same, but stores the string in a user-supplied buffer which should have room for at least 26 bytes:

```
char *ctime_r(const time_t *timep, char *buf);
```

Excellent! Did you notice that the key point here is that the ctime(3) API has been refactored (and renamed to ctime_r(3)) to become re-entrant- and thread-safe by having the user supply the buffer in which the result is returned? How will the user do this? Simple; here's some code showing one way to achieve this (we just require the concept here, no error-checking is shown):

```
// Thread Routine here
struct timespec tm;
char * mybuf = malloc(32);
...
clock_gettime(CLOCK_REALTIME, &tm); /* get the current 'UNIX' timestamp*/
ctime_r(&tm.tv_sec, mybuf); /* put the human-readable ver into 'mybuf'*/
...
free(mybuf);
```

Think about it: each thread that executes the preceding code will allocate a separate unique buffer and pass that buffer pointer to the ctime_r(3) routine. This way, we ensure that we do not step on each other's toes; the API is now reentrant- and thread-safe.

Notice in the preceding code how we achieved this refactoring trick in C: by passing the unique buffer to be written into as a value-result-style parameter! This is indeed a common technique, often employed by the glibc foo_r routines: we keep the routine thread-safe by passing one or more values to it (and even back to the caller, as a kind of return value) without using static or global variables (instead using value-result (or in-out) style parameters)!

The man page on ctime(3), and indeed on most other APIs, documents whether the API it describes are thread-safe: this is extremely important to note! We cannot over-stress this: the multithreaded application programmer must check and ensure that all functions being called in a function that is supposed to be thread-safe, are themselves (documented to be) thread-safe.

Here's a screenshot of a part of the man page on ctime(3) that shows, under the **ATTRIBUTES** section, this information:

```
ATTRIBUTES
       For an explanation of the terms used in this section, see attributes(7).
```

| Interface | Attribute | Value |
|---|---|---|
| asctime() | Thread safety | MT-Unsafe race:asctime locale |
| asctime_r() | Thread safety | MT-Safe locale |
| ctime() | Thread safety | MT-Unsafe race:tmbuf race:asctime env locale |
| ctime_r(), gmtime_r(), localtime_r(), mktime() | Thread safety | MT-Safe env locale |
| gmtime(), localtime() | Thread safety | MT-Unsafe race:tmbuf env locale |

Figure 1 : Screenshot of ATTRIBUTES section of the man page on ctime(3)

Quite obviously, MT-Safe implies the routine is thread-safe; MT-Unsafe implies it isn't. The man page on attributes(7) delves further into these details; it clearly notes that being thread-safe does not guarantee that the API is also atomic; do read through it.

We also note that the man page states that POSIX.1-2008 marks the `ctime_r` API itself as obsolete, and to use `strftime(3)` in its place. Please do so. Here, we have used the `ctime(3)` and `ctime_r(3)` APIs merely to illustrate an example regarding the thread-unsafe and -safe versions of a glibc routine.

## Some glibc foo and foo_r APIs

The `ctime(3)`, this being thread-unsafe, is now replaced by its thread-safe counterpart `ctime_r(3)`; this is just one example of a generic trend in modern glibc:

- The older, thread (MT-unsafe) unsafe function is called `foo`
- Has a counterpart, the newer, thread (MT-Safe) safe `foo_r` API

To give the reader an appreciation of this, we enumerate some (not all!) of the glibc `foo_r` style of APIs:

| | | |
|---|---|---|
| asctime_r(3)<br>crypt_r(3)<br>ctime_r(3)<br>drand48_r(3) | getpwnam_r(3)<br>getpwuid_r(3)<br>getrpcbyname_r(3)<br>getrpcbynumber_r(3)<br>getrpcent_r(3)<br>getservbyname_r(3) | seed48_r(3)<br>setkey_r(3)<br>srand48_r(3)<br>srandom_r(3)<br>strerror_r(3)<br>strtok_r(3) |
| getdate_r(3)<br>getgrent_r(3)<br>getgrgid_r(3)<br>getgrnam_r(3)<br>gethostbyaddr_r(3)<br>gethostbyname2_r(3)<br>gethostbyname_r(3)<br>gethostent_r(3)<br>getlogin_r(3) | nrand48_r(3)<br>ptsname_r(3)<br>qecvt_r(3)<br>qfcvt_r(3)<br>qsort_r(3)<br>radtofix_r(3)<br>rand_r(3)<br>random_r(3)<br>readdir_r(3) | ustrtok_r(3)<br>val_gethostbyaddr_r(3)<br>val_gethostbyname2_r(3)<br>val_gethostbyname_r(3) |

Table 3: Some of the glibc foo_r APIs

This list is not intended to be exhaustive; note that the `ctime_r(3)` API is in this list. At the risk of repetition, ensure you only use the `foo_r` APIs in an MT application as they are the thread-safe versions of the `foo` API.

## Thread safety via TLS

The preceding discussion was with regard to the already existing standard C library, glibc, and its API set. What about MT applications that are newly designed and developed? Obviously, the code we write for them must be thread-safe.

Let's not forget how we rendered our `testit_mt_refactored` function to become thread-safe by refactoring it – adding an `iobuf` parameter that passed along the address of the buffer to use for I/O—guaranteeing the buffer will be unique for each thread and thus thread-safe (without any need for locking).

Could we get such functionality automatically? Well, yes: the compiler (GCC and clang) does provide an almost magical feature to do something similar: TLS. With TLS, a variable marked with the `__thread` special storage class keyword will be instantiated once per thread that comes alive. In effect, if we use only local and TLS variables, our function will by definition be thread-safe, without any (expensive) locking required.

There do exist some ground rules and caveats; let's check them out:

- The `__thread` keyword can be used alone, or with (in fact, only with) the `static` or `extern` keywords; if used with them, it must appear after them:

  ```
  __thread long l;
  extern __thread struct MyStruct s1;
  static __thread int safe;
  ```

- More broadly, the `__thread` keyword can be specified against any global and file-or- function scope `static` or `extern` variable. It cannot be applied to any local variables.
- TLS can only be used on (fairly) recent versions of the toolchain and kernel.

Something important to understand: though it may seem akin to having a locked variable, this is certainly not the case! Consider this: given a TLS variable called `mytls`, different threads using it in parallel is fine. However, if a thread uses the address-of operator on the TLS variable, `&mytls`, it will have the address of its instance of the variable. Any other thread, if access to this address, can use this address to gain access to the variable; thus, it's not really locked in any real sense. Of course, if the programmer uses normal conventions (not letting other threads access a different thread's TLS variables), then all will work well.

It's important to realize that TLS support is only available from the Linux 2.6 kernel onward, gcc ver 3.3 or later, and NPTL. Well, practically speaking, this implies that pretty much any fairly recent Linux distribution will support TLS.

So, as usual, let's port our thread-unsafe function to become thread-safe via TLS. This is really simple; all we have to do is make the previously global buffer, `gbuf`, into a thread-safe TLS buffer (`iobuf`):

```
static __thread char iobuf[NREAD];        // our TLS variable

static void testit_mt_tls(FILE * wrstrm, FILE * rdstrm, int numio, int thrdnum)
{
  int i, syscalls = NREAD*numio/getpagesize();
  size_t fnr=0;

  if (syscalls <= 0)
    syscalls = 1;
  VPRINT("[Thread #%d]: numio=%d total rdwr=%u expected # rw
         syscalls=%d\n"
         " iobuf = %p\n", thrdnum, numio, NREAD*numio, syscalls,
```

```
iobuf);
...
```

The only important change to note is the declaration of the `iobuf` variable now as a TLS variable; everything else pretty much remains the same. A quick test run confirms that each thread receives a separate copy of the TLS variable:

```
$ ./mt_iobuf_tls 12500
./mt_iobuf_tls: using default stdio IO RW buffers of size 4096 bytes;
# IOs=12500
mt_iobuf_tls.c:testit_mt_tls:48: [Thread #0]: numio=12500 total
rdwr=6400000 expected # rw syscalls=1562
 iobuf = 0x7f23df1af500
mt_iobuf_tls.c:testit_mt_tls:48: [Thread #1]: numio=12500 total
rdwr=6400000 expected # rw syscalls=1562
 iobuf = 0x7f23de9ae500
 Thread #0 successfully joined; it terminated with status=0
 Thread #1 successfully joined; it terminated with status=0
$
```

Each `iobuf` is a per-thread TLS instance; each has a unique address. No locking, no fuss, job done. Real-world usage of TLS is high; the uninitialized global `errno` is a perfect example.

TLS seems such a powerful and easy-to-use technique to make a function thread-safe; is there a downside? Well, think about it:

- For every variable marked as the TLS storage class, memory will have to be runtime-allocated for every thread that comes alive; if we have large TLS buffers, this can cause significant amounts of memory to be allocated.
- Platform support: your Linux platform, if too old, will not support it (usually shouldn't be the case).

## Thread safety via TSD

Prior to the TLS technique that we just saw (that is, before Linux 2.6 and gcc 3.3), how did one guarantee writing a new API to be thread safe? A much older technology exists, called TSD.

In a nutshell, TSD is a more complex solution from the application developer's viewpoint—more work must be done to achieve the very same end result that TLS so easily gives us; that of making a function thread-safe.

With TSD, the thread-safe routine must invoke an initializer function (usually done with `pthread_once(3)`), which creates a unique thread-specific data key (using the `pthread_key_create(3)` API). This initializer routine associates a thread-specific data variable (such as the `iobuf` buffer pointer in our example) with that key, using the `pthread_getspecific(3)` and `pthread_setspecific(3)` APIs. The end result is that the data item is now thread-specific and therefore thread-safe. Here, we do not delve further into using TSD as it's an older solution that TLS easily and elegantly replaces on modern Linux platforms. Nevertheless, for the interested reader, please refer to the *Further reading* section on the GitHub repository—we provide a link to using TSD.

## Thread cancelation and cleanup

The pthreads design provides a sophisticated framework for achieving two other key activities for a robust multithreaded application: the ability to have a thread in the app cancel (effectively, kill) another thread, and the ability to have a thread that is either terminated normally (via the `pthread_exit(3)`) or abnormally (via cancelation) be able to perform the required resource cleanup.

The following sections deal with these topics.

## Canceling a thread

Visualize a GUI application running; it pops up a dialog box informing the user that it is now performing some work (perhaps displaying a progress bar as well). We imagine that this work is being carried out by a thread of the overall application process. For the user's convenience, a **Cancel** button is provided as well; clicking on it should cause the ongoimg work to be canceled.

How can we implement this? In other words, how does one kill off a thread? The first thing to note is that pthreads provides a framework for exactly this type of operation: thread cancelation. Canceling a thread is not sending it a signal; it is a way for one thread to request another a thread to die. Making this happen requires us to understand and follow the provided framework.

# The thread cancelation framework

To help bring clarity, let's take an example: let's say that the main thread of an application creates two worker threads, A and B. Now, the main thread wants to cancel thread A.

The API to request cancelation upon a target thread (A, here) is the following:

```
int pthread_cancel(pthread_t thread);
```

The `thread` parameter is the target thread—the one we are (politely) requesting to please go and die, thank you very much.

But, you guessed it, it's not as simple as that: the target thread has two attributes (that it can set) that determine whether and when it gets canceled:

- Cancelability state
- Cancelability type

## The cancelability state

The target thread is required to be in an appropriate cancelability state. The state is Boolean-cancelability (on the target thread, A) is either *enabled* or *disabled*; here is the API to set this up:

```
int pthread_setcancelstate(int state, int *oldstate);
```

The two possible cancelability states, the value provided as the first parameter, for a thread are as follows:

- `PTHREAD_CANCEL_ENABLE`  (default on creation)
- `PTHREAD_CANCEL_DISABLE`

Clearly, the previous cancelability state will be returned in the second parameter, `oldstate`.) The target thread can only be canceled if its cancelability state is enabled. A thread's cancelability state is enabled by default upon creation.

This is a powerful feature of the framework: if the target thread, A, is performing a critical activity and does not want to be even considered for cancelation, it merely sets its cancelability state to disabled, and, upon finishing the said critical activity, resets it to enabled.

## The cancelability type

Assuming the target thread has the cancelability state enabled is the first step; the thread's cancelability type determines what happens next. There are two types: deferred (the default) and asynchronous. When a thread's cancelability type is asynchronous, it can be canceled at any point in time (in fact, it should happen immediately, but is not always guaranteed to); if the cancelability type is deferred (the default), it can only be canceled (terminated) when it hits the next cancelation point.

A cancelation point is a list of (usually blocking) functions (more on this shortly). When the target thread—that, remember, is of the enabled cancelability state and the deferred type—encounters the next cancelation point in its code path, it will terminate.

Here is the API to set the cancelability type:

```
int pthread_setcanceltype(int type, int *oldtype);
```

The two possible cancelability types, the value provided as the first parameter type, are:

- PTHREAD_CANCEL_DEFERRED (default on creation)
- PTHREAD_CANCEL_ASYNCHRONOUS

Clearly, the previous cancelability type will be returned in the second parameter, `oldtype`.

Whew! Let's try to represent this cancelation framework as a flowchart:

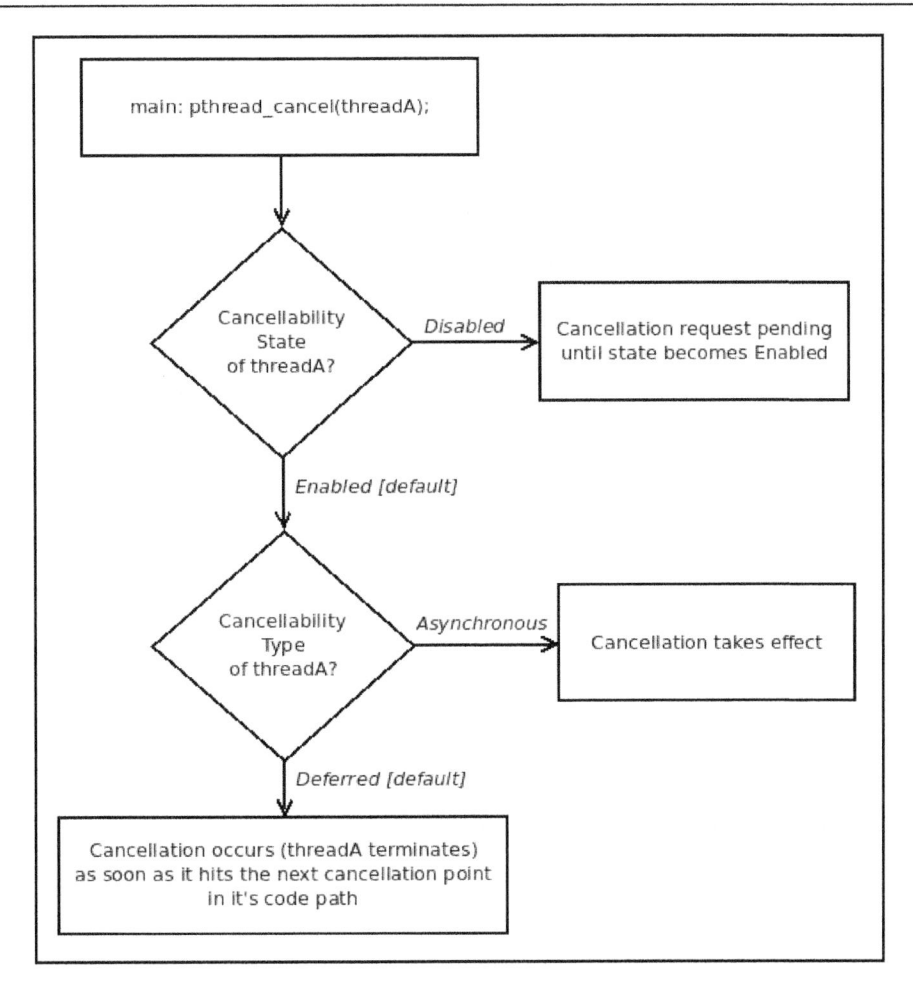

Figure 2: Pthreads cancelation

pthread_cancel(3) is a non-blocking API. What we mean is that, even if the target thread has its cancelability state disabled, or its cancelability state is enabled but the cancelability type is deferred and it has not reached a cancelation point, though the target thread might take some time to actually die,
the main thread's pthread_cancel(3) call will return with success (return value 0), implying that the cancelation request has been successfully queued.

Disabling the cancelation state for a short time while a critical activity is carried out is fine, but doing the same for long periods could cause the application to seem unresponsive.

Using the asynchronous value for the cancelability type is usually not the right thing to do. Why? Well, it becomes a race as to when exactly the thread was canceled; was it before it allocated some resource (such as memory via `malloc(3)`) or after? In such situations, even cleanup handlers are not really useful. Also, only APIs documented as being async-cancel-safe can be safely canceled in an async fashion; realistically there are very few—only the cancelation APIs themselves. For these reasons, it's considered best to avoid asynchronous cancelation. On the other hand, if a thread is predominantly highly CPU-bound (performing some mathematical calculation, say prime number generation), then using async cancelation can help guarantee the thread dies immediately on request.

Another key point: how does (in our example) the main thread know that the target thread has actually terminated? Remember that the main thread is expected to join upon all threads; hence, the target thread upon termination will get joined, and—here's the thing – the return value (status) from `pthread_join(3)` will be `PTHREAD_CANCELED`. `pthread_join(3)` is the only way to check that cancelation has actually occurred.

We have learned that, with the (default) cancelation type as deferred, the actual thread-cancelation will not occur until the target thread encounters a cancelation point function. A cancelation point is merely an API at which thread-cancelation is actually detected and made to take effect by the underlying implementation. The cancelation points are not limited to the pthreads APIs; many glibc functions serve as cancelation points. The reader can find a list of cancelation point APIs by following a link (Open Group POSIX.1c threads) provided in the *Further reading* section on the GitHub repository. As a rule of thumb, the cancelation points are typically blocking library APIs.

But, what if a thread is executing code that just does not have a cancelation point within it (say, a CPU-bound calculation loop)? In such cases, either one can use the asynchronous cancelation type or, even better, explicitly introduce a guaranteed cancelation point into the loop by invoking the `void pthread_test_cancel(void);` API.

If the to-be-cancelled target thread hits this function, and a cancelation request is pending, it will terminate.

## Canceling a thread – a code example

A simple code example demonstrating thread-cancelation follows; we have the main thread create two worker threads (think of them as thread A and thread B) and then have the main thread cancel thread A. In parallel, we deliberately have thread A disable cancelation (by setting the cancelation state to disabled), do some bogus work (we call our trusty `DELAY_LOOP` macro to simulate work), then re-enable cancelation. The cancelation request takes effect at the next cancelation point (as, of course, the type defaults to deferred), which, here, is simply the `sleep(3)` API.

The code demonstrating thread cancelation (`ch16/cancelit.c`) follows.

> For readability, only key parts of the source code are displayed here. To view the complete source code, build and run it. The entire tree is available for cloning from GitHub: https://github.com/PacktPublishing/Hands-on-System-Programming-with-Linux.

We pick up the code in `main`, after the thread creation loop is done:

```
int main(void)
{
...
  // Lets send a cancel request to thread A (the first worker thread)
  ret = pthread_cancel(tid[0]);
  if (ret)
      FATAL("pthread_cancel(thread 0) failed! [%d]\n", ret);

  // Thread join loop
  for (i = 0; i < NTHREADS; i++) {
      printf("main: joining (waiting) upon thread #%ld ...\n", i);
      ret = pthread_join(tid[i], (void **)&stat);
      ...
          printf("Thread #%ld successfully joined; it terminated with"
                 "status=%ld\n", i, stat);
          if ((void *)stat == PTHREAD_CANCELED)
              printf(" *** Was CANCELLED ***\n");
      }
  }
```

# Multithreading with Pthreads Part III

Here is the thread `worker` routine:

```
void * worker(void *data)
{
  long datum = (long)data;
  int slptm=8, ret=0;

  if (datum == 0) { /* "Thread A"; lets keep it in a 'critical' state,
          non-cancellable, for a short while, then enable
          cancellation upon it. */
      printf(" worker #%ld: disabling Cancellation:"
      " will 'work' now...\n", datum);
      if ((ret = pthread_setcancelstate(PTHREAD_CANCEL_DISABLE,
NULL)))
          FATAL("pthread_setcancelstate failed 0 [%d]\n", ret);
      DELAY_LOOP(datum+48, 100);    // the 'work'
      printf("\n worker #%ld: enabling Cancellation\n", datum);
      if ((ret = pthread_setcancelstate(PTHREAD_CANCEL_ENABLE, NULL)))
          FATAL("pthread_setcancelstate failed 1 [%d]\n", ret);
  }

  printf(" worker #%ld: will sleep for %ds now ...\n", datum, slptm);
  sleep(slptm); // sleep() is a 'cancellation point'
  printf(" worker #%ld: work (eyeroll) done, exiting now\n", datum);

  /* Terminate with success: status value 0.
   * The join will pick this up. */
  pthread_exit((void *)0);
}
```

A quick test run reveals that it indeed works; one can see that thread A has been cancelled. We suggest you run the debug version of the program, as shown here, as then the `DELAY_LOOP` macro's effect can be seen (otherwise it completes its job almost instantaneously as it's pretty much optimized away by the compiler):

```
$ ./cancelit_dbg
main: creating thread #0 ...
main: creating thread #1 ...
 worker #0: disabling Cancellation: will 'work' now...
0 worker #1: will sleep for 8s now ...
main: joining (waiting) upon thread #0 ...
000000000000000000000000000000000000000000000000000000000000000000
0000000000000000000000000000
 worker #0: enabling Cancellation
 worker #0: will sleep for 8s now ...
Thread #0 successfully joined; it terminated with status=-1
    *** Was CANCELLED ***
main: joining (waiting) upon thread #1 ...
```

[ 680 ]

```
    worker #1: work (eyeroll) done, exiting now
    Thread #1 successfully joined; it terminated with status=0

    main: now dying... <Dramatic!> Farewell!
    $
```

## Cleaning up at thread exit

Consider this hypothetical situation: a thread takes a mutex lock and allocates some heap memory. Obviously, once the critical section it is in is done, we expect it to free up the heap memory and unlock the mutex. Failure to do this cleanup will cause serious, if not fatal, application bugs (defects) such as memory leakage or deadlock.

But, one wonders, what if the poor thread is canceled prior to the free and unlock? It could happen, right? No! Not if the developer understands and uses the thread cleanup handler mechanism that the pthreads framework provides.

What happens when a thread terminates? The following steps are part of the pthreads cleanup framework:

1. All cleanup handlers are popped (reverse order of the cleanup handler push)
2. TSD destructors, if they exist, are invoked
3. The thread dies

This opens our eyes to an interesting fact: the pthreads framework provides a guaranteed way for a thread to ensure that it cleans up after itself—frees up memory resources, closes open files, and so on—before terminating.

The programmer can take care of all these cases by setting up a thread-cleanup handler – in effect, a kind of destructor function. A cleanup handler is a function that is automatically executed when a thread is canceled or terminates with pthread_exit(3); it's set up by invoking the pthread_cleanup_push(3) API:

```
    void pthread_cleanup_push(void (*routine)(void *), void *arg);
```

Clearly, the first parameter to the preceding routine is the cleanup handler function pointer, in other words, the name of the cleanup handler function. The second parameter is any argument one cares to pass to the handler function (often a pointer to a dynamically allocated buffer or data structure).

The reverse semantic is achieved via the corresponding cleanup pop routine; when invoked, it pops off the cleanup handler stack and thus in reverse order executes the cleanup handler(s) that were earlier pushed onto the cleanup handler stack:

```
void pthread_cleanup_pop(int execute);
```

One can also explicitly invoke the topmost cleanup handler on the cleanup stack by calling the `thread_cleanup_pop(3)` API with a non-zero argument.

> The POSIX standard maintains that the preceding pair of APIs—the push and pop cleanup handlers—can be implemented as macros that expand into functions; indeed, it seems to be implemented this way on the Linux platform. As a side effect of this, it becomes imperative that the programmer call both routines (the pair) within the same function. Failure to comply causes weird compiler failures.

As noted, TSD destructor handlers too, if they exist, get invoked; here, we ignore this aspect.

> You might think, fine, if we use these cleanup handler techniques, we can safely restore state as both thread-cancelation and -termination will guarantee that they invoke any registered cleanup handlers (destructors). But, what if another process (perhaps a root process) sends my MT app a fatal signal (such as `kill -9 <mypid>`)? Well, there's nothing to be done. Please realize that with a fatal signal, all threads in the process, and indeed the entire process itself, will die (in this example). It's an academic question—a moot point. On the other hand, a thread cannot just randomly get killed; there has to be an explicit `pthread_exit(3)` or cancelation carried out upon it. Thus, there is no excuse for the lazy programmer—set up cleanup handler(s) to perform the appropriate cleanup and all will be well.

## Thread cleanup – code example

As a simple code example, let's modify our earlier refactored program—`ch16/mt_iobif_rfct.c` by installing a thread-cleanup handler routine. To test it, we cancel the first worker thread if the user passes 1 as the second parameter to our demo program, the `ch16/cleanup_hdlr.c` program.

> For readability, only key parts of the source code are displayed here. To view the complete source code, build and run it. The entire tree is available for cloning from GitHub: https://github.com/PacktPublishing/Hands-on-System-Programming-with-Linux.

Here is the cleanup handler function and the re-worked wrapper routine – now with the cleanup handler push and pop APIs:

```c
static void cleanup_handler(void *arg)
{
    printf("+++ In %s +++\n" " free-ing buffer %p\n", __func__, arg);
    free(arg);
}
...
static void *wrapper_testit_mt_refactored(void *msg)
{
  struct stToThread *pstToThread = (struct stToThread *)msg;
  ...
  /* Allocate the per-thread IO buffer here, thus avoiding the global
   * heap buffer completely! */
  pstToThread->iobuf = malloc(NREAD);
  ...
  /* Install a 'cleanup handler' routine */
  pthread_cleanup_push(cleanup_handler, pstToThread->iobuf);

  testit_mt_refactored(pstToThread->wrstrm, pstToThread->rdstrm,
          pstToThread->numio, pstToThread->thrdnum,
          pstToThread->iobuf);

/* *Must* invoke the 'push's counterpart: the cleanup 'pop' routine;
 * passing 0 as parameter just registers it, it does not actually pop
 * off and execute the handler. Why not? Because that's precisely what
 * the next API, the pthread_exit(3) will implicitly do!
 */
  pthread_cleanup_pop(0);
  free(pstToThread->iobuf);

  // Required for pop-ping the cleanup handler!
  pthread_exit((void *)0);
}
```

Here, `main()` sets up the thread-cancelation as required:

```
...
  if (atoi(argv[2]) == 1) {
    /* Lets send a cancel request to thread A */
    ret = pthread_cancel(tid[0]);
  ...
```

A quick test run confirms that, upon cancelation, the cleanup handler is indeed invoked and cleanup performed:

```
$ ./cleanup_hdlr 23114 1
./cleanup_hdlr: using default stdio IO RW buffers of size 4096 bytes;
# IOs=23114
main: sending CANCEL REQUEST to worker thread 0 ...
cleanup_hdlr.c:testit_mt_refactored:52: [Thread #0]: numio=23114 total rdwr=11834368 expected # rw syscalls=2889
 iobuf = 0x7f2364000b20
cleanup_hdlr.c:testit_mt_refactored:52: [Thread #1]: numio=23114 total rdwr=11834368 expected # rw syscalls=2889
 iobuf = 0x7f235c000b20
+++ In cleanup_handler +++
 free-ing buffer 0x7f2364000b20
 Thread #0 successfully joined; it terminated with status=-1
  : was CANCELED
 Thread #1 successfully joined; it terminated with status=0
$
```

# Threads and signaling

In `Chapter 11`, *Signaling - Part I*, and `Chapter 12`, *Signaling - Part II*, we covered signaling in detail. We are still on the same Unix/Linux platform; signaling and its usage for the application designer/developer does not simply disappear just because we are now working on MT applications! We still have to handle signals (recall that you can list your platform's available signals with a simple `kill -l` on the shell).

# The issue

So, what's the problem? There is a significant difference in how we handle signals in MT apps. Why? The fact is that the traditional manner of handling signals does not really mix well with the pthreads framework. If you can avoid the usage of signals in your MT app, please do so. If not (often the case in real-world MT apps), then read on—we shall detail how to handle signals when within an MT application.

But why is signaling now an issue? It's quite straightforward: signals were designed and meant for the process model. Consider this: how does one process send a signal to another process? It's quite clear - using the kill(2) system call:

int kill(pid_t pid, int sig);

Clearly, the first parameter, pid, is the PID of the process to deliver the sig signal (number) to. But, and here we see it, a process can be multithreaded—which particular thread will receive, and which particular thread will handle, the signal? The POSIX standard cowardly states that "any ready thread cna handle a given signal". What if all threads are ready? Then who does? All of them? It's ambiguous, to say the least.

# The POSIX solution to handling signals on MT

The good news is that the POSIX committee has come up with a recommendation to the developers of MT applications for signal-handling. This solution rests on an interesting design fact; although a process has a table of signal dispositions (set up by the kernel and the sigaction(2) system call), every thread within the process has its own discrete signal mask (using which it can selectively block signals) and signal pending mask (by which the kernel remembers which signals are pending delivery to the thread).

Knowing this, the POSIX standard recommends that a developer handle signals in a pthreads application as follows:

- Mask (block) all signals in the main thread.
- Now any thread created by main inherits its signal mask, implying that signals will be blocked in all subsequently created threads—this is what we want.
- Create a special thread that is dedicated to performing signal-handling for the entire application. Its job is to catch (trap) all required signals and handle them (in a synchronous fashion).

Note that although it's possible to trap signals via the `sigaction(2)` system call, the semantics of signal-handling in MT apps often lead to using the blocking variants of signaling APIs—the `sigwait(3)`, `sigwaitinfo(3)`, and `sigtimedwait(3)` library APIs. It is usually a good idea to use one of these blocking APIs within our dedicated signal-handler thread to block all required signals.

Thus, whenever a signal does arrive, the signal-handler thread is unblocked, and it receives the signal; also (assuming we're using the `sigwait(3)` API), the signal number is updated in the second parameter to `sigwait(3)`. It can now perform the required signal-processing on behalf of the application.

## Code example – handling signals in an MT app

A quick demonstration of the POSIX recommended technique for handling signals in an MT application follows (`ch16/tsig.c`):

> For readability, only key parts of the source code are displayed here. To view the complete source code, build and run it. The entire tree is available for cloning from GitHub: https://github.com/PacktPublishing/Hands-on-System-Programming-with-Linux.

```
// ... in main:
/* Block *all* signals here in the main thread.
 * Now all subsequently created threads also block all signals. */
  sigfillset(&sigset);
  if (pthread_sigmask(SIG_BLOCK, &sigset, NULL))
      FATAL("main: pthread_sigmask failed");
...
  /*--- Create the dedicated signal handling thread ---*/
  ret = pthread_create(&pthrd[t], &attr, signal_handler, NULL);
  if (ret)
      FATAL("pthread_create %ld failed [%d]\n", t, ret);
...
```

The worker threads don't do much—they just invoke our `DELAY_LOOP` macro to simulate some work. Here, see the signal-handler thread routine:

```
static void *signal_handler(void *arg)
{
  sigset_t sigset;
  int sig;

  printf("Dedicated signal_handler() thread alive..\n");
  while (1) {
```

```
        /* Wait for any/all signals */
        if (sigfillset(&sigset) == -1)
            FATAL("sigfillset failed");
        if (sigwait(&sigset, &sig) < 0)
            FATAL("sigwait failed");

    /* Note on sigwait():
     * sigwait suspends the calling thread until one of (any of) the
     * signals in set is delivered to the calling thread. It then stores
     * the number of the signal received in the location pointed to by
     * "sig" and returns. The signals in set must be blocked and not
     * ignored on entrance to sigwait. If the delivered signal has a
     * signal handler function attached, that function is *not* called.
     */
        switch (sig) {
        case SIGINT:
            // Perform signal handling for SIGINT here
            printf("+++ signal_handler(): caught signal #%d +++\n", sig);
            break;
        case SIGQUIT:
            // Perform signal handling for SIGQUIT here
            printf("+++ signal_handler(): caught signal #%d +++\n", sig);
            break;
        case SIGIO:
            // Perform signal handling for SIGIO here
            printf("+++ signal_handler(): caught signal #%d +++\n", sig);
            break;
        default:
            // Signal <whichever> caught
            printf("*** signal_handler(): caught signal #%2d [unhandled]
***\n", sig);
            break;
        }
    }
    return (void *)0;
}
```

We leave it as a quick exercise to the reader to try it out, noting the output. By the way, how will you finally kill it? Just open another Terminal window and issue `kill -9 <PID>` from there.

> For the reader's convenience, we repeat an important tip originally shown in Chapter 12, *Signaling - Part II*.
> An important point to note: neither the `sigwait(3)`, `sigwaitinfo(2)`, nor `sigtimedwait(2)` APIs can wait for synchronously generated signals from the kernel—typically the ones that indicate a failure of some sort, such as the `SIGFPE` and the `SIGSEGV`. These can only be caught in the normal asynchronous fashion—via `signal(2)` or via `sigaction(2)`. For such cases, as we have repeatedly shown, the `sigaction(2)` system call would be the superior choice.

Also, to mask signals in a MT app, don't use the `sigprocmask(2)` API—it's not thread-safe. Instead, use the `pthread_sigmask(3)` library routine, which is.

Note that the following APIs are available to send signals to threads within the process:

- `pthread_kill(3)`: An API to send a signal to a particular thread within the same process
- `tgkill(2)`: An API to send a signal to a particular thread within a given thread group.
- `tkill(2)`: A deprecated predecessor of `tgkill`.

Look up the details on their respective man pages. Having said this, it's far better to kill a thread via the pthreads cancelation framework than by sending it a signal.

## Threads vs processes – look again

Right from the start of this trilogy (Chapter 14, *Multithreading with Pthreads Part I - Essentials*, Chapter 15, *Multithreading with Pthreads Part II - Synchronization*, and Chapter 16, *Multithreading with Pthreads Part III*) on multithreading with pthreads, with regard to the multiprocess (single-threaded) versus multithreaded argument, we have repeatedly said that it's not all advantages or disadvantages—there is always some of both, a trade–off.

*Table 4* and *Table 5* describe some of the pros and cons of the multiprocess (several single-threaded processes) versus the multithreaded (several threads within a single process) approaches.

# The multiprocess vs the multithreading model – pros of the MT model

Here are some pros of the MT model over the single-threaded process:

| Context | Multiprocess (single-threaded) model | Multithreaded (MT) model |
|---|---|---|
| Design for parallelized workloads | • Cumbersome<br>• Non-intuitive<br>• Using the fork/wait semantics repeatedly (creating a large number of processes) isn't simple or intuitive either | • Lends itself to building parallelized software; calling the `pthread_create(3)` in a loop is easy and intuitive as well<br>• Achieving a logical separation of tasks becomes easy<br>• The OS will have threads take advantage of multicore systems implicitly; for the Linux OS, the granularity of scheduling is a thread, not a process (more on this in the next chapter)<br>• Overlapping CPU with IO becomes easy |
| Creation/destruction performance | Much slower | Much faster than processes; resource-sharing guarantees this |
| Context switching | Slow | Much faster between the threads of a process |
| Data sharing | Done via IPC (Inter-Process Communication) mechanisms; involves a learning curve, can be fairly complex; synchronization (via the semaphore) required | Inherent; all global and static data items are implicitly shared between threads of a given process; synchronization (via the mutex) is required |

Table 4: Multiprocess versus multithreading model – pros of the MT model

# The multiprocess vs the multithreading model – cons of the MT model

Here are some cons of the MT model over the single-threaded process:

| Context | Multiprocess (single-threaded) model | Multithreaded (MT) model |
|---|---|---|
| Thread-safety | No such requirement; processes always have address space separation. | The most serious downside: every function in the MT application that can be run in parallel by threads must be written, verified, and documented to be thread-safe. This includes the app code and the project libraries, as well as any third-party libraries it links into. |
| Application integrity | In a large MT app, if any one thread encounters a fatal error (such as a segfault), the entire app is now buggy and will have to shut down. | In a multiprocess app, only the process that encounters a fatal error will have to shut down; the rest of the project keeps running[1]. |
| Address space constraints | On 32-bit CPUs, the VAS (virtual address space) available to user mode apps is fairly small (either 2 GB or 3 GB), but still large enough for a typical single-threaded app; on 64-bit CPUs the VAS is enormous ($2^{64}$ = 16 EB). | On a 32-bit system (still common on many embedded Linux products), the available VAS to user mode will be small (2/3 GB). Considering sophisticated MT apps with many threads, that's not a lot! In fact, it's one of the reasons embedded vendors are aggressively moving products to 64-bit systems. |
| The Unix everything's a file semantics | The semantic holds true: files (descriptors), devices, sockets, terminals, and so on can all be treated as files; also, each process has its own copy of a given resource. | Resource-sharing, seen as an advantage, can also be seen as a downside:<br>• The sharing can defeat the traditional Unix model advantage<br>• The sharing of open files, memory regions, IPC objects, paging tables, resource limits, and so on implies synchronization overhead upon access |
| Signal-handling | Designed for the process model. | Not designed for the MT model; can be done, but a bit clumsy to handle signals. |

[ 690 ]

| Designing, maintaining, and debugging | Quite straightforward compared to the MT model. | Increases complexity because the programmer has to track (in this mind) the state of several threads simultaneously, including notoriously complex locking scenarios. Debugging deadlock (and other) situations can be quite difficult (tools such as GDB and helgrind help, but the human still needs to track things). |
|---|---|---|

Table 5: Multiprocess versus multithreading model – cons of the MT model

[1] The Google Chrome open source project architecture is based on the multiprocess model; see their comic adaptation on why: `http://www.google.com/googlebooks/chrome/med_00.html`. From a software-design viewpoint, the site is very interesting.

# Pthreads – a few random tips and FAQs

To conclude this chapter, we provide answers to FAQs on multithreading as well as a brief note on how to debug a MT application using GDB. Do read on.

> Every function in your MT application that can be run in parallel by threads must be written, verified, and documented to be thread-safe. This includes your MT app code, your project libraries, as well as any third-party libraries you link into.

## Pthreads – some FAQs

- Q: What happens in a multithreaded process when a thread calls one of the `exec*()` routines?
  A: The calling application (the predecessor) is completely replaced by the successor process, which will be only the thread that called exec. Note that no TSD destructors or thread-cleanup handlers are called.
- Q: What happens in a multithreaded process when a thread calls `fork(2)`?
  A: It's OS-dependent. On modern Linux, only the thread that called `fork(2)` is replicated in the new child process. All other threads that existed prior to the fork are gone. No TSD destructors or thread cleanup handlers are called. Calling fork in a multithreaded application can lead to difficulties; it is not recommended. Find a link in the *Further reading* section on the GitHub repository regarding this very question.

[ 691 ]

- Think of it this way: calling `fork` in an MT application for multiprocessing is considered the wrong approach; invoking fork for the sole purpose of executing another program is okay (via the typical fork-exec-wait semantic we learned about). In other words, the newly born child process should only call functions documented as being async-signal-safe and/or the exec* routines to invoke another application.
  Also, you can set up handlers to run when fork is invoked via the `pthread_atfork(3)` API.
- Q: What is the effect on Resource Limits (see ulimit/prlimit) in a multithreaded application?
  A: All resource limits—except the stack size limit, of course—are shared by all threads in the process. On older Linux kernels, this was not the case.

# Debugging multithreaded (pthreads) applications with GDB

GDB supports debugging MT apps; almost all the usual commands work normally, just a few commands tend to be thread-specific. Here are the key ones to be aware of:

- See all visible threads:

```
(gdb) info threads
 Id     Target Id              Frame
<thr#>  Thread <addr> (LWP ...) in <function> [at <srcfile>]
```

- Switch context to a particular thread by using the `thread <thread#>` command.
- Apply a given command to all threads of the process: `(gdb) thread apply all <cmd>`
- Show the stack (GDB's backtrace or `bt` command) of all threads (the following example output is from our earlier MT app, `mt_iobuf_rfct_dbg`; first, we show the threads via the `thread find .` command):

```
(gdb) thread find .
Thread 1 has target name 'tsig_dbg'
Thread 1 has target id 'Thread 0x7ffff7fc9740 (LWP 24943)'
Thread 2 has target name 'tsig_dbg'
Thread 2 has target id 'Thread 0x7ffff77f7700 (LWP 25010)'
Thread 3 has target name 'tsig_dbg'
```

```
Thread 3 has target id 'Thread 0x7ffff6ff6700 (LWP 25194)'
(gdb) thread apply all bt

Thread 3 (Thread 0x7fffefff700 (LWP 21236)):
#0 testit_mt_refactored (wrstrm=0x603670, rdstrm=0x6038a0, numio=10,
thrdnum=1, iobuf=0x7fffe8000b20 "")
    at mt_iobuf_rfct.c:44
#1 0x00000000004010e9 in wrapper_testit_mt_refactored (msg=0x603c20)
at mt_iobuf_rfct.c:88
#2 0x00007ffff7bbe594 in start_thread () from /lib64/libpthread.so.0
#3 0x00007ffff78f1e6f in clone () from /lib64/libc.so.6

Thread 2 (Thread 0x7ffff77f7700 (LWP 21235)):
#0 testit_mt_refactored (wrstrm=0x603670, rdstrm=0x6038a0, numio=10,
thrdnum=0, iobuf=0x7ffff0000b20 "")
    at mt_iobuf_rfct.c:44
#1 0x00000000004010e9 in wrapper_testit_mt_refactored (msg=0x603ad0)
at mt_iobuf_rfct.c:88
#2 0x00007ffff7bbe594 in start_thread () from /lib64/libpthread.so.0
#3 0x00007ffff78f1e6f in clone () from /lib64/libc.so.6

Thread 1 (Thread 0x7ffff7fc9740 (LWP 21203)):
#0 0x00007ffff7bbfa2d in __pthread_timedjoin_ex () from
/lib64/libpthread.so.0
#1 0x00000000004013ec in main (argc=2, argv=0x7fffffffcd88) at
mt_iobuf_rfct.c:150
(gdb)
```

> Some miscellaneous tips and tricks with regard to MT programming with pthreads (including several we have already come across), are in a blog article mentioned in the *Further reading* section on the GitHub repository (Pthreads Dev - common programming mistakes to avoid); please do check it out.

## Summary

In this chapter, we covered several safety aspects of working with threads that the powerful pthreads framework provides. We looked at thread-safe APIs, what they are, why they are required, and how to make a thread routine thread-safe. We also learned how to have one thread cancel (effectively, kill off) a given thread, and how to have the victim thread deal with any required cleanup.

The remainder of the chapter focused on how to safely mix threads with the signaling interfaces; we also compared and contrasted – giving pros and cons (some food for thought, really)—the typical multiprocess single-threaded with several processes versus multithreaded (with one process) approaches. Tips and FAQs round off this trilogy of chapters (Chapter 14, *Multithreading with Pthreads Part I - Essentials* and in this chapter).

In the next chapter, the reader will be taken through details on CPU scheduling on the Linux platform, and very interestingly, how the application developer can exploit CPU scheduling (with a multithreaded application demo).

# 17
# CPU Scheduling on Linux

An often-posed question that people have about Linux is, how does scheduling work? We will address this question for user space application developers in this chapter in some detail. In order for the reader to clearly grasp important concepts regarding CPU scheduling on Linux and how you can powerfully use this in applications, we will cover essential background information (the process state machine, real time, and so on) as well. This chapter will end with a brief note on how the Linux OS can even be used as a hard, real-time OS.

In this chapter, the reader will learn about the following topics:

- The Linux process (or thread) state machine and, importantly, the POSIX scheduling policies that Linux implements under the hood
- Related concepts, such as real-time and CPU affinity
- How to exploit the fact that, on a per-thread basis, you can program threads with a given scheduling policy and real time priority (a sample app will be shown)
- A brief note on the fact that Linux can also be used as an RTOS

## The Linux OS and the POSIX scheduling model

In order to understand scheduling at the level of the application developer (and how you can leverage this knowledge in actual code), we must first cover some required background information.

The first and very important concept for the developer to understand is that OSes maintain a construct called the **Kernel Schedulable Entity** (**KSE**). The KSE is the granularity at which the OS scheduling code operates. In effect, what object exactly does the OS schedule? Is it the application, the process, the thread? Well, the short answer is that the KSE on the Linux OS is a thread. In other words, all runnable threads compete for the CPU resource; the kernel scheduler is ultimately the arbiter that decides which thread gets which CPU core and when.

Next, we present an overview of the process, or thread's, state machine.

## The Linux process state machine

On the Linux OS, every process or thread runs through a variety of definite states, and by encoding these, we can form the state machine of a process (or thread) on the Linux OS (do refer to *Figure 1* in the following section while reading this).

> Since we now understand that the KSE on the Linux OS is a thread and not a process, we shall ignore convention—which uses the word *process*—and instead use the word *thread* when describing the entity that cycles through various states of the state machine. (If more comfortable, you could always, in your mind, substitute the word process for thread in the following matter.)

The states that a Linux thread can cycle through are as follows (the `ps(1)` utility encodes the state via the letter shown here):

- **R**: Ready-to-run or Running
- Sleeping:
    - **S**: Interruptible Sleep
    - **D**: Uninterruptible Sleep
- **T**: Stopped (or suspended/frozen)
- **Z**: Zombie (or defunct)
- **X**: Dead

When a thread is newly created (either via the `fork(2)`, `pthread_create(3)` or `clone(2)` APIs), and once the OS determines that the thread is fully born, it informs the scheduler of its existence by putting the thread into a runnable state. A thread in the **R** state is either actually running on a CPU core or is in the ready-to-run state. What we need to understand is that in both cases, the thread is enqueued on a data structure within the OS called a **run queue** (**RQ**). The threads in the run queue are the valid candidates to run; no thread can possibly run unless it is enqueued on an OS run queue. (For your information, Linux from version 2.6 onward best exploits all possible CPU cores by setting up one RQ per CPU core, thus obtaining perfect SMP scalability.) Linux does not explicitly distinguish between the ready-to-run and running states; it merely marks the thread in either state as **R**.

## The sleep states

Once a thread is running its code, it obviously keeps doing so, until, typically, one of a few things (mentioned as follows) happen:

- It blocks on I/O, thus sleeping—entering state of **S** or **D**, depending (see the following paragraph).
- It is preempted; there's no state change, and it remains in a ready-to-run state **R** on a run queue.
- It is sent a signal that causes it to stop, thus entering state **T**.
  - It is sent a signal (typically SIGSTOP or SIGTSTP) that causes it to terminate, thus first entering state **Z** (zombie is a transient state on the way to death), and then actually dying (state X).

Often, a thread will encounter in its code path a blocking API—one that will cause it to enter a sleep state, waiting on an event. While blocked, it is removed (or dequeued) from the run queue it was on, and instead added (enqueued) onto what's called a **wait queue** (**WQ**). When the event it was waiting upon arises, the OS will issue it a wakeup, causing it to become runnable (dequeued from its wait queue and enqueued onto a run queue) again. Note that the thread won't run instantaneously; it will become runnable (**Rr** in *Figure 1*, Linux state machine), and a candidate for the scheduler; soon enough, it will get a chance and actually run on the CPU (**Rcpu**).

> **TIP**: A common misconception is to think that the OS maintains one run queue and one wait queue. No—the Linux kernel maintains one run queue per CPU. Wait queues are often created and used by device drivers (as well as the kernel); thus, there can be any number of them.

# CPU Scheduling on Linux

The depth of the sleep determines precisely which state the thread is put into. If a thread issues a blocking call and the underlying kernel code (or device driver code) puts it into an interruptible sleep, the state is marked as **S**. An interruptible sleep state implies that the thread will be awoken when any signal destined for it is delivered; then, it will run the signal handler code, and if not terminated (or stopped), will resume the sleep (recall the `SA_RESTART` flag to `sigaction(2)` from Chapter 11, *Signaling - Part I*). This interruptible sleep state **S** is indeed very commonly seen.

On the other hand, the OS (or driver) could put the blocking thread into a deeper uninterruptible sleep, in which case the state is marked as **D**. An uninterruptible sleep state implies that the thread will not respond to signals (none; not even a SIGKILL from root!). This is done when the kernel determines that the sleep is critical and the thread must await the pending event, blocking upon at any cost. (A common example is a `read(2)` from a file—while data is being actually read, the thread is placed into an uninterruptible sleep state; another is the mounting and unmounting of a filesystem.)

> **TIP**
>
> Performance issues are often caused by very high I/O bottlenecks; high CPU usage is not always a major problem, but continually high I/O will make the system feel very slow. A quick way to determine which application(s) (processes and threads, really) are causing the heavy I/O is to filter the `ps(1)` output looking for processes (or threads) in the **D**, uninterruptible sleep state. As an example, refer to the following:
>
> ```
> $ ps -LA -o state,pid,cmd | grep "^D"
> D 10243 /usr/bin/gnome-shell
> D 13337 [kworker/0:2+eve]
> D 22545 /home/<user>/.dropbox-dist/dropbox-
> lnx.x86_64-58.4.92/dropbox
> $
> ```
>
> Notice that we use `ps -LA`; the `-L` switch shows all threads alive as well. (FYI, the thread shown in the preceding square brackets, `[kworker/...]`, is a kernel thread.)

The following diagram represents the Linux state machine for any process or thread:

[ 698 ]

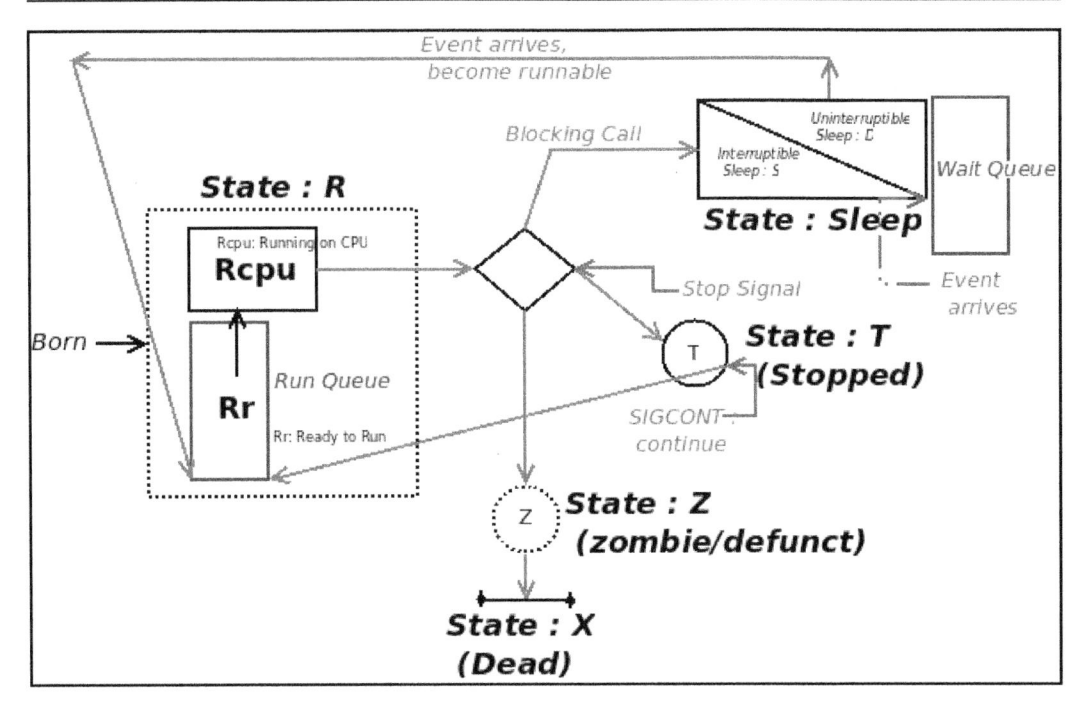

Figure 1: Linux state machine

The preceding diagram shows transitions between states via red arrows. Do note that for clarity, some transitions (for example, a thread, can be killed while asleep or stopped) are not explicitly shown in the preceding diagram.

# What is real time?

Many misconceptions exist regarding the meaning of real time (in application programming and OS contexts). Real time essentially means that not only do the real-time thread (or threads) perform their work correctly, but they must perform within a given worst-case deadline. Actually, the key factor in a real time system is called determinism. Deterministic systems have a guaranteed worst-case response time to real-world (or artificially generated) events; they will process them within a bounded time constraint. Determinism leads to predictable response, under any conditions—even extreme load. One way in which computer scientists classify algorithms is via their time complexity: the big-O notation. O(1) algorithms are deterministic; they guarantee that they will complete within a certain worst-case time, no matter the input load. True real-time systems require O(1) algorithms for implementing their performance-sensitive code paths.

Interestingly, real time does not necessarily mean real fast. A VDC survey (refer to the *Further reading* section on the GitHub repository for more details) shows that the majority of real-time systems have a deadline (real-time response time) requirement of 1 to 9 milliseconds. As long as the system can consistently and without fail service the event within its given deadline (which could be fairly large), it's real time.

## Types of real time

Real time is often classified into three types, as follows:

- **Hard real-time systems** are defined as those that must always meet all deadlines. Failure to meet a deadline even once results in the catastrophic failure of the system, including possible loss to human life, financial loss, and so on. A hard real time system requires a **Real-Time Operating System** (**RTOS**) to drive it. (Also, it's really important that the applications are written to be hard real time as well!). Possible hard real-time domains include human transportation vehicles of many types (aircraft, marine vessels, spacecraft, trains, and elevators) and some kinds of military grade or defense equipment, nuclear reactors, medical electronics, and stock exchanges. (Yes, stock exchanges are very much a hard real time system; do read the book *Automate This: How Algorithms Came to Rule Our World*—refer to the *Further reading* section on the GitHub repository for more information.)
- **Soft real-time systems** are all about best effort; deadlines do exist, but there is absolutely no guarantee that they will be met. The system will do its best to meet them; failure to do so is considered okay (often, it's just more of an annoyance to the end user rather than anything dangerous). Consumer electronics products (such as our smartphones, MP3 players, cameras, tablets, and smart speakers) are typical examples. While using them, it quite often happens that you will hear a glitch while listening to music, or a streaming video stutters, buffers, and jitters. While annoying, it's unlikely the user will perish.
- **Firm real-time systems** fall in-between the hard and soft real-time ones—deadlines are important and will be met as far as is possible, but again, no ironclad guarantees can be made. Performance degradation due to missing too many deadlines is an issue here.

# Scheduling policies

A key job of the **operating system** (**OS**) is to schedule runnable tasks. The POSIX standard states that a POSIX-complaint OS must provide (at least) three scheduling policies. A scheduling policy is really the scheduling algorithm used by the OS to schedule tasks. In this book, we will not delve into such details, but we do need the application developer to be aware of the scheduling policies available. These are as follows:

- SCHED_FIFO
- SCHED_RR
- SCHED_OTHER (also known as SCHED_NORMAL)

Our discussions on this, naturally, will be solely with regard to the Linux OS.

The first important thing to understand is that the vanilla Linux OS is not an RTOS; it does not support hard real-time and is classified as a **General Purpose Operating System** (**GPOS**), like the others—Unix, Windows, and macOS.

> Do read on, though; we shall see that while hard real-time is not possible with vanilla Linux, it is indeed possible to run an appropriately patched Linux as an RTOS.

Linux, though a GPOS, easily performs as a soft real-time system. Indeed, its high performance characteristics bring it close to being a firm real-time system. Thus, the predominant use of the Linux OS in consumer electronics (and enterprise) products is not at all surprising.

Next, the first two scheduling policies that we mentioned—SCHED_FIFO and SCHED_RR—are Linux's soft real-time scheduling policies. The SCHED_OTHER (also known as SCHED_NORMAL) policy is the non-real-time scheduling policy and is always the default one. The SCHED_OTHER policy is implemented on modern Linux kernels as the **Completely Fair Scheduler** (**CFS**); it's an implementation whose primary design goals are to provide overall high system throughput and fairness to every runnable task (thread), ensuring that a thread does not starve. This is quite the anti-thesis of a real-time policy algorithm, whose overriding motivation is priority of the thread.

# CPU Scheduling on Linux

For both the `SCHED_FIFO` and `SCHED_RR` soft real-time policies, the Linux OS specifies a priority range. This range is from 1 to 99, where 1 is the lowest real-time priority and 99 is the highest. The soft real-time scheduling policy design on Linux follows what is known as *fixed priority preemptive scheduling*, and this is important to understand. Fixed priority implies that the application decides and fixes the thread priority (and can change it); the OS does not. Preemption is the act of the OS snatching away the CPU from the running thread, relegating it back to its run queue, and context switching to another thread. The precise preemptive semantics with regard to the scheduling policies will be covered next.

We shall now briefly describe, in real-world terms, what it means to be running under these differing scheduling policies.

A running `SCHED_FIFO` thread can only be preempted under the following three conditions:

- It (in)voluntarily yields the processor (technically, it moves out from the **R** state). This happens when a task issues a blocking call or invokes a system call like `sched_yield(2)`.
- It stops or dies.
- A higher priority real-time task becomes runnable.

This is the key point to understand: a `SCHED_FIFO` task is aggressive; it runs with infinite timeslice, and unless it blocks (or is stopped or killed), will continue to run on the processor indefinitely. However, the moment a higher priority thread becomes runnable (state **R**, entering the run queue), it will be preempted in favor of this thread.

`SCHED_RR` behavior is nearly identical to that of `SCHED_FIFO`, except that:

- It has a finite timeslice, and thus has an additional scenario under which it can be preempted: when its timeslice expires.
- When preempted, the task is moved to the tail of the run queue for its priority level, ensuring that all `SCHED_RR` tasks at the same priority level are executed in turn (hence its name round robin).

Notice that on an RTOS the scheduling algorithm is simple, as all it really has to do is implement this semantic: the highest priority runnable thread must be the thread that is running.

All threads run under the SCHED_OTHER (or SCHED_NORMAL) scheduling policy by default. It is a decidedly non-real-time policy, the emphasis being on fairness and overall throughput. Its implementation from Linux kernel version 2.6.0 up until 2.6.22 (inclusive) was via the so-called O(1) scheduler; from 2.6.23 onward, a further improved algorithm called the **Completely Fair Scheduler (CFS)** implements this scheduling policy (actually a scheduling class). Refer to the following table for more information:

| Scheduling policy | Type | Priority range |
|---|---|---|
| SCHED_FIFO | Soft real-time: Aggressive, unfair | 1 to 99 |
| SCHED_RR | Soft real-time: Less aggressive | 1 to 99 |
| SCHED_OTHER | Non real-time: Fair, time sharing; the default | Nice value (-20 to +19) |

> Though not very commonly used, we point out that Linux also supports a batched mode process execution policy with the SCHED_BATCH policy. Also, the SCHED_IDLE policy is used for very low priority background tasks. (In fact, the CPU idle thread—(mis)named swapper with PID 0, exists for each CPU and runs only when absolutely no other task wants the processor).

## Peeking at the scheduling policy and priority

Linux provides the chrt(1) utility to view and change a thread's (or process) real-time scheduling policy and priority. A quick demonstration of using it to display the scheduling policy and priority of a given process (by PID) can be seen in the following code:

```
$ chrt -p $$
pid 1618's current scheduling policy: SCHED_OTHER
pid 1618's current scheduling priority: 0
$
```

In the preceding, we have queried the scheduling policy and priority of the chrt(1) process itself (with the shell's $$ variable). Try this for other threads; you will notice the policy is (almost) always SCHED_OTHER and that the real-time priority is zero. A real-time priority of zero implies that the process is not real time.

> You can always query a thread's scheduling policy and (real-time) priority by passing the thread PID (via the output of ps -LA or similar) to chrt(1).

## The nice value

So, now you may be wondering, if all non-real-time threads (the SCHED_OTHER chaps) have a priority of zero, then how can I support prioritization between them? Well, that's exactly what the nice value of a SCHED_OTHER thread is for: it's the (older) Unix-style priority model and now, on Linux, specifies a relative priority between the non-real-time threads.

The nice value is a priority range between **-20** to **+19** (on modern Linux), with the base priority being zero. On Linux, it's a per-thread attribute; when a thread is created, it inherits the nice value of its creator thread—zero being the default. Refer to the following diagram:

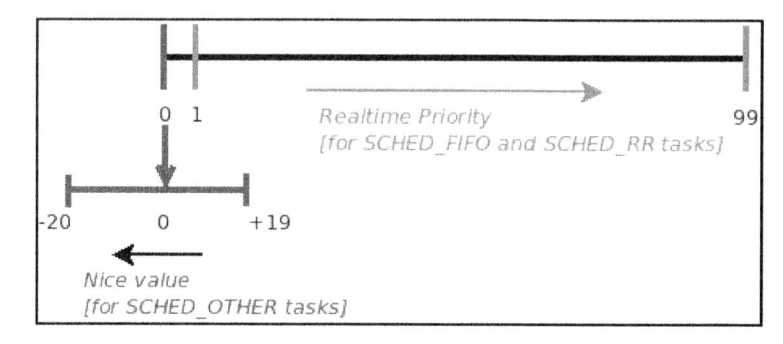

Figure 2: Linux thread priority ranges

From 2.6.23 (with the CFS kernel scheduler), the nice value of a thread has a large impact (a factor of 1.25 for each degree of nice value) on scheduling; thus, **-20** nice value threads get much more CPU bandwidth (this is good for CPU-sensitive applications like multimedia) and **+19** nice value threads get very little CPU.

An application programmer can query and set the nice value via the nice(1) command-line utility, and the nice(2), setpriority(2), and sched_setattr(2) system calls (the last being the most recent and correct one to use). We refer you to the respective man pages for these APIs.

Keep in mind that a real-time (SCHED_FIFO or SCHED_RR) thread is always superior to a SCHED_OTHER thread in terms of priority (thus pretty much guaranteeing that it will get a chance to run earlier).

# CPU affinity

Let's visualize a Linux system with four CPU cores and, for simplicity, one ready-to-run thread. On which CPU core will this thread run? The kernel will decide this; the key thing to realize is that it could run upon any of the four available CPUs!

Can the CPU(s) it could possibly be run upon be specified by the programmer? Yes, indeed; just this feature alone is called CPU affinity. On Linux, it is a per-thread attribute (within the OS). The CPU affinity can be changed on a per-thread basis by changing the thread's CPU affinity mask; this is achieved, of course, via a system call. Let's take a look at the following code:

```
#define _GNU_SOURCE /* See feature_test_macros(7) */
#include <sched.h>
int sched_setaffinity(pid_t pid, size_t cpusetsize,
                      const cpu_set_t *mask);
int sched_getaffinity(pid_t pid, size_t cpusetsize,
                      cpu_set_t *mask);
```

The kernel scheduler will honor the CPU mask—the set of CPUs the thread is allowed to execute upon—set by the programmer. We are expected to specify the CPU affinity mask as a `cpu_set_t` object. (We refer the reader to the man page on `sched_setaffinity(2)`, which helpfully provides an example program).

Note that the pthreads framework provides the wrapper APIs `pthread_setaffinity_np(3)` and `pthread_getaffinity_np(3)` to perform the same on a given thread (they internally invoke the `sched_setaffinity(2)` system call).

An interesting design is that of CPU reservation. On a sufficiently multi-core system (say we have a system with four CPU cores: 0, 1, 2, and 3), you can use the preceding CPU affinity mask model to effectively set aside one CPU core (say core 3) for a given thread (or threads) that are crucial to performance. This implies that you must set the CPU mask for that thread to the particular CPU (say core 3) and, importantly, set the CPU mask for all other threads to exclude core 3.

Though it may sound simple, it's really not a trivial exercise; some of the reasons why this is the case are as follows:

- You must realize that the CPU set aside is not really exclusively reserved for the thread(s) specified; for true CPU reservation, except for the given thread(s) running on that CPU, all other threads on the entire system must somehow be excluded from running on that CPU.
- As a general guideline, the OS scheduler best understands how to allocate CPU bandwidth among available CPU cores (it has a load balancer component and understands the CPU hierarchy); thus, CPU allocation is best left to the OS.

> **TIP**
> Modern Linux kernels have support for a very powerful feature: **control groups** (**cgroups**). (see Appendix B, *Daemon Processes*, for a note). With regard to CPU reservation, it can be achieved via the cgroup model. Please refer to the following Q&A on Stack Overflow for more details: *How to use cgroups to limit all processes except whitelist to a single CPU*: https://unix.stackexchange.com/questions/247209/how-to-use-cgroups-to-limit-all-processes-except-whitelist-to-a-single-cpu.

For convenience, Linux provides the taskset(1) utility as a simple way to query and specify the CPU affinity mask of any given process (or thread). Here, we shall query the CPU affinity mask of two processes. (we assume that the system we are running on has four CPU cores; we can use lscpu(1) to query this):

```
$ taskset -p 1
pid 1's current affinity mask: f
$ taskset -p 12446
pid 12446's current affinity mask: 7
$
```

PID 1's (systemd) CPU affinity mask is 0xf, which, of course, is binary 1111. If a bit is set 1, it implies the thread can run on the CPU represented by that bit. If the bit is cleared 0, it implies the thread cannot run on the CPU represented by that bit. Exactly as expected, on a four-CPU box, the CPU affinity bitmask is 0xf (1111) by default, implying that, the process (or thread) can run on any available CPU. Interestingly, in the preceding output the bash process appears to have a CPU affinity mask of 7, which translates to binary 0111, implying that it will never be scheduled to run on CPU 3.

[ 706 ]

In the following code, a simple shell script invokes the chrt(1) as well as the taskset(1) utility in a loop, displaying the scheduling policy, (real-time) priority, and CPU affinity mask of every process that's alive on the system:

```
# ch17/query_sched_allprcs.sh
for p in $(ps -A -To pid)
do
    chrt -p $p 2>/dev/null
    taskset -p $p 2>/dev/null
done
```

We encourage the reader to try this out on their own system. In the following code, we grep(1) for any SCHED_FIFO tasks:

```
$ ./query_sched_allprcs.sh | grep -A2 -w SCHED_FIFO
pid 12's current scheduling policy: SCHED_FIFO
pid 12's current scheduling priority: 99
pid 12's current affinity mask: 1
pid 13's current scheduling policy: SCHED_FIFO
pid 13's current scheduling priority: 99
pid 13's current affinity mask: 1
--
pid 16's current scheduling policy: SCHED_FIFO
pid 16's current scheduling priority: 99
pid 16's current affinity mask: 2
pid 17's current scheduling policy: SCHED_FIFO
pid 17's current scheduling priority: 99
pid 17's current affinity mask: 2
--
[...]
```

Yes! We find some threads. Wow, they are all of SCHED_FIFO real-time priority 99! Let's check out who these threads are (with a cool one-liner script, too):

```
$ ps aux | awk '$2==12 || $2==13 || $2==16 || $2==17 {print $0}'
USER PID %CPU %MEM   VSZ   RSS TTY STAT START   TIME COMMAND
root  12  0.0  0.0     0     0 ?   S    13:42   0:00 [migration/0]
root  13  0.0  0.0     0     0 ?   S    13:42   0:00 [watchdog/0]
root  16  0.0  0.0     0     0 ?   S    13:42   0:00 [watchdog/1]
root  17  0.0  0.0     0     0 ?   S    13:42   0:00 [migration/1]
$
```

> For clarity, the ps aux heading—which would not normally be displayed—is shown in the preceding code. Also, we use the ps aux style as, conveniently, kernel threads are displayed in brackets.

It turns out (here, in this particular example, at least) that they are all kernel threads (see the following information box). The important thing to understand is that they are deliberately SCHED_FIFO (real-time) priority 99, so that, when they want to run on the CPU, they will run pretty much immediately. In fact, let's take a glance at their CPU affinity mask: it's deliberately allocated (with values like 1,2,4,8) so that they are affined to a particular CPU core. It's important to understand that these kernel threads are not CPU hoggers; in reality, they will spend most of the time asleep (state S) and only spring into action when required.

> Kernel threads are not very different from their user space counterparts; they too compete for the CPU resource. The key difference is that kernel threads have no view of user space—they only execute in kernel virtual address space (whereas user space threads, of course, see both: userland in normal user mode and, upon issuing a system call, they switch to kernel space).

# Exploiting Linux's soft real-time capabilities

Recall that, earlier in this chapter, we stated: The soft real-time scheduling policy design on Linux follows what is known as fixed priority preemptive scheduling; fixed priority implies that the application decides and fixes the thread priority (and can change it); the OS does not.

Not only can the application switch between thread priorities, but even the scheduling policy (in effect, the scheduling algorithm used under the hood by the OS) can be changed by the application developer; this can be done on a per-thread basis. That's indeed very powerful; it implies that an application having, say, five threads, can decide what scheduling policy and priority to assign to each of these threads!

## Scheduling policy and priority APIs

Obviously, in order to achieve this, the OS must expose some APIs; indeed, there are a few system calls that deal with exactly this—changing a given process or thread's scheduling policy and priority.

Here's a list—a sampling, really—of some of the more important of these APIs:

- `sched_setscheduler(2)`: Sets the scheduling policy and parameters of a specified thread.
- `sched_getscheduler(2)`: Returns the scheduling policy of a specified thread.
- `sched_setparam(2)`: Sets the scheduling parameters of a specified thread.
- `sched_getparam(2)`: Fetches the scheduling parameters of a specified thread.
- `sched_get_priority_max(2)`: Returns the maximum priority available in a specified scheduling policy.
- `sched_get_priority_min(2)`: Returns the minimum priority available in a specified scheduling policy.
- `sched_rr_get_interval(2)`: Fetches the quantum used for threads that are scheduled under the round-robin scheduling policy.
- `sched_setattr(2)`: Sets the scheduling policy and parameters of a specified thread. This (Linux-specific) system call provides a superset of the functionality of `sched_setscheduler(2)` and `sched_setparam(2)`.
- `sched_getattr(2)`: Fetches the scheduling policy and parameters of a specified thread. This (Linux-specific) system call provides a superset of the functionality of `sched_getscheduler(2)` and `sched_getparam(2)`.

> **TIP**: `sched_setattr(2)` and `sched_getattr(2)` are currently considered to be the latest and more powerful of these APIs. Also, on Ubuntu, one can issue the convenient `man -k sched` command to see all utils and APIs related to scheduling (-k: keyword).

The astute reader will quickly notice that all of the APIs we mentioned previously are system calls (section 2 of the manual), but what about pthreads APIs? Indeed, they do exist and, as you may have guessed, are mostly just wrappers that invoke the underlying system calls; in the following code, we show two of them:

```
#include <pthread.h>
int pthread_setschedparam(pthread_t thread, int policy,
                          const struct sched_param *param);
int pthread_getschedparam(pthread_t thread, int *policy,
                          struct sched_param *param);
```

It's important to note that, in order to set the scheduling policy and priority of a thread (or process), you need to be running with root access. Recall that the modern way to bestow privileges to threads is via the Linux Capabilities model (we covered this in detail in Chapter 8, *Process Capabilities*). A thread with the capability CAP_SYS_NICE can arbitrarily set its scheduling policy and priority to any value it desires. Think about it: if this were not the case, then pretty much all apps could insist that they run as SCHED_FIFO priority 99, effectively rendering the whole concept meaningless!

pthread_setschedparam(3) internally invokes the the sched_setscheduler(2) system call, and pthread_getschedparam(3) invokes the sched_getscheduler(2) system call under the hood. Their API signatures are:

```
#include <sched.h>
int sched_setscheduler(pid_t pid, int policy,
                const struct sched_param *param);
int sched_getscheduler(pid_t pid);
```

Other pthreads APIs exist as well. Notice that the ones shown here help set up the thread attribute structure: pthread_attr_setinheritsched(3), pthread_attr_setschedparam(3), pthread_attr_setschedpolicy(3), and pthread_setschedprio(3), to name a few.

> The man page on sched(7) (look it up by typing man 7 sched in a terminal window) details the available APIs for controlling scheduling policy, priority, and behavior for threads. It provides details on current Linux scheduling policies, privileges required to change them, relevant resource limit values, and kernel tunables for scheduling, as well as other miscellaneous details.

## Code example – setting a thread scheduling policy and priority

To help solidify the concepts that we learned about in the previous sections of this chapter, we will design and implement a small demo program, illustrating how a modern Linux pthreads application can set an individual thread's scheduling policy and priority to make threads (soft) real-time.

Our demo app will have a total of three threads. The first is main(), of course. The following bullet points show what the application is designed to do:

- Thread 0 (main(), really):
  This runs as a SCHED_OTHER scheduling policy with real-time priority 0, which is the default. It does the following:
    - Queries the priority range of SCHED_FIFO, printing out the values
    - Creates two worker threads (with joinability state set to detached); they will automatically inherit the scheduling policy and priority of main
    - Prints the character m to the terminal in a loop (using our DELAY_LOOP macro; for a little longer than usual)
    - Terminates
- Worker thread 1:
    - Changes its scheduling policy to SCHED_RR, setting its real-time priority to the value passed on the command line
    - Sleeps for 2 seconds (thus blocking on I/O, allowing main to get some work done)
    - Upon waking up, it prints the character 1 to the terminal in a loop (via the DELAY_LOOP macro)
    - Terminates
- Worker thread 2:
    - Changes its scheduling policy to SCHED_FIFO, setting its real-time priority to the value passed on the command line plus 10
    - Sleeps for 4 seconds (thus blocking on I/O, allowing Thread 1 to do some work)
    - Upon waking up, it prints the character 2 to the terminal in a loop
    - Terminates

Let's take a quick look at the code (ch17/sched_rt_eg.c):

> For readability, only key parts of the source code are displayed here; to view the complete source code, and build and run it, the entire tree is available for cloning from GitHub here: https://github.com/PacktPublishing/Hands-on-System-Programming-with-Linux.

The following code is the code for `main()`. (We have omitted showing the error checking code):

```
#define NUMWORK    200
...
  min = sched_get_priority_min(SCHED_FIFO);
  max = sched_get_priority_max(SCHED_FIFO);
  printf("SCHED_FIFO: priority range is %d to %d\n", min, max);
  rt_prio = atoi(argv[1]);
...
  ret = pthread_create(&tid[0], &attr, worker1, (void *)rt_prio);
  ret = pthread_create(&tid[1], &attr, worker2, (void *)rt_prio);
  pthread_attr_destroy(&attr);
  DELAY_LOOP('m', NUMWORK+100);
  printf("\nmain: all done, app exiting ...\n");
  pthread_exit((void *)0);
}
```

The following code is for worker thread 1. We have omitted showing the error checking code:

```
void *worker1(void *msg)
{
  struct sched_param p;
  printf(" RT Thread p1 (%s():%d:PID %d):\n"
    " Setting sched policy to SCHED_RR and RT priority to %ld"
    " and sleeping for 2s ...\n", __func__, __LINE__, getpid(),
(long)msg);

  p.sched_priority = (long)msg;
  pthread_setschedparam(pthread_self(), SCHED_RR, &p);
  sleep(2);
  puts(" p1 working");
  DELAY_LOOP('1', NUMWORK);
  puts(" p1: exiting..");
  pthread_exit((void *)0);
}
```

The code of worker thread 2 is almost identical to that of the preceding worker thread; the difference, however, is that we set the policy to SCHED_FIFO and the real-time priority is bumped up by 10 points, thus making it more aggressive. We only show this snippet here:

```
p.sched_priority = prio + 10;
pthread_setschedparam(pthread_self(), SCHED_FIFO, &p);
sleep(4);
puts(" p2 working");
DELAY_LOOP('2', NUMWORK);
```

Let's build it (we definitely recommend building the debug version, as then the DELAY_LOOP macro's effect is clearly seen) and give it a spin:

```
$ make sched_rt_eg_dbg
gcc -g -ggdb -gdwarf-4 -O0 -Wall -Wextra -DDEBUG -pthread -c sched_rt_eg.c -o sched_rt_eg_dbg.o
gcc -o sched_rt_eg_dbg sched_rt_eg_dbg.o common_dbg.o -pthread -lrt
$
```

We must run our app as root; we use sudo(8) to do so:

```
$ sudo ./sched_rt_eg_dbg 14
SCHED_FIFO: priority range is 1 to 99
main: creating RT worker thread #1 ...
main: creating RT worker thread #2 ...
 RT Thread p1 (worker1():68:PID 18632):
 Setting sched policy to SCHED_RR and RT priority to 14 and sleeping
for 2s ...
m RT Thread p2 (worker2():101:PID 18632):
 Setting sched policy to SCHED_FIFO and RT priority to 24 and sleeping
for 4s ...
mmmmmmmmmmmmmmmmmmmmmmmmmmmmmmmmmmmmmmmmmmmmmmmmmmmmmmmmmmmmmmmmmmmmm
mmmmmmmmmmmmmmmmmmmmmmmmmmmmmmmmmmmmmmmmmmmmmmmmmmmmmm p1 working
1m1m1m1m1m1m1m1m1m1m1m1m1m1m1m1m1m1m1m1m1m1m1m1m1m1m1m1m1m1m1m1m1m1m
1m1m1m1m1m1m1m1m1m1m1m1m1m1m1m1m1m1m1m1m1m1m11m1m1m1m1m1m1m1m1m1m1m1
m1m1m1m1m1m1m1m1m1m1m1m1m1m1m1m1m1m1m1m1m1m11m1m1m1m1m1m1m1m1m1m1m1m
1m1m1m1m1m1m1m1m1m1m1m1m1m1m1m11m1m1m p2 working
2m12m1m2m12m12m1m2m12m1m2m12m12m12m112m12m12m12m112m12m12m
112m12m12m112m12m12m112m12m12m121m211m21m21m211m21m21m211m21m
21m21m211m21m21m21m211m21m21m21m211m21m21m21
main: all done, app exiting ...
$
```

[713]

# CPU Scheduling on Linux

In the preceding output, we can see the following characters:

- `m`: This implies that the main thread is currently running on CPU
- `1`: This implies that the (soft) real-time worker thread 1 is currently running on CPU
- `2`: This implies that the (soft) real-time worker thread 2 is currently running on CPU

But, oops, the preceding output really isn't what we expect: the `m`, `1`, and `2` characters are intermingled, leading us to conclude that they have been time-sliced.

But this isn't the case. Think about it—the output is as it appears in the preceding code for the simple reason that we have run the app on a multi-core system (in the preceding code, on a laptop with four CPU cores); thus, the kernel scheduler has cleverly exploited the hardware and run all three threads in parallel on different CPU cores! So, in order to have our demo application run the way we expect, we need to ensure that it runs on exactly one CPU core and no more. How? Recall CPU affinity: we can use the `sched_setaffinity(2)` system call to do this. There is an easier way: we can use `taskset(1)` to guarantee that the process (and thus all threads within it) run on only one CPU core (for example, CPU 0) by specifying the CPU mask value as `01`. So, let's perform the following command:

```
$ sudo taskset 01 ./sched_rt_eg_dbg 14
[sudo] password for <username>: xxx
SCHED_FIFO: priority range is 1 to 99
main: creating RT worker thread #1 ...
main: creating RT worker thread #2 ...
m RT Thread p2 (worker2():101:PID 19073):
 Setting sched policy to SCHED_FIFO and RT priority to 24 and sleeping
for 4s ...
  RT Thread p1 (worker1():68:PID 19073):
 Setting sched policy to SCHED_RR and RT priority to 14 and sleeping
for 2s ...
mmmmmmmmmmmmmmmmmmmmmmmmmmmmmmmmmmmmmmmmmmmmmmmmmmmmmmmmmmmmmmmmmmmmmm
mmmmmmmmmmmmmmmmmmmmmmmmmmmmmmmmmmmmmmmmmmmmmmmmmmmmmm p1 working
11111111111111111111111111111111111111111111111111111111111111111111
111111111111111111111111111111111111111111111111111111 p2 working
22222222222222222222222222222222222222222222222222222222222222222222
22222222222222222222222222222222222222222222222222222222222222222222
2222222222222222222222222222222222222222222222222222222 p2
exiting ...
11111111111111111111111111111111111111111111111111111111111111111111
11 p1: exiting..
mmmmmmmmmmmmmmmmmmmmmmmmmmmmmmmmmmmmmmmmmmmmmmmmmmmmmmmmmmmmmmmmmmmmmm
mmmmmmmmmmmmmmmmmmmmmmmmmmmmmmmmmmmmmmmmmmmmmmmmmmmmmmmmmmmmmmmmmmmmmm
```

```
mmmmmmmmmmmmmmmmmmmmmmmmmmmmmmmmmmmmmmmmmmmm
main: all done, app exiting ...
$
```

Yes, using the `taskset(1)` to ensure that the whole app—all three threads—runs on the first CPU core has the desired effect. Now, study the preceding output carefully; we can see that the `main()` thread – non-real-time—runs first for about 2 seconds; once 2 seconds have elapsed, the worker thread 1 wakes up, becoming runnable. As its policy and priority far outweighs that of main(), it preempts main() and runs, printing 1s to the terminal. Remember that worker thread 2 is also running in parallel, but, of course, it sleeps for 4 seconds. So, 2 seconds later—once a total of 4 seconds have elapsed – worker thread 2 wakes up, becoming runnable. As its policy is `SCHED_FIFO` and, more importantly, its priority is 10 points higher than thread 1, it preempts thread 1 and runs, printing 2s to the terminal. Until it terminates, the other threads cannot run; once it does, worker thread 1 runs. Again, until it terminates, main() cannot run; once it does die, main() finally gets the CPU and finishes, and so the application terminates. Interesting; do try it out for yourself.

For your information, the man page on `pthread_setschedparam(3)` has a fairly detailed example program: http://man7.org/linux/man-pages/man3/pthread_setschedparam.3.html.

## Soft real-time – additional considerations

A few additional points to think about: we have the power to associate threads with a (soft) real-time policy and priority (with the caveat that we have root access; or the CAP_SYS_NICE capability). For most human interactive application domains this is not only unnecessary, but it will cause disconcerting feedback and side effects to the typical desktop or server system end user. As a general rule, you should avoid using these real-time policies on interactive applications. Only when it is essential to highly prioritize a thread—typically for a real-time application (perhaps running on an embedded Linux box), or some kinds of benchmarking or profiling software (`perf(1)` being a good example; one can specify the `--realtime=n` parameter to `perf` to have it run as `SCHED_FIFO` priority n)—should you consider using these powerful technologies.

Also, the precise real-time priorities to be used are left to the application architects; using the same priority values for `SCHED_FIFO` and `SCHED_RR` threads (recall that both policies are peers, with `SCHED_FIFO` being more aggressive) can lead to unpredictable scheduling. Carefully think about the design and accordingly set the policy and priority of each real-time thread.

Finally, though not covered in depth in this book, Linux's cgroups model allows you to powerfully control the bandwidth allocation of a resource (CPUs, network, and block I/O) for a given process or group of processes. If this is what is required, consider using the cgroups framework to achieve your goals.

# RTL – Linux as an RTOS

The fact is, incredible as it may seem, the Linux OS can be used as an RTOS; that is, a hard real-time-capable RTOS. The project started out as the brainchild of Thomas Gleixner (of Linutronix), who wanted to port Linux to become an RTOS.

> Again, this is really the beauty of the open source model and Linux; being open source, interested, and motivated people take Linux (or other projects) as a starting point and build upon it, often coming up with significantly new and useful products.

A few points to note regarding this project are as follows:

- Modifying the Linux kernel to become an RTOS is a necessarily invasive procedure; Linus Torvalds, the de facto Linux boss, does not want this code in the upstream (vanilla) Linux kernel. Thus, the real-time Linux kernel project lives as a patch series (on kernel.org itself; see the links in the *Further reading* section on the GitHub repository for more information) that can be applied upon a mainline kernel.
- This effort has been successfully undertaken right from the 2.6.18 Linux kernel (from perhaps around 2006 or 2007).
- For many years, the project was called Preempt-RT (with the patches themselves called PREEMPT_RT).
- Later (from October 2015 onward), stewardship of the project was taken over by the **Linux Foundation** (LF)—a positive step. The name was changed from Preempt RT to **real-time Linux** (RTL).
- Indeed, the RTL roadmap very much has the goal of pushing relevant PREEMPT_RT work upstream (into the mainline Linux kernel; see the *Further reading* on the GitHub repository section for a link on this).

In effect, you can apply the appropriate RTL patches and then use Linux as a hard real-time RTOS. Industry has already begun to use the project (in industrial control apps, drones, and TV cameras); we can only imagine that this will grow tremendously. It's also important to note that having a hard real-time OS is not sufficient for true real-time usage; even the applications have to be written to conform to real-time expectations. Do check out the *HOWTO* documentation provided on this by the RTL project wiki site (see the *Further reading* section on the GitHub repository).

# Summary

In this chapter, we covered important concepts related to CPU scheduling on Linux and real-time. The reader has been taken through progressive topics on the Linux thread state-machine, real-time, CPU affinity, and the available POSIX scheduling policies. Furthermore, we have shown APIs—both at the pthreads and system call layers—to exploit these powerful mechanisms. A demo application reinforced the concepts that we learned. Finally, a quick note on the fact that Linux can also be used as a hard real-time (RTOS) was covered.

In the next chapter, the reader will be shown how to achieve the best I/O performance using modern techniques.

# 18
# Advanced File I/O

In `Appendix A`, *File I/O Essentials*, we covered how an application developer can exploit the available glibc library APIs as well as the typical system calls for performing file I/O (open, read, write, and close). While they work, of course, the reality is that performance is not really optimized. In this chapter, we focus on more advanced file I/O techniques, and how the developer can exploit newer and better APIs, for gaining performance.

Often, one gets stressed about the CPU(s) and its/their performance. While important, in many (if not most) real-world application workloads, it's really not the CPU(s) that drag down performance but the I/O code paths that are the real culprit. This is quite understandable; recall, from `Chapter 2`, *Virtual Memory*, we showed that disk speed, in contrast with RAM, is orders of magnitude slower. The case is similar with network I/O; thus, it stands to reason that the real performance bottlenecks occur due to heavy sustained disk and network I/O.

In this chapter, the reader will learn several approaches to improve I/O performance; broadly speaking, these approaches will include the following:

- Taking full advantage of the kernel page cache
- Giving hints and advice to the kernel on file usage patterns
- Using scatter-gather (vectored) I/O
- Leveraging memory mapping for file I/O
- Learning about and using sophisticated DIO and AIO techniques
- Learning about I/O schedulers
- Utilities/tools/APIs/cgroups for monitoring, analysis, and bandwidth control on I/O

# I/O performance recommendations

The key point when performing I/O is realizing that the underlying storage (disk) hardware is much, much slower than RAM. So, devising strategies to minimize going to the disk and working more from memory will always help. In fact, both the library layer (we have already discussed studio buffering in some detail), and the OS (via the page cache and other features within the block I/O layers, and, in fact, even within modern hardware) will perform a lot of work to ensure this. For the (systems) application developer, a few suggestions to consider are made next.

If feasible, use large buffers (to hold the data read or to be written) when performing I/O operations upon a file—but how large? A good rule of thumb is to use the same size for the local buffer as the I/O block size of the filesystem upon which the file resides (in fact, this field is internally documented as block size for filesystem I/O). To query it is simple: issue the `stat(1)` command upon the file in which you want to perform I/O. As an example, let's say that on an Ubuntu 18.04 system we want to read in the content of the currently running kernel's configuration file:

```
$ uname -r
4.15.0-23-generic
$ ls -l /boot/config-4.15.0-23-generic
-rw-r--r-- 1 root root 216807 May 23 22:24 /boot/config-4.15.0-23-generic
$ stat /boot/config-4.15.0-23-generic
  File: /boot/config-4.15.0-23-generic
  Size: 216807    Blocks: 424    IO Block: 4096   regular file
Device: 801h/2049d   Inode: 398628      Links: 1
Access: (0644/-rw-r--r--)  Uid: (   0/   root)   Gid: (   0/   root)
Access: 2018-07-30 12:42:09.789005000 +0530
Modify: 2018-05-23 22:24:55.000000000 +0530
Change: 2018-06-17 12:36:34.259614987 +0530
 Birth: -
$
```

As can be seen from the code, `stat(1)` reveals several file characteristics (or attributes) from the file's inode data structure within the kernel, among them the I/O block size.

Internally, the `stat(1)` utility issues the `stat(2)` system call, which parses the inode of the underlying file and supplies all details to user space. So, when required programmatically, make use of the `[f]stat(2)` API(s).

Further, if memory is not a constraint, why not just allocate a moderately-to-really-large buffer and perform I/O via it; it will help. Determining how large requires some investigation on your target platform; to give you an idea, in the earlier days, pipe I/O used to use a kernel buffer of size one page; on the modern Linux kernels, the pipe I/O buffer size is increased to a megabyte by default.

## The kernel page cache

As we learned from Appendix A, *File I/O Essentials*, when a process (or thread) performs file I/O by, say, using the fread(3) or fwrite(3) library layer APIs, they ultimately are issued to the underlying OS via the read(2) and write(2) system calls. These system calls get the kernel to perform the I/O; though it seems intuitive, the reality is that the read-and-write system calls are not synchronous; that is, they may return before the actual I/O has completed. (Obviously, this will be the case for writes to a file; synchronous reads have to return the data read to the user space memory buffer; until then, the read blocks. However, using **Asynchronous I/O (AIO)**, even reads can be made asynchronous.)

The fact is, within the kernel, every single-file I/O operation is cached within a global kernel cache called the *page cache*. So, when a process writes data to a file, the data buffer is not immediately flushed to the underlying block device (disk or flash storage), it's cached in the page cache. Similarly, when a process reads data from the underlying block device, the data buffer is not instantly copied to the user space process memory buffer; no, you guessed it, it's stored within the page cache first (and the process will actually receive it from there). Refer again to Appendix A, *File I/O Essentials, Figure 3: More detail—app to stdio I/O buffer to kernel page cache*, to see this.

Why is this caching within the kernel's page cache helpful? Simple: by exploiting the key property of a cache, that it, the speed discrepancy between the cached memory region (RAM) and the region it is caching (the block device), we gain tremendous performance. The page cache is in RAM, thus keeping the contents of all file I/O cached (as far as is possible) pretty much guarantees hits on the cache when applications perform reads on file data; reading from RAM is far faster than reading from the storage device. Similarly, instead of slowly and synchronously writing application data buffers directly to the block device, the kernel caches the write data buffers within the page cache. Obviously, the work of flushing the written data to the underlying block devices and the management of the page cache memory itself is well within the Linux kernel's scope of work (we do not discuss these internal details here).

Advanced File I/O

The programmer can always explicitly flush file data to the underlying storage device; we have covered the relevant APIs and their usage back in Appendix A, *File I/O Essentials*.

# Giving hints to the kernel on file I/O patterns

We now understand that the kernel goes ahead and caches all file I/O within its page cache; this is good for performance. It's useful to think about an example: an application sets up and performs streaming reads on a very large video file (to display it within some app window to the user; we shall assume the particular video file is being accessed for the first time). It's easy to understand that, in general, caching a file as it's read from the disk helps, but here, in this particular case, it would not really help much, as, the first time, we still have to first go to the disk and read it in. So, we shrug our shoulders and continue coding it in the usual way, sequentially reading in chunks of video data (via it's underlying codec) and passing it along to the render code.

## Via the posix_fadvise(2) API

Can we do better? Yes, indeed: Linux provides the `posix_fadvise(2)` system call, allowing an application process to give hints to the kernel on it's pattern of access to file data, via a parameter called `advice`. Relevant to our example, we can pass advice as the value POSIX_FADV_SEQUENTIAL, POSIX_FADV_WILLNEED, to inform the kernel that we expect to read file data sequentially and that we expect we shall require access to the file's data in the near future. This advice causes the kernel to initiate an aggressive read-ahead of the file's data in sequential order (lower-to-higher file offsets) into the kernel page cache. This will greatly help increase performance.

The signature of the `posix_fadvise(2)` system call is as follows:

```
#include <fcntl.h>
int posix_fadvise(int fd, off_t offset, off_t len, int advice);
```

Clearly, the first parameter `fd` represents the file descriptor (we refer the reader to Appendix A, *File I/O Essentials*), and the second and third parameters, `offset` and `len`, specify a region of the file upon which we pass the hint or advice via the fourth parameter, `advice`. (The length is actually rounded up to the page granularity.)

Not only that, the application, upon finishing processing upon a chunk of video data, could even specify to the OS that it will not require that particular piece of memory any longer by invoking `posix_fadvise(2)` with advice set to the value `POSIX_FADV_DONTNEED`; this will be a hint to the kernel that it can free up the page(s) of the page cache holding that data, thereby creating space for incoming data of consequence (and for already cached data that may still be useful).

There are some caveats to be aware of. First, it's important for the developer to realize that this advice is really just a hint, a suggestion, to the OS; it may or may not be honored. Next, again, even if the target file's pages are read into the page cache, they could be evicted for various reasons, memory pressure being a typical one. There's no harm in trying though; the kernel will often take the advice into account, and it can really benefit performance. (More advice values can be looked up, as usual, within the man page pertaining to this API.)

> Interestingly, and now understandably, `cat(1)` uses the `posix_fadvise(2)` system call to inform the kernel that it intends to perform sequential reads until EOF. Using the powerful `strace(1)` utility on `cat(1)` reveals the following:
> `...fadvise64(3, 0, 0, POSIX_FADV_SEQUENTIAL) = 0`
>
> Don't get stressed with the fadvise64; it's just the underlying system call implementation on Linux for the `posix_fadvise(2)` system call. Clearly, `cat(1)` has invoked this on the file (descriptor 3), offset 0 and length 0—implying until EOF, and with the advice parameter set to `POSIX_FADV_SEQUENTIAL`.

## Via the readahead(2) API

The Linux (GNU)-specific `readahead(2)` system call achieves a similar result as the `posix_fadvise(2)` we just saw in terms of performing aggressive file read-ahead. Its signature is as follows:

```
include <fcntl.h>
ssize_t readahead(int fd, off64_t offset, size_t count);
```

The read-aheads are performed on the target file specified by `fd`, starting from the file `offset` and for a maximum of `count` bytes (rounded up to page granularity).

*Advanced File I/O*

Though not normally required, what if you want to explicitly empty (clean) the contents of the Linux kernel's page cache? If required, do this as the root user:

```
# sync && echo 1 > /proc/sys/vm/drop_caches
```

Don't miss the `sync(1)` first, or you risk losing data. Again, we stress that flushing the kernel page cache should not be done in the normal course, as this could actually hurt I/O performance. A collection of useful **command -line interface** (**CLI**) wrapper utilities called linux-ftools is available on GitHub here: `https://github.com/david415/linux-ftools`. It provides the `fincore(1)` (that's read as f-in-core), `fadvise(1)`, and `fallocate(1)` utilities; it's very educational to check out their GitHub README, read their man pages, and try them out.

## MT app file I/O with the pread, pwrite APIs

Recall the `read(2)` and `write(2)` system calls that we saw in `Appendix A`, *File I/O Essentials*; they form the basis of performing I/O to files. You will also recall that, upon using these APIs, the underlying file offset will be implicitly updated by the OS. For example, if a process opens a file (via `open(2)`), and then performs a `read(2)` of 512 bytes, the file's offset (or the so-called seek position) will now be 512. If it now writes, say, 200 bytes, the write will occur from position 512 up to position 712, thereby setting the new seek position or offset to this number.

Well, so what? Our point is simply that the file's offset being set implicitly causes issues when a multithreaded application has multiple threads simultaneously performing I/O upon the same underlying file. But wait, we have mentioned this before: the file is required to be locked and then worked upon. But, locking creates major performance bottlenecks. What if you design an MT app whose threads work upon different portions of the same file in parallel? That sounds great, except that the file's offset would keep changing and thus ruin our parallelism and thus performance (you will also recall from our discussions in `Appendix A`, *File I/O Essentials*, that simply using `lseek(2)` to set the file's seek position explicitly can result in dangerous races).

So, what do you do? Linux provides the `pread(2)` and `pwrite(2)` system calls (p for positioned I/O) for this very purpose; with these APIs, the file offset to perform I/O at can be specified (or positioned) and the actual underlying file offset is not changed by the OS. Their signature is as follows:

```
#include <unistd.h>
ssize_t pread(int fd, void *buf, size_t count, off_t offset);
ssize_t pwrite(int fd, const void *buf, size_t count, off_t offset);
```

The difference between the `pread(2)`/`pwrite(2)` and the usual `read(2)`/`write(2)` system calls is that the former APIs take an additional fourth parameter—the file offset at which to perform the read or write I/O operation, without modifying it. This allows us to achieve what we wanted: having an MT app perform high-performance I/O by having multiple threads simultaneously read and write to different portions of the file in parallel. (We leave the task of trying this out as an interesting exercise to the reader.)

A few caveats to be aware of: first, just as with `read(2)` and `write(2)`, `pread(2)`, and `pwrite(2)` too can return without having transferred all requested bytes; it is the programmer's responsibility to check and call the APIs in a loop until no bytes remain to transfer (revisit Appendix A, *File I/O Essentials*). Correctly using the read/write APIs, where issues such as this are addressed). Secondly, when a file is opened with the `O_APPEND` flag specified, Linux's `pwrite(2)` system call always appends data to the EOF irrespective of the current offset value; this violates the POSIX standard, which states that the `O_APPEND` flag should have no effect on the start location where the write occurs. Thirdly, and quite obviously (but we must state it), the file being operated upon must be capable of being seeked upon (that is, the `fseek(3)` or `lseek(2)` APIs are supported). Regular files always do support the seek operation, but pipes and some types of devices do not).

*Advanced File I/O*

# Scatter – gather I/O

To help explain this topic, let's say that we are commissioned with writing data to a file such that three discontiguous data regions A, B, and C are written (filled with As, Bs, and Cs, respectively); the following diagram shows this:

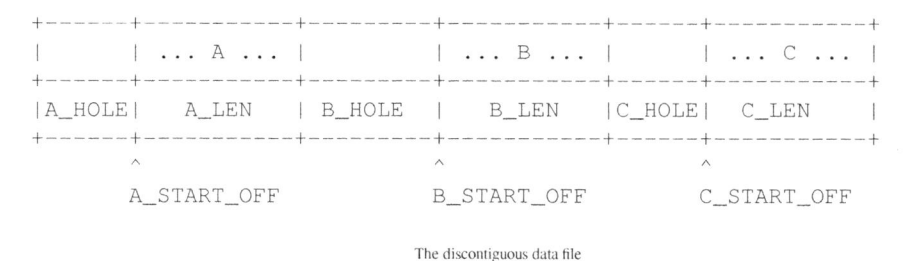

```
+------+-----------+---------+------------+------+-----------+
|      |   ... A ...|         |   ... B ...|      |   ... C ...|
+------+-----------+---------+------------+------+-----------+
|A_HOLE|   A_LEN   | B_HOLE  |   B_LEN    |C_HOLE|   C_LEN   |
+------+-----------+---------+------------+------+-----------+
       ^                     ^                   ^
       A_START_OFF           B_START_OFF         C_START_OFF
```

The discontiguous data file

Notice how the files have holes—regions that do not contain any data content; this is possible to achieve with regular files (files that are largely holes are termed sparse files). How do you create the hole? Simple: just perform an `lseek(2)` and then `write(2)` data; the length seeked forward determines the size of the hole in the file.

So, how can we achieve this data file layout as shown? We shall show two approaches—one, the traditional manner, and two, a far more optimized-for-performance approach. Let's get started with the traditional approach.

## Discontiguous data file – traditional approach

This seems quite simple: first seek to the required start offset and then write the data content for the required length; this can be done via the pair of `lseek(2)` and `write(2)` system calls. Of course, we will have to invoke this pair of system calls three times. So, we write some code to actually perform this task; see the (relevant snippets) of the code here (`ch18/sgio_simple.c`):

> For readability, only key parts of the source code are displayed; to view the complete source code, build, and run it, the entire tree is available for cloning from GitHub here: https://github.com/PacktPublishing/Hands-on-System-Programming-with-Linux.

```
#define A_HOLE_LEN    10
#define A_START_OFF   A_HOLE_LEN
#define A_LEN         20

#define B_HOLE_LEN    100
```

```
#define B_START_OFF  (A_HOLE_LEN+A_LEN+B_HOLE_LEN)
#define B_LEN        30

#define C_HOLE_LEN   20
#define C_START_OFF  (A_HOLE_LEN+A_LEN+B_HOLE_LEN+B_LEN+C_HOLE_LEN)
#define C_LEN        42
...
static int wr_discontig_the_normal_way(int fd)
{ ...
    /* A: {seek_to A_START_OFF, write gbufA for A_LEN bytes} */
    if (lseek(fd, A_START_OFF, SEEK_SET) < 0)
        FATAL("lseek A failed\n");
    if (write(fd, gbufA, A_LEN) < 0)
        FATAL("write A failed\n");

    /* B: {seek_to B_START_OFF, write gbufB for B_LEN bytes} */
    if (lseek(fd, B_START_OFF, SEEK_SET) < 0)
        FATAL("lseek B failed\n");
    if (write(fd, gbufB, B_LEN) < 0)
        FATAL("write B failed\n");

    /* C: {seek_to C_START_OFF, write gbufC for C_LEN bytes} */
    if (lseek(fd, C_START_OFF, SEEK_SET) < 0)
        FATAL("lseek C failed\n");
    if (write(fd, gbufC, C_LEN) < 0)
        FATAL("write C failed\n");
    return 0;
}
```

Notice how we have written the code to use an {lseek, write} pair of system calls three times in succession; let's try it out:

```
$ ./sgio_simple
Usage: ./sgio_simple use-method-option
 0 = traditional lseek/write method
 1 = better SG IO method
$ ./sgio_simple 0
In setup_buffers_goto()
In wr_discontig_the_normal_way()
$ ls -l tmptest
-rw-rw-r--. 1 kai kai 222 Oct 16 08:45 tmptest
$ hexdump -x tmptest
0000000 0000 0000 0000 0000 0000 4141 4141 4141
0000010 4141 4141 4141 4141 4141 4141 4141 0000
0000020 0000 0000 0000 0000 0000 0000 0000 0000
*
0000080 0000 4242 4242 4242 4242 4242 4242 4242
0000090 4242 4242 4242 4242 4242 4242 4242 4242
```

*Advanced File I/O*

```
00000a0  0000 0000 0000 0000 0000 0000 0000 0000
00000b0  0000 0000 4343 4343 4343 4343 4343 4343
00000c0  4343 4343 4343 4343 4343 4343 4343 4343
00000d0  4343 4343 4343 4343 4343 4343 4343
00000de
$
```

It worked; the file we created, tmptest (we have not shown the code to create the file, allocate and initialize the buffers, and so on, here; please look it up via the book's GitHub repository), is of length 222 bytes, although the actual data content (the As, Bs, and Cs) is of length 20+30+42 = 92 bytes. The remaining (222 - 92) 130 bytes are the three holes in the file (of length 10+100+20 bytes; see the macros that define these in the code). The hexdump(1) utility conveniently dumps the file's content; 0x41 being A, 0x42 is B, and 0x43 is C. The holes are clearly seen as NULL-populated regions of the length we wanted.

## Discontiguous data file – the SG – I/O approach

The traditional approach using the {lseek, write} pair of system calls three times in succession worked, of course, but at a rather large performance penalty; the fact is, issuing system calls is considered very expensive. A far superior approach performance-wise is called *scatter-gather I/O* (SG-I/O, or vectored I/O). The relevant system calls are readv(2) and writev(2); this is their signature:

```
#include <sys/uio.h>
ssize_t readv(int fd, const struct iovec *iov, int iovcnt);
ssize_t writev(int fd, const struct iovec *iov, int iovcnt);
```

These system calls allow you to specify a bunch of segments to read or write in one shot; each segment describes a single I/O operation via a structure called iovec:

```
struct iovec {
    void *iov_base; /* Starting address */
    size_t iov_len; /* Number of bytes to transfer */
};
```

The programmer can pass along an array of segments describing the I/O operations to perform; this is precisely the second parameter—a pointer to an array of struct iovecs; the third parameter is the number of segments to process. The first parameter is obvious—the file descriptor representing the file upon which to perform the gathered read or scattered write.

## Chapter 18

So, think about it: you can gather together discontiguous reads from a given file into buffers (and their sizes) you specify via the I/O vector pointer, and you can scatter discontiguous writes to a given file from buffers (and their sizes) you specify via the I/O vector pointer; these types of multiple discontiguous I/O operations are thus called scatter-gather I/O! Here is the really cool part: the system calls are guaranteed to perform these I/O operations in array order and atomically; that is, they will return only when all operations are done. Again, though, watch out: the return value from readv(2) or writev(2) is the actual number of bytes read or written, and -1 on failure. It's always possible that an I/O operation performs less than the amount requested; this is not a failure, and it's up to the developer to check.

Now, for our earlier data file example, let's look at the code that sets up and performs the discontiguous scattered ordered-and-atomic writes via writev(2):

```
static int wr_discontig_the_better_SGIO_way(int fd)
{
  struct iovec iov[6];
  int i=0;

  /* We don't want to call lseek of course; so we emulate the seek
   * by introducing segments that are just "holes" in the file. */

  /* A: {seek_to A_START_OFF, write gbufA for A_LEN bytes} */
  iov[i].iov_base = gbuf_hole;
  iov[i].iov_len = A_HOLE_LEN;
  i ++;
  iov[i].iov_base = gbufA;
  iov[i].iov_len = A_LEN;

  /* B: {seek_to B_START_OFF, write gbufB for B_LEN bytes} */
  i ++;
  iov[i].iov_base = gbuf_hole;
  iov[i].iov_len = B_HOLE_LEN;
  i ++;
  iov[i].iov_base = gbufB;
  iov[i].iov_len = B_LEN;

  /* C: {seek_to C_START_OFF, write gbufC for C_LEN bytes} */
  i ++;
  iov[i].iov_base = gbuf_hole;
  iov[i].iov_len = C_HOLE_LEN;
  i ++;
  iov[i].iov_base = gbufC;
  iov[i].iov_len = C_LEN;
  i ++;
```

*Advanced File I/O*

```
    /* Perform all six discontiguous writes in order and atomically! */
    if (writev(fd, iov, i) < 0)
        return -1;
/* Do note! As mentioned in Ch 19:
   * "the return value from readv(2) or writev(2) is the actual number
   * of bytes read or written, and -1 on failure. It's always possible
   * that an I/O operation performs less than the amount requested;
this
   * is not a failure, and it's up to the developer to check."
   * Above, we have _not_ checked; we leave it as an exercise to the
   * interested reader to modify this code to check for and read/write
   * any remaining bytes (similar to this example: ch7/simpcp2.c).
   */
    return 0;
}
```

The end result is identical to that of the traditional approach; we leave it to the reader to try it out and see. This is the key point: the traditional approach had us issuing a minimum of six system calls (3 x {lseek, write} pairs) to perform the discontiguous data writes into the file, whereas the SG-I/O code performs the very same discontiguous data writes with just one system call. This results in significant performance gains, especially for applications under heavy I/O workloads.

> The interested reader, delving into the full source code of the previous example program (ch18/sgio_simple.c) will notice something that perhaps seems peculiar (or even just wrong): the blatant use of the controversial goto statement! The fact, though, is that the goto can be very useful in error handling—performing the code cleanup required when exiting a deep-nested path within a function due to failure. Please check out the links provided in the *Further reading* section on the GitHub repository for more. The Linux kernel community has been quite happily using the goto for a long while now; we urge developers to look into appropriate usage of the same.

[ 730 ]

## SG – I/O variations

Recall from the *MT app file I/O with the pread, pwrite APIs* section, we could use the `pread(2)` and `pwrite(2)` system calls to effectively perform file I/O in parallel via multiple threads (in a multithreaded app). Similarly, Linux provides the `preadv(2)` and the `pwritev(2)` system calls; as you can guess, they provide the functionality of the `readv(2)` and `writev(2)` with the addition of a fourth parameter offset; just as with the `readv(2)` and `writev(2)`, the file offset at which SG-IO is to be performed can be specified and it will not be changed (again, perhaps useful for an MT application). The signature of the `preadv(2)` and `pwritev(2)` is shown here:

```
#include <sys/uio.h>
ssize_t preadv(int fd, const struct iovec *iov, int iovcnt,
               off_t offset);
ssize_t pwritev(int fd, const struct iovec *iov, int iovcnt,
                off_t offset);
```

Recent Linux kernels (version 4.6 onward for some) also provide a further variation on the APIs: the `preadv2(2)` and the `pwritev2(2)` system calls. The difference from the previous APIs is that they take an additional fifth parameter flag allowing the developer to have more control over the behavior of the SG-I/O operations by being able to specify whether they are synchronous (via the RWF_DSYNC and the RWF_SYNC flags), high-priority (via the RWF_HIPRI flag), or non-blocking (via the RWF_NOWAIT flag). We refer the reader to the man page on `preadv2(2)`/`pwritev2(2)` for details.

## File I/O via memory mapping

Both in Appendix A, *File I/O Essentials*, and in this chapter, we have on several occasions mentioned how the Linux kernel's page cache helps greatly enhance performance by caching the content of files within it (alleviating the need to each time go to the really slow storage device and instead just read or write data chunks within RAM). However, though we gain performance via the page cache, there remains a hidden problem with using both the traditional `read(2)`, `write(2)` APIs or even the faster SG-I/O (the `[p][read|write][v][2](2)`) APIs.

*Advanced File I/O*

# The Linux I/O code path in brief

To understand what the issue is, we must first gain a bit of a deeper understanding of how the I/O code path actually works; the following diagram encapsulates the points of relevance:

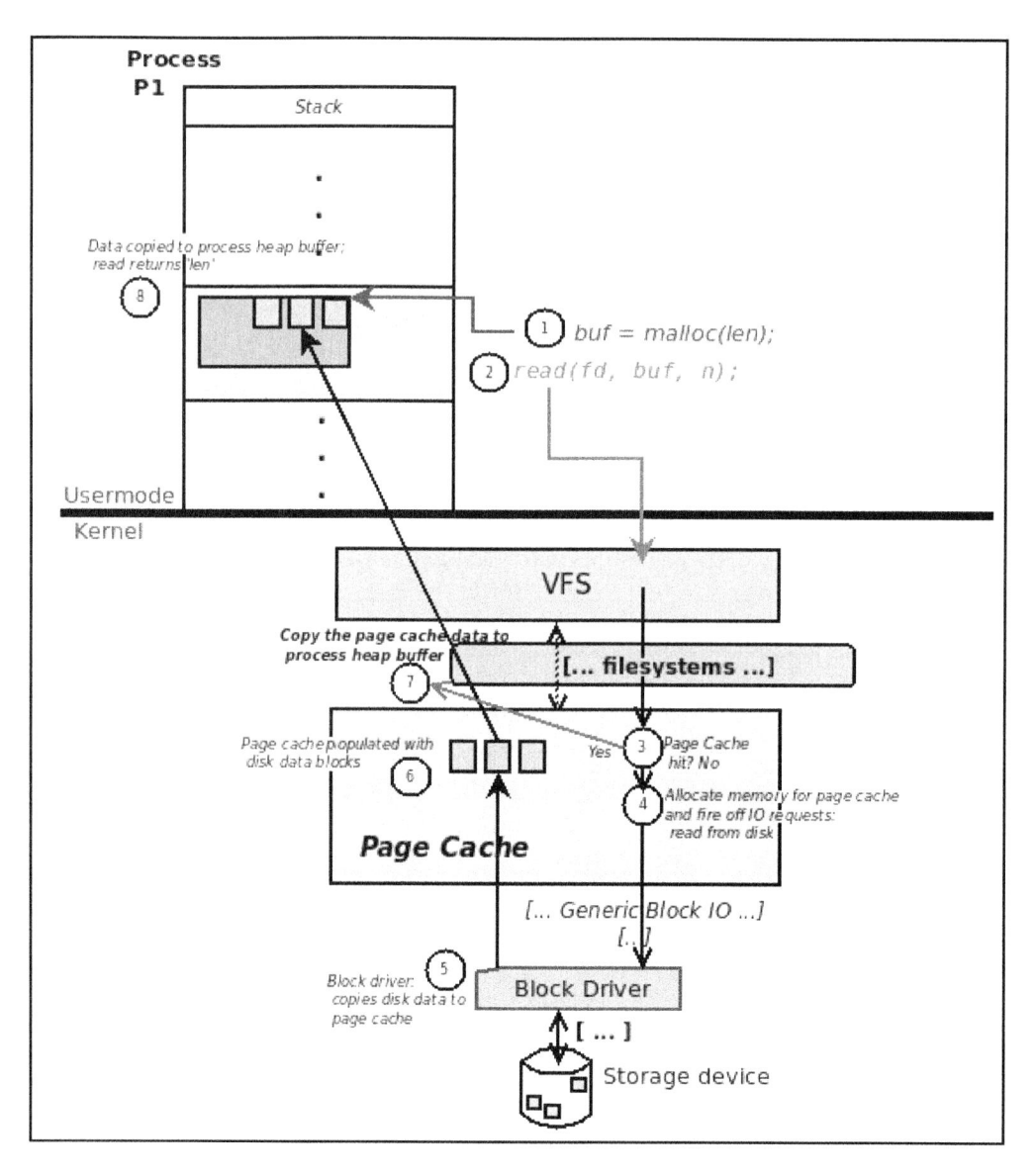

Figure 1: Page cache populated with disk data

> The reader should realize that though this diagram seems quite detailed, we're actually seeing a rather simplistic view of the entire Linux I/O code path (or I/O stack), only what is relevant to this discussion. For a more detailed overview (and diagram), please see the link provided in the *Further reading* section on the GitHub repository.

Let's say that a **Process P1** intends to read some 12 KB of data from a target file that it has open (via the `open(2)` system call); we envision that it does so via the usual manner:

- Allocate a heap buffer of 12 KB (3 pages = 12,288 bytes) via the `malloc(3)` API.
- Issue the `read(2)` system call to read in the data from the file into the heap buffer.
  - The `read(2)` system call performs the work within the OS; when the read is done, it returns (hopefully the value `12,288`; remember, it's the programmer's job to check this and not assume anything).

This sounds simple, but there's a lot more that happens under the hood, and it is in our interest to dig a little deeper. Here's a more detailed view of what happens (the numerical points **1**, **2**, and **3** are shown in a circle in the previous diagram; follow along):

1. **Process P1** allocates a heap buffer of 12 KB via the `malloc(3)` API (len = 12 KB = 12,288 bytes).
2. Next, it issues a `read(2)` system call to read data from the file (specified by fd) into the heap buffer buf just allocated, for length 12 KB.
3. As `read(2)` is a system call, the process (or thread) now switches to kernel mode (remember the monolithic design we covered back in Chapter 1, *Linux System Architecture*); it enters the Linux kernel's generic filesystem layer (called the **Virtual Filesystem Switch** (**VFS**)), from where it will be auto-shunted on to its appropriate underlying filesystem driver (perhaps the ext4 fs), after which the Linux kernel will first check: are these pages of the required file data already cached in our page cache? If yes, the job is done, (we short circuit to *step 7*), just copy back the pages to the user space buffer. Let's say we get a cache miss—the required file data pages aren't in the page cache.

*Advanced File I/O*

4. Thus, the kernel first allocates sufficient RAM (page frames) for the page cache (in our example, three frames, shown as pink squares within the page cache memory region). It then fires off appropriate I/O requests to the underlying layers requesting the file data.
5. The request ultimately ends up at the block (storage) driver; we assume it knows its job and reads the required data blocks from the underlying storage device controller (a disk or flash controller chip, perhaps). It then (here's the interesting thing) is given a destination address to write the file data to; it's the address of the page frames allocated (step 4) within the page cache; thus, the block driver always writes the file data into the kernel's page cache and never directly back to the user mode process buffers.
6. The block driver has successfully copied the data blocks from the storage device (or whatever) into the previously allocated frames within the kernel page cache. (In reality, these data transfers are highly optimized via an advanced memory transfer technique called **Direct Memory Access (DMA)**, wherein, essentially, the driver exploits the hardware to directly transfer data to and from the device and system memory without the CPU's intervention. Obviously, these topics are well beyond the scope of this book.)
7. The just-populated kernel page cache frames are now copied into the user space heap buffer by the kernel.
8. The (blocking) `read(2)` system call now terminates, returning the value 12,288 indicating that all three pages of file data have indeed been transferred (again, you, the app developer, are supposed to check this return value and not assume anything).

It's all looking great, yes? Well, not really; think carefully on this: though the read(2) (or pread[v][2](2)) API did succeed, this success came at a considerable price: the kernel had to allocate RAM (page frames) in order to hold the file data within its page cache (step 4) and, once data transfer was done (step 6) then copied that content into the user space heap memory (step 7). Thus, we have used twice the amount of RAM that we should have by keeping an extra copy of the data. This is highly wasteful, and, obviously, the multiple copying around of the data buffers between the block driver to the kernel page cache and then the kernel page cache to the user space heap buffer, reduces performance as well (not to mention that the CPU caches get unnecessarily caught up with all this trashing their content). With the previous pattern of code, the issue of not waiting for the slow storage device is taken care of (via the page cache efficiencies), but everything else is really poor—we have actually doubled the required memory usage and the CPU caches are overwritten with (unnecessary) file data while copying takes place.

## Memory mapping a file for I/O

Here is a solution to these issues: memory mapping via the mmap(2) system call. Linux provides the very powerful mmap(2) system call; it enables the developer to map any content directly into the process **virtual address space (VAS)**. This content includes file data, hardware device (adapter) memory regions, or just generic memory regions. In this chapter, we shall only focus on using mmap(2) to map in a regular file's content into the process VAS. Before getting into how the mmap(2) becomes a solution to the memory wastage issue we just discussed, we first need to understand more about using the mmap(2) system call itself.

The signature of the mmap(2) system call is shown here:

```
#include <sys/mman.h>
void *mmap(void *addr, size_t length, int prot, int flags,
           int fd, off_t offset);
```

*Advanced File I/O*

We want to map a given region of a file, from a given offset and for length bytes into our process VAS; a simplistic view of what we want to achieve is depicted in this diagram:

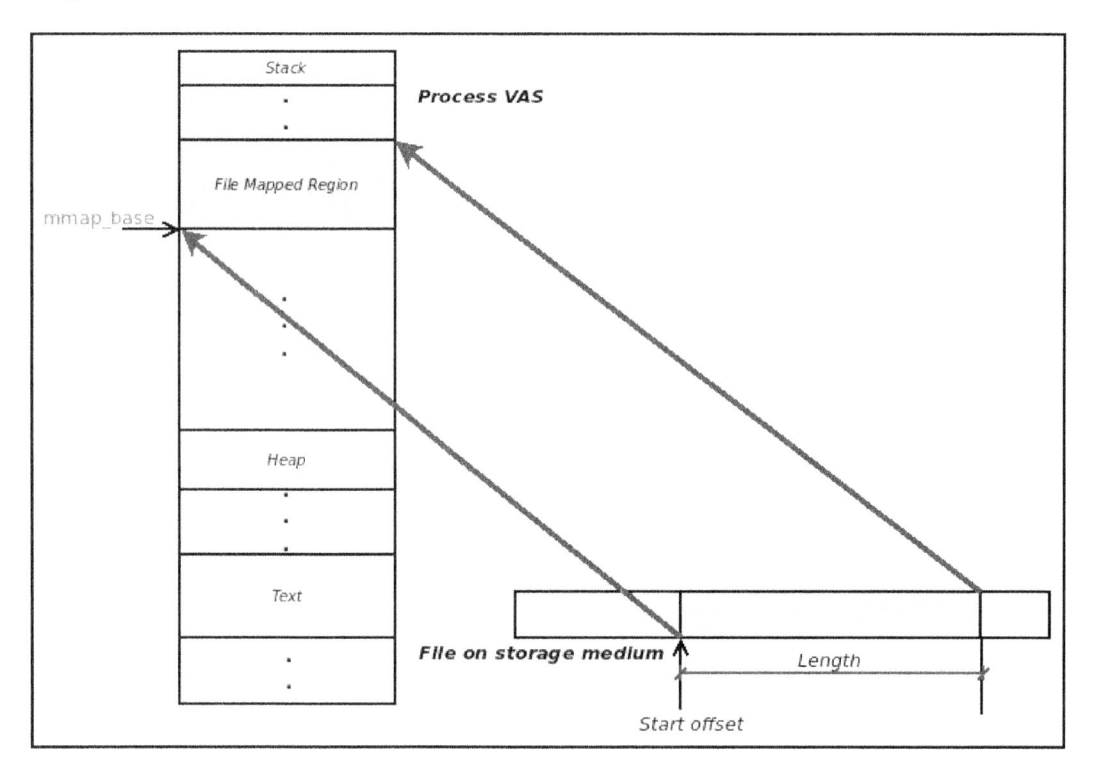

Figure 2: Memory mapping a file region into process VAS

To achieve this file mapping to process VAS, we use the mmap(2) system call. Glancing at its signature, it's quite obvious what we need to do first: open the file to be mapped via the open(2) (in the appropriate mode: read-only or read-write, depending on what you want to do), thereby obtaining a file descriptor; pass this descriptor as the fifth parameter to mmap(2). The file region to be mapped into the process VAS can be specified via the sixth and second parameters respectively—the file offset at which the mapping should begin and the length (in bytes).

The first parameter, `addr`, is a hint to the kernel as to where in the process VAS the mapping should be created; the recommendation is to pass 0 (NULL) here, allowing the OS to decide the location of the new mapping. This is the correct portable way to use the `mmap(2)`; however, some applications (and, yes, some malicious security hacks too!) use this parameter to try to predict where the mapping will occur. In any case, the actual (virtual) address where the mapping is created within the process VAS is the return value from the `mmap(2)`; a NULL return indicates failure and must be checked for.

> Here is an interesting technique to fix the location of the mapping: first perform a `malloc(3)` of the required mapping size and pass the return value from this `malloc(3)` to the `mmap(2)`'s first parameter (also set the flags parameter to include the MAP_FIXED bit)! This will probably work if the length is above MMAP_THRESHOLD (128 KB by default) and the size is a multiple of the system page size. Note, again, this technique is not portable and may or may not work.

Another point to note is that most mappings—and always file mappings—are performed to page granularity, that is, in multiples of the page size; thus, the return address is usually page-aligned.

The third parameter to `mmap(2)` is an integer bitmask `prot`—the memory protections of the given region (recall we have already come across memory protections in Chapter 4, *Dynamic Memory Allocation*, in the *Memory protection* section). The `prot` parameter is a bitmask and can either be just the PROT_NONE bit (implying no permissions) or the bitwise OR of the remainder; this table enumerates the bits and their meaning:

| Protection bit | Meaning |
| --- | --- |
| PROT_NONE | No access allowed on the page(s) |
| PROT_READ | Reads allowed on the page(s) |
| PROT_WRITE | Writes allowed on the page(s) |
| PROT_EXEC | Execute access allowed on the page(s) |

mmap(2) protection bits

*Advanced File I/O*

The page protections must match those of the file's `open(2)`, of course. Also note that, on older x86 systems, writable memory used to imply readable memory (that is, `PROT_WRITE => PROT_READ`). This is no longer the case; you must explicitly specify whether the mapped pages are readable or not (the same holds true for executable pages too: it must be specified, the text segment being the canonical example). Why would you use PROT_NONE? A guard page is one realistic example (recall the *Stack guards* section from `Chapter 14`, *Multithreading with Pthreads Part I - Essentials*).

## File and anonymous mappings

The next point to understand is that there are broadly two types of mappings; a file-mapped region or an anonymous region. A file-mapped region quite obviously maps the (full, or partial) content of a file (as shown in the previous figure). We think of the region as being backed by a file; that is, if the OS runs short of memory and decides to reclaim some of the file-mapped pages, it need not write them to the swap partition—they're already available within the file that was mapped. On the other hand, an anonymous mapping is a mapping whose content is dynamic; the data segments (initialized data, BSS, heap), the data sections of library mappings, and the process (or thread) stack(s) are excellent examples of anonymous mappings. Think of them as not being file-backed; thus, if memory runs short, their pages may indeed be written to swap by the OS. Also, recall what we learned back in `Chapter 4`, *Dynamic Memory Allocation*, regarding the `malloc(3)`; the fact is that the glibc `malloc(3)` engine uses the heap segment to service the allocation only when it's for a small amount—less than MMAP_THRESHOLD (defaults to 128 KB). Any `malloc(3)` above that will result in `mmap(2)` being internally invoked to set up an anonymous memory region—a mapping!—of the required size. These mappings (or segments) will live in the available virtual address space between the top of the heap and the stack of main.

Back to the mmap(2): the fourth parameter is a bitmask called flags; there are several flags, and they affect many attributes of the mapping. Among them, two flags determine the privacy of the mapping and are mutually exclusive (you can only use any one of them at a time):

- **MAP_SHARED**: The mapping is a shared one; other processes might work on the same mapping simultaneously (this, in fact, is the generic manner in which a common IPC mechanism—shared memory—can be implemented). In the case of a file mapping, if the memory region is written to, the underlying file is updated! (You can use the msync(2) to control the flushing of in-memory writes to the underlying file.)
- **MAP_PRIVATE**: This sets up a private mapping; if it's writable, it implies COW semantics (leading to optimal memory usage, as explained in Chapter 10, *Process Creation*). A file-mapped region that is private will not carry through writes to the underlying file. Actually, a private file-mapping is very common on Linux: this is precisely how, at the time of starting to execute a process, the loader (see the information box) brings in the text and data of both the binary executable as well as the text and data of all shared libraries that the process uses.

> The reality is that when a process runs, control first goes to a program embedded into your a.out binary executable—the loader (ld.so or ld-linux[-*].so). It performs the key work of setting up the C runtime environment: it memory maps (via the mmap(2)) the text (code) and initialized data segments from the binary executable file into the process, thereby creating the segments in the VAS that we have been talking about since Chapter 2, *Virtual Memory*. Further, it sets up the initialized data segment, the BSS, the heap, and the stack (of main()), and then it looks for and memory maps all shared libraries into the process VAS.
>
> Try performing a strace(1) on a program; you will see (early in the execution) all the mmap(2) system calls setting up the process VAS! The mmap(2) is critical to Linux: in effect, the entire setup of the process VAS, the segments or mappings—both at process startup as well as later—are all done via the mmap(2) system call.

Advanced File I/O

To help get these important facts clear, we show some (truncated) output of running `strace(1)` upon `ls(1)`; (for example) see how the `open(2)` is done upon glibc, file descriptor 3 is returned, and that in turn is used by the `mmap(2)` to create a private file-mapped read-only mapping of glibc's code (we can tell by seeing that the offset in the first `mmap` is 0) in the process VAS! (A detail: the `open(2)` becomes the `openat(2)` function within the kernel; ignore that, just as quite often on Linux, the `mmap(2)` becomes `mmap2(2)`.) The `strace(1)` (truncated) output follows:

```
$ strace -e trace=openat,mmap ls > /dev/null
...
openat(AT_FDCWD, "/lib/x86_64-linux-gnu/libc.so.6",
O_RDONLY|O_CLOEXEC) = 3
mmap(NULL, 4131552, PROT_READ|PROT_EXEC, MAP_PRIVATE|MAP_DENYWRITE, 3,
0) = 0x7f963d8a5000
mmap(0x7f963dc8c000, 24576, PROT_READ|PROT_WRITE,
MAP_PRIVATE|MAP_FIXED|MAP_DENYWRITE, 3, 0x1e7000) = 0x7f963dc8c000
...
```

> The kernel maintains a data structure called the **virtual memory area** (**VMA**) for each such mapping per process; the proc filesystem reveals all mappings to us in user space via `/proc/PID/maps`. Do take a look; you will literally see the virtual memory map of the process user space. (Try `sudo cat /proc/self/maps` to see the map of the cat process itself.) The man page on `proc(5)` explains in detail how to interpret this map; please take a look.

## The mmap advantage

Now that we understand how to use the `mmap(2)` system call, we revisit our earlier discussion: recall, using the `read(2)`/`write(2)` or even the SG-I/O type APIs (the `[p]readv|writev[2](2)`) resulted in a double-copy; memory wastage (plus the fact that CPU caches get trashed as well).

The key to realizing why the `mmap(2)` so effectively solves this serious issue is this: the `mmap(2)` sets up a file mapping by internally mapping the kernel page caches pages that contain the file data (that was read in from the storage device) directly into the process virtual address space. This diagram (*Figure 3*) puts this into perspective (and makes it self-explanatory):

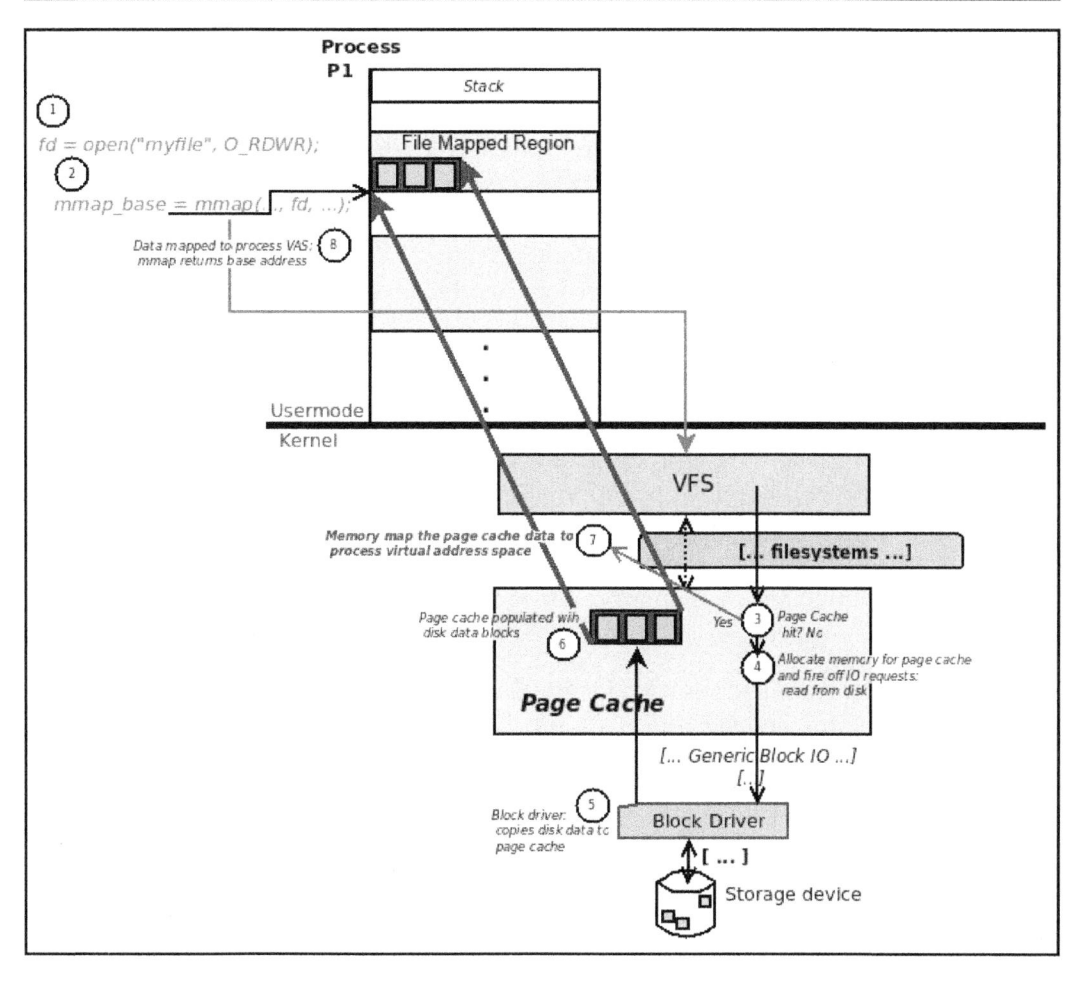

Figure 3: Page cache populated with disk data

A mapping is not a copy; thus mmap(2)-based file I/O is called a zero-copy technique: a way of performing work on an I/O buffer of which exactly one copy is maintained by the kernel in it's page cache; no more copies are required.

> The fact is that the device driver authors look to optimize their data path using zero-copy techniques, of which the mmap(2) is certainly a candidate. See more on this interesting advanced topic within links provided in the *Further reading* section on the GitHub repository.

Advanced File I/O

The mmap(2) does incur significant overhead in setting up the mapping (the first time), but, once done, I/O is very quick, as it is essentially performed in memory. Think about it: to seek to a location within the file and perform I/O there, just use your regular 'C' code to move to a given location from the mmap(2) return value (it's just a pointer offset) and do the I/O work in memory itself (via the memcpy(3), s[n]printf(3), or whatever you prefer); no lseek(2), no read(2)/write(2), or SG-I/O system call overheads at all. Using the mmap(2) for very small amounts of I/O work may not be optimal; it's usage is recommended when large and continuous I/O workloads are indicated.

## Code example

To aid the reader in working with the mmap(2) for the purpose of file I/O, we have provided the code of a simple application; it memory maps a given file (the file's pathname, start offset, and length are provided as parameters) via the mmap(2) and hexdumps (using a, slightly enhanced, open source hexdump function) the memory region specified on to stdout. We urge the reader to look up the code, build, and try it out.

> The complete source code for this book is available for cloning from GitHub here: https://github.com/PacktPublishing/Hands-on-System-Programming-with-Linux. The aforementioned program is here within the source tree: ch18/mmap_file_simple.c.

## Memory mapping – additional points

A quick summation of a few additional points to wrap up the memory mapping discussion follows:

- The fourth parameter to mmap(2), flags, can take on several other (quite interesting) values; we refer the reader to the man page on mmap(2) to browse through them: http://man7.org/linux/man-pages/man2/mmap.2.html.

- Directly analogous to how we can give hints or advice to the kernel regarding kernel page cache pages with the `posix_fadvise(2)` API, you can provide similar hints or advice to the kernel regarding memory usage patterns for a given memory range (start address, length provided) via the `posix_madvise(3)` library API. The advice values include being able to say that we expect random access to data (thereby reducing read-ahead, via the `POSIX_MADV_RANDOM` bit), or that we expect to access data in the specified range soon (via the `POSIX_MADV_WILLNEED` bit, resulting in more read-ahead and mapping). This routine invokes the underlying system call `madvise(2)` on Linux.
- Let's say we have mapped a region of a file into our process address space; how do we know which pages of the mapping are currently residing in the kernel page (or buffer) cache? Precisely this can be determined via the `mincore(2)` system call (read as "m-in-core").
- The programmer has explicit (and fine-tuned) control over synchronizing (flushing) file-mapped regions (back to the file) via the `msync(2)` system call.
- Once complete, the memory mapping should be unmapped via the `munmap(2)` system call; the parameters are the base address of the mapping (the return value from `mmap(2)`) and the length. If the process terminates, the mapping is implicitly unmapped.
- On `fork(2)`, a memory mapping is inherited by the child process.
- What if an enormous file is memory mapped, and at runtime when allocating page frames to hold the mapping in the process VAS (recall our discussion on demand-paging from Chapter 4, *Dynamic Memory Allocation*), the system runs out of memory (drastic, but it could occur); in cases such as these, the process will receive the `SIGSEGV` signal (and thus it's up to the app's signal-handling ability to gracefully terminate).

## DIO and AIO

A significant downside of using both the blocking `[p]read[v](2)` / `[p]write[v](2)` APIs as well as the `mmap(2)` (actually much more so with the `mmap`) is this: they depend on the kernel page cache always being populated with the file's pages (that it's working upon or mapping). If this is not the case—which can happen when the data store is much larger than RAM size (that it, files can be enormous)—it will result in a lot of meta-work by the kernel **memory management** (**mm**) code to bring in pages from disk to page cache, allocating frames, stitching up page table entries for them, and so on. Thus, the `mmap` technique works best when the ratio of RAM to storage is as close to 1:1 as possible. When the storage size is much larger than the RAM (often the case with enterprise-scale software such as databases, cloud virtualization at scale, and so on), it can suffer from latencies caused by all the meta work, plus the fact that significant amounts of memory will be used for paging metadata.

Two I/O technologies—DIO and AIO—alleviate these issues (at the cost of complexity); we provide a brief note on them next. (Due to space constraints, we focus on the conceptual side of these topics; learning to use the relevant APIs is then a relatively easy task. Do refer to the *Further reading* section on the GitHub repository.)

## Direct I/O (DIO)

An interesting I/O technology is **Direct I/O (DIO)**; to use it, specify the `O_DIRECT` flag when opening the file via the `open(2)` system call.

With DIO, the kernel page cache is completely bypassed, thereby immediately giving the benefit that all the issues that can be faced with the `mmap` technique now disappear. On the other hand, this does imply that the entire cache management is to be completely handled by the user space app (large projects such as databases would certainly require caching!). For regular small apps with no special I/O requirements, using DIO will likely degrade performance; be careful, test your workload under stress, and determine whether to use DIO or skip it.

Traditionally, the kernel handles which pieces of I/O (the I/O requests) are serviced when—in other words, I/O scheduling (it's not directly related, but also see the section on *I/O schedulers*). With DIO (and with AIO, seen next), the application developer can essentially take over I/O scheduling by determining when to perform I/O. This can be both a blessing and a curse: it provides the flexibility to the (sophisticated) app developer to design and implement I/O scheduling, but this is not a trivial thing to perform well; as usual, it's a trade-off.

Also, you should realize that though we call the I/O path direct, it does not guarantee that writes are immediately flushed to the underlying storage medium; that's a separate feature, one that can be requested by specifying the `O_SYNC` flag to the `open(2)` or of course explicitly flushing (via the `[f]sync(2)` system calls).

## Asynchronous I/O (AIO)

**Asynchronous I/O (AIO)** is a modern high-performance asynchronous non-blocking I/O technology that Linux implements. Think about it: non-blocking and asynchronous implies that an application thread can issue a read (for file or network data); the usermode API returns immediately; the I/O is queued up within the kernel; the application thread can continue working on CPU-bound stuff; once the I/O request completes, the kernel notifies the thread that the read is ready; the thread then actually performs the read. This is high-performance—the app does not remain blocked on I/O and can instead perform useful work while the I/O request is processed; not only that, it is asynchronously notified when the I/O work is done. (On the other hand, the multiplexing APIs such as `select(2)`, `poll(2)`, and `epoll(7)` are asynchronous—you can issue the system call and return immediately—but they actually are still blocking in nature because the thread must check for I/O completion—for example, by using the `poll(2)` in tandem with a `read(2)` system call when it returns—which is still a blocking operation.)

With AIO, a thread can initiate multiple I/O transfers concurrently; each transfer will require a context—called the *[a]iocb*—the [async] I/O control block data structure (Linux calls the structure an iocb, the POSIX AIO framework (a wrapper library) calls it aiocb). The [a]iocb structure contains the file descriptor, the data buffer, the async event notification structure `sigevent`, and so on. The alert reader will recall that we have already made use of this powerful `sigevent` structure in Chapter 13, *Timers*, within the *Creating and using a POSIX (interval) timer* section. It's really via this `sigevent` structure that the asynchronous notification mechanism is implemented (we had used it in Chapter 13, *Timers*, to be asynchronously informed that our timer expired; this was done by setting `sigevent.sigev_notify` to the value `SIGEV_SIGNAL`, thereby receiving a signal upon timer expiry). Linux exposes five system calls for the app developer to exploit AIO; they are as follows: `io_setup(2)`, `io_submit(2)`, `io_cancel(2)`, `io_getevents(2)`, and `io_destroy(2)`.

Advanced File I/O

AIO wrapper APIs are provided by two libraries—libaio and librt (which is released along with glibc); you can use their wrappers which will ultimately invoke the system calls of course. There are also the POSIX AIO wrappers; see the man page on `aio(7)` for an overview on using it, as well as example code. (Also see the articles in the *Further reading* section on the GitHub repository for more details and example code.)

## I/O technologies – a quick comparison

The following table provides a quick comparison to some of the more salient comparison points between the four to five Linux I/O technologies we have seen, namely: the blocking `read(2)/write(2)` (and the SG-I/O/positioned `[p]read[v](2)/[p]write[v](2)`), memory mapping, non-blocking (mostly synchronous) DIO, and non-blocking asynchronous AIO:

| I/O Type | APIs | Pros | Cons |
| --- | --- | --- | --- |
| Blocking (regular and SG-IO / positioned) | `[p]read[v](2)` `/[p]write[v](2)` | Easy to use | Slow; double-copy of data buffers |
| Memory Mapping | `mmap(2)` | (Relatively) easy to use; fast (in memory I/O); single copy of data (a zero-copy technique); works best when RAM:Storage :: ~ 1:1 | MMU-intensive (high page table overhead, meta-work) when RAM:Storage ratio is 1:N (N>>1) |
| DIO (non-blocking, mostly synchronous) | `open(2)` with `O_DIRECT` flag | Zero-copy technique; no impact on page cache; control over caching; some control over I/O scheduling | Moderately complex to set up and use: app must perform its own caching |
| AIO (non-blocking, asynchronous) | <Various: see aio(7) - POSIX AIO, Linux `io_*(2)`, and so on> | Truly async and non-blocking—required for high-performance apps; zero-copy technique; no impact on page cache; full control over caching, I/O and thread scheduling | Complex to set up and use |

Linux I/O technologies—a quick comparison

In the *Further reading* section on the GitHub repository, we provide links to two blog articles (from two real-world products: Scylla, a modern high-performance distributed No SQL data store, and NGINX, a modern high-performance web server), that discuss in depth how these alternative powerful I/O technologies (AIO, thread pools) are used in (their respective) real-world products; do take a look.

# Multiplexing or async blocking I/O – a quick note

You often hear about powerful multiplexing I/O APIs—the `select(2)`, `poll(2)`, and, more recently, Linux's powerful `epoll(7)` framework. These APIs, `select(2)`, `poll(2)`, and/or `epoll(7)`, provide what is known as asynchronous blocking I/O. They work well upon descriptors that remain blocked on I/O; examples are sockets, both Unix and internet domain, as well as pipes—both unnamed and named pipes (FIFOs).

These I/O technologies are asynchronous (you can issue the system call and return immediately) but they actually are still blocking in nature because the thread must check for I/O completion, for example, by using the `poll(2)` in tandem with a `read(2)` system call, which is still a blocking operation.

These APIs are really very useful for network I/O operations, the canonical example being a busy (web)server monitoring hundreds (and perhaps thousands) of connections. First, each connection being represented by a socket descriptor makes using the `select(2)` or `poll(2)` system calls appealing. However, the fact is that `select(2)` is old and limited (to a maximum of 1,024 descriptors; not enough); secondly, both `select(2)` and `poll(2)`'s internal implementations have an algorithmic time complexity of O(n), which makes them non-scalable.
The `epoll(7)` implementation has no (theoretical) descriptor limit and uses an O(1) algorithm and what's known as edge-triggered notifications. This table summarizes these points:

| API | Algorithmic Time-Complexity | Max number of clients |
|---|---|---|
| `select(2)` | O(n) | FD_SETSIZE (1024) |
| `poll(2)` | O(n) | (theoretically) unlimited |
| `epoll(7)` APIs | O(1) | (theoretically) unlimited |

Linux asynchronous blocking APIs

Advanced File I/O

These features have thus made the `epoll(7)` set of APIs (`epoll_create(2)`, `epoll_ctl(2)`, `epoll_wait(2)`, and `epoll_pwait(2)`) a favorite for implementing non-blocking I/O on network applications that require very high scalability. (See a link to a blog article providing more details on using multiplexed I/O, including the epoll, on Linux in the *Further reading* section on the GitHub repository.)

# I/O – miscellaneous

A few miscellaneous remaining topics to round off this chapter follow.

## Linux's inotify framework

While brilliant for network I/O, these multiplexing APIs, though they can in theory be used for monitoring regular file descriptors, will simply report them as always being ready (for reading, writing, or an error condition has arisen), thereby diminishing their usefulness (when used upon regular files).

Perhaps Linux's inotify framework, a means to monitor filesystem events including events on individual files, might be what you are looking for. The inotify framework provides the following system calls to help developers monitor files: `inotify_init(2)`, `inotify_add_watch(2)` (which can be subsequently `read(2)`), and then `inotify_rm_watch(2)`. Check out the man page on `inotify(7)` for more details: http://man7.org/linux/man-pages/man7/inotify.7.html.

## I/O schedulers

An important feature within the Linux I/O stack is a part of the kernel block layer called the I/O scheduler. The issue being addressed here is basically this: I/O requests are being more or less continually issued by the kernel (due to apps wanting to perform various file data/code reads and writes); this results in a continuous stream of I/O requests being ultimately received and processed by the block driver(s). The kernel folks know that one of the primary reasons that I/O sucks out performance is that the physical seek of a typical SCSI disk is really slow (compared to silicon speeds; yes, of course, SSDs (solid state devices) are making this a lot more palatable nowadays).

So, if we could use some intelligence to sort the block I/O requests in a way that makes the most sense in terms of the underlying physical medium, it would help performance. Think of an elevator in a building: it uses a sort algorithm, optimally taking people on and dropping them off as it traverses various floors. This is what the OS I/O schedulers essentially try to do; in fact, the first implementation was called Linus's elevator.

Various I/O scheduler algorithms exist (deadline, **completely fair queuing (cfq)**, noop, anticipatory scheduler: these are now considered legacy; the newest as of the time of writing seem to be the mq-deadline and **budget fair queuing (bfq)** I/O schedulers, with bfq looking very promising for heavy or light I/O workloads (bfq is a recent addition, kernel version 4.16). The I/O schedulers present within your Linux OS are a kernel feature; you can check which they are and which is being used; see it being done here on my Ubuntu 18.04 x86_64 box:

```
$ cat /sys/block/sda/queue/scheduler
noop deadline [cfq]
$
```

Here, `bfq` is the I/O scheduler being used on my Fedora 28 system (with a more recent kernel):

```
$ cat /sys/block/sda/queue/scheduler
mq-deadline [bfq] none
$
```

The default I/O scheduler here is `bfq`. Here's the interesting bit: the user can actually select between I/O schedulers, run their I/O stress workloads and/or benchmarks, and see which one yields the maximum benefit! How? To select the I/O scheduler at boot time, pass along a kernel parameter (via the bootloader, typically GRUB on an x86-based laptop, desktop or server system, U-Boot on an embedded Linux); the parameter in question is passed as `elevator=<iosched-name>`; for example, to set the I/O scheduler to noop (useful for systems with SSDs perhaps), pass the parameter to the kernel as `elevator=noop`.

There's an easier way to change the I/O scheduler immediately at runtime; just `echo(1)` the one you want into the pseudo-file; for example, to change the I/O scheduler to `mq-deadline`, do the following:

```
# echo mq-deadline > /sys/block/sda/queue/scheduler
# cat /sys/block/sda/queue/scheduler
[mq-deadline] bfq none
#
```

*Advanced File I/O*

Now, you can (stress) test your I/O workloads on different I/O schedulers, thus deciding upon which yields the optimal performance for your workload.

## Ensuring sufficient disk space

Linux provides the `posix_fallocate(3)` API; its job is to guarantee that sufficient disk space is available for a given range specific to a given file. What that actually means is that whenever the app writes to that file within that range, the write is guaranteed not to fail due to lack of disk space (if it does fail, `errno` will be set to ENOSPC; that won't happen). It's signature is as follows:

```
#include <fcntl.h>
int posix_fallocate(int fd, off_t offset, off_t len);
```

Here are some quick points to note regarding this API:

- The file is the one referred to by the descriptor `fd`.
- The range is from `offset` for `len` bytes; in effect, this is the disk space that will be reserved for the file.
- If the current file size is less than what the range requests (that is, `offset+len`), then the file is grown to this size; otherwise, the file's size remains unaltered.
- `posix_fallocate(3)` is a portable wrapper over the underlying system call `fallocate(2)`.
- For this API to succeed, the underlying filesystem must support the `fallocate`; if not, it's emulated (but with a lot of caveats and issues; refer to the man page for more).
- Also, a CLI utility called `fallocate(1)` exists to perform the same task from, say, a shell script.

> **TIP:** These APIs and tools may come in very useful for software such as backup, cloud provisioning, digitization, and so on, guaranteeing sufficient disk space is available before a long I/O operation begins.

[ 750 ]

# Utilities for I/O monitoring, analysis, and bandwidth control

This table summarizes various utilities, APIs, tools, and even a cgroup blkio controller; these tools/features will prove very useful in monitoring, analyzing (to pinpoint I/O bottlenecks), and allocating I/O bandwidth (via the `ioprio_set(2)` and the powerful cgroups blkio controller.)

| Utility name | What it does |
| --- | --- |
| iostat(1) | Monitors I/O and displays I/O statistics about devices and storage device partitions. From the man page on `iostat(1)`: The `iostat` command is used for monitoring system input/output device loading by observing the time the devices are active in relation to their average transfer rates. The `iostat` command generates reports that can be used to change system configuration to better balance the input/output load between physical disks. |
| iotop(1) | In the style of `top(1)` (for CPU), iotop continually displays threads sorted by their I/O usage. Must run as root. |
| ioprio_[get\|set](2) | System calls to query and set I/O scheduling class and priority of a given thread; see the man pages for details: http://man7.org/linux/man-pages/man2/ioprio_set.2.html; see its wrapper utility `ionice(1)` as well. |
| perf-tools | Among these tools (from B Gregg) is `iosnoop-perf(1)` and `iolatecy-perf(1)` to snoop I/O transactions and observe I/O latencies respectively. Install these tools from their GitHub repository here: https://github.com/brendangregg/perf-tools. |
| cgroup blkio controller | Use the powerful Linux cgroup's blkio controller to limit I/O bandwidth for a process or group of processes in any required fashion (heavily used in cloud environments, including Docker); see the relevant link in the *Further reading* section on the GitHub repository. |

Tools/utilities/APIs/cgroups for I/O monitoring, analysis, and bandwidth control

Note: the preceding mentioned utilities may not be installed on the Linux system by default; (obviously) install them to try them out.

> Do also check out Brendan Gregg's superb Linux Performance blog pages and tools (which include perf-tools, iosnoop, and iosnoop latency heat maps); please find the relevant links in the *Further reading* section on the GitHub repository.

*Advanced File I/O*

# Summary

In this chapter, we learned powerful approaches to a critical aspect of working with files: ensuring that I/O performance is kept as high as is possible, as I/O is really the performance-draining bottleneck in many real-world workloads. These techniques ranged from file access pattern advice passing to the OS, SG-I/O techniques and APIs, memory mapping for file I/O, DIO, AIO, and so on.

> The next chapter in the book is a brief look at daemon processes; what they are and how to set them up. Kindly take a look at this chapter here: https://www.packtpub.com/sites/default/files/downloads/Daemon_Processes.pdf.

# 19
# Troubleshooting and Best Practices

A brief overview on newer Linux troubleshooting tools and utilities, as well as industry best practices to follow when designing, developing, and deploying real-world Linux systems apps, is the focus of this chapter. We wish to make it very clear, though, that this is a book on Linux systems programming; the troubleshooting tips and best practices described here are exclusively with regard to the system-level development of applications (typically written in C/C++) on a Linux system; we do not deal with generic troubleshooting on Linux (topics such as troubleshooting network or configuration issues, system administration tips, and tricks).

For this chapter in particular (mainly due to the vast scope and size of the content it only mentions in passing), we have provided several useful online articles and books in the *Further reading* section on the GitHub repository. Please do browse through them.

This chapter serves to round off this book; here, with respect to Linux systems programming, the reader will be given the following:

- An overview of (newer) troubleshooting tools and techniques
- An overview of industry best practices—in terms of design, software engineering, programming implementation, and testing

# Troubleshooting tools

In this section, we will mention several tools and utilities that can help the application developer identify system bottlenecks and performance issues. (Note that here, to save space and time, we do not delve into the dozens of usual suspects—well-known system monitoring utilities on Linux such as ps, pstree, top, htop, pidstat, vmstat, dstat, sar, nagios, iotop, iostat, ionice, lsof, nmon, iftop, ethtool, netstat, tcpdump, wireshark—and instead mention the newer ones). Here is an important thing to remember when performing data collection (or benchmarking) for later analysis: take the trouble to set up a test rig and, when using it, change (as far as is possible) only one variable at a time for a given run so that you can see its impact.

## perf

Performance measurement and analysis is an enormous topic; the identification, analysis, and determination of the root cause for performance issues is no trivial task. In recent years, the perf(1) and htop(1) utility has emerged as the fundamental tool for performance measurement and analysis on the Linux platform.

Sometimes, all you need is to see what is consuming the most CPU; traditionally, we use the well-known top(1) utility to do so. Try, instead, the very useful perf variant, like so: sudo perf top.

Also, you can exploit some of the features with the following:

```
sudo perf top -r 90 --sort pid,comm,dso,symbol
 (-r 90 => collect data with SCHED_FIFO RT scheduling class and
 priority 90 [1-99]).
```

Essentially, this is the perf workflow: record a session (data files get saved) and generate a report. (See the links in *Further reading* section on the GitHub repository.)

Excellent diagrams available on Brendan Gregg's blog clearly show the dozens of tools available for performing observation, performance analysis, and dynamic tracing on Linux:

- Linux performance tools: http://www.brendangregg.com/Perf/linux_perf_tools_full.png
- Linux performance observability tools: http://www.brendangregg.com/Perf/linux_observability_tools.png

Due to its visual impact, Brendan Gregg's Flame Graph scripts are very interesting too; check out the links in the *Further reading* section on the GitHub repository.

Brendan Gregg also leads the development of a project called perf-tools. Here are some words from the project: performance analysis tools based on Linux `perf_events` (aka perf) and Ftrace. Several very useful shell script wrappers (over Perf, Ftrace, and Kprobes) make up the tools; do clone the GitHub repository and try them out. (https://github.com/brendangregg/perf-tools.)

## Tracing tools

In-depth tracing often has the desirous side effect of having the developer or tester spot performance bottlenecks as well as debug systems-level latencies and issues. Linux has a plethora of frameworks and tools available for tracing, both at user space and at the level of the kernel; some of the more relevant ones are mentioned here:

- **User space**: `ltrace(1)` (trace library APIs), `strace(1)` (trace system calls; also try doing `sudo perf trace`), LTTng-ust, uprobes.
- **Kernel space**: LTTng, ftrace (plus several frontends such as `tracecmd(1)`, kernelshark GUIm), Kprobes—(including Jprobes—up to Kernel Version 4.14), Kretprobes; SystemTaprm) eBPF.

## The Linux proc filesystem

Linux has a very rich and powerful filesystem called **procfs**—`proc` for process. It is usually mounted under `/proc`, and it contains pseudo-files and directories that contain valuable runtime-generated information on processes and internals information. In a nutshell, procfs serves as a UI for two key purposes:

- It serves as a viewport into detailed process, thread, OS, and hardware information.
- It serves as the place to query and set kernel-level tunables (switches and values for the core kernel, scheduling, memory, and network parameters).

Taking the trouble to study and use the Linux proc filesystem is well worth it. Pretty much all the user space monitoring and analysis tools are ultimately based on procfs. Find further information in the links provided in *Further reading* section on the GitHub repository.

# Best practices

In this section, we briefly enumerate what we consider to be industry best practices, though they are mostly generic and thus broad in scope; we will particularly look at them through the lens of the Linux systems programmer.

## The empirical approach

The word *empirical* (according to the *Cambridge English dictionary*) means based on what is experienced or seen, rather than on theory. This is perhaps the critical principle to be followed. A fascinating article by Gustavo Duarte (mentioned here: https://www.infoq.com/news/2008/02/realitydrivendevelopment) states: *"Action and experimentation are the cornerstones of empiricism. No attempt is made to subdue reality by extensive analysis and copious documentation. Reality is invited in via experiments. Instead of agonizing over market research, an empirical company hires interns and develops a product in one summer. A non-empirical company has 43 people planning an off-button design for one year."* Throughout this book, too, we have always tried to consciously follow an empirical approach; we definitely urge the reader to cultivate and embed the empirical principle in design and development.

## Software engineering wisdom in a nutshell

Frederick P Brooks wrote his famous treatise *The Mythical Man-Month: Essays on Software Engineering* back in 1975, and this book is to date billed as the most influential book on software project management. This is no wonder: certain truths are just that—truths. Here are a few gems from this volume:

- Plan to throw one away; you will anyway.
- There is no silver bullet.
- Good cooking takes time. If you are made to wait, it is to serve you better, and to please you.
- The bearing of a child takes nine months, no matter how many women are assigned.
- Good judgment comes from experience, and experience comes from bad judgment.

Interestingly, and, of course, the design philosophy of the venerable Unix OS indeed incorporates great design principles, principles that remain in effect to this day on Linux. We covered this in `Chapter 1`, *Linux System Architecture*, in the section, *The Unix philosophy in a nutshell*.

# Programming

Let's now move on to the more mundane but really important things to be kept in mind by the developer.

## A programmer's checklist – seven rules

We suggest seven rules as follows:

- Rule #1 : Check all APIs for their failure case.
- Rule #2 : Compile with warnings on (`-Wall -Wextra`) and eliminate all warnings as far as is possible.
- Rule #3 : Never trust (user) input; validate it.
- Rule #4 : Use assertions in your code.
- Rule #5 : Eliminate unused (or dead) code from the codebase immediately.
- Rule #6 : Test thoroughly; 100% code coverage is the objective. Take the time and trouble to learn to use powerful tools: memory checkers (Valgrind, the sanitizer toolset), static and dynamic analyzers, security checkers (checksec), fuzzers (see the following explanation).
- Rule #7 : Do not assume anything (*assume* makes an *ass* out of *u* and *me*).

Here are some examples of how serious failures can result from not following the rules: An Ariane 5 unmanned rocket crashed early in its launch (June 4, 1996); the bug was ultimately traced to a register overflow issue, a single type casting error (rule #5). The Knight Capital Group lost $460 million in 45 minutes. Don't assume the size of a page. Use the `getpagesize(2)` system call or the `sysconf(3)` to obtain it. Further along these lines, see the blog article entitled *Low-Level Software Design* (there are links to these in the *Further reading* section on GitHub repository).

## Better testing

Testing is a critical activity; thorough and continual testing (including regression testing) leads to a stable product in which both the engineering team and the customer have deep confidence.

Here is an often-overlooked truth: complete code coverage testing is critical! Why? Simple—there are often hidden defects lurking in sections of code that never actually get tested (error handling being the typical example); the fact is though, they will be hit one fine day, and this can cause terrible failures.

Then again, unfortunately, testing can only reveal the presence of errors, not their absence; nevertheless, good and thorough testing is absolutely critical. Most testing performed (test cases written) tends to be positive test cases; interestingly, the majority of software (security) vulnerabilities escape unnoticed by this kind of testing. Negative test cases help catch these failures; a class of software testing called **fuzzing** helps greatly in this regard. Testing code on different machine architectures can help expose hidden defects as well.

## Using the Linux kernel's control groups

Use the Linux kernel's **cgroups** (control groups) technology to specify and constrain resource allocation and bandwidth. The cgroup controllers on a modern Linux system include the following: CPU (limits on CPU usage), CPU set (the modern way to perform CPU affinity constraining a group of processes to a set of CPUs), blkio (limits on I/O), devices (limits on which processes can use which devices), freezer (suspend/resume task execution), memory (limits on memory usage), `net_cls` (network packets tagging with classid), `net_prio` (limit network traffic per interface), **namespaces** (**ns**), `perf_event` (for performance analysis).

Limiting resources is critical not only from a requirements angle, but from a security perspective too (think about malicious attackers dreaming up [D]DoS attacks). Incidentally, containers (essentially a lightweight virtualization technique), a hot topic nowadays, are largely a reality because of the combination of two Linux kernel technologies that have sufficiently evolved: cgroups and namespaces.

# Summary

Question: What's the biggest room in the world?
Answer: The room for improvement!

This, in general, should sum up the attitude you should have when working on enormous projects, and keep learning for life topics such as Linux. We, again, urge the reader to not only read for conceptual understanding—that's important!—but to also get their hands dirty and write the code. Make mistakes, fix them, and learn from them. Contributing to open source is a fantastic way to do so.

# Other Books You May Enjoy

If you enjoyed this book, you may be interested in these other books by Packt:

**Hands-On Linux Administration on Azure**
Frederik Vos

ISBN: 978-1-78913-096-6

- Understand why Azure is the ideal solution for your open source workloads
- Master essential Linux skills and learn to find your way around the Linux environment
- Deploy Linux in an Azure environment
- Use configuration management to manage Linux in Azure
- Manage containers in an Azure environment
- Enhance Linux security and use Azure's identity management systems
- Automate deployment with Azure Resource Manager (ARM) and Powershell
- Employ Ansible to manage Linux instances in an Azure cloud environment

## Practical Linux Security Cookbook - Second Edition
Tajinder Kalsi

ISBN: 978-1-78913-839-9

- Learn about vulnerabilities and exploits in relation to Linux systems
- Configure and build a secure kernel and test it
- Learn about file permissions and how to securely modify files
- Authenticate users remotely and securely copy files on remote systems
- Review different network security methods and tools
- Perform vulnerability scanning on Linux machines using tools
- Learn about malware scanning and read through logs

# Leave a review - let other readers know what you think

Please share your thoughts on this book with others by leaving a review on the site that you bought it from. If you purchased the book from Amazon, please leave us an honest review on this book's Amazon page. This is vital so that other potential readers can see and use your unbiased opinion to make purchasing decisions, we can understand what our customers think about our products, and our authors can see your feedback on the title that they have worked with Packt to create. It will only take a few minutes of your time, but is valuable to other potential customers, our authors, and Packt. Thank you!

# Index

## A

Address Sanitizer (ASan)
  cons 231
  pros 231
  reference 226
  summary table 230
  used, for building programs 216
  used, for executing test cases 217, 222, 230
Address Space Layout Randomization (ASLR) 131
Alarm API 487
alloca
  used, for allocating automatic memory 161, 163
alternate signal stack
  large (16 MB) 426
  small (100 KB) 425
  used, for implementing handle high-volume signals 423
  using 422
API interfaces
  about 105, 106
  code examples 107, 109, 111
APIs
  blocking 409
Application Binary Interface (ABI) 27, 443
ARM system 158
ARM-32
  memprot program, executing 159, 161
Asynchronous I/O (AIO) 721, 745

## B

backtrace ( bt) command 83
bash-builtins 92
benign race condition 345
big kernel lock (BKL) 644

Buffer Overflow (BoF) attacks 280

## C

C/C++ developer
  actions 237
capabilities
  embedding, into program binary 288, 289, 290, 292
  setting, programmatically 294, 295, 297, 299
capability bitmask 284
capability-dumb binary 292
capability-smart binary 292
CLI digital clock
  about 491
  trial runs 495
coarse granularity locking 610
code coverage
  in testing 236
command-line interface (CLI) 15, 24, 244, 483
Common Vulnerabilities and Exposures (CVE) 170
Common Weakness Enumeration (CWE) 170
Compile-time instrumentation (CTI) 214
Completely Fair Scheduler (CFS) 703
condition variable (CV)
  about 614
  broadcast wakeup 653
  CV usage demo application 649, 653
  naive approach 647
  using 647
control groups (cgroups) 706
control register 2 (CR2) 443
copy-on-write(COW) 352, 353, 538
credentials (cred) 302
Crude IPC 463

# D

daemons
  about 527
deadlock
  ABBA deadlock 612
  about 611
  avoiding 613, 614
  self deadlock (relock) 612
  types 612
debugging tools
  dynamic analysis tools 200
  key points 236
  static analysis tools 200
demand-paging
  about 139, 140
  mincore 141
denial-of-service (DoS) attack 91, 182, 366, 565
design motivation
  CPU, overlapping with I/O 548
  IPC 549
  logical separation 548
  manager-worker model 549
  potential parallelism 547
digression 362
Direct I/O (DIO) 744
Direct Memory Access (DMA) 734
Discretionary Access Control (DAC) 282
double-free
  test case 182
dumpcap 293, 294
dynamic analysis tools 200
dynamic binary instrumentation (DBI) 201

# E

Effective Group ID (EGID) 249
Effective User ID (EUID) 249
end-of-file (EOF) 14
errno
  about 447
  handling 447
  race 448
exec family APIs
  about 312, 315, 319

  code example 324, 326
  error handling 315
  execle API 321
  execlp API 319
  execv API 321
  OS level 322
  successor name, specifying 316
  summary table 323
  zero argument, passing 315
exec Unix axiom
  about 307
  exec operation, considerations 308
  experiment 310
  point of no return 311
  testing 309

# F

Fedora 27
  reference 10, 50
file descriptor (fd)
  about 346
file I/O
  file, memory mapping 735
  Linux I/O code path 732
First Come First Served (FCFC) 456
fork bomb
  about 366
  reference 367
fork system call
  using 333
fork
  atomic execution 343
  child process 330
  effect, on open files 345
  malloc 350
  multiple child, creating 366
  open files 349
  parent process 330
  rules 334, 335, 336, 337, 339, 340, 341, 343, 344, 345, 347, 348, 376, 377
  security 349
  working 330, 331
free API
  about 125, 126
  overview 126

Ftrace 158

## G

General Protection Fault (GPF) 445
General Purpose Operating System (GPOS) 701
getcap 292
glibc malloc API
  about 116
  calloc API 126
  free API 124
  malloc API 116, 118
  realloc API 127
Glibc mallop
  options, via environment 235
Glibc mallopt 233
GNU C library (glibc) 116
GNU Debugger (GDB) 81, 214
Graphical User Interface (GUI) 24, 305
Group Identifier (GID) 245

## H

hard limits 96
hardware-paging 61
hardware-segmentation 61
heap segment 116, 130
hyperthreading (HT) 569

## I

I/O performance recommendations
  about 720
  analysis 751
  async blocking I/O 747
  Asynchronous I/O (AIO) 744, 745
  bandwidth control 751
  Direct I/O (DIO) 744
  file I/O, via memory mapping 731
  I/O monitoring, utilities 751
  I/O schedulers 748
  I/O technologies 746
  kernel page cache 721
  Linux's inotify framework 748
  miscellaneous 748
  multiplexing 747
  pread, using 724

pwrite APIs 724
scatter-gather I/O 726
sufficient disk space, ensuring 750
incorrect memory accesses
  about 170
  out-of-bounds memory accesses 173
  uninitialized variables, accessing 171
  uninitialized variables, using 171
  use-after-free (UAF) bugs 179
  use-after-return (UAR) bugs 179
information node (inode) 246
Instruction Pointer (IP) 85, 334
Instruction Set Architecture (ISA) 604
Integer OverFlow (IOF) 121
Inter-Process Communication (IPC) 67
interval timers
  about 488
  CLI digital clock 491
  profiling timers 496

## J

Jet Propulsion Laboratory (JPL) 635
join
  using 578

## K

kernel build
  configuring (j4) 544
kernel documentation, on credentials
  reference 284
kernel page cache
  about 721
  hints, giving 722
  hints, giving via posix_fadvise(2) API 722
  hints, giving via readahead(2) API 723
Kernel Schedulable Entity (KSE) 696

## L

Last In First Out (LIFO) 78
Least Significant Bits (LSB) 234
Linux Foundation (LF) 716
Linux kernel 302
Linux OS scheduling model
  about 695
  process 696

real time  699
sleep states  697
state machine  696
Linux system
technical prerequisites  9, 49
Linux Tracing Toolkit next generation (LTTng)  469, 470
Linux's soft real-time capabilities
exploiting  708
scheduling policy APIs  708
scheduling priority APIs  709
soft real-time systems, considerations  715
thread scheduling policy, setting up  710
thread scheduling priority, setting up  710
Linux
about  10
as RTOS  716
performance tools, reference  754
locking
about  601
atomicity, checking  603, 607
considerations  607
granularity  610
guidelines  608
login shell  244
ls
binaries, displaying  300
LSM Logs  157

# M

malloc API helpers  237
malloc API
about  116, 118
FAQs  119, 122
overview  124
malloc
and program break  135
default options  135
freed memory  138
large allocations option  137, 138
statistics, displaying  136
working  134
mapping  74
Memory Checker tool ( Memcheck)  201
memory issues

about  168, 170
incorrect memory accesses  170
memory leakage  185
undefined behavior  195
memory leakage
about  125, 185
fragmentation  196
miscellaneous  197
test case  186, 187, 189, 190, 191, 193, 194
memory locking
about  142, 143
limits  143, 146
pages, locking  147, 148
privileges  143, 146
Memory Management Unit (MMU)  65
memory mapping, file
anonymous mapping  738
code example  742
considerations  742
MAP_PRIVATE  739
mmap advantage  740
memory protection
about  148
code example  149, 151, 154
keys  161
mincore
URL  141
mmap  134
modern POSIX capabilities model  280
multiprocess model
versus multithreading model, cons  690
versus multithreading model, pros  689
multiprocess, versus multithreaded
creation/destruction  536
kernel build  544
matrix multiplication  539, 542
multiprocess
versus multithreaded  535
multithreaded (MT)  657
multithreading  530
mutex attribute
attempt, timing out  639
usage  638
mutex lock
about  615, 618

attributes 621
busy-waiting (non-blocking variant) 640
checking 645
data race 618, 621
IPC 625
Mars 631
Mars Pathfinder mission 635
priority inheritance (PI) 636
priority inversion 631
process-shared mutex 625
reader-writer mutex lock 640
robust mutex attribute 623
semantics 639
spinlock variant 642
threads 625
types 621
usage guidelines 644
watchdog timer 633
mutual exclusion (mutex) 615

# N

nanosleep system call 451, 453
National Vulnerability Database (NVD) 184
Native Posix Threading Library (NPTL) 552
Next Generation Posix Threads (NGPT) 552

# O

older interfaces
  about 484
  alarm(2) system call 484
  interval timers 487
Open File Descriptor Table (OFDT) 346
operating system (OS) 701
orphans 374
out-of-bounds memory accesses
  about 173
  read overflow 173
  read overflow, test case 176, 177
  read underflow 173
  read underflow, test case 178
  write overflow 173
  write overflow, test case 174, 175
  write underflow 173
  write underflow, test case 175

# P

packcap 280
Page Table Entry (PTE) 435
pages 61
Paging Table (PT) 63
parameter
  passing 582
  structure, passing 583
  thread parameters 585, 587
pedagogical bank account example 597, 598
pentesting 281
performance motivation
  context switching 550
  creation and destruction 549
  modern hardware 549
  resource sharing 550
permanence 112
permission models layering 301
pipe 21
Portable Operating System Interface for
    Computing Environments (POSICE) 552
Portable Operating System Interface for Unix
    (POSIX) 552
POSIX (interval) timers
  about 498
  application workflow 499
  arming 502
  creating 499
  disarming 502
  mechanism, example programs 508
  overrun, figuring 507
  querying 504
  run walk interval timer application 517
  run-walk timer game 508
  timer lookup via proc 524
  using 499
  workflow 504, 507
POSIX capabilities model
  about 281, 282, 283
  file capability sets 287
  thread capability sets 286
POSIX scheduling model
  about 695
  CPU affinity 705

nice value 704
scheduling policies 701
scheduling policies, peeking 703
scheduling priority, peeking 703
POSIX threads (pthreads) 530, 551
Principle of Least Privilege (PoLP) 283
priority inheritance (PI) 636
prlimit utility
  about 102
  examples 103
proc filesystem 284
Process Control Block (PCB) 258
process crashes
  handling 430
  SA_SIGINFO, information detailing 430
process credentials
  about 249, 258
  code example 259
  hacking 262, 265
  querying 258
  saved-set ID 261
  setting up 261
  sudo utility 260
process descriptor 73
process execution
  about 306
  exec family APIs 312
  exec Unix axiom 307
  program, converting to process 306
Process Identifier (PID) 245, 308
process memory layout
  about 73
  mapping 74
  segments 74
  VM split 84
process model wait 579
process
  creating 330
  versus threads 688
procfs
  about 755
  process capabilities, viewing 285
profiling (perf) 331
program binary
  capabilities, embedding into 288, 289, 290, 292
program break 130
pthread APIs
  condition variable (CV) 646
  mutex lock 615
  using, for synchronization 614
pthreads
  about 691
  FAQs 691
  multithread pthreads applications, debugging with GDB 692

# Q
QEMU 158

# R
race condition 345
race
  critical sections 600, 601
  defeating, after fork 356
racing problem
  about 596
  atomicity 597
  concurrent execution 597
read-execute (r-x) 76
Read-Write (RW) 68
real and effective IDs
  about 248, 250
  password, changing 251, 253
  setgid bits 253
  setuid bits 253
Real Group ID (RGID) 249
real time signals
  about 454, 456
  priority 456, 458, 459
  standard signals, differences 455
real time
  about 699
  firm real-time systems 700
  hard real-time system 700
  soft real-time systems 700
  types 700
Real User ID (RUID) 249
real, effective and saved-set-ID (res) 275
real-time Linux (RTL) 716

Real-Time Operating System (RTOS) 700
realloc API
  about 127
  corner cases 128
  reallocarray API 129
reentrant functions
  about 398
  async-signal-safe functions 400
reentrant
  functions 398
  safety 398
resource limit values
  caveats 101
  changing 99
  prlimit utility 102
  querying 99
resource limits
  about 91, 93
  availability 94
  types 94
run walk interval timer application
  low-level design and code 520, 523
  trial runs 518
run-walk timer game
  about 508
  code view 513, 516
  trail 511
  working 509

# S

SA_NOCLDWAIT flag
  using 406, 407
SA_SIGINFO
  crash location, searching in source code 445
  information, detailing 430
  information, extracting 436, 440
  information, trapping 440
  information, trapping from crash 436
  register, dumping 441, 445
  siginfo_t structure 431, 435
  system-level details, obtaining on process crashes 435
Sanitizer tools
  about 214
  AddressSanitizer (ASan) 215
  Kernel AddressSanitizer (KASAN) 215
  LeakSanitizer (LSan) 215
  MemorySanitizer (MSan) 215
  reference 216
  ThreadSanitizer (TSan) 215
  UndefinedBehaviorSanitizer (UBSan) 215
saved-set ID 261
sbrk() API
  using 130, 133
Scatter – gather I/O
  about 726
  discontiguous data file 726
  SG – I/O approach 728
SEALS
  URL 160
security
  tips 302
segments
  about 61, 74
  data segments 76
  library segments 77
  stack segment 78
  text segment 76
setgid binary 254
setgid bits
  about 254
  hacking 255, 257
  setting up, with chmod 254
setgid installed programs
  identifying 266
  setres[u|g]id(2) system calls 275
setuid binary 252, 253
setuid bits
  about 254
  hacking 255, 257
  setting up, with chmod 254
setuid root binaries 253
setuid-root binary 253
setuid-root
  about 280
  example 268
  identifying 266
  privileges, giving up 271
  saved-set UID 272, 275
sigaction flags

about  404
alternate signal stack, using  422
interrupted system calls  409
SA_NOCLDSTOP flag  409
SA_NOCLDWAIT  405
SA_NODEFER flag  412
SA_RESETHAND flag  411
SA_RESTART flag, used for fixing interrupted system calls  410
sigaction system call
　used, for trapping signals  388
sigaction system
　sidebar  389
　structure  389, 392, 393
signal handler
　safety measures  400
　signal-safe atomic integers  401
signal-handling techniques
　alternatives  471
　pause  472
　signalfd API  479, 481
　sigtimedwait system calls  478
　sigwait library API  473, 475, 476, 478
　sigwaitinfo  478
　synchronously blocking, for signals via sigwait* APIs  473
　synchronously waiting, for signals  471
　waiting  472
signaling
　about  447, 684
　as IPC  463
　Crude IPC  463
　data item, sending  464, 465, 467, 469
　errno, handling  447
　handling, in MT app  686, 688
　issue  685
　LTTng  469, 470
　POSIX solution  685
　sleep state, using  450
signals
　about  383
　behavior, when masked  412
　example cases  380
　existence, checking  462
　handling  387

handling, at high volume  427
handling, within OS  398
kill system, calling  460
killing permissions  462
mask, querying  395
masking  394
masking, with sigprocmask API  394
mechanism  380, 383
need for  380
raise API  461
SA_NODEFER  414
SA_NODEFER bit, executing  418, 420
SA_NODEFER signal flag, avoiding  413
sending  460
standard or UNIX signals  384, 386
trapping, with sigaction system call  388
simpsh project  353, 357, 358, 359, 361
sleep state
　nanosleep system call  451, 453
　using  450
soft limits  96
Stack Pointer (SP)  587
stack segment
　process stack  78
　stack memory  78
　stack, peeking  81
standard or UNIX signals  385
static analysis tools  200
sudo  260
Symmetric Multiprocessor (SMP)  562
synchronization  345
system architecture, Linux
　ABI  27
　about  27, 38
　control register's content, accessing  33
　preliminaries  27
　register's content, accessing via inline assembly  31
system calls
　about  258
　process credentials, querying  258
　process credentials, setting up  261
　setgid installed programs, identifying  266
　setuid-root, identifying  266

# T

text 76
thread attributes
  querying 571
thread cancellation
  about 674
  cancelability state 675
  cancelability type 676, 678
  code example 679, 680
  framework 675
thread capability sets
  Ambient (Amb) 286
  Bounding (Bnd) 286
  Effective (Eff) 286
  Inheritable (Inh) 286
  Permitted (Prm) 286
thread cleanup
  about 674
  at thread exit 681
  code example 682, 684
thread join
  about 581
  life, checking 580
  using 574
thread model join 579
thread safety
  about 657, 659, 660
  APIs, avoiding 667
  approaches, for creating functions 662
  foo_r API 670
  glibc APIs, refactoring 668, 669, 670
  glibc foo API 670
  reentrant 660, 661
  standard C library 667
  thread-safe code, creating 660
  via function refactoring 665, 667
  via mutex locks 662, 664, 665
  via TLS 671, 673
  via TSD 673
thread stacks
  about 587
  guards 590, 593
  location 588
  size 587

threads
  about 530
  attributes 570
  counting 563
  creating 554, 564, 566, 568
  design motivation 547
  experimenting with 559
  features 547
  history 551
  managing 553
  parameter, passing 582
  performance motivation 549
  POSIX threads 551
  pthread APIs 553
  resource sharing 531, 535
  terminating, ways 562
  termination 557
  versus processes 688
timers
  via file descriptors 525
tracing tools
  kernel space 755
  user space 755
troubleshooting tools
  about 754
  Linux proc filesystem 755
  perf 754
  tracing tools 755

# U

Ubuntu Desktop
  download link 10, 50
ucontext 431
undefined behavior (UB) 125
uninitialized memory reads (UMR) 118, 171, 172
uninitialized variables
  accessing 171
  using 171
Unix fork-exec semantic 354
Unix permission model
  about 242
  access category, determining 246, 248
  at user level 243
  real and effective IDs 248, 250

security notes 277
  system calls 258
  working 243
Unix
  about 10
  cat utility 19
  command-line interface (CLI) 24
  design philosophy 12
  files 12
  mechanisms principle 25
  modular design 24
  philosophy 11
  plain text 23
  standard input (stdin) 18
  standard output (stdout) 18
  tools, assigning for specific task 15
  tools, combining 21
  word count (wc) 18
Use After Return (UAR)
  about 179
  test case 181
use-after-free (UAF)
  test case 179, 180
User Identifier (UID) 245
user interface (UI) 548

# V

Valgrind tools
  cachegrind 201
  callgrind 201
  drd 201
  helgrind 201
  massif 201
  Memcheck 201
  Memcheck, using 201
Valgrind
  summary table 213
  about 201
  cons 213
  Memcheck, using 205, 209
  pros 213
  reference 201
vfork 374
virtual address space (VAS) 58, 116, 307, 308, 530, 735
Virtual Filesystem Switch (VFS) 12, 733
virtual memory (VM), benefits
  memcpy() program, testing 69, 72
  memory-region protection 68
  physical memory 67
  process-isolation 66
virtual memory (VM)
  about 49, 50, 54, 56, 57
  address-translation 65
  benefits 66
  indirection 65
  objective 52
  paging 61
  problem 51
  simplified 64
  simplistic flawed approach 58, 60
virtual memory area (VMA) 740
VM split 85

# W

wait API 361, 363, 364
wait
  about 355
  actual system call 372
  performing 356
  scenarios 364, 365, 368
  variations 368, 370, 371
watchdog timer (WDT) 633
watchdog timers 527
white-hat hacking 281
Wireshark 293

# Z

zombies 375, 376

[ 774 ]

Printed in Great Britain
by Amazon